EDWARD MacLYSAGH

MORE
IRISH FAMILIES

MORE
IRISH FAMILIES

A new revised and enlarged edition of
 More Irish Families,
incorporating *Supplement to Irish Families*,
with an essay on Irish chieftainries

EDWARD MacLYSAGHT
MA, D Litt., MRIA

IRISH ACADEMIC PRESS

This book was set in Ireland for
IRISH ACADEMIC PRESS
Kill Lane, Blackrock, Co. Dublin, Ireland
and in North America for
IRISH ACADEMIC PRESS
c/o ISBS, 5804 N.E. Hassalo Street, Portland, OR 97213.

First paperback edition 1996

A catalogue record for this title
is available from the British Library.

ISBN 0-7165-2604-2

EDITORIAL NOTE

In 1957 Dr MacLysaght published *Irish Families* (Hodges Figgis &
Co., Dublin) which has been reprinted a number of times and is now
published by Irish Academic Press. In 1970 he brought out *More
Irish Families* (O'Gorman, Galway) which was followed by
Supplement to Irish Families (Helicon, Dublin, 1964). The present
work integrates and expands the material in the two last-mentioned
and forms effectively a single companion volume to *Irish Families*.
This 1996 printing is the first paperback edition of
More Irish Families.

Finally, Dr MacLysaght's, *The Surnames of Ireland*—a guide to over
4,000 Gaelic, Norman and Anglo-Irish surnames—is also published
by Irish Academic Press.

Printed in Great Britain
by Cambridge University Press, Cambridge.

CONTENTS

PREFACE

 preface is needed to explain the raison-d'étre of this book; and in addition to that I think it would be appropriate for me to refer to the series of books on Irish families and surnames of which this is definitely the final volume. In fact it is my validiction for, at the age of ninety-four, it is unlikely that I will write any more on the subject, beyond possibly a short article or two.

Over the past forty-five years I have published several books dealing with that subject. Those on surnames have taken their final form in *The Surnames of Ireland* (5th edition 1980): this consists of some 4,500 entries briefly summarizing essential facts – the form in Irish, derivation, location and numerosity (to use an American word), and thus includes many rarer names not to be found in any of the three volumes in the *Irish Families* series.

The fuller entries in those books focus attention on the historical and personal aspects of this subject. The first of these was *Irish Families* (with the sub-title 'Their names, arms and origins') published in 1957 and now in its fourth impression. This has entries on some eight hundred names chosen because they are the most numerous in the country or have produced famous people.

There has long been a demand for a new edition of the second volume of the series – *More Irish Families* (1960) – of which a mere 2,500 copies were printed, and it was followed in 1964 by *Supplement to Irish Families*. These accounted for a further thousand names, apart from incidental passing references.

The greater part of the present book consists of *More Irish Families* and *Supplement to Irish Families*, carefully revised and in many cased added to, all the entries being now alphabetically integrated in the text.

It is clear from correspondence received over the years and from conversations with interested people that very few were aware of the fact that *More Irish Families* included an appendix giving additional information on 170 names dealt with in the first volume of the series, in some cases, e.g. O'Higgins, Kennedy and Ussher, the new matter being considerably more extensive than the original article. This is now presented as Appendix I.

To complete this book an essay on the Chieftainries of Ireland is added. The *Bibliography of Irish Family History*, previously in *Surnames of Ireland*, was published separately in 1981. A few items in that bibliography as it appeared in earlier editions of *Surnames* have been omitted because letters from correspondents who were unable to locate the works in question led me to confirm that they were in fact pamphlets, printed often more than a century ago, and so are not now easily available.

A frequent disappointment or complaint expressed in the many letters I get from all over the world, especially from Irish-Americans, is that the name they bear is not dealt with by me. Nearly all these are from people who have only seen the first volume, *Irish Families*. The simple answer is that that work dealt (more than *en passant*) with less than a thousand well-known names and that theirs is probably to be found in the later volumes (now in this book). Even if that is not so, if it is in any way connected with Ireland there is almost certain to be a brief relevant entry in *Surnames of Ireland*.

I have come to the conclusion that only a small proportion of readers actually read an Introduction regarding it as a sort of elongated Preface. I think most people use my books as a source of information about some particular name or names rather than as works of general interest. This seems to apply to the six lengthy introductory chapters in *Irish Families* as well as to the introduction to *Surnames of Ireland*. These constitute a disquisition on the whole subject and it would be supererogatory to cover the same ground here again. I may mention, however, that the latter gives many little known facts of interest discovered, sometimes by chance, in the course of my researches. I will take three, almost at random, by way of illustration.

First the name Abraham. Like Father Woulfe, in his valuable *Sloinnte Gaedheal is Gall*, published in 1923 (how much we have learnt since then), I had regarded it as essentially Jewish until I happened to come across a MacAbraham in a thirteenth century document. Further research, as recorded in p. 21 *infra*, showed that it is an example of the way in which Gaelic-Irish names often become so distorted or corrupted that they are unrecognizable in their final anglicized form. My second is MacEneaney of which no less than 38 modern variants are recorded (see p. 91 *infra*). The use of Bird as one of these exemplifies the frequent occurrence of mis-translation in the process of anglicization, the Irish for bird being *éan* which was wrongly assumed to be the basic word in the name MacEneaney. Perhaps the most bizarre case of this type is Monday for Mac Giolla Eoin, due to the last part of the Irish form sounding like *Luain*, the Irish word for Monday. Then again the statistics quoted for the gradual resumption of the prefixes Mac and O, dropped during the period of Gaelic submergence, are certainly of general interest.

The Introduction to the 1960 edition of *More Irish Families* deals with several aspects of our subject not dealt with in those referred to above, and it is therefore reprinted now, with some slight revision, following this Preface. At the present time there is definitely a revival of interest in Irish family history, not only in Ireland but also in America and Britain. I wonder what caused it. I can remember well what, many years ago, did so in my own case. Away back before that treasure-house of historical records the Public Record Office in Dublin was destroyed in 1922, my father commissioned Tennyson Groves, the well-known genealogical researcher, to make a note of every reference to our own name which he found in the PRO, whether in its earliest anglicized form MacGillysaghta or later MacLysaght and Lysaght. A massive bundle of papers resulted. Among them was the certificate of transplantation of our ancestor Patrick MacLysaght as an Irish Papist under the Cromwellian 'settlement'. He had acquired by marriage a large farm in Co. Limerick, and an interesting point arises in that connexion. Though the strictest orders had been issued that families from Co. Limerick should go to Co. Galway and none be settled in Co. Clare, he in fact was transplanted to Co. Clare in which county his forbears had lived from the earliest recorded times (and we are there still). In the course of time I found that ours was not, as I thought, an isolated case, for some twenty other families from Co. Limerick were also moved to Co. Clare, which was then treated as part of Connacht. Though this aroused my interest in our past I did not envisage that twenty years later I would be making it the basis of the work which has mainly occupied me during the last forty years. Apart from one article, 'A forgotten blue-book', in the *Catholic Bulletin* in 1919, I wrote nothing on the subject of names and families until 1935, when I produced *Short Study of a Transplanted Family*, based on those PRO records and confined to the history of our particular family. Working on that stimulated my interest in social history and led to my writing *Irish Life in the Seventeenth Century* in 1939 (4th edition 1979).

Soon after that I was appointed to the staff of the Irish Manuscripts Commission. So my official work for the next thirty-four years, till I finally retired in 1973, was largely associated with kindred subjects, especially while I was head of the genealogical and manuscript departments of the National Library.

Well, if I am right about prefaces and introductions not being widely read, my parting admonition will fall on deaf ears: it is that this book should be a 'must' for nearly every one of the many thousands of libraries – not to mention individual booklovers – who have a copy of *Irish Families* as it is in effect an enlarged second volume of that work.

A léightheoiri, táim buidheach daoibh go léir.

E. MacL

INTRODUCTION

Most of the general questions relating to our subject, such as the origin, distortion and distribution of our surnames, and the effects on them of invasion and conquest, were discussed in the preliminary chapters of my book *Irish Families.* Some aspects of it might well have been given more attention; for instance the contribution of the Irish abroad to the countries in which they settled (in this connection cf. Appendix V). In the text of that work, as in the present volume, this is frequently referred to incidentally in the biographical notes, particularly in the case of France and the United States; but the importance of Irish exiles in South Africa and Australia was somewhat neglected. In South Africa they used to be spoken of as the three P's — priests, police and publicans: oddly enough the fourth P was not included, though elsewhere the Irish have been much associated with politics; but the number of Irishmen who have been preeminent in that country is not large. In Australia, on the other hand, their influence has been most marked. The extent of the Irish contribution to the building up of the Australian nation has hardly been fully recognized. In all phases of national activity Irish names have been prominent. In the Church (indeed I may say Churches, for the great Australian ecclesiastics include non-Catholics like Flynn of the Inland) such names as Mannix and Moran immediately occur to the mind; pioneering and exploration remind us of Durack and Collins; literature suggests Furphy and Browne; art Lindsay; industry Lysaght; law and medicine Gavan Duffy and Kenny; while in politics it is enough to say that, apart from the dozens of State ministers who have borne Irish names, six of the sixteen Prime Ministers of Australia have been of Irish stock.

One question, discussed in *Irish Families*, to which I could give no definite answer then, remains a matter of conjecture, viz. to what extent people of a certain name descend from one or more known eponymous ancestors. Where, as in the case of O'Kelly, at least seven such are recorded (and we know also that the ubiquitous Kelly has absorbed several somewhat similar but uncommon surnames, like Kilkelly, Kehilly and Keally) the great number of people now so called does not present the same problem as does the case of, say, O'Brien. The only recorded eponymous O'Brien ancestor is Brian Boru. There are now approximately 30,000 O'Briens in Ireland and, no doubt, more than that number in America, not to mention England, Australia and even the Continent. There is no doubt that the Norman Bryans of Leinster did become O'Brien to quite a considerable extent as did an appreciable number of Westmeath O'Breens; and this also obtained in the case of a number of families in various parts of the country who bore for a while the ephemeral surname MacBrien (i.e. son of a man whose Christian name was Brian). But even deducting these we are left with at least 50,000 genuine O'Briens (to whom must be added the Considines and other offshoots of the great O'Brien sept).

Canon O'Mahony discussing the origin of surnames in the *Journal of the Cork Historical and Archaeological Society* (Vol. 14, p. 16) considers that when Irish families began to be called after certain ancestors, not only the direct descendants but also those of cousins and remote relations acquired the same surname. It is certainly difficult to believe that so many O'Briens do actually descend from one man, although it is biologically quite possible; the other extreme is certainly true, for hundreds of surnames to be found in sixteenth century documents like the Fiants – not to go any further back – have died out; and this obtains to a marked degree in the case of names quite common in Ireland at a much later date. Take, for example, the Elphin diocesan census of 1749: an astonishing number of names which occur frequently in that document are now obsolete. Some, of course, have become absorbed in commoner surnames of a somewhat similar sound, but the fact remains that a great many once numerous surnames have died out. A striking illustration of diminution is to be seen, for example, in Forstall or Forrestal, which is by no means common today, yet in 1659 Petty found it numerous in no less than seven different baronies, all in or adjacent to Co. Kilkenny. Other examples of this from the Kilkenny area are Daton (which admittedly has since sometimes become Dalton) and Cuddihy, called Quiddihy in the seventeenth century, a form still occasionally found today. Similarly in Co. Cork de Courcy was once numerous in the barony of Courcies (named from the family).

De Courcy, indeed, was a name of great prominence in' the history of Ireland at the end of the twelfth century in the person of the famous John de Courcy, conqueror of Ulster, whose descendant Lord Kingsale (a title created in 1223) is the premier baron of Ireland. There are in fact quite a number of Irish families of Norman origin, once powerful (and often numerous too) whose descendants are still to be found in this country, but which, being no longer numerous, have received only a passing reference in this or the previous volume, e.g., Aylmer, Bagot, Cheevers, Everard, Herbert and Tuite. Similarly in the thirteenth century few names are of more frequent occurrence than Babe, Bathe, Blount, Fant, Lyvet and Netterville, but these, if not extinct, are now extremely rare in Ireland. Relevant entries will be found in *The Surnames of Ireland*.

I have discussed this question with several mediaeval scholars and, reverting to O'Brien, while still unable to speak with certainty, I think it can be accepted that, even though the surname was undoubtedly assumed at some period in the middle ages by families not of Dalcassian O'Brien stock, the great majority of people so called are of that descent.

Some names are recorded by officials to whom everything Irish was unfamiliar are so much distorted as to appear to be now obsolete, though actually they do survive. The well known Limerick-Tipperary name Berkery which appears in the Elizabethan Fiants under the following forms – Mac-Berrickerey, MacBirehagree, MacBirragra, MacBirrekry, MacBirryhaggery, MacByrracha and Mac-Byrryhaggery and later, in the Jacobite attainders, as Berhagrah – is perhaps recognizable in most or all of these; one soon learns that O'Thothele is O'Toole, MacYoughgan is MacGeoghegan and Inell and Ynell are O'Neill, but only internal evidence, to be gleaned from the document in which they occur, would identify MacUhuth with MacMurrough, Macheathisi with MacCassidy (not MacCasey). Some are not so difficult as they look at first sight – Goremyn Inyenyfaderan for example: Inyeny represents *inghean uí* i.e. Miss O'; but, knowing that the lady lived in south Munster, the best I can do is to guess that Faderan is a poor phonetic attempt at the obsolete Fordhane, now Foran and Ford.

For such elucidation a knowledge of the Irish language is essential. It is equally necessary when seeking surnames embodied in place-names. With it, it is not too difficult to recognize O'Tracy in Aghyrasy or O'Teigue in Clonyhague; but there are many pitfalls in this field of enquiry, not only in the phonetic approximation of Gaelic place-names (as I pointed out in *Irish Families*) but even in apparently straightforward English ones; Gilstown in Co. Meath, for example is not the townland of the Gill family but of the Gilberts. Many place-names which appear at first sight to be formed from the combination of a surname with Bally or other topographical prefix have in fact no such connotation. For example Ballycowan (Co. Offaly) is *Baile mhic Abhainn* and has no connexion with the surname Cowan; Rathnugent is *rath na bhfuinseán* (of the ash trees); Derrydrummond incorporates the word *dromán* (a ridge); while Ballymagowan, which commemorates the family of MacGowan elsewhere, is a corruption of *baile na gcanónach* (townland of the canons) in the case of the place near Derry.

Some strange examples of distortion are found in continental records. Godinez does duty for Wadding; and, to cite one of the most fantastic of such disguises, Cien-fuegos is made to represent Keating: the explanation of this absurdity is that Keating was assumed to be *céad teine* (i.e. hundred fires) and these words were translated into Spanish. Since the publication of *Irish Families*, in which I deplored the tendency outside Ireland to mispronounce many of our old surnames, I have been told of a number of grotesque distortions to be heard in America and Australia. The fate of MacLoughlin in one case is a good example of mispronunciation: Loughlin, first shorn of its Mac was later abbreviated to Lough which was pronounced to rhyme with rough or tough instead of equating with the Scottish loch thus creating the registered surname Luff. The most ridiculous — Ossil-eevan for O'Sullivan — though vouched for by a reliable correspondent is difficult to take seriously; but I believe it is a fact that a Mr Moynihan, who does not hail from either of those countries, has publicly insisted that his name should be pronounced Minion.

Reference was made in the previous book to the number of absurd translations, or rather mis-translations, of Gaelic surnames. Genuine translations, too, are not without their humorous aspect, as when families called Fox, Badger and Rabbit are found living close together in one parish — this is an actual case mentioned to me by Mr P.J. Kennedy of Galway. There might easily have been a Hare and a Woulfe there too. Among the many interesting facts relating to Co. Galway which he has given me I may refer here to the existence around Woodford of families locally termed 'Oultucs' i.e. *Ultaigh* (Ulstermen): these include O'Reilly, MacBride, MacCabe, MacAneany, MacGuire, Clarke, Finlay, Keon, Logue and Sheridan, who are believed to have come to the district in connexion with some mid-eighteenth century iron-mining operations.

Reference has frequently been made throughout this book and in the previous volume *Irish Families* to ephemeral surnames. By the fourteenth century, though many Mac and Fitz names were ephemeral, most of those with the prefix O had become hereditary. It cannot be taken for granted, however, that every mediaeval surname with the prefix O was hereditary; many such occur in the Annals relating to a period before hereditary surnames had come into existence at all.

O was seldom the prefix used in the case of surnames derived from trades or occupations e.g. MacAteer, MacInerney and MacGowan — the rare O'Gowan is one such. In *The Father of the Brontes* by Annette B. Hopkins, Professor Kemp Malone is quoted as suggesting that Bronte (which is of course an affected form of Prunty) is formed from the word *proinntighe*, i.e. the genitive case of *proinnteach* (refectory), a suggestion which was made by Fr Woulfe nearly sixty years ago. From this it could follow that Prunty is not really an O' name, the O being a corruption of the article — an, a'. Woulfe gives a similar explanation of the Co. Down name O'Prey, but this is not accepted by modern scholars. Neither Mac nor O is found in Irish surnames formed from places, which are rare in Ireland though they constitute the most numerous of all types of surname in England. The assumption of such names in mediaeval Ireland, except to the limited extent it was induced in the Pale by the Statute of Kilkenny (1367), was in fact almost entirely confined to Anglo-Norman families. The process is well illustrated in the case of Preston in England. As late as the middle of the fourteenth century, members of this great family were still known there as Adam son of Philip, Roger son of Adam and so on, but on coming to Ireland men so described were thenceforward called Adam or Roger de Preston; de Preston thus became a surname from which the *de* was in due course dropped. Most of the permanent Irish names of this class were towns and villages in France (e.g. Cusack, Nugent, Verdon) or in Britain (e.g. Hamilton, Morton, Trant). Many examples can, it is true, be cited of quasi-surnames taken from Irish towns, de Kilkenny, de Clonmel, de Callan, de Trim etc. etc., but these only survived as hereditary surnames in very few cases. I have found less than a dozen such, of which Athy, Corbally, Drumgoole, Finglas, Slane and Santry are the best known: of these Santry alone (with seven birth registrations, all in Co. Cork) is numerous enough to find a place in the statistical list officially published by Robert Matheson, who was registrar-general from 1900 to 1909. It is possible that some families called Bray may be named from the Co. Wicklow town, a few of our Nashes from Naas and our Carrs from Cahir, but the majority are no doubt respectively Ó Breaghaigh, Ashe and Ó Carra (or one of the other original forms of Carr – q.v. p. 50 *infra*). Ó Breaghaigh, though not formed from the name of a town, comes in the locative category, denoting as it does descendant of the inhabitant of the ancient Meath territory Bregia. Mac an Ultaigh (MacNulty) son of the Ulsterman and de Oirghill (Yourell), of Oriel, are similar formations in Mac and de. As I have remarked elsewhere, a number of names like Callan, Cavan, Derry, Ennis, Gorey, Kilcullen, Kilkenny, Limerick or Monaghan, without the prefix *de*, which are found as surnames in later records and in most cases are still extant, are not derived from place-names but are anglicized forms of some Gaelic patronymic of somewhat similar sound: Limerick, for example, appears as O'Limerick and O'Limbrick (i.e. Ó Luimbric) in the Hearth Money Rolls of Co. Derry (1665). The same is true of many non-Gaelic names formed from trades, employments, personal characteristics or nationality. The commonest of those found in thirteenth and fourteenth century records and still extant as surnames in Ireland today will be found in Appendix II.

The Macs present more curiosities than the O's, especially at the present day. A few long established names of English origin have fortuitously acquired an O prefix by local usage e.g. Gorham in Co. Galway – but it is very rarely that anyone has the audacity to tack on an invented O deliberately to his non-Gaelic surname. This does happen occasionally – witness a marriage recorded in 1794 between Mr P. O'Plunkett and Miss Swords. With Mac it is not so unusual, as a run through that section of a modern directory will show. Here again it is unwise to jump to conclusions. MacEvatt, MacFarrington, MacGeorge, MacGilton may be cases in point, but equally unGaelic-looking names can prove to be distortions of true Gaelic ones: MacStay (Co. Down), for example, bears little resemblance to its earlier anglicized form O'Mustey and still less to its Gaelic original Ó Maoilstéighe; or MacCluggage (Co. Tyrone) which Woulfe gives as Mac Lúcáis, but Mr T. Ó Raifeartaigh, whose knowledge of his native Co. Tyrone is profound, thinks may be the anglicized form of MacClogaid (from *clogad*, a helmet); or, again, if not actually of Gaelic origin, they may be names of long Gaelic usage, e.g. MacCutcheon, alias MacQuestion (i.e. Mac Uistin, for which Houston in Donegal is a synonym of MacTaghlin – Mac Giolla tSeachlainn. Mac Houston occurs among the names of the Derry Jacobites attainted after the defeat of James II. The form MacCutcheon had already come into use by 1663 as it so appears in the Donegal Hearth Money Rolls; MacQuiston was more usual especially in other Ulster counties as the anglicized form. MacKeeman (i.e. Mac Shíomoin, a Gaelic variant of FitzSimon) or MacKillop (i.e. MacPhilip) are other examples.

The improper assumption of O has occurred sometimes with Gaelic agnomina like Kinsella, and occasionally with Norman names such as Prendergast and Taaffe; but in most cases this has gradually arisen through the dropping of the M in Mac in the spoken language in many parts of the west and north. The Norman Jennings, *gaelice* Mac Sheoinín (in which the aspirated S is almost silent), will illustrate the changes such names underwent: Mac Sheoinin – 'ac Sheoinin – 'acHeoneen – 'acKeoneen – O'Keoneen. This tendency is not unknown in Gaelic surnames e.g. Costigan and Gannon. It must also be remembered that seventeenth century officials were inexact and frequently confused Mac and O. As we have seen elsewhere they entered the O'Connors of Co. Clare far more often as MacConnor than O'Connor in the 1659 'census'.[1] Such errors were usually not perpetuated by the families concerned, but many instances of permanent acceptance of such interchange could be given, such as MacLoughlin for O'Melaghlin or, conversely O'Gorman for MacGorman. Many examples, too, will be found, in this and *Irish Families*, of surnames with which both prefixes were almost indifferently used.

1. I have referred to this throughout the book as the census of 1659 as it was published under that title. In view of recent research, however, we can be sure that it was not actually a census but was compiled from the Poll Tax returns if 1660, made for Sir William Petty.

THE CHIEFTAINRIES

he use of the word 'The' as a prefix to a surname to indicate that the user is the head or chief of a sept comprising the bearers of that name is a comparatively modern practice, but the existence of the chieftainries so denoted makes an examination of its historical background essential.

To understand this one must glance back to the early mediaeval period when Ireland was administered by one legal system viz. the Brehon Code, Brehon being a word formed from the Irish *breitheamhan*, the genitive of *breitheamh*, meaning lawgiver or judge. That profession was of great importance and was usually the prerogative of certain families such as the MacClancys for the O'Brien dynasty and the well-known O'Dorans of Leinster. The Brehon Code differed in some essentials from the feudal system which obtained in western Europe. A class system, with degrees of status strictly laid down, was basic to it, but the idea of nobility as deriving from royal prerogative was absent, and so, as we will see later, was the concept of primogeniture. Briefly, the position was as follows.

There were more than a hundred petty 'kingdoms' in the country, that is to say their rulers were termed '*Rí*', the Irish word for king. They were in most cases no more than chiefs who were subject to overlords, to whom they paid tribute in the form of cattle, corn etc., and, in most cases, were liable to supply a certain number of armed men to assist the overlord when he was engaged in warfare with some other, usually neighbouring, *Rí*. The titular position of *Árd-Rí* (High King) was, generally speaking, more or less nominal. For much of the period under review the 'kings' of the northern half of the country (*Leath Cuinn*) recognized the hegemony of that O'Neill who was based on Tara and those of the southern half (*Leath Mogha*) the Rí who happened to be in power at Cashel. When one refers to an O'Neill or a MacCarthy in this connexion it is necessary to remember that surnames of the hereditary type did not come into being until the tenth century, and not widely until later. Thus the collective term Uí Néill denotes descendants of an ancestor named Niall. At one time the King of Connacht, O Connor, was paramount. The set-up of that kingship, whether as *Árd-Rí* or provincial king, may be taken as illustrating the position. The four provincial chiefs ranking as 'royal lords' under the O Connor Don, giving here the modern form of their names, were: O Mulrennan, O Finaghty, O Flanagan and MacGeraghty. Lesser chiefs associated with O Connor Don had traditional functions in his service. That these were of importance is clear from the inclusion of O Kelly (steward of the jewels), O Malley (naval), MacDermot (military) and O Mulconry (chief poet).

Actually the term Árd-Rí does not appear in the early Brehon law tracts which specify three grades of king, viz., (1) of the local *tuath* or tribal kingdom (2) of a larger territory and overlord of No. 1, (3) king of a province. Although the genealogists trace the high-kingship back to *Niall na naoi ngiallach* (referred to in English as Niall of the Nine Hostages) in the fifth century, it did not become an actuality until much later, and even such successful high-kings as Brian Boru (d. 1014), who stands 45th in their list, were far from exercising the undisputed authority associated with most monarchs in France and England. The effective kingship or principal overlordship was that of the *righte* of what were called the Cúig Cúigí, i.e. five fifths or provinces, Connacht, Leinster, Meath,

Munster and Ulster (to use the modern names) which in fact became seven due to the rise of Oriel and the further division of Ulster into two.

As might be expected, with so many semi-independent chieftainries, sporadic warfare was frequent and it sometimes occurred within the *tuath* or mini-state itself. I avoid the word tribe to translate *tuath* as it has connotations foreign to its use in this connection. In cases of that kind, fighting usually arose from the existence of rival claimants to succession after the death of the head of the group concerned. One of the main differences between the Brehon system and the feudal system was the non-existence of the principle of primogeniture in the former. The heir could be any one of the males comprised in the *deirbhfhine*, i.e. the descendants of a deceased chief to the fourth generation. The method of election varied. Tanistry, by which the heir or *táiniste* was chosen in the lifetime of the chief, was later introduced, but even so such disputes were by no means eliminated. However, it is not relevant here to explain the complicated rules which governed succession to the leadership in the various grades of social status. All were meticulously laid down in the written Brehon Code.

These minor wars had little effect on the cultural development of the country over a period of five or six hundred years before the coming of the Cambro-Normans in 1169. Poetry, art and genealogy flourished and missionary expeditions helped to keep Christianity alive in other countries where it had been threatened by the Goths and other marauders from northern Europe. Even the frequent incursions of the Norsemen, which caused much destruction especially to monastic buildings and treasures, did not at all affect the social system of Gaelic Ireland. The Norsemen, however, were responsible for one innovation in a community which was essentially rural, viz. the establishment of towns, as they founded several, notably Dublin, Waterford, Cork and Limerick. The introduction of this foreign element in the population — not throughout the country but in isolated coastal settlements — did little to unite the Irish kingdoms in opposition to it: in the famous battle of Clontarf, in which in 1014 the Irish forces under Brian Boru finally ended any hope the Norsemen had of dominating the country, it is to be remembered that some Irish septs actually fought on the Norse side against their own Árd-Rí.

Brian Boru (i.e. Boroimhe — of the tributes) was the first man of any lineage other than O Neill or O Conor to become High-King, and this position was obtained by force. His race, the Dál Cais, were originally a comparatively small population group located in Thomond (*Tuadh Mhumhain*, north Munster), mainly the present county of Clare.

Up to 1169, while predatory expeditions had from time to time been made by Irish raiders in Wales and even England, Ireland had seldom if ever been subjected to incursions by English forces. It was an Irish king, Dermot MacMurrough of Leinster, who was responsible for what was indeed a turning point in the history of the country, when he sought and obtained the aid of Henry II of England in his own struggle for the retention of his Leinster kingdom — it resulted in the invasion under Richard de Clare, Earl of Pembroke, known as Strongbow, and the subsequent permanent settlement of the Norman element in Ireland. These twelfth century invaders, it should be remembered, were French-speaking Cambro-Normans from Wales.

Their coming heralded the first significant change in the composition of the aristocracy in Ireland. Henry II of England, with the imprimatur of Pope Adrian IV (the only Englishman ever to become Pope), assumed the title of Lord of Ireland and many of the heads of the Irish states, regarding it as no more than a formality, acquiesced in this and continued to carry on as they had done previously. The high-kingship, however, was at an end: the last of their line was Ruaidhri Ó Conchobhair (Rory O Connor) who died in 1189.

The Norman element thus introduced became possessed of vast landed estates in various parts of the country — less in Ulster than elsewhere — but by a gradual process they became part of the Irish nation (though of course the modern concept of nationality was then as yet unthought of).

This process was threefold. Some became completely integrated, giving rise to the well known phrase 'Hiberniores Hibernis ipsis'. These formed septs on the Gaelic-Irish pattern, headed by a chief. Thus, the head of the Norman family of Wall in Co. Limerick was known as An Fáltach and the head of the Condons An Condúnach. Other families in this category were, inter alios, the Mandevilles who became MacQuillan, The Archdeacons Cody, the Berminghams Corish and the Nangles Costello. With the submergence of the Gaelic order in the seventeenth and eighteenth centuries they suffered the same fate as the indigenous septs.

Other great families which did not go so far as to adopt the Brehon system nevertheless became essentially Irish and were unaffected by the Statute of Kilkenny (1367) which vainly sought to prevent the descendants of the Norman invaders from dressing and riding in the Irish fashion or speaking the Irish language. To name the most notable of the Hiberno-Norman families, such as Barry, Dillon, de Lacy, Plunkett, Power, Prendergast and Roche would inevitably result in omitting some of equal importance, but I think it would be generally agreed that Fitzgerald, Butler and Burke were the most important.

There were two main branches of the Fitzgeralds, the head of both of which bore titles of nobility (Earls of Desmond and of Kildare) conferred on them by the King of England as Lord of Ireland. The Desmond branch were responsible in 1582 for the main Irish revolt against the extension of English power which resulted in defeat and the devastation of much of Munster. Apart from the earldom, there were two other hereditary titles borne by the Fitzgeralds of Kerry and Limerick, conferred in the fourteenth century, not by the King of England but by his representative in Ireland, which are unique and are still extent and fully recognized, viz., the Knight of Kerry and the Knight of Glin. The Fitzgeralds of Desmond (*Deas Mhumhain,* South Munster) eventually conformed and were prominent in the aristocracy of the eighteenth and nineteenth centuries. The Kildare branch found no difficulty in acknowledging the English sovereign's overlordship. One of them, Garret Fitzgerald, 9th Earl of Kildare, became the viceroy of Henry VIII (the first English soverign to be styled King, rather than Lord, of Ireland). So powerful did he become in that capacity that he was deemed a threat to royal supremacy in Ireland. Summoned to London, he languished in captivity till his death and his son, known as Silken Thomas, renounced his allegiance, went into rebellion and was eventually in 1537 executed in London with no less than five of his uncles. The family, however, was not thus entirely annihilated and later on regained their position as a leading one in the nobility of Ireland and, having become Dukes of Leinster, they occupied their mansion at Carton in Co. Kildare until quite recent times.

A third category are typified by the Butlers of Ormond (Co. Kilkenny and east Tipperary) whose titles (finally Marquis of Ormond) were equally the creation of an English monarch. While they made no attempt to become integrated, they perforce became Irish in many ways — in speaking the Irish language for example: one of them acted as interpreter at the Parliament of 1541 which was attended by the Irish-speaking chiefs as well as the English faction. For the most part, the Butlers regarded themselves as representing that section of the population having historical ties with England but distinct from the English people. To give a fair picture of them, it should be added that a number of individual Butlers are to be found in accounts of pro-Catholic activities and in the ranks of the 'Wild Geese' which will be dealt with later.

At this point it would, I think, be appropriate to refer to those prominent immigrant families who had no connection with the Cambro or Anglo-Normans and did not come to Ireland till the sixteenth century, such as the Bagenals, Edgeworths, Fleetwoods, Goldsmiths, Gwynns, Sigersons and Springs, to mention some of them. Perhaps the most remarkable of these were the Brownes. For the moment I am not referring to the Brownes of Camus, Co. Limerick, of whom were the famous Maximilian Ulysses Browne and other prominent 'Wild Geese', nor to those who in Connacht got the title Oranmore, nor again the Brownes who were one of the 'Tribes of Galway'. Those I have in mind are the Brownes of Kerry, Earls of Kenmare. They started as intrusive foreigners but following intermarriage with the O Sullivans, MacCarthys and other great Gaelic families of the area, they became before long uncompromising Catholics and suffered in their turn as such, though by reason of unusual circumstances related in *The Kenmare Manuscripts* regained and retained their vast estates in Counties Kerry and Limerick up to our own times. They, however, were never prominent in the political arena. Unlike the Brownes of Kerry, most of this class conformed at the Reformation and constituted a not inconsiderable element in the Anglo-Irish gentry of the eighteenth and nineteenth centuries. This category were in the seventeenth century termed the New English to distinguish them from the descendants of earlier invaders and settlers who had become hibernicized and espoused the Catholic cause in the wars of Cromwell and William of Orange. These were termed the Old-English.

Let us now consider the great Gaelic-Irish families and take Connacht as an example of the lordships of a province which had to a considerable extent fallen under the domination of Cambro-Norman invaders in the earlier period, these, however, having become hibernicized. Typical of the less important of these were the Nangles (de Angulo) who adopted the name MacOisdealbhaigh (modern Costello), incidentally the first non-Gaelic surname to use the Gaelic prefix Mac. At that time, Connacht included the modern county of Clare (Thomond) now in Munster, and much of Breifni (Co. Cavan) usually reckoned in Ulster. The families constituting these Lordships were, according to the *Anála Locha Cé*, Ó Ceallaigh (O Kelly) of Uí Maine, Ó Conchobhair (O Conor) in its three branches – Don (*donn*, brown) Roe (*ruadh*, red) and Sligo – MacDiarmada (MacDermot) of Moylurg, Ó Ruairc (O Rourke) of Breifni, Ó hEaghra (O Hara) of Leyney, Ó Dubhda (O Dowd) of Tireragh, Ó Flaithbheartaigh (O Flaherty) of Connemara and Ó Briain (O Brien) of Thomond, together with the three powerful branches of the de Burghs (Burke) – MacWilliam Iochtar, MacWilliam Uachtar and the Earl of Clanrickard, whose family were not so much hibernicized as the other Burkes of Connacht.

It would be helpful in presenting a picture of the Chieftainries in Ireland briefly to take one of those old Gaelic families as an illustration, and for that purpose the O'Briens of Thomond would be suitable because they were to some extent of divided allegiance. The lineal descendants of Brian Boru were hostile to the early invaders: Donal O'Brien, King of Munster, with his Dalcassian followers, was a leading figure in the successful battles against Strongbow in 1174 and Prince John in 1185. They retained the designation, King of Thomond (Tuadh Mhumhain, north Munster) and often King of all Munster, until 1543 when Morrough O Brien surrendered his 'captaincy and principality' to Henry VIII who, in accordance with the principle of 'surrender and regrant' created him Earl of Thomond. It may be noted that in the deeds conferring titles on chiefs who accepted that principle, the recipient was almost always referred to as 'chief of his name' or 'captain of his nation'. Murrough O Brien also conformed to the new Protestant religion, accepting Henry VIII instead of the Pope as head of the Church. The main branch were thereafter no longer champions of the Irish cause but, unlike many others similarly circumstanced, they did not become absentees but remained in Co. Clare, with the lesser title of Baron Inchiquin, to end as landlords of the better type. The junior branches, however, produced men who were notable as Irish patriots. Two were on the Supreme Council of the Confederation of Kilkenny (1642) and one of the most renowned regiments in the Irish army of Catholic James II against William of Orange was Clare's Dragoons – Clare being Daniel O'Brien, 3rd Viscount Clare. This regiment later became famous on the Continent and the O Briens in it, together with those who fought in the service of France at Fontenoy and elsewhere, can be counted among the more prominent of the exiles who constituted the "Wild Geese".

The flight of the Wild Geese began in earnest with the episode known as the 'Flight of the Earls' when Hugh O Neill (Earl of Tyrone) and Hugh Roe O Donnell (Earl of Tyrconnell) took ship with 99 other leading Ulster Gaels, going first to Flanders and then to Rome where the two great chiefs died. However, they left sons who, while remaining exiles, kept in touch with their own country.

From the beginning of the seventeenth century, the history of Ireland has been overshadowed by its religious or rather its denominational aspect. Up to that time, Ulster had been the most basically Irish part of Ireland, less affected than any other province by subversive incursions. The O Neills and O Donnells had maintained their real independence (even though they did accept titles of nobility from the English crown). Then, in spite of a remarkable victory over the English at the battle of the Yellow Ford in 1596, their defeat six years later at Kinsale, the last and conclusive battle of that campaign, resulted in the aforementioned "Flight of the Earls", the confiscation of their estates and the stttlement thereon of Scottish and English settlers, known as the Plantation in Ulster. This 'plantation' differed from the others inflicted on the country in that not only the land-owning class was wiped out but the smaller occupiers of land were forced to move from their holdings to patches of unprofitable mountain and boggy land.

Forty years after the destruction of the old order in Ulster came the Cromwellian Transplantation to Connacht and Clare which resulted in the confiscation of the estates of great numbers of Catholic landowners and their settlement in smaller holdings in the West or in many cases their exile. Though it was found impracticable to carry it out with the full severity originally intended, it did amount to a national upheaval and where the victims did not voluntarily find their way to exile in France and other European countries it inevitably resulted in a reduction of their social status in Ireland. This policy had first been attempted in the previous century with the Plantation of Leix and Offaly, then renamed Queen's County and King's County in commemoration of Queen Mary I and her Spanish husband, Philip. Though it caused much temporary disturbance it had little permanent effect on the majority of the inhabitants; and two chiefs concerned, O More and O Connor Faly never submitted, but the latter died and the O Mores went to Co. Kerry where they sank to minor importance.

The third war of the seventeenth century was fought between James II and William of Orange for the crown of England, and nominally of Ireland too. Patrick Sarsfield's heroic exploits, after James II had fled to France following his defeat at the Battle of the Boyne in 1690, secured the just Treaty of Limerick. Limerick was long called the 'city of the broken treaty' because its terms were not kept by England, and the enactment soon after of the very severe anti-Catholic Penal Laws completed the débacle. So Patrick Sarsfield, Earl of Lucan, and his men became yet another major contingent of the Wild Geese.

The overall position is thus concisely presented by Stephen Gwynn in his *History of Ireland* (p. 327) where he says 'what happened in the seventeenth century was not merely the transfer of property from certain persons to others; nor even the penalizing of one religion which was that of the vast majority, and endowing that of a minority at the general expense. It was the destruction of a ruling class in a country which was still aristocratic; it was depriving Ireland of its natural leaders — that is of those leaders whom Ireland willingly recognized'.

Literally hundreds of thousands of Irish men went to Europe, mainly to France, in the century and a half between the Cromwellian war in Ireland and the French Revolution; however, we are concerned here with the chiefs, not with the great majority who were of lesser rank, many of whom became officers of distinction in the armies of France, Spain and Austria.

We have now to consider the present Irish 'Chiefs of the Name'. I have discussed the question of these titles, or rather designations, in one of the introductory articles in *Burke's Irish Family Records* (1976) where I stated that those set out below are officially recognized as authentic, their descent by primogeniture from the last formally inaugurated chief having been exhaustively researched by the Genealogical Office, formerly the Office of Arms. That institution, which was founded in 1552, became during the period of the Union (1800-1921), a British Government office, and so did not recognize the Irish chieftainries except in one case: in 1900 O Connor Don was granted supporters and at the coronation of Edward VII he was officially appointed to carry the standard of Ireland in the ceremonies on that occasion.

The last official statement of authentic chiefs was made in 1956. It has been brought up to date in a work entitled *The Irish Chiefs* by C. Eugene Swezey (New York, 1974) where information regarding present addresses, heirs, arms etc., will be found. In that work the prefix 'The' before the surname is given because it has long been used in English to designate them (as it was in Irish in the case of hibernicized Norman septs). In their signatures, however, the surname alone is used without Christian name.

Briefly those now officially recognized are:

O'Brien of Thomond	Fox (An Sionnach)[1]
O Callaghan	MacGillycuddy of the Reeks
O Conor Don	O Grady of Kilballyowen
MacDermot of Coolavin	O Kelly of Gallagh
MacDermot Roe	O Morchoe
O Donell of Tirconnell	MacMorrough Kavanagh
O Donoghue of the Glens	O Neill of Clanaboy
O Donovan	O Toole of Fir Tire

Before the final submergence of the Brehon system there were, needless to say, many more recognized chiefs than the sixteen listed above who have actually substantiated their claim in recent times. Sixteenth century sources, such as the State Papers and the Fiants, show that, apart from the hibernicized Norman families already mentioned, the heads of the following families were there referred to as chiefs: MacArtan (now MacCartan), MacAuliffe, MacAuley, MacClancy, MacCarthy Mor, MacCarthy Reagh, MacCoghlan, MacDonagh, MacGeoghegan, MacGilpatrick (Fitzpatrick), MacGorman, MacGrath, MacGuinness, MacGuire, MacKenna, MacKiernan, MacKinnane (Ford), MacLoughlin, MacMahon, MacManus, Macnamara, MacRory, O Beirne, O Boyle (no connection with the English name Boyle, borne by the Earl of Cork), O Brennan, O Byrne, O Cahan (Kane), O Carroll, O Clery, O Connell, O Connolly, O Conor Faly, O Conor Roe, O Conor Sligo, O Daly, O Dempsey, O Devlin, O Doherty, O Dowd, O Driscoll, O Dunn, O Dwyer, O Farrell, O Flaherty, O Folane, O Gara, O Hagan, O Hanlon, O Hara, O Heyne, O Keeffe, O Kennedy, O Loughlin, O Madden, O Mahony, O Malley, O Mannin, O Melaghlin, O Molloy, O More, O Mulryan (Ryan), O Mulvey, O Nolan, O Phelan, O Reilly, O Rourke, O Shaughnessy, O Sheridan, O Sullivan Beare, O Sullivan Mór.

---

1. The original surname of this Fox family was Ó Catharnaigh (anglice O Kearney or Carney). The ancestor of 'An Sionnach' (The Fox) had the agnoman *Sionnach*, i.e. fox, and this in some places developed into a distinct surname Ó Sionnaigh.

ABBOTT This well-known English name is in Ireland since the fourteenth century and is now quite numerous in Dublin. It is usually of the nickname type. In Irish the form Abóid is used. Woulfe states that Abbott (a common Anglo-Irish surname) is a derivative of Abraham; but Reaney gives it its obvious meaning, adding that such surnames often originated as nicknames.

(Mac) ABRAHAM Woulfe correctly states that the surname Abraham has been in Ireland since the thirteenth century but gives the Irish form as identical with the English. The Jewish origin thus implied is seldom if ever applicable: the true origin in Ireland is from the Gaelic-Irish Mac an Bhreitheamhan, otherwise Bhreitheamhnaigh (son of the judge), which was first variously anglicized Macavrehan, Mac a' brehon and so to MacAbrehon. In speech the emphasis was on breh, not on A, but the Anglo-Norman clerks who kept most of the official records, being unaware of this, would be misled by the written word and so almost inevitably transcribed it as MacAbraham. In the long list of adherents of Rory O'Donnell who followed him from Tirconnell to Connacht in 1603 we find one Gillegroma MacAbrehan. The usual modern forms are Breheny and Judge, but as a surname Abraham is found today in small numbers in the south-eastern counties. Many examples of the name Abraham in mediaeval Ireland are to be found in such sources as the Ormond Deeds, Justiciary Rolls, Register of the Hospital of St. John the Baptist, Archbishop Swayne's Register etc. As early as 1287 there is a record of a grant to "Gilbert MacAbram, an Irishman" and his children to use English law, and a few years later the name MacAbraham appears again in the diocese of Cloyne.

A distinguished bearer of the name in modern times was William Abraham, Bishop of Waterford and Lismore from 1829 to 1837. Map

ADAIR The name Adair appears frequently in various Irish records since the beginning of the seventeenth century. It is said to have been used as the anglicized form of the old Irish surname Ó Daire, of which, however, there is little recorded in the mediaeval period. It occurs as O'Daury and O'Dawry in late sixteenth century Fiants in Co. Offaly. Dáire is an old Irish personal name.

Subsequently the name is associated mainly with Scottish families settled in Ulster. William Adair, of Wigtownshire, settled at Ballymacloss, Co. Antrim, and became a denizen of Ireland at Ballymena in 1614. There is a pedigree of this family in the Genealogical Office and many references are to be found to them and their estates in Ulster and Queens Co. (Leix) from the seventeenth century down to recent times: prior to the Land Acts of the late nineteenth century they possessed 25,000 acres in Donegal and Leix. Numerically the name belonged later to Antrim and adjacent counties throughout that period. In 1659 the "census" of that date recorded a number of tituladoes called Adair and Adaire there, and Adire (sic) is recorded in the same document as a principal name in the barony of Antrim,

Scottish and Irish being classed together in that case. The name is also of frequent occurrence in the Hearth Money Rolls for the north-eastern counties. Patrick Adair, the author of The True Narrative of the Rise and Progress of the Presbyterian Church in Ireland, came from Scotland to Co. Antrim about 1641. At that time Robert Adair held a small estate in Co. Antrim and a large one in Scotland. Archibald Adair, "a patriotic Scotsman," was made Dean of Raphoe in 1622, became Protestant Bishop of Killala in 1630, was prosecuted by Strafford for "incitement to rebellion" and deposed, later to be transferred to the see of Waterford. One may assume that the inclusion of Andrew Adaire among the 1641 Protestant proprietors in the parish of Templemurry, Co. Mayo, was not unconnected with the bishop's sojourn in that part of the country.

Robin Adair, made famous by the popular ballad set to the air of "Eileen Aroon," is regarded by many people as a more or less legendary Scotsman. Actually he was a real person, an Irishman of Leinster—indeed one might almost say he was two such persons. There were two authentic eighteenth century characters called Robin Adair and each has since been claimed as the hero of the ballad. One was Robin Adair of Hollybrook, near Bray, the head of a Dublin firm of wine merchants (Aldridge, Adair and Butler), a convivial sportsman whose harp was of sufficient interest to be described by Petrie in his essay on that instrument. His son John Adair (d. 1769), of Kilternan, is mentioned in another popular ballad "Kilruddery Hunt." Robert Adair M.P. (d. 1737) was of this family. The other Robin Adair for whom ballad fame is claimed was born about 1714 and died in 1790: at the age of 22 he got into trouble in his native city of Dublin where he was a medical student, rose to be surgeon-colonel in the British army and, having declined a baronetcy, ended his life as an honorary member of the College of Surgeons, Ireland. Lady Caroline Keppel, whom he eventually married, is said to have written the words of the ballad while well nigh heart-broken on account, of the opposition of her family to the match. Their son, Sir Robert Adair (1763-1855), was a notable member of the British diplomatic corps and close friend of Charles James Fox. James Adair (c.1709-c.1783), pioneer Indian trader and author of The History of the American Indians was born in Co. Antrim. Map

MacADAM MacCADDEN ADAMS At the present

time the name MacAdam is chiefly associated with Co. Monaghan where, as well as in Dublin city, it was also quite numerous in the seventeenth century. Prior to that we must look elsewhere for prominent persons of the name. In Co. Cork a branch of the Barrys of Rathcormac assumed this surname which was formed from the christian name of their ancestor. In the early seventeenth century we find them, for example in the Carew Papers, often called Barry alias MacAdam. In 1598 Barry of Rathcormac was styled MacAdam Barry. As MacAdam is now a name scarcely known in that county it can be assumed that these families resumed their original patronymic Barry. In the same way MacAdams, descendants of several Norman settlers called Adam, were widespread in Co. Mayo in the seventeenth century particularly in the barony of Clanmorris, but have since resumed their several original surnames. Some at least of the MacAdams of Dublin were of Scottish descent.

Two brothers, Robert S. MacAdam (1808-1895), Gaelic scholar and founder of the Ulster Journal of Archaeology, and James MacAdam (1801-1861), noted geologist, were born in Belfast.

The extent to which the name MacAdam was at various times distributed over widely separated parts of the country is exemplified by the location of various place names. Ballymacadam is found near Tralee and near Clogheen, Castlemacadam in the Rathdrum area, Cadamstown is in Co. Kildare, not to mention six Adamstowns in different counties which are presumably called after planter families of Adams having no connexion with Adam.

John O'Donovan, in his Ordnance Survey letters, mentions the name MacAdhaimh which he found in Co. Cavan. This is a variant of MacAdam pronounced and now spelt MacCaw.

Finally it should be mentioned that when MacAdam occurs in Co. Armagh it is nearly always a corruption of MacCadden. This is Mac Cadáin in Irish, and is derived from the obsolete Irish forename Cadán. This sept is entirely distinct from the MacAdams dealt with above. The MacCaddens of Co. Armagh were an old erenagh family and in the form MacCoddan it appears in the church lands inquisition of 1609 and it is one of the most numerous names in the Hearth Money Rolls for Co. Armagh. Father George Codan, O.F.M., Armagh, was the author of a Gaelic poem in honour of Ormond in 1680.

Adams is seldom used as a synonym of MacAdam. It has become numerous in modern times in Ulster, where it is also occasionally found as a variant of Aidy and Eadie. Its connection with Ireland goes back to mediaeval times. Fifteen placenames incorporating the surname Adams (all in Leinster or Munster) are listed in the modern townlands index—all named at latest in the seventeenth century—of which seven Adamstowns are mentioned in the sixteenth century Fiants; the "census" of 1659 lists three tituladoes (in Dublin, Cork and Coleraine); and the name Adams occurs fourteen times in the estate and army records of a few years later. Bibl.

ADRAIN, O'Drean ADRIAN The old Irish surname

Ó Dreáin, first anglicized O'Drean and O'Dreyne, became Adrain when the English language was widely introduced into Ulster after the seventeenth century Plantation, and in due course this in turn was usually shortened to Drain or Drean, or sometimes changed to Adrian; Adrian is normally of entirely different origin, being derived from the Latin Adrianus or Hadrianus. Adrain has for centuries been regarded as an Ulster name, but it originated in Co. Roscommon, where the O'Dreanes were chiefs of Calry and erenaghs of Ardcarne in the barony of Boyle until dispossessed by the MacDermotts. The last mention of them as such in the Annals is for the year 1241. By 1659 they were so well established in east Ulster that we find a townland in Co. Down in Petty's "census" called Ballydraine (i.e. Ballydrain in the parish of Tullynakill). Several families of the name, written in the Hearth Money Rolls of the 1660's as O'Drean and Adreane, were living in Co. Down and south Antrim at that time.

The best known man of the name was Robert Adrain (1775-1843), who was born at Carrickfergus, Co. Antrim: he was a noted mathematician in America, whither he had escaped after taking part and being wounded in the Insurrection of 1798.

AGNEW This name, which is a true Gaelic one, affords a good example of distortion in the process of phonetic anglicization. Originally Ó Gnimh, it was first written O'Gnive in English. The form O'Gnimh occurs as late as 1685 in a list of Irish Franciscan friars in which the names are all given in aglicized form (when not in Latin). A variant of O'Gnive, O'Gnyw, to be found in the Elizabethan Fiants, through the influence of the written word on pronounciation became O'Gnew; the northern tendency to slur or shorten the prefix caused this to be sounded a'Gnew, hence the modern form Agnew. In the Ulster Inquisitions it is always O'Gneeve, yet forty years later (1665) the Hearth Money Rolls for the north-eastern counties give 19 families of Agnew and no O'Gneeve. In the 1659 "census" Agnew, so spelt then, was one of the principal Irish names in the baronies of Glencarn and Belfast; and to-day ninety per cent of the Agnews in Ireland were born in Co. Antrim or in one of the other counties adjacent to the city of Belfast. It is somewhat surprising, therefore, to find that one Thomas O'Gnew was hanged for robbery and murder in Co. Waterford (in 1314). This O'Gnew was apparently of different stock: a family of Ó Gnimha was located near Doneraile, Co. Cork, from about 1200.

Dr. Hayes-McCoy states that Agnews came from Scotland as a family of mercenary soldiers and settled in Antrim, having presumably originally been among the Irish colonizers of Scotland. Their lands were around Larne and also in the north of the county. Their importance in Ireland, however, is in the cultural rather than the military sphere, since the O'Gnives were undoubtedly hereditary poets to the O'Neill chieftains in the mediaeval period, and the best known of these, Fearflatha O'Gnive (c.1580-c.1640), was still flourishing for some time after the Plantation of Ulster. The most distinguished of the name in modern times was Antrim-born Sir James Willson Agnew M.D. (1815-1901), who was Premier of Tasmania.

There was a Norman family of D'Agneaux which came to Ulster at the time of the invasion and acquired the lordship of Larne. This name in due course also became Agnew. One of them was a wholehearted adherent of Edward Bruce in his attempt to obtain the crown of Ireland (1315-1318). In 1641 Capt. Agnew fought against the Ulster insurgents but by that time the headquarters of his family had been removed to Scotland. Nevertheless the connexion with Ireland continued and prior to the Land Acts of 1870 to 1903 the Agnews held over 10,000 acres of valuable property near Larne.

Agnews of Ulster ancestry were prominent in the history of Pennsylvania in the eighteenth and nineteenth centuries. Bibl.

AIKEN Woulfe's treatment of this name illustrates a weakness in the work of that great worker in the field of Irish nomenclature. In his preliminary summary (p.79) he states that Aiken is Ó hAodhagáin in Irish, and in his article under that head (p.557) he gives Eakin as one of the anglicized forms of that name (O'Hagan). Incidentally he does not mention Aiken there, but that is immaterial. The weakness lies in the fact that he gives the impression that Aiken is of Irish origin, for he nowhere tells the reader that Aiken is an English name—or more accurately the Scottish form of the English Aitken. It is quite possible that a family called Ó'Hagan may have changed their name to Aiken, though I have found no evidence of this: it is, however, indisputable that the vast majority of Aikens of whom records were preserved were settlers in Ulster. The earliest reference I have found in past records is to William Ekyn, lessee on the Cunningham estate in 1613—all the other names in that list are English or Scottish. Next we meet an Englishman, Robert Akin, who was murdered at Sligo, in 1642. In 1676 Alexander Aicken, a soldier in the King's Guard of Horse, is stated to have been born in Co. Down about 1640. In 1659 Robert Ekin was a householder in Copper Alley, Dublin. From that on the name occurs fairly frequently in testamentary records etc., rarely outside Ulster.

The various forms of the name mentioned above are still extant to-day: Ekin occurs as synonymous with Aiken at Letterkenny, and Eakin is so found in both Counties Derry and Donegal.

The outstanding persons of the name are Dr. Joseph Aiken, author of "Londerias", a description in verse of the siege of Derry from the Protestant defender's point of view, published a few years after that event; and Frank Aiken, Irish Minister for External Affairs, whose work at the United Nations was notable.

MacALINDEN MacALINION (O) MULDERRIG
Woulfe considers MacAlinden (Mac Giolla Fhindéin) and MacAlinion (Mac Giolla Fhinnéin) to be variants, deriving both from St. Finian. Mr. T. O Raifeartaigh, however, states that the former is MacGiolla Fhiondain (the

saint there being presumably St. Fintan of Clonenagh) and the latter Mac Giolla Fhinnen (the saint honoured in that case being the famous St. Finnén of Clonard); in support of this view it may be observed that MacAlinden and MacAlinion are seldom if ever used as synonyms; and moreover MacAlinion belongs almost exclusively to Co. Fermanagh, whereas families called MacAlinden are located, or at any rate originated, in the eastern part of Oriel – Counties Armagh and south Down. The ubiquitous English surname Leonard has unfortunately largely superseded MacAlinion in modern times; formerly it was written MacEllinan, MacGillinan, MacLinnen etc., while the modern synonyms of MacAlinden include, besides mere variant spellings, Linden and Glendon, which in the Jacobite lists of the late seventeenth century is always given as MacLyndon. It is MacElenan and MacElynan in the Fermanagh Inquisitions taken in the 1620s and 1630s. They were an important sept in the heyday of the Gaelic order; like the O'Gallaghers and O'Dohertys of Tirconnell they claim descent from Niall of the Nine Hostages and their territory was in Co. Fermanagh, their chief being styled Lord of Lough Erne. Their eponymous ancestor was Giolla Finden O'Muldory.

O'Muldory (Ó Maoldoraidh), once a great name in Tirconnel, is now almost extinct—a few representatives of the sept (apart from the MacAlinions) may survive under the name of Mulderry. This, however, must not be confused with Mulderrig (Ó Maoildeirg), a Mayo name now often disguised under the anglicized synonyms Reddington and Rutledge. It would not be out of place to observe here that Mulderrig is quite distinct from another Mayo name Derrig (Ó Deirg) which is that of an old Ui Fiachrach family at Killala.

The Gaelic poet Padraig Mac Giolla Fhionndain (c. 1647-1732) is best known for his elegy on Séamus Mac Curta. There is a poem by his sister Máire Nic Alindon in Hyde's Love Songs of Connacht. Map

MacALISTER MacEllistrum The MacAlisters are usually regarded as a branch of the Scottish MacDonalds, and it is true that in historical times they did come to Ireland from Scotland. Nevertheless they are Irish Gaels by origin since they descend from Colla Uais, eldest of the famous three Collas of Oriel. The name does occur in Ireland occasionally in the early middle ages—a Mac Alister, for instance, was a witness to a deed of King Roderic O'Connor in 1176—but it was not until the fourteenth century that they became established as an Irish sept in north-east Ulster, having come over first as gallóglaigh (galloglasses), chiefly in the service of the MacDonnells. In 1578 a MacDonnell known as Turlogh óg MacAlexander appears as a leading galloglass captain in Leinster and in the previous decade MacAlister Gallda was similarly prominent in Ulster. The well known martial air "MacAllistrum's March" is believed to have derived its name from one of these.

In the 1659 "census" MacAlister is very numerous in Co. Antrim, and it also appears as a principal Irish surname in Co. Derry. In our own time over ninety per cent of the name come from that part of the country.

In Co. Down variants like MacCallister, MacLester and even Lester are found. The Kerry surname MacEllistrum has been sometimes recorded in the birth registers as MacAlister: these two surnames have a common origin etymologically, the Gaelic Mac Alastair and Mac Alastruim both meaning son of Alexander. The Munster branch has long been settled in Co. Kerry where in 1579 and subsequent years of Elizabeth I's reign several members of the family are included in the pardons of that period. The seat of the head of the family was Castle MacEllistrum, near Tralee.

Neither name is prominent in the disturbed years of the seventeenth century. One Archibald MacAlister was quarter-master in Tyrconnell's Regiment of Horse in King James II's army and two of the names are among the forfeiting proprietors of Co. Antrim after 1691. In the next century two are noteworthy: Oliver MacAlister, who was born in Co. Louth about 1715, occupied the unusual position of secret agent both for France and England at the same time; while Sam MacAllister, a deserter from the Antrim militia who was killed at the battle of Derrynamuch, took a heroic part in the 1798 Insurrection. In more modern times George MacAllister (1786-1812) church decorator, Alexander MacAlister (1844-1919), anatomist and Egyptologist, and his son Professor Robert Alexander MacAlister (1871-1950), the archaeologist, all born in Dublin but of Scottish ancestry, were men of outstanding attainments.   Map

ALLEN   MacELLIN   The majority of Allens in Ireland are doubtless of English or Scottish origin; but there are some families of the name who can claim to be indigenous Irish. Ó hAillín, anglicized as Hallion and Allen, was found formerly in counties Tipperary and Offaly, and Allen has also been used in the neighbourhood of Cashel as a substitute of Hallinan, Many of the English Allens came to Ireland under the Cromwellian régime, but of course there were earlier immigrants from England, notably Wolsey's creature John Allen or Alen (1476-1534) whose "Register," compiled when he was archbishop of Dublin, is a valuable source of information about mediaeval Ireland—he became Lord Chancellor of Ireland and was assassinated by the followers of Lord Thomas FitzGerald.

MacAilin is Scottish, being the name of a warlike branch of the Campbells, who were brought to Ulster by the O'Donnells in the stormy sixteenth century. These survive there as MacAllens and Allens today. Woulfe includes MacEllin among the anglicized forms of Mac Ailin, thus treating it as a galloglass origin. MacEllin, however, was a small distinct sept located on the borders of Mayo and Roscommon. The name in various spellings—MacEllen, MacAlyan etc.—occurs frequently in the Fiants of the 1580s dealing with that area. Contemporary references to Mac Ailin in the Four Masters are to the galloglass (Campbell) family in Ulster.

In addition to the archbishop mentioned above, the best known Allen in Irish history is probably William Philip Allen (1848-1867), one of the "Manchester Martyrs". Another adherent of the national cause was John Allen (d.1850) who was associated with Robert Emmet in 1803.   Bibl.

MacANDREW   ROSS   The MacAndrews, of Norman origin (in Irish MacAindriu), are a branch of the Barretts of Bac, Co. Mayo. In the course of time they became practically an Irish sept, having a well defined territory on the eastern side of Lough Conn. So numerous were they in the seventeenth century that they occupy half a column of the large page index of the Mayo Book of Survey and Distribution. They appear in it also under the synonym FitzAndrew. Similarly it is one of the most numerous names in Strafford's Inquisition of Co. Mayo, made in 1635. Though not so numerous now, they are still concentrated in Co. Mayo and all the sixteen Mac Andrew births registered in 1890 were in that county: the 1864-1866 registers reveal an almost similar position at that time.

Up to the end of the seventeenth century the name was also well known in Co. Kerry. In 1597 three Mac Andrews of that county were attainted, in 1622 we meet a MacAndrew of Ardfert, and their association with that part of the country is testified by the place-name Ballymacandrew in the Tralee area. They were presumably a branch of the Fitzgeralds who have since resumed their original patronymic. At one time MacAindréis, anglicized MacAndrew, was adopted as a Gaelic patronymic by the Scottish family of Ross; their descendants appear to have resumed the surname Ross, which is numerous in Ireland, especially in Ulster; of the 90 Ross births registered in 1866, 70 were in that province and in 1890 the proportion is much the same. The only county outside Ulster with any considerable number is Cork.   Map

ANGLIN, Anglim   This is an O name, Ó hAngluinn in Irish, but the prefix has long been discarded and I think never resumed. In Griffith's Co. Cork Valuation (1851-53) Angland is the most numerous form. In the Fiants we meet the early anglicized forms O'Hanglen, ny Anglyn etc. and also Angiant, Angyllant, Anglound. These are nearly all in Co. Cork, and it is in that county, and adjacent areas of neighbouring counties, the name occurs in wills, marriage licence bonds etc., of the seventeenth and eighteenth centuries, and there it is almost exclusively found today. The earliest relevant reference I have met is in the Four Masters, under date 1490, i.e. to Fionn Ó hAnghluinn, chief tympanist of Ireland, but his homeland is not there recorded.

ARCHER   Though prominently identified with Kilkenny from the middle of the thirteenth century, Archers were settled in Ireland before that; in Dublin, where Ralph Larcher (or le Archer) was a burgess in 1190, and a few years later in Westmeath, in which county the place-name Villa Archeriorum (Archerstown) is recorded in 1221. As well as another Archerstown, place-names in or near the city of Kilkenny include Archersgrove, Archersleas and Archersrath.   Bibl., Map

ARDAGH This is one of the small number of Irish surnames derived from a place-name. (Matheson was wrong in placing Kilkenny, Limerick, Cavan and Monaghan in this toponymic category.) There are parishes called Ardagh in five different counties, and, of course, the diocese of Ardagh and Clonmacnois. That in Meath is not far from Co. Louth. At present the name is rare and scattered, but formerly it was mainly associated with Co. Louth, where it occurs in legal and ecclesiastical records quite frequently from 1299, when Richard Ardagh, also called de Ardagh, was a Co. Louth juror. Several similar instances are to be found in the next century, e.g. in the Justiciary Rolls in the fifteenth century we find John Ardagh a chaplain in the diocese of Armagh, which includes Co. Louth, and a Walter Ardagh in the muster of archers at Mellifont in 1434. In 1541 again, Robert Ardagh of Disert, Co Louth, was another priest: and so on up to the seventeenth century, after which the name is found in all the provinces, but not at all numerous in any of them. Griffith's Valuation reveals that there were eleven families of Ardagh in Co. Waterford in 1850, one of which had a very considerable property there. And there General Sir John Charles Ardagh (1840-1907) was born: he distinguished himself in the British Service in India; while another Waterford man, Rev. Samuel Ardagh (1803-1869), was prominent in Canada.

ARDILL Apart from Dublin, where names from all the provinces are to be found, Ardill is mainly associated with north Tipperary. This location makes it unlikely that it is an abbreviation of MacArdle, though the townland of Ballyardell in Co. Down presumably derives from that surname. Matheson records Ardell and Ardhill as variant spellings of Ardill. The best authorities on the subject do not mention these.

In the list of United Irishmen returned by Thomas Collins, Mr. Ardill, an attorney of Longford St, Dublin, is mentioned.

MacARDLE CARDWELL MacArdle is the most usual modern spelling of this name, which is also written MacArdell and, in the Newry area, MacCardle. Woulfe mentions Cardwell as another variant but it is worth noting that in Co. Down the name Cardwell has been reported by local registrars as interchangeable with Carroll, not with MacArdle. Incidentally, it may be observed that the English name Cardwell is synonymous with Caldwell, a locative surname–at the cold well. There is only one form in Irish, viz. Mac Árdghail. By tradition a branch of the MacMahons of Oriel, the sept belongs by historical association to that territory; this is also the case to-day, for it is mostly found in Counties Monaghan, Armagh and Louth. The Hearth Money Rolls again indicate that MacArdill, with its variant spellings such as MacCardill, was one of the commonest names in those counties in the seventeenth century; this is confirmed by Petty's "census" of 1659, which indeed records the name as even outnumbering O'Hanlon in the barony of Dundalk.

James MacArdle (c. 1729-1765) is notable for his work as an engraver. Another James MacArdle (fl. 1700-1725) was a Gaelic poet of the Fews, Co. Armagh, a contemporary of Patrick MacAlinden (q.v), who married Siobhán nic Árdghail (Johanna MacArdle) herself a poetess. Map

MacAREE Woulfe gives MacHarry and Maharry among the synonyms of MacAree, but these are recorded by Matheson as having being used synonymously with Garry and MacIlharry, not with Mac Aree. Naturally Mac Aree appears to be Mac an Ríogh, son of the king, and consequently has been changed to King by translation or, if Woulfe is right, I should say by pseudo-translation. This change is recorded from Co. Monaghan and its vicinity, which is the part of the country in which the name Macaree is almost exclusively found. I presume Woulfe had some evidence for his statement that the correct Irish form of MacAree is Mac Fhearadhaigh but I am not able to confirm or refute that.

ARGUE This rare name has attracted considerable attention on account of the existence of a Sligo firm of solicitors called Argue and Phibbs–a remarkable enough title for members of the legal profession to be almost a tourist attraction. The founder of the firm was not a Sligo man but came from Co. Cavan, the place of origin of all Argue families, few of which today are to be found far from their original homeland. In Co. Leitrim, close to Co. Cavan, there is a place called Killargue or Killarga, but according to O'Donovan this is named not from the family but from an obscure Saint Fearga. I have little doubt that Argue is an anglicization of some Gaelic-Irish surname but cannot say for certain what is its original form, possibly MacGiolla Fhearga. A Fiant of 1591 mentions a Mahon O'Haraga but this man was from Co. Clare or Galway. In 1751 both Harachy and O'Harachy appear in a list relating to Stanorlar, Co. Donegal, which again is a long way from Co. Cavan. Argue is not an English surname, though Argument is found there (a corruption of the French place-name Aigremont).

MacATASNEY Sometimes this is spelt with an intrusive R – MacAtarsny and MacTarsney – without justification, since the original Irish of the name is Mac an tSasanaigh (son of the Englishman), giving such early anglicized forms as MacEntasny. It was probably derived from the circumstances or character of the eponymous ancestor rather than his race. It is an Ulster name always associated with Counties Armagh and Tyrone where it is on record from the sixteenth century, though never at all numerous.

**MacATEER, MacIntyre, Carpenter, Freeman
(O) SEERY** The Gaelic surname Mac an tSaoir belongs both to Ireland and Scotland. In Scotland it is always MacIntyre. In Ireland the MacIntyres slightly outnumber the

Mac Ateers, but a number of the former are Ulstermen of Scottish extraction. Taken together they are estimated in population statistics to number some 4,500 persons in Ireland: practically all the MacAteers are in Ulster (Armagh, Antrim and Donegal), while the MacIntyres are less concentrated in area, though chiefly in Ulster, with a considerable number also in Co. Sligo. Bally-macateer is a place near Lurgan; Carrickmacintyre is in Co. Mayo. The 1659 census tells us that they were numerous in Co. Donegal at that date, and the hearth money returns of somewhat later show that the name was also common in Co. Monaghan.

The belief that the name is uniformly Scottish in origin may, I think be discounted; the bishop of Clogher who held the sea from 1268-1287 was Michael Mac-an tSaoir and the famous St. Kieran, who flourished seven centuries earlier, before the era of surnames, was called Mac an tSaoir.

MacAteer, or MacIntyre, is one of those names which had been subjected to anglicization by translation. Saor is the Irish word for a certain type of tradesman such as a mason or a carpenter. The name has never become Mason, but Carpenter was fairly widely adopted as a synonym, so that the surname Carpenter in Ireland is often not English in origin but MacAteer in disguise. Similarly, since saor also has the secondary meaning of free, the English surname Freeman sometimes hides a MacAteer origin. It is not improbable that the English name Searson was also sometimes used in the same way. It has been used as the anglicized form of Ó Saorthaigh.

Freeman also does duty, in this case by mistrans-lation, for Ó Saorthaigh, the name of a small Westmeath sept normally called Seery in English. A branch of this, or possibly a distinct family of the same name, was also at one time located in Donegal, but its present day de-scendants are now found in small numbers in north Connaght, where some of its members are called Seery and some Freeman.

The adoption of Carpenter for MacAteer took place for the most part in the Dublin area, so that Most Rev. Dr. John Carpenter, Archbishop of Dublin from 1770 to 1786, who is remembered for his prominent part in the struggle for Catholic Emancipation, probably belonged to a branch of the sept under consideration. He was interested in Irish and in close touch with the Irish poet O'Neachtain; he wrote his name in Irish as Mac an tSaoir. However, Henry Carpenter (fl. 1790), poet and scribe, known in his native Irish language as Enri Mac an tSaoir, was a Clareman. The name also occurs in Co. Clare in a place-name—Cahermackateer, near Corofin; but as a surname it is very rare in that county in any of the forms given above.

ATKINSON ATKINS   These English names are de-rived from Adkin, a diminutive of Adam. Though not of early introduction Atkins became well established in Ireland in the seventeenth century, especially in Cork where the Atkins family, who had come from Somerset, were prominent in the commercial life of the city; they also established themselves in the Youghal area. It would appear, however, that the name was not unknown in Ireland before this time, because we find references as early as 1564 to land known as Atkinsacre, at Dunleek, Co. Meath—assuming of course that Atkins is in that case a surname.

Atkinson is much more numerous in Ireland than Atkins being found mainly in the three north-eastern counties. There was a family of the name in that part of Co. Offaly then called Fercall at the end of the sixteenth century.

AUGHMUTY   Four modern variants of this name are reported by local registrars, viz. Achmuty, Ahmuty, Auchmuty and Amooty. The last was in Co. Longford, in which county the family has been established since the middle of the seventeenth century: Arthur Aughmooty appears among the tituladoes for the barony of Longford, Co. Longford, in the "census" of 1659; the same man and also another of the name were Poll Tax Commissioners for Co. Longford in 1660 and again in 1661. The name sim-ilarly appears at Rathvilly, Co. Carlow. In the seventeenth century the variant spellings included also Aghmooty, Athmooty, Attamooty, Oughmooty and several more, all of which occur in the Irish army lists to be found in the Ormond Manuscripts for various dates between 1662 and 1680. One family came from Scotland at the time of the Plantation of Ulster and first settled in Co. Cavan: in 1611 John Aghmooty and Alexander Aughmooty each obtained one thousand acres in Tyllyhunco, Co. Cavan.

BAGENAL BEGLAN   Though perhaps at the present time the description might be misleading, after 1641 the Bagnalls or Bagenals were definitely counted as "Irish Papists," and with good reason. Col. Walter Bagenal (1641-1653), a prominent member of the Supreme Council of the Catholic Confederation of Kilkenny, was hanged by Cromwell and in the next generation his son Col. Dudley Bagenal (1638-1712) recruited and com-manded an infantry regiment for James II's army. He was a member of the 1689 "Patriot" Parliament and was attainted by the victorious Williamites. Col. Walter's Co. Carlow estate was recovered by the family after the Restoration (presumably through the influence of Ormond) and a considerable property in that county was still in Bagenal hands until quite recent times. These properties were Dunleckny and Bennekerry near Carlow, a few miles north of Bagenalstown which was named from the family under consideration. This has been superseded by the older Gaelic name Muine Bheag, but it is still used by many of the inhabitants in preference to the town's official name.

The Bagenals, however, are not one of the old Anglo-Norman families so many of whom became hibernicized, but first came to Ireland in 1539 in the person of Sir Nicholas Bagenal. He was of an influential Staffordshire family—the name is taken from a village in that shire. He left home in disgrace but, having been pardoned by Henry VIII, became a privy councillor and marshal of the English army and acquired estates around Newry.

One of his sons, Sir Henry Bagenal (1556-1598), the next marshal, was killed at the famous battle of the Yellow Ford; he wrote a description of Ulster in 1586 and is remembered as the bitter foe of Hugh O'Neill, who had eloped with his sister Mabel Bagenal. His half-brother, Sir Samuel Bagenal, commanded a regiment under Carew in the Munster campaign. A generation later, as we have seen, this family of English soldiers and settlers was to take its place among the most determined opponents of English aggression. The reversion of the family to Protestantism came about through Walter Bagenal's marriage to Eleanor Beauchamp, the children of this second marriage being brought up in their mother's religion. One of these, Beauchamp Bagenal (1735-1802), a picturesque character of the eighteenth century duellist M.P. type, was a consistent supporter of the Catholic cause. Philip Henry Bagenal (b.1850) was a prolific political and legal writer.

The Irish name Ó Beigléighinn, normally anglicized Beglan and Beglin, has assumed the form Bagnall in some isolated cases, e.g. in Co. Meath. In the Drogheda area Begney has been recorded as synonymous with Bagnall. The O'Beglins were one of the hereditary medical families of mediaeval Ireland; the Annals of Loch Cé record the death in 1529 of Maurice O'Beglin, "an adept in medicine". The sept was located principally in Co. Longford.   Bibl.

BALDWIN   This very English sounding name originated in Germany and came to England from Flanders. It was well established in the south-eastern counties of Ireland at least as early as 1500, being called both Baldwin and Baldon, as we know from the Fiants of Henry VIII and Edward VI. Many isolated instances of men named Baldwyn etc. in the Pale occur in much earlier records e.g. the Justiciary Rolls (1295-1307). Baldin and Baldon (both of which are recorded in our own time as synonyms of Baldwin in Ireland) are returned in the "census" of 1659 as principal Irish names in Co. Waterford; and in the same county five Baldwins are recorded as "tituladoes". The Tithe Applotment Books (c. 1825) and Griffith's Valuation (c. 1850) indicate that there were 68 Baldwin householders in Co. Waterford and 19 in Queen's Co. (Leix); in 1865 there were 23 Baldwin births registered, 16 of these being in or near Co. Waterford; by 1890 the birth registrations had fallen to ten, again mainly in the Waterford area. Of the 27 Baldwin wills (1627-1809) of which abstracts are in the Genealogical Office, 9 are Dublin, 8 Co. Cork, 7 Queen's Co. (Leix).

When the name occurs in Co. Donegal it is sometimes an anglicization of Mulligan, from a supposed translation of the Irish Maolagán (maol-bald).   Bibl.

BALLAGH   This name is one of the epithet types like Bane or Reagh: it is derived from the Irish ballach (speckled, marked). As might be expected, therefore, it has not been confined to a particular area. Thus we find Robert Ballagh a miller at Carlingford, Co. Down, in 1439, Patrick Ballagh a butcher at Kilkenny in 1509,

Edmund 'Ballaghe arraigned with two Butlers and others of equal standing as "common robbers" in Co. Tipperary in 1514, and Farrole Ballough one of the kern mustered by O'Byrne for service in England in 1544. Later in the sixteenth century people called Ballagh as a surname were to be found in Counties Clare, Galway, Kerry, Carlow, Kilkenny, Wexford, Meath and Dublin. In the past Ballagh was also common as a distinguishing agnomen added to christian name and surname. In quite modern times Ballagh is a rare surname associated chiefly with Ulster, especially Co. Monaghan. In the Hearth Money Rolls of Co. Monaghan (1663-65) it does not occur as a surname, but as an agnomen with Mac Kenna it does, e.g. Patrick Ballagh MacKennah: Mac Kennas were very numerous in parts of that county so that it is not unlikely that the agnomen Ballagh did become standardized as a surname there at the end of the seventeenth century. Similarly in the list of 1641 outlaws we find one of the Byrnes of Co. Wicklow described as alias Ballagh.

BALLESTY   Ballesty is derived from the old French balestier (cross-bowman) and in England took the form Ballester. In Ireland it was first Baliste, and as such occurs in mediaeval Dublin. In modern times it is mainly associated with Mullingar and Co. Westmeath.

BAMBRICK   Apart from a reference to one Oswald Banbrege, a cook, of Ballydowd, Co. Dublin, in 1514, who should perhaps not be regarded as a Bambrick, I have not met this name earlier than 1603 when Henry, Hugh and Thomas Bambrick were among a number of Irishmen of Queen's Co. (Leix) obtaining "pardons". In 1641 and the three following years four soldiers of the name are in the Irish army lists preserved in the Ormond Manuscripts. In 1659 two men of the name Bambrick are listed in the "census" of that date as tituladoes in Queen's Co. and as these have the same christian names (Henry and John) as two of the said soldiers it is not improbable that these soldiers are also Leix Bambricks. They multiplied considerably, for just two centuries later we find sixteen householders in Griffith's Valuation for that county (eleven of these in the barony of Slievemargy) and in Co. Kilkenny; three more are in the Tithe Applotment Books of the 1820's. They were located in the part of Leix contiguous with counties Kilkenny and Kildare; and Henry Bambrick, who was outlawed as a

Jacobite in 1691, is described as of Athy which, though in Co. Kildare, is close to the home of the two tituladoes mentioned above. Notwithstanding the fact that they were still fairly numerous a century ago the name is very rare now in Co. Leix and the other midland counties, but it is quite well represented in the city of Dublin. I do not know its origin: in view of the form it takes in the first example given above it might be a toponymic from Bambridge or more probably from the Scottish place-name Bambreich.

BANE Being familiar with Bane as a surname in Co. Clare I was surprised to find how rare it is outside counties Clare and Galway. For the benefit of readers who do not know Ireland well it should be mentioned that its pronunciation cannot be phonetically indicated by reference to any sound in English, nor is it as broad as the Irish word bán (white) from which it comes—the sound is the same as the bane in the town of Ferbane, quite different from Bayne. There is an English name Bayne or Baynes (sometimes written Bane in mediaeval documents). In Scotland Bayne has been used as an anglicization of bán: Reaney gives an instance where a man in 1623 is described as 'Bayne alias Quhyte'. Thus it originated as a distinguishing epithet, forming first an agnomen and sometimes being retained as a hereditary surname. But the extent to which families once so called reverted to their ancestral surname, or adopted White by translation, is indicated by statistics: in 1659 the "census" lists Bane as a principal Irish name in ten of the 27 counties which are included in what survives of that document; in 1793 the local census of Moycullen, Co. Galway, records 12 Bane families in that parish alone; yet in 1866 there were only eight births registered for Bane in all Ireland, by 1890 this fell below five. However the number of Bane entries in current directories may indicate that the tendency to diminish has been arrested.

(O) BANNON, Banim   (O) BANNAGHAN At the present time the name Bannon is widely scattered throughout the four provinces of Ireland, with a slight preponderance in Co. Tipperary and Co. Cavan. One of the several distinct mediaeval septs of Ó Banáin was seated at Léim Uí Bhanáin, now Leap Castle, in the barony of Clonlisk, i.e. the southern end of Co. Offaly near Roscrea, which is in Co. Tipperary. In 1659 Bannon is recorded as numerous in that barony and also in that of Lower Ormond, Co. Tipperary, where however Petty's census enumerators (erroneously) equated Bannon with Bane. It may be observed that Matheson records Banane as well as the obvious Bane or Bawn as synonymous with White in several widely separated parts of the country. Bane is simply the Irish word bán, white. Woulfe is mistaken in deriving Ó Banáin from bán. The Hearth Money Rolls of approximately the same date confirm the prevalence of the name Bannon in Co. Tipperary.

The census enumerators also found O'Banan numerous in Co. Fermanagh. The pedigree of Muintir Bhanáin is among the Fermanagh pedigrees (compiled about 1712) which occupy nearly 100 pages of Analecta

Hibernica No. 3. Of this sept, no doubt, were Maelpatrick O'Banan, Bishop of Connor from 1152 to 1172, and Gelasius O'Banan, Abbot of Clones, who was Bishop of Clogher from 1316 to 1319.

The Book of Lecan places Ó Banáin at Baile Uí Bhanáin, now Ballybannon, which is in the parish of Partry, on the western side of Lough Mask. In 1585 the Composition of Connacht found an O'Bannaghan possessed of an estate at Rathmullen, Co. Sligo and in 1659 O' Bennaghan appears as one of the principal names in the barony of Tirerrill, Co. Sligo. This is probably not a variant of Bannon but Ó Beannacháin (Ó Bethnacháin in mediaeval Irish manuscripts). O'Flaherty counts the O' Bannaghans as of Firboig descent.

Banim is believed to be a corrupt form of Bannon. It is made famous by the brothers Michael Banim (1796-1865) and John Banim (1798-1842), the novelists: they were born in Kilkenny and were presumably of the sept dealt with in the first paragraph above.

De Burgh's Landowners of Ireland (1878) includes the large and valuable estate of Bannon of Broughill Castle, near Frankfort (or Kilcormac), Co. Offaly.   Map

BARBOUR The name Barbour nowadays calls to mind big business in Northern Ireland and perhaps politics of the more broad-minded kind; it may therefore come as a surprise to learn that it is of frequent occurrence in Dublin since the year 1267 right down to the present day, though more often spelt Barber in modern times.

At first it was called le Barbour and frequently also Barbador. The place now known as Barberstown in the parish of St. Margaret, Co. Dublin, was formerly Barbedorstown. The two forms have the same meaning, one coming from the Norman-French barbier and the other from the Latin barbador. The spelling Barber is also found in quite early records, and occasionally Barbier e.g. the testator in a Dublin will of 1698. In the Middle Ages, just as the smith held a higher position in society than in modern times, so the barber is to be equated with the professional man of to-day, since he alone in the community practised surgery and dentistry.

Though more numerous in Dublin city and county than elsewhere in Ireland throughout the counties, it is recorded also several times in Co. Cork—William le Barbour was a man of substance in the city as early as 1299. In Co. Kilkenny, too, we find Barbours recorded in the Ormond Deeds as landholders from 1300 onwards: the last mention of them there is of one John Barbour, yeoman, in 1539.

A Mr Barber was one of the counsel retained on behalf of the Irish Catholics of Cork, Mallow and Youghal who in 1656 claimed, as "innocent Papists," to escape transplantation to Connacht. Mary Barber (1712-1757), wife of a Dublin woollen-draper, was one of the Dublin friends of Dean Swift who would probably be forgotten had she not got the dean into trouble by writing an anonymous letter to Queen Caroline which was attributed to him. Dr. Constantine Barbor (c. 1714-1783) was several times President of the Royal College of Physicians, Ireland. Rev. Samuel Barber (c. 1738-1811)

28

was a Presbyterian minister in Co. Down who, having been a colonel of the Volunteers in 1782, was imprisoned for high-treason in 1798.

At present the name is chiefly found in not inconsiderable numbers in Belfast and surrounding areas and in Dublin. The well known Ulster family, Barbour of Hilden, came from near Paisley in Scotland and settled at Lisburn in 1784. A member of this family emigrated to New York in 1849, and this branch is extant in America today. Bibl.

BARNEWALL, Barneville   This famous name, which, is now more often written Barnewell, survives also in its original Norman form of Barneville. Le Sieur de Barneville is said to have accompanied William the Conqueror to England from Normandy. No one of the name appears to have been among the earliest of the Anglo-Norman settlers in Ireland, but from about the year 1300 it is found in Co. Meath and in other parts of what was later known as the Pale, where the family became of great importance and influence. They were especially prominent in the sixteenth and seventeenth centuries. The head of the family was in 1461 created Baron Trimlestown (subsequently called Trimleston) of that place in Co. Meath and the most noteworthy Barnewalls have been of this line. Sir Christopher Barnewall was Chief Justice of the King's Bench in 1435 and John Barnewall, 3rd Baron Trimlestown, (1470-1538) was Chancellor of Ireland in 1534. Sir Patrick Barnewall (d. 1552) was Master of the Rolls and another Sir Patrick Barnewall (c. 1560-1622) was the leader of the Dublin Catholic recusants. None of the sixteenth and seventeenth century Irish parliaments was without one or more Barnewalls among its members. In the seventeenth century we find two of them superiors of the Capuchin order and many Barnewalls in James II's Irish army. Of these the most interesting perhaps was Nicholas Barnewall, 3rd Viscount Barnewall of Kingsland, whose outlawry after the siege of Limerick was reversed by William III: Nevertheless he protested bitterly against the violation of the Treaty of Limerick.

After the Jacobite débâcle many Barnewalls migrated to France and several had distinguished service in the French army, the most notable of whom were Col. Alexander Barnewall and Mathew Barnewall, 10th Baron Trimleston, (1672-1692), whose estates were confiscated in 1691 but restored to his brother.

Father Mathew Barnewall or Barneville (1656-1738), born at Swords and a close relative of the Trimlestown family, was a priest of marked Jansenist tendencies. The Trimleston lawsuit concerning the will of Nicholas Barnewall, 14th Baron Trimleston, (1726-1811) who had succeeded in getting the outlawry affecting the succession to the Trimlestown title reversed, was a cause célèbre for some years after his death.

BARRON   Apart from the use of Barron as the form in English of the rare Irish name Ó Bearáin (also anglicized as Barrington) the surname Barron came into existence quite independently in two widely separated parts

of the country. In both cases it is formed from the English word baron, but it had no connexion with English settlers. In Ulster the name was used, at first with the prefix Mac (MacBarron) for a branch of the Neills, who became numerous and important in Co. Armagh and north Louth. Art MacBarron, illegitimate brother of the Earl of Tyrone, was accounted one of the chief men of Co. Armagh in 1598. Two generations later families called Barron (the Mac was dropped as early as that) had so far increased in numbers that the name appears in Petty's census among the principal Irish surnames in the neighbourhood of Dundalk, where the parish of Barronstown is situated.

Many families called Barron in Co. Waterford and adjoining areas in Co. Kilkenny, south Tipperary and Wexford, are descended from a branch of the Fitz-Geralds, the leading man of whom was created Palatine Baron of Burnchurch in the fourteenth century. The title was not officially recognized. The attempt of the nephew of the last baron to recover the estates and honours at the Restoration failed; but a member of the family was created a baronet in 1841. Prior to the main Land Acts, in 1878 this and kindred families of Barron owned approximately 10,000 acres of valuable land, nearly all in Co. Waterford. Up to the seventeenth century they were often described in legal documents as Barron alias Fitzgerald e.g. Roland Barron, alias Fitzgerald, Archbishop of Cashel from 1553 to 1561 and Milo Baron alias Fitzgerald, Bishop of Ossory, who died in 1553, it is said of grief at the dissolution of the monasteries.

Baron or Barron as a surname, was, however, of quite frequent occurrence in that part of the country long before it was assumed by the Fitzgeralds. Instances abound in the Ormond Deeds as far back as 1270; and English settlers and merchants of the name were also in Dublin and the Pale in the thirteenth century, e.g. William Baron to whom in 1226 was made a grant of a fair at Naas, "his manor."

The roll of distinguished bearers of the name in the south of Ireland in considerable. The most noteworthy were: Geoffrey Baron (d. 1651) who was the representative of the Supreme Council of the Confederation of Kilkenny at the court of France in 1642 and nine years later was executed by Ireton after the surrender of Limerick, having refused to renounce the Catholic faith; and his brother Rev. Bonaventure Baron, O.F.M. (d. 1696), who had a long and distinguished career as author and professor at St. Isidore's, Rome. (Both these nephews of Fr. Luke Wadding were born at Clonmel.) As might be expected officers of the name were in James II's army. Philip Fitzgerald Barron (1797-c.1860) of Waterford was a forerunner of the Gaelic League in the work of the Irish language revival. In Irish, except when Ó Bearáin, mentioned above, is applicable, the name is gaelicized Barún. Bibl.

BARTON   The name Barton is now found scattered throughout all the provinces except Connacht, though nowhere in large numbers. It is on record in Ireland as far back as 1297 when Th. de Bartun was accepted by the seneschal at Drogheda as a surety, while in 1304 Lawrence Barton was a freeholder at Moycarkey in the barony of Eliogarty, Co. Tipperary. Before the middle of that century it was found at Kilcullen, Co. Kildare, and in the city of Kilkenny. The name is derived from a place, as the prepositional prefix de indicates. Following the mediaeval Norman form of the name in Irish it was written de Bartún.

The leading family of the name in Ireland is descended from Thomas Barton of Barton Hall, Lancashire, who came to Ireland with Essex in 1599 and obtained grants of land in Co. Fermanagh. At the end of the nineteenth century, before the break-up of the big estates under the Land Acts, his descendants were seated at Clonelly (Co. Fermanagh), Rochestown (Co. Tipperary) and Straffan (Co. Kildare): to the last of these the Bartons of Glendalough are most closely related. (Of this family is Robert Barton, reluctant signatory of the Anglo-Irish Treaty of 1921.) Another branch emigrated to Bordeaux where they are still prominent in the wine trade; one member of this family returned to Ireland and settled at Grove, Co. Waterford; Father Barton S.J. was with Father Peter Talbot associated with the negociations which took place between Charles II in exile and the King of Spain in 1653. Not all the Irish Bartons came to Ireland as Anglo-Normans or Elizabethans: there were, for example, two Bartons among the Cromwellian "adventurers." Barton does not occur in the 1659 "census" as one of the more numerous surnames but individual tituladoes are named in five counties – Fermanagh, Monaghan, Meath, Kildare and Kings Co. (Offaly). The many Barton wills proved in the prerogative and diocesan courts in the eighteenth century are mostly those of residents in Ulster or in Dublin. James Barton (fl. 1800-1820), a noted violinist, was born in Dublin. John Barton, governor of the Bank of Ireland and father of John Kellock Barton (b.1829), President of the Royal College of Surgeons, Ireland, came from Staffordshire, England.   Bibl.

BASTABLE   This name is well known in counties Kerry and Cork, but is not numerous. It is on record there since the seventeenth century, at Castleisland, Co. Kerry (will 1670) and Castle Magner, Co. Cork (birth 1698) after which many references to it in those counties have been noted. The name is derived from one of two English towns viz. Barnstaple in Somerset and Barnstable in Essex.

BATEMAN   This well known English name is on record in Ireland since 1292 when one William Bateman was fined for contempt, and since 1396 when John Bateman, born in Ireland, was appointed to a judicial position, the name occurs quite frequently in mediaeval Irish records such as the Ormond Deeds. It does not, of course, follow that all Irish Batemans of the present day are descended from these early immigrants. There was, for example, a John Bateman of Oxenham, England among the Cromwellian "adventurers", and one Rowland Bateman, a recent grantee, appears in the "census" of 1659 in the neighbourhood of Tralee, Co. Kerry, as a

titulado, in company with Trants, Dennys and Springs. Prior to that the name in Ireland occurs chiefly as holders of government office or as that of a settler in Co. Louth (Philip Bateman, 1422); but from the middle of the seventeenth century it became closely associated with south-west Munster – west Cork and Kerry, as the many wills recorded for Bateman testators show. The principal family there springs from Major Rowland Bateman, mentioned above, whose great-grandson, another Rowland, was Deputy-Governor of Kerry in 1779. Apart from this concentration in Munster, the name is not unknown in Ulster. It is of interest to note that contrary to the general tendency the total number of Batemans in the country has increased rather than decreased in the past century: the average number of Bateman births registered annually in the first years of compulsory registration (1864-66) was 12. This figure is surprisingly low having regard to the fact, revealed by Griffith's Valuation of 1851-53, that there were as many as 46 householders or landholders of the name in Co. Cork at that time; however, in 1890 there were 19 births registered. In both cases mainly in Co Cork–there are no statistics available for a later date. An annual birthrate of 19 represents a population of approximately 750 persons.

BATTLE   Though Battle or Battell – Old French de la Bataille – is a well known name in England, Irish families called Battle, who belong exclusively to Co. Sligo and the adjacent parts of the neighbouring counties, are of an indigenous Irish sept. Up to the seventeenth century their name, MacConcatha in Irish, was anglicized phonetically MacEncaha. This form was still used in 1662: the Co. Sligo hearth money rolls of that date list several families so called, but Battle does not appear. A still earlier anglicized form, closer to the original Gaelic, was MacConchaa which occurs in 1585 list of Co. Sligo "pardons"; Co. Sligo records of the next decade call them MacEncahe.

BAXTER   This is a Gaelic name of Scottish origin, viz Mac a' Bhacstair (son of the baker), and in Scotland the Mac is sometimes retained. The MacBaxters are a sept of the MacMillan clan. An early spelling of the name in Ireland was Bacstar and Backystre–the latter in 1341 as a burgess of Aherlow. In Ireland the name is quite numerous; 90 per cent of the births registered for Baxter are in Ulster, mainly Antrim. It has been found in that province since the beginning of the seventeenth century, Martin Baxter being one of the undertakers settled in Co. Fermanagh. The name, however, was not confined to Scottish Protestants, for among the Papists transplanted in 1656 was Garrett Baxter of Co. Sligo. One John Baxter was a lieutenant in the Co. Dublin troop of militia in 1659 and later a John Baxter, perhaps the same man, was captain in the Foot Guards (Leinster). The Ormond MSS. also record an Edmund Bagster among the army rank and file in 1644 and a William Baxter an officer in 1684. Two of the name are listed by de Burgh as extensive Irish landowners in Counties Mayo and Leix (Queen's) in 1878: both were resident in Scotland.

BEAMISH   The surname Beamish is of French origin, being derived from the place-name Beaumais (sur Dive). In Ireland it is not in the Anglo-Norman category, as that might suggest, nor is it Cromwellian as has been sometimes stated. The family, have been in Ireland since Elizabethan times, when the first of the name came from England to Co. Kerry, and has since been closely identified with that county and with Co. Cork. If, as seems probable, all Irish Beamishs spring from that source it presents an example of a family which not only prospered but also multiplied in the course of the four centuries it has been here: in 1851-53, when Griffith's Valuation was made, there were no less than 62 householders or landholders of the name in Co. Cork.

The leading landed families were seated in Co. Kerry: the several branches are fully described in Burke's Landed Gentry of Ireland (1912 and 1958 editions). De Burgh's Landowners records twelve of the name with extensive properties in Co. Cork in 1878, and numerically their association has been with Cork county and city rather than Kerry, as the many wills and other records from 1642 to the present day, as well as those of successful business enterprise, testify.

Major North Ludlow Beamish (1793-1872), author of works on military subjects, was born and died in Co. Cork. O'Donoghue in his Poets of Ireland includes two of the name, both natives of Co. Cork.   Bibl.

BEATTY, Betagh   There are many people called Beatty or Beattie in Ireland — an approximate estimate puts the number at 4,000. Eighty per cent of these are in northeast Ulster and are the descendants of Scottish settlers of the seventeenth century. According to Reaney Beatty is a Scottish form of Batey, which is a colloquial abbreviation of the christian name Bartholomew. In the rest of the country they may be of that origin, or alternatively belong to families formerly called Betagh (also spelt Betaghe, Beatagh, Bettagh etc.) This early form of the name is now almost extinct, though the birth registration returns for 1890 show that it was then still to be found synonymous with Beatty, around Athlone. The variant Beytagh has been noted in a Dublin will of 1839. Betagh is one of the not very numerous class of Gaelic Irish surnames derived from an occupation: biadhtach is a word (formed from biadh, food) denoting a public victualler; it was originally used in a complimentary sense, conveying the idea of hospitality as well as function, but in the thirteenth and fourteenth centuries, when the Anglo-Norman power was at its zenith, the betaghs, or betagii as they were called in the official Latin of the time, were persons of very inferior status whom Curtis described as comparable to the villeins in feudal England. This, of course, applies only to that half of the country under effective Anglo-Norman rule i.e. counties Dublin, Louth, Meath, Kildare, Kilkenny, Carlow, Wexford, part of Connacht and all Munster except Clare. The fourteenth and fifteenth centuries saw the reconquest by hibernicized Norman lords and Gaelic chiefs of the greater part of this territory and by 1500 the "English Pale" had shrunk to a small area in Counties Louth, Meath, Kildare and Dublin. The rest, including practically all Ulster, was still

Gaelic and unconquered. I do not think that the word was at all widely adopted as a surname. At the period referred to references to it in official records are almost all to persons of some standing, e.g. jurors and sureties in Co. Kildare and Co. Meath, and I have only noted one Betagh in the contemporary lists of hibernici, felons and outlaws. Betagh had certainly become a name of consequence in Co. Meath by the sixteenth century, for between 1570 and 1598 Betagh of Walterstown, Betagh of Rathalron, Betagh of Dunamore and Betagh of Moynalty all appear as gentlemen of that county, while William Betagh was chief serjeant of the adjoining Co. Cavan and Thomas Betagh was one of the gentlemen entrusted with the task of taking a muster of the inhabitants of Co. Cavan in 1587. The name occurs there and in the neighbouring Co. Monaghan in the Inquisitions of the next generation. Thomas Betagh of Laurencetown and William Betagh of Ballicashe, on the Meath-Cavan border, were transplanted to Co. Roscommon. Six of the name (Betagh or Bytagh) appear in the lists of outlawed Jacobites, 1689 to 1702. Five places called Betaghstown—three in Meath, one in Westmeath and one in Co. Kildare—are further evidence of their standing. Implying that the Betaghs were of Norman origin Woulfe mentions the fact that in early Hiberno-Norman records their christian names were Norman; this, however, is of little significance since in a list of outlaws in 1305 in which one Maurice Betagh appears, such forenames as Geoffrey, Henry, Nicholas, Richard, Simon and Thomas are as frequent with the many O's and Mac's cited as with men of Norman surnames.

In modern times Father Thomas Betagh, S.J. (1769-1811), who was born at Kells, Co. Meath, was notable for his activity in the revival of Catholic education at the end of the penal period. Thomas Edward Beatty (1801-1872), P.R.C.S.I., whose mother was a Betagh, was of a Co. Cavan family. Admiral David Beatty, Earl Beatty (1871-1936), famous as a naval commander in the First World War, came of a well known family in Co. Wexford. Betty is not uncommon as a variant of Beatty, especially in Co. Fermanagh, where MacCaffrey is recorded as having been used synonymously with those surnames as recently as 1890.

The cognate surname Mac an Bhiadhtaigh, anglicised MacVitty, is of Scottish Gaelic origin.   Map

BEGG, Beggs   Begg and Beggs are now about equally numerous in Ireland, the latter belonging mainly to north-east Ulster and the former to Dublin and adjacent Leinster counties. Ulster families so called may be of non-Irish origin—there is of course, an English surname Bigge—but it is reasonably certain that the Beggs of the rest of the country are of native Irish stock, their name being of the epithet class: the word beag (beg) means small. It has been used as a surname from very early times and occurs in every sort of record from the fourteenth century. These people belonged to every class from labourers to landlords: among the more interesting are four who were outlawed as Jacobites (two of these were from Galway, the only place outside Munster and

Leinster where they are at all prominent—their close association with Ulster was of later date. Two more, Matthew and George Begg, were among the Papists transplanted from counties Dublin and Meath in 1656.

(O) BEGLEY   MacCREADY   Ó Beaglaoich, first anglicized O'Begley, now Begley and occasionally Bagley, is the name of a Donegal sept located in the barony of Kilmacrenan where its present day representatives are still to be found. The place-name Tulloghobegley, a parish in the barony of Kilmacrenan, perpetuates their association with that area. References to Tulloghobegley occur in the Raphoe diocesan records, though the erenagh family there was not O'Begley but MacCready, a well known Ulster surname now plentiful in the three north-eastern counties. Of this erenagh family was Father Donogh MacReidy (also called MacCreedy), of Coleraine, Dean of Derry, who in 1608 suffered martyrdom by being pulled asunder by four horses. Monsignor Charles MacCready, Rector of the Church of the Holy Cross, New York, a century ago, was of the same stock. In Irish the name is Mac Riada, i.e. MacReedy, the initial C of MacCready being intrusive.

The name Begley is now almost as numerous in Munster as in Ulster. One of its principal modern locations is Co. Kerry: the 1911 census figures record 37 Begley families there. The O'Begleys of Munster are a branch of the Donegal sept; the first of them went to Co. Cork with the MacSweeneys as galloglasses at the end of the fifteenth century.

Conor Begley collaborated in the production of Hugh MacCurtin's English-Irish Dictionary, which was printed in Paris in 1732. The Abbé Thadé Begley, of that city, was largely responsible for the publication of that work for which he had a special fount of Irish type cast. In our own time John Canon Begley was the author of The History of the Diocese of Limerick, a work in 3 volumes of much value for secular as well as ecclesiastical history. Henry Begley (d.1895), of Limerick, was a landscape painter of note.

For some reason which I have yet to discover a few families of Begley around Enniskillen have been recorded as using the surname Morris as a synonymous alternative to Begley.   Map

(O) BEHAN   Behan is the usual spelling of the anglicized form of Ó Beacháin an older form of which is Ó Beacáin; Beahan, Beaghan and even Bean are occasional variants, while in Co. Kerry the Munster tendency to emphasize the last syllable has made it Behane there (not pronounced Behayne, of course, but Behaan). It is only in the course of the last two centuries that representatives of this Leinster sept settled in Kerry, though we do find one of them at the mouth of the Shannon in the person of Hugh O'Beaghan, who was Bishop of Iniscathy in 1188, before that small see was united to Limerick. Another notable ecclesiastic, the Franciscan Donat or Daniel Beaghan, also called O'Behechan (d.1541) was Bishop of Kildare at the beginning of the troubles which arose from the attempt to impose the Reformation on

Ireland. His diocese was near the homeland of the O'Behans, which covered a considerable area of the country lying at the juncture of Counties Kildare, Offaly and Leix.

The O'Behans were notable principally as a literary family, two of whom were thought worthy of mention in the Annals of Loch Cé, the Four Masters etc. as "eminent historians," viz. Conor O'Behan (d.1376) and Donal O'Behan (d.1411). Brendan Behan was a very successful playwright of the present day.

Very few, if any, present day representatives of this sept have resumed the prefix O which properly goes with the name.   Map

BELLEW   Though numerous enough in the seventeenth century to be listed in Petty's "census" of 1659 among the principal Irish (sic) names in the two baronies of Dundalk and Ardee, Co. Louth, the name Bellew is now comparatively rare. It is still extant in Co. Louth, with which county it has been associated since the thirteenth century. In that area it has been sometimes changed to Bailey. The earliest references to it in Ireland render the name Beleawe, which is close to the original French Bel Eau. The family went to England from Normandy with William the Conqueror, and settled in Co. Louth and the adjoining part of Co. Meath soon after the Anglo-Norman invasion. Up to the middle of the sixteenth century they were less in evidence than the majority of the great Hiberno-Norman families, but from then on we find them, particularly the family of Bellewstown, taking a prominent part in the affairs of the country as sheriffs, members of parliament and so forth. They were among the leading men on the Irish side in both the major wars of the next century: Sir John Bellew, who was on the Supreme Council of the Confederate Catholics, was specially exempted from pardon in 1652; three Bellew landowners were transplanted to Co. Galway under the Cromwellian régime; and four of the name served as officers in James II's army, but for various reasons they managed to save a portion of their estates from the wholesale Williamite confiscations. Though they did not conform, as so many of their kind did under the stress of the eighteenth century penal laws, they were in possession, when de Burgh published his Landowners of Ireland in 1878, of over 5,000 acres in Co. Louth while the Mountbellew (Co. Galway) family had some 23,000 acres. Capt Thomas Henry Grattan-Bellew, of Mountbellew, who is a Knight of Malta, is uncle and heir presumptive of the late baronet, Sir Christopher Grattan-Bellew. Dr. Dominic Bellew was Bishop of Killala from 1791 to 1812, and Rev. Paul Bellew V.G. administered the diocese of Waterford, the bishop, Richard Piers, who held the see from 1701 to 1735, being an absentee.   Bibl., Map

BENNETT   BUNYAN. Binane   The surname Bennett is derived from the christian name Benet, an early English form of the Old-French Benoit, Latin Benedictus. The earliest instances of it as a surname in Ireland are spelt Benet. Families of the name were established before 1250

in the barony of Moygoish (Westmeath) and in south Tipperary. They appear in all walks of life, as priests, officials, landowners and felons; one Nicholas Benett was hanged in 1295. The existence in 1312 of a place called Bennetstreet in Co. Kilkenny indicates that they were already of some importance there; and Bennettsbridge, of course, is a well known small Co. Kilkenny town. There is another Bennetsbridge, near Athy Co. Kildare. Other place-names formed from this surname are Bennettsmeadow (near Callan, Co. Kilkenny), Bennetstown (Dunboyne, Co Meath), Bennettstown (near Wexford), Bennettsknock (New Ross), Bennettsgate and Bennettslands (at Youghal). Later records show them to have been even more widespread. In 1486 Thomas Benet was bailiff of the city of Dyvelyn (Dublin). John Benet was Bishop of Cork and Cloyne from 1523 to 1536 and Benets or Bennetts appear in a number of sixteenth century Fiants relating to Co. Cork. Prof. Edward Halloran Bennet (1837-1907), a distinguished president of the Royal College of Surgeons Ireland, was the son of Robert Bennett, Recorder of Cork. A succession of Bennetts were sovereigns of New Ross from 1589 to 1632. Later in the seventeenth century we find the name, as MacBennett as well as Bennett, occurring frequently in Co. Armagh. Art Bennett (fl. 1825) the poet-satirist, was an Armagh man. Another Gaelic poet, William Bennett (fl. 1760) lived in Co. Clare but was born in Co. Kerry. He was known as Buineán in Irish rather than the normal gaelicized form Binéid. Buineán is actually a gaelicization of Bunyan or Bunion, the neme of an English family settled in Co. Kerry, whose association with that county is perpetuated in the place-name Ballybunion, called by the Four Masters Baile an Bhuinneanaigh. Nearly all these Bunion families have now become Bennett, but Binane and Banane were found by Matheson as synonyms of Bunyan in the neighbourhood of Castlegregory and Tralee. Elsewhere Banane is an occasional synonym of Bannon (q.v). One of the attainted Jacobites was William Banane of Loughmore, Co. Tipperary.

(O) BERGIN, Berrigan   John O'Donovan in his notes to O'Dugan and O'Heerin's Topographical Poems remarks that the form Mergin (O'Merriggyn in the sixteenth century Chancery Rolls) used by some families in Leinster, is a more correct anglicization of the Gaelic O hAimherigin than the usual Bergin. Actually Vergin would be phonetically more accurate than either, which are equally near to the Irish in sound, since both B and M when aspirated become V. By the end of the fifteenth century the B form had become generally accepted in English and Latin, as the records relating to the diocese of Ossory prove. O'Bergyn is given as the English form as early as 1314, in the official report in Latin of a court case in Waterford.

O'Dugan and O'Heerin place the sept in the barony of Geashill, Co. Offaly: it has always been associated with the Leix-Offaly area over which they spread from their original Geashill territory. Both now and in the sixteenth and seventeenth centuries Leix had been their principal homeland.

They were occasionally called MacBergin in English: Father Thady MacBergin several times prior of Lorrha, and a native of that place on the border of Co. Offaly, is an example of this. The most noteworthy of the many ecclesiastics of the name was the Cistercian abbot Luke Bergin, one of the many Catholic martyrs under the Cromwellian régime: he was hanged in 1655. Professor Osborn Bergin (1872-1950) of University College, Dublin, and later of the Dublin Institute for Advanced Studies, was a Celtic scholar of the first rank.

At least one case is on record of a family of Bergins in Co. Offaly assuming the non-Gaelic and aristocratic-sounding surname of Burgoyne.   Map

BERMINGHAM, Corish   Much has been written on the great Anglo-Norman families of de Bermingham. I can only give here a brief outline of the most important facts relating to them; readers desiring more detailed information, especially on their early history in Ireland, will find it in the sources indicated in my Bibliography, in addition to which they are recommended to consult Curtis's History of Mediaeval Ireland and also the index volumes of the Journal of the Royal Society of Antiquaries of Ireland which have many useful references; see also note under Preston, infra.

The first to come to Ireland was Robert de Bermingham of the Castle of Bermingham in Warwickshire, who accompanied Strongbow in the momentous Anglo-Norman invasion. By the year 1230 they were firmly established at Tethmoy in Offaly. In 1235 Peter or Piers de Bermingham took part with de Burgo in the conquest of Connacht, where the family acquired a great territory chiefly in the barony of Dunmore, Co. Galway, which came to be called Bermingham's country. This was also termed MacOrish's or MacHorish's country, the Gaelic patronymic MacOrish (now Corish) having been adopted by the Berminghams of Connacht who in due course, like the Burkes, became hibernicized. The eponym here is Piers de Bermingham, Feoras being the Irish equivalent of Piers. This was also used by the Berminghams of Co. Kildare where Castle Carbury, or the Castle of Mac Fheorais, was their principal seat. In the fourteenth century they were very prominent. John de Bermingham was the victor at the famous battle of Faughert, (1318) where Edward Bruce was defeated; and Richard de Bermingham (from whom the Bermingham Tower in Dublin Castle is named) won the decisive victory of Athenry "his town" in 1316. Later the Berminghams were to become Barons of Athenry. In the next century we find them coupled with the O'Connors when the parliament held at Drogheda in 1478 took protective steps "for the chastisement of the Berminghams." Even this indirect association with the O'Connors is ironical since in 1305 Sir Piers de Bermingham caused a large party of O'Connors who were his guests to be treacherously murdered—he himself and his family were afterwards similarly treated by the Verdons and the Gernons. The O'Connors were the principal sufferers by the defeat of Athenry. In 1584 Margaret Bermingham (Dame Bell) suffered death in prison as a result of her efforts on behalf of persecuted priests.

As might be expected officers of the name are to be found in King James II's army list. Since the seventeenth century, however, neither Berminghams (who are still numerous in Leinster and in Co. Cork) nor Corishes (who are less so) have played a very important role in the history of the country. Father Patrick Bermingham was warden of Galway in 1732. John Birmingham (1816-1884), who was a distinguished astronomer, was also a native of Co. Galway. George Bermingham, author of General John Regan and other well known novels and plays, is a pseudonym adopted by Canon George Hannay. Bibl., Map

BEST   The Bests in Ireland are of English stock. The name is probably of Norman origin: though Bardsley does in one of his earlier works suggest the English word best (superlative of good) as an alternative derivation, it is normally derived from the Old-French le beste (the beast—not necessarily in a derogatory sense), though sometimes it is an abbreviation of bester (herdsman). It cannot, however, be placed in the Hiberno-Norman category with Fitzgerald, Burke, Dillon, Roche etc., since its introduction into Ireland dates only from the seventeenth century.

In 1659 Robert Best was one of the 22 principal householders in Highfisher Street, Kinsale—all the 22 names are English except Courcy. In the same year Elias Best was an ensign in one of the Dublin Militia companies. At least six Bests are recorded between 1652 and 1687 in various deeds, wills and marriage licences as persons of substance in Dublin. The earliest reference I have met to the name in Ireland is the will of William Best of Parkgrove, Co. Kilkenny, gentleman, proved in 1640. He was the second son of Richard Best of Ashford, Kent, and was either the ancestor or a collateral of the Bests who were prominent in the next century as landed gentry in the adjacent counties of Carlow and Leix. They continued into the nineteenth century to possess property in Co. Kilkenny, but their principal seats were Dunganstown (the name of which they changed to Bestville), Anderston in Co. Carlow, and Knockbeg which, though actually situated within the borders of Co. Leix (Queen's Co.) is close to the town of Carlow. Their residence, Knockbeg House (prior to the Cromwellian upheaval the property of the Skelton family, who were transplanted as Papists), came into the hands of the Bests towards the end of the seventeenth century. They were related to William and Thomas Molyneux: the latter in his diary (1709) refers to a visit to "Cousin Best's at Knockbeg." Later it passed by marriage to the Maddens and in 1847 it was acquired by Dr. Francis Haly, Bishop of Kildare and Leighlin, who founded Knockbeg College in that year.

All the available evidence shows that in the eighteenth century the name Best in Ireland was seldom found outside Leinster. It is not until the beginning of the nineteenth century that it appears in appreciable numbers in Ulster. The earliest I have met is 1740: Richard Best, a "Protestant housekeeper" in the parish of Glendermot, Co. Derry. To-day it is quite numerous in Dublin and it is remarkable that, as recently as 1890,

of the 21 Best births registered in that year 19 were in Ulster (mostly in Counties Tyrone and Armagh) while none of them was in Leinster. This, according to the Registrar-General's computation, represents a Best population in Ireland at that time of approximately 950 persons. I may mention, by way of comparison, that a similar total is returned for Brett, Considine, Drennan, Dowdall, Fitzmaurice, Forbes, Lanigan, McErlean, Shanley, Tynan and some others. Notwithstanding the numer of people in Ireland called Best it may be regarded as essentially an English name: of the eight included in the Dictionary of National Biography none is Irish.

Dr Richard Irvine Best (1871-1959) the Gaelic scholar was born in Co. Fermanagh. Sir Robert Wallace Best (1856-1946) was a prominent minister in the first and subsequent parliaments of the Commonwealth of Australia.

BIGGAR   BICKERSTAFF   In Ireland this name may have either of two origins: it can be Lowland Scottish, derived from the place-name Biggar in Lanarkshire; or it can be a curious synonym of MacGivern, a Co. Down family, which for some reasons I have not learnt, in some cases in the Newry area changed their name to Biggar and Bickerstaff and in others around Downpatrick became Montgomery. The Mac Giverns, of course, are an indigenous Gaelic Irish sept, originally of Co. Tyrone, but before the end of the sixteenth century they were established in Co. Down. The Biggars are in the will indices of the seventeenth and eighteenth centuries in several Ulster counties; they have a long association with Co. Armagh for one of them, Alexander Biger, appears among the Co. Armagh householders in 1664 while a Biggar and a Bigger are among the large landowners in that county in 1878. Both Francis Joseph Biggar (1863-1927), the historian and antiquarian, and Joseph Bigger M.P. (1828-1890), the originator of parliamentary obstruction, were born in Belfast.

BINDON   The Bindon family settled at Ballyneelough, Co. Tipperary about 1580. They have however, been principally associated with Limerick and Co. Clare. Henry Bindon (d.1664) a grandson of David Bindon the first settler, was mayor of Limerick; in 1670, his grandson, David, acquired the property of Clooney, Co. Clare, which they retained until recent times: he was sheriff of Clare in 1694. All sources dealing with Co. Clare have many references to Bindons, but the name has now become very rare. It is perpetuated in Bindon Street, Ennis. There were two outstanding Claremen of the name, Francis Bindon (c.1690-1765), architect of many famous country houses of the Georgian period and also remembered particularly for his portraits of Swift and other celebrities. His father was M.P. for Clare and one of his brothers, David, was a writer on economics, while another was Dean of Limerick. Samuel Henry Bindon (1812-1879) barrister, was secretary to the Tenants League 1846; later he emigrated to Australia where, having distinguished himself at the bar, he became a cabinet minister and judge.

BLACKWELL   There are a number of places called
Blackwell in England, from one or more of which the
surname is derived. There were five Blackwells among
the Cromwellian "adventurers", one of whom obtained
5,800 acres in the Barony of Ikerrin, Co. Tipperary.
There were, however, Blackwell families in Ireland be-
fore that. Apart from two of the name who served in
Ormond's army in 1648, we find the will of James
Blackwall, a Co. Clare gentleman, proved in 1641.
Another, Col. Henry Blackwell, is listed in the 1659
"census" as a "titulado" in the barony of Moyarta, Co.
Clare, and there have been Blackwells in the county ever
since. The most notable of these was James Bartholomew
Blackwell (1764-1822) who was sent from his home in
Ennis to be educated in France; there he became a very
distinguished officer in Napoleon's army (an interesting
account of him will be found in Hayes, Biographical
Dictionary of Irishmen in France).

BLANCHFIELD   Though well known as Irish to readers of the sporting pages of newspapers Blanchfield is a
rare name. This is a modern form of the Norman-French
de Blancheville. As such it was associated prominently
with Co. Kilkenny from the early thirteenth century.
The Justiciary Rolls, the Ormond Deeds and other
extensive mediaeval records contain very many references to de Blanchvilles who frequently held such offices
as constable of Kilkenny, sheriff of the county and so
on. The extent of their influence is also illustrated by
the number of place-names called from the family: the
parish of Blanchvilleskill, and the townlands of Blanch-
fieldsland, Blanchvilletown etc.—eight in all, in Co. Kilkenny. There wholehearted adherence to the cause of
James II resulted in their final ruin, which had begun
with the Cromwellian confiscation in the previous generation. In the Jacobite outlawry records, in which three
of the name are listed, they are called both Blanchville
and Blanchfield.

BLANEY   Though now fairly numerous in east Ulster
this name was at first confined to the families of large
landed proprietors in Co. Monaghan, the first of these
being Sir Edward Blayney who settled there in 1598.
From then till the beginning of the nineteenth century
they, the. Leslies and the Dawsons were the leading
planter families in the county. One John Blayney was
among the officers who swore to defend the city of
Derry in 1689, and the name is prominent in such
records as the tituladoes of 1659, hearth money rolls,
the patentee officers, prerogative wills, nearly always in
or near Co. Monaghan. The Blayneys, indeed, as well as
becoming peers of the realm gave their name to a town—
Castleblayney.

Notwithstanding its Irish appearance the name Blaney
has no Gaelic background and has not been used as an
anglicized form of any indigenous Irish surname. It is
now rare in Co. Monaghan and is found to-day mainly in
Counties Antrim and Down.   Bibl.

(O) BLEHEEN (O) Melvin   Woulfe gives Ó Blichín as
the Gaelic-Irish form and only Bleheen as its anglicized
form. Bleahan is the spelling used by Mr. P.J. Kennedy,
an authority on Co. Galway names. He informed me that
in his lifetime some Bleahan families in the barony of
Kilconnel have changed their name to Melvin but he
could find locally no authority for the change.

The Registrar-General's report on the use of synonyms
shows that about seventy years ago Bleheen, Blehein and
Bleheine were interchangeable with both Melvin and
Melville in east Galway. Woulfe describes Ó Blichín as a
variant of Ó Maoilmhín (normally Melvin etc.) or of Ó
Maoilmhichíl (Mulvihil etc.).

The name Melvin is mainly located in Co. Mayo,
where Melville (probably there a corruption of Melvin) is
also found. Woulfe gives O Mullivine as an obsolete form
of Melvin. No doubt he refers to a Fiant of 1601 in
which this name occurs: no location is mentioned, but
the other people in the same document are of places in
the south of Ireland, so the equation must be accepted
with reserve.

BLOOD   The townland of Ballyblood near Tulla, Co
Clare, is named from the Uí Bloid, i.e. descendants of
Blod, son of Cas (from whom the collective word Dalcassian was formed). It is a coincidence that the family of
Blood, prominent among the gentry of Co. Clare from
1600 to the present time, have for centuries been seated
in the heart of the Uí Bloid country, for they have no
connexion at all with that group but are on the contrary
a family of English or Welsh extraction, having come to
Ireland from Derbyshire about the year 1595. (Reaney
says that Blood is a variant of Floyd (Lloyd)). They
were soon established in Clare, for one of them was M.P.
for Ennis in 1613. A Clare Blood was at Dublin University
in 1620. Neptune Blood is recorded as one of the Clare
Commissioners for the Poll Money Ordinance of 1661.
Many of the family were later named Neptune after him;
he is said to be so called because he was born at sea. Records dealing with Clare, e.g. The Inchiquin Manuscripts,
have many references to the Blood family from the
seventeenth century onwards. There were English Bloods
in Ireland before these, but they did not settle here. The
notorious Thomas Blood, whose father obtained an
estate in Co. Westmeath in 1640, was a nephew of the
above mentioned Neptune: though his unsuccessful
attempts to assassinate the Duke of Ormond and to steal
the crown jewels nearly brought him to the scaffold, he
was clever enough to live to enjoy the royal favour and
have his estate restored. His son, however, emigrated to
America.

A report on the family papers (1640-1845) is in the
National Library of Ireland.

BOAL O'BOHILL   Boal, sometimes spelt Boale, does
not appear to be an independent surname but is rather a
variant of two true surnames of very dissimilar origin,
viz: the Irish Ó Baoighill (Boyle) and the English Bowles
or Boles. Boal is almost exclusively found in Antrim and
Down and in those counties it has been widely used as a

synonym both of Boyle and Bowles. Bohill, found in Co. Down, is probably another anglicized form of Ó Baoighill; I think Woulfe's equation of it with the Gaelic Ó Baothghalaigh, a name mentioned by O'Dugan in his Topographical Poem among the Ulster septs, cannot be accepted: O'Donovan in his edition passes over the name without attempting to give it a modern equivalent.

BODEN   Ó Buadáin is the Irish form of this name and its Gaelic origin as an O name is corroborated by its appearance in the Elizabethan Fiants as O'Boden, the location in that case being Kilkenny. In the neighbouring county of Kildare, however, Boden or Bowden is an English surname and most of the Bodens in Ireland are of English origin, Bowden being the more numerous in all relevant documents from the sixteenth century to the present day. The earliest form of the name is Boudon. In the sixteenth century we also find Boding. Bodingstown alias Bodenston appears in a Fiant of 1569 relating to Co. Meath. The better known Bodenstown in Co. Kildare, birth-place and burial place of Wolfe Tone, was formerly also spelt Bowdenstown. In the place names Ballyboden and Bodenstown, Boden is a variant of Baldwin. In England Boden is of toponymic origin. There are few Bodens or Bowdens in the Ó Buadáin country; families so called are found mainly in Oriel today, and similarly in 1659, when Petty's "census" was taken, Boding was recorded as a principal Irish name in the barony of Ferrard, Co. Louth. (In that document the word Irish is used in a wide sense and is not confined to Gaelic-Irish.)

(O) BOGGAN, Bogan   These two forms appear to be synonymous, neither being confined to one of the two parts of the country in which the name is found. In the earliest official birth registrations Bogan was the most usual in north-west Ulster, Boggan or Boggin being the normal Co. Wexford form where a decade earlier Griffith's Valuation recorded no less than 39 householders called Boggan. In a map of Co. Donegal prepared for me by the late Mr. J.C. MacDonagh, Bogan appears as well established in the eastern part of the county. The Irish form is Ó Bogáin, derived presumably from the adjective bog (soft).

(O) BOGUE   BOWE   BOYCE   Bogue and Bowe are anglicized forms of the Gaelic Ó Buadhaigh, which is presumably derived from the adjective buadhach, victorious. Bogue is usual in Co. Cork and Bowe in the midland counties. The sept was located in the Corca Laoidhe country (south-west Cork) and O'Donovan says that they considered themselves to be a branch of the O'Sullivans who had adopted this alternative surname. Woulfe, however, states that there was no such kinship. The "census" of 1659 shows the extent to which the name was both numerous and scattered in the seventeenth century. In the returns of the principal Irish names, in addition to Buoige and O'Buoige in the part of Co. Cork referred to above, the "census" of 1659 gives: Buo, Co. Waterford (barony of Upperthird); Boe and O'Boe, Co.

Kilkenny (baronies of Galmoy, Gowran and Crannagh) and Co. Wexford; Bowe and O'Bowe, Queen's Co. or Leix (barony of Ossory). In the Tipperary Hearth Money Rolls of approximately the same date 40 families of Bowe are included in various parts of the county. In the Chancery Rolls for 1547 we find Thady Boee recorded as a cleric in the diocese of Limerick. In none of the records consulted does Co. Fermanagh appear, though nineteenth century birth registration returns indicate that Bogue—nowhere numerous—is mainly found in that county; and the same authority shows that the principal location of Bowe is Co. Kilkenny. There were many other variants of the name in English besides those mentioned above, e.g. Donough O'Bough, a Co. Cork witness in 1621; a Dermot O'Bowige, a Donough O'Boughaie and a Walter O'Boo illustrate the varieies of spelling used in the Fiants recording the names of men who received Elizabethan pardons, i.e. they were brought within the English law and ceased to be technically outlaws.

Ó Buadhaigh has also been anglicized Boyce, which is a surname fairly common in north-west Ulster (Donegal and Derry). Boyce is also an English name of Norman origin, derived from bois, a wood, and there is no doubt that some of the Irish Boyces of to-day are descended from English settlers: they appear as such at least as far back as the fourteenth century, when they were to be bound both in Co. Meath and in Co. Limerick (at first under the name de Boys) down to the time of the Cromwellian settlement when Joyn Boyce, an "adventurer" obtained 360 acres in the barony of Iffa and Offa, Co. Tipperary, and Henry Boyse, a London tallow-chandler, was also a large subscriber for lands. There is a Boystown in Co. Meath; and Boys of Gallgath, mentioned in the Meath muster of 1586 as one of the chief men of the barony of Deece, was also no doubt of Anglo-Norman stock. The Boyces of Donegal and Derry, however, are for the most part of Gaelic-Irish origin. It is of interest to note that Buie and Bwee, which are normally phonetic spellings of the adjective buidhe (yellow) are used in Donegal as synonyms of Boyce. Woulfe states that Ó Buadhaigh is the Irish form used by people called Bwee in English. Boy, of course, was the usual equivalent in sixteenth century English of buidhe as an epithet or agnomen, e.g. Sorley Boy. The use of Boy as an adjectival surname, comparable to Glass (glas) Reagh (riabhach) etc. has been noted in Counties Tipperary and Clare. A possible cause of confusion also lies in the fact that in the seventeenth century Boy was sometimes used as an abbreviated form of MacEvoy.

Rev. Dr. John Boyce (1810-1864), the priest who made his name as a novelist in America, was born in Co. Donegal, as was his nephew Jerome Boyce, a poet of some merit. Another poet, Samuel Boyce (1708-1747) was a Dublin man. Sir Rupert Boyce (1863-1911), whose work in connexion with tropical medicine was noteworthy, was born in London of Irish parents.   Map

(O) BOHAN, Bohane,   BOHANNON   Nowadays Bohan is a fairly common name, found chiefly in counties Galway and Leitrim, while Bohane, which is rare, is confined to families of Co. Cork origin. These modern spelling distinctions are fortuitous; in the "census" of 1659 Boughan appears as one of the principal Irish names in West Carbery, Co. Cork, while Bohane was numerous in Co. Leitrim. At that time the greatest number of people of the name were living in Co. Kildare: Boughan was, after Kelly, much the commonest name in the barony of Offaly in that county, having 40 families, compared with 26 for Byrne and 20 each for Dempsey, Doolin and Murphy, which came next in numerical order. This is the area to which the name Behan (q.v.) belongs. The enumerators in the 1659 "census" were careless about spelling and it is possible that Beaghan and Boaghan could have been confused by them. It is definitely not a misprint for Beaghan, because the "census" states that 37 of these were spelt Boaghan and 3 Boghan. In the Fiants of a hundred years earlier Beaghan and O'Beehan occur chiefly in Co. Kildare, O'Boughan is in Co. Cork, O'Bohen in Co. Leitrim, while the O'Boughans in the lists again introduce an element of uncertainty being from the Offaly and north Tipperary area.

Bohan is Ó Buadhacháin in Irish, the root word from which it is derived being doubtless buadh, meaning victory. This takes the form Bohannon in Clare and south Connacht. In Ulster Bohannon is a variant of Buchanan, a well known Scottish surname, which in that province has many synonyms including Mawhannon, MacWhannon and even sometimes Mawhinney.

Woulfe says that Bohane of Co. Cork is a nickname attached to a branch of the O'Sullivans and he suggests na mbothán, i.e. of the huts or sheds, as its Gaelic origin. Nevertheless, unless the clerks who recorded the Fiants mistook these two Irish words for O'Bohane, the existence of O'Boughan as a surname in Co. Cork in the sixteenth century does suggest that not all the Bohanes of that county were of O'Sullivan stock. In Co. Cork some families of Bohane have adopted the form Bowen. Bowen is normally Welsh (from Ap Owen) or a modern form of the Norman surname de Bohun.

The best known person of the name was Edward Bohane (1873-1940) who more than anyone else was responsible for the remarkable progress in our own time of the old-established Royal Dublin Society.   Bibl., Map

(O) BOLGER   Bolger is one of those Irish surnames which, in spite of its very un-Irish appearance in this anglicized form, presents no difficulty as to its origin. The name itself – Ó Bolguidhir in Irish – is certainly well disguised: the practice in modern English speech of pronouncing the G of Bolger soft adds to this; had it been written Bolgar the distortion would not have been so marked. Up to the end of the sixteenth century O'Bulgire was the usual form, though O'Boulger occurs at Ferns in 1541. Woulfe's derivation of Ó Bolguidhir from bolg odhar (yellow belly) seems not unreasonable, though it is not unquestioned.

The name Bolger is closely associated with south-east Leinster and is rarely found elsewhere. It is that of a sept which supplied many physicians to the chiefs in that area. There are frequent references to the name in the fifteenth and sixteenth centuries, to tenants, jurors and clergy as well as medical men, mainly in Co. Kilkenny; in the 1659 census it is recorded as a principal Irish name in three baronies of Co. Kilkenny, two of Co. Carlow and two of Co. Wexford. In the seventeenth century they are more prominent in Co. Wexford than elsewhere, as is the case today. Brassell and Dermot O'Bolger, both of Ballywalter, were among the chief gentlemen of the barony of Ballagheen in 1608, and in 1570 O'Bolgirs were of sufficient importance to be consulted by the Lord Deputy and Council on a matter relating to ancient rights, especially of the Colcloughs, in Co. Wexford. The family was well represented in James II's Irish army and, after the Jacobite defeat, in the Irish Brigade in France.

Although it is safe to say that almost all Bolgers in Ireland are of Ó Bolguidhir stock, it is possible that the soft G referred to above is to some extent attributable to the existence of the English surname Bolger or Boulger, which is derived from the Old-French word boulgier (maker of leather bags). It is of interest to note that in most (but not all) cases where the name Bolger appears in the sixteenth century it has no terminal R so the accepted derivation may be erroneous.   Map.

BOLTON   This is derived from an English place-name. It has been fairly numerous in Ireland since the seventeenth century. It appears frequently in the first half of that century and is still most numerous in Counties Antrim and Derry, though found in all the provinces with a fair number in Dublin. Members of these un-related families have held many prominent positions since Sir Richard Bolton was Solicitor-General in 1619. No less than 57 Boltons are in the register of students of Dublin University from 1611 to 1844 and it is worthy of note that only ten per cent of these were from Ulster. De Burgh in his Landowners of Ireland (1878) names fifteen with extensive estates in thirteen counties, only one in Ulster (Cavan). It will thus be seen that the name has never become closely identified with any particular locality in Ireland.   Bibl.

BOWDERN, Bowdren   A tradition exists in at least one branch of the Bowdern family that it owes its con-nextion with Ireland to the fact that one Nicholas Bowdern, a Swiss baker, was shipwrecked near Dun-garvan about the year 1650. It is certainly a fact that Bowdern, Bowdren or Budran families have been mainly located in the parts of Co. Waterford and east Cork not far from Dungarvan. If, however, the story of the alleged Swiss ancestor be true it must have been some gener-ations before the supposed date, since we know from Petty's "census" of 1659 that Bowdrans then were already numerous enough in Co. Waterford to be classed as one of the "principal Irish names" there: in the barony of Coshmore and Coshbride which is the portion of west Waterford which juts into east Cork, there were ten families of the name at that time. In 1601 Rick and William Budran of Dromadda obtained "pardons" – Dromadda is in the barony of Imokilly which adjoins Co. Waterford. Again in more recent times we find nine householders called Bowdren listed in Griffith's Valuation of Co. Waterford (1850). Though not then associated with these southern areas the name Boudran is to be found in Irish records of a much earlier date, for the Judiciary Rolls of 1297 and 11299 mention one William Boudran of Dublin.

I have not found any conclusive evidence of the origin of the name. I discount the Swiss theory though, Bourdon, which has both French and Germany affiliations, could well have become Boudron; nor does it appear to be an Irish Mac or O name. It is possible that it is one of the rare Norman toponymics viz. de Boderan from the place-name in Co. Wexford. It appears to be extinct now in the Dungarvan-Lismore area, where it was a century ago. It is extant in the United States.

BOWLER   This is a very old Kerry surname which according to evidence adduced by Miss M.A. Hickson was originally le Fougheler, Maurice FitzMaurice le Fougheler being coroner of Co. Kerry in 1320. In due course we find the name in an inquisition given as Fuller alias Bowler. By the sixteenth century it had become standardized as Bowler with Bowdler as a variant. The Desmond Survey of 1587 refers to Bowlerstown, which is situated near Dingle the homeland of the family, and other contemporary documents call the place Bally-bowler which is its present designation. Bowler is listed in the "census" of 1659 as a principal Irish name in the barony of Corcaguiney (in which Dingle lies). The name is still very closely connected with Kerry. According to the 1901 "census", of which an analysis is available for Co. Kerry, there were 54 families of the name then living there; in 1890 all the 14 births registered for Bowler in that year were in Kerry; and in 1865 there were 25 births, all but one in or near Kerry. People of the name were not, of course, entirely confined to Kerry, but spread to some extent into the neighbouring counties of Cork and Limerick – in 1710, for example, William Bowler was sovereign of Kinsale.

The name was gaelicized as Bóighléir: Father Thomas Bowler (Tomás Bóighléir) was the author of an elegy in Irish on Donogh MacCarthy, Bishop of Cork and Cloyne, who died in 1726.

BOYCOTT   The name Boycott is universally associated with Ireland, the famous Co. Mayo case of Capt. Charles Boycott having given a word to the English language. For that reason I include it in this book; but in fact it has no other connexion with Ireland. Captain Boycott (1832-1897) was the son of an English clergyman of an old Shropshire family: after a period of service in the British army he rented a farm in Co. Tipperary and later became agent for the vast estate of Lord Erne in Co. Fermanagh and bought a property at Lough Mask, Co. Mayo, for himself. A branch of the family lived for a while at Doneraile, Co. Cork, but there are none of the name there now.

BOYNE   Woulfe gives Mac Baoithín and Ó Baoithín as the Irish forms of Boyne and equates the latter with Ó

Baodháin (see Boyton) of Badhna in Co. Roscommon. MacBoyheen is listed in the "census" of 1659 as a principal Irish name in the baronies of Dromahare and Rosclogher, Co. Leitrim, and there can be no doubt that this is an anglicized form of MacBaoithin; it is probable, too, that Boyhan, found in Co. Westmeath in the eighteenth century, is a later variant of that name. I have, however, found no evidence that this became Boyne. None of the references to the name Boyne which I have met relate to Co. Roscommon or Co. Leitrim and only one of the province of Connacht (viz. a monument in the Dominican church at Athenry, dated 1697): all the rest, from John Boyn, who was outlawed in Co. Kildare in 1297, to the birth registrations of the last century, relate to Leinster, mainly the counties near Dublin.

BOYTON   Woulfe's statements in connexion with this name need further consideration. So far as the Tipperary Boytons are concerned he is quite correct in saying that they have been there since the thirteenth century and that their name is derived from an English village. In another place he asserts that O'Donovan was wrong in his belief that the name comes from the Gaelic Ó Baodáin. In my opinion they are both right. The de Boytons of Munster were already well established near Cashel before 1300 since they had given their name to the place names Boytonrath and Boytonstown by 1307. The first reference I have found to them is to a Richard de Boyton, successful plaintiff in a law case in 1297 at Cashel. From that time on there are many references to them in mediaeval documents and they were continuously associated with that part of the country until comparatively recent times. I may mention that their arms are displayed in Cashel Cathedral. Since the Reformation, however, not all these Boytons were Protestants: Father William Boyton S.J. was martyred for the faith at Cashel in 1647, and Patrick Boyton of Thomastown, Co. Tipperary, was among the transplanted Papists of 1657.

The Gaelic Irish records bring the Boytons of Connacht back even further than their Norman namesakes. Probably Woulfe did not realize how closely the name is associated with that part of the country in or near Co. Roscommon when he disputed O'Donovan's opinion, which, it must be remembered, did not specifically refer to the Munster Boytons. The Annals of Loch Cé record the death of Sanctus Mauricius O'Baedan in 1199. This name occurs occasionally e.g. in The Tribes and Customs of Hy Many but the Connacht Boytons were not very prominent. One appears in the "census" of 1659 as titulado in the parish of Clooncraffe, Co. Roscommon, and another of the same place was an officer of Clifford's Dragoons in James II's Irish army, though he does not appear in the lists of persons outlawed for that activity.

The name has now become rare but is still extant in the north-western part of the country.

James W. Boyton M.D. was the author of a work entitled An Authentic Narrative (1789) which gives an account of the cause célèbre of Mary Neal.

(O) BRACKEN   The name Bracken was, comparatively,

more numerous in the seventeenth century than it is to-day; it appears in the "census" of 1659 among the commoner Irish names in four baronies, three in Co. Offaly (then called King's County) and the fourth, barony of Offaly, in adjacent Co. Kildare; and all the references in the Fiants of the previous century in which the name O'Brackane or variants occur relate to the same part of the country, where, it may be added, families of the name (now without the prefix O) are still mainly found. In Irish the name is Ó Breacáin and is derived from the word breac, speckled.

Benedict O'Breacan was Bishop of Achonry from 1286 to 1312. Thomas Bracken (1843-1898), of Clones, emigrated from Ireland to Australia as a boy and after some years in that country became a prominent public figure in New Zealand as member of parliament and poet. The career of Brendan Bracken, 1st Viscount Bracken, (1901-1958) may be said to have begun when at the age of 15 he ran away from school at the Jesuit College of Mungret, Co. Limerick; it ended as a financial magnate and cabinet minister in the British government.

(O) BRANNELLY, Branley   This name, Ó Branghaile in Irish (branghal, raven valour), is peculiar to east Galway. It is not numerous. The cognate Ó Branghail appears to be obsolete now: it occurs as O'Branyll in a late sixteenth century Fiant relating to Co. Cavan.

(O) BRANNIGAN, Brangan   The Gaelic sept of Ó Branagáin is undoubtedly of the Cenél Eoghain and was located in Oriel, being found in the sixteenth and seventeenth centuries, as today, chiefly in the contiguous counties of Armagh, Monaghan and Louth. Families of the name associated with Ardee in the latter county have been confused with Norman Berminghams of the same barony. Thus Petty's "census" enumerators in 1659 regarded the two names as synonymous and totalled them together as one. The error was not an unlikely one for strange clerks to make, on account of the local pronunciation of Bermingham (cf. Brummagen for Birmingham in colloquial English). They are quite unmistakably O'Brannigan in the Hearth Money Rolls for Co. Armagh. A branch of the sept migrated to Galway (about the year 1400) where some of them became in due course O'Brangan. According to Dalton, Henry Branigan was warden of Galway in 1497, though the only reference to the name I found when examining the Wardenship MSS was to one Henry Brangan arbitrator in a dispute in 1525. Another Henry Branigan was an officer in Bellew's regiment (chiefly from the Louth-Monaghan area) in James II's Irish army. The townland of Ballybranagan in the barony of Kiltartan was presumably called after the Co. Galway branch. In Co. Armagh there is a Ballybranan which lends some colour to Father Woulfe's theory that the name Ó Branáin, that of the erenaghs of Derryvullan Co. Fermanagh, is merely a contraction of Ó Branagáin: be that as it may both are certainly derived from the forename Bran. Branigan, however, was the form used in Connacht at a comparatively recent date – three so called are in a Ballinrobe rental of 1783; at the present time Brangans

and Branagans are approximately equal in numbers in the east of Ireland – in the west it is now rare in any form.   Map

BRAY   The name Bray in Ireland is of dual origin: either de Bri (or de Bre) i.e. of a place called Bray – not usually Bray, Co. Wicklow; or alternatively Ó Breaghdha, a Munster sept mentioned by O'Heerin in the Topographical Poem. O'Donovan in his notes to that work states that this family is now unknown; but the name Bray occurs continually in mediaeval and early modern Munster records and it would appear to be a reasonable supposition that it is there sometimes, if not always, properly O'Bray. From the year 1207 onwards families called Bray are closely associated with Clonmel and several of the name were sovereigns of the town from the thirteenth to the sixteenth centuries; in the seventeenth the John Bray who was outlawed as a Jacobite in 1691 was an alderman of that town; a generation earlier there were eight families recorded in the Co. Tipperary Hearth Money Rolls; while Thomas Bray, Archbishop of Cashel from 1792 to 1810, was a notable churchman at that critical time; and finally, as regards Munster, the existence of Bray families in Co. Cork is attested by the frequent occurrence of the name in the Cork and Ross marriage licence bonds from 1697. It rarely appears with the prefix O: there is a county Tipperary Obrey in a 1295 Justiciary Roll (if one can accept this as a variant) and an O'Brahye is mentioned in a Co. Waterford Fiant of 1601. It cannot, however, be laid down that O'Bray is exclusively Munster and de Bray Leinster, because we do find an occasional de Bray in Co. Tipperary while a fifteenth century O'Bray is mentioned in an ecclesiastical case in 1433 and another in a Meath pardon of 1542. Brays are now fairly numerous in Offaly, but whether these had migrated northwards from Munster or southwards from Meath is uncertain.

Bree is a synonym of Bray, i.e. of de Bray: it does not appear as O'Bree. De Bray and de Bree belong mainly to Co. Dublin and the neighbouring counties of Meath and Louth.

(O) BRAZIL, Brassill   These two anglicized forms of the Irish surname Ó Breasail are now about equal in number: they are found mainly in Waterford and Offaly, but are not confined to those counties. A century ago they were located also in Counties Tipperary, Kilkenny, Limerick and Kerry, but more recent statistics indicate that the name has become rather rare outside of Co. Waterford. The name O'Brasil occurs there as early as 1308; the old name of Lysaghtstown in Co. Cork near the Co. Waterford border was Baile uí Bhreasail and O Bressyl occurs in Co. Cork in 1285. Sixteenth and seventeenth century records are rich in references to the name. The prefix O, now quite obsolete with Brazil, is retained in the Tudor Fiants, but even as early as 1537, when Brassell occurs among the commoners of Kilkenny, and in 1551, when Mahowne Brassill, a kern, was convicted at Clonmel of having stolen cattle, it is omitted. In the "census" of 1659 Brassell is returned as a principal Irish name in the Co. Waterford barony of Upper-third: as such it occurs ten times in the Tipperary Hearth Money Rolls of 1665-67 in various spellings also without the O. Other seventeenth century men of interest were John Brassell of Ballycargin, Co. Wexford, who was High Constable of the barony of Gorey in 1608, and Denis Brazill, of Ballyduff in the same county, attainted as a Jacobite after the failure of that cause. West Offaly was one of the homelands of the Brazils. However he was probably a MacBrassill, a name which occurs in the Elizabethan Fiants in Co. Galway and is that of a small but distinct sept almost if not quite extinct.

It should be added that the sept of Ó Breasail has no connexion with the Clann Bhreasail, which was the tribe name of the Uí Bhreasail of Oriel.

MacBREARTY, MacMurty   The name MacBrearty is numerous in Donegal and rare elsewhere. According to Woulfe it is a corrupt form of MacMurty (i.e. he says, Mac Muircheartaigh). This is to some extent corroborated by the fact that in Milford district MacMearty and Mac Merty have been recorded by local registrars as in use synonymously with MacBrearty and MacBrairty. However such usage is often due to ignorance rather than etymology or tradition: MacBrearty is a case in point, for the Glenties registrar reported that there some members of a MacBrearty family called themselves Brady. MacMurtry on the other hand is not so recorded in the years under review by Matheson. MacMurtry on the basis of its modern distribution must be classed as an Antrim surname; it is akin to the Scottish name Murdoch which is very numerous in Co. Antrim. MacMurdoch is a sept of the Scottish clan MacDonald; MacMurtrie of the clan Stuart of Bute.

(Mac) BREHENY, Judge   It seems a pity that the beautiful Irish name Mac an Bhreitheamhnaigh, first phonetically anglicized MacEvrehoona, MacVrehonne, MacBrehon etc., should have generally become Judge; though at least this is not one of the numerous cases of mistranslation, since the name means son of the judge. Today the form Judge outnumbers Breheny (and Brehony) by two to one. Many examples occur in the birth registrations for Co. Sligo and north Roscommon of a family using Judge and Breheny indifferently; and in a list of synonyms used by emigrants in the 19th century, recorded by the Cunard Company, Brehony, Brehon and Judge are equated, with the addition of Breen (which of course is an erroneous equation). That is the part of the country where Brehenys are now found; persons called Judge are not confined to Connacht. In 1659 Petty found MacBrehuny numerous in the barony of Tirerrill, Co. Sligo, and other records of the same century, such as Strafford's Inquisitions and the Books of Survey and Distribution, confirm that they were people of substance in north Connacht. The Four Masters record the death in 1483 of Cormac Mac an Brehon "intended ollave of Muintir Maelruain" i.e. the population group comprising the families of MacDermot of Moylurg, MacDermot Roe,

MacDermot Gall and MacDonagh of Tirerrill. In the next century Eugene MacBrehan was Bishop of Mayo (later Tuam) from 1541 to 1561, and Malachy MacBrehuna was Archdeacon of Kilmacduagh.

Peter Judge who died in 1947 was for many years regarded as the finest actor in the Abbey Theatre Company: his stage name was F. J. McCormack. William Quan Judge (1851-1896), theosophist, a well known character in America, was born in Dublin.

Mr. J.C. MacDonagh informs me that the Mac A Brehons of Co. Donegal have become Browne since about 1800. It is remarkable that Mac an Bhreithamhnaigh was also anglicized as Abraham — see separate entry for that name.   Map

BRERETON   On account of the prominence of the Parliamentary general Sir William Brereton and of Major Brereton, one of the disbanded officers of Col. Sadleir's regiment who settled in Co. Tipperary, Brereton is often regarded as a Cromwellian name in Ireland. Actually there were families of the name from Brereton in Cheshire established in Ireland nearly a century before the Cromwellian Settlement. The most notable of these were in Co. Down and Queen's County (Leix). In the former they were located at Lecale before 1550, and one Ralph Brereton was sheriff of Co. Down in 1591. The founder of the fortunes of this family in Ireland was the Sir William Brereton whose vigorous action enabled Lord Deputy Skeffington to crush the rebellion of "Silken Thomas" in 1535; four years later as Lord High Marshal he opposed Con O'Neill. His son and two of his nephews held high office and received large grants of land. According to family tradition the Breretons of Queen's County came from England at the time of the attempted plantation of Leix and Offaly under Philip and Mary; in fact the Loughteeog property was acquired by Sir William's grandson Edward in 1563. Grants in that county are recorded at various dates from 1563 to 1594. His youngest son John Brereton was constable of the castle of Wexford and seneschal of the county; he received a grant of land there under Edward VI, but the connexion with that county does not appear to have lasted long: the "census" of 1659 includes a number of tituladoes called Brereton in Queen's County (Leix) and elsewhere, but none in Co. Wexford, nor does the Civil Survey of Co. Wexford contain the name among English Protestant or Irish Papist proprietors. The principal Leix properties were Loughteeog and Shanemullen, and the families who owned them retained their influential position until quite recent times. Carew includes the Loughteeog family in his list of the principal gentry of Queen's County in 1600: one was M.P. for Ballinakill in 1613; and Father Edmund Hogan, editor of the MS. known as the "Description of Ireland in 1598", states that the Shanemullen family were in Co. Carlow when he wrote in 1878. They are not listed in Co. Carlow in de Burgh's Landowners of that date, though that work includes them as fairly extensive landlords in Co. Tipperary. Other families from the Queen's Co. settlers remained staunch Catholics throughout the penal times. The

Fiants likewise indicate that the Breretons of the sixteenth century, several of whom received pardons like their Gaelic neighbours, were not by any means all devoted to the English interest; and in the vital text of 1689-90 John Brereton of Loughteeog was found on the Jacobite side and was outlawed for "high treason" by William of Orange. Bibl.

(O) BRESLIN   Breslin, rarely O'Breslin in modern times, is primarily a Donegal name. The sept of O'Breislein, a branch of the Cenél Enda, possessed a district in the barony of Kilmacrenan called Fanad. The O'Breslins were one of the principal brehon families of Ireland. Their power as chiefs of Fanad, which up to the fourteenth century was such as to merit frequent mention by the Four Masters, was broken by the MacSweeneys about the year 1260, but the rank and file of the sept evidently remained in, or returned to, their homeland as it is there the name is principally found today, as it was in 1659. The leading families migrated to Co. Fermanagh, where they pursued their profession as brehons under the MacGuires. They also became erenaghs of Derryvullen in that county. John J. Breslin (c. 1836-1888), the Fenian who effected the escape of James Stephens from Richmond prison, was of a Co. Tyrone family.

There was also a distinct sept of the same name, a branch of the Hy Fiachrach, whose small territory lay on the east side of the river Moy at Killanley in the parish of Castleconnor, Co. Sligo. O'Donovan points out that they were of little importance compared with their Ulster namesakes, and they appear now to be extinct.

In Co. Donegal some families of Breslin have changed their name to Brice and Bryce which is a common English surname.

Canon Power in his History of Co. Waterford mentions O'Breslin with O'Brick, O'Foley and O'Keane as the great families of the Decies, and the name appears in the Justiciary Rolls of 1306 and 1307 dealing with Co. Waterford.   Map

BRETT, Britt   Brett is the more usual spelling in Counties Waterford and Tipperary; Britt in north Connacht. It appears as the latter among the principal Irish names in Counties Tipperary and Kilkenny in the "census" of 1659: though not a Gaelic name it had, like so many others of Norman origin, become hibernicized — it is derived from an old French word denoting a Breton and in mediaeval records usually appears as le Bret, le Brette or le Bryt. It occurs in some of the earliest of our Anglo-Norman records: in 1199 Milo le Bret obtained a grant of lands in Co. Dublin; a few years later a le Bret was in possession of the castle of Knocktopher; later we find them in Co. Tipperary at Cashel and Thurles and at Gowran and other places in Co. Kilkenny. Walter and Geoffrey le Bret were sheriffs of Co. Tipperary in 1295 and 1302 and if, as is probable, the barony of Ballybritt was named from them, it would appear that at least one influential family of the name settled beyond the bounds of Co. Tipperary in the neighbouring county of Offaly. William Britt was sheriff of Connacht in 1247.

Dr. John Brit O.F.M. was Bishop of Annaghdown from 1402 to 1421, but I have found no other evidence of more than a fleeting connexion with Connacht until 1636 when Joseph Britte was a tenant at Drumcolumb Co. Sligo; a man of the same name was a member of the Sligo Corporation in 1687. Another John Brett was a Connacht prelate: he was Bishop of Killala, but not till 1743 — he occupied the see of Elphin later (1748 to 1753). A few prominent men of the name were resident in the Pale: the Bretts were reckoned among the chief gentry of Co. Louth in 1598, and Richard Brett was sheriff of Co. Meath in that year. One, presumably of this family, was an officer in Slane's regiment of James II's army. Three, all described as merchants of Drogheda, are in the prerogative wills proved in the first half of the seventeenth century.

(O) BRICK, Badger   Except in Co. Kerry the name Brick is now very rare. All the Brick births recorded in 1864, 1865 and 1890 occurred in that county. Nevertheless the sept of Ó Bruic is not of Co. Kerry by origin, since it was first located in Thomond. The date at which this Dalcassian family was dispossessed of its ancient territory is uncertain, but the first authentic records of it are in Co. Kerry.

The name is derived from the Irish word broc meaning a badger, no doubt the sobriquet of the eponymous ancestor: Badger, indeed, has been sometimes used as an anglicized form of Ó Bruic and persons so called, at any rate in Ireland are in nearly all cases actually O'Bricks.

Another sept of a similar but philologically different Irish name, usually written Ó Bric but occasionally Ó Bruic, was in the mediaeval period, at least up to 1300, of great importance and distinction. Ó Bric is described in the Book of Rights and other early authorities as one of the chief septs of the Decies (Co. Waterford). In the Annals of Loch Cé two Ó Bric warriors, slain in 1103, are described as "royal heirs of the Decies." In 1203 O'Brick of the Decies was admitted to extensive knightly tenure by King John, but 50 years later the family were deprived of this by English influence; nevertheless they held out against the Norman conquerors for nearly a century longer, until finally overcome by the Powers of that area. In many cases great Gaelic-Irish families dispossessed by the Norman invaders remained in a subordinate position in their old homeland: these O'Bricks, however, despite, perhaps on account of their prolonged resistance appear to have died out soon after they were finally subdued.   Map

BRISCOE   Owing to the prominence of Alderman Robert Briscoe T.D., twice an outstanding Lord Mayor of Dublin in recent years, it might be thought that Briscoe is a Jewish surname of recent introduction in Ireland. It is not, it is true, of Gaelic-Irish origin, but it is on record in this country since the sixteenth century when in 1588 a Briscoe married a Kearney heiress and built the castle of Scraghe near Tullamore: the Briscoes of Riverdale, Killucan, are their descendants. John Briscoe of Sraigh (Scraghe) was transplanted as a Papist in

1656. Briscoes were still to be found in Co. Offaly in 1855: Griffith's Valuation records eleven families of the name mainly in the baronies of Ballybritt, Ballycowan and Garrycastle. In the next two centuries references to men of the name in different parts of the country are quite frequent: the "census" of 1659 records two titula-does in Co. Dublin, one of whom, Gabriel Briscoe, we know from another source was an official of the court of Chancery; about the same time a Thomas Briscoe, Crom-wellian "adventurer" of £100, obtained 540 acres in the barony of Clanwilliam Co. Tipperary; a few years later we find them as small householders in Kilbeggan town and less humbly as relatives of the Nugents of Farren-connell, Co. Cavan, while one was a brewer in Dublin. Seven of the name are in the lists of eighteenth century marriage licence bonds in Co. Cork. Then again there was William Briscoe of Sligo who was outlawed for his adherance to the cause of James II in 1690, and another place in which they appear in the period in question is Co. Waterford.

BRITTON MacBRATNEY Britton is the usual form of this name, which is to be found in most parts of Ireland, though nowhere very numerous; in Dublin it is sometimes spelt Brittain. Its origin is geographical but it is derived from Britany in France not from Great Britain. It occurs quite frequently in our mediaeval records such as the Justiciary Rolls and Ormond Deeds, with the prefix le — le Breton it is. — not de, though in England similar records have also de Bretagne. Though widely distributed it was first, in the thirteenth century, established in Co. Kildare and Co. Meath but by the seventeenth century Co. Tipperary was its main location, though fairly well established in Co. Wexford also. Thus it is listed in the "census" of 1659 as a principal name in the barony of Middlethird in that county and the Co. Tipperary Hearth Money Rolls of the next decade include no less than 32 householders of the name. The only reference to it in the Fiants of the previous century is one to James Brittyn of Milltown, Co. Tipperary, who obtained a "pardon" in 1567. During the eighteenth century it became scattered. Brittan is now numerous enough on the Donegal-Tyrone border to be included in the map of that area prepared for me by the late J.C. MacDonagh.

The "census" of 1659 also contains, as a principal Irish name, MacBritany, in the barony of Glencarne, Co. Antrim. It is possible that some families so called did later abbreviate this to Britain, but as a rule MacBritany can be taken as an earlier anglicized form of Mac Breath-naigh (i.e. son of the Welshman, and so akin to Brannagh and Walsh) now usually MacBratney and still located in north-east Ulster.

BROCAS This name is now very rare in Ireland. It occurs in the Patent Rolls relating to Co. Dublin in 1395, but there is no evidence that the family became estab-lished here at that early date. In 1625 a Thomas Brocas obtained a lease of silver and gold mines in Co. Kerry: the interesting conditions attached to this lease are out-lined in the Calendar of State Papers, Ireland, of that date. The name is of special interest to this country on account of the four distinguished artists Henry Brocas (1762-1837) and his three sons, Henry (c. 1798-1873), Samuel (1792-1847) and William (c. 1794-1868), all of Dublin. Before them there was Gabriel Brocas, also of Dublin, whose will was proved in 1747. The elder Henry was great-grandson of Robert Brocas of Derbyshire who came to Ireland as a cornet of horse in Cromwell's army. It is a name of antiquity in England where, according to Reaney, it (with its variants Brokus and Brochis) is synonymous with Brookhouse. It also appears among the names of Huguenot refugees from France. There are pedigrees of Brocas and Brokas in the Genealogical Office, Dublin Castle. Bibl.

(O) BROE BURY BURGESS BURROWES
Brugha (sometimes de Brugha) is used as the Irish equiv-alent of three surnames — Bury, Burgess and Burrows — while Ó Brugha (or Ó Brughadha) is the Irish original of the name now anglicized Broe and Brew, and also perhaps Broy, which, however, must be remembered occurs in mediaeval records as de Broy (i.e. of Broy, a place in Oxfordshire). Written by Elizabethan officials as O'Broe, O'Broghe, O'Broo etc., it is of frequent occurrence in sixteenth century records relating to Queen's Co. (Leix) and Kilkenny. In much the same part of the country we find Brew appearing as a Norman surname — de Berewa and de Bruth — as early as 1190; this is the de Brugha referred to above which is akin to the surname de Burgh and its English derivative Burrough or Burrowes. Brew is also a Manx surname, originally MacVriw, which, accord-ing to A.W. Moore (Manx Surnames), is cognate with the Irish MacBrehon.

Burgess, though the same in Irish, is of different origin: it is self-explanatory, meaning simply a citizen. An early alternative spelling of this was Burys; but it is improbable that this was modernized as Bury. At any rate the Bury family, which settled in Co. Limerick in 1666, consider that the origin of the name is locative and is taken from the Chateau de Bury in Normandy. Several place-names in England incorporate this word (which is a form of borough) e.g. Bury St. Edmund's. Burys of Norman descent came to Ireland with the Prestons: the name de Bury is to be found in records of the fourteenth century relating to Drogheda. One, Sir Simon de Bury, appears in Co. Wicklow as early as 1234. There were Burys in Co. Wicklow in the late eighteenth century: two of the 23 prerogative wills listed by Vicars under the name of Bury are for that county — the majority of these testators were of Dublin and Cork. According to Reaney in England Bury and Berry are synonymous. Berry is a not uncommon surname in Ireland: Matheson reports it as chiefly found in Counties Antrim, Mayo and Offaly. In the last it is a form of Beary. This is the angli-cization of Ó Beara, the name of a small Offaly sept akin to the O'Dempseys and O'Connors of that region. The name Burgess was quite common in mediaeval Ireland, nearly always in connexion with municipal or parlia-mentary affairs, e.g. a witness to the charter of Rosber-con (New Ross) in 1294, an assessor for Co. Kildare 1420 and so on. The records of the city of Dublin contain many references to persons called Burgess as members of trade guilds, churchwardens and the like. Broy occurs in Co. Kildare as early as 1297 when one Geoffrey Broy was outlawed as a robber.

Coming to the eighteenth century we read in James Freeney's graphic account of his adventurous life how Henry Burgess, sheriff of Co. Kilkenny, was mortally wounded in 1748 in an attempt to capture that celebrated highwayman. Of the Burys the best known was the distinguished scholar Professor John Bagenal Bury (1861-1927) who came of a branch of the Co. Limerick family which settled in Co. Monaghan. Peter Burrows (1753-1841) was an anti-Union M.P. and notable barrister who defended Robert Emmet at his trial. Cathal Brugha (1874-1922), the courageous and unyielding republican leader killed in the civil war, was of a Dublin family of Burgess long established in the city.

(O) BROGAN   (O) BROHAN, Banks   The sept of Ó Brógáin belongs by origin to the Hy Fiachrach group and possessed estates in the barony of Carra and also at Breaghwy in Co. Mayo, where, with Co. Donegal, the name is chiefly found in modern times. In the sixteenth century men of the name were to be found in both those counties: in the latter they were among the followers of Rory O'Donnell. Benedict Ó Brócáin was bishop of Leyney (i.e. of Achonry) from 1286 to 1312. The placename Ballybrogan suggests that they were also established in Co. Roscommon near Athlone. In 1504 Dom Dermicius O'Brogan was a member of the community of the priory of Kilkenny West near Athlone. This Kilkenny, it should be remembered, is a barony of Co. Westmeath and has no connexion with County Kilkenny. The 1659 "census" indicates that the O'Brogans were then chiefly located in Co. Westmeath but on the side farthest from Connacht. Charles Brogan, of Cavan, was one of the attainted Jacobites. There is in fact ample evidence to show that much earlier than the seventeenth century the name was not confined to Connacht. In Munster a Mahony O'Brogan was in 1300 among the tenants of Cahirconlish manor, Co. Limerick, and Stephen O'Brogan (d. 1302) was one of the more notable archbishops of Cashel; another example is the trial and acquittal at Waterford in 1312 of one Adam O'Brogan, charged with cattle stealing and protecting the king's enemies. In Ulster Nehemias O'Brogan was Bishop of Clogher from 1227 to 1240. Broganstown, Co. Wicklow, would seem to indicate a connexion with that county also.

Broghane, which occurs in the "census" of 1659 as one of the principal names in the barony of Geashill, King's Co. (Offaly) is not the same as Brogan, though it too is said to have originated in Connacht. It is Ó Bruacháin (Brohan in the anglicized form) and sometimes, by mistranslation, Banks. The Bankses in Ireland are mostly of this Gaelic stock; but the family of the best known of the name in Ireland, Sir John Thomas Banks (1816-1908), one of the most notable medical men of his time, though long connected with Co. Clare, is of English origin.   Map

(O) BROPHY   The name Ó Bróithe was formerly phonetically anglicized O'Brohy, but it later became Brophy. Both by the test of history and by present-day population statistics it belongs to the counties of Leix and Kilkenny. According to the "census" of 1659 Brophy was one of the principal names in five baronies of Queen's County (i.e. Leix) and in five of Co. Kilkenny: in other words it was numerous and widespread in those counties. In Clandonagh it is perpetuated in the well known Co. Leix place-name Ballybrophy. Originally situated in the barony of Galmoy, Co. Kilkenny, Anglo-Norman pressure drove many of the sept westwards into Upper Ossory, though the facts given above show that others were not uprooted from their homeland.

Daniel Brophy of Castlecomer, three times mayor of Ballarat, was a well known public figure in Australia in the 1870's. Hugh Brophy, a leading Dublin Fenian, was transported on the last of the convict ships and went to Melbourne (not Sydney) after his release from Freementle prison.   Map

(O) BROSNAN   Brosnan is essentially a Kerry surname. King's analysis of the 1901 census shows that there were then no less than 264 Brosnan families in Kerry. All the 66 births registered for the name in the most recent year for which detailed statistics are available were in Munster and 55 of them in Co. Kerry. In Irish it is Ó Brosnacháin, possibly derived from the Kerry place-name Brosna; its earlier anglicized forms, Brosnaghan etc., preserved the three syllables of the original. There are many variant spellings of the name recorded in the modern birth registrations including Bresnahan, Bresnane, Bresnehan, Bresnihan, Brosnahen, Brosnahin, Brosnihan, Brusnahan, Brusnehan and Brusnihan; Brestenehane occurs in the 1611 Inquisitions.

The earliest reference to the name I have met is for the year 1333, not however in Kerry but in east Munster, when the betaghs on a manor estate near Clonmel included O'Brosnanes.   Map

BROUGHALL   Several variant spellings of this have been recorded such as Brohal and Broughill, including Brothel in Co. Sligo: this occurs in a birth registration of 1866 and would seem to indicate a refreshing innocence in the Connacht of a century ago. Conor O'Brotall, who is mentioned among a number of Co. Roscommon men in a Fiant of 1584, was possibly of the small and little known sept in question. Connacht is not its modern homeland, if we take birth registrations of several years in the last century as a guide, since these were mostly in Co. Kildare. The earliest reference to the name I have met is to a Robert Brohale, a Co. Waterford juror in 1312, and in the next generation we find Philip Brohale resident in Co. Carlow in 1356; a John Brohale was assessor for the barony of Narragh, Co. Kildare, in 1420 and another of the same name (spelt Broghall) was of Moone in that county in 1402. Richard Broughall appears as a titulado in the barony of Castleknock, Co. Dublin in 1659; and in 1714 we meet the name again in Co. Dublin when Robert Broghill was brought to court as a Papist under the Penal Code. I have yet to find an early instance which might link it with an original form in Irish. The Broghil, from which Roger Boyle, later Earl of Orrery, took his title, is in Co. Cork; but I know of no evidence that the surname under consideration is derived from that place.

BROY   In the note on Broe the occurrence of this name as de Broy is mentioned. It should also be stated that it appears several times as O'Broy, notably in the sixteenth century Fiants, usually in or near Co. Kilkenny. There, and in the contiguous Queen's Co. (Leix), O'Broe, O'Broo, O'Brohe and O'Broha occur frequently in the same source: no doubt these are obsolete forms of the modern Brophy — formerly Brohy — (see Brophy), and it is probable that Broy, when it is O'Broy not de Broy, is also an anglicized form of Ó Bróithe not of Ó Brughadha.

(O) BRUEN   People of this name are mainly found in or near Co. Roscommon and most of these can with reasonable certainty be regarded as belonging to the sept of Ó Braoin, the principal family of which were erenaghs of St. Coman, Roscommon. (The other Ó Braoin septs are called Breen — see "Irish Families", p. 59). It was a coincidence that an English Cromwellian, James Bruen, settled at Abbeyboyle, Co. Roscommon, in the seventeenth century. His family did not long remain there: in the next century they moved to Co. Carlow and acquired there a very extensive family property — de Burgh's Landowners of Ireland (1878) states that it consisted of 16,477 acres in Co. Carlow and 6932 in Co. Wexford.

BRYAN   Bryan has inevitably been used at times as a synonym of O'Brien, but as a rule, particularly in the case of families from Co. Kilkenny and adjacent areas, it is of Anglo-Norman origin. The Christian name Brian, from which it is derived, usually regarded like Patrick as essentially Irish, was common in France and, after the Conquest, in mediaeval England. Practically all the Bryans who have been recorded as members of parliament, army officers, mayors etc. and landowners have been Kilkenny people, descendants of the first thirteenth century settlers there. In 1878 George Leopold Bryan, of Jenkinstown House, Co. Kilkenny, owned 12, 891 acres, while other Bryan estates, mostly in Counties Wexford and Kilkenny, amounted to another 13,000 acres.

BRYSON   There is an English surname Bryson or Briceson (i.e. son of Brice), but in Ireland it has an Irish origin in Ulster, particularly in Counties Donegal and Derry. This is clearly indicated in its earlier anglicized forms: the seventeenth century Hearth Money Rolls for the northern counties list many householders whose name is written Mrieson and similar variants, which is an approximate phonetic rendering of Ó Muirgheasáin. The "census" of 1659 gives O'Mrisane as a principal Irish name in the barony of Inishowen, Co. Donegal. As might be expected this has been largely absorbed by the better

known Morrison. Even as early as 1606 O'Morison was not unknown in Co. Donegal, at any rate by the non-Gaelic authorities: for example Bishop Montgomery in his survey of the Diocese of Derry called the erenagh of Clonmany in Inishowen Donatus O'Morison. Nevertheless Bryson is the modern form adopted and usually retained in the counties mentioned above. Woulfe states that it has become Price in Co. Mayo; but of course this is normally a Welsh name (viz. Ap Rhys). Price is a very numerous name in Ireland, found in all the provinces and on record since early mediaeval times.

(O) BUGGY   Woulfe says nothing about this name except that is is Ó Bogaigh in Irish and is derived from bog (soft) and is rare. It is in fact not rare in Leinster, being found mainly in Counties Kilkenny and Wexford.

BUGLER   This name in Ireland is peculiar to the barony of Tulla in east Clare, particularly the parishes of Mynoe (Scariff) and Ogonneloe. It is not an anglicization of a Gaelic Irish surname, nor is it derived from the English word bugler (bugle player); but, according to Weekley, it is taken from the place-name Bugley in Dorset, to which county it exclusively belongs in England. This, no doubt, accounts for the fact that it is pronounced "Buggler" not "Bewgler".

BULFIN   Much searching and enquiry has failed to discover any positive evidence regarding the origin of this name. I provisionally accept the suggestion that it is a variant of the surname Bullfinch now extant in America but, according to Bardsley, obsolete in England. Nor can I state when it first came to Ireland. Since the beginning of the nineteenth century it has been continuously in Co. Offaly. Thence came William Bulfin (1862-1910) who was born and died at Birr. He is best known for his Rambles in Erinn but spent most of his life as a journalist in Argentina where he lost no opportunity of furthering the cause of Ireland.

BUNTING   The name Bunting is, of course, intimately associated with Ireland in the person of Edward Bunting (1773-1843) who spent his life collecting Irish music. At the age of 19 he organized a great harp festival in Belfast; 3 years later he published the first of his three large collections of Irish airs. He himself was born at Armagh and his father was the manager of a coal mine at Drumglass in Co. Tyrone. The name is principally found in those counties, being of the affectionate nickname type of surname. The earliest example of it in Ireland I have met is James Bunting a trooper in Ormond's own regiment in 1640; there was another Bunting also in the army in 1647. The name was established in Ulster by the middle of the seventeenth century. Two of the name are in the Tyrone Hearth Money Rolls of 1664, and presumably the five householders who appear in the Antrim Rolls as Buntin, Buntine and Buntaine are also Buntings.

In 1672 the will of Anthony Bunting, yeoman, of Co. Antrim was proved.

MacBURNEY, Birney   This is a Scottish name of comparatively recent introduction into Ireland but now numerous in and around Belfast. Woulfe gives Mac Biorna as the Gaelic form.

BURNS   While the majority of families called Burns in Ireland are either of Scottish immigrant stock or Byrnes in disguise, when this name is found in north Connacht it is usually the anglicized form of Mac Conboirne, which was first anglicized phonetically as MacConborney.

BUSTEED   This name, well known in Co. Cork, is very rarely met with elsewhere. It is of Cromwellian origin in Ireland. In the so-called census of 1659 four Busteeds are recorded as tituladoes, one in the city and three in the county of Cork. At least twelve Cork wills are listed for the name between 1666 and 1793 and a Cork man Jephson Busteed (born 1678), recorder of Kinsale and M.P. for Midleton etc., was closely related to the powerful family of Jephson of Mallow Castle. Modern birth registrations indicate that, while the name is not numerous, it still, as formerly, belongs almost exclusively to Co. Cork. The marriage licence bonds for the diocese of Cork and Ross include no less than 41 Busteeds between the years 1682 and 1750.

BUTTIMER   This may fairly be described as a Co. Cork name for ever since it first appeared in Irish records until the present day it has been found there and rarely elsewhere. I have not been able to ascertain the origin of this name. The exact date of its introduction into Ireland is uncertain but it was at least as far back as the Elizabethan period. In 1601 it appears as Botymer in a Fiant giving a long list of "pardons" to O'Mahony of Castlemahony Co. Cork and his followers. This Maurice Botymer was son of Robert Botymer. Mr. John T. Collins tells me that Maurice and Robert are still favourite christian names with the Buttimers of today. In Griffith's Valuation (1851-3), in which the name occurs frequently in all parts of Co. Cork, it is spelt in seven different ways including Buttamore and even Buttermore; Buttimer, however, was the most usual.

CADOGAN   This is familiar by reason of the fame of William Cadogan (1675-1726), first Earl Cadogan, who was closely associated with Marlborough in his military campaigns. He was born in Dublin, but was of a Welsh family of whom Prince Cadwugaun (d. 1112) was the most notable. Several of these held official positions in the sixteenth and seventeenth centuries and the correspondence and activities of Major William Cadogan, who was governor of Trim from 1647 to 1661, occupy more space in the later Ormond Manuscripts than almost any other individual other than one of the Butler family.

The name is still extant in fair numbers, but seldom met outside Co. Cork (apart of course from migrants from Co. Cork). These families are of quite different origin, being native Irish, Ó Ceadagáin by name. It was first anglicized O'Kadegane and O'Keadagan as is known from the Elizabethan Fiants and was found then as now in the O'Sullivan country.

The Gormanston Register records that Thomas and Bartholomew Cadigan were considerable landholders in Co. Limerick in 1341, their place being called Martyncadyganestown. These were probably of the O'Cadigan sept. The Patent Rolls also record several people of the name in Co. Limerick between 1345 and 1360.

(O) CAHALANE, Callan CULHANE   Writing over a century ago O'Donovan remarks that Ó Cathaláin, correctly anglicized Cahalane, was then generally shortened to Callan; fifty years later Matheson, though he found both used interchangeably with other commoner surnames such as Cullen, Collins and Callanan, records no instance of Callan and Cahalene occurring as synonyms. Nevertheless it would appear that they are basically the same: Ó Cathaláin was in some places shortened to Ó Cathláin, whence arose the form Culhane in English. The form Cahalane is that mainly used in Counties Kerry and Cork, but Culhane is almost peculiar to Co. Limerick, which is the original homeland of the Munster sept of Ó Cathaláin: their chiefs appear in O'Heerin's Topographical Poem, the Four Masters and elsewhere as chiefs of Owney Beg, of which territory they were dispossessed in the late twelfth or early thirteenth century by the O'Mulryans.

Callan is usual in Louth and Monaghan where the Oriel sept of Ó Cathaláin were and still are located. The eponymous ancestor, in this case, is said to be Cathalan, King of Farney, who was slain in 1028. In Co. Monaghan especially we find them frequently in such sixteenth and seventeenth century records as the Fiants, Monastic Extents, Hearth Money Rolls, Petty's "census" etc. Sometimes there they are called MacCallan, but as a rule in other parts of Ulster this, with MacCallion, is to be regarded as the name of the Scottish galloglass family MacCailin which served the O'Donnells of Tirconnell. A third distinct sept of Ó Cathaláin was to be found in what is now Co. Roscommon in early mediaeval times, but the name is rare there today. Father Nicholas Callan (1799-1864), one of the most distinguished professors at Maynooth (where he spent his whole adult life), was a

Louth man, while Fr. Bernard Callan – Brian Ó Cathaláin (1750-1804) – a noted Gaelic poet and scholar, was one of many learned priests of the diocese of Clogher.

In mediaeval records, e.g. the Justiciary Rolls of the thirteenth and fourteenth centuries, de Callan (i.e. of the town of Callan) occurs as a surname: David de Callan, for example, was mayor of Dublin in 1280; but this, like de Cashel, de Clonmel, de Naas, de Kildare etc., must be treated as one of the ephemeral type.

MacCAHERTY Woulfe gives Mac Eachmharcaigh as the Gaelic-Irish form. This name was noticed in Irish Families, p. 70 under the anglicized form MacCafferky, which is that of a Mayo sept; MacCaherty, however, definitely belongs to the Oriel country especially the Castleblaney area of Co. Monaghan and the Irish form suggested by Woulfe cannot be accepted without definite evidence.

(O) CALLINAN The old proverb 'O'Callanan himself cannot cure him' is an indication of the reputation acquired by this medical family of Carbery – MacCarthy's country – in Co. Cork. One of them, Angus O'Callanan, wrote a medical treatise for MacCarthy Reagh in 1403; another Angus (fl. 1475), was the chief scribe of the Book of Lismore (otherwise called the Book of MacCarthy Reagh). Six of the name appear in King James II's army list, one being surgeon in Hon. Nicholas Browne's regiment. Though most of these were of the sept referred to above, it must not be forgotten that another of the same name was located west of the Shannon. Today, as in 1659, its members were mostly to be found in Co. Clare, but their actual homeland was in Co. Galway. O'Callanans were coarbs of Kilcahill. It will be observed that two spellings of the name have been used above: Callinan is usual in Co. Clare, Callanan in Counties Galway and Cork. Calnan and Calnane are variant spellings. The prefix O, allowed to lapse in the period of Gaelic depression, has not been widely resumed.

Joseph Jeremiah Callanan (1795-1829), the Co. Cork poet, is buried in Lisbon. The best known of his works in Irish and English is "Gougaune Barra."

MacCALMONT MacCalmont was listed in Petty's "census" of 1659 as one of the "principal Irish names" in the barony of Belfast; but that list includes several surnames such as Bell, Miller and Eccles which cannot be so described. MacCalmont is in fact of Scottish origin, being a sept of the clan Buchanan. It has since its introduction into Ireland been continuously associated with Co. Antrim. Woulfe says that the Gaelic form Mac Calmáin is a variant of MacColmain, which would make it cognate with the Irish name Coleman (Irish Families p. 83): that could be so etymologically, but may be discounted genealogically.

MacCAMBRIDGE In most cases a surname remains basically the same with or without its prefix Mac or O; but this is not so with MacCambridge. With the Mac it is an anglicized form of the Gaelic Mac Ambróis (son of Ambrose) mainly found in north-east Ulster and of Scottish origin; without the prefix it is normally an English toponymic taken from the town of Cambridge, though of course there may also be isolated instances of a MacCambridge family dropping the prefix Mac. Mac Giolla Domhnaigh states that Mac Ambróis has also been anglicized Chambers in north Ulster.

CAMPBELL, MacCawell In the Hearth Money Rolls for Co. Tyrone (1665) this name is given as MacCampbell.

Mr. T. Ó Raifeartaigh has given me the following interesting note on them: 'About the Donegal Campbells (Mac Ailín on the lips of present day native Irish speakers in Donegal) I have no doubt that Woulfe is correct in saying that they were Scottish galloglasses. The transfer from "Mac Ailín" to "Campbell" arises from the most famous of the line being Dubhghall Caimbél, just as in Donegal one says "Pádraig Ó Domhnaill" but referring to the same person without using his christian name one calls him "An Dálach" (not "Ó Domhnaill").

'Mac Firbis gives the Mac Ailín genealogy, wherever he got it, back to Dubhghall Cambél and beyond. Curiously, he gives it "Mac Ailín," the present Donegal pronunciation, though the original was Mac Cailein.

'However, the "Campbells" I have in mind are the Co. Tyrone "Campbells'. The Tyrone "Campbells" are usually not the Scottish Campbells (Mac Cailein) but the indigenous Tír Eoghain sept, Mac Cathmhaoil.

'The sept MacCathmhaoil got their name from Cathmhaol, descended from Feradhach son of Muireadhach son of Eoghan (son of Niall Naoighiallach). Their genealogy is given in detail by Ó Cléirigh.

'As the MacCathmhaoils were the leading sept of Cenél Fearadhaigh, they are often called Cenél Fearadhaigh, but sometimes Cenél Fearadhaigh Theas, to distinguish them from the offshoots of Cenél Fearadhaigh who remained in (the present) Inishowen or thereabouts.

'The MacCathmhaoil sept were fixed in the Clogher area of Co. Tyrone, which it was their function to hold as a bastion for Cenél Eoghain against Cenél Conaill on the northwest and the descendants of the Colla on the south-west and south. They later became an important church family.

'They receive honourable mention in Ceart Uí Néill being, together with MacMurchaidh and O'Devlin, classed as "fircheithearna" (i.e. "true kerns") of O'Neill, but their importance is obvious from a glance at the events listed in connexion with them under MacCathmhaíl in the index to the Annals of Ulster.

'Now the strange thing is that MacCawell is a rare surname in Co. Tyrone to-day, although the county is full of Quinns, Devlins, Hagans, Donnellys, Gormleys and the rest of the Cenél Eoghain septs. There are, however, quite a number of "Campbells" in Tyrone, and although they are officially "Campbells" the local colloquial name is "MacCawell." A certain family who have used the name "Campbell" for at least three, and probably more, generations, I have heard referred to colloquially as "the

MacCawells." It is accepted generally that the rarity of this once important surname is simply that its bearers adopted the similar sounding Scottish name of Campbell. Incidentally, Dr. Séamus Ó Ceallaigh, who knew Tyrone pre-plantation family history better than anyone ever before or probably ever again, says in "Gleanings from Ulster History" (p. 7) "From him [Fearadhach] came the powerful Cinéal Fearadhaigh – Mac Cathmhaoil, who became MacCawell and Campbell."

'There are Mac Caileins in Tyrone as well, but not many. Also of course, as you point out in the book, a particular bearer of a particular surname is of no significance. A particular Campbell might easily be of Scottish or Donegal origin, but Mac Cathmhaoil was one of the seven powerful septs supporting Cenél Eoghain and that sept alone could not virtually disappear while the other surnames continued to flourish.' Bibl.

CAMPION Apart from the English Jesuit historian, Edmund Campion, who came to Ireland in 1569, the first mention of the name in this country I have met is William Campyon, a soldier who obtained a "pardon" in 1578. The particular Fiant in which he appears is of special interest because the first name in the list is that of Miler Magra (sic), Archbishop of Cashel. In 1590 William Campion (alias Champion) was appointed dean of Ferns and archdeacon in 1608. By 1659 the family had become so firmly established that Campian appears in Petty's "census" of that date as one of the principal Irish surnames in the barony of Ossory, Queen's County (Leix). Ossory is no longer a barony name: that territory is covered by Upper Woods and Clandonagh. when Griffith's Valuation was made in the 1850s there were 74 householders named Campion in Leix and 118 in Co. Kilkenny, and there are still mainly located in these counties. On the other hand Thomas Campion given in the 1659 "census" as titulado of Leitrim near Fermoy, Co. Cork, is clearly regarded as English. In this connexion it must be noted that there are 21 Campions in the marriage license bonds for the three Co. Cork dioceses from 1639 to 1800.

As early as 1295 and 1297 several Champaynes and de Champagnes appear in law cases, and it is possible that this name may have become Campion in England, though it is normally Campain or Campen; but there is no reason to believe that it has survived here in the descendants of these mediaeval figures. The derivation of Campion given by Reaney is interesting: old Norman French campion "a combatant in the arena . . . In the ordeal by battle . . . in disputes about the ownership of land the actual parties to the suit were represented by 'champions', in theory their free tenants, but in practice hired men, professional champions and very well paid". In an early Ormond deed (c. 1275) I came across an isolated case of de Campione but there the de may be a mistake for le. I have met an isolated instance of an O'Kempan in Co. Kilkenny (in a Fiant of 1602): if further examples of this should be found it would suggest an alternative Gaelic-Irish origin, but it may well have been a clerk's error.

(O) CANAVAN Like the O'Lees the O'Canavans were hereditary physicians to the leading O'Flahertys of Connemara, and are mentioned as such by the Four Masters under the date 1416; one, indeed, was the constant medical attendant of the O'Flahertys of Lemonfield right up to the end of the eighteenth century. O'Canavan, now almost always without the prefix O, is not of frequent occurrence in the records, but it may be regarded, both historically and at the present day, as primarily a Co. Galway surname. Though in the seventeenth century the O'Canavans were domiciled almost exclusively in counties Galway and Mayo they later became scattered, and today the name is distributed throughout the four provinces, in none of which, however, is it common. It is found in Co. Waterford sometimes as Guinevan; and in several places Whitehead has been used as a synonym of it. This is a peculiar case of mistranslation because the Irish surname Ó Ceanndubháin is formed from the root words ceann (head) and dubh (black): the final bháin was mistaken for bán, white. Canavan has been anglicized as Whitelock in Co. Armagh. Map

MacCANDLESS This name is very numerous in the three north-eastern counties of Ulster. According to Woulfe the Gaelic-Irish form of it is Mac Cuindlis. In Co. Down, its main location, the variants MacAndless and MacAnliss are also found.

CANNING The famous George Canning is sometimes thought to have been of an ancient Irish family of Co. Derry: his father, George Canning (1733-1771), a poet, was of that county, and for a century before his time the Cannings of Garvagh, Co. Derry, had been landowners of standing, but in fact they came from Wiltshire, England; while another George Canning, who was very active in organizing the Plantation of Ulster in 1615, was from Warwickshire. These were thus not connected with any of the Gaelic-Irish families whose names have at some time been anglicized as Canning. One of these is Ó Cainin of Westmeath and Offaly, called O'Cannine and O'Cannyn in the sixteenth century Fiants. It is recorded in official birth registrations as having been used synonymously with Cannon (see Irish Families p. 73) in Donegal, Leitrim and Mayo, and with Cunnane in Mayo. Canning is now quite a numerous name in Ireland, being found chiefly in west Ulster and north Connacht.

MacCANNON, MacConnon Woulfe describes Mac-Cannon (Mac Canann in Irish) as rare and scattered. It is not very rare, being quite numerous in its homeland, viz Oriel, outside which it is seldom found. He does not mention MacConnon at all, though this name is still extant, and as it appears in nineteenth century birth registrations in the same parts of the country as MacCannon the two names may be regarded as synonymous. Mac-Cannon is also found occasionally in Co. Donegal as an erroneous synonym of O'Cannon (see next entry). The sept of MacConnon was located originally in the Clones area, but in the eleventh century they moved southwards to south Monagahan where, with the adjacent Co. Louth, they are mainly found today. In 1659 the "census" of that date records them as numerous in the part of Co. Meath nearest to Co. Louth. In Co. Louth some families of MacConnon have changed their name to MacConnell, an example of the not uncommon process whereby comparatively rare names become absorbed in better known ones of a somewhat similar sound. According to Woulfe the same thing happened in the case of MacCannon and the well known name MacCann. There are some families of MacCannon in Dublin now — the metropolitan area always contains names belonging to all the four provinces — and have long been there: George and William Mac-Cannon were well known tailors who carried on their business in Dublin between 1730 and 1760. John Mac-Cannon was Sheriff of Co. Monaghan during the brief Catholic régime under James II. This name has no connextion with O'Cannon.

(Mac) CANNY   (O) CANNY   The plain form Canny now does duty for MacCanny and O'Canny, two quite distinct septs. The O'Cannys (Ó Caithniadh) of the Uí Fiachrach Muaidhe were predominant as chiefs of Erris until subjugated by the Barrets in the thirteenth century. They were then largely but not entirely dispersed, for Cannys are still found in Co. Mayo. The other sept Mac Annaidh (later this became Mac Cannaidh), which belongs to Thomond, is to be distinguished from the northern sept of MacCann (see "Irish Families" p. 72). Though nowhere numerous it is extant in east Clare: in the sixteenth century they appear in that part of Thomond near the city of Limerick, MacCanny of the Castle of Drumbanny being the most notable of the family in 1598. Later they were of Ballycasey (now called Firgrove) in the barony of Bunratty. This family is now extinct. The most remarkable of them was the deaf and dumb Mr. Canny who was an expert steeplechaser: he was killed while so engaged at Scariff about the year 1850.   Map

CANTILLON   In early mediaeval deeds the Cantillons are called de Cantelupo, the Latin equivalent of the Norman de Cauntelo from the place in northern France. As early as 1302 the form de Cantelowe was in use in Ireland. Before coming to this country they settled for a time in England: the shrine of St. Thomas de Cantelupe, the last saint in England to be canonized before the Reformation, is in Hereford Cathedral. By the middle of the thirteenth century the family was well established in Counties Kerry and Limerick and for the next four centuries they were prominent in Co. Kerry. During most of that time their principal seat was at Ballyheigue, which they held until it was forfeited in the seventeenth century. They lost their Kerry estates as a result of their supporting first the Catholic Confederation and a generation later James II — the list of officers in that king's Irish army includes two Cantillons, one of whom was chaplain to Kilmallock's (Sarsfield's) regiment. James Cantillon of Ballyheigue, who followed James II to France, took a notable part in the battle of Malplaquet

in 1709 where he led the Irish troops. His brother Richard Cantillon (c. 1675-1734), who was born at Ballyheigue, was a man of international reputation: he has been called "the father of political economy"; going to Paris after the end of the Williamite war he prospered as a banker and gave much financial assistance to James III (the "Old Pretender") and to impoverished Irish gentlemen in France. The family has many associations with France. As early as the sixteenth century we find an Irish priest called Cantillon there and in more recent times Napoleon in his will left Lt. Cantillon 10,000 francs with the comment "Cantillon has as much right to assassinate Wellington as that oligarch had to send me to perish on the rock of St. Helena." Col. Antoine Cantillon, President of the Council of War in Paris (1843), had been created Baron de Ballyheigue by Louis Philippe a few years earlier: he was the grandson of the Thomas Cantillon who distinguished himself serving in the Irish Brigade in 1747.

Though the Cantillons had long ceased to be one of the great Kerry families they were still among the landed gentry in 1878 when John Heffernan Cantillon of Mannister House, Croom, was the owner of a valuable estate in Co. Limerick.   Bibl., Map

In order to clarify as far as possible the confusion which exists regarding the Cantillon family in France I add here a note kindly given to me by Mr Antoin E. Murphy of the Department of Economics, Trinity College, Dublin: 'The background of Richard Cantillon, who died in 1734 is difficult to disentangle because of (a) the "cooked" and totally unreliable family tree of the Cantillons produced by the "Baron of Ballyheigue", Count Antoine Sylvain de Cantillon — the Notice Historique, Genealogique et Biographique de la Famille de Cantillon ... (Paris 1844); (b) the fact that Cantillon's mother came from the Cantillon family in County Limerick and was a cousin of her husband; and (c) the further complication that Cantillon's wife married her stepmother's brother within a short time of the death of the economist.

'Cantillon, one of the founding fathers of modern economics wrote the Essai Sur La Nature Du Commerce En General, a book published in Paris in 1755. The views on the relationship between changes in the money supply and the balance of payments found in the Essai may be regarded as pre-dating those of Hume and forming the basis of the modern Monetary Approach to the Balance of Payments.'

'Cantillon's date and location of birth are still not known. What is known is that his father Richard Cantillon married his third (or fourth) cousin Bridget Cantillon of Kilgobbin, County Limerick. This intermarriage explains some of the problems that genealogists have met in explaining the economist's complicated family relationships. A namesake, the Chevalier Richard Cantillon, a banker in Paris, who died in 1717, seems to have been a first cousin once removed of Richard Cantillon. Through his mother Cantillon had a further banking connexion. His mother was a niece of Sir Daniel Arthur who had a banking business in both London and Paris.

'Cantillon arrived in Paris in 1714. By 1715 he was

running the bank founded by the Chevalier – in one transaction he discounted a bill of exchange of $20,000 for Lord Bolingbroke. By 1716 he had purchased the bank. In 1718 Cantillon was involved in business transactions with the Scottish adventurer John Law. During Law's famous "System" (1718-20) Cantillon amassed a considerable fortune, estimated by Du Hautchamp, in the Histoire du Visa (1743), as amounting to 20 million livres tournois.

'In 1722 Cantillon married Mary Anne O'Mahony daughter of Count Daniel O'Mahony and Cecily Weld. Her mother died when she was young and Daniel O'Mahony re-married to Charlotte Bulkeley, a sister-in-law of James Fitzjames, Duke of Berwick – the "fills naturel" of James II. To add to the complications Mary Anne O'Mahony/Cantillon married her stepmother's brother, Count Francois Bulkeley, a year after Cantillon's death.

'The Cantillons came from Ballyheigue. The economist's grandfather, Thomas "The Cantillon" forfeited lands under the Cromwellian plantations. It is difficult to trace the family after this forfeiture though there is a document signed by a Richard Cantillon (the economist's father?) of the Barony of Clanmaurice contributing funds to the building of a chapel in Killurie, Barony of Clanmaurice. This document is dated April 1681 (Crosbie of Ardfert Papers, Mss. 3821+32, Trinity College). There is therefore the strong possibility that Richard Cantillon was born in Ireland. Richard Cantillon was murdered in his bed in London in 1734.'

CANTWELL   The Cantwells, who came to Ireland following the Anglo-Norman invasion, are one of the English families which became hibernicized. Though they have produced no outstanding figure in Irish history they have played a prominent part in the life of the country since the beginning of the thirteenth century, when they appear as de Kentenall, de Cantwell etc. (of Kentwell in Suffolk) in the records of the Ormond country, the first I have met being a witness to the foundation charter of Owney Abbey in 1200. Their estates lay chiefly in the baronies of Knocktopher and Gowran, Co. Kilkenny, Cantwell's Court, four miles north of the city, being their principal seat. In 1598 they are listed among the principal gentlemen both in Co. Kilkenny and Co. Tipperary bordering on Co. Kilkenny. Though they appear as soldiers and officials – two were officers in James II's army and one was sheriff of Kilkenny and three were attainted in 1691 – the most notable men of the name were ecclesiastics. As early as 1208 we find a Cantwell in the registry of the monastery of Kells (Ossory). Two John Cantwells were Archbishops of Cashel (1405 to 1440 and 1440 to 1452), Richard Cantwell was Bishop of Waterford and Lismore from 1426 to 1446 and Oliver Cantwell (d. 1527) was Bishop of Ossory for almost forty years. In the same century Patrick Cantwell was Abbot of Navan and Richard Cantwell Prior of St. John's Kilkenny, and later there was John Cantwell (b. 1797) Bishop of Meath from 1850 to 1866, who was very prominent in his support of O'Connell and later of the Tenants League. In France, Tipperary-born Professor

Andrew Cantwell (c. 1705-1764) was a noted physician and writer and his son Andrew Cantwell (1744-1802), a Paris librarian, was also an author of repute.

All works dealing with the history of Counties Kilkenny and Tipperary contain abundant references to the Cantwells, but in the past hundred years they have somewhat diminished in numbers and importance in Ireland.

The diocese of Los Angeles was advanced to an archbishopric during the episcopate of Dr. Cantwell in 1936.

(O) CANTY   O'Encantie, one of the early anglicized forms of this name found in sixteenth century records, gives a link between the modern Canty and the Irish original Ó an Cháintigh. This surname is of an unusual type, since those formed from professions and occupations usually have the Mac not the O prefix. In this case it denotes descendant of the satirist, an cháintigh being the genitive of an cáinteach. It is the name of a bardic family belonging to west Cork; Canty is given in the "census" of 1659 as one of the principal names in the barony of Kinalmeaky, Co. Cork. It produced some well-known poets such as Fearfasa O'Canty (fl. 1610) who was concerned in the celebrated "Contention of the Bards" in the early seventeenth century. His name in Irish is usually spelt Ó an Cháinte. The sept spread from Co. Cork into Co. Limerick where they had already become numerous by the seventeenth century, then usually under the name of O'Canty and sometimes County: County, though nowhere numerous, is found in Kerry and Limerick at the present time.

In the survey of Armagh made in 1618 the name Canty rather surprisingly occurs.

(Mac) CARBERY   (O) CARBERY   The principal sept of Ó Cairbre belonged to Co. Westmeath where they were chiefs in the barony of Clonlonan. They remained there in a leading position up to the end of the seventeenth century. Hugh Carbery of Ballymore, Co. Westmeath, was outlawed for his activities on the side of James II, in whose army another of the family was an officer. At that period, however, the name Carbery was much more numerous in Co. Waterford, but it is probable that the people there so called were of different stock and that in Irish they were Mac Cairbre not Ó Cairbre: the existence of the place Ballymacarbry in Co. Waterford corroborates this. In fact MacCarbery occurs more often in the earlier records than O'Carbery, but such references relate to places so widely scattered as to be of little use as a guide to location. For example the Four Masters mention, inter alios, Dermot MacCarbry, an Ultonian harper in 1490; while Eneas MacCarbery of the Clogher diocese appears in Archbishop Swain's Register in 1427 both as Mac and O. In the next century the Fiants record many MacCarberys in Counties Monaghan and Longford as well as in the parts of the country in which we would expect to find them. In the Fiants the O'Carberys, much fewer in number, are all in the midland area around Co. Westmeath; but in 1659 some families were found in Co. Armagh. Finally it should be mentioned that a Norman family deriving its name from the place Carbury, i.e. the parish of Carbury in the barony of Carbury, appears in early records, e.g. as a tenant of the manor of Cloncurry, Co. Kildare, in 1304, i.e. the parish of Carbury in the barony of Carbury, Co. Kildare. There is also a barony of Carbury in Co. Sligo and of Carbery in Co. Cork, while in Co. Meath near Trim, there is a Carberrystown.

At the present time the name is a scattered one, but it is safe to say that it is found most often in Dublin, north Leinster and south Ulster and seldom in Connacht. A family of O'Carbery were erenaghs of Galloon in Co. Fermanagh.   Map

(O) CAREY   (Mac) KEIGHRY   In Irish Families, p. 73 the Gaelic surname Mac Fhiachra is described as nearly extinct. This is true so far as its earlier and phonetic anglicizations – Keaghry, Keighry and Keahery – are concerned, very few families so called being now extant, though they are not unknown in east Galway and the neighbourhood of Athlone. It would appear, however, that the Co. Galway sept of Mac Fhiachra does survive in considerable numbers, but under the alias of Carey. At the same time it must be remembered that Carey has been adopted as the anglicized form of several other Irish surnames; to those given on pp. 73, 74 (op. cit.) the Norman name Carew may be added,·which in fact is often pronounced Carey by the people bearing it. The majority of the numerous families called Carey belong to the Ó Ciardha sept of the southern Uí Néill, originally located in south Ulster and north Leinster, not to that of Mac Fhiachra. This probably applies to some extent also to the Mac Fhiachra sept of the Cinel Fearadaigh (of the northern Uí Néill) who were still called MacKeaghery, and also MacGeaghery, in the seventeenth century, as the Hearth Money Rolls attest. An Armagh Inquisition taken in 1444 before Primate Mey found one Nemeas MacKeaghery, a nativus, to be the rightful heir to the lands commonly called the lands of MacKeaghery.

(O) CARMODY   Carmody is an old and honourable Thomond surname found now chiefly in its original habitat, east Clare, but also in Kerry and Limerick. It is one which has been unfortunate in the spelling of its anglicized form: the Irish Ó Cearmada might just as well and indeed more accurately have been standardized Carmady as Carmody. The ocular effect of the latter has produced the erroneous pronunciation Carmoady in America (the stress of course should be on the first syllable); nor is this faux pas unknown in Ireland: I have actually heard the name so pronounced at the Abbey Theatre, of all places, and a synonym noticed by Matheson in his birth registration report is Kermode.   Map

MacCARNEY   According to Woulfe this name is Mac Cearnaigh and the family was originally seated at Ballymaccarney, Co. Meath. According to·records from the sixteenth century to the present day it must be regarded as belonging to Ulster: in the Fiants we find a MacCarney among the followers of Rory O'Donnell; in the Hearth Money Rolls of the 1660's the name appears frequently in Counties Monaghan and Armagh; and comparatively recent sources indicate that they are still mainly located in that part of Ulster. It would appear, however, that the prefix Mac has been widely dropped, the name being now registered as Carney or Kearney.

Probably the most remarkable person of this name was Susan MacKarney who died in Dublin in 1751 reputedly 120 years of age. She was a beggarwoman who had £250 secreted in the mattress of her death bed.

(O) CARR, Kerr   (O) KERRANE   (Mac) CARRY (O) CARRY   MacILHAIR   MULCAIR, Wilhair
Nine synonyms of Carr were reported to the Registrar-general by local registration officers. First there is the obvious Kerr. This equation was noted in the Coleraine and Lisburn districts and its spelling variants Ker and Karr in Co. Down. Kerr is a very common name in northeast Ulster. Their distribution is illustrated by the following figures which give the birth registrations for 1890, with those for 1866 in brackets:

Carr

Ireland	Leinster	Munster	Ulster	Connacht
90 (114)	21 (31)	10 (10)	35 (54)	24 (19)

Kerr

| 142 (192) | 12 (11) | 2 (4) | 123 (171) | 5 (6) |

Kerr is among the forty most numerous surnames in Scotland and the majority of the Irish Kerrs of today are of Scottish origin. Isolated cases occur in Munster even as early as 1375: in that year Richard Kerr was a collector of taxes in Co. Tipperary.

The second synonym to be noticed is Kerrane (also Kirrane). The birth registrations for these combined were 15–13 in Co. Mayo and two in Co. Galway. The synonymous use of Carr did not occur in Mayo but in Counties Galway and Sligo. Mr. P.J. Kennedy, of Galway, tells me that Kerrane and Kirrane are quite common in north-east Galway and around Loughglynn and Frenchpark, Co. Roscommon. In the parish of Ballymacward he has in his own lifetime observed the gradual change from Kerrane to Carr. While this is clearly the origin of some of the Carrs of Connacht we must not overlook the fact that the name O'Carr was found in Connacht in the sixteenth century before the pressure of anglicization, which converted Kerrane into Carr, was noticeable. The Fiants and the Composition Book of Connacht prove that they were then numerous and not unimportant in that province, chiefly in Co. Sligo but even down to the borders of Clare. O'Dugan in the Topographical Poem mentions the sept of O'Carthaigh of Clancahill, for which O'Donovan gives O'Carthy as the anglicized equivalent, adding that the name was then (1862) unknown there: I think it more likely that it had by that time become Carr, and this view is supported by the fact that in the Fiants for the counties in question the name is spelt O'Carhy as well as O'Carre.

In the Fiants we also find, in Co. Armagh, O'Care and

O'Carr – which are indistinguishable in their anglicized form from the Connacht name dealt with above. This is the sept of Ó Cairre. The Annals of Loch Cé note under 1095 the death of Muirchertach Ua Cairre, "steward of Cenél Aengusa and royal heir of Oilech" (i.e. one of a number of eligibles for the kingship of Ulster). Donal O'Cairre was one of the Ulster chiefs killed at the battle of Downpatrick in 1260; and seventeenth century records such as the Hearth Money Rolls and Petty's "census," record the name O'Carr as numerous in Oriel. It is manifest, therefore, that while most Kerrs are British, a great many of the Ulster Carrs are, like those of Connacht, of Gaelic-Irish origin.

Having regard to the forms of these names in Irish it is inevitable that confusion has arisen between Carr and Carry, especially as the latter also belongs to Oriel, not only as Ó Cairre but as a Mac name too. Mac Carry occurs in the 1664 Hearth Money Rolls for Co. Armagh and the census of approximately the same date found MacCarry (bracketed with MacCarey) one of the most numerous names in the barony of Moycashel, Co. Westmeath, and at the same time Carr was similarly recorded for Duleek, Co. Meath. Woulfe gives two Irish surnames for MacCarry viz. Mac an Charraigh and Mac Fhearadaigh, while modern synonyms of MacCarry recorded by Matheson are MacGarry, MacHary, Maharry, Magarry etc.

Reverting to synonyms of Carr we come now to MacElhar, MacIlhair and Wilhair, all from Co. Donegal. The two former are Mac Giolla Chathaoir (from St. Cathaoir) also anglicized Kilcar(r) in Co. Donegal. Wilhair, however, is a different name, viz Ó Maoilchéire (from St. Ciar) called MacKerry, Mulcair or Mulhare in Munster and Wilhair in Co. Donegal. The Donegal surname Carr, however, is generally given the Irish form Mac Giolla Cheara.

Finally as further examples of the complexity of this subject I may mention that among the gentlemen of the barony of Ballagheen on the grand panel of Co. Wexford in 1608 was Edmond MacCarr of Tomduff; and finally Woulfe states that de Cathair (i.e. of Cahir, a place-name) anglicized Carr is found in many parts of Ireland.

They are not very prominent in the political or cultural history of the country. Rev. George Whitmore Carr (1779-1849), pioneer in the cause of temperance, was a remarkable character who served in the Yeomenry in 1798 and later gave vigorous support to Father Mathew and Daniel O'Connell. In recent times Dr. Thomas Joseph Carr (1840-1917), Archbishop of Melbourne, formerly Bishop of Galway, and perhaps I may add Joseph Carr, an outstanding champion amateur golfer, are well known names.

(Mac) CARRAGHER, Caraher   This Oriel names, MacFhearchair (man dear), usually without the prefix Mac in the anglicized form, is fairly numerous on the Armagh-Louth-Monaghan border. Woulfe states that it is a variant of the Scottish Farquhar i.e. MacFearchair. MacFhearchair, however, with the initial F aspirated, is indigenous in Ireland: in early mediaeval times a branch migrated to Scotland where the name has become Caraher. The Scottish Farquhar is of similar derivation, the F in that case

being unaspirated. Whether there is any common blood-kinship origin I do not know. (Perhaps in due course the Caraher Family History Society in Perthshire may have an answer to that question). Coming to comparatively modern times it is on record as MacCarehir at Dysart, Co. Louth, as early as 1616, well outside the territory affected by the Plantation of Ulster; in 1663 MacCarraher occurs in the Co. Monaghan Hearth Money Rolls in the barony of Dartree. Several eighteenth and early nineteenth century wills of Co. Louth testators of the name are on record.

(Mac) CARRIG(Y), Carrick, Rock   This Clare surname, Mac Concharraigh in Irish (con, hound; carraig, rock) was first anglicized MacEncarigy, of which many odd variants such as MacCarrigoyne, Karracky etc. occur in the 'Inchiquin Manuscripts. In the course of the seventeenth century the initial MacEn, and usually also the final y, were dropped leaving the abbreviated form Carrig (sometimes Carrigy). Carrick was used as a synonym of this. This may also be de Carraig, referring to some notable rock, or, in the case of the Anglo-Norman family, de Carrick in Ayrshire. Carrig is confined to counties Clare and Limerick and MacCarrick is found in Ulster and Co. Roscommon.

CARTMILL   Though this name is not dealt with in any of the standard works on surnames its frequent occurrence in mediaeval Irish records with the prefix de indicates that it is a toponymic, and a Fiant of 1563 shows the place to be Cartmell in Lancashire. The earliest reference to it which I have met is to John Kertmel, a Drogheda juror in 1306, and the Justiciary Rolls of the same year contain a strange case in Co. Kildare where one deKertmel was concerned in the rescue of the murderer of another deKertmel. The family in due course became established in Co. Armagh and are to be found in the 1664 Hearth Money Rolls for that county. Modern birth registrations show that they are still there and in some adjacent areas.

MacCARTNEY   There are many families of MacCartney in Ulster and they were well established in that province more than three centuries ago: MacCartney is listed in Petty's "census" of 1659 as a principal Irish name in the barony of Belfast, and in the Co. Monaghan Hearth Money Rolls of 1666 a James MacCartney appears in the parish of Mucknoe (barony of Cremorne), though in that of 1664 a different proprietor is given for that townland. According to family tradition two George Macartneys came to Ireland in the seventeenth century, one in 1630 and the other in 1649. In the Williamite war they took the Orange side and after the Jacobite debacle they flourished and several were High Sheriffs of Antrim. In 1878 the MacCartneys of Lissanure Castle, Ballymoney, owned 12,532 acres of valuable land in Co. Antrim; and another of the name (spelt in this case MacArtney), resident in Co. Tyrone, had considerable property in counties Antrim and Armagh. As stated above the name is now numerous: it is no longer confined to the landlord class. MacCartney is Scottish, being a sept of the clan Mackintosh. Two curious synonyms recorded by registrars of births are Mulhartagh (Ballyshannon area) and MacCaugherty (Newtownards area).

Among the distinguished men of the name (five find a place in Crone's Dictionary of Irish Biography), George MacArtney, 1st Earl (1735-1808), distinguished himself in the British foreign service and perhaps less so as an Irish politician – his letter books from 1768 or 1804 are preserved in the Public Record Office, Northern Ireland, and a microfilm copy of these is in the National Library; another, James MacCartney (1770-1843), was a member of the United Irishmen, but is better known as a noted surgeon.

CARUTH   I have not discovered the origin of this name: it may possibly be an abbreviation of Carruthers which is a north of England surname taken from the place in Dumfriesshire, Scotland. In Ireland Caruth has been in Ulster since the seventeenth century and it appears in the Rolls for Antrim, Armagh and Donegal (1664–9) while Carruthers will be found in the Inquisition for Co. Armagh some thirty years earlier.

CASEMENT   Attention has been widely drawn to Casement as an Irish name since the execution of Roger Casement (1864-1916), the most picturesque and also the most controversial of the outstanding men of 1916, and before that world-famous for his exposure of the atrocities in the Congo and Putamayo. He himself was born at Sandycove, Dublin, but the family to which he belonged was of Co. Antrim. Actually the family, though Gaelic, was Manx not Irish: they only came to Ulster from Peel in the Isle of Man in the eighteenth century. Roger Casement's father and grandfather were both named Roger Casement: the latter, who died in 1832, was a solicitor at Ballymena. They were already established as landed gentry in the previous generation: Leet's Directory (1814) lists three such. By 1878 they had extended the area of their estates greatly for in that year there were six landed families of Casement in Co. Antrim owning between them over 11,000 acres. The name Casement has never become numerous and is not found among the ordinary folk of the country. It is derived from the Norse Asmundr and in Manx was first MacAsmundr then MacCasmonde. I have met the name occasionally in early Hiberno-Norman records: Thomas MacAssemond, for example, was one of a large number of persons in Co. Cork listed in a Justiciary Roll of 1311 as taking the part of Edward II against some Norman rebels who were allied with the Irish of Leinster. The list comprises Norman and Gaelic names in about equal numbers.

(Mac) CASHIN O'CASSIN   The MacCashins were hereditary physicians in Upper Ossory. The Queen's County Book of Survey and Distribution tells us that many MacCashins were 1640 Irish Papist proprietors in

that county (now Co. Leix). As early as 1304 the name occurs in nearby Co. Kildare and in 1331 in north Tipperary, which also adjoins Co. Leix. The Hearth Money Rolls of 1666 indicate that it was then common in Co. Tipperary. The Hearth Money Rolls for Co. Leix are not extant, but Petty's "census" of approximately the same date found Cashins very numerous there. The most notable of the aforesaid physicians was Conly Cashin who wrote a medical tract in Latin in 1667. There are many references to the name in Carrigan's book Ossory and O'Hanlon's book Queen's County. The latter states that the Cassans of Sheffield House (Capoley) were properly de Cassagne, a family which, having left France on the Revocation of the Edict of Nantes, went to Flanders whence they came to Ireland, their ancestor being an officer in the army of William of Orange. At the end of the eighteenth century there was a notable firm of shipowners in Waterford, viz. Cashin, Wyse and Quan. This family of Cashin came from the parish of Kilshane in Co. Tipperary.

MacCashin is Mac Caisín in Irish. Woulfe states that Ó Caisín is a variant thereof, in use in the south of Ireland. An alternative theory is that Cashin should there be equated with Cashman (Ó Ciosáin: see Kissane). Every early reference I have found to the name with the O prefix relates to south Munster, as do all the sixteenth century Fiants. It is true that in a Judiciary Roll of 1295, relating that Kenedi carach O'Cassin was one of a party which slew six Englishmen (and that the official, who should have arrested them, kissed them and let them escape) the alleged crime took place in north Tipperary, but the men were apparently natives of the Clonmel area. Placenames of interest in this connexion are Ballycasheen, near Killarney, and Ballycashin in Co. Waterford. Ballycasheen, in Co. Clare near Corofin, is nearer to Connacht than to South Munster. This is not very far away from the Sodhan country with its sept of Ó Casáin (see Cussane under Kissane). To this, I suggest, the bishop John O'Cassin, who resigned the see of Killala in 1490, belonged.   Map

(Mac) CASSERLEY   Cassily and Cushley are noticed in Appendix I (sub Costello); another name which may be confused with them is Casserley i.e. Mac Casarlaigh which has long association with Co. Roscommon and now (without the prefix Mac) is found there and in the adjoining county of Galway. The confusion is the more likely because in Co. Roscommon some families so called spell the name without the R, viz. Casseley. Cumumhan Mac Casarlaigh is mentioned by the Four Masters as one of the Connacht chiefs slain at the battle of Athenry in 1249 and another of the name was a canon of Tuam in 1462.

MacCAUGHAN, MacCahon   These two anglicized forms of Mac Eacháin are fairly numerous in Co. Antrim, but very rare outside north-east Ulster. The cognate Mag Eacháin is usually made MacGahan, which is a well known Co. Louth name: it is often written Magahan.

Woulfe says that Mac Gaoithín has also MacGahan as

one of its anglicized forms, but this is usually MacGeehin (q.v.).

MacCAUGHEY

In Irish this name is Mac Eachaidh. Variant spellings of its anglicized form are MacAghy, MacCaghey and MacCahy and three centuries ago we find it as MacCahee in the Co. Tyrone Hearth Money Rolls. There it has remained since, as is proved by modern birth registrations.

MacCAUL, MacCawell, Caulfield
(Mac) CORLESS, Carlos

Caulfield is a surname of several origins, some of which were briefly dealt with in Irish Families (pp. 153 and 305). The majority of our Caulfields are actually MacCawells — Mac Cathmhaoil in Irish, a Cenél Eoghain sept traditionally descended from Niall of the Nine Hostages and located in the barony of Clogher (Co. Tyrone). Few Irish patronymics have acquired so many different anglicized forms as this: in addition to those given above there are Campbell, Howell, MacCarvill, MacCowhill, Callwell, MacCall and MacHall. The last two, it should be observed are also used for Mac Cathail of Hy Many, which, however, when found in its original homeland in Connacht is now Corless, Carlos or Charles; and here I must prolong this parenthesis by adding that Corless and Carlos are often rendered Mac Carluis in modern Irish. Turning to present day distribution we find that MacCaul and MacCall now belong chiefly to the Armagh-Monaghan-Cavan area, while Caulfield (apart from metropolitan Dublin) is most numerous in north-east Ulster and in Mayo. Petty's "census" (1659) indicates that Cawells and MacCawells were then numerous in Armagh and Louth, two of the counties comprised in ancient Oriel: the abbreviated form MacCall had not yet been adopted and Caulfield appears only as a planter family.

This was established as a leading Ulster landlord family by Sir Toby Caulfield. Born at Oxford in 1565 and registered at baptism in the name of Calfehill, he had come to Ulster in the service of Queen Elizabeth; in 1607 he obtained a large grant of abbey lands in Co. Armagh and also in Co. Derry, and he acted for the government as collector of rents and fines on the forfeited O'Neill estates from 1608 to 1611. He was the first Baron Charlemont and ancestor of the present peer. One of the seats of this family, Castlecaulfield (formerly Alconecarry), was the nucleus of the town of that name in Co. Tyrone. They were active always in the English interest. William, the 5th Baron, captured Sir Phelim O'Neill in 1652 and in the next generation they took the side of William of Orange. They retained until recent times their extensive estates and in 1883 held over 26,000 acres in Counties Armagh and Tyrone. Another Lord Charlemont, James Caulfield, 1st Earl, (1728-1799), first president of the Royal Irish Academy, was commander-in-chief of the Irish Volunteers as well as being a scholar. Another James Caulfield was Catholic Bishop of Ferns from 1785 to 1810. Richard Caulfield (1823-1887) was noticed in Irish Families (p. 153).

As the Charlemont family lived in the same territory as the Gaelic sept of MacCawell some confusion must arise as to the origin of individuals since the partial adoption by the MacCawells of the surname Caulfield. Prior to the eighteenth century identification presents no difficulty. MacCawells are to be found frequently in early seventeenth century Ulster records, e.g. in the 1606-1609 inquisition juries, most of whom were of Gaelic-Irish stock. It is of interest to recall the recorded fact that in 1609 of 15 Limavady jurors (including two MacCawells as well as MacAttagarts, O'Heaneys and a MacGilligan) no less than 13 "spoke good Latin." The MacCawells are principally noteworthy as ecclesiastics: two were Bishops of Clogher between 1390 and 1432 and many others held lesser positions in the diocese between 1356 and 1612; and there was also the Franciscan historian and philosopher, Hugh MacCaughwell (1571-1626), who was appointed Archbishop of Armagh the year he died; but possibly he was not of this stock as in Irish he is usually called MacAingil.   Bibl.

MacCAVANA

Woulfe's conjecture that this is Mac Caomhanaigh in Irish cannot be accepted; it would appear to be Mac an Mhanaigh, which is anglicized MacEvanny in north Connacht. In the adjacent Ulster county of Fermanagh Mac A Vinny (sic) is listed in the "census" of 1659 as a principal Irish name. MacCavana is now fairly numerous in Co. Antrim.

MacCAY

This is a variant of MacKay (Mac Aodha) which is now, and has long been, numerous in Ulster. As Mac Cay alias MacKay it appears in the "census" of 1659 as a principal Irish name in the northern baronies of Co. Antrim and as MacCay a few years later in the Hearth Money Rolls of Co. Armagh. No doubt this and similar variants were also found elsewhere e.g. Mortagh MacCae was one of the Papist transplantees from Co. Clare in 1657; and the list of synonyms published by Matheson from reports received from local registrars shows that it has also been equated with MacCoy and with Mackey.

CHAMBERS

This name first appears in Ireland in the thirteenth century as de la Chambre, i.e. chamberlain, (the cognate surname Chamberlain also occurs in thirteenth century Irish records but is now rare); but it is unlikely that any families called Chambers today are descended from those early Anglo-Norman settlers. Some, we know, were immigrants in the seventeenth century, first under the Plantation of Ulster and later the Cromwellian Settlement. Many families of the name were established here, however, before that: the existence of the placename Chamberstown in Co. Meath in the previous century is proof of that. This was not the Chambers family prominent in Co. Meath in the eighteenth century, for they had previously long been large landowners in the New Ross area of Co. Wexford where the townland of Chambersland perpetuates their name. The name occurs frequently in the lists of government officials, from 1592 when Thomas Chambers was housekeeper at Kilmainham and in 1609 when George Chambers was Chief Chamberlain of the Exchequer, down to quite modern times. It is less prominent in the political and military sphere: no Chambers appears in the Jacobite outlawries, but one was in Stanley's predominantly Irish regiment in 1593 and John Chambers, a Dublin printer and book-seller, was a member of the Dublin Society of United Irishmen just two centuries later.

The name is now numerous in the northern counties of Ulster and in Dublin; a century ago there were many families of Chambers in west Cork; outside those areas the only county in which it is found in considerable numbers in recent times is Mayo. There Chambers does not seem to be a synonym of any Gaelic-Irish name nor is it long enough established to appear for example in Strafford's Inquisition of Mayo (1635). The ancestor of the Chambers of Killoyne, Co. Mayo, who obtained a grant of arms in 1724, came from Hertfordshire, England.

CHERRY   This is an English name of comparatively recent introduction into Ireland – the first I have noted is Edward Cherrye "gent" of Dublin whose will was proved in 1613. Though isolated families of the name were living in Counties Tipperary, Kilkenny and Water-ford during the seventeenth and eighteenth centuries it has always been rare outside east Ulster, where it has been fairly numerous since 1680. Two well known persons of the name were Andrew Cherry (1762–1812) dramatist, actor and writer of popular songs – "the Dear Little Shamrock" etc. – and Judge Richard Robert Cherry (1859-1923).

CHESNEY CHEYNEY, Cheney   The earliest refer-ence I have met to Chesney in Ireland is in 1251; de Chaeny (presumably the same name) occurs as that of the seneschal of Leinster in 1246; while Ralph Cheyny was Lord Deputy in 1372 – he is also called O'Heyne in the Liber Munerum, but this is clearly a mistranscrip-tion of Cheyne. These men can be disregarded, I think, so far as Cheneys of later centuries are concerned. In 1610, under the Plantation of Ulster, Thomas Cheyney obtained 1,000 acres at Drominishen, Co. Fermanagh. A generation later there were two Cheneys among the English Cromwellian "adventurers", but I have found no evidence that they ever took up possession of any land in Ireland, though there was a John Cheney of Dublin in the army in 1648 and a Robert Chaney appears as a city of Cork titulado in 1659. The name subsequently became established in Co. Cork: six are mentioned in the will of James Cheney dated 1775. Other eighteenth century wills indicate that they were then mainly to be found in east Leinster, particularly Co. Kildare. The name is now rare and scattered.

Reaney links Cheyney and Cheney with Cheyne and Chesny, all deriving from the Old-French chesnai, Latin casnetum (i.e. an oakgrove) whence also the French place-name Quesnay. Chesney is a surname not un-common in Ulster, sometimes with the prefix Mac. I state the fact: I have yet to learn the explanation of it. Three Chesnys, born in Co. Down, who distinguished themselves abroad, including Francis Rawdon Chesney (1789-1872) of Suez Canal fame, find a place in the Dictionary of National Biography; the Cheyneys therein have no connexion with Ireland.

CHINNERY   The first Chinnery to appear in Irish records, as far as I know, was Quartermaster John Chinnery, described as of Cnocktane Castle, Co. Lim-erick, who was one of the 1654 Inquisition jury in con-nexion with the Civil Survey for the baronies of Owney-beg and Clanwilliam. According to family tradition a George Chinnery of an ancient Essex family settled in Co. Cork before 1641, and John Chinnery of Mallow obtained a grant of Castlecor, Co. Cork, in 1666. Subse-quently the name is almost entirely associated with Counties Cork and Limerick, as wills, family papers and birth records indicate. George Chinnery was Protestant Bishop of Cloyne in 1780. He with nine others of the name appears in the register of students of Dublin University: the earliest of these was born in Co Cork in 1652, the son of John Chinnery of Ballyadam. London-born George Chinnery (1774-1852), a notable portrait painter, is reckoned among Irish artists having lived in Dublin and being related to the Chinnerys of Co. Cork. The head of that family was created a baronet in 1799. Extensive records of Chinnery families, collected by James Welply, are in the manuscript collection of the Genealogical Office, Dublin Castle.   Bibl.

CHRISTOPHER   This English name is included here because, though never numerous in Ireland, it has been consistently located in Co. Waterford since the thirteenth century. No less than eleven men of the name appear in the cases recorded in the Justiciary Rolls for Co. Water-ford in or before 1295 and an even earlier instance of the name there occurs in the person of Griffin Christopher, who was Bishop of Lismore from 1225 to 1245. In the "census" of 1659 it appears as a principal Irish name in Co. Waterford; and coming to comparatively recent times we find nearly all the Christopher birth registra-tions have been in the same county, where indeed their descendants are still represented by a number of families.

CHURCH, Aglish   Among the synonyms officially re-ported by local registrars and recorded by Matheson when he was Registrar-General were Aglish and Church. I think this is one of the few cases where an English name has been translated into Irish (eaglais, pronounced aglish, is the Gaelic for a church). The name Church is English, from atte churche, that is dweller near the church, and has been established in Ulster since the seventeenth cen-tury – families of Church will be found in the Hearth Money Rolls of several northern counties, Derry being their main location, while two tituladoes called Church appear in the "census" of 1659 in the barony of Lough-insholin in that county. In the next century we begin to find them also in Munster, particularly in Co. Cork and Co. Kerry, not in large numbers but always in promin-ent positions. However, they were still large landowners in Co. Derry up to the time of the Land Act of 1903. Matheson omits to state where the name Aglish occurred and I have never met an instance of it myself, except as a place name in Co. Waterford and Co. Tipperary.

(Mac) CLAFFEY, MacClave   Mac Laithimh, anglicized MacClave and MacLave in Ulster, and made by pseudo-translation Hand in Co. Monaghan, has become Claffey in the midlands. It is found mainly in the country around Athlone.

(O)CLAVIN SWORDS   There are a number of families called Swords in Dublin at the present time. The name has, however, now usually no connexion with the Co. Dublin village of Swords, but derives from two quite distinct Gaelic-Irish surnames both of which belong to the counties of Offaly and Leix: in the former it is numerous to-day, as it is also in the neighbouring county of Kildare, as also is Clavin. Clavin is Ó Claimhín in Irish and was sometimes anglicized Swords in the mistaken assumption that the root word is claidheamh (a sword). The other derivation is simple viz. from Ó Suaird, which in a Fiant of 1562 is anglicized O'Sword, while two others of about the same date have O'Swerte: all three relate to the Leix-Offaly area. As early as 1016, probably before the era of fixed hereditary surnames, Ó Suairt is mentioned by the Four Masters as the name of the then successor of St. Brigid (i.e. abbess of Kildare). The names Swords, Swoordes and Sourdes all occur in the Ulster inquisition of the first half of the seventeenth century. Apart from these every reference I have met to these two names relates to their midland homeland; but they are evidently not unknown in Co. Mayo, for Matheson's list of synonyms reported to him by local registrars includes Claveen and Swords at Ballinrobe. In the fourteenth century, the surname de Swerdes (derived from the village) was recorded in several places in Ireland; and in the Ulster inquisitions of the first half of the seventeenth century we find Swords, Swoordes and Sourdes in Co. Down.

MacCLEAN, MacLean   This is a Scottish name which has become very numerous in Ireland. Of the 106 Irish births recorded in 1890 (mostly in Ulster) 54 were spelt MacClean and 43 MacLean, the remaining 9 being Mac-Alean, MacClane etc. In Scotland it is the name of the clan Maclean. Their connexion with Ireland, which began with their employment by the MacDonnels as mercenary soldiers, dates from the fifteenth century. Flower in his catalogue of Irish manuscripts in the British Museum mentions Eoghan Macgilleoin (Ewan MacLean) as a Scottish scribe writing Irish in Argyllshire in 1698. In Ireland it is Mac gilla Eáin or Mac giolla Eoin. The fashionable London highwayman James MacLaine (1724-1750), who was executed after robbing Horace Walpole, was a Co. Monaghan man.

CLEAR, Clare   Except when used as a synonym of

O'Clery – examples of this are referred to below – Clear and Clare are names of Norman origin formerly written de Clare. The most famous, of course, was Richard de Clare (d. 1176) better known as Strongbow, the leader of the great Anglo-Norman invasion, whose sister married the almost equally famous Raymond le Gros and whose daughters made important alliances. Nicholas de Clere or Clare was Treasurer of Ireland in 1290. They were at first associated chiefly with Co. Wexford where Cleres-ton commemorates their occupation, and the name recurs frequently in mediaeval records relating to the whole south-eastern part of the country. Cleeres and Cleares indeed were prominent up to the end of the seventeenth century in Co. Kilkenny and in south Tipperary. As might be expected one of these, Simon Clear, was an officer in Col. Edmund Butler's regiment of James II's army which was recruited from that area. Clear and Clare are now numerically about equal. There are a great many Clare wills (seventeenth to nineteenth century) recorded in the reports of the Deputy Keeper of Records.

The name is derived from a place in Normandy as the preposition de implies; it does appear as le Clere occasionally, e.g. in a Kells deed of the year 1289, but possibly this is an error for le Clerc. The form de Clare may sometimes be derived from the place Clare in Suffolk, England, and Clare is an English surname too – it is to be found in the lists of Cromwellian "adventurers"; but at the present time, in the absence of an authentic pedigree or at least a strong family tradition, it cannot now be differentiated from Clear.

In the sixteenth and seventeenth centuries there was apparently a tendency to turn this Norman name into Clery. In the 1659 "census", which shows it to have been very numerous in Co. Tipperary, Clear and Cleary are bracketed as one name and in episcopal deeds of the Ormond Collection two sixteenth century ecclesiastics – James Clere, Dean of St. Canice's Kilkenny, and Mgr. Thomas Clere, Chancellor of Lismore, are both also called Clery.

Rev. Fr. Wallace Clare, (1895-1963), founder of the Irish Genealogical Society, did much valuable work in that field.

MacCLELLAN(D), MacLellan, Leland   There was a sept of the Uí Fiachrach seated in Co. Sligo called Mac Giolla Fhaoláin. The name was first anglicized Mac-Gillilan(d) which is a phonetic approximation to the Irish form. This in due course became MacClellan, Mac-Lellan, Leland etc. Writing a hundred years ago John O'Donovan stated that this sept was then extinct and that all persons of the name in Ireland were Ulster Scots. This may well be true since not only did the great majority of the births registered for the name in all the years for which we have detailed statistics in the nineteenth century take place in north-east Ulster but also Petty's "census", made some two centuries earlier, indicates that the name was then found chiefly in Co. Derry (baronies of Keenagh and Coleraine) and in Antrim (barony of Belfast). It appears there with and without the final D but always with initial C not L. It should be added that MacClelland is included by the enumerators as an Irish not a Scottish name in those two counties; but since such obviously non-Irish names as Boyd, Bell, Eccles, Fulton and Miller are classed by them as Irish I think this fact may be disregarded.

The most notable man of the name in Ireland was Thomas Leland (1772-1785), the historian and donor of the MS. of the Annals of Loch Cé (a primary source frequently mentioned in the pages of this book) to the library of Trinity College, Dublin. John Leland (d. 1552), the earliest of the modern English antiquaries, does not appear to have had any connexion with Ireland.

MacCLEMENT, MacLamond   CLEMENTS   The English surname Clements, formed from the Christian name, has long been associated with Counties Donegal and Leitrim, the head of that family being the Earl of Leitrim; and in the seventeenth century there were settler families of the name in Co. Antrim. It is therefore sometimes difficult to distinguish between them and the Irish family formerly known as MacLamond as this, though still retained in some parts of Co. Derry, has now become MacClement, from which the prefix has often been dropped and replaced by a suffix S. The Irish form of this name is MacLaghmainn. The Scottish Lamont is of the same Ulster (O'Neill) origin.

MacCLENAGHAN, MacLenaghan   The former of these, with minor variations (e.g. MacClenahan), is about twice as numerous as MacLenaghan, which also has similar variants. Both are anglicized forms of Mac Leannacháin. It belongs almost exclusively to Ulster, particularly Counties Antrim and Derry. It appears, as one might expect, in the Elizabethan Fiants in the O'Neill country and once, rather strangely, among the Co. Cork "pardons" of 1601. Two testators of 1783, Mac Clenahan and Mac Clenachan, lived in or close beside north Tyrone. In 1878 de Burgh's Landowners shows that at that date both MacClenahans and MacLenahans held considerable estates in other Ulster counties.

MacLennan may occasionally be a contracted form of MacLenahan, though normally this is either the well known Scottish surname or a rare variant of MacAlinion (q.v.). MacLenahan is quite distinct from O'Lenahan (Irish Families, p. 209).   Bibl.

CLIFFORD, (O) Cluvane   In dealing with the name Clifford in Ireland we must not be misled by the fact that it is indigenous and very common in England. The most famous individual of the name in Ireland, Sir Conyers Clifford (d. 1599) President of Connacht, was of course an Englishman; but it is safe to say that almost all the Cliffords in Ireland, particularly in Counties Kerry and Limerick where they are very numerous, are of Gaelic-Irish ancestry. The name is an example of the barbarous way in which some Gaelic names were anglicized: originally O'Clovane (Ó Clumháin in Irish), it was given as its synonym a well known English surname

vaguely resembling it in sound. Fifty years ago there were a few families around Dingle and Killarney who were still called Cluvane but even with them Clifford was already being accepted as correct. Today, in fact, Clifford has almost entirely superseded Cluvane and Clovane, though the latter was the usual form at the time of the 1659 "census", when it was numerous in Co. Limerick, while Clifford only appears in that document in the person of the representative of the English Cliffords of Co. Sligo.

Prior to that time the name was not unknown in Ireland. A Walter de Clifford appears in an Ulster de Lacy document in 1213. The bishop of Emly from 1286-1306 was William de Clifford and several other de Cliffords are to be found in the contemporary Justiciary Rolls, Gormanston Register etc.

The first Cliffords to settle permanently in Ireland were this Sligo family who came to that county at the end of the sixteenth century. Unlike most of the Elizabethan settlers they became Catholic and one of them, Col. Robert Clifford, commanded a regiment of dragoons in James II's Irish army, though his reputation for courage and leadership was much inferior to that of the English Sir Conyers Clifford who died heroically on the battlefield in 1599, much regretted by the Irish people on account of his conciliatory policy towards them.

In the very county in which this family acquired estates lived a sept of Ó Clumháin whence sprang the Kerry Cluvanes and Cliffords dealt with above. The name, however, does not seem to have been anglicized Clifford in Co. Sligo. Though scarcely to be found in north Connacht now this family of Ó Clumháin were noteworthy in mediaeval times, for they supplied poets to the O'Haras, several of whom figure in the Book of O'Hara and the Book of Magauran. Of the same stock were Angus Ó Clumháin, Bishop of Achonry, (res. 1250 and d. 1264) and Malachy O'Clowan or O'Cluan, Bishop of Killala (d. 1508).

The name Ó Clumháin is not to be equated with Clune (q.v.).

CLINCH   Though not Gaelic in origin – Clinch derives from the Old-English word clenc meaning a lump or low hill, and was formerly spelt Clench – families of the name have been located in Ireland since 1305 when John Clenche appears in a law case in Dublin. Dalton in his King James's Army List states that about this time they were established in Ormond; but they did not remain there, for in the whole series of Ormond Deeds from 1172 to 1603 the name does not appear even once. In the Leinster counties nearer to Dublin, however, they are the subject of frequent notice in all kinds of records from the thirteenth century onwards – in social standing they range from leading gentry, in Counties Dublin and Meath, to small tenants; in religious affairs from Catholic martyrs to subservient Reformation clergy; but in the sphere of war and politics, at any rate since 1600, any who are at all noteworthy have been on the patriotic side: four of the name, for example, were outlawed as Jacobites; one was "titular" Dean of St. Patrick's in

1743 in defiance of the Penal Laws; and at least one was a member of the United Irishmen half a century later.

Perhaps the most distinguished individual of the name was James Bernard Clinch (1770-1834), of Maynooth College, Catholic pamphleteer as well as a classical and Gaelic scholar.

CLINTON It is true that MacClinton has been recorded as a synonym of MacAlinden (q.v.) but the use of Clinton in this way is so rare that we may disregard it in this note. Clinton itself is a rare name in Ireland to-day, but it is so frequent in our records from the thirteenth century that it deserves a place in any book dealing with Irish families. This is not the place to give specific references but as a guide to anyone wishing to obtain detailed information I may mention that it is obtainable in inter alia the Calendar of Documents, Ireland (1171-1307) the Justiciary Rolls (1295-1314), the Ormond Deeds Vols III-VI (1419-1603), Swayne's Register (1428-35), the Fiants (1541-1603), Chancery Rolls (1538-1629), Wills – Prerogative, Diocesan and Genealogical Office (1597-1820), 56th and 57th Reports of the Deputy Keeper of Records (chiefly 18th century) etc. The name is of special interest on account of the prominence of three Irish Clintons in the history of the United States viz. Charles Clinton (1690-1773) born in Co. Longford and his two sons General James Clinton (1733-1812) and Governor George Clinton (1739-1812).

As Canon Leslie has pointed out, Charles Clinton, the father of James and George, was not the descendant of a Williamite settler, as has been alleged, but of the old Hiberno-Norman family of Dowdstown and Clintonstown, Co. Louth. The names of three Clintons, all of this family, appear in the lists of Jacobite outlawries. Twenty-two are mentioned in the Dowdall Deeds (c. 1250-1691) and many in other records dealing with Co. Louth and adjacent territory. Families of the name were also established in other parts of the country notably County Kilkenny. Clinton is the family name of the Duke of Newcastle: this family is English not Irish, but in 1878 a member of it was the owner of a property of 13,563 acres in Co. Cork. Bibl.

(O) CLOGHERTY This is more often spelt Cloherty nowadays, the prefix O being omitted except in Irish (Ó Clochartaigh). This is not just an academic observation, because the name belongs to an Irish-speaking part of the country, being numerous throughout Connemara but very rare elsewhere. It is said to have been changed to Stone by quasi-translation (cloch means a stone), but, apart from the few cases of this which may exist in Co. Galway, Stone is an English name of obvious derivation. For the use of Stone for Mulclahy see Irish Families, p. 232.

(O) CLOONAN, Clunan This name, Ó Cluanáin in the Gaelic-Irish form, belongs almost exclusively to Co. Galway.

MacCLORY This Ulster name is mainly found in south Co. Down. It occurs once in the Co. Armagh Hearth Money Rolls of 1664. The Irish form is Mac Labhradha, which is akin to Ó Labhradha (Lavery) q.v.

CLOSE This is a fairly numerous name in Counties Antrim, Down and Tyrone, but Woulfe is misleading in implying that it is of Gaelic-Irish origin: he rightly equates it with Ó Cluasaigh and does not mention that it is also a well known English name. In fact the principal families of Close in the counties mentioned above are known to have descended from settlers from Yorkshire, the earliest being Richard Close an officer in the English army in 1640. He first acquired property in Co. Monaghan whence the family moved to Co. Antrim, and William Close appears in the "census" of 1659 as one of the tituladoes at Lisnagarvy Co. Antrim. The Hearth Money Rolls of approximately the same date record seven families called O'Cloase, O'Closs and O'Closse in that county. Two centuries later one of them was a very extensive landowner in Co. Armagh, for which county he was High Sheriff in 1854 and M.P. at various times between 1857 and 1878.

CLOSSICK This name is peculiar to Connacht and is mainly found in the Swinford area of Co. Mayo. It is not of English origin but its Gaelic form has not been determined. Mac Lusaigh, derived from the Middle-Irish (and modern) lus (strength, also herb) has been suggested as a possibility.

(Mac) CLUNE (O) CLONEY Clune is properly a Thomond surname. The Clunes or MacClunes of Ballymaclune near Quin, Co. Clare, are called Mac Glúin in a deed of 1542 in the Irish language and this may be accepted as the correct original form of the name, Mac Clúin being the accepted form today. As well as Ballymaclune there is a place called Tiermaclune in Co. Clare. It appears in the Inchiquin MSS. as MacClune. Families of the name still live in and near Quin, and two of them have been prominent in recent times, viz. Conor Clune, who was murdered in Dublin Castle with Dick MacKee and Peadar Clancy in November 1920, and Father George Clune, the author of "Réilthíni Óir". Dr Patrick Joseph Clune, consecrated Bishop of Perth (Australia) in 1910 – raised to archbishopric in 1913 – was actively concerned in endeavouring to effect a peaceful settlement of Anglo-Irish relations after the breakdown of the Irish Convention in 1918. John Clune was the leading Clare Fenian in 1867.

Confusion with the name Ó Clumháin is inevitable (see under Clifford), particularly because in the "census" of 1659 Clovane is given as one of the principal Irish names in east Clare. At the same time O'Cluvan is similarly given from Co. Limerick and O'Clovan for Co. Carlow. MacClune does not appear in the document, but all MacClownes, MacClones etc., in the Fiants of the previous century belonged to Co. Clare or to a place adjacent to it.

We can only assume that Clovane is a clerk's error for Clune since none of the Fiants contain this O name and all its Mac variants relate to Co. Clare; nor is there any evidence that the Gaelic name Ó Clumháin was to be found in Co. Clare. In this connexion it may be observed that in the Franciscan records in Brussels relating to Ireland O'Cluvan and O'Cluan are used in different places to denote the same person.

Finally it should be noted that occasionally MacClune has been used as a synonym of MacGloin (see MacGlynn) and Clune for Cloney. Cloney is actually quite a distinct name, being Ó Cluanaigh in Irish and belongs both historically and by present day location to Co. Wexford. Petty recorded it in 1659 as one of the more numerous Irish names in the Co. Wexford barony of Bantry and also in the nearby barony of Gowran. Thomas Cloney (1772-1850) took a notable part in the Rising of 1798. Map

MacCLURE   There is a Scottish family of MacClure from which many of the MacClures of Ulster are descended. There was also a small Oriel sept so called, their name in Irish being Mac Giolla Uidhir (from odhar duncoloured) also called Mac Aleer. MacClures appear frequently in the Hearth Money Rolls for Co. Armagh and occasionally in those for Co. Monaghan which were compiled in the 1660s. In Ulster the variant form MacLure is sometimes found. Sir Robert John Le Mesurier MacClure (1807-1873), a pioneer arctic explorer, was born in Wexford. Samuel MacClure (b. 1857), the American publisher, was born in Co. Antrim. John MacClure (b. 1846) took a leading part in the 1867 Rising: it is probable that he belonged to the family of MacClure which had settled in south Tipperary earlier in the century.

COAKLEY, MacKehilly   COLCLOUGH
Coakley is the usual modern form of the fine old West Cork surname MacKeighley – Mac Caochlaoich in Irish— which still survives around Dunmanway and Bandon in the more Irish sounding form of Kehilly. This has in some cases inevitably been absorbed by Kelly. In 1584 the MacKeighelys were among the followers of Florence MacCarthy. In one Fiant of 1601 there are no fewer than 19 of the name ranging in station from gentleman to labourer and shoemaker. The majority are described as yeomen and husbandmen, some of their names being veritable pedigrees in themselves e.g. Diermod Oge MacDermody MacTeige Cowy MacKeioghely. Having regard to the number referred to therein it is somewhat surprising not to find the name figuring in the 1659 "census", either as MacKeighley or Coakley. The latter form, however, was of more recent invention. Miss Cecile O'Rahilly in her edition of Five Seventeenth Century Poems suggests that the name of the poet Donnchadh Mac Maoilfhiaclaigh alias Mac an Chaoilfhiaclaigh may be a form of that which is now Coakley.

Coakley may also be a phonetic rendering of the name Colclough which is so pronounced. The family of Colclough, which was established in Co. Wexford in the sixteenth century, came to Ireland from Staffordshire in England. Anthony Colclough acquired Tintern Abbey in 1575: during the seventeenth and eighteenth centuries they were very prominent in that county and, though newcomers compared with the earlier Anglo-Normans and faithful servants to the crown under Elizabeth I, they were classed as "old English" and no less than 14 Colcloughs suffered under the Williamite confiscation as "Irish Papists." Occasionally, however, one was found on the other side, as for example Capt. Thomas Coakley who was rewarded in 1656 for his activity in "apprehending" tories. Several of them held important offices in Counties Wexford and Kilkenny in the reign of James II and two at least were officers in his army. John Colclough (b. 1769), a Catholic landlord, was hanged on Wexford Bridge for his leading part in the Insurrection of 1798. Caesar Colclough (1766-1824), son of Sir Vesey Colclough of Tintern Abbey and M.P. for Wexford, was in France at the time of the Franch Revolution which he supported; another distinguished himself while serving with the Irish Brigade at Fontenoy. The family was still in possession of Tintern Abbey at the end of the last century when they possessed an estate of 13,000 acres in Co. Wexford.

CODY, Archdeacon   CODD   Although originally all Codys were Archdeacons the patronymic Mac Óda assumed by that hibernicized Norman family in the course of time superseded it so that now Cody is a numerous surname and Archdeacon rare. The name Cody, (in Irish Mac Óda) is derived from Odo le Ercedekne, whose family had settled in Co. Kilkenny at the beginning of the thirteenth century. They were prominent in the history of that county until the final conquest of Ireland by England in the seventeenth century. The Ormond Deeds and the mediaeval ecclesiastical records have a great many references to them first as Lercedekne etc., later as Archdeken and Archdeacon, the latter frequently being described as alias MacOdo, MacOde, MacCood, MacCoda or MacCody. The peculiar transition which occurred in the name of the well known Jesuit Father Richard Archdekin (d. 1693) was noted in Irish Families, p. 161. Archdeacon did survive quite extensively until the eighteenth century, and even later one or two notable people have borne it, e.g. Nicholas Archdeacon who was Bishop of Kilmacduagh and Kilfenora from 1800 to 1824, Matthew Archdeacon (c. 1800-1853), the poet and novelist, and Joseph Archdeacon who was a leading Fenian and I.R.B. man in Liverpool in the 1860s. Archdeacon, not Cody, was the surname used by the families which settled in France after the Jacobite collapse: one became and long remained leading merchants at Nantes, while the descendants of Edmond Archdeacon, who went to Dunkirk and attained high rank in the French navy, are still a family of importance in that country.

In 1659, when Petty's "census" was taken, both Archdekin and Cody were listed among the principal Irish names, the former in the barony of Slieveardagh (Co. Tipperary) and the latter in the four baronies of Galmoy, Gowran, Iverk and Ida (Co. Kilkenny) and in the city of Kilkenny, and also in Queen's Co. (Leix). The

Tipperary Hearth Money Rolls of a few years later name twenty-two families of Cody and three of Archdeacon. There were also twenty-two of Cuddihy, which Woulfe thinks was a synonym of Cody though in modern Irish it is rendered Ó Cuidighthigh: probably it is one of the many cases of confusion in regard to names of somewhat similar sound.

Notwithstanding the numerical superiority of Cody, since 1650 the only one of the name to attain fame was William Frederick Cody (1845-1917) known to all the world as Buffalo Bill, whose family was of Co. Tipperary origin.

In the Elizabethan Fiants Codd as well as Cody and Coddy is used as a synonym of Archdekin. The Codds however are a distinct family. The first in Ireland is believed to have come over with Fitzstephen in 1169 and built Castletowncarne in the barony of Forth. Since then the Codds have long been closely associated with Co. Wexford: in the Elizabethan and Cromwellian wars they were on the English side but from the Williamite period onwards they have been Catholic and nationalist.

COGAN, Gogan, Goggin   (O) COOGAN
(Mac) COGGAN, Cogavin   KEOGAN   KEOHANE

The outstanding figure in the history of the Cogan family is the first of them to come to Ireland, Milo de Cogan (d. c. 1183), who was Strongbow's right-hand man in the Anglo-Norman invasion of 1171. He was granted a huge area in Co. Cork by Henry II. Milo left no surviving son and the great territorial family thus founded, though reinforced by grants to Richard de Cogan in 1207 and still of sufficient importance to be listed among the chief gentry of the barony of Kinelea in 1591, was practically extinct as such by the end of the seventeenth century. Minor branches of it, however, survive up to the present day, usually under the name of Goggin and sometimes Gogan. In the sixteenth century the name was in the transition stage: the earlier Fiants gave as a rule Cogan, Cogane and Coggain, the later ones Gogan and Goggan. Among the Co. Cork place-names in the same source we find Goganrath and Gogganshill, the latter being also given as Knockgogan and a few years earlier as Knockcowgan. The form Cogan, however, did not become obsolete. Philip Cogan sailed to Spain with del Aquila in 1602; two Cogans and a Coggan were officers in southern regiments of James II's Irish army, Richard Cogan was a "doctor of physic" in Co. Cork in 1707 and in 1798 Pascho Coggin was a witness to a deed relating to Charleville. Charleville, by the way, was formerly known as Rathgoggan – Rathgoggan, indeed, is the name of the civil parish embracing the town of Charleville. Another Philip Cogan (1750-1834), a composer of some note, was also a Cork man. A very valuable study of the various families of Cogan has been made by Mr. Dermot Murphy, which was presented at University College, Cork, in 1957 as a thesis.

In addition to the Cogans of Norman origin there is a sept of the Uí Maine whose name is sometimes anglicized as Cogan, though Coogan is more usual and nearer the Gaelic-Irish form Ó Cuagáin. They are of the same stock as the O'Maddens. And finally the small sept of

Mac Cogain (the Book of Fenagh and the Topographical Poem spell it Mac Cagadhain), who were located in Glanfarne on the shore of Lough Allen in Co. Leitrim, dropped the prefix Mac in the eighteenth century and became Cogan and Coggan. Neither of these, however, is at all numerous today. The variant Cogavin is also rare.

Matheson's Synonymes, published in 1901, mentions Cogan and Keogan as synonymous in Co. Cavan; and I have noticed in a Co. Meath will of 1834 the testator described as Cogan alias Keogan. Keogan, however, is properly quite a different name from those we have considered above. Woulfe, mentioning that it is Ó Ceogáin in the spoken Irish language, gives Mac Eochagáin as the correct Irish form of it, which is a variant of the better known Mag Eochagáin (MacGeoghegan) – see Irish Families p. 158. Keohane or Keoghane, in Irish Mac Eocháin, and corruptly Ó Ceocháin, is almost peculiar to west Cork. Bibl., Map

COLBERT   This name is well known in south Munster and the prominence of Cornelius Colbert, one of the signatories of the Irish declaration of the Irish Republic, who was executed by the British after the 1916 Rising, has familiarized it widely in Ireland. Although one of the most famous characters in French history bore this name it came to Ireland from England. According to Ewen it occurs in Domesday Book (1066) as Colbeorht, a combination of Old-English words meaning calm and bright; Reaney says it is Colbert in Domesday Book giving it an Old-German origin. In Ireland it appears at least as early as 1417 when one Thomas Colbert was involved in a trespass case at Tipperary. Griffith's Valuation found Colberts very numerous in Co. Waterford in 1850, no less than 55 householders of the name being recorded there.

COLFER   As Calfer this appears in the old Wexford rhyme quoted sub Devereux, this variant being due no doubt to the Forth dialect. Coylefer is a name met with in records of the early fourteenth century dealing with the southern counties. Though Wexford is not actually one of these, it is in Co. Wexford we chiefly find the name both in official records of the past and such useful sources as birth registration and voter's lists of the present day. A Co. Wexford testator of 1666 signed himself William Culpher, but as a rule the spelling is consistently Colfer. There are no less than 75 Colfer householders in Griffith's Valuation for Co. Wexford (c. 1853).

(Mac) COLLEARY   (Mac) CALLERY   This is a case where I cannot accept Woulfe's suggestion that Collery (he does not mention Colleary) is an anglicized form of Mac Giolla Arraith, which is normally MacAlary (q.v.), sometimes MacLary or MacClary, and belongs to Co. Derry. Colleary and its variants Collary and Colary are almost exclusively found in north Connacht. There Irish speakers use Mac Giolla Laoire as the Irish form. Callery and Callary are also found in the same part of the country but not exclusively – both occur also in counties Meath

59

and Cavan where MacClearys (now usually called Clarke) are numerous; these are probably offshoots of the Derry sept mentioned above. Woulfe also confuses Callery with Gallery, a Clare name. There can be no doubt, however, that in Connacht Callery is a synonym of Colleary since we find a MacCallery among the landholders of Co. Sligo in 1633. In the previous century MacCallery occurs four times in the Fiants, always in Co. Sligo. At the present time, apart from metropolitan Dublin, the name is confined to Co. Sligo and north Mayo.

(O) COLLERAN   I am informed by Mr. P.J. Kennedy that Gaelic speakers in Co. Galway use the form Ó Callaráin and in the north eastern part of the county it is so pronounced also by English speakers; that and Co. Mayo is its main location. In 1785 the parochial census carried out by the parish priest found eleven families of the name in Ballinrobe, Co. Mayo; in 1866 all the 17 births registered for it were in north Connacht and again in 1890 all the births were in Counties Mayo and Galway, while the statistics of the present day show that they are still there. Woulfe makes the tentative suggestion that Ó Callaráin is a corrupt form of Mac Allmhuráin. As we meet O'Calleran as far back as 1602 I prefer to accept it as an O name. That reference is, however, not to a place in Connacht but to the barony of Fertullagh in Co. Westmeath and in the seventeenth century we do meet occasional references to Collerans in Leinster.

COLLIER   This well known English name is included here because it has been in Ireland at least since 1305, when Thomas Colyere was one of a guard appointed by the seneschal of Trim, Co. Meath. In that barony there is a place called Collierstown; in another part of Meath there is another Collierstown and a Colliersland. The latter is mentioned in a Fiant of 1543. The name is found intermittently up to the late sixteenth century when the Elizabethan Captain Collier was prominent. In the next century, though historically it is connected with Co. Derry, we find it listed by Petty as a principal Irish (sic) name in the barony of Dunleek, Co. Meath. Coluer is similarly returned for the barony of Shelbourne, Co. Wexford but I am assuming that this, i.e. Coluer, is a variant of Colfer. In this connexion it should be noted that Co. Wexford and the adjacent counties of Carlow and Kilkenny are its present main location. In the middle of the last century it was also quite numerous in Queen's County (Leix).

A recent Bishop of Ossory is Dr. Collier; Father Anthony Collier, who was shot by Communists in Korea in 1950, was from Co. Louth. The derivation of the name is simple: it means a charcoal burner. In the form Colyear it is counted as a branch of the Scottish clan Robertson.

COLLIS   Though this name, now rare but formerly much more numerous, is well known in Ireland it does not appear in Woulfe. It is of English origin, deriving from the christian name Nicholas. Apart from John

Collis who appears in a Co. Tyrone land transaction in 1638, its establishment in Ireland dates from later in the seventeenth century, two army officers obtaining land under the Cromwellian Settlement when the family became established in Co. Sligo and in Co. Kerry. The former appears to have died out, though possibly some of the name now to be found in Dublin may be of that descent. The Kerry family increased and prospered. Already by 1661 one Collis had become provost of Tralee and another is listed as a Co. Kerry titulado in the "census" of 1659. From that time until the revolution effected by the Land Acts of 1870 to 1903 the Collises of West Munster frequently occupied prominent positions such as High Sheriff of Kerry, and the number of Collis wills proved in the Prerogative court between 1685 and 1857 testified to their continued prosperity; in 1878 they owned 12,000 acres in Counties Kerry, Cork, Limerick and Tipperary. From 1670 others of the name have been merchants in the city of Dublin.

An interesting diary commenting on current events in Ireland and gossip in Dublin from 1685 to 1690, kept by A.M. Colles, can be consulted in the Ormonde Manuscripts (H.M.C. 2nd series VIII). John Day Collis (1816-1879) a noted educationist in England, was born in Ireland. Abraham Colles (1773-1843) was a Dublin surgeon of international reputation.

(Mac) COLUM   For the Irish Mac Coluim, Woulfe gives the modern forms MacColum, MacCollom, Colum etc.: he derives this from colum, dove. Elsewhere he states that Mac giolla Choluim is son of the follower or devotee of St. Columcille. For this name he gives only one modern form viz. the very rare MacElholm, obsolete forms being MacGillacollom etc. I find this in a Fiant dated 1601 and relating to Co. Wexford and Mac Gil Colum (prior of Ardstraw, Co. Tyrone 1179) in the Four Masters. Woulfe's statement that MacColum is an Ulster surname chiefly found in Antrim, Tyrone and Donegal is correct both for the present day and for the seventeenth century when Petty's "census" listed MacColum as one of the principal Irish surnames in Co. Antrim; but I am not convinced that these families are basically Mac Coluim rather than Mac Giolla Choluim. In modern times the name is approximately equally numerous with and without the prefix Mac. As Colum (or the variants Collum, Columb) it is found in appreciable numbers in Co. Longford. Proof may be forthcoming that these represent a small distinct midland sept and are not part of the larger Ulster one.

In the seventeenth century Collum occurs as a synonym of the English name Colme e.g. in the lists of regimental personnel in the Ormond Manuscripts.

The best known of the name is a Co. Longford man, the poet Pádraig Colum (1882-1972).

MacCOMB   This surname came to Ireland from Scotland, being that of a sept or branch of the Clan Mackintosh. It is numerous in Counties Antrim, Down and Derry. It was already well established in Ulster in the seventeenth century for Petty's "census" of 1659 classes it then as an Irish name: it was then among the more numerous names in Co. Down. In addition to the three Ulster counties mentioned above it appears also (five times) in the Hearth Money Rolls of Co. Armagh. In these seventeenth century documents it is spelt MacCome as well as MacComb and MacCombe. As MacCom and MacCome it appears in the Fiants for 1571 and 1596 in Counties Louth, Sligo and Leitrim. Woulfe gives Mac Thom as the Gaelic form of the name and this is corroborated by Reaney. MacComie and MacCombie are cognate names.

COMERFORD   This name looks English and is in fact that of an English village in Staffordshire. Nevertheless it is not now found as a surname in England (except perhaps among Irish emigrants) — at any rate it does not appear in Reaney or Bardsley as such. It has been in Ireland since 1210 and in the 770 years which have since elapsed has been one of our most distinguished Irish families, particularly in the counties of Kilkenny and Waterford where they first settled. By the seventeenth century they had become numerous there and in parts of Co. Tipperary also. The head of the family was Baron of Danganmore, Co. Kilkenny, a Palatine title; junior branches were seated at Ballymacka, Ballybur, Callan and Inchebologhan Castle. Thomas Comerford of Ballymacka was attainted in 1572 for his part in resistance to Elizabethan aggression, and a century later we find no less than 14 Comerfords serving as officers in James II's Irish army. After the Jacobite defeat many Comerfords were outlawed and several settled in France and Spain, while seven were Wild Geese officers in the Irish Brigades of the eighteenth century. The best known of these exiles was Joseph Comerford, Baron of Danganmore and afterwards Marquis d'Anglure. At home the most distinguished, at any rate in the sixteenth and seventeenth centuries, were the Comerfords of the Waterford branch, or, to give them the name by which they were more often then known, the Quemerfords. This family was outstanding for its adherence to the old faith at the time of the Reformation. The celebrated Louvain lecturer and controversialist Dr. Nicholas Quemerford (c. 1542-1599) was the first of sixteen Waterford Jesuits of the name living in the half century between 1590 and 1640. His nephew, Patrick Comerford, O.S.A., who was Bishop of Waterford from 1625 to 1652, was an ardent supporter of the Nuncio and as such was the cause of his native city's opposition to the Ormond peace in 1646. Other bishops were Edmund Comerford or Quemerford (Ferns 1505 to 1509) and Edward Comerford (Archbishop of Cashel 1695 to 1710). The name is prominent too in the municipal records of Waterford and Kilkenny and also of Clonmel. John Comerford (c. 1762-1832), a noted miniature portrait painter, was born in Kilkenny.

In Irish speech and documents the Comerfords or Quemerfords were called Comartún. It may be noted that in Counties Cavan and Longford the name Comerford has been used as an anglicized form of Mac Cumascaigh, a Breffny surname normally MacCumiskey or Cumesky in English.   Map

(Mac) COMISKEY   Woulfe states that this name, Mac Cumascaigh in Irish, is peculiar to Counties Westmeath, Longford and Cavan, and this is substantially true of the present century, as birth registrations and voters lists attest; but historically speaking the statement is misleading because the name belongs basically to Co. Monaghan. Originating in the Clones area, this was one of the septs which moved thence to south Monaghan in the eleventh century. Having regard to its frequency in the Hearth Money Rolls of Co. Monaghan in 1664-66 it is remarkable that Comiskey in any of its forms does not appear in the Petty "census" of almost the same date as a principal Irish name in any barony of that county, the explanation probably being that, although numerous, it was not concentrated in one particular district. The only man of the name appearing in the list of army personnel in the seventeenth century, found in the Ormond Manuscripts, was Roger Commoskey, of Dundalk, which is near the homeland of the sept. This is one of the many variant spellings of the name, others being Comaskey, Comesky, Commiskey, Cummiskey etc., etc., with and without the prefix Mac, which was sometimes retained, especially in south Down, a century ago and is still extant though rare. Matheson in his report on synonyms in 1890 records the use of Comerford by some families also known as Comiskey.

(O) CONAN, Coonan   Though the name Conan is now rare, it is very well known on account of the Conan Doyle family (see Irish Families, p. 129) — the Conan came from the marriage of John Doyle (grandfather of Arthur Conan Doyle) to Marianne Conan of Dublin, of a family which claims to be of Breton descent. According to O'Donovan Ó Cuanáin of Dunbeakin in the parish of Kilmacshalgan, Co. Sligo, is to be equated with the modern form Conan. One might expect this to be anglicized Coonan or Coonane, and in the 1659 "census" O'Cunane does appear as a "principal Irish name" in Co. Sligo, though not very numerous. However, in the same document O'Conan is similarly listed for the two baronies of Co. Leitrim which adjoin Co. Sligo. The Fiants show that the name was somewhat scattered even in the previous century, several being located in Kilkenny and neighbouring counties, a fact corroborated by the Ormond Deeds and by the Hearth Money Rolls of 1666, which show Conane to have been a fairly common name in Co. Tipperary at that time. Cornelius Conan of Co. Kildare was an officer in Eustace's Regiment in James II's army in Ireland. From 1161 to 1168, Isaac Ó Cuanáin was Bishop of Roscrea, a see which disappears shortly after his death. In modern times the name Coonan has been associated with the area between Roscrea and Birr. In counties Offaly and Tipperary the usual form now is Coonan.

(O) CONATY, Connaghty
Mac CONAGHY, MacConkey
The Breffny name Conaty, peculiar to Co. Cavan, is definitely an O name, viz. Ó Connachtaigh, although another somewhat similar Mac name, MacConaghy, has been

used there as a synonym of Connaghty which is a variant of Conaty, as also is Connoty.

MacConaghy is, in fact, entirely different: it is Mac Dhonnchaidh, a branch of the Scottish Clan Robertson, and is very numerous in north-east Ulster both as Mac-Conaghy and as MacConkey.

(Mac)CONHEADY   Rev. John Ryan, S.J. suggests Mac Con Éidigh as a probable Irish original of this Co. Clare surname. In that case the H is intrusive, cf. Mac Con Aonaigh, sometimes anglicized Conheeny.

(Mac) CONLEY   Conly has been fairly widely used as a variant of Connolly in the Oriel counties and to a less extent in Munster (for these septs see Irish Families, pp. 87f) but when found in Offaly it is the name of a sept belonging to that midland area. There it is Mac Connla. It has now become very rare there, but in the sixteenth century it was quite prominent among the followers of O'Caherney (The Fox).

The name has also Ulster connexions: Patrick O'Connley of Dublin, merchant, acquired lands in Co. Donegal in 1626 and Thomas Conley was one of the signatories of the "thanksgiving" manifesto issued at the conclusion of the Siege of Derry in 1688; and in 1632 John Conly obtained grants in Counties Donegal and Fermanagh.

(O)CONNAUGHTON   As mentioned in Irish Families, p. 237 Connaughton is sometimes abbreviated to Naughton and so is liable to be confused with Ó Nachtáin. Connaughton, however, is Ó Connachtáin in Irish. This is the name of an important sept originally located in the north of the present Co. Sligo, where they were of importance, as we know from the Annals and other sources for mediaeval times. Later they migrated to Co. Roscommon. Its proximity there to the homeland of the O'Naughtens of Uí Maine adds to the chances of the two names becoming confused. At the inauguration of the kings of Connacht on the Hill of Carnfraoigh, near Tulsk, it was the hereditary duty of the Connaughtons to guard the entrance to the carn. People of the name are still found mainly in Counties Roscommon and Sligo: the deplorable practice of spelling the name Connerton or Connorton, which was quite common in the last century, appears to have been given up and the intrusive R dropped in most places, though it is still occasionally retained in Co. Galway.

(Mac)CONNULTY   This name is found in west and mid-Clare and is a form of the Donegal surname MacNulty peculiar to Co. Clare.

(O)CONOLE   This name, Ó Coineoil in Irish, is now perhaps too rare to justify its inclusion in this book, being confined to a district around Ennistymon, Co. Clare. It was sometimes called O'Connowe in English at first: a Fiant of 1600 refers to O'Connowe of Ballyconnowe (near Ennistymon), while the Wadding correspondence mentions Father James Conoyl of Kilfenora in 1630. In 1576 it appears unexpectedly in Co. Leix. The Fiant in which it occurs presents a good example of this type of document: it is a "pardon to Eugene MacPheolim riough MacMicke Morrishe O'Knogher of Irree in the county called Leix, gent, James MacKnocker MacShane vic Connole, of the same, Rory MacFarreill MacCohee of Towwyannee in Ferraile and Thady MacEe of the same, kerns." In and before the fifteenth century the family was of some note in north Connacht, being coarbs of Drumcliffe, Co. Sligo, and according to the Four Masters also to be found around Killala. Bernard O'Coneoil was Bishop from Killala from 1432 to 1461. It would appear that, as has happened with so many of our rarer surnames, it has to some extent been absorbed by a commoner one — in this case Connolly.

(O)CONRAN, Condron   Condron and Conran are anglicized forms of the Irish surname Ó Conaráin. Condron, now more usual than Conran, is a comparatively modern variant, all the references to the name before 1700 which I have met being to Conran, O'Conran and O'Coneran. These are frequent in the sixteenth and seventeenth centuries and all relate to Leinster. Munter Coneran are mentioned in the survey of Co. Fermanagh, made in 1603, as coarbs of the "parish church of the Mill" in the barony of Tirkennedy, but as a surname Coneran does not seem to have survived there. The sept, which originated in Co. Offaly, was to be found there in considerable numbers and also in the adjoining counties of Leix and Kildare as evidenced by the Ormond Deeds, the Tudor Fiants, Petty's "census" etc. The modern birth registration returns indicated that they are still chiefly located in the same part of the country. The place name Ballyconran suggests that they were also at one time influential in the Leinster county of Wexford.

(Mac) CONVERY   Woulfe states that Mac Ainmhire is the Gaelic-Irish form of Convery but gives no further information on the name. Convery, without the prefix Mac is fairly numerous in Ulster, being particularly associated with the country lying on the west side of Lough Neagh. With further reference to the prefix it is of interest to note that in the Armagh Hearth Money Rolls of 1664 the name appears as O'Convery. This does not necessarily mean that Mac Ainmhire should be rejected, as it was not unusual for Mac names beginning with a vowel to be recorded in such documents as O names, the final C of Mac becoming the initial of the anglicized form. Mac Ainmhire must be accepted, at any rate so long as no evidence of an alternative is forthcoming.

MacCONVILLE   The alternative form of this name, MacConwell, is now almost obsolete, but MacConville is numerous especially in Oriel, its homeland, being found now mainly in Counties Down, Armagh and Louth. Six of the name from Co. Down were among the Irish Jacobites attainted after the defeat of James II. The Gaelic-Irish form of the name is Mac Conmhaoil. See also Mac-Gonigle.

CONYERS   When this name is met in Ireland it is often an anglicized form of O'Connor – one of those cases of the assumption of an aristocratic sounding surname of Norman origin like D'Evelyn for Devlin, Hastings for O'Hestin and Melville for Mulvihill. In England Conyers was originally de Coignieres. This family was represented in Ireland by Ralph Conyers of Tarbert, who was a poll-money commissioner for Co. Kerry in 1660 and 1661. Thence also came the place name Castletown-Conyers in Co. Limerick, which was formerly Castletown-MacEneiry. Conyers has been reported in fairly recent times as in use synonymously with Connor in Co. Roscommon while Cunnyer was similarly reported for Co. Derry. Turning to the seventeenth century we find both O'Conier and O'Cunier in the Co. Monaghan Hearth Money Rolls. It is unlikely, however, that these are synonyms of O'Connor.

MacCOOEY   Woulfe gives the Gaelic-Irish form of this as Mac Cobhthaigh. I prefer, however, the form Mac Cumhaighe which Father Paul Walsh uses in his Irish Chiefs and Leaders. The name appears to be less numerous now than it was a century ago, when it was found in all the Oriel counties, especially Armagh. It is quite distinct from MacCoy.

COOKE   There are three distinct origins for the name in Ireland. In Leinster it is mainly an English occupational name, in many cases long established there: nine place-names in the province (Cooks-town, Cooksland etc.) attest this. In Ulster it is usually Scottish – MacCook or MacCuagh, a branch of the clan MacDonald of Kintyre. Cookstown, Co. Tyrone, was founded by Alan Cook in 1609. In Connacht Cooke is the modern anglicized form of Mac Dhabhoc (also called Mac Uag) the name of a branch of the Burkes: it is anglicized MacCooge in some places. The MacCoogs of south Co. Galway were first named MacHugo from Hugo Burke.

COOLEY   There are two quite different origins for this name: in Clare and Galway it is an abbreviation of Kil-cooley (Mac Giolla Chuille), which is by no means as rare as Woulfe suggests; and in Ulster it is usually a synonym of either Colley or Cowley, two well known English names. Cowley, it may be added, is also the Manx form of MacAuley.

COOLING   At first sight this would appear to be a variant of the English name Couling (derived from a place in Yorkshire); but this may not be so, since the traditional pronunciation of the name in Ireland, preserved by the family in spite of its being invariably pronounced by strangers in accordance with the spelling, is Culling, with the emphasis on the second syllable. Richard Foley suggests (N.L.I.Ms.G.841) that it is a Gaelic-Irish name viz. Ó Cúilfhinn. I make no comment on this. If John Cullyng, described as of Ardee in 1450, was a mediaeval member of the family now called Cooling, they are established in this country over five centuries: they are now counted as a Co. Wicklow family.

CORBETT, O'Corbane   In Ireland the English surname Corbett is usually the Irish Ó Corbáin, formerly anglicized and still occasionally found as O'Corbane or Corban, and now corrupted to Corbett. Nevertheless Anglo-Norman families of Corbett did settle in Co. Meath and even as far from Dublin as Offaly – there are two Corbetstowns named from them situated in Westmeath and Offaly, one of which, it is interesting to note, was also called Ballycorbet in the sixteenth century. Miles Corbett the regicide, who was prominent as Chief Baron of the Irish Exchequer in the Cromwellian régime, was of course an Englishman, as was John Corbett, Constable of the Castle of Limerick in the reign of Edward III.

The present day distribution of the name Corbett corresponds fairly closely to the original habitat of the two Irish septs whose names are now usually so anglicized. O'Corbane, mentioned above, which has many variant spellings such as O'Corribane, was in the sixteenth and seventeenth centuries to be found in all the Munster counties except Kerry. The other is Ó Coirbín, which is still extant as Corribeen and O'Cuiribeen in Counties Galway and Mayo (though there, too, more often changed to Corbett).

Several Corbetts served with distinction in the Irish army of James II – Thomas Corbett was colonel of the Lord Grand Prior's Regiment – and in the Irish Brigades in France. General William Corbet (1779-1842), a Co. Cork man, having been expelled from Trinity College Dublin, was with Napper Tandy in 1798, was associated with Robert Emmet, and received the order of St. Louis as a final reward in the French service. His brother Thomas, another officer in the Irish Brigade, was killed in a duel. Later the poet William John Corbet (1824-1899) was M.P. for East Wicklow: there is a memorial to him in Delgany church.

It should be added that in Co. Limerick Corbett and Conba (Ó Conbagha) have been found as synonymous. Conboy, the normal anglicization of this name, however, occurs chiefly in counties Sligo and Roscommon. Conboy is normally Ó Conbhuidhe in Irish (see Irish Families p. 92).

MacCORD   This numerous Co. Antrim name is stated by Woulfe to be a variant of MacCourt (q.v.)

CORDUE   This name is found in east Clare. It is possibly of Spanish origin. Don Louis de Cordua was one of the Spaniards from the Armada captured in Connacht in 1588; or it can be a corrupt form of Cardew, an English surname taken from a place in Cumberland.

(O) CORRIDON   In the anglicized forms of this name (Ó Corradáin in Irish) the prefix O is seldom if ever retained to-day. Variant spellings are Corrodan and Corridan; Cordan has also been noted as a synonym at Listowel. It is now definitely a Co. Kerry name; King's analysis of the 1901 census shows that there were then 40 families of the name in that county. Originally, however, it belonged to Co. Clare being located on the north side of the Shannon not far from the present Shannon Airport. Though seldom to be found in Irish records Ó Caradáin appears in the Book of Ballymote.

All the evidence available confutes Woulfe's suggestion that Corridon is a variant of Corrigan.

(O) CORRY   (Mac) CORRY   (MacGil)   CORR (O) CORR Reference was made in Irish Families to O'Curry of Thomond. Curry is sometimes used as a variant of Corry. Where the name Corry occurs in Co. Clare, as it not infrequently does, it can be equated with Curry (Ó Comhraidhe). Elsewhere Corry is usually Ó Corraidh (or Ó Corra) and in modern times is often abbreviated to Corr. All the forms Corr, Corry and Curry are much more numerous in Ulster than elsewhere. There they can be of more than one origin. The majority no doubt are Ó Corra, descended from the sept of that name located in the Tyrone-Fermanagh country and numerous in central Ulster in the seventeenth century as the Hearth Money Rolls show. Many of the Corrs of Tyrone and Derry are, however, descended from the Gilla Corr, mentioned in the Annals of Ulster (1186), whose son is perpetuated in the townland of Ballykilcurr, near Maghera. One of the anglicized forms of Mac Gothraidh — a branch of the MacGuires of Fermanagh — is MacCorry, often without the prefix Mac; others are MacCorry and Godfrey. Mac Corra, too, has been noted in Ulster but this is possibly a modern form of Mac Gothraidh. Both O'Cor and Mac-Cor occur in the Armagh Hearth Money Rolls, O'Cor being the more numerous there. (Woulfe suggests that in Co. Leitrim it is a variant of MacCorraidhin, anglice Curreen or sometimes Curren.)

The prevalence of the name Corry in Co. Waterford and south Tipperary in the seventeenth century might suggest that some of the O'Currys of Thomond migrated but this theory is not borne out by numerous mediaeval records (e.g. the Ormond Deeds and the Justiciary Rolls) which show that people called Cor and Corre were established in Counties Tipperary and Kilkenny as early as 1270 (Richard Corre was Bishop of Lismore from 1279 to 1308): this may well be an unidentified Norman name unrelated to Corry, for migration from Thomond to Ormond was unusual before the fourteenth century.

The Ulster Corrys are also hard to trace: they spread south and east and Corry is one of the principal Irish names in Co. Meath in the 1659 "census", and a century earlier we meet the name in Co. Louth. Moyntercor (Uí Chorra) mentioned in 1609 as a sept holding Armagh church lands are presumably of this origin. In a note to a reference to Muintir Uí Charra (J. Arm. D.H.S., I., 1, 86) Mr. Michael Clancy describes them as stewards of the mensal lands of Glenaul. An interesting controversial case, which is quoted by Dr. J.G. Simms in his Williamite Confiscation, indicates that at that period one James Corry obtained a very considerable estate in Co. Fermanagh at the expense of the Maguires. Burke's Peerage describes him as John Corry: at any rate he was a Scotsman, ancestor of the Earls of Belmore and this family possessed nearly 20,000 acres in Counties Fermanagh and Tyrone prior to the break-up of the great estates under the Land Acts of 1870 and 1903. It was merely a coincidence that these Scottish Corrys settled in that part of the country much of which formerly belonged to the Irish Corrys.

Isaac Corry (1755-1813), Chancellor of the Irish exchequer and leading opponent of Grattan, was born at Newry, and John Corry (1770-1827), a prolific but forgotten author, was also from that area.   Bibl., Map

CORSCADDEN   I think Corscadden is a synonym of Garscadden, which is an old English surname formed from the root word gart, a field (cf. Irish gort). Apart from the Dublin district Corscadden is found in Co. Leitrim and I have met it also as Garscadden, in Ulster; but I know of no reference to it before the beginning of the nineteenth century. Possibly Cuscadden is a variant form. Dr. G. Cuscaden (1857-1933), the notable Melbourne surgeon, was born at Wexford.

(O) COSGRAVE, Cosgrove   (Mac) COSGROVE, Mac-Cusker   The Cosgraves and Cosgroves are mainly to be found now in three areas, roughly corresponding to the territories in which the several distinct septs now so called originated. For Cosgrave we must look to the east coast of Leinster, from Dublin to Wexford, where dwell most of the modern representatives of the Leinster sept of Ó Cosraigh. Before it was dispersed by the O'Tooles and the O'Byrnes this sept was in possession of part of north Wicklow not far from the present town of Bray. In the sixteenth century, though no longer concentrated there, they are often mentioned as people of standing, particularly in Co. Wexford.

In Ulster and Connacht the name is more usually spelt Cosgrove. In Connacht the sept, again Ó Coscraigh (or its shortened form Ó Coscair), is of the Uí Maine and was located on the eastern shore of Galway Bay. Presumably Coningus Ó Coscraigh, Bishop of Clonmacnois (d. 997) and Benedictus O'Cascry, Bishop of Killaloe (d. 1325) were of this sept. In Ulster Cosgrove is the modern form of three distinct Irish surnames, Ó Coscraigh once more — but not of the same stock as those mentioned above — was the name of the chiefs of Feara Ruis (near Carrickmacross) hard to distinguish, with the prefixes Mac and O discarded, from the neighbouring family of Mac Coscraigh, who were erenaghs of Clones. These were called MacCosguyr, MacKuesker etc., in sixteenth century records in English; they appear as MacCosker among the principal Irish names in Co. Fermanagh in 1659 and in our own time this is preserved in the form MacCusker still found in or near Co. Tyrone. MacIlcosker, found in the Co. Armagh Hearth Money Rolls (1664) is not quite the same, being MacGiolla Coscair in Irish. Finally we come to the third distinct origin in Ulster, viz Mac Cosracháin, MacCosrichen in Tudor English, e.g. in the Fiants, now abbreviated to Cosgrove and indistinguishable from the others. The modern synonyms of Cosgrove also include Cuskery (Co. Armagh) and Cosker (Co. Wexford). The local pronunciation of the name in West Limerick — Cosgree — is much nearer phonetically to the original Irish than is Cosgrave.

William T. Cosgrave, a Dublin man, was the first Taoiseach of the Irish Free State, and his son, Liam Cosgrave, was Taoiseach of the Republic from 1973 to 1976. Map

(Mac) COSTIGAN   This name which is now rare was formerly both numerous and important in Co. Leix and all the references to it I have met are to people in that or adjacent counties, the furthest away being Naas, Co. Kildare, where in 1540 Patrick MacCostykyen was a juror. MacCostigan, the present form, was used as early as 1544 when it appears in a list of Irish kern mustered by the Earl of Ormond. The variant spellings of the name such as MacCostigane (Queens Co. 1562) and Mac-Costygyn (rector of Durrow 1516) include O'Costigan. This is an example of the not unusual substitution of O for Mac in names which in the Gaelic form begin with a vowel; in this case it is Mac Oisticin, the C of Costigan being carried over from the Mac (cf. Costello, Coulihan etc). The confusion of Mac and O is evident as early as 1601 when both forms occur side by side in a Queen's Co. Fiant. In a deposition of 1650 we find Dermot O'Costigan, a dispossessed gentleman turned rapparee, accused of acting as a "tory," a term which was introduced officially at that time. The family was unaffected by the attempted plantation of Leix and Offaly and retained their main seat at Grange, Queens Co. (Leix) until the débâcle of the seventeenth century.

MacCOURT   COURTNEY   (O)CURNEEN
Woulfe makes the suggestion that this name, Mac Cuairt or Mac Cuarta in Irish, is a corruption of Mac Mhuircheartaigh. The latter, anglicized MacKurdy or MacCurdy, is a variant of Mac Muircheartaigh i.e. MacMurtry in Antrim, MacBrearty in Donegal and Murtagh in some places. MacCourt, however, should be treated as a surname of independent origin. It belongs now, and has belonged as far back as records are available, to counties Louth and Armagh. In the Hearth Money Rolls of the latter county (1664) it is spelt MacQuorte. Father Ronan in his Irish Martyrs gives the anglicized form of Mac Cuarta (Co. Armagh) as MacWorth. In Co. Cork this name has been found curiously equated with Rothe, e.g. in a lease of 1584, to Ellis Rooth alias MacWoorthe (Tanner Letters, p. 519). The name has been made famous in the literary history of Ireland by James MacCourt or Séamus Mac Cuarta (1647-1732) whose poems were collected and published by Rev. L. Murray. He was a friend of Turlough O'Carolan and has been described as "the greatest of the northern Gaelic poets." He was known as Courtney as well as MacCourt.

Courtney, however, usually of quite different origin from this, is a common name in several parts of Ireland. It is principally found in Kerry and adjoining areas, where it is the normal anglicized form of the Gaelic Ó Curnáin, sometimes more properly called Cournane in English around Killarney and Tralee. It has been claimed that his family was a branch of the O'Curneens (Ó Cuirnín in Irish) who were poets and chroniclers to the O'Rourkes of Breffny. The Courtneys who are now to be found in north-east Ulster (sometimes under the form of Mac-Courtney) may possibly be descendants of this Breffny sept, but are more probably either MacCourts (the Irish name of the village of Cappagh, near Dungannon, is Ceapach Mhic Cuarta); or alternatively settlers from England; for it must not be forgotten that Courtney is a well known Norman name: one de Courtenai took part in the Anglo-Norman invasion under Henry II, and in 1383 Sir Philip de Courtney was the King's lieutenant in Ireland. The Earls of Devon, who owned 33,000 acres in Co. Limerick in 1878, were of this family.

(O)COWAN   MacCOAN   Cowan is an alternative form of two surnames dealt with in Irish Families — see Coyne (p. 98) and MacKeown (p. 200). Where it occurs in Connacht records it is a substitute for the former but now nearly all families of this Hy Fiachrach sept are called Coyne or Coen. In modern times Cowan is (apart, of course, from the metropolitan area of Dublin) almost confined to Ulster. In that province — at any rate in the Oriel country — it is a modernized form of MacCone, a name which was very numerous in Co. Armagh in the seventeenth century as evidenced by the Hearth Money Rolls and also by the exhaustive analysis of Co. Armagh surnames published by George Paterson and by Michael Clancy in Seanchas Ardmhacha. At the beginning of the century we find in a Fiant relating to the Fews, Co. Armagh, the spellings MacCowan and MacCowane. James MacKowen (1814-1889), poet, was born near Lisburn and James C. MacCoan (c. 1829-1903), political and historical writer, in Co. Tyrone. To a large extent MacCowan has since been altered to MacKeown, thus presenting an example of a surname, uncommon outside a certain limited area, being absorbed by attraction in a much commoner one. Many instances of this tendency were given in Irish Families, e.g. Sullahan to Sullivan, Mulclohy to Mulcahy etc.

There was evidently also a sept of south Kilkenny and Waterford whose name was anglicized O'Cowan. The Justiciary Rolls, which seldom refer to the Gaelic population except as felons, outlaws or serfs, record the case of one Walter O'Cown, associate of highwaymen, who was beheaded in 1305; and in the same area the name occurs too often in the records from that time until 1600 to be that of occasional migrants from Connacht or Ulster. Nor are these references by any means confined to the lower order of society: in 1582, for example, John Cowan was Chancellor of Christ Church, Waterford; and even a horseboy of that county in 1567 is not without pedigree being imposingly described in an official Fiant (not in a Gaelic-Irish production) as John MacTeige MacEe O'Kowan. I have not yet found any evidence of what the surname of this particular sept was in Irish.

It is of interest to note that there is a place-name Ballycowan, that of a barony in Co. Offaly; this however is not formed from the surname Cowan but from an obsolete personal forename.

COYLE, MacIlhoyle   Mac COOL, MacCole

The relative numerical strength of the names given above is indicated by the nineteenth century birth registration returns, taking the two years 1890 and 1866, the latter being printed in brackets: viz Coyle 90 (112) Cole 37 (40) MacCool 22 (15) MacCole 12 (6) MacIlhoyle not registered. Coll registered 28 (26), of which the majority were in Co. Donegal. (For Coll see under Mac Cullagh.)

Cole is a numerous English surname and no doubt some Irish families so called are of that origin, while more are properly MacCole, but with the prefix dropped. Though MacCole (or MacCool) and Coyle are both of Co. Donegal they do not seem to have been used synonymously there, presumably because there is a considerable difference in the Gaelic forms of these names, and Donegal is one of the counties where the Irish language is still fairly widely spoken. Coyle — Mac Giolla Chomhghaill — was formerly anglicized MacIlhoyle, a form still extant in the barony of Kilmacrenan and particularly in the parish of Meeragh, the homeland of the sept. For Mac Giolla Chomhghaill Woulfe gives MacCool, MacCole, Cole and Gilhool, but not Coyle, as the modern anglicized equivalents; he tells us that Coyle is Mac Dhubhghaill in Irish, which he also equates with MacCool and MacCole. So far as Donegal is concerned, however, that is to say in the part of the country where the name is most numerous, Coyle is MacIlhoyle as above. Woulfe states that MacIlhoyle is Mac Giolla Choille in Irish, but beyond saying that it is a rare Ulster surname, sometimes perhaps abbreviated to Hoyle or translated Woods, gives no information. In a very useful map of the county showing the present distribution of Donegal families, prepared for me by Mr. J.C. MacDonagh of Ballybofey, Coyle and Coll appear in the barony of Kilmacrenan while MacCool is in that of Raphoe — MacCole is not shown separately. In this connexion the existence of the place-name Ballymacool in the barony of Kilmacrenan should be remembered.

I think Fr. Woulfe is wrong with regard to Mac Dhubhgaill. It is true that when the initial D is unaspirated this name is MacDowell in English — a well known family in Co. Roscommon. Nevertheless a perusal of the Fiants reveals the fact that the following all appear in or near Co. Roscommon in the sixteenth century; Macgillecoell, Macgillehole, Macgilleholly, Macgillelcole, MacGillyole, MacGillekolle, MacCooil and MacCowle, indicating that in Connacht too the name Coyle is chiefly if not entirely Mac Giolla Chomhghaill rather than Mac Dhubhgaill. These Fiants relate to a period prior to the large scale migration from Donegal to north Connacht, and I assume therefore that the Coyles of that province are of a separate sept, or if a branch of the former that the

division took place at an early date. In Petty's "census" (1659) Coyle is returned as a principal Irish name for Co. Roscommon and MacIlchole for the barony of Kilmacrenan in Co. Donegal.

The most notable man of the name was Most Rev. Anthony Coyle, who was Bishop of Raphoe from 1782 to 1801: he was a Gaelic-Irish poet, yet he is best remembered not as such, nor for his voluminous religious works, but rather as the author of the poem on the finding of Moses in the rushes, which was popularized by the celebrated character known as Zosimus (Michael Moran). Map

CRADDOCK

Craddock is the anglicized form of the Welsh Caradawg of Caradoc (Caractacus in Latin) and it appears in Irish records fairly frequently from the thirteenth century onwards. The earliest references relate to Munster, a number of those in the fourteenth century being in Co. Kerry. At the same time, however, the name became closely associated with Co. Kildare, where the place-name Cradockstown, near Naas, perpetuates the family. It is so called in a deed dated 1319. This property passed into the hands of the Eustaces before 1560. There is also a Cradockstown in Co. Meath and a Craddockstown in Co. Kilkenny. The latter is also called Rathcradock in deeds of 1343 and 1348. Craddocks were also found elsewhere in Ireland e.g. William Cradoc a landholder at Dundalk in 1321. In 1577 Stephen Craddock was one of the surgeons named in the charter incorporating the guild of the Blessed Mary Magdalene of Dublin which amended the barbers' charter of Henry VI. In his will, dated 1577, he is described as a barber of Dublin. Another prominent men of the name was Roger Cradock who was Bishop of Waterford from 1350 to 1363. Philip Craddock was High Sheriff of Co. Wicklow in 1682 and John Francis Craddock, formerly of Kinsale, was quartermaster-general in 1792. John Cradock, Protestant Archbishop of Dublin from 1772 till 1778, was not an Irishman; he came to Ireland as chaplain to the Lord Lieutenant and was appointed Bishop of Kilmore in 1757. His son, the first Baron Howden, was born in Dublin and was a member of Grattan's Parliament from 1785 to 1800 and later changed his name to Caradoc. The Township of Cradock, in the Cape of Good Hope, was named after him.

CREAMER, Cramer

Creamer is not the same as Cramer of Co. Cork, which was originally Von Kramer: for particulars regarding this name see J.C.H.A.S. No. 16, and Burke's Landed Gentry of Ireland 1912. It is also associated with Co. Kilkenny where, since 1682 when Balthasar Creamer was High Sheriff of the county, the family have been extensive landowners. Five of the name are in the Kilkenny School register between 1685 and 1750. It is presumably from this family that the place-name Cramer's Grove in that county was derived. There is also a townland of Cramer's Valley near Naas in Co. Kildare. Cramer does occur in the birth registration returns as having been used as synonymous with

Creamer, but for the most part Creamer and Creamor belong principally to Co. Leitrim, though occurring also in Counties Tyrone and Fermanagh, seventeenth century records, e.g. the Co. Armagh Hearth Money Rolls of 1664-5, present instances of MacCramir being used for the more usual MacCraner or MacCreanor, which is an older form of the Ulster name Traynor dealt with in Irish Families (p. 278). In the absence of any other explanation of the origin of the name Creamer in Co. Leitrim it appears probably that this is a corrupt anglicized form of Mac Thréinfhir, borne by migrants from Co. Armagh or Co. Tyrone. At the same time it must be observed that Creamer is also an English surname, which Bardsley explains as being derived from the word creamer, a pedlar, a crame being a pedlar's pack. Cramer has definitely been used as a variant form of Creamer and thus has three different origins in Ireland. Bibl.

CREEDON, Creed   Creedon, a west Cork name, is now called Ó Criodáin in Irish (e.g. Tomás Ó Criadáin, the nineteenth century Gaelic-Irish scribe) but formerly and properly it was Mac Criodáin. It appears in the late sixteenth century Fiants dealing with Counties Cork and Tipperary as MacCredon and MacCridan, and in 1564 in the person of Donagh MacCrydon of Swynome, Co. Tipperary, harper. The O prefix was occasionally used even in the sixteenth century, at least by the clerks who compiled the official records as this same man appears in a later Fiant of 1582 as O'Kredane. Creedon has been abbreviated to Creed to a considerable extent – even as early as 1659 when Francis Creed was a titulado in the parish of Kilquan, Co. Limerick. About that time the name occurs as MacCreed in the Irish army lists preserved in the Ormond manuscripts. Both Creed and Creedon appear in the marriage licence bonds of the diocese of Cork, Ross and Cloyne from 1682 and among the names of larger landowners in Co. Cork in 1878. In 1866 there were 40 Creedon, Creedan and Creeden births registered (37 in Co. Cork) while Creed was only 8; the figures for 1890 were Creedon 15 (all Co. Cork or near) Creed 9 (5 Co. Cork). In the Macroom districts, where these names are most numerous, cases have been recorded of their synonymous use by one family in registering births.

MacCREESH   According to Woulfe this is Mac Raois, a corrupt form of Mac Aonghuis (MacGuinness). This may be accepted: the substitution of R for N is not uncommon – compare MacGreal for MacNeill or Limerick for Luimneach. It follows that MacCreesh families are a branch of the MacGuinness sept. Their location in Co. Down and adjacent Oriel counties corroborates this.

(O)CREMIN   Ó Cruimín, Cremin in English, is exclusively a west Munster surname; almost all the families so called are resident in counties Kerry and Cork or have recently migrated therefrom, though in the 1659 "census" they were more numerous in the Co. Limerick barony of Connelloe, which adjoins these two counties. The tradition is that they are a branch of the MacCarthys,

and in that connexion it is interesting to note that in the Bantry district Matheson found the name Cremin interchangeable with MacCarthy.

In various sixteenth century records such as the Fiants and the Composition Book of Connacht the name MacCremon, MacKremin etc., often appears in Co. Galway. This, however, must not be confused with Cremin of Munster, being in fact a clerk's misspelling of MacRedmond, one of the many aliases of the Burkes of Connacht, and still extant.

(Mac)CRILLY, Crolly   Though the prefix Mac is now obsolete in this case the records for the counties comprised in the ancient territory of Oriel show that Crilly is definitely a Mac name. Several variant forms of the surname, as well as the place-names Ballymacreely, occur in the sixteenth century Fiants for Monaghan and south Down; MacCrolly, MacCroley and Crolly are among the principal Irish names in Co. Louth in the 1659 "census"; MagCrolys are found in the Co. Armagh Hearth Money Rolls of 1664; two Crellys and a MacCrolly, priests located in different parts of Oriel, are prominent in the Rinuccini correspondence (1653-1660); MacCrylly appears in the Farney (Co. Monaghan) rentroll of 1695. Crelly and Creely without prefix appear among the attainted Jacobites of Co. Down about the same date. Nevertheless the prefix O was sometimes used with this name. Friar O'Mellan, writing in 1647 in Irish, gives O Crili as the name of a Maghera priest, and it occurs with O as well as Mac in the Armagh Hearth Money Rolls. Reeves calls the erenaghs of Tamlaght (Co. Derry) O'Crilly not MacCrilly and the modern name of the parish formerly called Drumgarvan is Tamlaght O'Crilly. There was, too, a James O'Crilly in one of the O'Neill regiments of James II's army. By some authorities the erenagh family of Tamlaght is considered to be a branch of the MacDermots of Moylurg.

Abbot Patrick Creely acted for Owen Roe O'Neill in negotiations with London on behalf of the Ulster Catholics. Dr. William Crolly (1780-1849) was Bishop of Down and Connor from 1825 to 1835 and Archbishop of Armagh until his death: he was a supporter of the establishment of national schools and, within certain limits, of the Queen's Colleges. His nephew Rev. George Crolly (1813-1878), the theologian, wrote a life of the archbishop. Rev. George Croly (1780-1860), poet and famous preacher, had two sisters, a daughter and a son, all of whom were also poets of some merit.

O'Croly, which is of frequent occurence in the Fiants, has no connexion with the name now under consideration, being merely an older form of that now written Crowley. Thus several of the name have been prominent in the U.S.A. but they too, were Crowleys from Co. Cork. (For the O'Crowleys of Co. Cork see Irish Families, p. 100). That is Ó Cruadhlaoich in Irish. MacCrilly is Mac Raghallaigh.   Map

(O)CROFFY   This name is extant in the eastern part of Co. Galway where, Mr. P.J. Kennedy informed me, it is pronounced Craffy, and Ó Crabhthaigh is used as its

Gaelic-Irish form. A century ago Craffy was actually an accepted form of the name and it so appears in Griffith's Valuation of King's Co. (Offaly) which is not far from east Galway.

CROFTON   Though this is a surname taken from one of the several places so called in England it has been quite undistinguished in the country of its origin, but very prominent in Ireland since it became established here. The name is on record as early as the thirteenth century – e.g. a permit of 1232 to a London merchant to travel to, and remain in, Ireland – but no family of the name appears to have settled permanently here before the sixteenth century. Since then they have been closely identified with north Connacht. Like many Anglo-Irish families they are found on both sides in the wars and rebellions which occurred in the next two centuries. John Crofton of Ballymote is included in O'Flaherty's book Iar-Connaught with the O'Haras, O'Dowds, Mac-Donoghs etc., among the Irish chiefs of Co. Sligo in 1586, and John Crofton of Canvoe, Co. Roscommon, was one of the leading men associated with O'Conor Don in signing the agreement with Sir John Perrot in 1585. A closer connexion with O'Conor Don was to follow through intermarriage resulting in some of this hitherto Protestant family becoming Catholic and so adherents of James II. Among the public positions held by Croftons were auditor-general, deputy escheator-general, provost of Sligo and sheriffs of four counties (Leitrim 5, Sligo 3, Roscommon 3, Longford 1). Edward Crofton was deputy-lieutenant of Co. Sligo and Henry Crofton M.P. for Sligo during the short reign of James II. He was outlawed in 1690 as a Jacobite. This attainder was reversed in 1693 so I presume the Henry Crofton who attained the rank of major-general in the service of Philip V of Spain and distinguished himself in the war of the Spanish succession was his cousin. Two other Croftons who were in James II's Irish army at the siege of Derry were from Co. Armagh. At the same time three brothers of the name were among the defenders of Derry. One of them, Col. Richard Crofton, was among the Protestant officers cashiered by Tyrconnell prior to the Revolution. They were of Lisdorn, Co. Roscommon.

The name occurs so frequently in Irish records – Fiants, State Papers, Composition Book of Connacht, Books of Survey & Distribution, wills etc., etc. – that it is impossible to do more in this article than pick out a few of them almost at random. In addition to those referred to above I should mention Thomas Crofton who in 1671 murdered Dubhaltach Og, the last of the Mac-Firbis scholars, in circumstances described by O'Curry in his Manuscript Materials of Irish History.

The Croftons, however, were not indifferent to Irish culture: the manuscripts of the Annals of Boyle, which eventually went to the British Museum in 1734, was preserved by them for a period in the preceding century. Francis Blake Crofton (1842-1911), poet and novelist, was born in Co. Mayo; he emigrated to Nova Scotia after graduating at Dublin University and became a leading literary figure in Canada.   Bibl.

MacCROHAN, Croghan   (O)CREHAN   CREIGHTON
These are three distinct surnames of quite different origin, but liable to be confused. MacCrohan, with which the prefix Mac is almost always retained, is a Kerry name, the sept being a branch of the O'Sullivans with whom they were regularly associated: they were recorded, for example, as providing 40 men for O'Sullivan's army in 1596. Their seat was the castle of Letter, near Cahirciveen. In the penal times they were reduced to obscurity in Ireland, but as exiles they rose to prominence in Spain. As late as 1657 the MacCreohins are included in a state paper of the day among the Munster families "plotting for trouble"; and in the next generation we find Denis MacCroghan an officer in O'Donovan's regiment of James II's army, while Jeremiah Croghan was in Creagh's regiment. Two MacCroghans of Kerry were subsequently attainted as Jacobites.

Croghan, however, is listed both by Matheson and Woulfe as a distinct name, the latter giving Mac Con-chruachan as the form in Irish and explaining it as "son of the hound of Croghan": Croghan, the ancient royal seat of Connacht, is a place in Co. Roscommon, to which county he assigns this minor sept.

Older anglicized forms of the Kerry name as found in the Fiants, Monastic Extents etc., are MacCriohin, Mac-Cruhen, MacCrughen; MacCriffon, however, which would be an approximate phonetic rendering of the Irish Mac Criomhthainn, occurs in the Fiants only in Co. Wexford and some other Leinster counties. The name of the Kerry seanchaidhe, Thomas Ó Criomhthainn, so well known for his An tOileánach (The Islandman) is so printed in that and other books. As this is always a Mac not an O name, this form is remarkable.

The MacCrohans of Kerry sometimes appear also as MacCrehan, e.g. in a patent of James I wherein the chief is called MacCrehan alias O'Sullivan. Crehan, however, normally without a prefix in modern times, is entirely different, being usually Ó Creacháin in Irish: this sept belonged to the Hy Fiachrach group and was located in the barony of Tirawley, Co. Mayo, its modern representatives being almost all found in that county and Co. Galway. Another Crehan, Ó Croidheáin of counties Sligo and Donegal, is dealt with in Irish Families (see Crean.)

All this, however, does not exhaust the possibilities of confusion, for Ó Críocháin of Ardstraw, Co. Tyrone, the name of an Oriel sept, has also been anglicized Crehan; but, in accordance with the unfortunate tendency, especially in Ulster, to adopt English names approximating in sound to earlier and more Irish forms, Creighton has largely superseded Crehan in the north. Indeed it was common in Donegal and Tyrone in the mid-seventeenth century as the Hearth Money Rolls show. Creaton is another synonym of it. Creighton is also a variant of the Scottish surname Crichton. It appears as Creichtown among the Scottish applicants for lands at the time of the Plantation of Ulster. Creighton is the surname of the Earls of Erne. John Creighton (1768-1827) who introduced the practice of vaccination into Ireland was one of this family: he was born at Athlone. Edward Creighton (1820-1874) was a telegraph pioneer in the United States. William Croghan (1752-1822) was a major in the U.S. revolutionary army in 1778 and his son, Col.

George Croghan, was also a distinguished American soldier. Another Irish-American, George Croghan (c. 1710-1782), was a most successful Indian agent. The famous American actress Ada Rehan (1860-1916) was actually Crehan by name. She was born in Limerick. (See Crowne).   Map

CROMIE   Woulfe gives two alternative Irish forms for Cromie viz Ó Cromtha and Cromtha, the latter a simple adjective meaning crooked. I think, however, that some Irish Cromies and Crummys, who belong almost exclusively to Down and adjacent Ulster counties, are of Scottish descent. In Scotland the name Cromie (with six variants) is well known. There it derives from the place Crombie in Aberdeenshire: the B is not pronounced. Similarly in Ulster the Scottish surname Abercrombie is sometimes abbreviated to Crombie, which is pronounced and sometimes even written Cromie. One such was John Cromie who was prominent among the defenders of Derry in 1689. That the Cromies may also be Irish Gaels is indicated by the fact the Petty's "census" of 1659 records five families of O'Cromy in the barony of Armagh. A Fiant of 1602 mentions Teig McConnogher O'Cromy, yeoman, of Dromkarra (Co. Cork). In the same source for the previous century O'Crome and O'Croyme occur in counties Meath and Galway and these may be earlier forms of the same surname.

CROMWELL, Grummell   It will come as a surprise to many people to learn that this name, usually written Gromwell, was well known in Ireland more than two centuries before Oliver Cromwell left his permanent mark on this country. No less than six Gromwells were mayors or bailiffs (i.e. sheriffs) of Limerick between 1426 and 1598. They were of an old Anglo-Irish family whose name, it is usually stated, was taken from a place in Nottinghamshire. Reaney equates Grumell not with Cromwell, but with another English surname viz Grimble or Gribble, which, it is accepted, derives from the forename Grimbald; but the fact that de Cromyll appears in Limerick as early as 1307 would seem to corroborate its locative origin. If we consider modern synonyms we find that Cromwell, Crummell and Grummell have all been officially reported as such, the last named in Co. Kerry. In the birth registrations of the 1860's Grummell appears in Co. Kerry but Cromwell and Crumwell in counties Armagh and Down. In this connexion it may be mentioned that the Poll Money Commissioners for Co. Down in 1661 included two Cromwells (one named Oliver) among the local gentry who were appointed in this capacity. In that year also the will of Lord Cromwell of Ardglass was proved. The name has now become very rare in Ireland.

While it is only of academic interest the fact that in the sixteenth century the Gaelic-Irish surname MacGillegromell was found in Co. Antrim: this could of course, have been abbreviated later to Gromell but there is no evidence that the Cromwells of Ulster were of that stock.

(O) CRONIN   Cronin, with which the prefix O is very

seldom retained today, is one of our most numerous surnames, just failing to be included in the list of the hundred commonest (which of course includes those of Scottish and English origin located in Belfast and its neighbourhood): actually Cronin has the 101st place. The great majority of people so called belong to west Munster, particularly Co. Cork. In 1659 it was recorded as a principal name in Co. Limerick (barony of Connello) and Co. Kerry (barony of Magunihy) as well as in two baronies of Co. Cork – curiously enough in the north and east of the county, not the west as might be expected, since the sept of Ó Cróinín is one of the Corca Laoidhe located as indicated in the sept map. The name is derived from the word crón, meaning saffron-coloured. A leading family of O'Cronin were erenaghs of a church near Gougane Barra.

Of 176 births registered in 1890, 161 were in Munster, and of these 102 were in Co. Cork and 42 in Co. Kerry. In the 1901 census 261 householders called Croinin were returned in Co. Kerry. Their names, with some genealogical information of interest, are listed in Jeremiah King's book Co. Kerry Past and Present. No comparable publication exists for Co. Cork.

Croneen was formerly a common spelling of the name: it is met in the place-name Ballycroneen in east Cork which Joyce makes Croneen's town, but it is also said to commemorate St. Cronin.

Father Donogh O'Cronin, teacher of O'Sullivan Beare, was hanged at Cork in 1601. Rev. Patrick Cronin (1835-1905), the Irish-American poet-priest, was born at Adare.

A number of Cronins appear in the Kenmare Manuscripts.   Map

MacCROSSAN, Crosbie   There were two distinct septs of Mac an Chrosáin. The one which is now easily indentified is that of Tirconnell, whose present day representatives are to be found more numerous in Tyrone and Co. Derry than in Donegal: in Tyrone the prefix Mac has been retained but in Co. Derry it has been to a large extent dropped. From this sept came Henry Mac an Crossan and Richard MacCrossan, both of whom were Bishops of Raphoe in the fourteenth century.

The other main family were hereditary bards to the O'Mores and O'Connors of Leix and Offaly. In the Chancery Rolls of 1550 we find a pardon for Owen Oge MacCrossan of Ballymacrossan (King's Co.), rymer. These MacCrossans, however, have long disguised their name under the English form of Crosby or Crosbie. The first to do so is said to be Patrick Crosbie, who, having deserted the O'Mores and thrown in his lot with the English, obtained lands at Ardfert, Co. Kerry, in the late sixteenth century. His family became extensive landlords in that county, possessing among other properties the historic estate of Ballyheigue. As early as 1610 Pierce Crosbie, already described as "a very powerful Kerry landlord" and also as a noted intriguer, was one of the Commissioners for the Plantation of Ulster, just at the time the aforesaid Patrick was offering lands in Co. Kerry on which to settle the transplanted "seven septs of Leix," while another, John Crosbie, was Protestant Bishop of Ardfert (from 1600 to 1620). Intermarriage with the MacGillycuddys, MacElligotts and other Kerry families soon established them in the county. As was so often the case with families which were at first zealous in the English interest, the Cromwellian and Williamite invasions found them on the Irish side. In the Queen's County Book of Survey and Distribution it is stated that Sir Pierce Crosbie, a Protestant proprietor in 1640, "turned Papist and led a troop of horse with the Irish." In 1657, too, Crosbies were officially included with Mac-Carthy Mór in a list of Kerry families "plotting for trouble," and thirty years later Sir Thomas Crosby was an officer in James II's army. They were, however, more fortunate or more astute than most Jacobites, for prior to the Land Acts the estate of Crosbie of Ballyheigue Castle extended to 13,422 acres and that of Talbot-Crosbie of Ardfert to 9,913 acres. The family papers of the last named are now in the National Library (MSS. 5033-5042). The first part of Hickson's Old Kerry Records, 2nd series, is devoted to an account of the Crosbies of Kerry.

In this age of air travel it is of interest to recall that one of the first men to devote attention to aeronautics was Richard Crosbie (1755-c.1800) who made a successful balloon trip across the city of Dublin in 1785.

The first of the MacCrossan family (now spelt Macrossan in the country of their adoption), which has been very prominent in Australia, was John Murtagh Macrossan (1832-1891) who left his native Co. Donegal in 1853.

(O) CROTTY   The family of Ó Crotaigh is traditionally believed to be a branch of the O'Briens of Thomond which at an unspecified date settled in west Waterford and east Cork, where both in the sixteenth century (as the Fiants testify) and at the present time persons of the name Crotty (or O'Crottagh as it was first anglicized) were and are chiefly found. In the seventeenth century Petty's "census" found them numerous in the baronies of Decies and Coshmore & Coshbride in the western half of Co. Waterford. At that time the prefix O had already been dropped and it has since seldom been resumed.

The two most prominent persons of the name were noteworthy in very different walks of life, for Bartholomew Crotty (d. 1846), appointed rector of the Jesuit College at Lisbon in 1790, was afterwards Bishop of Cloyne and Ross, while William Crotty, who was hanged in 1742, was a famous highwayman. Canon Power in his Short History of County Waterford asserts that the traditional view of him as a hero is misguided.   Map

(Mac) CROWNE   The name Crowne, associated with Manorhamilton and adjacent areas, is a form of Croghan (q.v.), a name chiefly found in Co. Roscommon, alias Croan. Croghan is listed in the "census" of 1659 as a principal Irish name in the barony of Ballintubber, Co. Roscommon. In the Fiants we find MacCrowane in Co. Roscommon; Brian Keogh macBrien MacCroughen occurs in a Fiant of 1591 with a numer of O'Beirnes in Mayo, near Co. Roscommon; and again in 1601 there is Croghan "alias O'Beirne", which, taken in conjunction

with their location, suggests that the MacCroghans or Crownes were a branch of the O'Beirne sept. Woulfe gives MacConchruacháin as the Gaelic-Irish form which is corroborated by a Fiant entry of 1582 in which Mac-Encroghan appears as a Co. Roscommon name.

(Mac) CRYSTAL   As this name is derived from the diminutive of Christopher it is more properly spelt Mac-Christal, but the form given above is now the more usual. It is seldom met outside Ulster. Woulfe says it is a Co. Down name but in fact it belongs rather to Counties Armagh and Tyrone as modern birth registrations testify. The Hearth Money Rolls of the 1660's record it in those counties and also Co. Derry, with one family in Co. Antrim. The name is of Scottish origin and was introduced into Ireland in the seventeenth century.

(O) CUDDIHY, Quiddihy   Although the very earliest reference to this name – in Co. Cork in 1214 – gives it the Mac prefix calling in Mac Cuidithe, it appears as O'Codihie, O'Kuddyhy etc., in the sixteenth century Fiants several times. Subsequently it is Cuddihy, Cudahy, and Quiddihy with no prefix. Woulfe makes the suggestion – it is not a positive statement – that this O name, which he calls Ó Cuidighthigh (i.e. Ó Cuidithe in modern spelling) is a corrupt form of Mac Óda: for one account of this name see Irish Families, p. 161. Beyond the fact that O'Cuidithe and Mac Óda both belong to Co. Kilkenny there seems little evidence to support that view. It is true of course that Mac followed by a vowel has sometimes become O'C, but that two syllables should be lengthened to three with an intrusive H is most unlikely.

Cuddihy was mentioned here as an example of a name once numerous which has in the past century or less become quite scarce. Twenty-two Cuddihy householders appear in the Co. Tipperary Hearth Money Rolls (these are not extant for Co. Kilkenny) and later records find them in fair numbers almost always in the Ormond country, quite a number as far south as Carrick-on-Suir.

CUDMORE   This name came to Ireland from the west of England where it was formerly of note in Devon and Somerset. Paul Cudmore was Controller of the Pipe in 1655 and from that time there have been Cudmore families in Co. Cork: Cork, Ross and Cloyne wills and marriage licence bonds indicate that the majority of these were Protestants of standing in different parts of the county from Kinsale to Doneraile: in the latter place they had a family burial place in the churchyard. In the course of time, however, Cudmores ceased to be all of that class and persuasion. At the present time the name is found mainly among the professional and commercial community in the city of Cork and, I may add, we have Catholic farmers called Cudmore in east Clare.

(Mac) CUGGERAN   COCHRANE, Coughran   In this name, also spelt Coggoran, we have an example of the substitution of the prefix O for Mac, which is not unusual with names beginning with C, G and K (cf. Costigan, Creedon, Gogarty, Keegan). In this case the change took place at an early date. In 1585 it was still Mac – in a Fiant of that date a Co. Clare carpenter is recorded as Donogh MacCogerane; fifteen years later we meet in the same source two other Claremen called O'Cogran. The prefix is now obsolete. Cuggerans are not at all numerous today: those extant are either resident in Clare or their forbears came from that county. They are mainly found in its western baronies; but the east Clare place-name Ballycuggeran indicates their original homeland, situated as it is near Killaloe, the seat of King Brian Boru, in whose employment the eponymous ancestor of the sept is said to have been. (It has been suggested that, since his position was a confidential one, the surname may be derived from the word cogar, the secondary meaning of which is confidant.) The equation of Cochrane as a synonym of Coggeran is untenable. Cochrane is a Scottish name very numerous in Ulster. Coughran appears to be a synonym of Cochrane not of Coggeran, since it is also an Ulster name.

MacCULLACH, MacCullough   COLL   While not in the list of the hundred most numerous surnames in Ireland, MacCullagh, MacCullough and other spelling variants such as MacCollough combined constitute one of our most numerous names, with an estimated population in Ireland of nearly 5,000 persons. As regards location the same conclusion can be drawn from the birth registrations for all the years for which statistics are available, namely that 80 to 90 per cent of the name belong to Ulster, principally Antrim, Down and Tyrone. Petty's "census" reveals a similar position in 1659, when MacCullough and variants was listed as among the principal Irish names in the baronies of Antrim, Belfast, Carrickfergus and Toome in Co. Antrim and Lower Iveagh in Co. Down. In the previous century the Annals of Loch Cé tell us that Séamus Mac Con Uladh was killed at Dunbo (near Coleraine) in 1532. This name is given by the learned editor in his index as MacCullagh. Treating of Mac Con Uladh (son of the hound of Ulster) Woulfe gives MacAnully, MacNully, MacAnaul, MacCullow etc., but not MacCullagh as a modern or early anglicized form. According to him the Irish form of MacCullagh is Mac Colla (sometimes Mac Collach) derived from Colla, a personal name in use in MacDonnell and MacSweeney families. Woulfe's opinion cannot be accepted here. There is no doubt that the Irish form of MacCullagh is either Mac Con Uladh or Mac Cú Uladh. The reason for the alternative forms is that in later times Cú Uladh was regarded as one word and so cú did not change in the genitive. From the later form came the pronunciation which gave the anglicization MacCullagh. Dr. Hayes-McCoy considered that the MacCollas were galloglass families.

The most exhaustive source for sixteenth century Irish surnames is the Fiants: therein we find MacAnulla (Belfast); but MacColla, MacCullo(e) and MacCullowe were mainly Connacht, though occasionally Ulster. The Composition Book of Connacht (1585) records Rory MacCollo of Becklone, Co. Galway, and Rory MacHugh MacCullogh of Bollindrone, Co. Sligo, as men of substance. As the large scale migration from north-west Ulster to north Connacht did not take place until the next century it would appear that there was an independent sept of MacCullough originating in north Connacht, though it must be observed that there is no mention of such in the Tribes and Customs of Hy Fiachrach or in the Annals of Connacht, except for the 1532 death recorded in those of Loch Cé and noted above.

The name MacCulloch is also that of an important Scottish family originally of Argyleshire and later of Galloway, whence came the Ulster Plantation undertaker who was the ancestor of some of the MacCulloughs of Ulster. The first of them settled in Co. Donegal. This name is traditionally derived from the Scots-Gaelic word culach, a boar, and in this connexion it is interesting to note that in Co. Sligo, within living memory, Boar and Bower were in use as synonyms of MacCullagh.

The best known people of the name were Ulstermen: James MacCullagh (1809-1847), born at Strabane, an eminent mathematician and physicist; John Edward MacCullough (1837-1885), born at Coleraine, a leading tragedian in the U.S.A.; and Joseph Burnbridge MacCullagh (1843-1896), born in Dublin, who has been called "the father of the interview."

In addition to the MacCollas the Fiants have several references to the names O'Collo and O'Colle, located in much the same areas as the MacCollas; O'Colle appears also as well as Colle in the list of the Earl of Tyrone's kern in 1544. Colle or Coll without a prefix, however, is, at any rate in Munster and Leinster, a different name altogether, being of English or possibly Norman origin: it appears in the Ormond Deeds intermittently from 1360 onwards (occasionally with an O prefix even in the Ormond country). The first mention I have met of the Co. Limerick family of Coll is at Kilmallock in 1598: they are well known now on account of their intimate association with the late President Eamon de Valera. The name Coll is, however, chiefly found in Co. Donegal today and it is probable that there it is an abbreviated form of MacColla. (v. sub Coyle supra). In Belfast MacColl has been recorded as used synonymously with MacCaul.

(Mac) CULLETON, Colletan   The above is the usual modern spelling of the anglicized form of Mac Codlatáin. Colleton, Culliton and even Cullington are recorded by district registrars as synonyms of it in our own time. There were twelve births registered for the name in the last year for which I have consulted statistics – mostly in Co. Wexford. A century ago, when compulsory registration of births was introduced there were 23 registrations, 17 as Culleton, mostly again in Co. Wexford, Colleton being the spelling in Counties Kilkenny and Carlow.

The surname as Colletan, Coltane etc. has been associated with south-east Leinster (counties Kilkenny, Carlow and Wexford) for many centuries: it is of frequent occurrence in records dealing with that part of the country since 1500. In the sixteenth century it was most often given as MacColletan in English, though in the Ormond Deeds it usually appears without the prefix. In this connexion I may mention that O'Colletan is often found side by side with MacColitan and MacCulletan in the same parish. This can be explained by the fact that many Mac surnames beginning with C were often corrupted to O, due to the tendency in speech to slur the Mac making it 'ac: this MacColletan – 'ac Colletan – a Colletan – O'Colletan.

Many of the numerous entries relating to MacColletans to be found in the Tudor Fiants are of special interest being miniature descriptions in themselves e.g. (Fiant 2231, AD 1573) pardon inter alios to Edmund duff Macgilpatrick MacCollytan; (4036, A.D. 1582) Donell and Donagh duff O Colletan mac Teige. As a rule their place of abode (always either in Co. Kilkenny, Carlow or Wexford) is given, together with their status or occupation— yeoman, husbandman, kern etc.

Though there are more than 20 thus recorded in the Fiants as well as some in the Ormond Deeds, Liber Primus Kilkenniensis, Carlow Inquisitions etc., the name does not occur in later records such as the "census" of 1659 (which however is only a summary of the population not a complete list of names); nor, to my surprise, do I find it in the index of the Journal of the Royal Society of Antiquaries (which began as the Journal of the Kilkenny Historical Society). In 1608, however, Piers and Edmund Collatan are mentioned with four others of Gaelic-Irish stock, as the chief gentlemen of the barony of St. Mullins, Co. Carlow (close to Co. Wexford) in a comprehensive official report on the leading men of certain Leinster counties. There is a Culleton family burial place in the parish of Carrick-on-Bannow, Co. Wexford. The townland of Ballycolliton in north Tipperary is said to be named from a family of Colliton, but I have no proof of this.

(O) CULLIGAN, Quilligan   Both these variants of Ó Cuilleagáin are Clare names and are mainly found in that county and of course the city of Limerick, part of which lies on the Clare side of the Shannon. A century ago Culligan was much more numerous than Quilligan but the numbers are now about equal. Woulfe regards the name as an attenuated form of O'Colgan (which is more correctly MacColgan – see Irish Families p. 83): this implies that the sept migrated westwards from Offaly which is to some extent corroborated by a Fiant of 1588 where one of the name living in Kings Co. (Offaly) obtained a pardon. An earlier Fiant shows another O'Collegan among the many O'Connors whose location is not mentioned. They were, however, well established in West Clare in the seventeenth century, as we know from the fact that Cullegane is returned in Petty's "census" as a principal name in the barony of Clonderalaw.

Mac CULLOW   The birth statistics showing the location of this name are interesting. Taking the three years 1864-5-6 we find that 46 MacCullow births took place: of these no less than 39 were registered at Gortin, Co. Tyrone, and 6 at Strabane in the same county, the odd one being in Co. Cavan. In Co. Tyrone MacCullow is a variant of MacCullagh.

Woulfe includes Culloo among the anglicized forms of Mac Con Uladh, but the only place I have met it is around Tulla, Co. Clare.

(Mac) CUNNIFF, MacNiff, Caddo, MacAdoo   CANNIFF Cunniff, also spelt Cunneffe, Coniffe etc., is the most usual anglicized form of the Irish surname Mac Conduibh (cu: hound; dubh: black) and belongs almost exclusively to Counties Galway and Mayo. Another form of the same name, MacNiff or MacNeeve, is similarly associated with the adjacent Co. Leitrim and when Strafford's Inquisition of Co. Mayo was made in 1636 MacEniffe with MacNuff appear in that county; a few years later MacConniffe and MacCunniffe were among the Irish Papist transplantees in Counties Galway and Mayo. MacAniff and MacEniffe and their spelling variants, however, are now found chiefly in Counties Cavan and Tyrone, where Cadoo, Caddow and MacAdo or MacAdoo are also found; and these, strange as it seems at first sight, are also anglicized forms of Mac Conduibh. It would be hard to find any Gaelic-Irish surname with more different anglicized forms: in addition to those mentioned above there are many rare forms occasionally found e.g. MacKiniff, MacEndoo, Caddy and Quinniff, numbering 22 in all. In the form Cadie and Caddy it occurs in the 1659 "census" (Co. Monaghan) and in the Jacobite attainders of the next generation (Navan), and in Co. Cavan wills of a century later. In a manuscript in the National Library (G. 841) Risteárd Ó Foghlú suggests an alternative basic form for MacNeeve, MacAniff etc., viz Mac Naoimh; but I think we may accept Mac Conduibh as given by Woulfe in both cases. Another possibility is that Caddy is not a variant of Caddo but is MacCady (gaelice Mac Ada), or even perhaps the English name Cady.

In this connexion references must be made to the Co. Cork name Canniff or Canniffe, which Woulfe says is rare though in 1852 Griffith found as many as 25 Canniffe families in west Cork. Woulfe gives Ó Ceannduibh for Canniff, treating it as entirely different from MacAniff. The fact that MacAniff belongs almost exclusively to Co. Leitrim and the adjacent parts of Cavan supports its differentiation from Cunniff.

(Mac) CUOLAHAN, Coolahan
(O) CUOLAHAN, Coolican
Cuolahan or Coolahan is a surname about which there has been confusion, not only because it now does duty in English both for Mac Uallacháin and Ó Cúlacháin but also because it has been mistaken for MacCoughlan. It is easy to understand how this mistake arose, because the homeland for many centuries of the sept of Mac Uallacháin has been the parish of Lusmagh in the barony of Garrycastle, Co. Offaly, and the MacCoughlans occupied the remainder of that barony. Lusmagh borders on that part of Co. Galway known anciently as Síl Anmchadha and the MacCuolahans were sometimes lords thereof, though usually O'Kelly or O'Madden held the dominant position there. As not infrequently happens in the case of Mac names beginning with a vowel, Mac Uallacháin, tended to become Ó Cullacháin in speech and sometimes to be so written – by so doing O'Dugan in the Topographical Poem gave literary currency to this error. In the

seventeenth century the MacColleghans were extensive landholders in east Galway, one Brien MacColleghan being in 1617 seised in fee of Ballymaccoulighan, so called by reason of this family's long association with the place. At the end of the century they were still in Co. Offaly – thence came Lt. Daniel Cuolaghan of James II's army – and they are there today, though nowhere in large numbers.

The O'Cuolahans are of different stock, being of the Hy Fiachrach group and located around Carra, Co. Mayo. Diarmid Ó Cúlacháin (b. 1221), professor of history and scribe of the mass-books of Knock and Aghagower, was the most distinguished member of this sept. The forms Coolihan and Coolican are modern variants of this ancient name.   Map

MacCURDY   This name has long been associated with Co. Antrim: it is listed as a principal Irish name in the northern half of Co. Antrim in 1659, being exceeded only by MacNeill, MacCay and the Scottish Stewart there. Woulfe gives Mac Mhuircheartaigh as the Gaelic form adding that this is abbreviated to Mac Guirtigh.

CURRAGH   This name, which for the past two centuries has been found in south Down and the north Louth area, appears near there as early as 1428 when Thomas Curragh a farmer, of Kilpatrick, was mentioned in a case recorded in Archbishop Swayne's register. In the next century we find it mentioned occasionally in or near Dublin, e.g. in 1561, Richard Curragh, farmer, of Raheny, and, in 1589, another Richard Curragh a member of the Merchant Tailors' Guild who was made a freeman of Dublin city.

I have not ascertained the correct derivation of the name: it may be a toponymic from one of the many places in Ireland called Curragh; the rare Irish word curach, meaning champion or hero, has also been suggested as a possible alternative; or it may be an Irish form of MacCurrach, which is a sept of the Scottish clan MacPherson.

CURRID   This name must find a place in this book because it is very closely identified with one place, viz. Sligo. It does not appear to be of English origin but I have failed to find an authentic Gaelic-Irish form. Woulfe says that he heard Ó Corthaidh used by a local native speaker in Co. Sligo.

CUSSEN, Cushing   Although not among the first of the Anglo-Norman invasion settlers, the Cussens have been in Ireland since 1295, if not earlier, and may be regarded as hibernicized Normans. At the beginning of the fourteenth century they were to be found in Counties Cork and Tipperary and also in the Meath-Louth area. Their principal seat was at Farrahy, near Kildorrery, Co. Cork, which was renamed Bowenscourt when the Welsh family of Bowen (Ap Owen) acquired the property subsequent to the ruin of the Cussens under the Cromwellian régime. It would appear, however, that they were not all remarkable for their resistance to aggression for we find Mrs.

Cushin of Fermoy in 1654 notable for her "good affection" and "utterly refusing to forsake the English". (It has been suggested that this lady was really a Cashin – q.v.). At that time and even later the name was often written Cushine or Cooshin; it appears as Coshin and Coosheene in King James II's army list. Coosheene is phonetically the same as the form used in Irish – Cúisín. In the Fiants of the previous century there are a number of other variants including Quyshen – Robert oge Quyshen of Grange, Co. Limerick, was attainted in 1593. The majority of these are in Co. Limerick, but a family of the name was evidently well established in Co. Westmeath, for among the 1582 pardons we find Edmond Cushene, of Cushenstown in that county, and Edward Cushine of the same place in the 1659 census. Families of Cussen etc., were formerly numerous in Leinster (there was another Cushenstown alias Cosinestown in Co. Wexford and Cussin is listed in 1659 as a principal name in the barony of Forth, but these have to a large extent died out and Cussen, the usual form today, is chiefly found in Counties Limerick and Cork.

The form Cushing survives in Co. Wexford and is prominent in the person of Cardinal Cushing, a recent Archbishop of Boston, though not all Cushings in U.S.A. are of Irish descent.

Apropos of variants it may be mentioned that Cushion is not unknown as a synonym of Cussen in Co. Tipperary, while the tendency to adopt English names has also turned it into the English Cousins. This is at least etymologically correct as Cussen is derived from the Old-French le cosin, meaning the kinsman.

Adam Cussin (fl. 1395) was one of the scribes of the Book of Uí Maine. A Cussyn was M.P. for Athy in 1560. Since the submergence of the Gaelic order the name has not been prominent in Irish public life.

MacCUTCHEON   This name is nowhere mentioned by Woulfe though it is quite numerous in Ulster, its estimated population figure being approximately one thousand, mainly found in Tyrone and Antrim, but also in adjacent counties. It is originally a Scottish surname, being formed from the Scottish christian name Hucheon: this in turn came from the Old French Hueçon, which in England became Hutchin, forming the surname Hutchings, while in Scottish Gaelic Hucheon became Huisdean or Uisdean. From this came the surname Mac Uisdin which may be rendered Mac Uistín in Irish Gaelic. Woulfe does treat briefly of this, but though he gives nine anglicized forms of it (Mac Question, MacQuiston, Houston etc). MacCutcheon is not among them. (He also records Mac Oistín, with Costin and Costen as equivalents, deriving this from the English Hodge.) MacCutcheon occurs in the Donegal Hearth Money Rolls of 1663. The wills proved in the diocese of Derry take the name back to 1684 in that area. No doubt it was there from the time of the Plantation of Ulster. It may be added that in the Newry-Poyntzpass area Kitchen and Kitson are both used synonymously with MacCutcheon, while examples of the latter have also been recorded from Enniskillen. MacCutcheon, MacHutcheon, MacQuisten and Houston are all branches of the Scottish Clan MacDonald.

DAGG   During the past hundred years this name has become quite numerous in Dublin and is also found in north Tipperary and in Cork. Before that families of Dagg were established in Counties Wicklow and Wexford. The first I have met with in Ireland was John Dagg whose marriage licence bond was lodged in Cork in 1679 (four more such bonds are recorded for the eighteenth century). Another was a student of Dublin University from 1714 to 1719: he was born in Cornwall in 1686. Authorities differ as to the origin of the name: Reaney, the most reliable, derives it from Old-French dague, a dagger, i.e., one who carries a dagger.

DAHILL   Woulfe says that according to MacFirbis Ó Dathaill was a sept of the Silmurray, Co. Roscommon, but is now peculiar to Co. Tipperary. The latter part of this statement is incorrect as it belongs as much to Co. Cork as to Co. Tipperary. If we may identify O'Daal with O'Dahill it appears in Co. Cork records very early. Walter O'Daal, charged with many thefts, was delivered to Philip de Rupe as his hibernicus at Cork gaol delivery in 1295. In the sixteenth century we meet John Roe MacDonagh O'Dahill of Bruree, Co. Limerick, in 1579 and Knogher O'Deaghill, who was born in 1529, appears as a deponent before the commission appointed to determine the bonds of the Earl of Ormond's ancient estates in 1590 and the evidence of others of the name is cited in this Co. Kilkenny case. An analysis of several years of birth registrations shows that in modern times Dahills are found in all Munster counties except Kerry and Clare but seldom in other parts of the country. Daile and Deale may occasionally have been used as anglicized forms of O'Dathail but normally these are English names both derived from the word dale i.e., valley. MacDeale and MacDeele, and in one case O'Deele as well as Deale and Dale occur frequently in the Armagh Hearth Money Rolls of 1664-5: I do not know the origin of this name in Ulster.

MacDAID, MacDevitt, Davitt, Cavey   Mac Daibhéid (son of David), variously anglicized as above, is the name of an Inishowen sept whose eponymous ancestor was David O'Doherty (d. 1208) a chief of Cenél Eoghain. Voters lists and birth statistics indicate that both Mac-Daids and MacDevitts are numerous in Co. Donegal and adjacent parts of Derry and Tyrone, but seldom found elsewhere, 75 per cent of the registrations being for Mac-Daid and 25 per cent for MacDevitt. The third variant, MacDavitt, is that in use in Co. Mayo, whither a branch of the sept (some of whom have become Davy) migrated in the seventeenth century. In Mayo Davitt, without the prefix Mac, usually denotes a family of Burke origin. Richard Foley (NL. MS. G. 841) states positively that Michael Davitt (1846-1906), the founder of the Land League, should be so described. Similarly references to MacDavid in Co. Mayo in the seventeenth century and earlier have no relation to the sept now under consideration but denote Burkes, Philbins etc., whose father's name was David. MacDavid is also of frequent occurrence in other seventeenth century records, e.g. Petty's "census", which lists it as numerous in south Leinster and east Munster, where no doubt it denotes a Norman

origin, as does the cognate FitzDavid appearing in the same part of the country. In the same way the MacDavids in the Elizabethan Fiants dealing with Co. Wexford are not MacDavitts but Kavanaghs (alias MacDavymore). The 1659 "census" found MacDevet located in the baronies of Raphoe and Loughinsholin and particularly numerous in Inishowen. A return I received from Mr. J. C. MacDonagh of Ballybofey indicates that MacDevitts are now chiefly located in the western part of Co. Donegal. In this connexion I may mention the townland of Ballydevitt in the barony of Banagh, Co. Donegal, and another in Co. Derry.

Notable persons of the name in addition to Michael Davitt, noticed above, were Dr. Daniel Philip MacDavit, Bishop of Derry from 1773 to 1789; Dr. James Mac-Devitt (1832-1879) Bishop of Raphoe and author of The Donegal Highlands; his brother Dr. John MacDevitt, chaplain to the Papal Irish Brigade and author of works of a religious character; and Neil MacDevitt, one of the poets who contributed to The Nation from 1844 to 1851. Neal Devitt, the 1798 man, came from a family long established in Co. Wicklow with a burial place at Glendalough, but whether they sprang from the MacDavymores or were migrants from Co. Donegal I do not know.

The surname Cavey is the anglicized form of Mac Dháibhidh which is a variant of Mac Dáibhidh the initial D being aspirated.   Map

(O) DALLAHER   This is a Co. Limerick name which was formerly more often written Dollagher or Dollaher. The prefix O appears to have been entirely discarded in modern times. An early anglicization of Ó Dalachair was O'Dologher: in 1587 three men of the name, of Foynes, Co. Limerick. obtained "pardons" (see Appendix IV.)

(O)DANAGHER (O)DENNEHY DENNY DEENY
Reference has frequently been made in this book and in the previous volume (Irish Families) to the absorption of rare surnames in more common ones of somewhat similar sound (e.g. Sullivan for Sullehan) and also of widespread names absorbed in others considered to be more aristocratic (e.g. D'Evelyn for Devlin). We have now under consideration three surnames which exemplify one or other of these tendencies. From the eastern part of Co. Cork Danagher has been reported as being changed to Dennehy; and in the same area some families formerly Dennehy have become Denny.

Danagher, however, may be said now to belong not to Co. Cork but to Co. Limerick: it actually originated in north-west Tipperary, where the chief of the name was lord of a territory near Nenagh until dispossessed following the Anglo-Norman invasion. Woulfe, following O'Donovan, gives the Irish form of the name as Ó Duineachair, but I prefer to accept Ó Danachair as correct, on the authority of Captain Kevin Danaher of the Irish Folklore Commission: he informs me that his forbears, who have been Gaelic literates for many generations, have always so spelt their name. Possibly they are distinct names, but more probably variants of one name: that of the eighteenth century shepherd and Gaelic scribe Timothy Dinagher is an approximation of the form given by O'Donovan and Woulfe.

Dennehy (Irish Ó Duineachdha), an O name with which the prefix has seldom if ever been resumed in English, is (apart from the inevitable migrants to Dublin) rarely found outside Counties Cork and Kerry, in both of which counties (especially Cork) is is now numerous. The earliest reference I have found to the name is to Donall O'Denaghie of Cloghlea, Co. Cork, who in 1585 is described as vestarius, the primary meaning of which is keeper of monastic wardrobe, later being used for keeper of a vestry.

It appears that Denny was used as a synonym of Dennehy at least as early as the mid-seventeenth century: in 1657 the family of Denny is included in an official report relating to the Kerry families which with Mac-Carthy Mór were "plotting for trouble." This was certainly not the Denny family of Tralee: the first of these was Sir Edward Denny (d. 1599), one of the principal Munster "undertakers" who distinguished himself as a soldier at Fort del Ore in 1580. His namesake Sir Edward Denny, Bart., (1796-1889) of Tralee Castle, still possessed no less than 21,000 acres of good land in Co. Kerry three centuries later: he was, it may be mentioned, a poet as well as a county magnate. The most notable of the Dennehys were Major-General Sir Thomas Dennehy (1829-1907), born in Co. Cork and educated in Paris, who was a distinguished administrator in India and author of topographical works, and Daniel Henry Deniehy (1828-1865) who was born in Sydney of Irish parents and was a prominent figure in Australian journalism and politics.

Denny, it must be mentioned, is sometimes used also for Deeney i.e., Ó Duibhne, a sept of Tirconnell very strongly represented in the priesthood of the diocese of Raphoe from the year 1400 to the present day and seldom met with outside the counties of Donegal and Derry.   Map

(O) DANE   The English surname Dane (which is not derived from Denmark but from an old English word meaning a valley) has inevitably been confused with Dean (q.v.). In Ireland, however, Dane is primarily the name of a Connacht sept Ó Déaghain. In the "census" of 1659 it appears as one of the principal Irish names in Co. Roscommon; and two centuries later we find it largely concentrated around Belmullet in the adjoining county of Mayo.

(Mac) DARBY   (O) DERMOND   DORMER
The Christian name Diarmuid is anglicized Darby as well as Dermot, and similarly the surname Mac Diarmada, normally MacDermott, became MacDerby in Munster and south Leinster as early as the sixteenth century and was returned in the "census" of 1659 as one of the principal Irish names in the barony of Iffa & Offa, Co. Tipperary. As Darby it appears very frequently in eighteenth century records relating to that part of King's County (now Offaly) nearest to Co. Tipperary. In that case, however, it was an English family, the first of whom was John Darby, who, according to family tradition, came from Leicestershire with the Earl of Sussex

in 1559 and took part in the siege of the O'Carroll stronghold, Leap Castle, which he subsequently acquired by marriage with an O'Carroll heiress. Judging by the modern distribution of surnames it would appear that Gaelic-Irish Darbys also survived as Darmody in that part of the country. Two men named Derby appear frequently in the Co. Cork Justiciary Rolls of 1311 as jurors etc: judging by the other names in the same context they were of English descent.

According to MacGiolla Domhnaigh Darby in Ulster is an anglicized form of Ó Duibhdíorma. This is the name of a once numerous Co. Donegal sept, now known under many variants such as Dermond, Deyermott, Diarmod as well as Dermott, sometimes with the prefix O or even Mac. Ó Duibhdíorma occurs ten times in the Annals of the Four Masters between 1043 and 1454: the head of the family was chief of Breadach in Inishowen. The same name has also been anglicized as Dormer, which, however, is normally an English name (of French origin) associated with Co. Wexford, especially New Ross, since 1590. Six Dormers, of different families, appear in the Co. Wexford Inquisitions of the early seventeenth century; and of the six Dormers who suffered outlawry for their adhesion to the Jacobite cause three were of New Ross and three of Co. Kilkenny.

DARDIS   Though not actually an uncommon name — there are 15 Dardis entries in the current Dublin City Directory and some families in several Leinster counties — it has never been numerous. Birth returns indicate that it is one of the few surnames which has held its own numerically since compulsory registration was introduced in 1864, notwithstanding the fact that the population of Ireland was then much higher than it is now. There are few names, even of those which are far more numerous, which occur more often through the centuries in every record dealing with north Leinster since 1250, e.g. the Justiciary Rolls, ecclesiastical registers, Dowdall Deeds, the Fiants, the Chancery Rolls, testamentary records, and so on. Five of the name appear on the roll of Jacobites who were outlawed after the defeat of James II. There are four places called Dardistown — two in Co. Meath, one in Westmeath and one in Co. Dublin — and another called Dardisrath in Co. Louth, and these testify to the importance of this family and indicate the localities in which they were mainly established, though by the end of the sixteenth century the Meath and Westmeath properties had largely fallen into the hands of the Talbot and Nugent families. The name hardly occurs at all in English records: it is said to be derived from the Ards (in Co. Down) and certainly appears in medieval Irish documents as Dardes and Darditz: Woulfe gives de Ardis as an obsolete form.

DARLEY   With a few exceptions, e.g. Dr. John Darley (1799-1884) Protestant Bishop of Kilmore, who was born in Co. Monaghan, the Darleys, since they came to Ireland in the seventeenth century, have been continuously associated with Dublin and adjacent counties.

The best known family of the name was that which produced six prominent Dublin builders and architects in the second half of the eighteenth century; George Darley (1795-1846), the poet, was born in Dublin and Sir Frederick Matthew Darley (1830-1910) Australian statesman, in Co. Wicklow. The earliest reference to the name I have met is to Bryan Darley who is mentioned in Cromwellian Settlement papers as a surveyor in 1652 and a few years later Petty's "census" includes Daniel Darley as a titulado in Cork; but there appears to have been little further connexion with that city.

The name is taken from Darley, a place on the borders of Derbyshire and Yorkshire but is not noteworthy in England: the only Darleys included in the Dictionary of National Biography are Irish.

DARRAGH, Oakes   Darragh, formerly MacDarragh – it is still occasionally found with the prefix – is essentially a name belonging to north-east Ulster. Taking the statistics for two different generations since compulsory registration was introduced in 1864 we find that the number of births were respectively 21 and 18, nearly all in Co. Antrim and the remainder in an adjacent county. Going back to the first record of a census character which we have – that of 1659 – we find MacDarragh among the twenty most numerous surnames in the barony of Glencarne, Co. Antrim. It does not appear in that document as Oakes, which is recorded by Matheson in 1901 as a fairly widespread synonym of Darragh, MacAdarra and MacDara, particularly in the Dundalk area, which is somewhat further south than their main habitat. In the Hearth Money Rolls of Tyrone (1664) and Antrim (1669) the name appears as Dorragh, Dorah etc.

While I am not able to support the statement by any first-hand evidence I might mention that Mac Giolla Domhnaigh in his Some Anglicized Surnames in Ireland says that the name Darragh is of Scottish origin, having been assumed in the seventeenth century by a branch of the MacIlwraiths of Rosshire, who in repelling a raid by the MacLeods against their kinsmen the MacDonalds, used oak-stocks, (dair, gen. darach, is the Irish for oak). On the other hand Johnston's book Scottish Clans states that Darroch is a branch of the clan MacDonald. Before reading these books I had thought the MacDarraghs to be of native Irish stock: if Woulfe is right in equating the early form MacDwdara with MacDubhdara, which he says is the Irish form of MacDarragh, then it certainly was in Ireland before the extensive immigration of Scots at the time of the Plantation of Ulster: the reference in

question is in a Fiant of 1585 dealing, however, with Co. Galway.

Dermitt Darreagh of Callagh, Co. Cork, was outlawed as a Jacobite in 1690; other instances of the rare occurrence of the name outside Ulster are a Kerry will (1797), two Dublin wills (1744 and 1785) and one Wicklow (1808). It is also in the Hearth Money Rolls of Co. Wicklow (1668). In this connexion the fact that it is found today in Dublin may be disregarded, since the metropolitan population in every country is composed of families originating in all its provinces. James Darragh was one of the Fenian prisoners transported to Australia who, after many adventures, escaped to New York in 1876.

(Mac) DAVOCK   Woulfe treats Davock as obsolete, giving Doake, Doag and Doig as the modern forms of MacDabhóc. In that he is wrong: these names, as Reaney states, are abbreviated forms of Gille Dog, i.e. follower of St. Cadoc, and are quite distinct from Davock; I may add that in Ireland they are not found in Co. Galway, but are not uncommon in east Ulster. Woulfe mentions, correctly, MacDavock as an earlier form. Mr. P.J. Kennedy tells me that, though it is very scarce, there are families of Davock in the Athenry district today, and birth registrations show that it was in east Galway in small numbers during the past century. It is of the same origin as Mac Cavock and MacCooke i.e. a branch of the Burkes of Connacht. MacCavock is also found in Mayo, in which county the place name Ballydavock, indicates the presence of the family in the Castlebar district.

Arthur Gerald Davock (d. 1675) of Athenry was a distinguished missionary priest. Two other seventeenth century priests of the name, Fathers John and James Davock, were also from Co. Galway.

DAWSON   DORRIAN   Occasionally Dawson has a Gaelic not an English origin. A district registrar's report from Ballyshannon states that in that part of Co. Donegal the same family has been known both as Dawson and Durrian. Durrian, however, like Dorrian, is normally a variant of Doran, i.e., Ó Deoráin (one of the Seven Septs of Leix). In Co. Down this is sometimes anglicized Adorian, as well as the more usual Dorrian, noticed in Irish Families, p. 125.

The Dawson family of Ulster came to Ireland in the time of the Elizabethan wars and settled in Co. Monaghan, becoming Earls of Cremorne and Dartrey. Another Dawson family acquired large estates around Portarlington, Co. Laois, and a third got possession of the Glen of Aherlow in Co. Tipperary – hence the appellation Dawson's Table in connexion with the mountain, Galtee More.   Bibl.

DEANE   Reference was briefly made to this name as one of the Tribes of Galway in Irish Families, p. 49 n. According to Hardiman the first of that family in Ireland was William Den of Bristol, and ever since there have been Deanes in Galway and Mayo. Deanes were among the 1641 proprietors in Co. Mayo, as we know from the Books of Survey and Distribution, and Dane was a principal Irish name in the 1659 "census" for Co. Roscommon – both of these were presumably offshoots of the "Tribe" as certainly were the Deanes of Balrobuck near Tuam, about whom Hardiman in his History of Galway tells a very interesting anecdote regarding secret information they possessed about one of the 1649 regicides. The name Deane, though rare now in Co. Kilkenny, was in the seventeenth century numerous in that part of Ireland. It appears, as de Dene and de Denne, in the Ormond Deeds frequently from 1270 – always de not le, indicating that it was derived from the English word dene, a valley, not from the ecclesiastical or scholastic word dean. There were two mediaeval Irish bishops surnamed Denn. As it appears as O'Deane as well as Deane in the Fiants for Counties Kilkenny and Tipperary it is probable that the Deanes of that area were of dual origin i.e. de Denne and Ó Deagháin. This surname is derived from the Irish word for a dean. So also is the Irish surname Mac an Deagáin or Mac an Deagánaigh – the ultimate derivation is the Latin decanus. This name, too, has become Deane in modern times and as such is found in Co. Donegal: in the sixteenth century it was there and in some other parts of Ulster, the forms then used being approximations to the Irish such as MacAdegany. MacIdegany, MacDegana etc. In 1871 when the Annals of Loch Cé were published the editor (William M. Hennessy) mentioned that it was then extant in Co. Tyrone as MacDigany or Deane, but the former is now very rare. Woulfe also notes Digney and Dagney as extant synonyms. Curiously he omits all reference to the Galway Deanes.

The most celebrated of the name was Sir Thomas Deane (1792-1871), who was the architect of many of the finest buildings in his native city of Cork, of which he was at one time mayor. His son Sir Thomas Newenham Deane (1828-1899) was architect of the National Library, Dublin, and other well-known buildings. The purchaser of the ancient Co. Cork estates of the Lords Muskerry was Sir Matthew Deane who came from Suffolk early in the seventeenth century. His great-great-grandson was created Baron Muskerry in 1781. Henry Deane (d. 1503), who was Chancellor of Ireland and built a wall to protect the Pale in 1496, was not an Irishman. He was later Archbishop of Canterbury.

DEASY DEASE   The name Deasy, first anglicized as Deasagh (a phonetic approximation to the Irish Déiseach), is now numerous in Co. Cork and also, to a less extent, in Co. Mayo. Déiseach is a topographical adjective signifying a native of the Decies (a barony in Co. Waterford) bestowed upon some immigrant family or families which came from Co. Waterford, this epithet superseding the surname they bore in their original homeland. In the "census" of 1659 it is written Dacy and Dacey in the Co. Cork returns. Dacy, indeed, occurs as early as 1313, being the name of a Drogheda juror, but this may be of English origin. A few years later we find the spelling Deshay in the Ormond Deeds. Petty's men in 1659 found O'Dacy numerous in the barony of Corren, Co.

Sligo, which is contiguous to Co. Mayo; they also record Dacey and Dacy as a principal Irish name in the barony of Barrymore, Co. Cork. The O in the former case is clearly an enumerator's error, for this name never had the prefix O, though it was sometimes greated in Connacht as a Mac name – Mac as Déisigh, i.e. the son of the Decies man. Co. Galway is missing from the 1659 "census", but in 1793, when Father Francis Xavier Blake compiled a parochial register for Moycullen, there were twelve families of Deasy in that parish.

Mr Basil O'Connell, who made a special study of the Deasy family, told me that according to a tradition current at least as long ago as 1800, the Deasys of Co. Cork derived their name from a child rescued from a massacre in the barony of Decies about the year 1620: protected by the O'Donovans of the Island the child lived to have seven sons and it is claimed that he was the ancestor of all the Co. Cork Deasys. It is certainly true that the name was very rare before that date: it only occurs once in all the many thousands of persons specified in the Fiants, but it is significant that the one instance is a Co. Cork man, Donell Degseach of the Downings.

Dease is also of topographical origin, in this case the barony of Deece, Co. Meath. It appears as Dece in 1583 when Richard Dece of Turbotstown was appointed one of the commissioners for musters in Co. Westmeath. Earlier, e.g. in the fourteenth century Justiciary Rolls, we find it as Desse. This Norman family is one of the few which remained continuously resident on the same estate from the time of their settlement there in the thirteenth century until almost the present day, for it is only a few years since the Turbotstown property passed out of their hands.

Of distinguished men produced by this family the best known was Thomas Dease (1568-1652) who, after a period as a priest in France, became Bishop of Meath in 1622 and was noteworthy for his uncompromising opposition to the Nuncio Rinuccini in the counsels of the Confederate Catholics. Rev. Oliver Dease was another prominent priest of the same period. The family were strong supporters of James II, five of the name being officers in his Irish army and four attainted after 1691. William Daase (c.1750-1798) was a noted surgeon and medical writer; according to Madden, he was a sworn United Irishman, though Cameron refutes this. His son Richard Dease (1774-1819) was also an eminent surgeon.

The Deasys, though much more numerous than the Deases, have been less prominent. Rickard Deasy (1812-1883), Lord Justice of Appeal, belonged to the Co. Cork family. He was the author of "Deasy's Act" which formed the basis of subsequent land reforms. His son Henry Hugh Peter Deasy (1866-1947), who explored and surveyed for the first time eastern Turkestan, was a pioneer in motor-car construction and traffic control. Mr. Basil O'Connell believed that the name "Capt. Deasy," one of the prisoners rescued by the "Manchester martyrs" Allen, Larkin and O'Brien, was a pseudonym. John Devoy treats it as a genuine name, calling him Timothy Deasy.   Map

(O) DEEGAN, Duigan The most usual modern form of the name Ó Duibhginn is Deegan. Duigan and Deighan are also found in Leix and Offaly where the name is most numerous today, as it was in 1659, when Petty's "census" was taken, and equally a century earlier as evidenced by the Fiants. In the last named it appears as O'Doygan and O'Diggan, while Petty's enumerators wrote it down as Duigen. According to Woulfe, families of the name originated in three separate parts of the country – two west of the Shannon, in Clare and Galway, and another in Co. Wexford. He gives no explanation of how they became almost extinct in those places yet numerous in the midlands – migration of Gaels was usually westwards not eastwards.

Actually they should be counted as belonging to the barony of Clandonagh (Co. Leix). The most remarkable family of the name was that of Cloncouse, in the parish of Kyle, who were keepers of the Bell of St. Molua. Their lands, amounting to some 2,000 acres, were granted to the notorious Sir Charles Coote (Earl of Mountrath) in 1667. First coming to Ireland in the army of Elizabeth I the Cootes settled in Co. Leix and became one of the most influential of the Anglo-Irish families. The town of Cootehill in Co. Cavan is named from them.

James Robertson Duigan (1882-1951), the pioneer Australian airman, whose flight in a plane he built himself in 1910 is commemorated by a monument at Lancefield, Victoria, came of a Co. Kilkenny family. Map

(O) DEENIHAN, Dinaghan Both these anglicized forms of Ó Duinneacháin are found today in Co. Kerry: there were sixteen families called Deenihan in Kerry in 1901 according to the census of that date; and a 1666 tombstone at Rattoo in that county bears the name Dinighan. The name is that of a small sept located in the barony of Owney, Co. Limerick. In Griffith's Valuation of Co. Cork (1851-3) it appears in small numbers as Denihan, Deenihan and Dynahan.

DEERING (O) DIRRANE O'Hart's statement that the Irish Deerings are an ancient Munster family called in Irish Ó Dirighe is quite untenable. It is possible that some families of Ó Dirín may have anglicized their name Deering, though I have found no evidence of that. There is no doubt that Ó Dirín is normally Dirreen: Woulfe considers this rare name (so rare indeed is it that it is not to be found in the birth registrations for the three years 1864 to 1866) to be a variant of Dirrane (Ó Diréain) which is quite numerous in and around the city of Galway and rarely found elsewhere.

Deering is the name of a very old Kent family (spelt Dering there). In Ireland they date back to 1577 and in 1585 Antony Deeringe, queen's pensioner, obtained grants of land in Counties Dublin and Kildare. In 1623 John Dearing or Dering "gent" lived at a place called Moat in Co. Kildare and in 1667 Thomas Deering was of Newtown in the same county as we know from their wills: and about the same time the family had considerable property in Co. Wexford as the Civil Survey attests.

From that time references to the family are numerous in seventeenth and eighteenth century Leinster records. A Col. Daniel Dearing served with the Danish forces in the Williamite war: none of the name is recorded as fighting on the Jacobite side. No less than eleven of the name appear as state officials between 1667 and 1732, holding such posts as auditor-general and clerk of the Privy Council. Later they acquired property outside Leinster: the Charles Deering, who was M.P. for Monaghan in 1695 and 1699, was of Dublin; but one branch settled in Co. Fermanagh and another at Dunmore, Co. Galway, where their estate extended to 11,206 acres in 1876. Griffith's Valuation of the 1850's records 16 families of Deering in King's Co (Offaly), 9 in Co. Carlow and 8 in Co. Kildare.

(O) DEERY (O) DERRY Though originating in and subsequently closely associated with Co. Derry, the derivation of the names Deery and Derry, which are generally synonymous, has no connexion with the county and city of Derry. It is Ó Daighre in Irish. This is properly O'Deery, but is sometimes corrupted to Derry. Derry however is the correct anglicization of another name viz. Ó Doireidh.

Confusion has understandably arisen between these two families, not only on account of the similarity of their names but also because both were erenagh families located in north-west Ulster, Ó Daighre of Derry church and Ó Doireidh of Donaghmore in the nearby diocese of Raphoe. Even as late as 1609 the Derry Visitation reports Ó Doireidh as erenagh of Columbkil in that diocese, of which Maeliosa Ó Doireidh was bishop in the 13th century.

Two other bishops of the name ruled over western sees – Denis O'Diera (Mayo 1574 to 1576) and John Derry (Clonfert 1847-1870) – but nearly all the references to the name which I have met relate to Ulster and north Connacht. For example Father Patrick O'Derry was hanged at Lifford in 1609; Father Patrick O'Deery (who is also called O'Deary and O'Dyry), a friar of Derry Abbey, was specially mentioned by St Oliver Plunket in 1671 as an exceptionally good man and a great preacher; and in the Hearth Money Rolls for Counties Armagh and Monaghan (1663-1666) O'Deery and O'Deary occur quite often, one entry as MacDeery is probably a clerical error: this substitution of Mac for O (and vice versa) being not unusual in seventeenth century records. Edmund Derry was Bishop of Dromore from 1801 to 1820.

An exception is Donough O'Derry, the rapparee, who in 1655 was described as the "tory governor of Leinster." It is probable, however, that he was of Ulster stock.

Modern birth registrations indicate that Deery is seldom found outside Ulster and Co. Louth and that the forms Deary and Derry are comparatively rare. Map

(O) DELAHUNTY, Dulanty Delahunty is one of those true Gaelic Irish surnames which have a foreign appearance. This name, which has been also anglicized Delahunt and Dulanty, is Ó Dulchaointigh in Irish. Old forms

78

in English are O'Dolleghenty, O'Dulleghyntie and many other somewhat similar variants, under which persons of the name appear frequently in the Ormond Deeds from 1441 onwards, as well as in the Tudor Fiants and other mediaeval and early modern Irish records. In the "census" of 1659 the spellings are Dullahunty and Dullchanty, the former being one of the principal names in the barony of Crannagh, Co. Kilkenny, and the latter in the barony of Ballybritt, Co. Offaly (then called King's County).

In the King's Co. Book of Survey & Distribution (c. 1670) the spellings are Dolochanty and Dulohonty. In the same decade there were 27 families of the name included in the Hearth Money Rolls of the adjoining County Tipperary, and twenty years later we find three officers so called in a regiment of James II's Irish army. The sept was always closely associated with that part of the country and was of the same stock as the famous O'Carrolls of Ely O'Carroll. A branch migrated to Co. Kerry in the sixteenth century but the name is seldom found there now, the Ely O'Carroll country being still their principal habitat. The best known of the name in Ireland is probably the John Whelan Dulanty, (d. 1955) for 18 years Irish High Commissioner (later ambassador) in London. In America, as Delahunty, it recalls great feats in the game of baseball. Delahunty has taken the form Dulhunty in Australia.   Map

(O) DELARGY   Though the name Delargy is not numerous it is given here for several reasons. It is a surname about which the usually dependable John O'Donovan makes an inaccurate statement: meeting it in The Book of Lecan, where Ó Duibhlearga of Dunfeeny in the barony of Tirawley is described as "loving not the Galls" (i.e. the Anglo-Norman settlers in North Mayo), O'Donovan remarks that the name was obsolete then (1844). It is true that it is no longer found in north Connacht, the Delargys having no doubt been driven out by the Barretts and the Burkes; but it is not obsolete, for it reappears later on in the Glens of Antrim. We know that they were at one time tributary to the O'Dowds in territory near that of the O'Haras, and it is not unreasonable to suppose that the migration was contemporaneous with that of a branch of the O'Haras to Antrim. The Delargys being comparatively obscure, their fortunes cannot be traced continuously before the middle of the seventeenth century; but from 1666, when they appear in the Hearth Money Rolls for the Cushendun area, onwards they have been found until the present day in the Glens of Antrim.

The name presents a good example of a Gaelic patronymic assuming a French guise (though it has not, like some similar names, been carried so far as to be written De Largy).

Finally it was borne by a distinguished Irishman of the present day, Professor Séamus Delargy, whose work in the field of folklore earned him an international reputation.

The surname Largey has been in Dublin for a considerable time. I have not yet been able to discover whether this is an abbreviation of Delargy or that of an immigrant family from England.

DENVIR   Assuming that Dvenir is a copyist's error for Denvir the earliest reference I have found to the name in that form is in the Co. Monaghan Hearth Money Rolls 1663, parish of Donaghmoyne, viz Patrick Denvir of Laragh; in 1665 the taxpayer for the same holding was named MacIlmartin. Any references to the name I have met for a later date also relate to places in Ulster, but further north, chiefly Co. Down. Most Rev. Cornelius Denvir was Bishop of Down and Connor from 1835 to 1865. Cardinal Cullen described him in 1856 as a very good man but timid in dealing with the plight of the underprivileged Catholic population of Belfast, then rapidly becoming urbanized. The frequent references to him in the Kinsly Correspondence (Archivium Hibernicum No. 31) take a more favourable view of this.

Family tradition traces the Irish Denvirs back to D'Anver of Norfolk (temp. William the Conqueror) and makes the family of Sir John Denvir, the regicide, settle in Ireland at a place near Strangford, Co. Down, the United Irishman Patrick Denvir (1747-1831) being his descendant. The latter went to America in 1799. John Denvir (1834-1916), author of Life Story of an Old Rebel etc., and a notable figure among the Catholic Irish of Liverpool, was born in Co. Antrim.

DERRIG   This, Ó Deirg in Irish, is the name of an old Uí Fiachrach family at Killala. It is quite distinct from O'Mulderrig which is also of Co. Mayo.

(O) DERVAN   This, without the prefix O, is the usual spelling. Woulfe only gives Derivin and Derwin which are rare and variants rather than synonyms of Dervan. According to Woulfe the Irish form is Ó Doirbhin. Dervan would be Ó Doirbheáin and this is corroborated by the early anglicized form O Dirrevane found in a sixteenth century Fiant for the barony of Rathconrath, Co. Westmeath, adjacent to Co. Longford and not far from Co. Roscommon. An earlier Fiant has O'Durvin in Co. Roscommon. The name is very rare except in east Galway and south Roscommon where Dervan, Dervin, Dervine and Derwin are all extant.

(O) DESMOND   Desmond is an O name, though the prefix has long been dropped and has not been resumed. It is Ó Deasmhumhnaigh in Irish, denoting descendant of the Desmondman, i.e. native of Desmond, the old name of south-west Munster (deas, south; Mumha, gen. Mumhan, Munster). The early anglicized form O'Dassuny was a phonetic approximation to the Irish form given above. O'Deason was another early form in English. It has always been closely associated with Co. Cork and seldom found outside that county. It was presumably acquired by migrants from Desmond to the northern and eastern parts of Co. Cork, the country around Mallow being its main habitat. Kingwilliamstown, in the Newmarket district of Co. Cork, has of late years been renamed Ballydesmond. This name is a recent invention: the old name of the place is Tooreenkeogh. The surname appears in 1659 as MacDesmond in the list of principal Irish names in the barony of Kinalea, Co. Cork. This no doubt is one of the many examples of confusion on the part of Petty's enumerators between the prefixes Mac and O. Possibly Mac an Deasmhumhnaigh (on the analogy of Mac an Déisigh) may have been occasionally used in Irish, but I have met no instance of it.

Desmond, when used as a title not as a surname, is one of the most prominent names in Irish history on account of the leading position of the southern branch of the Fitzgeralds, of whom between 1329 and 1583 fifteen were Earls of Desmond.

(O) DEVANY, Devenney   The mention of this name immediately calls to mind one of the best known of the Irish Catholic martyrs, Conor or Cornelius O'Devany, Bishop of Down and Connor from 1582 to 1612, whose capture, torture and execution are described at unuaual length by his contemporaries the Four Masters. In the many records and commentaries which deal with his case his name is written in a number of different ways: O'Devany, O'Duvany, O'Dovany, O'Deveney, O'Devenny etc., in English, all still extant in Ireland or America — but usually without the prefix O — while in Irish he is called both Ó Duibheannaigh and Ó Duibheamhna. According to Woulfe these are distinct names, the former of Co. Down, the latter being that of the ancient chiefs of Uí Breasail in Co. Armagh; but O'Donovan places Ó Duibheamhna in Co. Down near Lough Neagh. It is open to doubt whether these were two separate septs at all, but we can be sure that, whether of the same stock or not, they belonged to east Ulster.

The fame of one member has imparted a disproportionate importance to the Ulster sept to which he belonged. It must be remembered that there is another — in this case unquestionably distinct — sept, called Devany etc. in English. This is Ó Dubhanaigh of Connacht and Donegal. As Devenny it is often met with in the records of the Diocese of Raphoe; Matheson's modern statistics show it to be most numerous in Mayo and Leitrim. It is reasonable to conclude that the O'Devannys pardoned with Rory O'Donnell and his followers in 1602, the O'Devenys of Inishowen in the 1659 "census" and the Devennys of Raphoe were all of this sept, which was formerly of Donegal rather than of Connacht. Another difficulty arises in connexion with the name Devany in Connacht: Devane and even Devine have been recorded as synonyms in the birth registration returns for Mount Bellew and other places in Co. Galway.

DEVEREUX   This name is formed from the Norman place-name Ev(e)reux and remains unchanged today except for the dropping of the apostrophe, d'Evereux having become Devereux. Matheson gives Devery, Deverill and Deevey as synonyms used in Co. Offaly and Duvick around Mullingar, but all these variants are very rare. Devereux itself is chiefly found in Co. Wexford. Coming from France to England in the eleventh century, a hun-

dred years later the chief men of the family took part in Strongbow's invasion of Ireland and, having obtained large estates in Co. Wexford, became the most powerful of the Norman settlers in that county.

In an old rhyme in the Forth dialect on Co. Wexford families that of Devereux (spelt Deweros there) is labelled proud, others being stiff Stafford, dogged Lamport, gay Rochford, laughing Cheevers, obstinate Hore, cross Calfer, false Furlong, showy Synnot and gentlemen Brune. The name figures among the great landed proprietors in the early Ormond Deeds and other thirteenth century records; as early as 1229 John d'Evreux obtained extensive grants of lands in the Decies (Co. Waterford). In the 15th century they begin, in the person of Alexander Deverous, Chief Sergeant of Co. Wexford, to assume a prominent part in the government of that part of Ireland which was under the control of Henry VI of England; after which time references to leading men of the name are very numerous. In 1520, for example, Alexander Devereux was Abbot of Dunbrody and in 1589 Richard Devereux was Archdeacon of Ferns. In 1599 the then John Devereux was knighted by his namesake the Viceroy Robert Devereux, Earl of Essex, who paid a state visit to Balmagir, the chief seat of the family in Co. Wexford.

In 1689 Col. James Devereux was M.P. for Enniscorthy. His son, Rev. Francis Devereux, was Superior of the College des Lombards in Paris; another of the branch which emigrated to France was Robert Devereux, a well known advocate of Catholic Emancipation. In 1634 the name Devereux was conspicuous as that of the Irish captain the the pay of the Emperor Ferdinand who assassinated the famous General von Wallenstein.

Though harassed by their neighbours the Kavanaghs, especially in the sixteenth century, and for the most part resisting inducements to forsake the Catholic faith, they managed to retain fairly extensive estates in Co. Wexford until comparatively recent times.   Bibl., Map

(O) DEVILLY, Diffley, Devally   These are anglicized forms of Ó Duibhghiolla, the name of two distinct septs — of the southern Uí Fiachrach and of the Síol Anmchadha — both of Co. Galway. Diffley and Deffely are more usual in the adjoining county of Roscommon. In Co. Galway Deely too is a well known synonym; and another is Duffley. Devally is a modern variant. Devilly is pronounced with the emphasis on the first syllable — its variants Diffley etc., illustrate this so that the I of the second syllable is almost silent, and a century or more ago, when the spelling of names was not consistent, a Devilly birth could thus be registered as Devally, and later the influence of the written word resulted in this becoming De-valley in speech.

Among the synonyms reported by local registrars and recorded by the registrar-general in 1901 Duvalley is noted as interchangeable with Diviney in the Ballinrobe, Co. Mayo, district. This is a form of Ó Duibheannaigh, normally anglicized as Devanny, Divenney etc. (See Devany). I presume the rare name Diffney is another variant of Diviney.

(O) DEVIN   This is the form usual in Co. Louth of the surname elsewhere called Devine, which was dealt with in Irish Families, p. 115: further investigation confirms O'Donovan's opinion that it is Ó Daimhín in Irish. When met in Co. Tipperary Devin is a variant of Davin.

(O) DEVOY, Deevey   The name Devoy is very well known on account of the famous Fenian John Devoy (1842-1928); and it is surprising to find it so rare that in none of the years for which we have detailed statistics was there more than a combined total of 19 birth registrations for Devoy and its synonym Deevey. Judging by up-to-date directories and voters' lists this low figure would appear to be somewhat misleading. The O'Devoys or O'Deeveys were one of the "Seven Septs of Leix", the chief men of which were transplanted to Co. Kerry in 1607. This transplantation had little success with any of these septs and least of all with the O'Devoys since that name is not located in Co. Kerry now, nor was it in 1659. It has always been associated with Leix and adjoining midland counties. As regards the Gaelic form of the name, O'Donovan places the sept from time immemorial in the barony of Maryborough and says that when surnames came into existence it took that of Ó Duibh which, he says, in due course became the well known Leix name of Deevy or Devoy. This is supported by an entry in the Annals of the Four Masters (1071) where the lord of Creamhthainn (i.e. Maryborough) is called Ó Duibh. Woulfe, however, gives Ó Dubhuidhe as the Irish form: the early anglicizations, written down phonetically from the spoken Gaelic, support this: O'Dyvoy, O'Dyvoie, O'Dywy, O'Dewy, O'Devy, O'Divie are some of these, all of Leixmen in the 16th century. A later example of the equation of Devoy with these other forms is afforded by the Ossory will of Edmund Divey "alias Devoy" of Smithstown (1681). On the other hand Woulfe's statement that Ó Dubhuidhe is a form of Ó Dubhuidhir (O'Dwyer) can hardly be admitted in the absence of the evidence for it. Duff being practically unknown in Co. Leix, where Deevey and Devoy do exist, I think that O'Donovan's opinion must be accepted, with the qualification that Ó Duibhidhe or Ó Dubhuidhe was the surname adopted, or possibly that Ó Duibh in the course of time became Ó Duibhidhe.

(O) DIGGIN   In dealing with Deegan, the Gaelic-Irish form of which is stated by Woulfe to be Ó Duibhginn, no reference was made to another anglicized form of that name viz. Diggin which is almost peculiar to Kerry and quite numerous in that county. Diggin does not appear to have been used synonymously with either Deegan or Duigan.

(O) DILLEEN   (O) DILLANE   Dilleen, a Gaelic O name (Ó Duillín), is entirely distinct from Dillon though sometimes confused with it. Dilleen is chiefly found in south Galway and Clare, though not numerous anywhere.
    Dillane (Ó Duilleáin) also tends to be absorbed by Dillon. It is also distinct from Dilleen, being concentrated in the country between Tralee and Glin in Counties Kerry and Limerick.

(O) DINAN   Though sometimes used synonymously with Dinneen in Co. Cork, Dinan is actually quite a distinct name, viz. Ó Daghnáin in Irish. It belongs to Munster, particularly Counties Cork and Clare. Griffith's Valuation (1851) found it mainly in east Cork, but it appears as a principal Irish name in the west Cork barony of Carbery in the "census" of 1659, where there were 13 Dinane families, with whom were bracketed Buoige (16) and Roe (35), making a total of 64 in that barony. Such equation is unusual in that statistical document and it must be assumed that Buoige and Roe were epithetal names which were already at that date tending to supersede the original name. It was not then sufficiently numerous in any one barony of Co. Clare to be classed as a principal name; but by 1821 there were 23 forty-shilling free-holders in Tulla barony besides a considerable number in other parts of the county. In Bishop Montgomery's survey of the diocese of Raphoe (1606) O Dinan is given as the name of the erenagh family of Aghadowney, but it is evident that this is properly O'Dunan (see Doonan). Dinan is now very seldom met with its prefix O; the variant spelling Dynan is also rare. Bibl., Map

DISNEY   This is a name which was formerly quite well known in Ireland but has almost died out in recent generations. It is, of course, familiar to everyone today in the person of Walt Disney whose connexion with Ireland is remote. It is not, however, a Gaelic-Irish name, being derived drom a French place-name and originally written D'Ysni, d'Isigny etc. I have not discovered when the first family of Disney was established in Ireland, but the number of references to the name in surviving records of the second half of the seventeenth century make it reasonably certain that this was prior to the Cromwellian settlement when Capt. Disney of Col. Clarke's regiment was rewarded for his services by a considerable grant of land in the barony of Moycashel, Co. Westmeath. Another Disney appears in the army lists of 1644. There is a Dublin Disney will of 1658 (Vicars Prerogative Wills gives the date of this as 1650) recorded in the Genealogical Office where there are also some Disney pedigrees, and 14 of the 19 entries of students of Dublin University are of that period. The "census" of 1659 records two Disney (and one Desney) tituladoes seated respectively in Counties Louth, Tipperary and Westmeath – the last-named in the barony of Corkaree not Moycashel. We find it also, some six years later, in the Hearth Money Rolls of Monsea, near Nenagh. It is of remarkably frequent occurrence, for a rare name, in the eighteenth century will records: I have noted at least a dozen in eight different counties. They are less numerous in the nineteenth century: Griffith's Valuation found a few families of the name in north Tipperary and also in Leix, Offaly, Carlow and Waterford. Other references worthy of mention are Moore Disney, sheriff of Waterford in 1763 and another (Sir) Moore Disney (c.1766-1846) also of Waterford, a soldier of note in the Peninsular War: William Disney was Commissioner of Prisons in Ireland in 1808. An interesting letter from Col. (then Lt.) Brabazon Disney (d. Dublin 1833) of a Co. Cork family, written from Waterloo in 1815, is quoted in full in Jnl. Cork Hist. & Arch. Soc. X 134-6.

DOBBYN   Although some of the earliest references to this name in Ireland, i.e., those in the thirteenth century, find it in Cork and Limerick, it became firmly established in Co. Kilkenny during the next century as the Patent and Chancery rolls, Ormond deeds, and other such records attest. Dobbyn of Dobbynswood, Co. Kilkenny, was prominent from 1500, Dobbyns appear among the leading gentry of the country in 1537 and 1598. The "census" of 1659 found Dobbyn a principal Irish name in the barony of Gowran; Nicholas Dobine of Ballymarey, Co. Kilkenny, was transplanted to Connacht as a papist in 1657. From Co. Kilkenny they spread to the nearby city of Waterford and perhaps the best known family of the name is that of Waterford. Two of them were mayors (1460 and 1589) and their prosperity can be measured by the fact that all the eight Dobbyns whose wills were proved in the Prerogative court between 1663 and 1808 were of Waterford. This statement raises the question of the spelling of the name. Eight Dobbin wills also passed through the Prerogative court (from 1718 to 1795) and none of these was of Waterford, 5 being of Ulster. If we now consider the distribution of the name in modern times we find that 75 per cent belong to Antrim or an adjacent Ulster county – all Dobbin – and only a small number of Dobbyns are still to be found in counties Waterford and Kilkenny. The Dobbins of Antrim first appear as Constable of Carrickfergus Castle in 1400: seventeen of them were sheriffs and eight mayors of Carrickfergus between 1571 and 1666.   Bibl.

(Mac) DOCKERY   This name is seldom found outside its original habitat viz. Co. Roscommon, where before the destruction of the Gaelic order it was the duty of O'Flanagan, O'Beirne and Clan Dail-re-deacair (branches of the Silmurray) to guard the preys or spoils of O'Conor, the last named being specially charged with the provision of straw for encampment and furniture and beds for O'Conor's house. In its original form the surname, MacDail-re-Deachair, is of a rare and interesting type. It was first anglicized as MacGallredocker – in 1582 and again in 1591 several men of that name received pardons with others in Co. Roscommon; in 1585 in a similar official document it appears as MacGilldogher, which is presumably a clerk's attempt to write down Mac Giolla Deacair phonetically, for even as early as that this synonym was coming into use. According to Woulfe the corrupt modern form is Ó Dochraidh, and O'Dockery is now used as the anglicized form when the prefix is not omitted; but there is no doubt that Dockery is properly a Mac not an O name.

Sir Henry Dowcra, the Elizabethan commander in the war against O'Neill, whose name was sometimes spelt Dockewray in contemporary documents, was of course English and had no connexion with the Roscommon sept. This, no doubt, is the same name as Dockerey, which was found in the Pale in the fifteenth century.

Matheson records the use in Meath of Harden as synonymous with Mac Dacker. Woulfe states that Hardy and Hardiman are also so used. Such cases are very rare.   Map

DOLPHIN   We have here an example of an old English name, in this case of Norse origin, which became thoroughly hibernicized. The Four Masters mention one John Dolifin, a follower of Walter Burke in his campaign against the O'Connors in 1270. Isolated references to it in Ireland occur from the early thirteenth century, and from the sixteenth onwards we find it firmly established in Co. Galway whence it spread to north Connacht. In a list of leading men of Co. Galway in the sixteenth century given in O Flaherty's book Iar Connacht we find Redmond Dolphine of Rarroddy "chief of his name"; at the same time Dolphin of Turoe and Dolphin of Brackloonmore and Dolphin of Galboly were other important landed families in Co. Galway. I give these in modern spelling: the last named for example appears in a Fiant of 1582 as Walter Dolphinn of Galweyle and in another of 1585 as Walter Dolfin of Galbwoly. They seem to have been especially identified with the Loughrea area wherein lies Raroddy or Rathruddy: Mr. P. J. Kennedy said that this was the centre of a deBurgo feudal district known as the Dolphinage. Eight Dolphins from this east Galway country were among the transplanted Papists of 1656-7. Though largely uprooted from their ancestral homes they did not lose their position in the social scale in Connacht. Several Dolphins were among the largest landowners in Co. Galway at the end of the nineteenth century and one indeed held Turoe. This result was not attained by conforming, as the families in question were Catholics. Four were students at Dublin University, all born in Co. Galway.

(O) DONEGAN, Dungan   Considering the fact that Ó Donnagáin is the surname of at least four distinct septs of mediaeval Ireland, the number of their present day representatives is less than might be expected; nineteenth century birth statistics, which may be taken as approximately representing the present position, record an average of 50 registrations for Donegan and its variants, 18 of which were in Leinster, 13 in Munster, 15 in Ulster and 4 in Connacht. The best available sources of comparison in this respect for previous periods are the "census" of 1659 and the Fiants of 1540 to 1601. These show that in the seventeenth century the name was numerous in the barony of Rathconrath, Co. Westmeath and in the neighbouring barony of Athlone, while there were an appreciable number in Co. Sligo also; whereas two or three generations earlier O'Donegans were found not only in west Leinster but also to an equal extent in Co. Cork and adjacent parts of Munster. The latter, no doubt, were of the once powerful sept of Muscraidhe Tri Maighe, alias O'Donegan's country, which lies in the baronies of Orrery and Duhallow in the north-western part of the county. In the thirteenth century their territory passed for the most part into the possession of the Norman Barrys. In south-west Cork the small sept of Ó Donnagáin became tributary to O'Sullivan Beare; while that of Ara, in north Tipperary, was dispersed by the O'Briens whose chief there became Mac I Brien Ara.

The origin of the O'Donegans of Co. Sligo is obscure: it may be conjectured that they are a branch of the Westmeath sept. Those of Ulster, however, are distinct. The Annals of Loch Cé record the death in 1029 of Donnchadh Ó Donnagáin King of Fernmhagh (Farney, Co. Monaghan) and in 1113 of Ó Donnagáin "royal heir" thereof (the same annalists describe O'Boylan as king of Farney in 1093). Notable Ulstermen of the name were John Dongan, Bishop of Down from 1394 to 1412 and Dr. Edmund Dunnegan, Bishop of Down & Connor, who died in prison in 1629.

The Westmeath O'Donegans, who held the manor of Kildrought, Co. Kildare, from the Earls of Kildare, were also established in Leix and Offaly, where their territory was formerly known as Críoch Dungan (i.e. Dungan's or O'Donegan's country). Of this family was Thomas Donegan or Dongan Earl of Limerick, framer of the celebrated New York Dongan Charter of 1686 (his house on Broadway had a garden of several acres); his elder brother the first Earl was attainted as a Jacobite in 1691: their father was Sir John Dongan, Bart., of Castletown, Co. Kildare. Another distinguished member of the Castletown family was Thomas Dongan (c. 1595-1663), a lawyer who, after being reduced to dire poverty by the aftermath of the Rising of 1641, became a Baron of the Exchequer at the Restoration.

Dunegan Castle in Co. Westmeath is a few miles northeast of Athlone.

Reference was made in Irish Families (p. 105) to the Co. Down sept of MacDonegan.   Map

(O) DONNAN   (O) DOONAN   Woulfe regards these two names (Ó Donnáin and Ó Dúnáin in Irish) as variants; and it is certainly a fact that their similarity has led in some cases to their synonymous use. They should, however, be treated as distinct. They are in modern times definitely associated with two widely separated areas: Donnans are mainly located in Co. Down and Doonans in Counties Roscommon and Leitrim; in neither is the prefix O retained. The fact that Maelmuire Ó Dunáin was Bishop of Meath (from 1096 to 1117) is little evidence of his family origin; but the existence of an Adam O'Dounan, who appears in a Co. Roscommon land case in 1299, indicates that the family was there at that early date. When we consult the sixteenth century Fiants we find the name spelt O'Donayne as well as O'Donnane in Co. Leitrim; though this does no more than present an example of the inconsistency which was normal in the early anglicization of Irish surnames. The Fiants, however, record a Donnanstown in Co. Cork and an O'Donnane in the same county. As Donane also appears in the Tipperary Hearth Money Rolls of the 1660s it would appear that the name was formerly to be

found in Munster; but I have no knowledge of its origin and if it is still there it is very rare.

O'Donovan in his introduction to the Topographical Poem of O'Dugan and O'Heerin says that Ó Donnáin is derived from the adjective donn (brown), but he does not mention Ó Dúnáin.

(O) DOORLEY   O'Doorley was undoubtedly the name of one of the smaller septs of Corca Laoidhe, but appears to be now almost extinct there. The east Galway (Uí Maine) sept, whose original territory lay between Loughrea and the Shannon, were from the sixteenth century onwards more generally established on the other side of the river in Co. Offaly, though still to be found on the Connacht side also. The name, given by Woulfe as Ó Dubhurthuile, has also been anglicized Dufferly in Connacht.   Map

(O) DORNEY   (O) TORNEY   Dorney, a name found in modern times almost exclusively in Counties Cork and Tipperary, is associated with that part of the country for the past four centuries: O'Dorney occurs, with the normal spelling variants, a number of times in the sixteenth century Fiants relating to Co. Cork; in the next century an O'Dorney of Co. Cork was among the men outlawed for their participation in the Rising of 1641 and the "census" of 1659 records it among the principal Irish names in the barony of Kerrycurrihy, Co. Cork, and the name appears five times in the Tipperary Hearth Money Rolls of the following decade; a generation later, according to Dalton, Owen O'Dorney of Clondullane, Co. Cork, was attainted as a Jacobite, but his name does not occur in the Jacobite outlawries listed in Analecta Hibernica No. 22 by Dr. J.G. Simms; while in Griffith's Valuation of 1851-3 there are 15 Dorney families in east and 19 in west Cork. In just one late Fiant of 1602 an O'Dorney is found in Co. Monaghan. It is possible that this was clerical error for O'Torney, for five families so called in the neighbouring county of Fermanagh are recorded in the "census" of 1659. Torney, as distinct from Dorney, is not found in Munster, but according to O'Curry the sept of O'Torna inhabited that part of north Kerry in which the village of Abbeydorney lies, Abbeydorney thus being called after a family of O'Torney (Ó Torna) not O'Dorney. As we have no traditional genealogy giving the origin of O'Dorney, the obvious inference is that O'Dorney is a later form of O'Torna. I can offer no evidence regarding the existence of the name Torney in Ulster.

(O) DOROHY   The name Dorohy is associated mainly with Kerry, particularly the Kenmare area. It is not, nor was it ever, numerous. Formerly it was found in other parts of Munster as well as Kerry e.g. (in Fiants between 1552 and 1601) in Counties Limerick and Tipperary as O'Doroghie. At the same time and in the same source (Fiants) we find O'Dorrechy in Clare, but this is presumably Dorcy (now usually Darcy) not Dorohy. Dorohie occurs, too, in the Hearth Money Rolls of 1667 for

Co. Tipperary. Though unconnected in origin toponymically they may be similar etymologically – Ó Dorchaidhe in Irish (from dorcha, dark). Another form of the name, now obsolete, was Dorogho which I have met in a Co. Cork deed of 1593. This suggests the Irish form Ó Dorchadha as a variant of Ó Dorchaidhe.

Other surnames which might be confused with Dorohy are Dorothy and Dorrity both of which are found occasionally in northern Ulster.

(O) DOUGHAN   (O) DOOHAN   As might be expected confusion arises with these two names. Doughan (Ó Dubhchon in Irish, presumably dubh, black; con, hound) though it originated as a Corca Laoidhe sept in Co. Cork, belongs in modern times to north Tipperary and the adjacent areas of Co. Offaly. As Doghon and O'Doghon it is listed as one of the more numerous names in the baronies of Eliogarty and Ikerrin in the "census" of 1659. It has spread also into Co. Clare where, however, it is spelt Doohan. Doohan is primarily a Tirconnell name (Ó Duacháin in Irish).

DOWDALL   Families of this name are now mostly located in the counties of Dublin and Louth, as was the case in 1659 when Petty's "census" was taken. This was true indeed long before that, for they were established there not long after the Anglo-Norman invasion and have been prominent in the activities of the Pale ever since. Woulfe derives the name from a parish in Staffordshire; Bardsley from another in Yorkshire – it can be accepted that it comes from an English place-name, though MacFirbis includes it among the families of Norman-Welsh origin. Its earlier spelling is Dovedale. Much detailed information is available in the calendar of Dowdall Mss., published by the Irish Manuscripts Commission. This collection is perhaps second only to the Ormond Deeds in value and importance, dealing as it does with estates in Co. Louth from the thirteenth to the seventeenth century. There was a branch of the family in Counties Mayo and Sligo in the seventeenth and eighteenth centuries but few of these are now extant.

Among the many distinguished persons of the name who have adorned the pages of Irish history perhaps the most noteworthy were George Dowdall, Archbishop of Armagh from 1543-1558 (with an interval of retirement during the reign of Edward VI) and William Dowdall (natural son of Hussey Burgh, Chief Baron of the Exchequer) who, having been out in 1798 and later joined Emmet, served with great distinction on the Continent in the Irish Legion, finishing his career with severe wounds at the siege of Flushing in 1809.

(O) DOWDICAN   Dudican is a variant of this name, which is Ó Dubhdacáin in Irish, a family said to be of the Cenél Eoghain. Both forms are almost entirely confined to the two counties of Sligo and Donegal.

DOWSE   Though never numerous this name is in Ireland continuously since the end of the thirteenth century. In 1305 it appears in the Justiciary Rolls among citizens of Dublin as Dowse; in the same year it occurs in a Co. Kildare law case as Douez, i.e., Old French le Douz (from Latin dulcis). By 1326 it had become Dousse and Douce, the former a juror at Shankill, Co. Dublin, the latter a freeholder at Rathcoole on the border of Co. Dublin and Kildare. The name was in England too; among the Cromwellian "adventurers" we find the name Dowse and Dowys, and in 1642 a Mr. Dowse was one of the Commissioners for the Affairs of Ireland. Seventeenth and eighteenth century wills place them in counties Wicklow and Wexford, and more modern statistics indicate that they are still found in those counties as well as in the city of Dublin.   Bibl.

(O) DRADDY, Graddy   Draddy is a name which should have been included in Appendix F of Irish Families since not only do modern statistics show that it is almost exclusively a Co. Cork name, but as far back as it appears in records it is invariably associated with Co. Cork. The prefix O was dropped very early. The Cork and Ross wills, the earliest of which is 1629, are signed Draddy and even in the sixteenth century Fiants, six of which list Draddys (all in Co. Cork), only one is given the O. John Draddy, the Co. Cork Gaelic scribe, whose work was done mainly between 1820 and 1840, used the form Ó Dreada in Irish.

Woulfe treats Graddy either as a variant of O'Grady or as the anglicized form of Ó Greada; Richard Foley (Nat. Library MS. G. 841) suggests that it is a variant of Draddy and the fact that Graddys are found almost exclusively in counties Cork and Kerry is worth noting in that connexion. It is inevitable that a rare name like Graddy should be swallowed by the well known Grady and this has been recorded as occurring more than once in the Listowel area. Draddy has also been used as a synonym of Drudy (Ó Draoda), a north Connacht surname.

DRAKE   The ancestor of the Drakes of Stokestown, Co. Wexford, came to Ireland as a Cromwellian official. Drakes, however, were in Dublin in the thirteenth century and the Drakes of Drakerath were one of the leading families in Co. Meath from 1386. The name actually occurs in that county as early as 1311. Drakerath is near Kells. There is a Drakestown in Co. Meath in the barony of Morgallion, also named from the Drake family – in this case a parish as well as a townland. Another Drakestown, yet again the home of Drake family in mediaeval times, is in Co. Louth (bar. Ardee). Their prominence up to the time they lost their estates under the Cromwellian régime is indicated by the frequency with which their name occurs in all kinds of records relating to Leinster (and to a small extend also to Co. Cork): there are for example 65 references to Drak and Drake in the Patent Rolls from 1318, when the first in that source occurs, down to 1509. A very remarkable man of the Drakerath family was Peter Drake (1671-1755). His Memoirs published in 1755 (and recently re-issued under the title of Amiable Renegade) vividly describes his adventurous life as a soldier in Ireland and in the service of France. At the present time the name is found in Dublin and Belfast and in small numbers in counties Meath and Cork.

(O) DREA DREW (O) DROUGHT   It is quite possible that some Drews are of Gaelic-Irish origin since there was a minor Thomond sept of Ó Druadh or Ó Drae which survives (in Co. Kerry) as Drea. Even in the Thomond country, however, Drew is usually of English stock: the descendants of Capt. Drew, who settled in Co. Waterford in 1598, were living in the present century at Drewscourt, Co. Limerick, and a will of 1781 locates them at Drewslodge in that county. The family of Drewsboro (at Tuamgraney, Co. Clare) are said to be of similar origin, but it is worth noting that O'Dree appears in a Fiant of 1601 relating to that area.

Drought, though some early and even modern forms of the name may give rise to confusion with Drew, is quite distinct. In Co. Westmeath, for example, Drew and Drough are recorded as synonyms. The latter appears in the Fiants as O' Droughie as well as O'Drought and belonged primarily to Offaly and Westmeath – Ó Drochtaigh in Irish, a minor Gaelic sept of which little is known. Woulfe considers that the Droughts of this region were immigrants from England of Frankish origin and Father Hogan, editor of The Description of Ireland in 1598 remarks that the Droughts of Offaly and Carlow "seem to have been in Ireland since the thirteenth century." I think these authorities were confusing Drought with Drew. The Annals relate that David Drew (Triu in the Gaelic original) was killed in action in Co. Sligo in 1249, being one of Bermingham's advance guard in his campaign against the O'Connors of Connacht. Druy appears in the Ormond Deeds in 1244 and Dru in 1302. Hugh Dru and Thomas Dru were convicted of cattle stealing in Westmeath and Kildare in 1295-7. The Annals record Drews among the "Galls" fighting in Connacht in 1249 and 1307. Another origin for Drought is suggested by O'Hart, viz. Drouet, a Huguenot name. This may possibly be an authentic alternative but I have met no corroborative evidence of it. Mr. Edward Keane states that a family of Droett (later spelt Drought) came to Ireland from the Netherlands in the thirteenth century. I think, however, that there is little doubt but that the Droughts of Leinster are of the sept of Ó Drochtaigh.

Another somewhat similar surname in Irish is Ó Droichid. This rare name was found at Kenry, Co. Limerick, in 1587. It was then anglicized as O'Drehitt, but has since become Bridgeman by semi-translation (droichead means a bridge). There were families of Bridgeman in Co. Clare in my youth who came from England to Clare early in the seventeenth century.

Dublin-born John Drew (1825-1862) was a leading actor in America, as was his son John Drew (1853-1927), while his daughter Louisa, herself a noted actress, was the mother of John, Lionel and Ethel Barrymore, all famous on the American stage and screen. Of the Co. Limerick family, though living in Belfast and Dublin, were Rev. Dr. Thomas Drew, (1800-1870) the Orange leader, and his son, Sir Thomas Drew (1838-1910), the noted architect. Bibl.

(O) DRENNAN SKEHAN THORNTON, Torrens The number of synonyms of Thornton revealed by the birth registrations recorded at the beginning of the present century is remarkable. Apart from occasional instances of Tarrant (Tarrant in Co. Cork and Torrens in Antrim and Derry are normally anglicized forms of the Gaelic Ó Toráin), Thorn, Torrens etc., being so used, Drennan, Dreinan, Drinane, Drinan and also Meenagh and Meenaghan were interchangeable with Thornton in counties Galway and Mayo, where at the present time Thornton is fairly numerous and Drennan etc., are not. These are translations or pseudo-translations. Drennan is Ó Draighneáin in Irish (draighneán means a blackthorn); Meenagh and Meenaghan are Muimhneach and Ó Muineacháin, neither of which have any connexion with the word muineach (thorny). In the same way the word sceach (a briar – sceach geal is white-thorn) is the cause of making the Monaghan - Louth name Mac Sceacháin into Thornton as well as the normal MacSkeaghan, Skehan etc. Incidentally it may be observed that the Tipperary surname Skehan (Ó Sceacháin in Irish) does not appear to have been similarly translated.

It is usually accepted that the sept of O'Drennan belonged to the Síol Anmchadha group, located in the barony of Longford, Co. Galway, where it now survives as Thornton. At the end of the eighteenth century Drynan was still fairly widely used both in Galway and Mayo. The name has very early associations with Co. Westmeath: the Four Masters record the death of Gillachiarain Ó Draighnen at Fore in 1163 and from various sources we learn that families of O'Drennan were living in other Leinster counties, particularly Kilkenny, and also in Co. Tipperary. There are two Ballydrinans in the latter county and a Dreynanstown in Co. Kildare. The United Irishman Dr. William Drennan (1754-1820), the poet, who was the first to call Ireland "the Emerald Isle," was the son of a Belfast dissenting minister. His two sons John and William were also poets.

Matthew Thornton (1714-1803), who was a signatory of the American Declaration of Independence, was also from the north of Ireland and a medical doctor before he became a judge. Another of the name worth mentioning was Robert Thornton, who established the Dublin News-Letter in 1685. At that time there were a number of prominent citizens of Dublin called Thornton, who were mostly of English origin, for it must not be forgotten that Thornton is a common English name and many of our numerous Thorntons outside Connacht are no doubt Anglo-Irish. George Thornton, the Provost Marshal of Munster in 1598, was an Elizabethan undertaker in Co. Limerick and we find Thorntons among the Cromwellian soldiers.

Sir Robert Richard Torrens (1814-1884) was the originator in South Australia in 1857 of a simplified land title registration known as the Torrens System, subsequently adopted by many other countries. He was born in Co. Cork. The River Torrens in South Australia is named after his father, Colonel Robert Torrens. Map

(O) DROHAN   This is Ó Druacháin in Irish: though

never prominent it has always been well known in and near Co. Waterford. The "census" of 1659 records it as a principal Irish name in the baronies of Upperthird and Galtire in that county; similarly Griffith's Valuation tells us that there were 67 householders of the name there in 1850 and 12 in Co. Wexford a few years later; and the latest available birth registration statistics corroborate this distribution, as also do the current voters' lists. We find it in Co. Wexford in 1565 when Maurice O'Droughane, husbandman, of Ballincolane, obtained a "pardon"; and Daniel Drohan (generally known at the time as James Walsh) was vicar-apostolic of Ferns from 1588 to 1624. Dame Elizabeth Druhan, a native of Lady's Island, Co. Wexford, succeeded as Lady Abbess of Ypres, Kylemore, Co Mayo, in 1940.

DRUM   The family of Ó Droma (anglice Drum) were erenaghs of Kinawley, a parish which lies on both sides of the Cavan-Fermanagh boundary. This is the homeland of the sept: O'Drum appears as a principal Irish name in south Fermanagh in the "census" of 1659 being also called Mac-Dromma in the area around Enniskillen; the eighteenth century penal law records include several Fermanagh and Cavan priests of the name; and modern birth registrations indicate that it is still fairly numerous in the same part of the country. There it has sometimes been changed to Drummond. This equation is found as early as 1663 in the Derry Hearth Money Rolls where O'Drummond is the form used; while in those of Armagh and Fermanagh we find it as O'Drum and O'Drome, and in one case in Co. Fermanagh as MacDruma.

The Drummys of Co. Cork are probably of similar origin: some early references to the name relate to Munstermen. Possibly Gregory Drome, a minor Co. Cork official in 1299, may not have been a Gael, but Solamh Ó Droma, chief compiler of The Book of Ballymote, was of Corca Laoidhe. There are other examples of the name O Droma or Drummy in Munster in the sixteenth and early seventeenth century.   Map.

DRUMGOOLE   This is also spelt Dromgoole and formerly Drumgold and other variants. It is one of the small class of Irish toponymics, in this case taking the name of a place called Dromgabhail, and the surname so formed gave rise to the place-name Dromgoolestown, near Ardee in Co. Louth. That is the county with which families of the name have been chiefly identified. The original Dromgabhail was probably in Co. Louth. We find Robert de Drumgol going pledge for another man in a Co. Louth law case in 1299 and Robert de Dromgol coroner for the same county in 1311-13. From that on Louth records, such as the Hearth Money Rolls and the Dowdall Deeds, have many references to the name. It was to be found in adjacent counties also: for example of the four Drumgooles who were outlawed for their adhesion to the Jacobite cause in 1690 one was of Porterstown, Co. Meath, and two were of Newry.

Several of the name are worthy of individual mention, notably Dr. Edward Dromgould (c. 1635-c. 1695) who was vicar-apostolic of Armagh and close friend of St

Oliver Plunkett; Col. John Dromgoole (1720-1781) Paris-born writer of note, the son of a Louth man; and Dr. Thomas Dromgoole (c. 1750-1826), Dublin physician and a leading supporter of Daniel O'Connell.

(O) DUCEY, Dufficey   Ó Dubhghusa, anglicized Ducey, Ducy, Ducie and Doocey, though nowhere very numerous, is found mainly in Munster, particularly in Counties Tipperary and Waterford. It occurs eleven times in the index to the only record now extant of the Hearth Money Rolls for Co. Tipperary viz Thomas Laffan's edition, the unreliability of which is exemplified by the fact that eight of these eleven references are in the text not to Ducey or any variant thereof but to Duby, Duhy, etc. We have not the Hearth Money Rolls for Waterford, but in Griffith's Valuation (c. 1855) for that county there are 21 householders called Doocey. These names occur very rarely in other Irish records, though Ducie does appear occasionally in Great Britain. The form Doocey has been occasionally reported as in use as a synonym of Duffy in the Milford district of Co. Donegal, I presume that the Co. Roscommon name Dufficey is also a form of Ó Dubhghusa.

(O) DUFFIN   DUFF   There are early references to Ó Duibhin (bishop of Kildare 1148), O'Duffyne (Cork, 1311), O'Doghwyn (Co. Waterford, 1573) and O'Duffyn (Co. Cork, 1601) but from the middle of the seventeenth century the name Duffin, by that time already beginning to be deprived of its O, became closely associated with the Oriel country and the adjacent parts of Ulster. In the 1659 "census" it appears as a principal Irish surname in Co. Louth; in 1664 it was in the Co. Monaghan and Co. Armagh Hearth Money Rolls; and in the same decade it occurs also in those of Antrim and Tyrone; in 1689 we find it at Carlingford. By the end of the eighteenth century the location had moved more definitely to Antrim, particularly the Ballymena area. There have also been a number of Duffin families in Co. Wexford and Co. Waterford, deriving no doubt from the early Munstermen of the name referred to above; some of these, however, lost their identity by adopting Duff as a synonym, and that seems also to have happened to some extent in the case of the northern Duffins.

Duff, as an epithetic surname from dubh (black) has no distinct location. As the almost extinct O'Duff it is cognate with Devoy (see Irish Families, p. 89). As MacDuff it is Scottish

(O) DUIGENAN, Deignan, Dignam   There are several anglicized forms of the Irish surname Ó Duibhgeannáin (the root word of which, no doubt, is dubh, black): none of these retains the prefix O in modern times. It is that of one of the more important literary families of Ireland, who were bards and ollavs to the leading septs of the country now comprised in Counties Leitrim, Roscommon and Longford – the MacDermots, the MacRannells and the O'Farrells. Their principal residence was at Kilronan, Co. Roscommon, of which parish they were erenaghs. They had a bardic school at Castle Fore, Co. Leitrim. The best known in this category was Peregrine O'Duigenan (d. 1664), one of the Four Masters. Magnus O'Duigenan was the chief compiler of the Book of Ballymote (c. 1415); Dubhthas óg Ó Duibhgeannáin annotated the original Book of O'Hara, which was compiled in 1597; and they produced a similar work of their own – the Book of the O'Duigenans. The O'Duigenan family is recorded as resident at Castle Fore in 1636. The literary tradition may be said to have been carried on by Patrick Duigenan (1735-1816) a notable polemical writer in his day. One of the most remarkable of the eighteenth century harpers was Jerome Duigenan (b. Co. Leitrim 1710). They produced distinguished churchmen too: in the Book of Magauran one of these, Maelpeadar O'Duigenan (d. 1290) is described as "that holy man, peer of saints, who surpassed even Paul". In the military sphere we find the names O'Duigenan, Duigenan, Duigenane and Deignan among the officers of James II's Irish army.

Throughout the centuries up to the present time the name O'Duigenan has been intimately associated with Connacht and particularly Counties Leitrim and Roscommon.

(O) DUNLEA, Dullea   Woulfe equates Dunlea with Dunleavy. MacDuinnsléibhe, as the Gaelic form of Dunlea, must, however, be accepted with reserve as there is no record of that sept migrating from one end of the country to the other. All the numerous references to Dunlea and its synonyms I have met from 1583 up to quite modern times relate not to Ulster or north Connacht but to the south western counties of Munster. As far back as the sixteenth century in the Fiants we find variants which elide the N and correspond to the modern Co. Cork synonym Dullea (sometimes written Delea): O'Dullea (Corkbeg) occurs in those Fiants, as do Donlea and O'Donlegh: the former in the persons of Donell and Owen MacDermodie O'Donlegh, who were among a number of Cork men "pardoned" in 1586; the latter of Cloyne, Co. Cork. There it may lead to confusion, for in the very part of the country in which those names are indigenous we meet in Cork, Cloyne and Limerick wills of the seventeenth and eighteenth centuries Douly and Dully, and these at first sight suggest the Offaly name Dooly rather than Dullea. Having regard, however, to the consistency with which they appear in Munster, it would seem more likely that they originate in the Ó Dubhalla sept of Muskerry, Co. Cork. Possibly O'Doly, which appears in a Justiciary Roll of 1307 for Co. Cork is a very early anglicized form of Ó Dubhalla. Here are a few instances of a later date than the Co. Cork Fiants mentioned above: O'Dule is recorded in the "census" of 1659 as a principal Irish name in Limerick city; in 1664-66 Dunlea and Dynlea are frequent in the Tipperary Hearth Money Rolls; in 1704 Father Owen Dunlea was parish priest of Kilcomin, Co. Kerry (the same I presume as Father Eugene Dunlea, parish priest of Killarney in 1725). The place called Dunlea's Hill, near Glenstal, Co. Limerick, marks the home of one branch of the family:

to this belongs Father Thomas Vincent Dunlea, P.P., the founder of Boystown, New South Wales.

DUNSEATH   Variant forms of this name are Dunsheath, Dunshea, Dunshee and Dunseith. Older forms, as found for example in the Tyrone and Antrim Hearth Money Rolls (1664 and 1669) were Dunsith and Dunsheesthe. Since it first appears in our records in the seventeenth century it has been found principally in Ulster, particularly in the Ballymena area, though a few appear in the eighteenth century Cork marriage licence bonds. One James Dunsayer acquired property at Mount Stewart, Co. Tyrone, under the Plantation of Ulster, but as he appears also in the Ulster Inquisitions with the name so spelt, Dunsayer is probably not synonymous with Dunsay.

DURACK   This is Ó Dubhraic in Irish. Woulfe's derivation from rath, prosperity, is improbable. The Duracks who are of east Clare were perhaps the greatest of the pioneer pastoral families of Australia. The story of their two and a half year trek across the continent (1883-1885) makes enthralling reading. Two members of this family have distinguished themselves in modern Australian literature; and Fanny Durack (1891-1955), Olympic Games swimmer, was the holder of eleven world records.   Bibl., Map

(Mac) DURKAN   The only Gaelic-Irish surname to have an anglicized form beginning with the letter Z is Mac Dhuarcáin, normally Durkan or Durkin, but also sometimes spelt Zorkin and Gurkin. Zorkin I may add is recorded by Matheson as having been used also as a synonym of Bodkin. The word duarcán, from which Durkan is presumably derived, means a pessimist. Durkan is a very numerous name in Mayo and Sligo: it is estimated that there are well over 2,000 persons so called in north Connacht and very few elsewhere. It originated in Co. Sligo and is said to have been adopted by a branch of the O'Haras: a Duarcán who died in 1225 does appear in the O'Hara pedigree. In an Inquisition made in the reign of James I the name appears as MacDurcan, several so called being landholders in the barony of Gallen. In the Strafford Inquisition of Co. Mayo (1635) there is one MacDurkain, while MacCurkan is of frequent occurrence in the barony of Gallen and it is unquestionably the same name. A modern representative of these was Most Rev. Patrick Durcan, Bishop of Achonry from 1852 to 1875.   Map

(O) DURNIN   (O) DORNAN   It is mentioned in More Irish Families p. 251 that Ó Duirnín, normally anglicized Durnin, had become Cuffe in some places (a far-fetched "translation", dorn meaning a fist). The fact that Dornan as well as Durnian and Durnan, are also recorded as synonymous with Durnin in Louth and east Ulster makes differentiation between Ó Duirnín and the cognate Ó Dornáin difficult. As Durnian it is perpetuated in the place-name Ballydurnian, Co. Antrim. Durnion is the more usual form in Tyrone, Fermanagh and Donegal. In the latter Durning is also found, no doubt in that case also a variant of Durnin; but Durning occurs in sixteenth and seventeenth century records as Exchequer officials, army officers etc., presumably of English origin. There is at least one seventeenth century record of the native Irish family being found outside Louth and Ulster for Farrell and Ennis O'Durnyne were landowners in the barony of Tirawley, Co. Mayo, when Strafford's inquisition was taken in 1635, but nevertheless Ulster was their homeland and we must usually consult such records as the Hearth Money Rolls for the northern counties to find them. Dornan is the usual form in Down and Antrim today, and we meet O'Dornans with the O'Neills in Co. Antrim in the sixteenth century Fiants.

(O) DURR, Durey DORE   Durr must be distinguished from Dore alias Dower (Ó Doghair), which is a name belonging to counties Kerry, Limerick and South Tipperary and was sometimes written O'Dure in mediaeval times (though this may be a foreign clerk's attempt to write O'Dwyer); and we even find it taking the form O'Durey in Co. Limerick as late as 1679. About that time in the form of Dowyer or O Dower it was listed in Petty's "census" as a principal Irish name in the barony of Decies (Co. Waterford) and in the Co. Tipperary Hearth Money Rolls we find nine families called Dower. One O'Dower appears among the 1641 outlaws: he was of Co. Wicklow. Without the prefix O, Dore and Dorey are still more difficult to identify in the absence of a family pedigree or tradition, for Dorey is an English toponymic and Dore may be an anglicized form of the French Doré. As long as these names are found in Munster we can be fairly confident of their Irish origin; but elsewhere these various forms have appeared in many widely separated places. In the seventeenth century Hearth Money Rolls Dury and Dorre are in Co. Derry, and Dury in Antrim; and in the Fiants we meet Dorre in Co. Carlow. Durr and Dury (gaelice Ó Doraidh) belong by origin to counties Leitrim and Roscommon where, however, these have sometimes been registered as Dorr and even occasionally Dore. The Patent Rolls of 1373, in a list of leading septs of Thomond and Tipperary, includes the O'Dures. This may be taken as O'Dwyer.

DWANE, Devane, Duane, Downes   All these surnames, the first three of which are also found without the final E., are anglicized forms of the Irish Ó Dubháin and taken together represent a not inconsiderable section of the population. Downes is the most numerous form and this is found chiefly in Clare and Limerick; next comes Duane, mainly in Connacht; Dwane (or Dwan), of west Munster, and Devane, which occurs both in Kerry and Connacht, are comparatively rare. In the 1659 "census" O'Devane is recorded as a principal name in Co. Clare and Devane in Co. Tipperary. Several Gaelic septs were called Ó Dubháin. That of Knowth (Meath) mentioned in O'Dugan's Topographical Poem was dispersed soon after the Anglo-Norman invasion; that of Corca Laoidhe gives us the families of counties Cork and Kerry today; that of Connemara the families of Duane now found in Connacht and possibly some of the Downeses of Co. Clare, who however are more often descendants of a Co. Cork sept of the name. The use of these variants in different counties must not, however, be regarded as constant and invariable, particularly in the pre-registration period. In Kerry, for example, David Duane was prominent in the management of the extensive Kenmare estates in the early eighteenth century. In a Fiant of 1585 O'Dwane is the spelling in Co. Galway and a little later O'Duan is used in Munster.

According to Ms. T.C.D. H. 2. 17, quoted by Hardiman in his edition of O'Flaherty's book Iar-Connacht, the Connacht family of Duane (Ó Dubháin) were erenaghs of Killursa, which is in the barony of Clare, Co. Galway: the MS. adds "agus do aiscin Fursa i Dubain," which Hardiman quaintly translates "and St. Fursa cursed O'Dubháin," whereas this sentence actually conveys the idea that the saint loved the erenaghs of this particular church. The Dwanes of Munster are primarily a sept of Corca Laoidhe, as shown in the sept map (written O'Duane there). Dwan, however, was one of the more numerous names in Co. Tipperary in the seventeenth century. It occurs 19 times in the Hearth Money Rolls for that county, and O'Devane, a synonym of it there, occurs 8 times. Dwaine, Dwayne, and O'Dwayne are among the principal names in Co. Tipperary in the 1659 "census" Though thus written by an English clerk, Dwane is never so sounded, being always pronounced Dwaan. Woulfe considers that the Dwanes of Co. Limerick are of different stock. There are townlands called Ballyduane in Co. Limerick and Co. Cork.

A secondary meaning of dubhan is kidney, so by "translation", Kidney has been used as a surname synonymous with Dwane. James Duane, son of Anthony Duane of Cong, Co. Mayo, was the first mayor of New York after the Revolution. William Duane, of Philadelphia, a pioneer newspaper man in America, was born in Clonmel.

MacDYER, MacDwyer   MacDyer is the more usual spelling, MacDyre being another variant. It is now mainly associated with Glenties in Co. Donegal though it is found also in the northern parts of Connacht. The first reference to the name I have met is to three MacDyers who obtained "pardons" in Co. Sligo in 1593. I think it is cognate with the well known Donegal name Devir, which, it is true, usually occurs as an O name, but not always: witness, for example, in an inquisition of 1632, a Co. Donegal landowner called Phelim MacDavir a "meere" or native Irishman who, it may be of interest to note, had tenants. MacDuibhir, the Gaelic-Irish form given by Woulfe (who offers no further information on the name), may be accepted as correct. MacDwyer, it would be added, has no connexion with O'Dwyer and it is quite distinct from it.

The English occupative surname Dyer appears frequently in mediaeval Irish records as le Deyer etc., but it has no connexion, of course, with the name now under consideration.

EAGER Eager and Egar are the spellings usual in Kerry, Eager in Co. Down and north Louth: these are the two areas in which these names are mainly found. In the latter Agar has been recorded as a synonym, but for the most part this is a surname of different origin: according to Reaney it is an abbreviated form of Elgar, whereas Eagar is a form of Edgar. A family of Agar was very prominent in Co. Kilkenny in the eighteenth century having come from Yorkshire to Gowran following an earlier matrimonial alliance with the Blanchfields: two of this family, both sons of Henry Agar M.P. were created peers, Charles, Earl of Normanton, also becoming Archbishop of Dublin in 1801. These people, however, had no connexion with the Eagars now under consideration.

The Eagars of Co. Kerry have been prominent among the gentry of that county since 1660 when Alexander Eagar left Queen's County, where his father (Major Robert Eagar an officer in Charles I's army) had acquired an estate. Two centuries later they are listed among the extensive landowners of Co. Kerry, by which time they had intermarried with many of the principal families of that county. In the 1660's, however, the name was by no means confined to Munster: we find it for example among the householders in Co. Armagh at that time. Nor indeed was it, or is it, confined to the Protestant "ascendancy" in Kerry for it is quite numerous among the Catholic population there.

Though unconnected with the families referred to above it is of interest to note that as early as 1356 the name occurs in the Ormond Deeds as that of an attorney at Ardmayle. In the Elizabethan Fiants we find an O'Eger in Leix. This is perhaps a form of the name which appears about the same time (1589) in the Ormond Deeds for Co. Kilkenny in the person of Anstace ny Egher, but this cannot be equated with Eager: I take it to be O'Hegher, an early anglicized form of Ó h-h-Aichir (mod. O'Hehir). Bibl.

EARLS EARLE Mr. P. J. Kennedy, whose mother was an Earls, says that their tradition is that the name is of Bristol origin. "The Earls family", he states, "was one of the earliest settlers in Athenry and the name occurs there in the thirteenth century (see Blake Family Records, Vol. I). The name is still quite common in the mid-Galway parishes of Grange and Killimordaly and the only other places in which it occurs in the Republic are in Limerick (an undertaker), one family in Sixmilebridge, Co. Clare, one in Clones and one in Arklow. It is entirely distinct from Earle and Errol." This is borne out by birth registrations: those I have checked show that Earl and Earle are found mainly in Ulster, Earls and Earles in Co. Galway. I noticed an Earls in the patent rolls at Lucan dated 1416. The Fiants have a Mac Inierligh in the Ormond country, which may have been anglicized Earl.

EARLY, O'Mulmohery The form O'Mulmohery, given above, is I think almost obsolete now: the Irish surname Ó Maolmocheirghe was phonetically so anglicized at first, then abbreviated to Mulmoher. There is not one entry in the birth indices for the three years 1864 to 1866 for O'Mulmohery or Mulmoher. The substitution of Early and Earley for these by a kind of translation — moch means early and éirghe rising — took place during the period of Gaelic submergence in the seventeenth and eighteenth centuries.

The family is notable as an ecclesiastical one: they were coarbs of Drumlane, Co. Cavan, and of Drumreilly, Co. Leitrim. As well as these coarbs, the Four Masters mention a bishop of Breffny (Kilmore) and an abbot of Kells (Co. Meath) in the twelfth and thirteenth centuries whose name in O'Donovan's translation is given as O'Mulmoghery. In the Composition Book of Connacht (1585) it is O'Mulmoher: the important family so called was seated in Co. Leitrim, which modern statistics show to be the chief homeland of the Earlys today. In the Jacobite attainders of Co. Leitrim the name is spelt Mulvogherry. A branch of the sept was also established in Co. Donegal: in 1659 there were several families of O'Mulmoghery in the baronies of Banagh and Boylagh (west Donegal) and there are priests of the name, in one form or another, in the records of the diocese of Raphoe. The Prior of Kells (Co. Kilkenny) in 1361 was Robert Erley and as early as 1305 the place-name Erleystown in Co. Tipperary is on record. At that time the use of Early as an anglicized form of a Gaelic surname was unknown and the Erleys of Kilkenny and Tipperary were of Norman origin, as is evident from the fact that they were often called d'Erley.

Dr. John Early S.J. (1814-1874) founder of St. Ignatius College, Worcester, Mass., was of the O'Mulmohery sept. General Early of the Confederate army in the American Civil War, who, after several successful engagements was eventually defeated by an Irishman, General Sheridan, at Winchester and Hatchers River, was not of an Irish family.

It appears that O'Mulmoghery was first abbreviated to O'Mohery in Co. Armagh and subsequently "translated" as Fields, from the mistaken belief that Moghery represented the Irish word machaire, a plain or extensive field. For a curious use of Early as a synonym of Loughran, q.v. Map

EBRILL   This is a rare name now associated with Co. Limerick. As Abrill it occurs in the Co. Tipperary Hearth Money Rolls of 1666 and in 1755 the will of John Ebrell of Darlinghill in the same county was proved. John Averill, possibly another form of the same name, was bishop of Limerick in 1771 and dean of Limerick prior to that, but he was born in Co. Antrim. Averell is among the names introduced by the Plantation of Ulster.

Abril is a French surname cogante with Latin aprilis and is probably the origin of our Ebrill.

MacELDERRY   This name, now numerous in Antrim, belongs to the area around Magherafelt and the western shore of Lough Neagh. Woulfe suggests that it is the modern form of Mac Giolla Dorcha, an early anglicized form of which was Macgilledoroughe: this occurs as the name of a tenant of lands at Grangeclare, Co. Kildare, in 1592 which is a long way from Co. Derry. Edmund Mac-Elderry was an officer in James II's Irish army at the time of the siege of Derry (1689).

MacELHERON   Woulfe is right in giving the Gaelic-Irish form of this name as Mac Giolla Chiaráin (son of the devotee of St. Ciaran), but the only other information he offers, viz. that it belongs to the midlands, cannot be accepted as correct. All the sources to be consulted in this connexion leave no doubt but that this small sept is one of east Ulster, e.g. Elizabethan Fiants (Co. Armagh), wills of succeeding centuries and modern birth registrations. In the latter (all in Antrim and Down) the forms MacIlheron and MacLeheron occur as often as Mac-Elheron; and MacKlern has also been registered as a synonym of it: these forms draw attention to the current pronunciation of the name in Dublin where the emphasis is on the El, instead of on the her, an unfortunate departure from the original Gaelic.

Gillacam Macgillachiarain, "distinguished professor of poetry and literature", whose death occurred in 1259, was considered of sufficient importance to be mentioned both in the Annals of Loch Cé and the Four Masters.

It may be added that MacElheran is recorded also as a branch of the Scottish clan MacDonald.

MacELLIGOTT   The origin of this name is controversial but the fact that it is borne by a family long established in Co. Kerry and not found indigenous elsewhere is not in dispute. Dr. John O'Brien, writing in 1768, asserted that they were of the same stock as the MacCarthys. Mrs Hickson, who did much valuable research in records relating to Kerry (though not always sound in her conclusions) states that they descend from a Scotsman called MacLeod who about the year 1295 acquired lands in Co. Kerry by his marriage to the heiress of Maurice, second Lord of Kerry, and that the name MacLeod passing through various stages such as MacAlliod and MacElgott eventually became MacElligott. In this connexion a fact not referred to by her may be mentioned viz. the name of the seneschal of Connacht killed in 1247 was MacElget. O'Donovan states that he was the progenitor of the Kerry family. Woulfe, again, giving Mac Uileogóid as the Gaelic form, derives it from Wilecot (i.e. little Ulick, a double diminutive of William) and ascribes to it an Anglo-Norman origin. Ballymacelligot, near Tralee, is named from them and they have, since the sixteenth century at least, been prominent residents of north Kerry. Though not recorded in Matheson's synonyms I have personally met cases of MacElligott and Cliggot being used interchangeably by the same family. Perhaps the most probable, is that of the late Prof. E. Curtis for which Mr. K.W. Nicholls has recently found further evidence. It is that they were a Cambro-Norman family first called FitzElias. As such they were in Kerry from the middle of the thirteenth century. There are a number of indications suggesting this identification. The surname FitzElyoth, which appears in Kerry in 1455, would represent a transitional form and, of course, the tendency was for Fitz to be changed to Mac. The Fitz-Elias family was associated with the same area as were the MacElligotts at a later date. There were 103 families called MacElligott in Kerry in 1901 and very few elsewhere.

Probably the most distinguished bearer of the name was Col. Roger MacElligott (c. 1650-1701) – spelt Mac-Ellicott in King James's army list. In the subsequent attainders we find the barbarous alias MacCullcoate recorded. There were five other MacElligotts in his regiment. He and his sons served with distinction on the Continent after 1691, one being killed at Fontenoy and others rising to high rank in Austria and Spain. Rev. James Elligott, procurator of Cloyne, was a member of the Provincial Synod of Cashel in 1685. A generation earlier (1657) the MacElligotts are mentioned in a state paper as one of the Munster families "plotting for trouble"; and in the previous century they are a recognized Irish sept, for Thomas MacKelgot or MacKelgot (so spelt in the Elizabethan Fiants) "slain in rebellion" is called "chief of his nation."   Map

ELLISON   Woulfe gives Ó hEilgheasáin as the Irish form of Ellison with no further information. He does not mention that Ellison is a well-known English name. All the Ellison families of whom I have any knowledge came to Ireland from the north of England, the earliest settling in Mayo about 1620 and others comparatively recently. The name Ó hEilgheasáin appears in the Annals of Loch Cé under date 1230 when the death of a canon and anchorite called Gilchrist O hEilghisan is recorded, without however any mention of his abode or background. This isolated reference hardly justifies the bald statement that our Ellisons are of that descent, especially with no mention of an alternative English origin. They are now numerous in and around Belfast. Two of the name were prominent Church of Ireland clergymen in the eighteenth century, one at Castlebar, the other at Kilkenny.

MacELMEEL   MacILMOYLE   Though Woulfe treats

them as synonyms MacElmeel and MacElmoyle are in fact distinct names. The latter, modern variants of which are MacIlmoyle, MacIlmoil and Macklemoyle, is from the Irish Mac Giolla Mhaoil (maol, bald); it is fairly numerous in counties Antrim and Derry. MacElmeel, on the other hand, is confined to Co. Monaghan and the adjoining part of Co. Tyrone. Outside that area the variants MacMeel and MacMeal are occasionally found.

As far back as records are available, MacElmeel has always been an Oriel name and its identity with Mac Giolla Mhichil is confirmed by the fact that in the Co. Monaghan Hearth Money Rolls we find the man returned as Phelim MacIlmeel in 1663 called Phelim MacIlmichele two years later. This name means son of the devotee of St. Michael; it has also been anglicized as MacMichael. In that form it is found in the more northerly parts of Ulster.

ELVERY   Reaney states that Elvery, with its synonyms Alfrey, Affray etc., is derived from one of the old English christian names beginning with AE, e.g. Aelfreth or Aelfrith, which can be accepted where the surname is English. I have not found any early Irish reference to the name Elvery unless Albrey is a mediaeval form of it – the Justiciary Rolls for 1307 mention a Robert Albrey, of Kells, Co. Kilkenny and in 1311 a Thomas Albrey, a Co. Carlow juror, but there is on record the will of Beatrix Alfrey of Dublin, 1649, which at once recalls Beatrice Elvery (Lady Glenavy), the well-known artist of our own time.

In the days when origins were often assigned to suit the taste of the enquirer the Spanish Alvarez and the Irish MacAlivery might both have been suggested, but I fear we cannot accept either of these without definite evidence. Elverstown in Co. Kildare has no connexion with Elvery: it is an obsolete form of Aylwardstown.

MacENEANY   A study of this name which appeared in the Clogher Record in 1960 (see Bibliography) presents evidence, which I have verified, to prove that its Irish form is not the generally accepted Mac Conaonaigh but Mac an Dhéaghanaigh, earlier Mac an Déaganaigh (déagnach, dean).

MacAneany, also written MacEneany and sometimes MacNeany, was changed to Bird by some families in counties Monaghan, Louth and Meath. The Irish form of this is Mac Con Aonaigh, derived from con, genitive of cu, a hound, and aonach, a fair, was accepted up to quite recent times but it has now been verified that it is Mac an Dhéaghanagh, earlier Mac an Déagaraigh (déaganach, dean). There were two distinct septs so called: that of Oriel, originally of the Clones area, and another of Co. Roscommon where the place-name Kilmacananneny may indicate their homeland. Representatives of both these appear in the Elizabethan Fiants. In 1365 John MacAneany, canon of Clogher, was appointed coarb of St. Tighearnach of Clones and in 1393 another Clogher priest of the name was appointed coarb but was displaced in 1398. In the next century the MacAneanys surrender-

ed this office to the MacMahons, who in turn gave way to the MacGuires. Dr. John Barry, of the Genealogical Office, who supplied me with notes on the coarbship of Clones, considers that after the above-mentioned reverse the MacAneanys ceased to be an ecclesiastical family; but, as we know from the 1659 "census", the Hearth Money Rolls, Griffith's Valuation and modern statistical records, they clung tenaciously to what they had left and are now to be found in considerable numbers in counties Monaghan, Lough, Armagh and Tyrone.

Possibly no Irish surname has been spelt in so many different ways as this. These are notable enough in Ireland; in America their number is quite remarkable. Mr V. X. McEnaney of Toronto has sent me a list of no less than 38 variants which appear in official telephone and other directories, all but four of which are American or Canadian. Still more remarkable is the fact that the tombstones of six members of one family all record the name in a different form. Four were buried in the cemetery at Caledon, Ontario, viz. Peter MacEneaney, the father, Mary McAneaney, the mother, Francis McAneney and Patrick McEnaney, sons; the other two children went to New York, where they were buried at St. Mary's monastery, Dunkirk) under the names of John Bird and Catherine McEneany. Peter and his wife Mary were both born in Co. Monaghan in 1792. Five of their six children were also born there, before they emigrated about the year 1829. See also Heany.   Map

The recorded variations of this name are McAnaney McAnany   McAnanny   McAneaney   McAneany McAneeney McAneeny McAneney McAneny McAniney McAnneeney   McAnnenny   McAnneny   McAnney McEaneney McEnaney McEnanie McEnany McEneaney McEneany McNeaney McNeany McNeeney McNeney McNenney McNennie McNenny.

The list included also some cases where the prefix Mac not Mc is used, but these cannot of course be regarded as variant spellings.

ENGLISH, England   (Mac) GALLOGLY, Inglis, English There are a considerable number of families called English belonging both to Munster and Ulster. The former, located for the most part in counties Tipperary and Limerick, are, as the name implies, of English extraction if we go back to the twelfth century, but they are of course as completely hibernicized as their Norman comrades of the invasion – and indeed may well have been themselves of Norman origin. In the thirteenth and fourteenth centuries we find the name as L'Englys, L'Angleys, Lenglais etc., already well established: there were landowners so called in counties Dublin and Louth and also in several counties of Munster. References to the name in Leinster continue to be fairly frequent up to the middle of the seventeenth century: chiefly scanty information such as the plundering in 1428 of the convent of Fore, of which William Englonde was prior; the outlawry of James English, Co. Wicklow, 1450; Elizabethan pardons; or the appointment of John Englishe alias Ynglysshe as Abbot of Bective at the date of the suppression of the monastery in 1536. By that time, however, they were much more closely identified with Munster, as indeed they are now. There was already an Englishtown in Co. Limerick, also called Ballyengland, showing that it was formed from the surname, England being a rare synonym of English. The majority of the many references to the name in the sixteenth century Fiants are to people living in Munster. The Carew calendar names English of Cloghemenecode and English of Rahine among the principal gentlemen of Co. Tipperary in 1600.

In mediaeval times the name appears less frequently in Ulster, at any rate as English. There, however, English is a mistranslation of the Irish surname Mac an Gallóglaigh (son of the galloglass) which, as well as English and Inglis, is also properly anglicized as MacGallogly or Gallogly and ridiculously as Ingoldsby and Golightly. This is a sept of Co. Donegal origin, the modern representatives of which are more numerous in the adjacent county of Tyrone; the three forms English, Ingoldsby and Gallogly are all to be found today in Co. Monaghan. In 1458 a MacGillogly appears as one of the older residents of Balmartin, Co. Meath.

Distinguished persons of the name English or England have nearly all been Munstermen. Father William English (d. 1778), a Limerick man associated with Co. Cork, was one of the best of the eighteenth century Gaelic poets. Rev. Thomas England P.P. (1790-1847), the biographer, and his brother Dr. John England (1786-1849), one of America's most illustrious bishops, were born in Cork; while Richard England (1750-1812) and his son Sir Richard England, both notable soldiers, were Claremen. I do not know to which family the notorious eighteenth century Buck English belonged. The Inglis family, on the other hand, two of whom were Protestant bishops of Nova Scotia, and one, Sir John Inglis, the defender of Lucknow, were from Co. Donegal.

ENNIS   Since the sixteenth century, when the general anglicization of Gaelic-Irish names began, at any rate for official purposes, the surname Ennis has been closely associated with Co. Kildare and the adjoining parts of Meath and Offaly. Ennis was formerly O'Hennis, which is Ó hAonghuis in Irish. That is a variant of Ó hAonghusa i.e. O'Hennessy. Those septs which concern us in dealing with Ennis are O'Hennessy of Moyfenrath, a Meath barony contiguous with north Kildare, and O'Hennessy of the barony of Philipstown, Co. Offaly, which adjoins both counties Meath and Kildare.

In both those areas we find Ennis, then written Enos, Ennous (to mention only two of the many variants) very frequently in sixteenth century records; and in the next century the "census" of 1659 returns it as one of the most numerous names in four baronies of Co. Kildare and in one of the baronies of Co. Offaly adjoining Co. Kildare. The spellings in that document are Ennis, Ennos, Ennes and Enos. By that time it had to some extent died out in Co. Meath where, however, it is perpetuated in the place-name Ennistown in that part of the county associated with the sept of O'Hennessy. This occurs in a Fiant of 1568 as Enostown. As Enos it was

well known in Dublin as the records of the city guilds from 1550 to 1650 show.

The form Enos is, I think, now obsolete but it was used at least as late as 1720, as we know from a Registry of Deeds will of that date. Before the general relinquishment of the Gaelic prefixes Mac and O, Ennos was often written O'Hennos. MacEnnos also occurs in similar records. In Ulster this may well be an English official's mis-spelling of MacGennis, but when it is found in Leinster it is more probably an error for O'Hennos: much confusion existed — not among the Gaels themselves but among officials with no Irish background — between Mac and O. This question has been discussed elsewhere in this series and need not be further considered here.

The Ennis family suffered under both the Cromwellian and Williamite regimes. In 1642 three of the name were attainted — two of Grennagh, Co. Wicklow, one of Hacketstown, Co. Carlow, and also James Ennis, of Clane, Co. Kildare. A Lieutenant James Ennis was a Royalist soldier of note of that time. In the next generation we find John Ennis, who had previously risen to the rank of major in the French army, as lt. colonel of Edmond Butler's Infantry Regiment in James II's Irish army; and following their defeat Edmund Ennis, of Athy, Co. Kildare, was outlawed as a Jacobite.

In Ireland Ennis must not be confused with the Scottish name Innes. It should be added that as a surname it has no relation to the town of Ennis; though early English records, e.g. the Hundred Rolls (1273) contain the name del Ennesse, which Reaney states is derived from the Irish word inis, island, as is the town of Ennis.

Two ecclesiastics of the name are notable: Rev. Walter Enos, S.T.D. author of Survey of the Peace (1646) and a severe critic of Clanrickarde; and Dr. John Ennis, the Dublin parish priest prominent for his part in the opposition to those bishops who were not in favour of the establishment of the Queen's Colleges in 1848.

ENRIGHT, Erraught   Though Woulfe equates Erraught with O'Heraghty I prefer the opinion of Rev. John Ryan, S.J., that Erraught is actually a form of the name which was formerly Enraght and is now usually anglicized as Enright. The substitution of Err for Enr is not unusual. Woulfe mentions that in the spoken Irish language Mac Ionnrachtaigh is pronounced 'a Ciúrrachta, which is closer to Erraught than to Enright. Woulfe derives Heraghty, an O name, from oireachtas (holder of assemblies) and Enright, a Mac name, from ionnrachtach (unlawful). Father Ryan considers that Enright comes from an adjectival form of indrecht which seems to mean "attack." As a personal name Indrectech (later Inrechtach) is found in the early Annals. From this personal name comes the family name Mac Ionnrachtaigh. Airechtach occurs also in the early records as a personal name and from it, I am informed by Father Ryan, is derived the family name Mac Oireachtaigh (Geraghty). In the sixteenth century Fiants we find both MacErachta (Co. Longford) and O'Heraght (Co. Roscommon); MacEnryckty and Kinraght occur at Kilmallock, Co. Limerick.

The Erraughts to-day are located chiefly in Co. Kerry,

where we would expect to find Enright rather than Her-aghty, for the latter is not connected with Munster. Dean Donal A. Reidy has suggested to me that Erraught in Kerry is an abbreviation of Irraghty-connor. Matheson records Erought as synonymous with Haroughten near Tralee, where the latter has inevitably been absorbed by the commoner Harrington. Of this family was Father Maurice MacKenraghty, chaplain to the Earl of Desmond, who having given himself up to save another man's life, was beheaded at Clonmel in 1585 in the most gruesome circumstances. The Guardian of the Franciscan convent at Quin, Co. Clare, in 1685 was Father Anthony Kenraghty. Map

MacENTAGGART   Though now chiefly located in Co. Antrim where they are numerous, persons of this name were formerly widespread throughout Ulster. Under various synonyms – MacEtegart, MacTaggart, Ateggart etc., – it appears frequently in sixteenth and seventeenth century records of counties Antrim, Derry, Fermanagh, Donegal and Armagh and also in Louth. Among a number of rectors and erenaghs of the name mentioned in the Derry diocesan visitation of 1606 William Mac-Teggart, Dean of Derry, was specially praised as a worthy man "speaking Irish and Latin." From this document it would appear that the name was sometimes abbreviated to MacTegg. At the same time we find two MacIteggerts among the Armagh jurors and a Mac-Atagairt and a MacEtegart on a Limavady inquisition jury. Ballymactaggart is a place in the barony of Lurg, Co. Fermanagh, which is in the centre of the territory originally occupied by the sept. In Irish the name is Mac an tSagairt (sagart is derived from the Latin sacerdos, a priest).

In addition to the many earlier variants of the name given above several rather odd ones are recorded in Matheson's lists of modern synonyms taken from the official birth registrations, e.g. Teg (at Newtown Butler) and Teggarty at Castleblayney, where MacIntyre was also so recorded, while Tiger was registered for a Mac-Entaggart birth in Co. Meath.

Moses Taggart (1854-1909), the Ulster poet, was born in Co. Armagh; and Thomas Tagart (1856-1929), one of those Irishmen who began life in impoverished circumstances and became one of America's big business men, was a native of Co. Monaghan. Map

MacENTEE MacGINTY   Though occasionally recorded as synonyms these two surnames are of quite different origin. MacEntee is one which presents little difficulty, for even its derivation is not open to doubt – it is Mac an tSaoi (pronounced Mac un tee as in the anglicized form). The Irish word saoi is used to denote s scholar or simply a cultured person. The MacEntees, who were formerly more numerous than at present, were always located in Oriel, and the name occurs there as MacEntee, MacEtye, MacYntie, MacAtee etc., in the Chancery Rolls, Fiants, Hearth Money Rolls, and other sixteenth and seventeenth century records, especially in counties Monaghan and Armagh. Woulfe says that Mac-

Ginty (Mag Fhinneachta in Irish) was almost peculiar to Co. Armagh in the sixteenth century. I think he must have confused MacGinty and MacEntee because the former is a Donegal surname, now found chiefly in the south-eastern part of that county bordering on Tyrone and Fermanagh. It is also (without the prefix Mac) fairly numerous in Co. Mayo; this presumably represents the result of the great migration of Donegal families to north Connacht at the time of the Plantation of Ulster. It is remarkable that the name is a rare occurrence in the records and it does not appear, for example, in the 1659 "census" or in the Elizabethan Fiants.

Jervis MacEntee (1828-1891), a noted American landscape painter, was of Irish ancestry.   Map

MacERLEAN   MacErlean is a phonetic approximation to the Irish Mac Fhirléighinn, the full form of which – Mac an Fhirléighinn – means son of the learned man or "lector." This family appears in the fifteenth century near Sligo town and a Patent Roll of 1603 relating to Dermot Dale MacEnyrline shows him also to be of that place. This was no other than the poet Dermot Dall. A branch of the family settled in Co. Derry, where as MacErlen and MacErlyn the name occurs in the Hearth Money Rolls of the 1660s, particularly in the parish of Tamlaght. O'Crilly, and modern statistics show that it is in counties Derry and Antrim the name is now chiefly found. Rev. J.C. MacErlean S.J (1870-1950), editor of O'Bruadair's works, was a distinguished Irish scholar.   Map

EUSTACE   This is one of the most distinguished of the names which came to Ireland at the time of the Anglo-Norman invasion. While not multiplying to the same extent as the Burkes, Butlers, FitzGeralds, Powers and other great Hiberno-Norman families, the Eustaces were numerous enough to be classed in Petty's "census" of 1659 among the principal Irish names in four baronies of Co. Kildare. Yet the name is by no means common today – in 1864 there were 20 Eustace birth registrations, in 1865 and 1866, 18 for each year; while in 1890 the figure was 9, compared with 330 for FitzGerald and 272 for Power or, to take a few less numerous ones at random, Bermingham 40, Comerford 30, Cusack 46. Whatever may be the cause of this numerical reduction since 1659 the elimination of the great families of the name is due of course to their constant support of the Irish side in the struggles of the late sixteenth and seventeenth centuries. So long as the English connexion with Ireland was no more than a suzerainty and the effective control of the country was in the hands of the Hiberno-Normans, as was the case up to the middle of the sixteenth century, the name Eustace was prominent in the sphere of government. There were many of them sheriffs, constables of castles and the like from 1200 onwards; in the fifteenth century Sir Richard Eustace was Lord Chancellor (a position held at different times by four other Eustaces); in 1454 Sir Edward FitzEustace was Lord Deputy; his son, Sir Roland, also Lord Chancellor, was created Baron of Portlester; he founded the Franciscan monastery of New Abbey in Co. Kildare – just a century earlier, in

1356, another Eustace founded the Dominican priory at Naas; Sir Roland died in 1496, having occupied the position of Lord Treasurer for 38 years.

In the next century the first of the many Eustace attainders occurred: James Eustace 3rd Viscount Baltinglass, who with the Gaelic septs of Co. Wicklow had signally defeated Lord Grey in 1580, shared in the general ruin following the collapse of Desmond's rebellion. The 1642 attainders include about 20 Eustaces mostly of Co. Kildare, with a few on its eastern border in counties Dublin and Wicklow. On the Kildare-Wicklow border the name is perpetuated at Ballymore Eustace. One who, always notably loyal to Charles I and Charles II, escaped any penalty for his public activities was Maurice Eustace (c. 1590-1665) — he was speaker of the Irish House of Commons in 1639 and Lord Chancellor in 1660. His nephew and co-heir, Sir Maurice Eustace (d. 1693) commanded one of the infantry regiments in James II's army, in which there were six officers named Eustace, as well as several in other regiments. Sir Maurice was one of the 22 attainders and forfeitures in 1691 (on this occasion 12 were in Co. Kildare, 8 in Co. Carlow and 2 in Co. Wicklow). Many of these whole-hearted Jacobite Eustaces followed James II to France.

The Eustaces have been notable chiefly as soldiers, lawyers and administrators; Rev. John Chetwode Eustace (c. 1760-1815) who was one of the first professors in Maynooth College, is worthy of mention in the field of literature.

Eustace, primarily a christian name, is derived from the Latin eustacius, of Greek origin, meaning fruitful. It is written Iústás in Irish.   Bibl., Map

MacEVILLY, Staunton   This important Hiberno-Norman sept — for sept they became after the manner of their Gaelic neighbours — has already been briefly noticed in Irish Families, p. 52.

The family of Staunton was among the early settlers in Connacht after the Anglo-Norman invasion: at the beginning of the fourteenth century under the famous "Red Earl" (Richard de Burgo) they acquired territory in the baronies of Clanmorris and Carra. The ancestor of the MacEvillys (Mac an Mhílidh — son of the knight) was Sir Bernard Staunton, or de Sdondon as it was formerly spelled, whose son, Philip Mór de Sdondon was among the first invaders. In 1585 Mylie MacEvily of Kinturke, Co. Mayo, was described in the Composition Book of Connacht as chief of his name, yet a century later the Mayo Book of Survey & Distribution mentions many Stauntons as land-holders in that county, but has no MacEvilly or MacAvealy, which were alternative forms of that name. It is a fact that the MacEvillys have to a very large extent reverted to the name Staunton. In the birth registrations for 1890 there were 67 Stauntons or Stantons (chiefly in counties Mayo and Galway, but 14 were in Co. Cork) and MacEvilly had less than 5 entries. Even a generation earlier we find but one in 1864 and 5 in 1865. In this connexion it may be noted that Mac-Evely and Staunton were used indifferently in recent times by the same families in Co. Sligo and the former was prominent in the second half of the nineteenth century in the person of John MacEvilly, Bishop of Galway, Kilmacduagh and Kilfenora from 1857-1881 and Archbishop of Tuam from 1881 to 1902. Castle Stanton is a place near Castlebar, Co. Mayo.

Three Stauntons from west of the Shannon were prominent in their day — Sir George Staunton (1737-1801) and his son George Thomas Staunton (1781-1859) were notable for their activities in China, while Michael Staunton (1788-1870), Lord Mayor of Dublin and editor of the Freeman's Journal, was at first an associate and later an opponent of the Young Irelanders.

Not all Stauntons, however, are of this early Hiberno-Norman stock. There have been a number of English immigrants of the name including two Cromwellian "adventurers."   Map

EWING   Ewing is quite a numerous surname in Ireland: in 1866 there were 27 births registered for it, including a few for the synonyms Ewings and Ewin, while in 1890 the number was 24, in both cases almost entirely in Ulster. In that province it has since the seventeenth century been especially associated with the counties of Donegal, Derry, Tyrone and Antrim. Many Ewing wills are recorded for the dioceses comprising these northern areas. The "census" of 1659 is one of the earliest Irish documents to include the name — in it Alexander Ewing appears as one of the leading inhabitants of Letterkenny, Co. Donegal. A few years later it appears frequently in the Hearth Money Rolls for that county. It is probable that Dublin Ewings, such as the notable printing and publishing family of the mid-eighteenth century, came to the capital from the north.

The origin of the name is interesting. According to Reaney it goes back to the Greek eugenes (well-born), cognate with the Gaelic Irish eoghan. Mac GiollaDomhnaigh, too, states that Ewing, also found as MacEwing, is a form of the well known Scottish name MacEwen, gaelice Mac Eoghain, i.e. our Irish MacKeown.

EYRE, Codyre   Codyre is found in the parish of Rahoon near the city of Galway. Mr. P.J. Kennedy informs me that its origin is unknown with certainty, but that it is believed locally that it is an anglicization of cuid Eyre, i.e. the illegitimate children of the Eyre family. Eyre might well have been included in the Anglo-Irish section of Irish Families, since they were an influential Cromwellian family seated since the seventeenth century at Eyrecourt and Eyreville, Co. Galway, five of whom were sheriffs of Co. Galway between 1675 and 1809. The first of them, Col. John Eyre, accompanied Ludlow and, having obtained extensive grants in Co. Galway, built the castle and village named Eyrecourt after him. The place was formerly called Cillinithe. From them descended the Co. Cork family of Hedges-Eyre. Elsewhere Eyre has been reported as a synonym of Ayres. It is derived from the Old-French word for heir and was first written le Eir and le Eyer.   Bibl.

(Mac) FADDEN   Though, when not Scottish, Mac-Fadden is and has always been primarily a Co. Donegal name, it has also a long standing connexion with Co. Cavan. Charles MacFadin was one of the commissioners for that county charged with the administration of the Poll Tax Ordinance of 1660. Another Charles MacFadden acquired through the Williamite confiscations the Quilca (Co. Cavan) property, so well known on account of Dean Swift's connexion with it when it was in the possession of the Jacobite Sheridan family. He was a Protestant of the liberal type and was largely responsible for the continuance without molestation of Father Peter Garrigan's classical school at Moybolge. Three centuries later another of the Co. Cavan Garrigans Rt. Rev. Philip J. Garrigan (1840-1919) was outstanding in the sphere of education. He was Vice-Rector of the Catholic University of America before becoming first Bishop of Sioux City in 1902. Garrigan or Gargan (Mac Geargáin and sometimes Ó Geargáin) is a comparatively rare surname belonging to the Breffny country. The Quilca property reverted to the Sheridans on the marriage of the MacFadden heiress to Dr. Thomas Sheridan in 1710.

Sir Arthur Fadden, one of Australia's most colourful Prime Ministers, was the son of Richard John Fadden who was born at Roundstone, Co. Galway. His mother, née Hannah Morehead, came from Cookstown, Co. Tyrone.   Map

(O) FALVEY   Although Falveys are found in counties Cork and Clare this must be regarded as essentially a Kerry name. From the eleventh century, when hereditary surnames came into existence, until the present day Kerry has been their homeland. The O'Falveys, O'Sheas and O'Connells were three branches of the same stock tracing their descent to Conaire I, King of Ireland at the beginning of the Christian era. Passing from legendary to historical times we find O'Falveys chiefs of Corcaguiney from the twelfth century to the final destruction of the Gaelic order. Father Donough O'Falvey was one of the many west-Munster priests hanged in Cork during the Elizabethan religious persecution. In 1657 they are mentioned with the MacCarthys, O'Sullivans, O'Donoghues and MacElligotts and other well known Kerry families as "plotting for trouble." Even after the upheaval of the Cromwellian Settlement they still held considerable lands around Cahirciveen, some of which remained in their hands in unbroken succession until in quite recent times the property of this branch of the family passed by alliance to the Morrogh-Bernards.

In 1690 at least four Falveys were serving as officers in King James's army. Thereafter, like other formerly great Catholic and Gaelic families living in the more inaccessible parts of the country, they were content to remain in obscurity until Catholic Emancipation.

The name is Ó Fáilbhe in Irish. It has almost invariably been anglicized Falvey, but occasionally in north Kerry it has become Fealy (not to be confused with Feely: q.v.) while in the Tulla district of Co. Clare Fallaher is recorded as a synonym. Fallaher, however, is stated by Woulfe to be properly the anglicized form of Ó Faolchair, a very rare name the origin of which is obscure. It would seem,

however, more likely that the equally rare Co. Limerick name Falahee or Falihey (Ó Faolchaidh) might be confused with Falvey.   Map

(O) FARREN   (O) FEARON   (O) FARNAN
Farren is a name closely associated with Co. Donegal where it is normally the anglicized form of Ó Faracháin. In O'Dugan's Topographical Poem and in the Book of Fenagh Ó Furadhran is described as Lord of Finross (now called the Rosses, in Co. Donegal) and the editors of both those works (John O'Donovan and William Hennessy) give Farren as the modern equivalent of that name, which however is distinct from Ó Faracháin. Ó Fearáin, a sept of the Cenél Eoghain, correctly anglicized Fearon in the counties of east Oriel (Armagh etc.), has tended to be changed to Farran in the case of families of the name living in Co. Donegal. O'Farran is listed as a principal name in the barony of Inishowen, Co. Donegal, in the 1659 "census", but the prefix O has since then been dropped and rarely resumed.

Farnan or Farnon is another Ulster surname somewhat similar in sound. It was formerly Ó Forannáin in Irish (it is so spelt in the Annals of Loch Cé) and is now Ó Farannáin. This was an erenagh family of Ardstraw, Co. Tyrone.

The best known person of these names was Elizabeth Farren (1759-1829), a celebrated actress who at the age of 38 married the 12th Earl of Derby. She was born in Co. Cork, far from the country of the O'Farrens.   Map

FARRINGTON   Farrington is a well-known name in England and our Irish Farringtons came from that country at various times, some comparatively recently and some as early as the fourteenth century. The derivation of the name is simple: it is "of Farrington" a place in England; and it was originally written de Faryngton. A Simon de Feringdon or de Farindon (which are possibly earlier synonyms of Farrington) occurs more than once in lists of Co. Louth jurors in 1306. In 1399 we find one de Faryngton Lord Treasurer and another a Baron of the Exchequer; by 1400 when Hugh Farrington was commissioned to conduct a sworn enquiry into duties paid on wines etc., at Drogheda, the prefix de begins to be regularly dropped — even the juror of a century earlier referred to above is mentioned once without it. There is reason to doubt whether descendants in the male line of any of these mediaeval officials are still extant. The name, however, was kept from dying out in Ireland by the arrival of later immigrants (for example the garrison at Trim in 1647 included Capt. Farrington's company of Col. Fenwick's regiment) but it has never become numerous. While not very closely associated with any particular place it is better known in Co. Cork than elsewhere. The most prominent family of the name there came from Lancashire about 1850.

(O) FAUGHNAN   Apart from stating that Ó Fachtnáin is the Gaelic form of Faughnan Woulfe gives no information about this name. Nineteenth century birth statistics indicate that it belongs to counties Leitrim and Longford; and comparative statistics suggest that it is one of the few names which was as numerous at the end of the century as it was in the middle.

It is possible that an early anglicization of the name was Faughey, a form which seems to be now quite obsolete. If we accept this as synonymous with Faughnan it follows that the sept was of considerable importance in the sixteenth century as a Fiant of 1588 shows. This document is of some general interest and the abstract of it, printed in the 16th Report of the Deputy Keeper of Public Records Ireland, is therefore given in full: "Grant (under commission, 7 Dec. xxviii) to Gillernewe Ó Faghny or m'Faghny of Rathclyne, Co. Longford, esq., captain and chief of the territory of Calloe same co.: of all manors, castles, lands, and services, in Rathklen, Forkill, Dromharfe, Aghadain, Agholughan, Cooleteggell and Ferrinegiragh or Ferrenkragh, and elsewhere within the territory of Callo, surrendered by his deed of 20 May, xxx.; also half the goods of fugitives and persons attainted of treason or felony, and all goods of waifs and strays, and fines within the territory. To hold for ever, by the service of a twentieth part of a knight's fee. This grant not to alter any rent or service reserved by composition, nor shall it pass any possessions vested in the crown otherwise than by the surrender of Gillernew. He may once in each quarter hold a court baron, and twice a year a court of view of frank pledge at Rathklen, or elsewhere within the premises, before his seneschal. This grant shall not prejudice the rights of the heirs of N. Malby, knt, or any other of the queen's subjects, except to the title of captain or chief of the Callo, which title is abolished.– 22 June, xxx".

FAVERTY   This is, I believe, an American form of Faherty, the pronunciation of which in U.S.A. as Farty offended the susceptibilities of some people. Faherty (three syllables, not two), i.e. Ó Fathartaigh, is a surname almost peculiar to Co. Galway, especially Connemara. The sept was originally located on the shore of Lough Corrib, where it is still numerous: it is now even more so further west in and around Clifden.

FEDDIS   This rare name belongs to Co. Fermanagh, as is clear from the pedigree in the Genealogical Office and numerous testamentary records, only one relating to a place outside that county. The earliest of the wills is dated 1742. I have not discovered the origin of the name. According to a list of fourteenth century Latin forms of English surnames given by Ewen, Fiddes is equivalent to de Sancto Fide. I presume he had adequate authority for that statement. It may well be also that origin of the rare south Leinster name Sanfey (also spelt Sanphy). We know from another source (Ball's "Judges") that De Sancta Fide occurs in a list of chancellors under date 1235.

(O) FEDEGAN   Though by no means numerous now this name has been continuously associated with the barony of Ardee since the sixteenth century: in 1659 Petty's "census" recorded them as a principal Irish family in that barony. The sept originated in the Clones area, where the Co. Monaghan place-name Tiredigan and Ballyviddegan on both sides of Clones indicate the location, whence they moved in the eleventh century to south Monaghan and in due course over the Co. Louth border. In 1425 Neyll O'Fedegan and others were charged with abducting the chaplain of Nobber and were threatened with excommunication by the Bishop of Clogher. The Irish form of the name is Ó Feadagáin.

(O) FEE, Ó Fiaich   (derived from fiach, raven, rather than from fiadhach, hunt) is widely regarded as a Co. Armagh name, perhaps because of the prominence of Cardinal Tomás Ó Fiaich (affectionately known to many in south Armagh as Tom Fee) now Archbishop of Armagh and formerly President of Maynooth College. His family has long been established in north Louth, from which they moved into south Armagh. By origin, however, they belong to Fermanagh and are on record in the Annals of the Four Masters as erenaghs of Derrybrusk, near Enniskillen, as far back as 1482. O'Fee is listed as a principal name in that area in the "census" of 1659.

The name Fay (q.v.) usually of quite different origin, has been used as a synonym of Fee in Ulster so that some confusion may thus arise. The statistics given in Griffith's Valuation of the 1850s illustrate this. Thus in Co. Cavan one finds 15 entries for Fee in one barony (Tullyhaw) and in the barony of Tullygarvey, where Fee is rare, no less than 52 Fay or Fey entries occur. Co. Cavan adjoins Meath where Fays were numerous. So without close research on individual families it is not possible to say whether many of these Fays are actually Fee. The same source shows that Fee was about equally numerous in counties Fermanagh, Cavan, Leitrim, Monaghan and Tyrone and (presumably because it includes Belfast) slightly more so in Co. Antrim. It is interesting to note that 7 of the 27 relevant entries for that county appear as O'Fee. Elsewhere the prefix O had been generally discarded. That this is still the case is evidenced by a glance at the modern telephone directories where of approximately 50 of the name listed only two appear as O'Fee. The Griffith's Valuation figure for Co. Armagh is 8; the other three Ulster counties together only total five.

(O) FEEHAN (O) FEGAN Woulfe treats Ó Fiacháin (Feehan, Fehane) and Ó Feichín (Feeheen, Feen) as Connacht variants, but the latter is in fact distinct, being the name of a small west Cork sept. Fegan has been recorded as a synonym of Fehan, but in fact Fegan is basically a different name: it, Ó Faodhagáin, is numerous in the Oriel country — Louth, Armagh etc., — (see Irish Families, p. 137). Feehan has for many centuries been associated with the Ormond country, particularly counties Tipperary and Kilkenny. The early anglicized spelling of Irish surnames as set down in legal records is very corrupt and may be misleading. Probably Muirihirt and Thomas O'Fechan, who appeared before a court held in Clonmel in 1295 were of this sept; as no doubt was Philip MacShoan O'Fethan who was convicted of robbery in Co. Tipperary in 1359, while another, equally picturesquely named, Conghor Leith O'Fean, was fined at Clonmel in 1380. By 1601 the name had assumed a form nearer to the modern Feehan: in that year Teige MacNicholas O'Fehin was one of a number of men belonging to the Ormond territory who were granted "pardons", i.e. immunity from the current anti-Irish legislation. Coming to modern times, there were 57 householders of the name in Co. Tipperary in 1855 and birth registrations of the 1860s indicate that Feehan was then found mainly in the Munster-Kilkenny area to which they traditionally belong — only 3 of the 22 births registered in an average test year were outside it and those were in or near Co. Louth. A generation later the same source shows the name in all the provinces, less than half being recorded in the O'Feehan homeland and the majority of the rest being in Co. Louth. As a rule names closely identified with a locality continue to be mainly found there always, and it therefore appears probable that Feehan has sometimes been substituted for Fegan in Co. Louth.

(Mac) FEERICK This is Mac Phiaraic in Irish, and was first anglicized, e.g. in the sixteenth century Fiants, as MacFeyrick; but the prefix Mac is quite obsolete in modern forms of the name. Few surnames are more closely identified with a particular place than Feerick, the homeland of which is Ballinrobe, Co. Mayo. There were eleven Feerick families in Ballinrobe in 1783, but none appears among the large landowners at any time: it does not, for example, occur in the Composition Book of Connacht (1585), in the Strafford Inquisition of County Mayo (1635) or in the Book of Survey and Distribution, Co. Mayo. The latter gives the proprietors in 1641 and the subsequent grantees under the Cromwellian Settlement and the Williamite forfeitures at the end of the century. Unfortunately Counties Mayo and Galway are missing from the "census" of 1659.

Other names numbering eleven or more householders in Ballinrobe in 1783 were Flannelly, Hennelly, Meay, Mellott, O'Mealy, Sheridan and Walsh, but all of these were also found elsewhere.

(O) FEHILLY, Fihelly, Feeley, Field This name is Ó Fithcheallaigh in Irish, which is said to be derived from the Gaelic word fithcheallach, meaning a chess-player. Chess was a game much in vogue in ancient Ireland. During the past century the normal forms Fehilly and Fihelly have been increasingly corrupted to Feeley. The substitution of the English name Field for these dates back to the sixteenth century. Thomas O'Fihelly, Bishop of Leighlin from 1555 to 1567, is described in contemporary documents as "alias Field," and a Co. Cork Fiant of 1584 names two O'Fihellys alias Field. In the 1659 "census" Field appears as one of the principal Irish names in the Youghal area of Co. Cork. A sept of the Corca Laoidhe, the O'Fehillys were chiefs of a district comprising the parish of Ardfield and other territory in the neighbourhood of Clonakilty, Co. Cork. Families of the name, more often Field in Co. Cork, have remained constantly in south-west Munster to this day; Fealy (pronounced Fayley) in north Kerry, however, is to be equated with Falvey rather than with Fehilly. For Fehilly, since the beginning of the seventeenth century we must look rather to north Connacht and Donegal than to Co. Cork. Dr. A. Moore states that in Connacht O'Fihelly is a Silmurray sept.

The famous Archbishop of Tuam, Maurice O'Fihily (d. 1516), called Maurice de Portu, professor at Padua and editor of the works of John Scotus, was not a Connacht man — he was born at Baltimore, in the heart of the original habitat of the sept; another Maurice O'Fihelly (d. 1559) was Bishop of Ross, a diocese approximately co-extensive with the ancient territory of Corca Laoidhe, whence also came Donal O'Fihelly (fl. c. 1500), the annalist. Another noteworthy O'Fehilly whose name was disguised was Father Thomas Field or Filde, S.J. (1548-1626), a Limerick-born priest famous for his missionary work conducted under conditions of great hardship in Brazil and Paraguay, where he remained for more than 50 years. In more recent times a notable man of the name was a Donegal priest, Rev. James Feeley (1799-1875), the Dean of Raphoe. John Arthur Fihelly (d. c. 1930) "the stormy petrel of the Queensland Labour Party" was a pioneer in workmen's compensation legislation.

A curious transition in nomenclature may be noted here: in Co. Roscommon Feeley was sometimes changed to Foley which in turn was equated with Sharry — searrach, genitive searraigh (pronounced Sharry), is the Irish word for a foal.

The rare Co. Limerick name Fehill, also alias Field, is simply an abbreviated form of Fehilly.

The Anglo-Irish surname Field was briefly noticed in Irish Families (p. 291). Map

(O) FEIGHNEY, Feeheny, Hunt
(O) FEIGHREY, Feehery, Hunt
(O) FEY, Hunt (O) FEENEY I have frequently referred to the slavish but understandable practice, which prevailed during the period of Catholic and Gaelic submergence, of changing Irish surnames into English ones by a process of supposed translation. The difficulties which arise from this are illustrated in the case of the name Hunt, the Irish word for which is fiadhach. Hunt is a very common name in England and no doubt many of

the Hunt families established in Ireland, at any rate in Leinster, are of English origin. However, since the name Hunt is much more numerous in Mayo and Roscommon and other parts of Connacht than elsewhere, it is not surprising to find that in that province Hunt is not English but was adopted as an anglicized form of Ó Fiachna, which was formerly Feighney, Feeheny, Fagheny etc., a name still found in Co. Sligo. This minor sept was a branch of the Síol Muireadhaigh (Silmurray) located in Co. Roscommon. In the same way Ó Fiachra of Co. Tyrone, first O'Feighry, Feehery, Feery etc., became Hunt; as did the family of Ó Fiaich (or Ó Féich) who were erenaghs of Derrybruck, near Enniskillen, though in this case the normal anglicized form Fey (with variants such as Fee, Fay, Foy) was not widely superseded by Hunt. Finally we find Hunt fairly numerous in Co. Waterford, and there it takes the place of Fee or Fye — Ó Fiacha or Ó Fiaich in Irish. See also O'Fee supra.

There is a tendency for three syllable names with an internal H to be shortened to two. Fehily reduced to Feeley and Garrahy to Garry are examples, similarly Geoghegan is often pronounced Geagan and in place-names Glenbehy has become Glenbeigh. It is therefore rather remarkable that Feeney has not, as far as I can ascertain, been used for Feheny (also spelt Feeheny). The Connacht name Feeney is more numerous than any of the Gaelic names mentioned above, indeed it almost equals Hunt which, as we have seen, has many origins; and if Finney, its Ulster variant, be added, it outnumbers Hunt. Feeney is Ó Fiannaidhe in Irish, now abbreviated to Ó Fianna. This sept of the Hy Fiachrach was located in the parish of Easkey, Co. Sligo. I cannot say whether the Feeneys of Co. Galway (who write their name Ó Fidhne in Irish) are a distinct family or a branch of the sept of Ó Fiannaidhe. Dr. Thomas Feeny was Bishop of Killala from 1847 to 1873.

(O) FENELON, Fenlon   Owing to the fame of a succession of French Fénelons in the sixteenth, seventeenth and eighteenth centuries it might be thought that this name is of French origin in Ireland. It is a fact that some Huguenot immigrants so called did settle in Ireland. The great majority, however, of our Fenelons and Fenlons (both spellings occur in about equal numbers) are of Gaelic stock. The surname, Ó Fionnaláin in Irish, was that of the chiefs of Delvin in Co. Westmeath, many of whom are mentioned in the annals up to the end of the twelfth century, when they were dispossessed by the Norman Hugh de Lacy. The sept, though dispersed, was not driven out of Leinster and today the name, without its prefix O, is chiefly found in Counties Carlow and Wexford. The poet, Rev. Timothy Brendan Fenelon (d. 1923), was a native of Co. Carlow.

(O) FENNELL   (O) FENNELLY, Hennelly   These names are treated together because in the past they have often been confused. Fennell is more numerous than Fennelly. According to Woulfe the former is Ó Fionnghail or Ó Fionnghaile and the latter Ó Fionnghalaigh. Ó Fionnghaile, however, would anglicize as Finnelly or Fennelly rather than Fennell. As he so often does, Woulfe ignores the fact that Fennell is an English surname as well as the anglicized form of an Irish one. Reaney states that the English name is derived from the plant fennel and suggests alternatively that it is a corruption of FitzNeel. It has been associated with the Ormond country since the fourteenth century, if not longer; it appears from time to time in the Ormond Deeds from 1324 onwards as Fynnel, Fenell etc., and the context suggests that these men were of Anglo-Norman not Gaelic stock, as certainly some of the Finnellys were; for we find the name in the Justiciary Rolls in 1295 as de Fynaly. On the other hand O'Fynewil occurs in Co. Dublin in 1295. With the prefix O both names appear in the Fiants between 1570 and 1600, always in Co. Kilkenny or near it, e.g. in King's Co. (Offaly).

In the next century Petty's "census" lists them both as principal Irish names in King's Co. Dr. Gerald Fennell, friend of the Marquis of Ormond, is recorded as taking a lease of Athassal, Co. Tipperary in 1634. He is also described as of Ballygriffin in the same county, again adjacent to Co. Kilkenny. He was a member of the Supreme Council of the Confederation of Kilkenny in 1647 and was a strong opponent of the Nuncio's party. Another of the name, Col. Edward Fennell, has been branded as a traitor at the Siege of Limerick in 1651 — probably wrongly, since he was hanged by Ireton with four others of the defenders of Limerick. Two Fennells appear in King James's army list a generation later. The Ballygriffin estate, confiscated under the Cromwellian regime, was recovered at the Restoration. The attainders of 1642 include the name of Patrick Fennell, of Kilrush, Co. Clare, in 1680, in which county the name is still extant. The "census" of 1659 returns Robert Fennell of Ballymoryhy, Co. Limerick, as English.

Some of the Fennells of the Kilkenny-Tipperary area were undoubtedly O'Fennellys. This name has in more recent times been corrupted to Finlay (also spelt Finley and Findley). Several people so called are to be found in the biographical dictionaries, but these were chiefly of Scots descent from the north of Ireland. Father Thomas Finlay S.J. (1848-1940), ardent advocate of the co-operative movement and for many years president of the Irish Agricultural Organization Society, was born in Co. Cavan of Scottish ancestry. In this connexion it is interesting to observe that in a Co. Cavan Inquisition of 1629 John and Patrick Fenley of Tullylurkan are included among the tenants not described as "meere Irishmen."

The name Hennelly, which has for many centuries been found in Co. Mayo, is said to be a variant of Fennelly, the initial F of the Gaelic form being aspirated there. I have not been able to trace the origin of this family. According to a register made by Father F. X. Blake in 1783 Hennelly was one of the most numerous names in the parish of Ballinrobe at that time. It has also been used as a variant of O'Hanley. It should be added that O'Fennelly and variants of the name appear in the Hearth Money Rolls of Co. Monaghan, (1663-65).

(O) FERGUS, Ferris, Ferguson   The name Ó Farghuis

or Ó Fearghusa takes several forms in English. Apart from Farrissy, which in modern times occurs only occasionally, the two usual forms are Fergus and Ferris. Fergus or O'Fergus is seldom found outside Connacht. Persons so called, who are mainly in Co. Mayo at the present time, are of the sept of Ó Fearghuis, which provided hereditary physicians to the O'Malleys. Knox in his History of Mayo tells us that O'Fergus held the parish of Burrishoole in 1303 and ranked then as a minor chief, a status no longer obtaining in 1585, since they do not figure in the Composition Book of Connacht, though we know from the Strafford Survey that they were still considerable landholders in Burrishoole and Carra about the year 1635. In that document the name is spelt Farregish, Faregesie and O'Farressie, while in the Mayo Book of Survey & Distribution, compiled some 50 years later, it occurs frequently as O'Farrissy. It must also be remembered that in the Connacht county of Leitrim there was an ecclesiastical family of the same name who were coarbs of St. Mogue and erenaghs of Rossinver: O'Connell in his work on the diocese of Kilmore calls them O'Ferguson. It was in the northern end of that county, adjacent to Co. Sligo, that Petty's "census" shows them, as O'Fergussa, to have been most numerous in 1659. In the Fiants of the previous century they appear chiefly in Co. Sligo. In the form of O'Fergus or O'Fargus it occurs there only once — at Spiddal, Co. Galway. It may be of interest to add that in 1362 an O'Fergus was vicar of Omey, an island off the coast of Connemara.

Ferris (alias O'Farris etc.) is more numerous both in the old records and today than Fergus. The name Ferris is now very numerous in north-east Ulster where it is that of a branch of the Scottish clan Ferguson — Fairy and even O'Ferry have been used as synonyms of it there but these are properly anglicizations of Ó Fearadhaigh, a Cinel Conaill sept. Ferris is also well known in Kerry. W.F. Butler in his Gleanings from Irish History states that Ferris there is traditionally believed to be the cognomen of a branch of the O'Moriartys. There were 27 families of Ferris in the 1911 census of Co. Kerry and the name was there at least as early as 1586. It occurs five times in the diocesan wills of Ardfert and Aghadoe in the eighteenth century. From Tralee came three interesting characters. The amazing and chequered career of Richard Ferris (1750-1828), ex-priest, spy, politician and business man, is outlined in Richard Hayes's Biographical Dictionary of Irishmen in France; his brother, Edward Ferris (1738-1809), was a distinguished priest who, after many vicissitudes in France and Rome, became the first president of Maynooth College; while a kinsman of theirs, another Edward Ferris, was also a political agent in France.

Other notable men were the exile Father Cormac O'Fergus, who came to Cork from Lisbon in 1571 and, while preaching at Clonmel, was captured and thrown into prison; the two O'Fearghusas of the O'Naghten poetic circle about 1725; and Dr. Fergus the well known patron of Gaelic learning at the same period. The late Bishop of Achonry and secretary to the hierarchy was Dr. James Fergus. O'Farys etc., was also in Co. Wexford

in 1659 and is still there, but as Vargus and Vargis, until quite recently used interchangeably with Ferguson. Ferguson, of course, is itself a Scottish name and is numerous in the north-eastern counties of Ireland, whence came Sir Samuel Ferguson (1810-1886), one of the best poets of the Irish literary renaissance and founder of the Protestant Repeal Association.

There was also a Norman name occurring occasionally in mediaeval records which must not be confused with O'Farys: Mgr. de Farys, for example, was canon of St. Patrick's Cathedral in 1302.

Carrickfergus in Co. Antrim is said to have been named after Fergus mac Roigh, the "Red Branch" hero of the Táin and reputed ancestor of several Ulster septs. This legendary personage is not to be confused with Fergus Mac Erc, Prince of Dalriada in north Antrim, who in A.D. 470 crossed to Scotland and founded the Gaelic kingdom there.   Map

MacFERRAN   Woulfe says that the Gaelic-Irish form of this name is Mac Mhearáin and that it was first anglicized as MacMeran. This form does appear in a Fiant of 1586, the location being Co. Roscommon. He is wrong however in stating that MacFerran is extremely rare: it is in fact found in not inconsiderable numbers in Counties Antrim and Down today and that was equally the case more than a century ago.

(O) FERRIGAN   This name is now mainly found in south Down and north Louth. It is Ó Feargáin in Irish. In 1544 Cahir O'Feregan was one of the kern mustered by the O'Reilly of the day for service abroad.

MacFETTRIDGE   Woulfe gives the Gaelic form of this name as MacPheadruis (son of Petrus, the Latin of Peter); I presume he had some authority for adding that the family was "not improbably an offshoot of the O'Breslins". It is essentially an Ulster name. It occurs in Co. Antrim in the "census" of 1659 as MacPhetrish; and MacPhatricks which is also there, is probably a variant of the same name not of MacPatrick (q.v.). From Co. Antrim, too, came Lieut. MacPhedris and his relative William MacFetrick, two of the defenders of Derry at the siege of 1689. Woulfe distinguished between MacFettridge (Mac Pheadruis) and MacFetrick, which he makes MacPhadraic: they are, however, usually synonymous. MacFettridge is numerous to-day in Counties Antrim and Derry but not elsewhere.

FIGGIS   The original form of this name le Fykeis, which is derived from the Old French ficheis meaning faithful, is found in English records as early as the thirteenth century, but does not appear to have been established in mediaeval Ireland. In this country it is of comparatively recent introduction being chiefly associated with Dublin, where it has been prominent in the publishing and bookselling business since 1809. Darrell Figgis (1882-1925), the author who was active in the revolutionary movement from 1914, was born in Dublin. Richard Foley suggested that Ballyviggis in Co. Down was named from a family of Figgis, but O'Donovan derives the place-name from one called Viggs. Reaney equates the name Vigus with Vigors but does not mention Figgis in this connexion.

(O) FINAGHTY, Finnerty, Fenton   It is regrettable to have to say that the deplorable English practice of substituting R for H has prevailed in the anglicizing of Ó Fionnachta (spelt Ó Fiannachta in Munster), even though it is chiefly found in Co. Galway, which until recently was largely Gaelic-speaking. We have already noticed (Irish Families, p. 237) the same thing in the use of Norton for Naughton, but in that case the barbarism was not extensively adopted; Finnerty and Finerty, however, have almost entirely superseded Finaghty.

O'Donovan, who wrote many notes about the O'Finaghtys in the numerous antiquarian works he edited, points out that they were not only of the same stock as the O'Connors of Silmurray but were actually senior to them, and in consequence enjoyed many privileges under the King of Connacht. Dr. A. Moore states that there was also an Uí Maine sept of O'Finaghty. Before the upheaval resulting from the Anglo-Norman occupation of Connacht O'Finaghty was chief of a considerable territory called Clanconway lying on both sides of the River Suck, i.e. in both Co. Galway and Co. Roscommon: his seat was at Dunamon.

A branch of one of these, or possibly a distinct sept, was located in Co. Kerry. There the English name Fenton has largely superseded Finaghty. King, in his analysis of the census of 1901 for Co. Kerry, found 38 families of Fenton there. However, a few families in north Kerry retain the normal form and, moreover, the correct not the corrupt spelling of it. Sir Geoffrey Fenton (d. 1608), an Englishman who held important government positions under Elizabeth I, lived at Dunboyne, Co. Meath. His daughter was the wife of the famous Richard Boyle, Earl of Cork.

Of the sept Ó Fionnachta was John O'Finaghty (d. 1354), Bishop of Elphin. Simon O'Finaghty is described by the Four Masters as erenagh of Elphin in the previous century. (The Annals of Loch Cé term him archdeacon). Peter Finnerty (1766-1822), the printer who was imprisoned for refusing to divulge information about the United Irishmen, was a Loughrea (Co. Galway) man. Michael J. Finnerty (d. 1908), Young Irelander and Fenian and subsequently United States soldier and politician, was the son of Galway-born John Frederick Finnerty, founder of The Chicago Citizen.   Map

O'FINAN FANNING   Ó Fionnáin, reasonably anglicized Finan in north Connacht, has also been anglicized Fanning. Fanning itself is a name of Norman origin early established in the south of Ireland: Woulfe says it is derived from the forename Panin and adds that the surname Panneen is extant in Co. Limerick. Fanning is particularly associated with that county. Fanningstown, earlier called Ballyfanning and Ballynanning (i.e. Baile an Fhaininn) is in Co. Limerick in the Knockainy area: in 1540 Nicholas Fanning occupied "the Lordship of Aine" (Knockainy). Of the Fannings who have been prominent in Limerick and Clare the most famous was Dominick Fanning, the mayor of Limerick who greatly distinguished himself at the siege of that city in 1651 and was hanged by Ireton as a result of his patriotic and uncompromising stand. In the next war three Fannings served as officers in King James II's army. The name, however, was by no means confined to that part of Munster: it appears as early as 1300 in Co. Kilkenny and in later centuries also there and in Co. Waterford. Fannin and Fenning are modern variants of Fanning.

The O'Finans were of the Uí Fiachrach Muaighe (Moy) group and chiefs of Coolcarney in Co. Mayo, but by the seventeenth century they were to be found mainly in Co. Roscommon which, with Co. Sligo, is also their principal homeland today. They are called Finane and Finan in the 1659 census, which also recorded O'Finan as established in Co. Armagh at that time. The most notable of the Hy Fiachrach sept was Dr. Francis Joseph O'Finan O.S.D. (d. 1847) Bishop of Killala.

St. Finan (d. 661), who was noted for his missionary work in England, sheds lustre on the name, but he lived of course several centuries before the introduction of surnames. The name Finan is derived from the Irish word fionn meaning fair.   Map

FINGLAS   This is a toponymic derived from the village of Finglas, now a suburb of Dublin, and is on record ever since the Anglo-Norman influx in the thirteenth century. From that time families of the name have been mostly located in Dublin or in the counties of the Pale. They are not numerous now, but from mediaeval to early modern times individuals of the name have been constantly in prominent positions. At first we only meet them in the law-courts of Co. Dublin as jurors or sureties or litigants, e.g. four men called de Fynglas who appeared in the archbishop's court at Finglas in 1256. Similar references occur in the fourteenth and fifteenth centuries. In the sixteenth they become more numerous. In that century Patrick Fynglas, author of the Breviat of Ireland, was chief justice of the King's Bench in 1534 and four others of the name held high legal office. In 1560 Thomas Finglas of Westphalstown was M.P. for Co. Dublin, while in the Perambulation of the Pale in 1596 Finglas of Tobersool (alias of Tobertown) was one of the "men of name" in Co. Dublin. At the same time some of them occupied much humbler positions, as for example Patrick, Peter and Roger Fynglas who were among the Irish kern mustered for service in England in 1544. Coming to the seventeenth century we have a Finglas mentioned several times in official correspondence of 1646 to 1648 and described as "lieutenant-colonel of the rebels" and four Co. Dublin men of the name were outlawed for their participation in the Rising of 1641. From that on they were less prominent and lost their status as large landowners; though a document of the Penal Code informs us that Andrew Finglass, 80 year old parish priest of Balrothery, was living at Tobertown, presumably on some portion of the ancestral property in 1698. They were to be found thenceforward in the professional and commercial classes and notably, too, in the ranks of the established clergy.

(O) FINNERAN Ó Finntighearn occurs in the Leinster section of O'Dugan & O'Heerin's Topographical Poem as chief of Uí Mealla, the location of which O'Donovan was unable to determine. All records of the past century or so find the modern form Finneran in Counties Galway and Roscommon, so that we may perhaps assume that Uí Mella was in the part of Leinster nearest thereto, viz. Westmeath.

FINUCANE Woulfe makes this name Ó Fionnmhacháin and says it is a rare Munster name of which he can find no early form. It is found chiefly in Co. Clare, where the form Kinucane is recorded as having been used synonymously with Finucane. This suggests that it is a Mac not an O name viz. Mac Fionnmhacháin or Mac Fhionnmhacháin.

FITZELLE Now found mainly in Dublin and Kerry it was formerly numerous in Ulster: the name occurs eleven times in the Antrim Hearth Money Rolls (1669) with a few more in adjacent counties. In Kerry it is used as a synonym of the Palatine name Fizzell.

(O) FLAHAVAN, Flavahan Flavahan might well have been included in Appendix F. of Irish Families since it belongs almost exclusively to west Waterford and the adjoining part of Co. Cork. There also are found the variants Flahavin, Flavahan and – in east Cork and west Waterford – Flavin. It is not very numerous now, but a century ago Griffith's Valuation recorded 46 householders in Co. Waterford, and three centuries earlier fourteen O'Flahavans of the same locality are to be found in the Elizabethan Fiants.

(O) FLANNELLY Though located in Co. Mayo, not far from one of the septs of O'Flannery (Ó Flannabhra, dealt with in Irish Families, p. 147) Flannelly (Ó Flannghaile) is quite distinct from Flannery. Owing to the similarity of the names and also to the proximity of their location Flannelly and Flannery have inevitably become to some extent interchangeable in common usage. Flannelly was first anglicized O'Flanhill and O'Flanill, and it so occurs in the sixteenth century Fiants at Rosserk, Co. Mayo, and also at Kilglass nearby in Co. Sligo. The Four Masters record the death of Ó Flannghaile (i.e. O'Flannelly), vicar of Skreen, in 1395. Skreen is in Tireragh, the Sligo barony adjoining Tirawley in Mayo, the homeland of the sept.

Dealing with the barony of Tirawley Strafford's Inquisition of Co. Mayo found an O'Flannel there in 1636 and according to the Book of Survey and Distribution for Co. Mayo the name so spelt was there also in 1655.

By 1793, when a local census was taken, the name had been standardized as Flannelly, 17 families so called being then resident in Ballinrobe parish alone. Map.

(O) FLATLEY   (O) FLATTERY These two names are said to be basically the same, originally Ó Flaithfhileadh in Irish, this being contracted to Ó Flaithile and Ó Flaitile anglice Flatley. O'Donovan's suggestion that this is in turn was corrupted to Flattery is no doubt sound up to a point. It would appear, however, that while the two names are to a large extent synonymous they represent nevertheless at least two distinct septs. We must not overlook the authority of the Four Masters in whose Annals the name Ó Flaithre occurs four times in entries relating to Ulster between 971 and 1166, the men in question being termed King of Ulidia and Lord of Lecale; while in the same early period we find Ó Flaithfhileadh in Offaly. Now Offaly is the part of the country with which the name Flattery is chiefly associated – in the "census" of 1659 it is returned as a principal Irish name in three different baronies of King's County (Offaly). In modern times Flatley is numerous in north Connacht where the O'Flatleys of Moy were one of the Hy Fiachrach septs and Carrowflatley is a place in Co. Sligo. Flattery is also found there as well as in Offaly. At the present time both names are found in Co. Galway and Mr. P. J. Kennedy informed me that there Flattery is definitely a corruption of Flatley, the former being now the more numerous.

Further confusion may arise from the fact that in some old records O'Flattery has been equated with O'Flaherty through clerical error.   Map

FLOYD Floyd has been used in Ulster sometimes as a synonym of Flood, but it is normally a variant of Lloyd, the Welsh Ll being pronounced Hl, an attempt at phonetic spelling which easily became Fl. Floyd is not a numerous name: it is mainly found in Munster. It is derived from the Welsh word llwyd, meaning green.

(O) FOLAN The extent to which this name is confined to Connacht is illustrated by the birth registrations: 63 were recorded in 1866, 62 of which were in Co. Galway; in 1890 the number was much less, only 28, but 23 of these were in Co. Galway and the other 5 in Co. Mayo. Disregarding the metropolitan area of Dublin, which of course comprises families from all the provinces of Ireland, this concentration of the name in Connacht still obtains. Woulfe, who is usually reliable, states that the name is Mac Fualláin in Irish; but I think in this case he is wrong, and that it should be Ó Fualláin. It is true that in one case in a Fiant of 1584 relating to Co. Galway the name MacFolane appears, but this is the only instance I have met of it, whereas O'Folane is frequent: in a Fiant of 1577 an area in Co. Roscommon called Grange O'Folan is specifically termed O'Folan's country. O'Folan and O'Fallon have been much confused in records: "O'Folan's country" was in Co. Roscommon, "O'Fallon's country" in Co. Galway. In the Composition Book of Connacht eight years later several O'Folanes of Co. Galway are mentioned. While the evidence in this respect is convincing it is easy to be misled in another direction because O'Phelan (in Irish Ó Faoláin) was often entered in early mediaeval records as Offolan and later as Follon, Follan etc., e.g. in Petty's "census", thus giving the impression that Folane is a Waterford or Kilkenny name. A good example of this is to be seen in the person of the Bishop of Limerick (1489-1521) whose name is given by Canon Begley as John Folan alias Whelan (Whelan, as stated in Irish Families, is the same as Phelan). Eugenius O'Folan, Bishop of Kilmacduagh from 1409 to 1418 and subsequently Bishop of Killaloe, was no doubt of the Ó Fualláin sept.

(O) FORAN   FORTUNE   Ó Furtháin, now Ó Fuaráin, was first anglicized as O'Forhane etc., which was subsequently contracted to Foran and unfortunately sometimes changed to Ford. Ford or Forde, however, is usually of quite different origin (see Irish Families, pp. 150, 151). Forhan and Fourhane are still extant in the country between Millstreet (Co. Cork) and Killarney; Foran is fairly common in Limerick and Waterford, the latter county being that in which it appears earliest, though it occurs occasionally in the sixteenth century in some parts of Leinster also. The most notable of this sept was Most Rev. Nicholas Foran who was Bishop of Waterford and Lismore from 1837 to 1855. Lawrence Foran was one of the eighteenth century Irish scribes in Co. Waterford. He compiled the Book of Portlaw in 1780.

O'Donovan in his edition of the Four Masters states that Ó Foirtchern, the leader of the Ossory men who slew the son of the King of Leinster in 1175, was of a family whose name was subsequently anglicized Forehan and Foran. O'Donovan is usually right, but in this case I think he made a mistake and that Ó Foirtchern is the original form of the well known Wexford surname Fortune, which is almost peculiar to that county. This appears in 1253 in a letter from Henry III to the Irish Judiciary as Offorthiern and was later anglicized as O'Fortyn etc. In this connexion it should be added that the Irish Fairsing has been made Fortune in English as well as Farshin, both of these being found as synonyms of MacCarthy in the Dunmanway district. Fairsing is the Irish word for generous and is used as a rare surname of the epithet class. It is quite unconnected with the Fortunes of Co. Wexford.   Map

FORESTALL   This name, of which Foristal, Forristal, Forestal and Forrestal are variants in use today, is not found in England except in the case of families which migrated from Ireland. It is, however, of English origin and is considered to be a variant of the surname Forester. The Forstalls, as they were usually called until modern times, may be classed as Anglo-Norman since they came to Ireland shortly after the Invasion and were prominent in the activities of their new homeland from the thirteenth

century. They appear very frequently in all mediaeval records dealing with the counties of Kilkenny and Wexford and also in Co. Kildare, where Geoffrey, William and Patrick le Forstal were living in 1297. They are occasionally described as de Forrestal but I think this de is a clerical error for le. Not only did they become fully hibernicized; they also multiplied exceedingly and by the middle of the seventeenth century they were recorded by Petty as among the principal Irish inhabitants of the baronies of Ida, Knocktopher and Fassadinin in Co. Kilkenny, Bantry and Shelbourne in Co. Wexford and Cullenagh (Queen's Co. i.e. Leix). There were four main branches of the Forrestall family seated respectively at Forrestallstown, Carrickloney, Kilbride and Mullinahar, all in the southern part of Co. Kilkenny. The most distinguished of the family, Dr. Mark Forstall O.S.A., Bishop of Kildare and Leighlin from 1676 to 1683, was especially praised by St. Oliver Plunket in his correspondence with the Holy See: he had previously been a man of note in Vienna. Four of the name appear in the list of Irish Jacobites attainted or outlawed after 1691.

Having regard to its numerical strength in the seventeenth century it is remarkable that the name is comparatively rare now.   Map

FOYLE   Though apparently Irish — perhaps through association with the Ulster lough and river and other Irish place-names so called — as a surname Foyle is not Irish in origin, but is derived from the French fouille (excavation) and first appears in mediaeval England as Atte Foyle. As Foyle and Foyll it occurs in early Dublin city records at least once in the thirteenth century and quite frequently in the fourteenth but less often in the fifteenth and sixteenth: throughout that period the family had continuous association with the parish of St. Werburgh's. In the nineteenth century it was well established in Queen's County (Co. Leix) particularly in the neighbourhood of Abbeyleix: there are 14 Foyle householders in Griffith's Valuation for that county (1855). It is now rather rare.

The name O'Foyle occurs once in the Co. Antrim Hearth Money Rolls of 1664. As I have met no other instance of this apparently Gaelic form I think it may be a mistranscription of O'Fryle, an early anglicized variant of O'Friel.

(O) FRAHER, Farraher   These two names are basically the same, both being anglicized forms of the Gaelic-Irish Ó Fearchair. Farraher is almost peculiar to counties Galway and Mayo while Fraher is mainly found in counties Waterford, south Tipperary and Limerick. Fraher appears to be a comparatively modern form: a county Limerick family is given as O'Farragher in a Fiant of 1601, and the Co. Tipperary Hearth Money Rolls of 1666-67 have a number of Farrahers but no Fraher. Neither occurs in any of the usual sources such as the Four Masters, An Leabhar Muimhneach, Ormond Deeds, Prerogative and Diocesan will abstracts, nor were they numerous enough to be included in the 1659 "census" summary (from which it must be remembered Co. Galway is missing). The earliest reference to the name I have found is to Thomas O'Fareghyr, of Cahirduggan in north Co. Cork, who in 1307 suffered distraint, having given pledge for a man who absconded: in another document relating to the same case his name is spelt O'Ferther. The register of the householders in Ballinrobe, Co. Mayo, made by Father Francis Xavier Blake in 1783, includes seven families of Farraher. Modern birth registrations, which are officially recorded from 1864, indicate that that area and north Galway are still their homeland, while those for Fraher also confirm the statement as to locality made above.

Other recorded anglicizations of the name are Harragher and Raher. The latter is extant in Co. Waterford.

(O) FRAHILL (O) FREHILL These two names are quite distinct. Both, according to Woulfe, are metathesized forms of better known names: Frahill (Ó Freathail) of Farrell, and Frehill (Ó Frithil) of Friel. Frahill belongs to west Munster, while Frehill, also spelt Freghill, is principally found in Co. Mayo. Fraul is a corrupt form of Frahill.

FRAIN, Freyne, Freeney The earlier form of the names given above is de la Freigne (with many variant spellings) and as such it repeatedly occurs in every collection of documents relating to counties Kilkenny and Tipperary from the year 1302 when Fulk de la Freigne was seneschal of Kilkenny, an office held frequently by members of the family, as was the similar post in Co. Tipperary. The form used in mediaeval deeds in Latin is usually de Fraxineto. It is thus etymologically akin to the better known surname French: Latin fraxinus, French frêne (ash). The surname of the Barons de Freyne, of Frenchpark, Co. Roscommon, is French (see Irish Families, p. 152).

Freney, to which numerous references appear in the Elizabethan Fiants for counties Kilkenny, Tipperary, Waterford and Wexford, and in the Hearth Money Rolls for Co. Tipperary in 1666, does not seem to have been used before the sixteenth century, though I should mention that the name of the treacherous Linebéd a Frende, who betrayed O'Connor Faly in 1419, is equated by William Hennessy, in his notes to the Annals of Loch Cé with the modern Freyne or Freney. The latter, of course, is very well known on account of the exploits of the celebrated Co. Waterford character James Freney, whose career as a highwayman modern commentators think was less glamorous and heroic than popular tradition suggests. His autobiography, written about 1750, is a remarkable document. In later life he received a pardon and settled down as a respectable minor official at New Ross. Freney of Ballyreddy is recorded as one of the chief gentlemen of the barony of Ida (Co. Kilkenny) in 1608. Later in the same century the Book of Survey & Distribution shows Freneys to have been old proprietors in that barony. James Freeney, of Ballyreddy, was

one of the prominent people attainted after the Jacobite defeat.

Frain (Frayne etc.) is now more numerous than Freeney. The former is most often met with in Mayo and Roscommon; while Freeney, scarce in its mediaeval homeland, is chiefly found in Dublin. Mother Ursula Frayne (d. c. 1886), notable for her work with missionary priests in Canada and Australia a century ago, was from Co. Carlow.

There is much information relating to families of Frayne in Carrigan's History of the Diocese of Ossory.

FRAME Though nowhere numerous even in England, and in Ireland not associated with any particular locality, the name Frame is on record in this country since the sixteenth century when one Robert Frame of Carrick-on-Suir was in the employment of the Earl of Ormond and in 1577 was a lessee on the Ormond estate. We meet it again 1664, this time in Co. Armagh where John Frame was a householder at Derrycughan, and twice in the Donegal Hearth Money Rolls of the next year. A little later we find them in Cork, as three marriage licence bonds (the first is 1700) and wills of 1719 and 1726 attest. In the next century they are located in various parts of Ulster and in our own time the name has been prominent in the industrial life of Dublin.

(O) FRAWLEY Woulfe's statement that Frawley (Ó Freaghaile) is a metathesized form of O'Farrelly is correct but he gives no further information about these names. In Irish Families (p. 140) I mentioned that a century ago O'Donovan commented on the fact that the Co. Limerick sept of O'Farrelly had disappeared from that county. It is true that the name in that form is no longer there but as Frawley it is numerous there, and even more so in the neighbouring county of Clare. The change from Farrelly to Frawley dates from the seventeenth century, Fraly and Frally being the usual forms in the eighteenth; many testators so called are in the diocesan wills for Killaloe and Limerick and in rentals such as that of Lord Kenmare's Co. Limerick estate.

FRIZELL Woulfe devotes eleven lines to this name but beyond stating that it appears (as Fresel) in Dublin in 1216 gives little information. He derives it from Norman Frisel i.e. native of Friesland. Weekley, an authority on British surnames, says that the root word is A-S. frithu (peace) and describes as "unaccountable" the change from Frizell to Frazer which has undoubtedly occurred quite often in Scotland: it would appear to be simply a case of attraction, of which we have so many examples in Ireland (e.g. Blowick to Blake, Sullahan to Sullivan etc.).

Families of the name were early established in Munster and the Justiciary, Patent and Chancery Rolls record a number of cases in which they are concerned between 1295 and 1305. There was, for example, a dispute between two Freisels regarding their property at Freisels-town in Co. Limerick in 1297, and the same year Nicholas Freysel was excommunicated by the Bishop of Cork in circumstances which appear extraordinary by modern standards. Nearly all these many early mediaeval references are to Cork city and county – in the former Freyzel's Castle was still so called in 1519, but it was no longer the property of that family. Later the name became scattered. Its distribution in the seventeenth century, when it was chiefly found in Antrim and adjacent counties, suggests that it had then almost died out in Munster – there was one family of Frizell in Kerry in 1901 – and that quite different families of the name had subsequently settled in Ulster. Modern statistics indicate that it is now associated with north Connacht as well as Co. Tyrone. The Arthur O'Frizil mentioned in Knox's History of Mayo as appointed Archbishop of Tuam by the Pope in 1536 may be disregarded as he was an O'Friel, the Gaelic G having been mistaken for Z.

FULLAM   This is an old Dublin name. It has been in Co. Dublin continuously since the thirteenth century when John de Fullam held land at Swords in 1294. The family was still there in 1519 when Simon Fullame, yeoman, of Swords, obtained a "pardon". The numerous wills and other records in which we meet Fullams in the seventeenth and eighteenth centuries indicate that they were for the most part merchants in the city of Dublin or farmers in its vicinity, though not confined to Co. Dublin, as the sixteenth and seventeenth century Leinster inquisitions testify. One of the former, Patrick Fullam "woollen draper", was a member of the Dublin United Irishmen in 1793.

FULLERTON   This, like MacCloy, is a sept of the clan Stuart of Bute, Fullarton being a town in Scotland. Fullertons are numerous in Ulster, particularly in Antrim and Down. In the birth registrations for 1865, 23 are recorded (17 spelt Fullerton and 6 Fullarton) 19 of these being in Ulster; in 1890 the returns were much the same – 25 births, 22 in Ulster, mostly in Antrim and Down. According to Burke the founder of the best known family of the name in this country was Nicholas Fullerton, of Drummond, Co. Derry, whose nephew Col. Adam Fullerton acquired more property in the same county. Burke also states that the first of the family in Ireland was Fergus Fullerton who came from Scotland in the reign of James I. The earliest of note was James Fullerton who first appears on the Irish scene as master of the Free School, Dublin, in 1588 when he taught James Ussher: he was one of the first Fellows of Dublin University. He later became a commissioner for the Plantation of Ulster in 1607 and died in 1631. I presume this is the same James Fullerton who got a grant of the Wardenship of Youghal College, with the lands appertaining to it, in 1603. A James Fullerton is also mentioned in a Fiant of 1593 as standing bond for a number of Roscommon men in that year.

(O) FUREY, Feore   According to Woulfe the modern Irish form of Furey is Ó Fiodhabhra; in the Annals of Loch Cé it is given as Ó Furreidh and the Four Masters spell it Ó Foirreith. In any case it can be accepted that the sept was early located in the barony of Clonlonan, Co. Westmeath, and was a branch of the royal O'Melaghlins. They were still there in 1659 in considerable numbers, but by the end of the sixteenth century families of the name had already crossed the Shannon and settled in east Galway, where they are mainly located today. It is seldom indeed found elsewhere, though a few are still in Westmeath. Feore is the anglicized form of a variant of the same Irish surname: O'Feore appears in a Westmeath Fiant of 1578. It is rare now, but there are some families of the name in Co. Limerick.

The sept has produced several distinguished churchmen, the most notable of whom was Donat Ó Fidhabhra (d. 1237) who was successively Bishop of Clogher and Archbishop of Armagh. Magnus Ó Fiodhabhra O.F.M. (d. 1591) of the convent of Multyfarnham was one of the earlier Irish Catholic martyrs.

The name has been somewhat oddly changed to Fleury in the Ballymahon area. For Ferry, Feery etc., distinct surnames, see under Feighry and Fergus.   Map

FURLONG   According to Bardsley this name, of English origin, is derived from the word furlong which formerly had the meaning of an unenclosed field. Reaney develops this, showing that in the fourteenth century it had acquired the meaning of the Latin stadium, the surname being first Atte Furlong. Families of the name were settled in Co. Wexford at least as early as 1343, when eleven Furlongs took part in a military expedition against O'Brien of Thomond; and since then they have been numerous and influential in that county and neighbouring districts of Co. Kilkenny, though seldom found in other parts of Ireland. Furlongstown in Co. Wexford is named after them, but their principal seat was at Horetown. In one Fiant listing many pardons in the year 1559 no less than twelve Furlongs are named, of different places in Co. Wexford, ranking from gentlemen to kern; and in another of 1572 Matthew Furlonge is indicted for his "open rebellion" in the same county. No doubt he was one of those Furlongs officially described about the same date as "malefactors matched with the Cavanaghs."

In modern times three Furlongs have been notable as poets: Thomas Furlong (1794-1827), Mary Furlong (1868-1898) and Alice Furlong (c. 1870-1945).

An interesting sidelight on the position of the Irish language as the vernacular towards the end of the eighteenth century is afforded by the cancellation in 1764 of the appointment of Father Peter Furlong as guardian in the Irish College of Lille, because he could not speak Irish, which was the habitual language of the students.
Map

FURPHY   The surname Furphy is very rare. It occurs occasionally in the birth registers for Co. Armagh. Professor M.A. O'Brien suggested to me that it is probably Ó Foirbhthe, derived from the adjective foirbhthe, meaning complete or perfect. It is of interest because a tenant farmer of the name from Tanderagee, Co. Armagh, emigrated to Australia in 1840 and in so doing added a word to current Australian speech, "furphy", there signifying a rumour without foundation. Actually the word is derived from his son Joseph Furphy who was also known by his nom-de-plume, Tom Collins. Joe was not himself a disseminator of rumours, but the water-carts his firm manufactured, which were in use all over the country and were called "furphies", were frequently the meeting place of gossips.

FYAN The name Fyan is on record in Dublin since the fifteenth century: John Fyan was mayor in 1472 and 1479, and others of the family were later mayors and altermen of the city, one of whom was outlawed as a Jacobite, though this outlawry was later reversed. From them was named Fyan's Castle (subsequently renamed Proudfoot's Castle) on the Quays: it would appear that like many successful merchant families the Fyans became in due course landed gentry, for two townlands in Co. Meath are called Fyanstown. Woulfe gives Faghan for Fyan, and treats Paghan (Poyne, Pyne) and Phaghan (Fyans, Foynes) and even the better known Fagan as variants of the one name, deriving them all from the Latin paganus. He makes a slip in stating that Fyans occurs several times in the list of mayors of Limerick in the thirteenth and fourteenth centuries, for the mayors in question were named Poines.

As Fyans the name survives in small numbers in Dublin and neighbouring counties.

(O) GAHAN, Gaughan, Gavaghan   (O) GEEHAN, Guihen   MacGEEHAN, MacGahan   WYNNE, (O) Mulgeehy
As in the case of Crehan (q.v.) we have in Gahan and variants a name about which confusion is apt to arise. Gahan is used as the anglicized form of three distinct Irish surnames, which are quite different in the original Gaelic.

First there is Ó Gaibhtheacháin, shortened now to Ó Gacháin, the name of a sept of the north Connacht Hy Fiachrach who possessed a territory situated around Crossmolina, Co. Mayo. The Annals mention them frequently as chiefs of Calry (or half Calry), barony of Tirawley in that county. The usual spelling of this particular Gahan is Gaughan; the statistics of 1866 show 34 of the 35 Gaughan births in Co. Mayo (the Belmullet area predominating) the other being in Co. Sligo, while nearly all the Gahans were in east Leinster. The 1890 summary indicates that practically no change had taken place in the intervening period. Gavahan or Gavaghan (which is more or less a phonetic rendering of the older Irish form given above) is also a synonym of Gaughan in Co. Mayo.

The sept called Ó Gaoithin anglicized Geehan, Guihen and sometimes Gahan, also belongs to north Connacht. This was originally located in Co. Roscommon. A sept of the same name, now called Gahan, is associated with the

country of the Wicklow-Wexford border: Ballygahan, near Arklow, perpetuates this association.

Ó Gaoithín must be distinguished from Mac Gaoithin which is anglicized as MacGeehan, Mageean etc., and is found principally in Co. Donegal. In that area MacGahan is synonymous with MacGeehan; but MacGahan is usually found in Co. Louth and the adjacent Ulster counties where the Irish form is said to be Mac Eacháin.

Another Tirconnell (Donegal) name which may add to the confusion is Ó Maolghaoithe, i.e., O'Mulgeehy of Clondavaddock, for this has almost universally become Wynne (from the word gaoth, wind, embodied in it) and even Wyndham. The cause of confusion here is not apparent at first sight: it arises from the fact that each of the Gaelic surnames mentioned, except Ó Gaibhtheacháin, has in some places become Wynne. In this connexion I may mention that Wynne has also been used as a synonym of MacGee in Co. Cavan and occasionally also as a variant of the Welsh Gwynn.

The Wynnes of Co. Sligo derive their name from Gwynn. Coming from Wales in the seventeenth century Owen Wynne was High Sheriff of Co. Leitrim in 1659, and two centuries later another Owen Wynne of Hazelwood owned over 18,000 acres in counties Sligo and Leitrim. Just a century earlier yet another Owen Wynne of Hazelwood was notable for his progressive agriculture. Father Wynne O.P. was remarkable for his missionary work in the Western Isles of Scotland, from which he was finally driven by the laird in 1774. All the many Wynnes appearing in the Dictionary of National Biography were Welsh or English: it might well have included Florence Wynne who was responsible for the establishment of the first tuberculosis hospital in Ireland in 1891.

Finally I may add that Wynne can also be a modern form of the earlier de Vin, which occurs in lists of Irish names in the seventeenth century, e.g. in the Franciscan records printed in Liber Lovaniensis.

Father William Gahan O.S.A. (1730-1804) is remembered not only as the author of devotional works but especially for his trial and conviction in connexion with the reconciliation to the Church of Dr. John Butler (of the Dunboyne Maynooth Foundation) sometime Catholic Bishop of Cork.   Map

MacGAHEY   (Mac) GAFFEY   According to Woulfe MacGahey (with its variants MacGaughy etc.) is Mag Eachaidh in Irish, this being another form of Mag Eochadha (MacGeough) which in turn is etymologically akin to Mac Eochadha (Mac Keogh). MacGahey is definitely an Ulster name and its location is approximately the same as that of MacGeough. Woulfe regards Gaffey as another variant of MacGahey. It is certainly not used as a synonym: Gaffey belongs almost exclusively to the country around Athlone. The Gaffeys cannot be regarded as one of those septs which migrated from Ulster to Connacht in the wake of the O'Donnells in the early seventeenth century since they did not come from Donegal nor did they settle in north Connacht. O'Dugan in the Topographical Poem mentions a sept called Mac Gaibhidh whose location in Connacht O'Donovan was unable to determine, but as the poet describes their habitat as a land of fruit it was clearly not in Connemara or on the Atlantic coast. I think, therefore, that we may regard the Gaffeys as a distinct south Connacht sept whose name in Irish is Mac Gaibhidhe.

MacGAHERN   Though MacGauran has frequently been recorded as a modern synonym of MacGahern and though both belong by origin to the same part of the country – Co. Cavan – these names are basically quite distinct. MacGahern is Mag Eachráin in Irish and this is also anglicized MacGaughran, with or without the prefix Mac. The cognate Irish form Mac Eachráin – anglicized Mac Cahern etc. – is also found occasionally.

GAMBLE   Though English in origin and in Ireland only since the seventeenth century Gamble is sufficiently numerous to merit a place in a work on Irish families – 40 births were registered in 1890 and 48 in 1865. The great majority of these were in north-east Ulster. The name first appears here in the Ulster inquisitions in Co. Armagh (1618) and Co. Cavan (1629); it is in the army lists of the 1640s; two Gambles are specified in Petty's "census" of 1659, one a merchant in Derry, the other in Cork city. The Hearth Money Rolls for the northern counties (1663-9), contain 18 Gamble families: and the Cork marriage licence bonds have the name 13 times from 1670. Those in Munster gradually died out though a few remain, but in Ulster the reverse was the case, as any modern directory or voters' lists show. The principal landed family was in Kilooly in Co. Offaly: de Burgh lists four others, all in Ulster. John Gamble (c. 1770-1831) was an author who wrote some admirable descriptions of life in his native Ulster.

Gamble, with its variants Gambell, Gammel and Gamel, is derived from the Old-Swedish gamal (old).

GARLAND, Gernon   Though there is an English surname Garland (of dual derivation – from garth land or a nickname) in Ireland it is a synonym of Gernon, which it has almost entirely superseded. Gernon is, according to Reaney, itself in the nickname category, from Old-French grenon or gernon, a moustache. The transition from Gernon to Garlan and thence to Gartlan is curious – the final d is intrusive (like Bolan-Boland) – but that it took

place is indisputable: thus, to give but two of many examples, Roger Gernon, sheriff of Co. Louth in 1578, was known both officially and colloquially as Gernon and Garland, and the well-known Patrick Gernon of Gernonstown is described in a deed in 1642 as Patrick Garland of Garlandstown. The Gernons of Gernonstown, Co. Meath and Killincoole Castle, Co. Louth, descend from Roger de Gernon, who accompanied Strongbow in the Anglo-Norman invasion of 1172; and this suggests that in that case Gernon was a French place-name. Other examples of the use of this de occur in such records as the thirteenth and fourteenth century Justiciary Rolls, so it is unlikely that de is a substitution for le, as has happened quite often with other surnames. In the Dowdall Deeds, which deal with counties Louth and Meath from the thirteenth century, the variants Gernon, Garnon, Gernin, Gearlon, and Garland occupy nearly two columns of the index. In the 1598 manuscript preserved at Clongowes we meet Gerlone and Gerlonstown as well as Garland of Garlandstown and Garland of Killincoole. The Co. Armagh Hearth Money Rolls have Gernon and Garnan but no Garland. Similarly the Jacobite outlawries, which include eleven members of this family, are all in the name Gernon not Garland. Occasionally we find the form MacGartlany and O'Gartlany, e.g. in the Co. Monaghan Hearth Money Rolls of 1663-5 (in which Gartlan and Gernon also appear): presumably these Gaelic prefixes are not authentic, for many examples can be cited of their addition to non-Gaelic names. MacGartland and MacGartleny are, however, still found in Co. Tyrone. The main location of the Garlands in modern times is around Carrickmacross, in Co. Monaghan, near the border of counties Louth and Meath. The Franciscan Anthony Gearnon (d. post 1667) author of "Parrthas an Anma" was an Irishman, but Luke Gernon (d. 1673), who was appointed judge in Munster in 1619 and was the author of the treatise, A Discourse of Ireland, came to this country from England. According to Dr. Richard Hayes the Gernoons of Bordeaux are descended from Christopher Gernon of Drogheda.

(Mac) GARRAHAN   This family (Mag Aracháin in Irish) belonged originally to Lisgoole in Co. Fermanagh – an ecclesiastical family according to Woulfe; it has since moved southwards and westwards and is now mainly found in the adjacent counties of Cavan and Leitrim and also in Roscommon. As early as 1577 we find Owen MacGaraghan in a Co. Galway Fiant, but as he was a kern he was not necessarily a native of that county. The prefix Mac is fairly often retained with this name. Birth registrations indicate that it is also spelt Garahan, Garaghan and Garraghan, with and without the Mac.

(Mac) GARRAHER   Originating in Donegal this family migrated to Roscommon. Their name, Mag Fhearchar, is said to derive from fearchar, man dear. John Garragher, the blind travelling harper, taught Denis O'Hempsy, the musician. It is called Mac Garragher in the list of O'Donnell's followers in 1601. See Carraher.

(O) GATELY   Woulfe in a two line note on Ó Gatlaoich gives Keatley, Keitley and Keightley, as well as Gately, as the anglicized forms of it. There may have been a few isolated instances of this; but in fact Keightley and its variants are English names taken from a place in Yorkshire. None of them appears as a synonym of Gately in Matheson's lists. Birth registrations indicate that the few Keightley families in Ireland are almost all found in Ulster or Dublin; Gately on the other hand, the true modern form of Ó Gatlaoich, is peculiar to Co. Roscommon and adjacent areas, particularly the town and barony of Athlone. Any references to the name Gately I have met in records earlier than 1800 are to the part of the country mentioned above, e.g. to John Gately, a miller, of Ahascragh, in 1746. The fact that MacGattely, not O'Gattely, appears in the "census" of 1659 as one of the principal names in the barony of Athlone can be disregarded, as the clerks who compiled that document frequently confused these prefixes in the case of names beginning with C or G. Keightly references are fairly numerous owing to the prominence of the family of Lord Justice Thomas Keightley (c. 1650-1719): these, however, were definitely not of the Ó Gatlaoich sept: the family came to Ireland from Hertfordshire.

(O) GAVAN, Gavin   There were two entirely distinct septs called Ó Gabháin, of which Ó Gaibhín is a variant, and these spellings are reflected in the anglicized forms Gavan and Gavin. The prefix O, dropped in the seventeenth century, has seldom been resumed. One of these septs was a branch of the Corca Laoidhe, located in south-west Cork, as shown in the sept-map. These spread into other Munster counties. In 1428 we find Walter O'Gawane in Clonmel; in 1584 Gavin of Ballynerine, Co. Limerick, was "in rebellion"; eleven families of Gavan appear in the Co. Tipperary Hearth Money Rolls of 1665-7, about which time, according to Petty's "census", there were also six families near Mullingar. Though a few O'Gavan entries in the Fiants of a century earlier do relate to Westmeath that is an area with which they do not appear to have any historical connexion. These may have been of some unrecorded minor but distinct sept; or possibly they came from Connacht, though migration from Mayo to Westmeath was unusual. It is to Mayo the Gavans of the present day principally belong. Statistics of birth registrations in 1890 give 66 births for Ireland, 42 of which were in counties Mayo and Galway. A comparison with the 1864-1866 returns shows approximately the same preponderance of Connacht people. There are occasional references to the name in Mayo records of the seventeenth century. Rather surprisingly Gavan does not seem to have been used as a synonym of another Mayo surname, Gavaghan (q.v.).
Perhaps the most notable personality of the name was Father Cormac O'Gavane O.F.M. (d.1617) to whom there are many references in Analecta Hibernica No. VI. The conjunction of the name Gavan with Duffy was noticed in Irish Families (p. 131).   Map

(Mac) GAYNOR   (O) GERANE, Guerin   All the old

records agree in placing the territory of Mac Fhionnbhair, chief of Muntergeran, on the west side of Lough Gowna in the present county of Longford. Muntergeran is a shortened anglicized form of Muintir Geradhain and the eponymous ancestor of the family of Gaynor, or MacGinver as it was formerly more phonetically rendered, was Fionnbhair (Finbar) Ó Geradhain, who was lord of that area in the eleventh century. Writing a century ago O'Donovan found the normal anglicization then to be Maginver with the synonym Gaynor already coming into more general use. The Gin sound is preserved in the form MacGinty found synonymous with Gaynor in south Ulster. The latter, however, was no innovation as it appears as a principal name in Co. Westmeath in the "census" of 1659. Westmeath and Cavan, with both adjoin Co. Longford, are the counties in which the name is chiefly found today. The prefix Mac, as is often the case with names beginning with a vowel or aspirated F, becomes Mag, first in speech and later in the written word, so that Mag Fhionnbhair is now the normal form in Irish.
Woulfe identifies the Ó Geradhain mentioned above with Ó Géaráin, a Hy Fiachrach sept located in Erris (Mayo), and regards MacGinver (Gaynor) as an offshoot of it.
This sept of Ó Géaráin appears to be now almost extinct. There was another sept of the same name, anglicized O'Gerane and later Geran, which is listed among the principal names in that county in 1659. This survives there today as Guerin. Some of our Guerins, however, may be of quite different origin, Guérin being a French Huguenot surname.   Map

(Mac) GEANEY   (O) GEANEY, Gaine   From the second of these names the prefix O has been almost entirely dropped: the Gaelic-Irish form of it is Ó Geibheannaigh (see Keaveney): this Geaney has always been found mainly in counties Cork and Kerry, where the abbreviated variant Geane or Gaine is not uncommon. Early anglicized forms of the name were O'Giany etc. – Father Roger O'Giana, for example, was captured by the English in 1599 and thrown into Cork prison whence he managed to escape. The Mac prefix, on the other hand, has been usually retained. MacGeany, which is much less numerous than (O) Geany, and quite distinct from it, belongs now to south Ulster. Woulfe suggests as a possibility that MacGeany is an anglicized form of Mag Éanna which he says is a variant of Mac Éanna (i.e. MacKeaney): Mac Geibheannaigh might be considered more likely, but the only early anglicized from of this I have found, viz. MacGebenay, is the name of a man who obtained a "pardon" in 1590 in Co. Roscommon.

(O) GEARY, Guiry   When a branch of the sept Ó Gadhra migrated in the fifteenth century from north Connacht to west Munster the usual anglicized form O'Gara was dropped and they became Geary in counties Limerick and Kerry. Another Co. Limerick form is Guiry.

MacGETTIGAN, MacEttigan   The latter of the spellings given above is the more correct, since the G is carried over from the prefix Mag (=Mac) in the Gaelic Mag Eiteagáin. MacGettigan however is the usual form today. O'Donovan in his edition of O'Heerin and O Dugan's Topographical Poem states that the name, originating in the Tyrone end of Oriel and at first Ó hEitigen, became a Mac name by a common commutation. The Four Masters used both Mac and O: their earliest reference, under date 1132, is to Diarmid Mac Eitigen, Chief of Clann Diarmada (now Clondermot, Co. Derry). The name is said to be of Norse origin. The sept so called unquestionably belonged originally to that district, but they gradually moved westwards into Co. Donegal where the name is chiefly found today. The sept has produced many distinguished churchmen, including William O'Etigen (d. 1444) Bishop of Elphin, Tomás Ó hEidigein, Dean of Elphin (1487), Patrick MacGettigan, Bishop of Raphoe, from 1861 to 1870, when he became Archbishop of Armagh. It should be added that some authorities consider the O'Hetigans of Elphin to be distinct from the O'Hetigans, or MacEttigans of Oriel.

Two curious modern synonyms of the name Mac-Gettigan are recorded in Co. Donegal viz: Gaitens and Gattins. Gethin, on the other hand is now a synonym of it; the landed family of Gethin, of Co. Sligo, formerly of Co. Cork, is of Welsh origin: Reaney suggests that this name is derived from the Welsh word cethin meaning swarthy.

(O) GIBLIN   The chief distinction of the O'Gibellans, or Giblins to give the name its usual modern form, is in the ecclesiastical sphere. They are frequently mentioned in the Annals as priests, anchorites or brehons in the diocese of Elphin. The most noteworthy of these was Maurice O'Gibellan (d. 1328) who is described as "chief professor of the new law" i.e. the Brehon code as modified by Christianity. Hiw knowledge of Ogham is the subject of special mention.

The sept has remained undisturbed throughout the centuries and, apart from families which have settled in the metropolitan area of Dublin, are scarcely to be found at the present day outside their original habitat in Co. Roscommon and its immediate vicinity in Co. Mayo.

In Irish the name is written Ó Gibealláin.

It has been stated that some families of this sept have deplorably changed their name to Gibson.   Map

(O) GIBNEY   The name Gibney is fairly numerous in the counties of Meath and Cavan. Though it is that of an ancient Irish sept, there are few references to it in the early records. In 1574 Dionysius Gibney of Loughcrewe, Co. Meath, obtained a "pardon" and other sixteenth and seventeenth century references indicate that they were then located in Meath and Cavan. In Grace's regiment of James II's army there was a Thomas Guibenny, doubtless of the same family. In 1590 there was an Irgas MacGabenay of Ardcarne, Co. Roscommon, which is a considerable distance from Co. Cavan; but as Gibney is an O name (Ó Gibne in Irish) possibly this man was not a Gibney at all

but a MacGibbon. The Statistical Survey of Co. Meath, prepared for the Royal Dublin Society in 1802, contains much useful information about the Gibney family.

Dr. Matthew Gibney (1838-1925) is remembered perhaps less for his fine work in the diocese of Perth (Australia), of which he was bishop from 1887 to 1910, than for his courageous attempt to rescue the outlaw Ned Kelly from a burning building in which he lay seriously wounded. Actually in the incident mentioned, though some of the bushrangers lost their lives in the fire, Ned Kelly escaped from it. He was later captured and hanged. The extent of which Ned Kelly (1854-1880) ranks in Australia as a national figure of the Robin Hood type is not generally recognized. His father was a Tipperary man who was transported to Australia in 1841; his mother was a Cody, a relative of "Buffalo Bill". Sir John Gibney, physician to George IV, by his advocacy of the salutary effects of sea bathing, was largely responsible for the subsequent popularity of Brighton, till then a little known village, as a seaside resort.   Map

GILBEY   (O) GILBOY   Gilbey is a surname of dual origin. The majority of families so called are English, the name being derived from one of several place-names in England known as Gilbey or Gilby. It may also be a form of Ó Giolla Bhuidhe, which, however, is usually anglicized as Gilboy. There may be cases of Gilbey being used for Mac Giolla Bhuide (see MacKelvey). As one of the early anglicized forms was O'Gilvie it might be expected that it is the same as the Scottish Ogilvie. That, however, has no connexion with O'Gilvie (except occasionally when Ogilvie may have been made to look Irish, as in the case of Odell, written O'Dell): the Scottish Ogilvie is taken from a Scottish place-name, the Glen of Ogilvy in the County of Angus. This may be the origin of Oglebee, a name which occurs in the Antrim Hearth Money Rolls of 1669. Neil and Terlagh O'Gilevoy were among the followers of O'Donnell in 1602. Many Donegal families migrated to north Connacht soon after that, which probably accounts for the fact that Gilboy has in modern times been found mainly in Co. Mayo. The prefix O, now I think quite obsolete with this name, was retained by at least one family up to 1839, when the will of Robert O'Gilby was proved in the Derry Diocese. John Ogilby who was appointed Master of the Revels in 1661 and may be described as the founder of the modern Dublin theatre was not a native Irishman.

(Mac) GILCHRIST   This is Mac Giolla Chríost in Irish, i.e. son of the servant of Christ. In the "census" of 1659 it is returned as MacIlchrist among the principal Irish names in the three northern baronies of Co. Antrim and one titulado in that county is given as Gilcrist. Woulfe considers most of these Gilchrists of north Ulster (where the name is most numerous today) to be of Scottish origin. Certainly MacGilchrist is a sept of two Scottish clans, MacLachlan and Ogilvie. Be that as it may, there is no doubt that the Gilchrists of Co. Longford and north Connacht are true Gaelic-Irish in origin. The name appears in the modern birth registrations in many variant spellings, including Kilchrist in Co. Longford and Kilchrist and Kilcrist in Tyrone.

(Mac) GILDEA, Kildea   This name, which is Mac Giolla Dhé in Irish (i.e. son of the servant of God), is also called Kildea; in some places it has been corrupted to Gay, while in others by a curious semi-translation it has been changed to Benison. It is primarily a Tirconnell sept, but like so many of the followers of the O'Donnells some of its families migrated to Mayo, where, with Donegal, it is chiefly found today. Among the adherents of Rory O'Donnell in 1601 were Conor, Owen, Brien and Edmund MacGillegea, this being an early anglicization of the name in Co. Donegal. In 1624 Daniel Guilday was vicar-general of the diocese of Killaloe; as Gildea it is not unknown in Clare today. Ballykildea in Co. Clare and Bally-killadea in Co. Galway are presumably named from this sept. Sir James Gildea (1838-1920), co-founder of St. John's Ambulance Association, was born in Co. Mayo.

A peculiar fact, illustrating the way in which erroneous gaelicizations as well as anglicizations can arise, may here be mentioned. A boy called Holden when at school at St. Enda's, where the pupils were expected to use the Gaelic forms of their surnames, was told by Pádraig Pearse to call himself Mac Giolla Dhé, which has given currency, quite erroneously, to this equation. (For Holden see under Howlin.)

(O) GILGAN   As the prefix O is seldom retained with Gilgan it might be supposed that it is a variant of Mac-Gilligan, but in fact the two names are quite unrelated.

O'Gilgan, or O'Gilligan, i.e. Ó Giollagáin, is that of a small sept located in north Leitrim and Co. Sligo, far from the MacGilligan country.

(Mac) GILHOOLY   The family of Gilhooly, or Mac-Gillehowley as it was first anglicized, has been prominent in Leitrim and Roscommon since records have been kept. Three parish priests of Kiltoghert, Co. Leitrim, between 1461 and 1505 were named Gilhooly and, to come to modern times, another was bishop of Elphin eighty years ago. Teig MacGillgooly of Granard, Co. Longford, was a transplantee to Connacht in 1657. O'Donovan in his note to the Four Masters reference to one of the name under date 1243 says that the sept of MacGilhooly is an offshoot of that of O'Mulvey. Mac Giolla Ghuala is probably the earlier Gaelic form but Mac Giolla Shúiligh, which Woulfe treats as a corruption of the former, is of sufficient antiquity to appear in The Annals of Loch Cé. Apart from migrants to Dublin the name Gilhooly is seldom found outside Connacht but a branch was established at Ballynagally, Co. Limerick, in the eighteenth century.   Map

(Mac) GILLEECE   Gilleece is a variant form of the better known MacAleese (Mac Giolla Íosa) and is used as

such in Co. Fermanagh, MacAleese being more usual in Co. Derry and other parts of Ulster. The spellings Gilleese and Gillice are also found occasionally.

(Mac) GILLESPIE   Mac ANESPIE, Bishop
Gillespie is the usual modern form of the surname formerly written MacGillespick etc., in English and Mac Giolla Epscoip in Irish, the latter being Mac Giolla Easpuig in its modern form. The meaning of these words is "son of the servant or follower of the bishop." Aspig as a surname may be an abbreviation of this or merely a translation of the common English surname Bishop. Matheson's book Synonymes indicates that Clusby and Glashby are alternatives in Co. Louth and that Glaspey was used by one family in Westport who were formerly Gillespie.

Almost all the Gillespies etc., to be found in the Annals, Fiants, county and diocesan histories and other records were Ulstermen. Mac Giolla Epscoip was chief of Aeilabhra (barony of Iveagh, Co. Down) up to the end of the twelfth century; later the family appear as erenaghs of Kilraine (Killybegs, Co. Donegal). The leader of the Scots who slew Shane O'Neill in 1567 was William Gillespie. The Fiants and Petty's "census" indicate that the name was chiefly found in north Ulster in the sixteenth and seventeenth centuries, while in our own time the birth indexes show that it still is numerous in the same northern counties. Sir Robert Rollo Gillespie (1766-1814), born in Co. Down, had an adventurous and distinguished career as a soldier in India, where he was killed in action.

An allied name, MacAnespie, now rare or surviving as Bishop, is Mac an Easpuig (son of the bishop): it appears as MacNaspuk in the Red Book of Ormond in 1320, in the Four Masters (sub 1440) in Tirconnell, and in Perrot's Chronicle of Ireland (1584-1608) as MacEnespick, who was then accounted one of the leading men of Connacht and Thomond.   Map

(Mac) GILLIGAN   (O) GILLAN, Gillen
(O) GALLIGAN (Mac Gil) GUNN, MacElgunn
Although Gilligan and Galligan are properly quite distinct, one being a Mac name of Ulster and the other an O name of Connacht, they are dealt with together here because in practice, since the time these prefixes fell into disuse, they have been much confused, and many families originally O'Galligan have become Gilligan.

Mac Giollagáin, usually Gilligan to-day but sometimes MacGilligan or Magilligan, belongs to Co. Derry, where in the sixteenth and early seventeenth centuries their territory was known as MacGilligan's country and where Magilligan Strand is still a feature marked on modern maps. In 1608 Sir Arthur Chichester in an important official despatch mentions the MacGilligans as one of the three chief septs of Co. Coleraine (Derry) under the O'Cahans – the others were O'Mullane and MacCluskey. The parish of Tamlaght Ard, Co. Derry, was in the sixteenth century known as Ard MacGilligan. By the middle of the seventeenth century the Mac had already been widely discarded. The families we find entered in

Petty's "census" as Gillgon and Gillgun in Co. Fermanagh are Mac Giolla Ghunna, of whom was Cathal Buidhe Mac Giolla Ghunna, the eighteenth century Gaelic poet. This name is now usually abbreviated to Gunn; a century ago it was Gilgunn, Gilgunn and the variant MacElgunn, which was more usual a century ago, were at that time almost peculiar to west Ulster.

Galligan is chiefly found to-day in Co. Cavan, where it is undoubtedly often merely a synonym of Gilligan. O'Galligan appears also as O'Gilligan in the Fiants, chiefly in Connacht but with a few in Clare and Limerick. This is Ó Gealagáin in Irish, originally the patronymic of a sept of the Uí Fiachrain in Co. Sligo; but in 1850, when O'Donovan wrote, the head of this family was called Gilligan not Galligan; he lived at Grange, in the barony of Carbury, Co. Sligo. Peter Galligan (1793-1860), a Co. Cavan schoolmaster, was a great collector of manuscripts: these are now preserved in the Royal Irish Academy, University College Dublin, Belfast Municipal Library and elsewhere.

It should be observed that the term Muintir Gilligan has no connexion with the sept of MacGilligan but denotes a clan or group of septs of whom the O'Quins of Co. Longford were the most important.

Woulfe draws attention to MacFirbis's statement that O'Gillan (Ó Giolláin) is an abbreviated from of O'Gilligan. If that is so it must be distinguished from Ó Gilín, which in its anglicized from of Gilleen is now very rare. O'Donovan, treating of Hy Fiachrain families, suggests that it may be synonymous with Killeen (q.v.), though I think this unlikely. Nineteenth century statistics show that Gillan was chiefly found in counties Sligo and Antrim, while Gillen was concentrated in north Ulster and as we know the distribution pattern is still substantially the same. Ó Gilín undoubtedly belongs by origin to north Connacht.

Enog Ó Gilláin translated a Latin life of St. Catherine into Irish in 1484.

Gillan is also found as a synonym of Gillilan (q.v. under MacCleland).   Map

GILLMAN   The reason for including this name here is its close association with one restricted area in west Cork and the extent to which an immigrant family has multiplied: their pedigree is on record for a long period before they came to Ireland. The first to do so took part in the Essex expedition of 1599. Though not so numerous now, in 1853, when Griffith's valuation of Co. Cork was carried out, he recorded no less than 73 Gillman householders or landowners in the western part of the county, the great majority of them in the barony of East and West Carbery. In this respect they are comparable to another rather similar family, the Kingstons. (q.v.).

The name derives from Guillemin, the diminutive of Guillaume, the French form of William.   Bibl.

GILMARTIN, Kilmartin   These two anglicized forms of Mac Giolla Mhartain (devotee of St. Martin), the sept being a branch of the O'Neills of Tyrone and Fermanagh, are equally numerous today, principally in east Connacht.

Both are among the principal Irish surnames in Co. Fermanagh in the 1659 "census".   Map

(Mac) GILMORE, MacIlmurray   There are a great many Gilmores in north-east Ulster and the name is also not uncommon in Connacht. The latter are no doubt descended from the Hy Fiachrain sept of Mac Giolla Mhir of Finnure in the parish of Skreen, Co. Sligo, mentioned by O'Donovan in his notes to The Tribes & Customs of Hy Fiachrain, who says that they were then (1844) called Gilmer and Gillmor. The Ulster sept of Mac Giolla Mhuire (son of the servant or devotee of Bl. Virgin Mary) is historically of considerable importance. Of the famous race of O'Morna, they took their surname from Mac Giolla Mhuire Ó Morna who died in 1276. He was chief of the name and lord of an extensive territory in north-east Ulster. At one time their sway extended over the baronies of Lecale, Castlereagh and Antrim and though they were reduced by the incursion of O'Neills, MacCartans, Whites and Savages, they continued (with the O'Neills) to be among the most consistent opponents of English aggression in Ulster up to the end of the fifteenth century. In the seventeenth century they were numerous in Co. Armagh being recorded there as MacGillamura and MacGilmoory as well as Gilmore.

Occasionally they were called O'Gilmore, in the "Book of Rights" for example. Patricius Palladius O'Gilmore is mentioned as a leading man in the parish of Bredagh in 1442 and Bagnall, in his Slender Description of Ulster (1586), says that the ancient proprietors of Great Ards in Down were the O'Gilmores, a rich and strong sept always followers of the O'Neills of Clandeboy. These, however, are merely isolated examples of the frequent confusion between Mac and O. Gilmore is quite definitely a Mac name. Even in the seventeenth century they were still to the fore: Charles Gilmore was a prominent member of the Confederation of Kilkenny in 1646 and Daniel Gilmore was an officer in Col. Felix O'Neill's regiment of James II's Irish army.

In quite recent times several people of the name have been noteworthy. Richard Gilmore (1824-1891), of Scottish ancestry, was in the forefront of the controversy relating to American Catholic schools in 1853; Patrick Sarsfield Gilmore (1829-1892) was a celebrated bandmaster and composer, whose daughter Marie Louise Gilmore was a patriotic poetess of some note.

Although the name Gilmore has little association with Munster it should perhaps be added that several references to MacGilmur and MacGilmor as owners of land, burgesses, and officials occur in documents relating to Co. Waterford as early as 1329 and as late as 1597.

Another anglicized form of Mac Giolla Mhuire is MacIlmurray (alias, MacElmurry, MacKilmurray, Kilmurry etc.). These variants, which are found in Ulster, are nowhere common.   Map

GILPIN   According to The Tribes & Customs of Hy Fiachrain, taken from the Book of Lecan, the sept of Mac Giolla Finn was located at Dromard in the barony of Tireragh, Co. Sligo: they are there described as a "noble comely-faced people". Assuming that the statement that this name was anglicized Gilpin is true, it is surprising to find it concentrated in modern times in Co. Armagh and the adjacent parts of Co. Cavan. In this connexion it should be observed that there is also an English name Gilpin, derived from a river in Westmoreland; and this is well known in England – there are six Gilpins in the Dictionary of National Biography, all of whom were English.

GILTRAP   The second syllable of this name – trap – is a form of the English word thorpe, and occasionally the surname is actually Gilthorpe. In East Anglia it also takes the form Gilstrap. In Ireland, though nowhere numerous, it is quite well known in the eastern counties from Dublin to Wexford. I have not found it on record here earlier than the latter part of the eighteenth century.

Mac GIMPSEY   The interesting thing about this name, the Irish form of which Woulfe gives as Mac Dhiomsaigh (derived from diomasach, proud), is the fact that it belongs almost exclusively to a small area in Co. Down around Newtownards. In 1865 there were 13 births registered for it and in 1866 there were 10: everyone of these 23 were in that registration district. In 1890, when there were 8 births registered, 7 of these were in Co. Down and one in Antrim. MacJimpsey occurs occasionally as a variant spelling. A man called MacGimpsey (his christian name is forgotten) was one of the heroes of the defence of Derry in 1689: he lost his life in a brave attempt to convey a message from the garrison by swimming the Foyle.

Mac GINLEY, Ginnell   Mac KINLEY
MacGinley and MacKinley are both numerous names in Ulster, the former, now as in the seventeenth century, belonging predominently to Co. Donegal, the latter being more widespread in that province. In spite of their similarity and proximity they do not appear to have been often used as synonyms. MacGinley is true native Irish. MacGinnelly is a spelling sometimes found and this is approximately how the Irish form Mag Fhionnghaile is pronounced: the initial G comes from the carry over of the last letter of the prefix Mag, which, as we have already noticed elsewhere, is a form of Mac used with names beginning with vowels or aspirated F. Reeves in his notes in the "Visitation of Derry Diocese" states that Ó Cionnfaolaidh was first anglicized O'Kynnele, which in time became MacKinely and MacGinley in Donegal and Tyrone; but this opinion is now discounted.
    MacKinley or MacKinlay on the other hand is usually of Scottish origin (Mac Fhionn Laoich); but it can also be Irish Gaelic viz: Mac an Leagha (son of the physician): Maelechlainn Mac an Leagha – anglicized MacKinley – (the death of whose son an "eminent" man in his own art, i.e. medicine, in 1531 is noticed in the Annals of Loch Cé) was the author, or perhaps only the transcriber, of an Irish medical manuscript now in the King's Inns Library, Dublin.
    The MacKinlays are mentioned as physicians in J. F. Kenney's list of famous families with whom hereditary professions are associated.
    MacGinleys have been chiefly notable as churchmen. The records of the diocese of Raphoe contain many clergy of the name including John MacGinly who was Bishop of the Philippines. Dr. John B. MacGinly (Consecr. 1922) was first Bishop of Monterey Fresno, California. Peter MacGinley (1857-1942) another Donegalman, better known perhaps by his pen-name Cú Uladh, was for many years a leading figure in the activities of the Gaelic League.
    The best known of the MacKinleys were the Presbyterian family of Conagher near Ballymoney, Co. Antrim. One of these was Francis MacKinley who was hanged for his part in the 1798 insurrection. William MacKinley (1843-1901), President of the United States, who was assassinated in his fourth year of office, was not (as has been stated) the direct descendant of Francis MacKinley but was of the same family, as also was John MacKinley (fl. 1819-1834), the Ulster poet.
    The surname Ginnell is akin to MacGinley being Mag Fhionnghail in Irish: it is the form used by the Donegal MacGinleys who settled in Co. Westmeath in the sixteenth century. It was well known during the lifetime of Lawrence Ginnell (1854-1928) M. P. for Westmeath, on account of his active participation in the cattle-driving campaign and his early support of Sinn Féin.

MacGINN   MacGinn and its composite form Maginn are approximately equally numerous and are now found respectively in counties Tyrone and Down. MacGinn, or MacGinne, is listed in the "census" of 1659 as a principal Irish name in the barony of Oneilland, Co. Armagh, i.e. the territory which lies between Tyrone and Down. The name is Mag Fhinn in Irish. This is anglicized MacGing, or Ging without the prefix, in the three Connacht counties of Mayo, Leitrim and Galway. In Mayo, according to Woulfe, the variant Mac Fhinn, which becomes MacKing, is also found, but if extant this is very rare. I have found no evidence to determine whether MacGing of Connacht is a branch of the Ulster sept.
    William Maginn (1793-1842) left Dublin in 1828 and became one of the foremost personalities in the literary and journalistic field in London. Edward Maginn (1802-1849), a Tyrone man, was coadjutor Bishop of Derry and a staunch supporter of the more extreme Nationalists of his time.

MacGIRL MacGARRIGLE   Variants of MacGirl are MacGarrell, MacGorl and MacGurl: all these are anglicized forms of Mac Fhearghail (which Woulfe says also has become MacCarroll – normally a different name, viz Mac Cearbhaill). Mac Fhearghaill is written Meg Fergail in the Annals of Loch Cé – one of the name was among the notable men slain by the O'Doghertys in 1196. This would suggest that the sept is of the Cenél Conaill, not a branch of the O'Farrells of Annaly but this may be the

111

modern MacGarrigle. The aspiration of the G gives the sound resulting in MacGarrell and the other forms given above. Unaspirated the same name becomes MacGarrigal, or MacGarrigle, hence the variants MacErrigle and even Cargill and Carkill. These latter are mainly associated with Co. Donegal: in 1659 MacGargill was listed in Petty's "census" as a principal Irish name in the barony of Tir-hugh. MacGirl, however, belongs in modern times to Leitrim and Cavan. None of these names is numerous.

MacGIRR   This is the most usual form of the name Mac an Ghirr and as such it belongs to Co. Armagh and the adjacent part of Co. Tyrone. In the former it occurs as a "principal Irish name" in the "census" of 1659 and it is also in the Hearth Money Rolls (1664) of that county; three families of the name also appear in the Hearth Money Rolls of Co. Monaghan. It was in Co. Armagh before the plantation of Ulster, recorded in 1602 as Mac-Eghir; as MacGhir and MacGerr we meet it in the Ulster inquisitions (Co. Tyrone) in 1628 and 1639; Shane Mac-Girr of Fintona, Co. Tyrone, was one of the Jacobites outlawed after 1690; and so to modern birth registrations which show Tyrone to be its location. These also indicate that the variant MacGeer is found in north Leinster. There are a few families of the name in Connacht but not enough to justify any form of it being regarded, with Woulfe, as belonging to that province. He mentions Short, Gayer and MacGarr as synonyms of MacGirr. Short is a semi-translation of Mac an Gheairr (Geárr, short, earlier giorr) sometimes used in Co. Tyrone; Gayer is very rare and usually unconnected with MacGirr, being a variant of the English toponymic Gare; MacGarr, when not an abbreviated form of MacGarry, belongs, like Mac-Geer, to north Leinster and it occurs in the 1659 "census" in Co. Westmeath (bar. Delvin).

GIRVAN   Woulfe suggests as a possibility that Girvan may be an anglicized form of Ó Gairbhín and a variant of the well known Munster Ó Garbháin (Garvan). No evidence to support this supposition is forthcoming, and I prefer the alternative suggestion that it came from Scotland as a toponymic formed from the place-name Girvan. The fact that Girvan and Girvin are exclusively Ulster surnames, mainly found in Co. Antrim, where they are quite numerous, would seem to coroborate this.

In Co. Armagh Garron has been reported as equated with Girvin — one of the many strange synonyms recorded by Matheson. That is no proof of etymological connexion and even if it were it would link Girvin with Garrahan (q.v.), an entirely untenable theory and in any case in no way supporting Ó Gairbhín as the Gaelic form.

(Mac) GIVEN   The fact that this was formerly often spelt Giveen corroborates Woulfe's statement that the Irish form is Mag Dhuibhín, a variant of Mac Dhuibhín, anglicized MacKevin and MacAvin. These are not names which occur frequently in our records but, apart from a few Dublin wills, Given and Giveen have been associated almost exclusively with northern Ulster (particularly Glenties in Co. Donegal), while MacAvin — much less numerous than Given — belongs to counties Donegal and Sligo. Thomas Givens (1864-1928), who was a prominent labour leader and President of the Australian Senate, was the son of a Co. Tipperary farmer, but the name is rare in Munster.

(Mac) GIVERN   In Irish Mac Uidhrin (derived from odhar, meaning dun-coloured). Strangely used as a synonym of both Biggar and Montgomery.   Map

Mac GIVNEY   Variants of this Co. Cavan name, also seldom found elsewhere, are MacEvinney, MacAvinue, MacGivena, Magivney etc. In the Annals of Loch Cé it appears as Mac Dhuibhne, in the person of Mathew Mac-Givney, Bishop of Kilmore, from 1286 to 1307, who they state died in 1314. The Four Masters give his name as Maguibhne; later they mention two other ecclesiastics as MacDhuibhne, John, arch-deacon of Drumlahan, 1343, and Farsithe (d. 1464) as Bishop of Kilmore, though the Handbook of British Chronology points out that he died without provision or consecration. MacDuibhne is the form used in Irish today. As Mac Avynny it is given in the "census" of 1659 as a principal Irish name in Co. Fermanagh. A notable modern member of the sept was Michael Joseph MacGivney (1852-1890) of Connecticut, son of an Irish exile, who founded the Knights of Columbus in 1882.

(Mac) GLADDERY   Mac GLADE   This name is found now and during the past century in the neighbourhood of Belfast, usually but not always with the prefix Mac and sometimes spelt MacGlathery. We know from The Tribes and Customs of Hy Many that it originated in Co. Galway, but there appears to have been a migration northwards, since it is now very rare in Connacht but extant in Co. Donegal. In Uí Maine the family was called Ó Gleadra as well as Mac Gleadra, and even in Ulster the O prefix was also sometimes used: an O Gleather is recorded in the Tyrone Hearth Money Rolls of 1664. O'Donovan considered O'Gladdery and MacGladdery to be quite distinct.

The use of MacGlade, which is quite numerous in the northern counties, as an abbreviated form of MacGladery has been officially reported from Co. Down to the Registrar-General. That is a definite fact. Woulfe, however, makes MacGlade Mag Léid: I have found no evidence to support his suggestion that it is an Irish variant of the Scottish MacLeod.

(Mac) GLASGOW   GLASSCOCK   According to Reaney, a reliable authority on British surnames, Glasgow is derived from the city of that name. Possibly some of the not inconsiderable number of people so called who reside in the northern counties of Ulster may be of that origin, but there is little doubt that Glasgow is also, and more usually, an anglicized form of Mac Bhloscaidh, (for

which see MacCloskey)especially in Co.Tyrone, the homeland of that sept. Glasgow does not appear ever to have
been used as a synonym of Glasscock, which was numerous in Co. Kildare in the seventeenth and eighteenth centuries. There were several officers named Glascoe in the
Irish Brigade during the century following the siege of
Limerick in 1691. This appears to have been a variant of
Glasscock not of Glasgow.

(Mac) GLORY   (O) GLORNEY   The early forms
O'Gloerne, O'Gloiairn and Gloryn occur fairly frequently
in mediaeval records relating to Co. Kilkenny, e.g. the
Justiciary Rolls and the Ormond Deeds. The first reference I have met is to one William O'Gloerne convicted as
"a felon" in Co. Tipperary in 1292; eight years later
several O'Gloernes ambushed an Englishman at Callan,
Co. Kilkenny. It is also in the famous Topographical Poem
of O'Dugan and O'Heerin: in a note to this O'Donovan
says this name, formerly anglicized Glory, was obsolete,
but this was not the case as four Glory householders
appear in Griffith's contemporary Valuation of Co.
Kilkenny and it is definitely stated by the editors of the
Journal of the Royal Society of Antiquaries in 1853 that
families of the name were then in Kilkenny city.

A more phonetic anglicization is Glorney, which is
also still extant in Munster and in Dublin. Although the
origin of Glory in mid-Leinster seems to be that given by
O'Donovan, Glory in the northern half of the country is
properly MacGlory, being derived from Mag Labhradha
(Lavery). This appears in our records somewhat later
than O'Gloerne and belongs to Ulster. The most interesting of such references is that to Donatus MacGlory
who "held a bishop's court before the O'Neill and the
Savage" in Lecale in 1447; another ecclesiastic of the
Archdiocese of Armagh is called in Swayne's Register
(1436) MacGlory alias MacClory. By the end of the sixteenth century the name was found south of the Ulster
border in Co. Meath and the "census" of 1659 tells us
that there were six families of MacGloyre (presumably a
form of MacGlory) in the city of Dublin at that date.
John Glorney was one of the Jacobites whose outlawry
was reversed on appeal in 1699: he is described as of Co.
Cork.

(Mac) GLYNN   (Mac) GLENNON   GLENN
MacGLOIN   The initial G of Glynn and MacGlynn
comes from the prefix Mag (a variant of Mac often used
with names beginning with vowels or aspirated F) the
Irish being Mag Fhloinn. The root word, as in the cognate surname Flynn, is the adjective flann, meaning
ruddy. At the present time Glynns and MacGlynns together number some four thousand of the population of
Ireland, in the proportion of about two to one, the
majority of the Glynns being found in the western
counties from Sligo to Clare. The main sept of Mag
Fhloinn originated in the Westmeath-Roscommon area,
whence they spread west of the Shannon and even as far
north as Donegal. Several priests of the name are notable
in the history of the diocese of Raphoe, and one of the
same stock was famous in America, viz. Dr. Edward Mac-

Glynn (1837-1900), the New York priest who was
suspended for his support of socialism and successfully
appealed to Pope Leo XIII against this sentence. Other
notable ecclesiastics were Rev. Bonaventure Maglin, who
was Franciscan vicar-provincial of Ireland in 1654; and
Rev. Martin Glynn (1729-1794) who, going from the
diocese of Tuam to France, became superior of the Irish
College at Bordeaux, of which he was the last rector, and
was guillotined during the French Revolution. The Mac-
Glynns (or Glynns) were well established in Mayo and
Galway in the seventeenth and eighteenth centuries as
the Books of Survey & Distribution, diocesan MSS and
other records testify; but the name was by no means
confined to the west even then: for example in 1617
James Glynn, one of the grand jurors of Co. Tipperary
was fined and imprisoned for refusing to present recusants. In addition to outstanding personalities of the
name already noticed, I may mention two pioneers of
the Gaelic cultural revival, viz. John Glynn (1843-1915)
and Joseph Glynn (1865-1907); and Martin Henry
Glynn (1871-1924) the son of humble Irish parents who
became Governor of New York.

John O'Donovan states that the surnames Glynn and
Glennon have absorbed the Hy Fiachrach Ó Gloinín. As
we have seen, Glynns are certainly numerous in north
Connacht, but Glennon (Mag Leannáin) is a Leinster
name. It is of interest to note that in the 1659 "census"
it is placed in the same counties (Westmeath and south
Roscommon) as Glynn and MacGlynn though for the
most part in different baronies, which subbests that confusion may have existed there too. At the present time
the name Glennon is chiefly found in Leinster and
Connacht. In Co. Roscommon Glennon may also be
MacGiolla Fhionnáin of the Uí Maine.

Finally the surname Glenn should be considered in
this section. Apart from occasional confusion with
Glynn which is known to have occured in Co. Derry, it
has two distinct origins: the English surname Glen is
one; the other is the Irish a Ghleanna (i.e. of the glen),
one of the very few residential Gaelic surnames. This is
also anglicized Glenny and Glanny but is rare in any
form.

MacGloin is not to be mistaken for MacGlynn. It is
quite a different name, formed as it was from the Irish
MacGiolla Eoin (son of the follower of St. John) and
chiefly found in Tyrone and Donegal. It has many synonyms in English e.g. MacGlone, MacAloon, Gloon, including one which is a particularly unfortunate mistranslation — Monday (from Dia Luain!): this has been
quite widely used in counties Fermanagh and Derry. A
very prominent Texas pioneer was named James Mac-
Gloin.

(Mac) GOGARTY   As stated in Irish Families this is
Mag Fhógartaigh in Irish. In the sept-map in that book it
appears as O'Gogarty. As this is a modern corruption, it
should be written MacGogarty in a map dealing with
medieval times. The transition from Mac to O is not unusual especially with Mag names followed by a vowel or
an aspirated F or Mac names followed by a vowel or
initial G (cf. Costigan, Gannon etc.). The belief that the

Gogartys were an independent sept not a branch of the O'Fogartys of Eliogarty is corroborated by the fact that all the somewhat scanty records of them show them located in a part of the country far away from Co. Tipperary, viz north-east Leinster and South Ulster or, to be more precise, counties Louth, Meath and Monaghan.

The earliest reference to the name I have met is in the Four Masters, who record the death of Ruaidhri Mac Fógartaigh, Lord of South Breagh (in Meath), in 1027. This is somewhat early for a hereditary surname, but having regard to its location may well indicate the location of the eponymous ancestor of the family. I have found nothing further until 1647 when one Patrick Gogarty was a soldier in Col. Bagly's regiment: he is returned in that document as of Dublin, which of course is of no help as a guide to his original abode. The best known man of the name was Oliver St. John Gogarty (1878-1957) physician, poet, wit and hero of the Liffey swans incident.   Map

(O)GOHERY   This is Ó Gothraidh in Irish. It is derived from the personal name Gothfrith or Godefrid (god peace) said to have been introduced into Ireland by the Norsemen. As this became Godfrey in England and was subsequently adopted as a surname Gohery and Godfrey tend to become confused in Ireland, the latter being equally distributed throughout the four provinces while the rarer Gohery (also met as Geoghery and Gohary) is found in the district between Portumna and Birr, i.e. Offaly and north Tipperary. In the Co. Tipperary Hearth Money Rolls (1664-6), Gohery, Godfry and Godfrey are all listed. Goffrey again can cause confusion because it may also be a truncated form of MacGoffrey which has no connexion with Gohery but is Mac Gofraidh: Mac-Goffrie is entitled "Chief of his name" in a Fiant of 1591 relating to the Maguire country (Co. Fermanagh). A somewhat similar name Gahery is among the Co. Leitrim Jacobites outlawed after 1690 but this is probably a synonym of MacGaffrey which is also in the same list (see note on MacCaffrey in Irish Families, p. 70).

GOING   People called Going may be of different origins. Woulfe equates this name with MacGowan and Smith (Mac an Ghobhann); Going and Gowen have been recorded as synonymous in the Fermoy area; Weekley states that Going is an anglicized form of the French Gouin. The Co. Tipperary landed families of the name do not trace their pedigree further back than the end of the seventeenth century, but before that time Goings were located in Co. Tipperary: there are ten recorded as householders there in the Hearth Money Rolls of 1664. In 1850, when Griffith's Valuation was made, there were 21 Going householders and two Gowings in South Tipperary, while in north Tipperary the number of Going householders was 13. Compared with these considerable figures the present numbers are small.

In 1822 Capt. Richard Going, of Newport, Co. Tipperary, was shot by Whiteboys in Co. Limerick in revenge for his implacable campaign against their organization.

This incident, as well as the events which led up to it and its sequel, are related in Begley's The Diocese of Limerick, Vol. III.

MacGOLDRICK GOULDING, Golden   The surname Goulding is used in Ireland as the modern form of several distinct patronymics. First there is the English name Goulding or Golding, which was introduced by migrants from England who settled around Dublin and Cork soon after the Anglo-Norman invasion. An early reference to this family is to Nicholas Goldinges, of Castleknock, the king's victualler in 1314. There were, of course, subsequent immigrants of the name e.g. Nicholas Goulding who was a quartermaster-sergeant in Cromwell's army in Ireland. The name, it may be mentioned, appears in a 1598 list of the chief gentlemen of counties Dublin and Kildare.

Goulding and Golding also take the form Golden. These, which are to be found quite frequently in Co. Cork and in Connacht (where the spelling of the former is usually Golding) have an alternative and probably more unusual origin viz as an anglicized form of the Irish Ó Goillín, which Woulfe states is a variant of Ó Gaillín. This is a family of the Cenél Eoghain called Gallen in English and extant today in that territory (which comprised part of Co. Donegal as well as Tyrone and Derry). O'Gullin appears in the Elizabethan Fiants, both in Co. Cork and Co. Kerry, O'Geallan in Co. Sligo alongside MacCollrick.

Golden and Goldrick are recorded as synonymous around Carrick-on-Shannon and Boyle. This leads us to MacGoldrick, now fairly numerous in Co. Fermanagh, where it is recorded in the Hearth Money Rolls of 1665-66. As MacGolrick and MacGoulrigg it appears in the similar document for Co. Donegal. This was anciently a sept of some consequence in and around the county of Leitrim which adjoins Fermanagh. The Four Masters in an entry dated for 1054 describe Mac Ualghairg as Lord of Cairbre. The sept derives it name from Ualgharg (Ulrick) O'Rourke, Lord of Breffny, who died in 1231 as a pilgrim on his way to the Holy Land. The form Mac-Goldrick was widely used in Co. Mayo (where Golden has now largely superseded it) at least up to the end of the eighteenth century, as records of householders and the like attest; it also occurs several times in the ecclesiastical records of Raphoe. John Golden, alias Golding, was a privateer captain in the legitimate service of James II, who nevertheless was condemned for treason and piracy in 1692 and duly hanged by order of an English court.

Peadar Mac Ualghairg, the Nobber (Co. Meath) weaver, who had a reputation as a Gaelic poet about the year 1800, was known in English as Peter Coalrake.

MacGONIGLE MacCONVILLE, Conwell   The principal thing to be noted about the MacGonigles (or Magonagles) is their constant association with Co. Donegal. Apart from the adjacent parts of Co. Derry they were very seldom to be found elsewhere. Some of the sept were counted among the warlike followers of O'Donnell;

but they were primarily an erenagh family, their church being at Killaghtee. It is as ecclesiastics they are best known in history. As well as many priests they have given two bishops to the diocese of Raphoe, Patrick and Malachy (Gams has Donat) Magonigail (d. 1589). The name is Mac Congail in Irish which is also used in English, so spelt, as a synonym of MacGonigle.

In his history of the diocese of Raphoe Canon Maguire speaks of the Magonagle or Conwell sept. I presume he has some authority for equating these two names, but I think it is indisputable that Conwell is MacConmhaoil in Irish. A more usual anglicization of this is MacConville. In Co. Down the variant MacConwell is found and in the Elizabethan Fiants MacConwall is the spelling. The form MacConwell is now almost obsolete but MacConville is numerous especially in Oriel, its homeland, being found now mainly in counties Armagh, Down and Louth. Six of the name from Co. Down were among the Irish Jacobites attainted after the defeat of James II. In all cases the references relate to Ulster. I have met Conwill and Conwyll in early fourteenth century Munster deeds but I presume these names represent a clerks clumsy attempt to write (O) Connell and have no relation to the Armagh sept. One of the most interesting characters of the latter was Most Rev. Henry Conwell (1748-1842), who after 40 years ministry as a priest in Ireland (he was Vicar-General of the diocese of Armagh) was in 1820 appointed Bishop of Philadelphia, a choice which caused much friction and difficulty.   Map

GOOLD, Gould   In a previous article (see MacGoldrick and Golden) we saw that Goulding etc. are associated with Co. Cork. Another somewhat similar name, quite unconnected with these, but closely identified with the city of Cork since the fourteenth century, is Goold or Gould. Coming to Dublin some time before 1226 the family moved to Munster, first to Kilmallock and finally to Cork. No less than thirty times, men of the name were mayors of Cork between 1442 and 1640, a record only exceeded by the Galweys and the Skiddys. Though chiefly associated with the city as men of business, they also became landed proprietors in the county: in 1591 a Goold was among the leading gentry of Kinalea, and earlier in the century the head of the family in the county was so far hibernicized as to be officially described as "captain of his nation" like any Gaelic chief.

Members of these southern families were also much to the fore in military and political activities in the seventeenth century. John Goold of Cork was a member of the Supreme Council of the Confederate Catholics in 1647; three of the family were attainted in 1642 and six after 1691 (a seventh was from Galway); at least six were officers in Munster regiments of King James II's Irish army; and one in the Ultonia regiment in the Spanish service was prominent in the next century in support of James's grandson the "Young Pretender". Other notable Cork exiles were Father Thomas Gould (1657-1734), the distinguished priest and writer whom Louis XIV specially praised for his mission work; and Father Richard Goold, Professor of Theology in Spain, who about 1630 was postulated for several sees in Ireland by the King of Spain, O'Sullivan Beare and other influential persons but never actually became a bishop.

About the same time Father John Goolde, collaborator of the Four Masters and scribe of the "Lives of the Saints" in 1627, was Guardian of the Franciscan community at Cashel. Dr. James Alipius Goold (1812-1886), Archbishop of Melbourne, was born in Cork.   Map

(O) GORRY, Gorey   The above and also Gurry are anglicized forms of Ó Guaire. Gorry is the most usual form and this is mainly found in Co. Offaly. Tadhg O'Guaire who was slain in 1032 is described by the Four Masters as Lord of Uí Cuilinn: O'Donovan in his notes to that work says that Uí Cuilinn was in Leinster, which I suggest was probably on the border of Offaly and Meath. Apart from a reference by the Four Masters to an anchorite at Devenish, Co. Fermanagh (1058) and another to a householder in Armagh in 1659 all I have met are to Leinster. I give some of these. In 1406 Richard Gowery acquired English liberty at Maynooth; in 1618 "white lights" were specially provided at the wake in Dublin of Walter Gorry of the Merchant Tailors Guild; four of the name appear in the Co. Meath Inquisitions between 1619 and 1638; Henry Gory of Trim, Co. Meath, was among the first Jacobites outlawed in 1669; Seaghan Ó Guaire was the author of the Jacobite song "Ar maidin inde". There are remarkably few to be found in the eighteenth century but in the nineteenth we meet them again, mainly in Co. Offaly e.g., in Griffith's Valuation. In the 1865 birth registrations there are ten Gorrys, all in the Tullamore area – the two Goreys in the same year were born respectively in Waterford and Dublin.

The surname Gorey is never a toponymic derived from the town in Co. Wexford.

GOUGH   MacGEOUGH   Gough, formerly pronounced Goch, is now called Goff and often so spelt. There are two Irish septs whose name has sometimes been anglicized as Gough. Ó Cuacháin, of the Hy Fiachrach group and located in Mayo, is one, formerly O'Cowhane, O'Quohane etc., now obsolete as such and rare as Gough. The other is Mag Eothach (recte Mag Eochach), which is said to be one of the many branches of the great MacKeogh sept: it is now found as MacGeough, MacGeogh and MacGoff in counties Armagh, Monaghan and Louth, and seventeenth century records indicate that this was also the case at that period.

The great majority of Goughs in Ireland, however, are of Welsh origin. Families called Coch (coch is the Welsh work for red or ruddy) came to Ireland in the thirteenth century, settled mainly in Dublin and Waterford and have been identified with those counties since – in the former principally as merchants, in the latter as administrators and landed gentry. In 1329 Henry Goghe, of a family already in Munster, obtained a grant of land and houses at Dungarvan; and west Waterford has since been the homeland of many Gough families. In 1607 Sir James Gough purchased the Kilmanahan Castle estate from Sir E. Fitton, to whom it had been granted in 1586 after the Desmond rebellion, thus further consolidating their position in Co. Waterford. They were also in the city of Waterford: Nicholas Gough was mayor in 1435 and 1441 and Sir Edward Gough was mayor in 1660. Sir James Gough was one of the Catholic M.P's imprisoned by James I. In 1641 the Goughs were listed with the Ronans, the Coppingers and the Fitzgeralds as the leading families of Youghal. Alderman Edward Gough was M.P. for that town in 1634 and 1639, and another Alderman Edward Gough was its member in the Parliament of 1689.

In the nineteenth century the Goughs of Munster were chiefly notable as high-ranking officers in the British army: one of these, Field-marshal Hugh Gough (1779-1869), was created a viscount in 1849. These were of a Wiltshire family which came to Co. Limerick in the seventeenth century and are now resident at Lough Cutra, near Gort, Co. Galway. One, however, of quite different type, was Wexford-born John William Goff (1847-1924), a noted jurist in America, whose connexion with the Fenian organization – not always harmonious – is elucidated in the Devoy correspondence. (Devoy's Post Bag is a valuable source of information on matters relating to Fenianism and the I.R.B. and the people who participated in those movements.)   Bibl.

(Mac) GOURLEY   This exclusively Ulster surname is a variant of MacTurley, the prefix Mag being substituted for Mac and the T aspirated, giving Mag Thoirdhealbhaigh. It occurs in the Tyrone Hearth Money Rolls of 1664 and probably earlier, though I have not met it before that date. It is now quite numerous and is located mainly in Co. Antrim.

GOVERNEY   This name is now associated with Carlow and a century ago was found in small numbers in Co. Leix. Its origin has not been finally determined. I do not think Woulfe's tentative suggestion that it may be a corrupt form of Coveney can be accepted. A more probable origin is the Huguenot name Gouvernet. In this connexion, however, it must be observed that the Governeys of the present day are nearly all Catholics: as a rule Huguenot families have remained for the most part Protestant.

GRACE   The Grace family is one to which many pages might be devoted. Readers wanting further and more detailed information than is given in the following brief summary will find this in the works mentioned in the Bibliography.

The Graces are descended from Raymond le Gros, or le Gras, one of the three outstanding figures of the Anglo-Norman invasion. He married Strongbow's daughter and was viceroy in 1176. The territory which they acquired in consequence was in what is now Co. Kilkenny and it was called Grace's country. The head of the family was known as Baron of Courtstown (a place to be distinguished from Courtown in Co. Wexford). In 1690 the extent of this property was 32,000 acres: the then owner, Robert Grace, was exempted from confiscation

by an article of the Treaty of Limerick, but his son was dispossessed in 1701 on a technical legal point. The Graces, like almost all the great Hiberno-Norman families, remained Catholic and espoused the Jacobite cause. Col. John Grace raised and commanded one of the regiments in James II's army, in which at least ten of the name served as officers. Col. Richard Grace (1620-1691) was one of the most notable personalities of seventeenth century Ireland: he was prominent in both the Cromwellian and the Williamite wars, and in the latter he was killed in action at the siege of Athlone at the age of 70. Up to the time of the Courtstown confiscation the Grace connexion was mainly, but by no means entirely, with Co. Kilkenny, in which county, indeed, the name is still quite numerous – in 1659 it was recorded as a principal Irish name in four baronies of Co. Kilkenny and also in the adjoining Tipperary barony of Eliogarty. A number of places in the four midland counties of Kilkenny, Carlow, Leix and Kildare have taken their names from the Grace family: Castle Grace, Grace Castle, Grace's Wood, Graceland, Grace's Court and Gracefield – the last named, near Athy, was formerly called Shanganagh.

The Ormond Deeds, the Justiciary Rolls and every mediaeval record which deals with that part of the country abound in references to the Grace family, who held many public administrative positions and were closely associated with the monastery of Jerpoint, of which two Graces were abbots. James Grace (fl. 1538), the annalist, was of Gracefield, the home of a branch of the Courtstown family. Another very notable member of the Gracefield branch was John Grace (1734-1811) who, while serving with the Austrian army, was detailed as the special escort of Marie Antoinette on her journey back to France; on retiring from foreign service he returned to Ireland and was the first Catholic since 1689 on the Grand Jury for Co. Roscommon. The Co. Roscommon estate at Mantua, near Elphin, formerly in the possession of the Dowell family, was acquired by marriage in the eighteenth century. Another worthy of mention was Sheffield Grace (c. 1788-1850), the antiquary. The mission of Father John Grace to the West Indies (1667-1669) is described in Analecta Hibernica, No. 4. The Grace baronetcy, held by direct descendants of Raymond le Gros, descended by special remainder in 1818 from Sir Raymond Grace Gamon.   Bibl., Map

(O)GREANEY   MacGRANE, McGranny   These two names are fairly numerous: Greany in south-west Munster and MacGrane around Dublin, and so cannot be ignored, though I have little positive information about them (in the 1901 census there were 36 Greaney families in Co. Kerry). In modern times the prefixes Mac and O have been dropped and it was inevitable that some confusion would consequently arise between Greaney, Graney and even Granny. When these occur in Munster they are of the Ó Gráinne sept. As a Cork-Kerry surname Greany is O'Greany, Ó Gráinne in Irish – Woulfe derives it from the christian name Gráinne and thus makes it one of our few matronymic surnames. As O'Granie and O'Grane it appears in the Co. Cork sixteenth century Fiants. More than two centuries earlier in 1313 the Justiciary Rolls record the acquittal by a jury in Co. Cork of Rawenyld O'Grayne, charged with aiding a convicted robber. In Connacht they are usually basically MacGraney, but whether this is a distinct family of Mac Gráinne or an off-shoot of the Ulster sept I cannot say. There the initial G comes from the prefix Mag (a form of Mac), the Gaelic-Irish form of the name being Mag Ráighne. No doubt Rory MacGraney, of Tullylish, Co. Down, who was one of the Jacobites outlawed after the battle of the Boyne, was of this origin. In the form Granny it belongs exclusively to Co. Donegal (mainly Inishowen) and adjacent parts of Co. Derry. The fact that O'Granny is the form used in the Donegal Hearth Money Rolls adds to the confusion, but I think this can be regarded as a case of the not infrequent substitution of O for Mac with names beginning with C, G and K. Mac Granny and MacGraney, now extant in Co. Armagh as MacGrana, occur quite frequently in the same records in two areas, Co. Armagh and Co. Roscommon, and can I presume be equated also with the modern MacGrane. Mr. George Paterson, curator of the Armagh Museum, is of this opinion and he says that MacGrane, locally pronounced MacGran, is still prevalent in Co. Armagh. As MacGran it appears in the Hearth Money Rolls for Co. Tyrone (1664). A Fiant dated 1559 records a pardon to "Johanne MacGrane, late of the Shepe Grange, Co. Louth, wife of Richard Cardife, especially for the murder of Neil O'Gialghous, mason". MacGreene is listed in Petty's "census" of 1659 as a principal Irish name in the barony of Ardagh, Co. Longford, which is close to Co. Roscommon, MacGrean being at the same time a principal name in Co. Donegal. In this connexion the reader is referred to the note on Magreena and Greene in Appendix I. It is not unlikely that the ubiquitous Greene has superseded one or more of these names in some places, as indeed has Grant occasionally in Ulster.

Mrs. A.S. Greene, quoting Holinshed, refers to a Dublin schoolmaster named MacGrane who wrote carols and ballads: he flourished about 1550.

GREER Most people of this name in Ireland spell it as above, though occasionally the variant Grier is used: these and also Grierson are basically the same, being anglicized forms of the Scottish MacGregor, which is found unchanged in Co. Derry. Greer is very numerous in Co. Antrim now and it occurs many times in the Hearth Money Rolls for that county (1669) and to some extent also in the rolls of other Ulster counties. The principal families of the name came to Ireland in the seventeenth century, the earliest in the Plantation of Ulster and others a generation later. Derry-born Samuel McCurdy Greer (1810-1880), who ended as county court judge of Cavan and Leitrim, was co-founder of the Tenant League in 1850 with Charles Gavan Duffy.

MacGREEVY The chiefs of the name Mac Riabhaigh were lords of Moylurg (Co. Roscommon) until in the thirteenth century they were subdued by, and became tributary to, the MacDermots. The last to be mentioned by the annalists is Cathal Mac Riabhaigh, who died in 1238. A century later O'Dugan in the Topographical Poem refers to Mag Riabhaigh as one of the old chiefs of Moylurg: by that time their decline was already taking place. The Fiants, however, prove that many of the rank and file of the sept were still to be found in their home territory in the sixteenth century.

It will be observed that the prefix used by O'Dugan is Mag not Mac. O'Donovan, in his notes to O'Dugan's work, mentions that, though then (1862) it was little known, it was still extant in its original habitat and in Co. Sligo. In his notes to The Tribes and Customs of Hy Fiachrach O'Donovan states that Mac Giolla Riabhaigh of Skreen Co. Sligo was then (1844) anglicized Kilrea there and MacIlrea elsewhere. It does not appear to have ever become MacGreevy. He writes the anglicized form as Magreevy. One would expect MacGreevy, for the contraction of MacG to Mag is unusual in Connacht though common in Ulster. The initial G of MacGreevy comes, of course from the prefix Mag, and the surname would be philologically more correct if anglicized MacReevy — Matheson indeed does note the use of MacReavy, (see Gray) and also MacCreevy, as synonyms of MacGreevy and Magreevy, but he does not state the locality in which those forms were found. In 1659 Petty's "census" enumerators recorded Crevy as a principal Irish name in the barony of Moycashel, Co. Westmeath, which is a considerable distance from the territory of Moylurg. In quite modern times the name is more numerous in Ulster than in Connacht.   Map

(O) GRENNAN   (Mac) GRANAHAN, Grenahan
Grennan, an O name, Ó Grianáin in Irish, must not be confused with Grenaghan, which is a Mac name, viz. MacGreannacháin. The O'Grennans are a Connacht family mainly found in Co. Mayo. There is also a family of Grennan or Grenan of Norman origin, at one time much in evidence in the Pale of Leinster. As early as 1205 we find a Robert de Grenan witnessing a deed in Co. Kildare, and the several Grenanstowns, in Meath and elsewhere, are named from these families not from O'Grennans. There are five Ballygrennans in Co. Limerick and a Ballygrenane in Co. Kerry, but these are derived from the Gaelic word grianán, (summer house) not from a proper name.

Grenahan or Granahan, as I have said, is of entirely different origin. The sept of Mac Greannacháin or Mag Reannacháin (both forms are found in Irish) was seated in the parish of Mevagh, diocese of Raphoe. Maguire in his history of that diocese states that they are still influential in the district.

(O) GRIBBEN   (Mac) CRIBBEN   Although Cribben occurs in the official registration returns as having been used as a synonym of Gribben these two names are actually quite distinct. O'Gribben (i.e. Ó Gribín in Irish) belongs almost exclusively to Ulster but is fairly widespread in that province. In 1866 there were 47 births registered for Gribben, Gribben and Gribbon (none with the prefix O) all except two in Ulster, mainly in the five north-eastern counties – the other two were in Co. Mayo; and in 1890, the last year for which such detailed statistics are available, 27 out of the 28 births were in Ulster, 24 of these in Down, Antrim and Armagh. The family has not been prominent in the history of the country, but those who have left their mark belong to those counties: there are, for example, five O'Gribbens among the Jacobites outlawed in 1690 and following years all of Down or Antrim; and two Gaelic scribes of some note in the seventeenth and eighteenth century called Ó Gribín were from Co. Down.

O'Gribbin appears in the Co. Armagh Hearth Money Rolls of 1664-65, as also does MacGribben. The latter may of course be an example of the not uncommon official confusion between Mac and O (especially with names beginning with G, C and K), or it may possibly be an anglicized form of Mag Roibín, a variant of Mac Roibín, whence Cribben. MacRobin as an anglicized form is very rare, if not obsolete, but it occurs in the Galway Book of Survey & Distribution (temp. Charles II) and Cribben, which is rare, is found in Co. Mayo, where no doubt Gribben (referred to above in relation to Mayo) is a substitute for it. It may be added that Mac-Roben and MacRobyn occur in the Fiants of 1566 to 1573 as kern in Co. Louth (twice), and in counties Carlow and Wexford, though these may not be hereditary surnames; they also appear occasionally in the Inquisitions for Queen's County and Wexford (1604-1628).

(O)GROGAN   The O prefix of this name – Ó Gruagáin in Irish – was dropped in the seventeenth century and does not appear to have been resumed at all in recent times. We hear first of the sept in 1265 under which date the Four Masters and other annalists record the death of Maelbrighde Ó Grugáin (or Ó Grocan) of Elphin.

In the sixteenth and seventeenth centuries references to the name in our surviving records are plentiful, but by 1550 the sept had been dispersed from their homeland in Connacht to an unusual degree. In the Tudor Fiants, in which the name appears usually as O'Grogan, but with variants such as O'Grugane, O'Growgane and O'Gruogan, six of the relevant dozen relate to Co. Limerick, the others to counties Kildare, Offaly and Tipperary, and only one is placed near the sept's original habitat. None is from Co. Westmeath, yet less than a century later, when Petty's "census" was compiled in 1659, Grogan is listed as one of the principal Irish surnames in the barony of Farbill in that county and also in the barony of Ballyboy, Co. Offaly.

Some of the names by which these men and women were recorded are brief pedigrees in themselves: e.g. Molaghlin MacEe MacCoin O'Gruagan of Castleton, Co Limerick, who in 1579 was with many of his neighbours fined 20s., pardoned and ordered to find security for his peaceful behaviour. Katherine nyne Tyaung, alias Katharin ny Gruagaine, of Gortaclecane, Co. Kerry, provides another intriguing entry. Most of these people are described as husbandmen and yeomen, though we have also a horseman, a tailor and even a labourer. Unlike most of our earlier records the Fiants are not concerned solely with landholders, soldiers and officials.

Few townlands were named later than the early seventeenth century so that Ballygrogan in Co. Tipperary and Derrygrogan in Offaly, near Tullamore, presumably called after branches of the family, provide corroborative evidence of their establishment in those areas. Modern statistics also indicate their wide distribution in recent times: birth registrations show approximately the same number in three provinces with considerably fewer in Ulster: in the northern province the variants Groggan, Groogan and Grugan are found, the last of these being apparently almost peculiar to the Omagh district.

In the seventeenth century (individual references are too numerous to be enumerated in this brief account) we find, for example, one as a witness to the will of Nugent, Baron of Delvin, in 1602, another Dominican Prior of Urlagh in 1631, another in the list of 1649 officers; and in this century begins the authenticated pedigree of the principal landed family of the name, Grogan of Johnstown Castle, Co. Wexford, which is registered at the Office of Arms, Dublin Castle. In 1878 the Grogan estates totalled upwards of 13,000 acres in counties Wexford, Wicklow, Westmeath and Offaly.

Of this family was Cornelius Grogan (1738-1798) one of the Co. Wexford gentry who joined the United Irishmen: he was executed for his prominent part in the Insurrection; his brother Thomas, who fought on the other side, was killed in action. Sir Edward Grogan, Bart., (1802-1891), who was M.P. for Dublin City for 25 years, was also of this family. Nathaniel Grogan (1740-1807), a painter of note, was a Cork man.

GUBBINS   This name in Ireland is of dual origin. In Ulster it is native Gaelic, Ó Goibín, now found usually but not always without the final s and mainly concentrated in the Inishowen peninsula of Co. Donegal. This survived in an anglicized form as O Gobban which is of frequent occurence in the Donegal Hearth Money Rolls of 1665 and was found in the parish of Stranorlar at least as late as 1751. The first reference to it I have met in Ulster is to John O'Gubuin, Bishop of Derry in 1445. There is, however, an isolated reference to one Maurice O'Goban who was in possession of land in Co. Kilkenny in 1307. In the form Gubbins it is chiefly associated with Co. Limerick where the Gubbins family of Kilfrush has long been prominent particularly in connexion with racing. They have been established there since the middle of the seventeenth century. I am not absolutely certain but I think they are not of the Ulster Ó Goibín stock, their name being derived from the Old-French Giboin or Old-German Gebawin (gift-friend) and so is akin etymologically to Gibbons. From the eighteenth century onwards such sources as wills indicate that Co. Limerick and adjacent territories may be regarded as the homeland of the Gubbinses, though, as stated above, its continued indigenous association with Inishowen must be remembered.

John Gubbins (fl. early 19th c.), a portrait painter of distinction, was a native of Co. Limerick; Henrietta Gubbins (fl. mid. 19th c.) was also a well known portrait painter.

GUIDERA, Guider   The synonyms collected by Matheson from returns by local registrars (i.e. forms used indifferently by the same family), in this case Guidera, Guidra and Guider, are a guide to the correct pronunciation of this name, which is neither Guddeera nor Gyder but approximately Giddera and Gidder. A note by the late Richard Foley (Fiachra Éilgeach) — admittedly not a reliable authority — (Nat. Lib. MS. G 841) mentions that Aodh de Blacam thought the name to be Mag Fhuadaire (fuadaire, rambler) in Irish: I think this most unlikely, but having discovered no Irish form myself I give it for what it is worth. Foley also states that there is a family of Guidera in Co. Derry and I am informed that they use Mac Giodaire as the Gaelic form of their name. Though this G is slender it does approximate to the correct pronunciation of Guidera but it may only be a modern gaelicization.

So far as my research has gone I have met no early example of the name. The Tipperary Hearth Money Rolls have Daniel Gedery or Gidery (parish of Kilmore) and Donnaigh Gidder (parish of Aghnameadle) both in the barony of Upper Ormond. These are presumably alternative forms of Guider etc. In the nineteenth century it was fairly numerous in Co. Tipperary, as evidenced by the Tithe Applotment Books (1815-1827) and a generation later by Griffith's Valuation. In almost every case in those records the form given is Guider. It appears to have been then associated particularly with the north of the county around Roscrea, though it also occurs in the south at Clogheen and Clonmel. All the three forms recorded by Matheson as synonyms in 1890, occur in the registrations for 1864 to 1866: only one birth took place outside Co. Tipperary and that was in Dublin, the name there being spelt Guidera. Mr. P. J. Kennedy informs me that the name in that form is not unknown in east Galway.

MacGUIGAN, MacGuckin   Though I am unable to give much definite information regarding this name I include it for two reasons. First because of its numerical strength: there are, it is estimated, approximately 1,750 persons of the name in Ireland, the great majority of them in counties Tyrone and Antrim. Secondly, this is a case where Woulfe's view cannot be accepted. He believed MacGuigan to be either a variant of MacGahan, which is untenable, or of MacGeoghegan wherein he was probably misled by the fact that Geoghegan was reported from the Newry area to have been used in registering births for one or more families known as MacGuigan: this, however, was almost certainly one of the many instances of absorption. Matheson records no less than 15 modern synonyms of MacGuigan, viz. Gavigan, Geoghegan, Guigan, Maguigan, MacGoogan, MacGookin, MacGuckian, MacGuiggan, MacQuiggan, MacWiggan, MacWiggin, Meguiggan, Wigan and also Fidgeon and Pidgeon.

The pronunciation of the name in its homeland, Co. Tyrone (especially around Omagh), is MacGwiggen, which suggests Mag Uigin as the Irish form. Surnames formed from Norse words or forenames are quite common in the Cenél Eoghain. In 1602 a Fiant relating to Co. Tyrone spells the name MacGuigine and in the same

year one of O'Donnell's following was Conor MacGugyne. At the end of that century Hugh Magwygin of Co. Down is among the attainted Jacobites.

William MacGuckin (Baron de Slane) (fl. 1837-1868), the orientalist, was born in Co. Antrim and Barton MacGuckin (b. 1853), tenor, was born in Dublin. An important modern representative of the name is Cardinal MacGuigan, Archbishop of Toronto.

(O) GUNNING   In spite of its English appearance Gunning is not an indigenous English name. It is usually the anglicized form of Ó Conaing. This was a sept of the Uí Bloid situated at Castleconnell: this presents an example of the faulty anglicization of place-names since a correct rendering of the original would be Castlecunning or Castlegunning. The Gunnings are descended from a brother of Brian Boru; they retained their Castleconnell territory until the middle of the thirteenth century when they were dispossessed by MacWilliam Burke. Prior to that they were important and influential in that part of Munster. The Annals of Loch Cé speak of Edmund O'Conaing as the "royal heir of Munster" in 1032, and of Domhnall O'Conaing "chief bishop of Leath Mogha" (i.e. Cashel), who died in 1137, in the highest terms of praise, while in 1195 the death of Dermot O'Conaing, Bishop of Killaloe, is recorded. Peter O'Conyng was Abbot of Holy Cross in 1297. The name is rare now. In the eighteenth century it was familiar on account of the celebrated Co. Roscommon sisters: Elizabeth Gunning (1734-1790) who married successively two dukes and was the mother of four dukes, Maria (1733-1760), who also married into the English peerage, and Catherine (d. 1773) the youngest of the three: all were women of exceptional beauty.

The Clare name Goonane (Ó Gamhnáin) has sometimes been made into Gooney and even Gunning.   Map

HAIDE   This name is also spelt Hade and Hayde. It is not an English name and is probably an anglicized form of some Gaelic-Irish surname. Richard Foley (Fiachra Éilgeach) considered that it is an abbreviation of Ó hÉidin. This is the only opinion on the origin of the name I have heard. I give it without comment, beyond saying that it certainly belongs to the same parts of the country as Hayden, viz. south Leinster and Co. Tipperary. It is found also in Co. Kildare, where there is a place-name Ballyhade, in the Castledermot-Athy area. It is not numerous anywhere: there were eight births registered for the name in 1866 and less than five in 1890.

The English family of Head, associated with Co. Tipperary since the end of the seventeenth century, is not, I think, to be confused with Hade.

(O) HALLAHAN, Hallighan   (O) HALLIGAN

Hallighan must be clearly distinguished from Halligan. The former is more usually spelt Hallahan or Hallihane and is the name of an old but not very numerous Munster family (Ó hAileacháin in Irish) belonging primarily to Co. Cork, but well established as O'Hallaghan, also in Co. Waterford in the sixteenth century, as evidenced by the Tudor Fiants and Chancery Rolls. Professor John Halahan (1753-1813), an original member of the Dublin College of Surgeons, was of a Co. Cork family. It was inevitable, however, that in records largely compiled by officials who were strangers to Ireland, Halligan and Hallighan should be confused. In the Co. Tipperary Hearth Money Rolls, for example, Halligan not Hallighan is the spelling used. Halligan is actually the modern form of Ó hAileagáin, an Oriel sept of Louth and Armagh: it is to be found there as early as 1042 when the death of one of the name, who was lector of Armagh, is recorded in the Annals of Ulster and elsewhere. It is also written Ó hAllagáin, and was found as O'Hallagan and O'Hollegan in north Connacht in the sixteenth century, as it is today. The latter form has been recorded, as Olligan, in Co. Kildare in modern times. It would appear that the family has long associations with that county since William O'Halegan was among a number of leading gentlemen of Co. Kildare who received "pardons" in 1597.

(O) HALLINAN

According to the Four Masters MacBeathadh Ó hAilgheanáin, who died in 1106, was Bishop of Cork. The surname Hallinan is still so spelt in Irish. It was never numerous in any part of the country, and has always been practically confined to the province of Munster. The name occurs once in the Justiciary Rolls (Co. Limerick 1313) where Hugh and Henry O'Halinan are acquitted of sheltering one Robert Bettagh Russell who had killed several Englishmen. In the Chancery Rolls of the first half of the sixteenth century and in the Elizabethan Fiants, in which it appears frequently, the references are almost all to counties Waterford, Limerick and Kerry; in the 1659 "census" we find it in the barony of Decies, Co. Waterford; a few years later the Hearth Money Rolls show it to have been fairly numerous in Co. Tipperary. In recent times (1918-1923) the see of Limerick was occupied by Most Rev. Denis Hallinan.

Hallinan is one of those surnames which have unfortunately tended to be absorbed by other commoner names of a somewhat similar sound: it has been partially superseded by Allen and Hanlon in some parts of Munster.

(O) HALPIN, Halpeny

As long ago as 1602 Halpeny was alternatively written Halfpenny in English: at that date five of this name, both spellings being used, were (with a number of O'Kirwellans) excepted from an intensive pardon to MacMahons and other families of Co. Monaghan. The sept originated there, being called Ó hAilpín in Irish, an older form of which was Ó hAilpéne, whence came the three syllable pronunciation Halpenny. Halpin was and is usually found in counties Limerick and Clare, where another sept of the name originated.

A distinction between Halpin and Halpeny has existed since the anglicization of Irish surnames took place: in the sixteenth century Fiants, for example, most of the Halpins are from Co. Limerick and most of the Halpenys from Co. Monaghan; and (disregarding the metropolitan area of Dublin) the same thing applies now except that today the neighbouring parts of Meath and Louth are as much the home of the Halpenys as Co. Monaghan. Other records corroborate this: thus for example John Halpeny appears as a juror in north Meath (near Co. Monaghan) in 1541; in the list of Irish kern mustered for service under the king in England in 1544 of the 27 recruited from the Meath-Monaghan area 14, including the captain, were Halpenys; in 1539 Robert Halpenny is described as hereditary standard bearer to the Flemings (Lords Slane); another John Halpeny was an officer in Bellew's regiment of James II's Irish army; a Dermot Halpin appears in a Co. Limerick Transplanter's Certificate of 1653, a Denis Halpin in the Kinsale presentments of 1659 and Halpin is among the more numerous Co. Limerick names in the "census" of that year. However, while Halpeny is almost entirely confined to south Ulster and north Leinster, Halpin cannot be treated as an exclusively Munster surname because in modern times there has been a tendency to abbreviate Halpeny to Halpin. All the best known men of the name have in fact been Leinstermen and have all borne the surname Halpin not Halpeny: e.g. Thomas Halpin the 1798 insurgent who was a close associate of Michael Dwyer and eventually turned informer to save his life; Thomas Mathew Halpin, the '48 man; General William Halpin (b. 1825) the Fenian who distinguished himself in the American Civil War, as did Charles Graham Halpine (1829-1868) humorous author, whose father Nicholas John Halpine (1790-1850), the Shakespearean critic, was a bitter opponent of Daniel O'Connell. Others were Patrick Halpin (fl. 1755-1787) engraver, and his son John Halpin (b. 1764), miniature painter; and George Halpin, senior (1779-1854), architect and inspector of lighthouses.

(O) HAMILL

The O'Hamills, whose name in Irish is Ó hAghmaill, were a branch of the Cenél Eoghain with territory in south Tyrone and the neighbouring parts of Oriel, where from the twelfth century onwards they were noteworthy as poets and ollavs to the O'Hanlons. They were to be found engaged in warlike as well as literary activities: Donnell O'Hammoyle, for example, was among the adherents of Rory O'Donnell at the end of the sixteenth century. In the course of time they became more closely identified with that part of Oriel comprised in the present counties of Armagh and Monaghan than with Tyrone. In Petty's "census" (1659) they are most numerous in Co. Monaghan, where a few years later the name appears often in the Hearth Money Rolls;

while in the modern birth registration statistics counties Armagh and Louth (with Belfast) are their main location. In addition to poets the O'Hamills also produced a number of distinguished ecclesiastics, particularly sixteenth and seventeenth century Franciscans. In Archbishop Swayne's Register (1418-1439) the name appears as that not only of a dignitary of the archdiocese of Armagh but also of laymen who distrained the goods of the monastery at Armagh.

The full form O'Hamill is still used by a few families in Co. Derry, but elsewhere the prefix O, dropped in the period of Gaelic submergence, has not been much resumed. In the Derry area it has in some cases been changed to Hamilton, while in Dublin Hammond has occasionally been substituted for it.   Map

HAMPSON, (O) Hamsey   The name Hampson has a very English look and indeed there is such a surname indigenous in England, but in Ireland, or at any rate in and near Co. Derry, it presents an example of the deplorable tendency, especially marked during the penal times, of corrupting good Gaelic-Irish names so as to give them an English appearance. The small Derry sept of O'Hampsey had become O'Hamson by 1659, at which time it is thus recorded in the so called census of 1659 as one of the principal Irish surnames in the barony of Keenaght, and as O'Hampson and O'Hanson it will be found in the contemporary Hearth Money Rolls for Co. Derry. From 1700 we seldom meet the name except as Hanson or Hampson, though the Irish musician Denis Hempson (b. 1695 Co. Derry, d. 1793) used O'Hempsey as an alternative form. Wills and other records indicate that for the past two centuries members of the sept were to be found to some extent in other Ulster counties as well as Co. Derry. A Charles Hampson was among the purchasers of forfeited estates in Co. Cavan in 1700 and a Capt. William Hampson is also listed in the same connexion. There is a pedigree of Hampson of Cavan in the Genealogical Office, but it does not go back far enough to indicate whether this family was of Irish or English origin.

(O) HANAHOE   Though this name is quite well known in north Mayo it is not mentioned in Woulfe's "Sloinnte". He gives the Co. Galway name Heanue with the Gaelic form Ó hEanadha. Heanue belongs particularly to the north-west part of Connemara, where it is quite numerous. I suggest that Hanahoe is Ó hEanchadha (though I have no evidence for this or any other Gaelic-Irish form) just as Horahoe is Ó hEarchadha.

HANNA, Hannay   Although Hanna and Hannay do not appear as synonyms in Matheson's collection there is no doubt that they should be treated as such. Harrison's fanciful derivations (Hanna: Hebrew; Hannay: an English place-name) may be disregarded. The name is Scottish and it belongs by origin to the county of Galloway in that country, whence it came to Ireland in 1621, when Robert Hannay (alias Hanna and Hana) was among the planters in Co. Longford: he was made a baronet of

Scotland in 1630. Practically all the Hannas today belong to north-east Ulster, where they are numerous, as indeed they were about 1665 as we know from the Hearth Money Rolls for the several counties there; and all the notable men of the name in Ireland (there have been many in Scotland) were Presbyterian divines from Belfast and neighbourhood. These do not appear to descend from Sir Robert Hannay or from his brother Patrick, who was also an early seventeenth century settler, but from Scottish immigrants, who came to Ulster after 1691. Hanna was formerly written A'Hannay which is said to be a corruption of O'Hannay (Ó hAnnaidh) and to be one of the few examples of a Scottish Gaelic surname with the prefix O.

Notwithstanding the clear evidence that Hannay in Ireland today is of Scottish origin, the fact that a similar name was to be found here long before the immigration referred to above cannot be overlooked. As early as 1313 an O'Hanni was tried for robbery and acquitted in Co. Cork; in 1540 both O'Hanney and Hanye occur in Cashel, as well as Hanny at Ardee in 1541 and 1570. I have however, found no evidence that these families have any surviving descendants today. The place-name Ballyhanna occurs in counties Donegal and Derry.

George Bermingham, author of many popular Irish novels and plays, is the nom-de-plume of Canon Hannay (1865-1950).

(O) HANNIGAN   Birth registration statistics show 30 for the year 1890, chiefly in counties Dublin, Waterford and Tyrone – only one was recorded in Connacht. In 1864, 53 births were registered for Hannigan (including Hanagan and other spelling variants); then, too, though rather more scattered than in 1890, the majority were in the Tyrone-Fermanagh area or in east Munster. Woulfe gives Ó hAnnagáin as the Irish form and says it is an old Co. Limerick name; he surmises that it is a variant of O'Hannon but I have found no evidence to corroborate this suggestion – later variants tend to be shorter rather than longer than the original form. The earliest reference to the name I have met is 1556 when John Hannigane of Waterford city obtained "English liberty." A generation later the name occurs among jurymen and trade guild officials in Dublin and also in Inishowen pardons, so that in the sixteenth century it was to be found approximately in the areas assigned to it by modern statistics. Later we find it as a principal Irish name in the barony of Decies, Co. Waterford, in the 1659 census and in eighteenth century wills in Waterford, south Tipperary and Limerick. In Dublin James Hannigan was warden of the Guild of St. John the Baptist (merchant tailors) in 1752-53. David Henegan, who helped in the revision and publication of O'Brien's Irish dictionary in Paris in 1768 was a Cork man: in 1774 he founded the course for Cork students in the Lombard College, Paris.

I have no information as to the origin and early location of the sept or septs of O'Hannigan. O'Hart says they were one of the Corca Laoidhe, but O'Donovan's edition of that part of the "Book of Lecan" does not mention them in text or notes.

Ó hAnnacháin, anglicized Hannahan, is no doubt a variant of Ó hAnnagáin. The name appears in the Fiants in the person of Conor McShane Y Haneghan of Clonlare, Co. Limerick, who was pardoned and fined one cow in 1577. It is very rare now.

HARDIMAN, Hargadan, Harman   The Irish surname Ó hArgadáin has three anglicized forms in use today. Hargadan is the more usual in Co. Sligo and Hardiman in Co. Galway. In the sixteenth century Fiants the form O'Hardegan appears as well as O'Hargedan. The prefix O, discarded in the period of Gaelic and Catholic depression, has not been resumed to any extent.

The most notable man of the name was James Hardiman (1782-1855) of Galway, author of Irish Minstrelsy, History of Galway, etc.

Harman is sometimes a synonym of Hardiman in Connacht, but Harman and Harmon are chiefly found now in east Leinster. There is a modern form of Hereman, an Old-German name meaning warrior, and as such it occurs in Ireland in the late thirteenth century – the place-name Heremanstown, alias Harmanstown, in the barony of Upper Slane, Co. Meath, is recorded in the Justiciary Rolls of that period; in 1584 Nicholas Harmon appears in a list of Maryborough tenants; in 1608 the name occurs among the principal gentry of Co. Carlow, and the "census" of 1659 records several tituladoes in counties Kildare and Carlow. The well known family of King-Harman, of Co. Longford, is descended from these Co. Carlow Harmans who, they state, came from England and settled in Co. Carlow at the beginning of the seventeenth century. The most prominent of these was Sir Thomas Harman M.P., of Athy, who was a trustee for the '49 officers.

A family of the name has been prominent in Co. Cork in recent times, but whether they are descended from Richard Harmon, an English M.P. who was a Cromwellian adventurer (for £300) or from the Kerry family, one of whom appears in the Elizabethan Fiants in company with many native Irishmen, I do not know.

Woulfe treats the Antrim name Herdman as of similar origin to the Teutonic Harmon, but it is in fact English, meaning a herdsman.

HARDY   The ubiquitous English surname Hardy in Ireland often conceals an ancient Gaelic-Irish name viz. MacGiolla Deacair. Deacair is the Irish word for hard. The early anglicized form of this name was Macgilledogher. This is now obsolete and in the absence of a reliable pedigree, or at least of a well established family tradition, it is not possible to distinguish between Hardys of English and Hardys of Irish origin. In this regard it is of interest to remember that the sept of Macgilledogher was located in Co. Roscommon. I am informed by Mr. P. J. Kennedy that some families formerly Hardiman in mid-Galway are now called Hardy. See Dockery. .

HARFORD   Harford is a fairly numerous name in Dublin and adjacent areas. Derived from the English place-name Hereford (it may also, rarely, be from Hertford) it has been in Ireland since the thirteenth century. Mediaeval and early modern records contain many references to the name in Leinster, especially in Co. Kilkenny. In the "census" of 1659 it actually appears as a "principal Irish name" in the barony of Balrothery, Co. Dublin, where, it is of interest to note, it was also numerous in quite recent times. However, it was not confined entirely to Leinster, for we find a Harford mayor of Youghal in 1618 and the only entry in the Jacobite outlawries is of a Co. Monaghan man.

(O) HARKIN, Harkan   ARKINS   Ó hEarcáin, now usually anglicized Harkin, is a very numerous name in Co. Donegal and this was also the case in the seventeenth century, the 1659 "census" specifying O'Harkan as a principal Irish surname there, particularly in the barony of Inishowen where it also appears in the Fiants of the previous century. It occurs also in the Inquisitions for Co. Donegal and very frequently in the Hearth Money Rolls for that county compiled in 1665. Their association with Inishowen is recorded long before that, for the O'Harkans were erenaghs of Clonska, which is a parish near Malin Head. One appears as such in Bishop Montgomery's diocesan survey of 1606. Daniel O'Harcan (d. 1581) was one of the many Ulster martyrs for the faith.

There is a Clare name Arkins which is said to be the modern form of the Gaelic surname Ó hOrcáin. It is also found in Co. Mayo. Woulfe conjectures that it is of the same origin as Harkin, but I have found no evidence either to support or refute this suggestion.

Michael Harkin (b. 1830) did much to collect Co. Donegal folklore: he was the author of Inishowen: its History, Traditions and Antiquities under the nom-de-plume Maghtochair. Peter Harkan (c. 1780-1814) the "resurrectionist" was an interesting character who is described in Fleetwood's History of Medicine in Ireland.

(O) HARTNETT, Harnett   (O) HARNEY   Other forms of this old west Munster name are Harknett and Harnedy. Its early anglicized form O'Hartnedy, which occurs frequently in the sixteenth century Fiants, is closer to the Irish Ó hAirtnéada: Hartnetty is occasionally found in Co. Cork today. Families of these names are mainly located in counties Cork, Kerry and Limerick, Harnet being more usual in Co. Limerick and Hartnett in Co. Cork, while both are found in Co. Kerry, where the 1901 census recorded 55 families so called. In each of those counties before the transfer of ownership of land from landlords to tenants there were four large proprietors called Harnett.

Harney is a different name (Ó hAthairne, according to Woulfe) alias Haherney, which belongs originally to south Roscommon, but is now also found in counties Tipperary and Waterford.   Map

(O) HARTY   The older form of this name was

O'Haherty, a phonetic anglicization of Ó hAthartaigh; the elimination of the internal H with Irish names in their English form (cf. Fehilly – Feely, Cahalane – Callan etc.) is not unusual but it is rare to find it taking place in the Gaelic form, as has happened in this case; Ó hAthartaigh has been abbreviated to Ó Hartaigh or Ó Harta, whence Harty. The name may be regarded as peculiar to Munster – when it occurs elsewhere it will be found that the family in question came from the southern province, though it should be noted that MacGeoghegan counted them of Offaly origin.

Two of the most notable men of the name were from counties Limerick and Tipperary, viz. Dr. John M. Harty, (1867-1946) Archbishop of Cashel; and Lt. Gen. Oliver Harty (1746-1823) who, after nearly 30 years in the Irish Brigade, remained in the service of France following the Revolution and was ennobled by Napoleon as Baron de Pierreburg.

It is somewhat surprising to find no entry for the name in the "census" of 1659 nor in the Hearth Money Rolls for Co. Tipperary compiled about the same time – unless the eleven Harte families recorded are a clerk's error for Harty. It is surprising also to find O'Heartye in the Co. Armagh Hearth Money Rolls, but this is then possibly an abbreviated form of O'Haverty (q.v.) H. Hamilton Harty (1879-1941), the composer, was born at Hillsborough in Co. Down, not far from Co. Armagh.

The name Hartry has been recorded in south Leinster as used synonymously with Harty. This is probably an error in registration. The names are quite distinct; Hartry being Ó hAirtrí in Irish: it is mentioned in the Annals as of importance in Connacht in the twelfth century.

(O) HASSAN   Hassan may have an eastern look but in Ireland it is the anglicized form of Ó hOsáin. It is to be distinguished from Ó hOisín and Ó hOiseáin (see Hession and Hishon). In Co. Derry, where it is numerous, it is spelt Hassan, Hassen and Hasson. In the Monaghan Hearth Money Rolls of 1663 it appears as O'Hessan. There was a Hasson of Wexford among the "principal gentlemen" of that county in 1598, but that family was no doubt of non-Gaelic stock and a John Hassane was an influential merchant in Wexford fifty years earlier.

(O) HASSETT BLENNERHASSETT (O) HAHESSY
The ancient Thomond sept of Ó hAiseadha were formerly called O'Hassia and also O'Hessedy in records in the English language, whence came the modern form Hassett. This was adopted in the seventeenth century: it appears as such in the Hearth Money Rolls for Co. Tipperary (1665-1667) but is still O'Hashea in the 1659 "census", where it appears as one of the principal Irish names in the barony of Bunratty, Co. Clare. This was their original homeland, for they were a branch of Clancullen and are mentioned in "Caithréim Thoirdhealbhaigh" as one of the septs fighting in alliance with their kinsmen the Macnamaras at the Battle of the Abbey in 1317. After the middle of the seventeenth century it is not always easy to distinguish the families of this Gaelic sept from the better known English settlers called Blennerhassett. One

family of this name was descended from Sir Edward Blennerhassett, a leading undertaker in the Plantation of Ulster, who acquired lands in Co. Fermanagh and called his residence Castle Hassett. More prominent, however, were the Blennerhassets of Co. Kerry who came to that county at the end of the reign of Elizabeth I and for centuries after remained among its leading gentry. Those of Ballyseedy, near Tralee, were the most extensive landlords: in 1878 they held 12,621 acres, while others of the name possessed about 22,000 acres in Kerry as well as over 4,000 acres in the neighbouring counties of Cork and Limerick. Harman Blenner-Hassett (c. 1764-1831), an Irish-American lawyer and politician, notorious for his part in Aaron Burn's rebellion, was heir of Castle Conway (Killorglin) and having sold his land to Lord Ventry in 1796 emigrated to U.S.A. The Blennerhassetts came from Norfolk in England where they were established in the fifteenth century, having previously been located in the border country between England and Scotland. Blennerhassett, from which they take their name, is a place in Cumberland. Having regard to their affiliations it can be assumed that the family of Assett, referred to in an official report of 1657 as one of the Kerry families "plotting for trouble," was the Gaelic O'Hassett rather than Blennerhassett. I presume that Thomas Henry Hassett, who was born at Doneraile, Co. Cork, in 1841, and was a very active Fenian, was also of that stock. Downe Hassie, of Fenit, in a Co. Kerry pardon of 1586, an associate of O'Sullivans and MacCarthys, was clearly before the time the Blennerhassets came to Kerry. A Hussae is among the signatories of a petition from leading Kerry families to Rome in 1631.

O'Hassie, however, which occurs in the Fiants, as a rule denotes quite another family or sept viz. that known as Hahessy, a name long found in Co. Waterford, but rare even there. Hahasie is recorded as a principal name in Co. Waterford in the "census" of 1659. This is Ó hAitheasa in Irish. In The Tribes & Customs of Hy Many it is reckoned as of the Síol Anmchadha, located in the O'Madden country in the south-eastern part of Co. Galway, but in his notes to that work O'Donovan says that when he wrote (1843) the name was no longer there.

(O) HAUGHEY   This name belongs to two areas in Ulster: Donegal-Fermanagh and the Oriel country around counties Armagh and Monaghan. It is normally an O name. (Ó hEachaidh) but occurs occasionally with the Mac prefix, e.g. in the Armagh Hearth Money Rolls of 1666, where, however, the O form predominates. Mac Eachaidh is usually anglicized Mac Caughey and Mac-Caghy of Co. Tyrone. Synonyms of Haughey recorded by the Registrar-General are Hoy in Antrim and Haffey in Co. Armagh. Hoey (q.v.) is also an occasional variant. Haughey, as Ó hEachadha, is mentioned as a sept located in the Glenard area in the 1609 Armagh church lands inquisition. The best known of the name is Charles J. Haughey, Taoiseach (Prime Minister) of Ireland 1979-1981.

HAUGHTON (O) HAUGHIAN   Though presenting no difficulty in England, where Haughton, alias Houghton, is a toponymic, as an Irish surname its origin cannot be determined except where a family has a certified pedigree or at least a well established tradition. Haughtons in Ireland can be the descendants of English settlers or alternatively of Gaelic ancestry, more than one Irish surname having been so anglicized. Ó hEacháin is anglicized Haghan, Haughton and even Hawkins. In the list of synonyms recorded by the Cunard Company met with among their emigrant passengers to America, Haughton is equated with Hutton, and even Naughton, as well as Houghton. This presents an example of the inadvisability of accepting such casual usage (often no more than the result of clerical error) as evidence of a genuine synonymity. Again Ó hEacháin is often hard to distinguish from Ó hEachaidhín, usually Haughian: these are Ulster surnames, of Down and Tyrone. O'Donovan equates this with Ó hEochagáin which Woulfe says was changed to Ó hEacháin. Then we find Haughton in the south and in the midlands. A number of Haughtons appear in Griffith's Valuation of Counties Waterford, Wexford, Wicklow, Kildare and Offaly. John Haughton, alias Houghton, was mayor of Waterford in 1659, presumably of an English family, and another Haughton appears in that document as titulado in south Wexford in which county a few years later a Haughton obtained a confirmatory grant of 1600 acres. Laffan's edition of the Hearth Money Rolls for Co. Tipperary in the next decade gives a number of Haughtons, but it is probable that these were really O'Haghtirs which, as Gleeson's Last Lords of Ormond reminds us, was formerly of importance in north Tipperary. That name is now normally anglicized Hoctor.

Two notable Haughtons were born in Carlow: James Haughton (1795-1873), worker with Father Matthew in the cause of temperance, and his son Rev. Samuel Haughton, M.D. (1821-1897) the scientist. In connexion with Carlow I may mention that the seneschal of that town in 1292 was a de Hochton.   Bibl.

(O) HAVERTY   This old Connacht name is now, and indeed always was, rare: it is, however, I am informed by Mr. P.J. Kennedy of Galway, fairly well represented in a small area around the Co. Galway parishes of Kilmordaly and Craughwell. It is not often met with in the records. The Annals of Innisfallen mention Ó hÁbartaig, as Abbot of Mayo in 1095; William O'Havorta is included in a list of Co. Galway "pardons" in 1584; and one O'Havarta occurs in the Strafford Inquisition of Mayo in 1635. Ó hAbhartaigh is the modern Irish form of the name.

It is included here on account of the distinguished careers of Joseph Patrick Haverty (1794-1864), the portrait painter, and his half-brother Martin Haverty (1809-1887), the historian. The name of the former is perpetuated in the Haverty Trust, which provides funds for the purchase of works by Irish artists. Patrick Martin Haverty (1824-1901), the Galway born American publisher of many Irish historical and musical works, who took part in the Young Ireland movement at home and in the Civil War in America, has been described as the "best known Irishman in America".   Map

(O) HEADON, Hayden, Hadian   Though Headon with its variants is well known in Co. Tipperary today, as it was in the past, the name must be regarded primarily as belonging to Co. Carlow and neighbouring areas. As O'Headon, Headon and Heydon it was one of the principal Irish surnames in that county at the time of the 1659 "census", in which it also occurs in the same category for the contiguous Kilkenny barony of Gowran as Heiden, and was very numerous as Hedien in the Kildare barony of Kilkea (near Carlow town). William O'Hedian, who was Bishop of Emly from 1449 to 1475, went there from Kells, Co. Kilkenny, and John O'Hedian or O'Hayden, Bishop of Ossory from 1481 to 1486, was another prominent churchman of the same sept; so, no doubt, was Peter Hydden of Boleycarrigeen, Co. Wicklow, who, at first elected captain of the insurgents in preference to Michael Dwyer, was with 35 other prisoners killed by Yeomanry in 1798.

Reverting to Co. Tipperary, the name O'Hedian, O'Hedyane etc., is of frequent occurrence in the Ormond Deeds from the year 1374 (it occurs in Co. Kilkenny, barony of Gowran, in 1303 in the Red Book of Ormond), the Bishop of Ossory, mentioned above, being a landed proprietor in the Clonmel area. It is also of frequent occurrence in the history of Clonmel and in the ecclesiastical records of the archdiocese of Cashel. No less than 43 families called Hayden appear in the Co. Tipperary Hearth Money Rolls of 1665-67; the fact that Petty's "census" does not list it as a principal name in that county is presumably due to its being scattered throughout the various baronies of the county and so not being particularly numerous in any one of them. The form O'Hedian mentioned above is now obsolete, but Hadian is found around Athlone. George Thomas Hayden (1798-1857) and Thomas Hayden (1823-1881), distinguished medical men, were both from Co. Tipperary.

In addition to this Gaelic-Irish sept – Ó hÉideáin, sometimes Ó hÉidín in Irish – there were also Haydens of Norman stock who came to Ireland shortly after the Invasion and whose names are to be found in early Dublin and Wexford records. As de Heddon etc., they held Adamstown and Ballymalgir in 1231 (these estates came later into the possession of the Devereux family). It is an open question whether any Haydens in our present population are surviving representatives of Norman families of the name.

Joseph Timothy Haydn (1786-1856), editor of Lewis's Topographical Dictionary and author of The Book of Dates, was born in Limerick. Dr. William Hayden (1868-1936), Archbishop of Hobart, and his brother, Mgr. Thomas Hayden (1864-1945), equally prominent in Australia, were born and educated at Kilkenny.   Map

(O) HEANY, Hegney, Bird   (O) HENAGHAN, Bird   MacANEANY, Bird   There is no connexion between these three surnames except the fact that they have all been often absurdly anglicized as Bird. This arose from the supposed incorporation of the Irish word éan (bird) in these names. None of them, however, is so derived.

Heany is the anglicized form both of Ó hÉanna (i.e. descendant of Enda) and also of Ó hÉinigh, which was formerly Ó hÉignigh, a form still extant as Hegney. There were several septs of both these names, now all Heany or Heeney. Since these are now found mainly in counties Armagh and Louth, the ancient sept of greatest interest to people of the name today will be that of Oriel: Ó hÉignigh was chief of Fermanagh until they became tributary to the MacGuires in 1202; some of the annalists give them the title of king of Fermanagh and others king of Oriel prior to that date. There were also O'Heaneys, chiefs of Clann Chearnaigh (in Co. Armagh) whom some authorities consider to be a distinct sept. Also in Ulster there were the O'Heanys who were erenaghs of Banagher, Co. Derry. The tomb of St. Muireadach O'Heaney is, or was, in the church which he is reputed to have founded there in 1121. O'Heanys and Heneys were found by Petty's enumerators to be numerous in both Louth and Derry in 1659 and the Hearth Money Rolls of Co. Armagh, compiled about the same time, list a considerable number of them. At that time the former recorded Heany, Heeney and Heney as among the principal Irish names in Co. Tipperary, and in the Hearth Money Rolls of that county it appears no less than 44 times. It is, however, rare now in Munster, as also is Bird. One may assume that these Co. Tipperary O'Heanys were of the Eoghanacht sept of Ó hÉanna mentioned by Woulfe, who differentiates it from a Dalcassian sept whence, he says, sprang three mediaeval archbishops or bishops of the name. There were, in fact, five: three of Killaloe in the early thirteenth century and two of Cashel, notably Matthew O'Heney (d. 1205), a Cistercian monk of Holy Cross, who became archbishop in 1196, was Papal legate, founded many churches and wrote a life of St Cuthbert. The Four Masters mention another bishop, Maelfinnia Ó hAenigh, who filled the see of Luighne (Meath). O'Donovan treats Ó hAenigh in this case as a hereditary surname: if that was so it furnishes a very early example, as the bishop died in 922 A.D. There is yet another important O'Heany sept, one of the Hy Fiachrach group, seated in Co. Mayo. Here again it is probably that these O'Heanys of north Connacht are of dual origin, one being Ó hÉighnigh and the other Ó Héanna. The name, however, is not numerous there today. In modern times one of the north Tipperary-Offaly O'Heanys was very well known in America, namely Cornelius Heeney (1754-1848), who went to New York at 30 years of age, became a multi-millionaire and devoted practically all his immense fortune to charity. Seamus Heaney is a distinguished contemporary poet.

The second surname to be widely changed to Bird is Henaghan, other forms of which in use today are Heanaghan, Henehan, Henihan, Henekan and occasionally Heenan – the last is properly a different name associated with Offaly and north Tipperary. This sept of O'Henaghan, called Ó hÉineacháin (sometimes Ó hÉanacháin) in Irish, was also of the Hy Fiachrach and located in Co. Mayo – originally in the parishes of Balla and Manulla. Henaghan is a very numerous name now in counties Mayo and Galway. In 1635 when Strafford's Inquisi-

tion of Co. Mayo was carried out there were many of the name in the adjacent baronies of Carra and Clanmorris – in that document the G is treated as hard, the spellings being O'Henegan and O'Henigan. We find Henecan, too. Fr. Patrick Henecan, parish priest of Ballysodare, was Dean and Vicar-General of the diocese of Achonry in 1743. A few families, usually spelt Henehan or Henihan, are to be found also in west Munster; these may well be a distinct sept, at any rate they were in Kerry at an early date, for Tayg O'Henehan was arraigned as a robber there in 1295.

(O) HEARTY   Though I have no alternative suggestion to offer, I hesitate to accept Woulfe's statement that Hearty is Ó hAghartaigh and a variant of Ó Faghartaigh, which as we know from The Book of Lecan was of Carra (Co. Mayo) and has since been confused with Faherty. Not only do the birth registrations of the past century indicate that the name now belongs almost exclusively to counties Louth and Monaghan; three centuries ago O'Hearty appears in the Oriel country several times in the Co. Armagh Hearth Money Rolls.

HEASLIP   This name has many spelling variants: Hazlip, Heslip, Heyslip and Hyslop were all reported by local registrars and recorded in Matheson's Synonyms (1901); in the 1866 birth registrations, Haslip, Heslip and Heslop as well as Heaslip occur (13 births were registered in that year, all in counties Cavan and Down) while in earlier centuries we find many other variants.

The remarkable fact about Heaslip families is that, though since the late eighteenth century the great majority of them have been located in south Ulster, prior to that the name was almost exclusively associated with Munster. At the present time there are 15 families of Heaslip living in or near the parish of Denn, which is between Cavan town and Ballyjamesduff.

The earliest reference I have met is the deposition of Francis Haslopp, described as of Ballyharaghan Castle (which is in the parish of Ruan, Co. Clare), a Protestant deponent, in 1642. Thirty years later a Francis Hasclopp of Killeedy (Co. Limerick) appears as referee in a bounds dispute near O'Brien's Bridge, Co. Clare, and as late as 1831 we find another Francis Huslop (sic) in the Inchiquin estate records for Co. Clare. As Haselope and Heaslip the name appears in the Cork & Ross wills for 1675 and 1695, and I have noticed one or two other Co. Cork references in the late seventeenth century. Finally to give one more variant spelling, and at the same time another county in which they have settled, I may mention William Heslep, who was described in 1725 as a farmer of Ballymorane, King's County (Offaly).

According to Reaney the name is derived from the Old English words haesel (or possibly Old-Norse hesli) and hop, forming heslihop, i.e. dweller in a hazel valley.

O'HEAVY HEAPHY   In the sept map in Irish Families O'Heavy is placed in Co. Armagh. This is a misprint for O'Heany. It is corrected in the said map elsewhere. Heavy is a name now found in small numbers in all the provinces except Ulster; its main location being in the Athlone area. Its origin is obscure. The earliest instance I have found of it is a husbandman of Tristernagh, Co. Westmeath in 1601. The cognate surname Heaphy (Ó hÉamhthaigh) belongs to counties Waterford and Cork.

(O) HEDERMAN   The older form of this name, O'Hedroman is nearer the original Ó hEadroman than the present Hederman which, though it looks English, is a Gaelic-Irish surname belonging to counties Clare and Limerick. Dr. Dermot Hederman (b. c.1629), who was superior of the Irish scholars in the College of St. Barbara, Paris, in 1657, was later proposed as bishop of Limerick and became vicar-general of that diocese where he was prominent in church affairs for many years, particularly at the time of the alleged "Popish Plot". Traditionally the family is of west Clare. Eugene O'Curry in a note to John O'Donovan says: "The O'Hedromans are still numerous in the parish of Moyarta and are traditionally remembered as the ferry and fishermen of Saint Seanan, who, it is said, left them the privilege that none of the name should ever be drowned between Inis-Cathaigh and Kilcardain, nor was any of them remembered to have been drowned within that limit, though they are almost all boatmen". There is also a tradition that St. Senan appeared to a certain husbandman Senanimus O'Hettromain in the same part of Co. Clare. The modern variant spelling Hetherman is found in east Cork.

(O) HEELAN, Hyland   This name is Ó hAoileáin in Munster and Ó hOileáin in Connacht, both of these being variants of Ó Faoláin which was dealt with under the heading of Phelan — Whelan in Irish Families, pp. 245-246.

I have not found early references to them in Connacht, but the name Hyland is fairly common in Mayo now, as it was in the second half of the eighteenth century. Though frequent in the 1659 "census", none therein relates to Connacht nor does it appear in the Mayo Book of Survey & Distribution. I have not yet discovered when this branch of the sept was established in Mayo, but as it does not appear in the Annals or genealogical manuscripts dealing with north Connacht it can safely be assumed that it was not a distinct sept.

References to Hiland, O'Hilane, Hylan, O'Huylan (and many other variant spellings) are numerous in the Ormond Deeds, the Fiants and other mediaeval documents, as well as those of a later date, and all are to persons dwelling in the O'Phelan country, i.e. primarily Co. Waterford, but stretching into Leinster through Kilkenny into Leix and even (in 1659) as far as Co. Kildare. They first come into prominence, as Hyland rather than Phelan, in connexion with Carrick-on-Suir, beginning with Philip Hywlan, a burgess of the town in 1338, followed by other citizens in the fifteenth and sixteenth centuries. In 1508 John Hilan was public notary in Waterford; in 1592 Father Maurice O'Hillane is described in a State Paper as "one of the chiefest maintainers" of Dr. Creagh, Bishop of Cork. The christian names Philip and David seem to have been much in favour with these Waterford and south Kilkenny families, who frequently

used, and use, the form Heelan as their surname.

A notable churchman of Irish birth was Dr. Hyland O.P. (d. 1884), Archbishop of Port of Spain.

(O) HEFFRON, Haverin   Hefferan and Haverin (with other minor spelling variations) are variants of Heffron, which is the usual modern form in Co. Mayo — in a 1783 Ballinrobe list of householders, in which there are six of the name, they are all given as Hevrin. In the Fiants of two centuries earlier they are O'Heverin, O'Heveron, etc. Most of these, however, are of quite different stock from the Heffrons of Co. Mayo who are a branch of the Cenél Eoghain called Ó hEimhrin in Irish. The great majority of the numerous people referred to in the sixteenth century records as O'Heverin etc., belonged to the Offaly sept of Ó hUidhrin, which is anglicized O'Heryne and O'Herin in the earliest examples. The bard Giolla na Naomh Ó hUidhrin (d. 1420), who completed O'Dugan's famous Topographical Poem, is usually called O'Heerin in English. Families of this sept were very numerous in the seventeenth century also; they appear among the principal Irish names for three baronies of King's County (Offaly) in 1659; but as the name has been widely changed to O'Heffernan, a sept of the neighbouring county of Tipperary, the two in and near Offaly are now indistinguishable. In the "census" of 1659 we also find O'Heveran among the principal Irish names in Co. Antrim. These were yet another distinct sept whose surname in Irish is Ó hAmhráin. If the name is still extant in north-east Ulster it is very rare.

O HEHIR   Though by origin probably belonging to the Uí Fidhgheinte group, this family has been for so many centuries established in Co. Clare in the heart of Thomond that it is now usually counted as Dalcassian. The name is fairly numerous in counties Clare and Limerick, but rare elsewhere. It is Ó hAichir (from aichear, bitter, sharp) in Irish.   Map

HEMPENSTAL   This name was formerly spelt Hepenstal, and still is in the case of the family of Dopping-Hepenstal (until recently of Derrycassan, Co. Longford). It is derived from a Yorkshire place-name. The Hepenstals have been prominent among the landed gentry of Co. Wicklow since the early eighteenth century and references to the name are almost entirely confined to that county and to the neighbouring counties of Wexford and Dublin. The earliest I have met is to a family living at Templeogue towards the end of the seventeenth century. In 1855 there were fourteen householders in Co. Wicklow and seven in Co. Wexford, according to the returns in Griffith's Valuation. The best known individual was the gigantic Lieut. Jack Hepenstal of the Yeomanry, whose activities in supressing the Rising of 1798 made him notorious and earned for him the soubriquet of "the walking gallows". His savagery, however, was quite uncharacteristic of the family.

HENDRON   This name is particularly associated with Co. Armagh. The births of 1865, for example, reveal that of eleven registered in that year eight were at Lurgan, two in other Co. Armagh towns and one in Co. Antrim. Other years for which statistics are available present a similar picture though the numbers were smaller and there was less concentration at Lurgan itself. An interesting fact also emerges from this source, viz., that the name Hendry also belongs to Co. Armagh. It appears that while not used as synonyms, both these names are of the same origin as Henderson, which in fact is recorded by the Registrar-General as interchangeable: cases where one member of a family was reported as Hendron and another as Henderson are cited. Reaney, usually a reliable authority, differentiates between Hendry and Hendra, deriving the former, like Henderson, from the Old-French Henri and the latter from a Cornish place-name, Hendra being a modern form of hen dref i.e. old homestead. Hendry and MacHendrie are a branch of the Scottish clan MacNaughton. It is thus clear that these two Irish-sounding surnames, Hendron and Hendry, are in fact of British origin – or, if one goes back far enough, of Norman origin (except in the rare case of MacHendry being used for MacHenry). Hendron does not appear to be of any great antiquity in Ireland: at any rate I have found no instance of it before the eighteenth century. All the references I have met have been to families located in Ulster, except for Dublin in which, of course, being the capital of the country, people from all the provinces are found. Hendry, however, occurs earlier, e.g., William Hendry is recorded in Pynnar's survey as a tenant on the manor of Fortcunningham, Co. Donegal, in 1618.

(O) HESLIN   This sept belongs by tradition to Breffny and its representatives are still mainly located in the western part of that territory, particularly around Mohill, Co. Leitrim. The Gaelic-Irish form of the name is now Ó hEislin: it was formerly Ó hEisleanáin and the anglicized form of this is illustrated in the person of Father Heslenane OFM (Louvain, 1664). A century earlier we find the name in Leitrim and Longford Fiants given as O'Hislenane and O'Hiselunane. It is occasionally met elsewhere, e.g., Cormack O'Heslenan who was arrested for suborning a witness against Phelim O'Byrne in Co. Wicklow in 1629.

HESTER   Woulfe gives the Gaelic-Irish form of this name as Ó hOistir, but this appears to be little more than a guess on his part. According to Bardsley Hester is an English name derived from the Anglo-Norman estre, which means a street or town.
    Perhaps John Estret of Co. Meath, who is mentioned in Archbishop Alen's Register under date 1504, may be an early form. Another name introduced in the Dowdall Deeds, which might possibly be a form of Hester, is Colm Heycetir, provost of Dundalk in 1340-41. Neither of these is anywhere near counties Mayo and Roscommon which is the part of the country associated with the name Hester in modern times.

(O) HESTIN, Hastings   Ó hOistín, formerly Hestin in north Connacht and Histon in Co. Limerick, has now been widely corrupted to Hastings, an English name having no connexion whatever with Ireland. The sept was one of those associated with the powerful Mac-Dermots of Moylurg and their present day representatives are mainly found in Mayo. A branch migrated to Clare and thence to Co. Limerick: the name is found today in both those counties.

HEWITT   This is, of course, a well known English name: it is derived from a diminutive of the Christian name Hugh. In Ireland it is now generally regarded as belonging to Ulster, perhaps owing to its prominence in the athletics of that province and possibly from the fact that it is the surname of the Viscounts Lifford. Modern statistics, too, indicate that the name is now found predominantly in Ulster. It is therefore interesting to find that, though there are some Hewitts in the Ulster Hearth Money Rolls of the 1660's and Humphery Hewett was then an officer in the Tyrone militia, early references to the name all relate to Munster, from 1295 when John Heued, late "sargeant of the King", and his wife Alice were found not guilty of fraud and larceny. There is not one Ulster Hewitt among the eleven who appear in the list of Prerogative wills – they are practically all Cork and Dublin. Diocesan wills record seven between 1652 and 1795 in the diocese of Cork and Ross, one in Cloyne and two in Cashel. Similarly the register of Dublin University students has eleven Hewitts or Hewetts mostly from Co. Cork, none from Ulster. In the "census" of 1659 there are two tituladoes called Hewett both in Munster. From 1522 they begin to appear in Co. Dublin and the 1598 "Description of Ireland" includes Hewitt of Garriston among the "men of name" in Co. Dublin.

HILLERY   The surname Hillery is closely associated with west Clare, especially since Dr Patrick Hillery, a prominent member of the Lemass cabinet, became President of Ireland in 1976. His other three grand-parents were of Gaelic-Irish stock, but Hillery, still sometimes spelt Hillary, is of Norman origin, being derived from the Latin word hilarius (cheerful), whence St. Hilaire and Mt St. Hilary in Co. Cork. As Hillary it appears in wills and other Leinster records of mid-eighteenth century with an East Anglia background, but I have found no evidence indicating a connexion between those Leinster families and the Clare Hillerys. The latter have long become well established in the west Clare baronies of Ibrickan and Corcomroe and are there regarded as just as Gaelic-Irish as any indigenous Clancy, MacMahon or O'Brien. Ó hIrghile has been used officially as the Irish form of Hillery but this appears to be based on no authentic evidence. In Co. Clare it has locally been gaelicized as Hilaoire.
    Ó hIrghile is properly anglicized (O') Hirelly, a rare variant of the Donegal name Hirrell, both of these being synonyms, locally aspirated, of Ó Frighill, i.e. (O') Friel.

HILLIARD   This is a name of German origin (from Old-

German hildegard, meaning war stronghold) which came to Ireland from England in the seventeenth century: there are five officers and men of the name (spelt Hild-yard, Hilliard and other variants) in the Irish army lists between 1644 and 1685; and Robert Hilliard, whose will was proved in 1678, was a distiller in Dublin. From that on, apart from Dublin, they have been mainly associated with Co. Kerry. In the 1901 census 19 families of Hilliard are recorded as resident in Co. Kerry.

(O) HINGERTY   Woulfe regards Hingerty as a variant of O'Finaghty. I do not accept this. I think Hingerty derives from one of the early Gaelic surnames which for the most part became in due course Harrington. Fairly conclusive evidence of this is afforded by Elizabethan Fiant 3082 in which John MacTeige O'Hengertye of Dunbeacon, Co. Cork, is described as alias Harrington: that was in 1577. Hingerty occurs twice in the Co. Tipperary Hearth Money Rolls of 1664. It is now rare.

HIPWELL   One Isaac Hipwell served in Dongan's Regiment of the royalist army in Ireland about the year 1665. A family of the name became established in Queen's Co. (Leix) subsequently and is still well known around Portlaoise.

(O) HOBAN   According to MacFirbis the sept of Ó hÚbáin was a branch of the Ulster Cenél Eoghain settled in Mayo. Mayo is the county in which the name is chiefly found today and the only two pre-seventeenth century references to the name I have met are both to persons in that county, viz., in 1584 to David O'Hubane of Burrishoole, a cleric, and in 1592 to Shane O'Howbane of Togher, a carpenter. In the next century the Book of Survey & Distribution for Co. Mayo mentions several Hubans. Even then the prefix O appears to have been generally discarded from this name. It was also in counties Tipperary and Kilkenny. In the former five families of Hubbane are listed in the Hearth Money Rolls of 1665; in the latter three Hobans are included in the Ossory wills (1754-1771), and in Co. Kilkenny, too, the place called Hoban's Bridge recalls the inexplicable explosion in 1826 whereby a carrier called Hoban lost his life.

The most noteworthy man of the name was John Hoban (1762-1832), who was the architect of the White House and other important buildings in the United States. He was born in Carlow.

(O) HOLLERAN   This is a form of the well known surname Halloran. Holleran is almost peculiar to counties Mayo and Galway.

HOLLY MacCULLIN   Disregarding the English name Holley or Holly which, if found at all in Ireland, is very rare, Holly is located in two widely separated areas and in these its origin is different. In Co. Kerry it was first anglicized MacCullin, i.e. Mac Cuilinn (cuileann is

the Irish for holly), and this form occurs in the Fiants for Co. Kerry in the person of Teig MacCullin of Gortinsearnie who received a "pardon" in 1601, but this soon became Holly. Of the seven births registered for Holly in 1865 six were in the Glin-Listowel area (the other was at Kilmacthomas) and in 1901 there were 15 Holly families in Co. Kerry. We also find Morogh MacRorye MacOwen O Holowe in Co. Kerry in a Fiant of 1574; I have found no evidence that this became Holly, but even if it is not relevant I like to record it as an example of a name which is a pedigree in itself. The other habitat of the Hollys is Ulster. In modern times it has been recorded by local registrars as used synonymously with Quillan. In that case no doubt the Gaelic form is Mac Uighilin (see MacQuillan). MacCullin is in the Elizabethan Fiants relating to Co. Monaghan and in the next century Petty's "census" lists it as a principal Irish name in that county. MacCullin, however, does not appear to have become to any extent Holly by translation there. It is still MacCullin where it has not been absorbed by the better known MacQuillan.

(O) HONAN   Honan is a rare name, but it is well known on account of the fame of the beautiful Honan Hostel Chapel in University College, Cork. Though like many more of our uncommon Irish surnames it does not appear in Matheson's modern birth registration records, since less than 5 births were registered in 1890, there were 16 registrations in 1864, 17 in 1865 and 22 in 1866, more than half of these being in Co. Clare. It is not in the "census" of 1659, which, of course, as presented by Petty, or at least as it now survives, does not purport to give the name of every person dwelling in the country. Nevertheless it occurs frequently in the Co. Tipperary Hearth Money Rolls of 1665 and 1667. Robert Honan, of Limerick, was one of those whose outlawry as a Jacobite was reversed in 1699. In the previous century we find it not only as O'Honan and Honyn but in such forms as O'Honounne in various parts of Munster, especially counties Cork, Limerick and Tipperary. Earlier an interesting entry appears in the Justiciary Rolls for 1307 when Adam le Blound received 5 marks and 40d. as compensation for the slaying of his hibernicus John O'Honan by Henry de Midia in Co. Cork. Woulfe gives the Irish form of Honan as Ó hEoghanáin, and Ó hUaithnín for Honeen, thus sharply differentiating these two surnames both of which are of Thomond origin. Honan is still prominent though not common in Co. Clare, while Honeen (earlier O'Huonyn) has become Greene, (from Irish uaine, green). They have inevitably been confused: Herbert, for example, in his Worthies of Thomond refers to Admiral O'Huonyn (mentioned in the article on O'Huoneen in Irish Families, p. 185) as Honan. I am by no means convinced that in Co. Clare they are not of common origin.

HONE   The best known family of this name came to Ireland from Holland. It has also been used for Howen i.e., Ó hEoghain in Co. Fermanagh. O'Hone and O'Howen both appear in the Co. Monaghan Hearth Money Rolls (1664).

128

(O) HOOD, Mahood   The name of the legendary outlaw Robin Hood (whose historical authenticity is ill supported) is so well known to young and old that the surname Hood is usually assumed to be purely English. In Ulster, however, it is less likely to be borne by a British settler than by a descendant of the Ó hUid sept. They were hereditary bards to the O'Neills of Clandeboy and produced several mediaeval Gaelic poets of sufficient importance to be mentioned in the Annals. Hood and also Mahood are names found almost exclusively in Ulster and chiefly in Antrim and Down today. Mahood is, of course, simply MacHood (analagous with Mahaffy, Mahollum etc.), which as MacHudde is to be found in seventeenth century records, e.g. the Co. Armagh Hearth Money Rolls. Hood, without a prefix, occurs in those for Co. Donegal. I think that this is a case of erroneous substitution of Mac for O and that the Mahoods or Mac-Hoods are really O'Hoods. Elsewhere in Ireland their origin is English. The name Hudde, an earlier form of Hood, is very common in early English records, and in Ireland, though not actually Norman, it goes back to the thirteenth century. Several people so called are recorded in the Justiciary Rolls and Ormond Deeds as early as 1297: these were mostly in Co. Tipperary and one of their homes, in the Cashel area, was called Huddeston. By the seventeenth century they had become more numerous in south Kilkenny and Wexford, where the place-name Hoodsgrove perpetuates the memory of one branch. The name occurs very frequently in the records of the city of Dublin, too, especially in connexion with the trade guilds.

John Hood (1720-1772), inventor of Hood's compass theodolite, came from Co. Donegal.

HOPKINS   Hopkins is, of course, a well known English surname derived from Hobb, a colloquial form of Robert; and no doubt some families of Hopkins in Ireland, including those from whom the townlands of Hopkinstown (Co. Meath) and Hopkinsrea (Co. Tipperary) are named, are of English origin. But the prevalence of the name in Connacht, particularly in Co. Mayo, and the fact that Habbagan is recorded in our own time as synonymous with Hopkins there, suggest a different and more Irish background. This is corroborated by a search of seventeenth century records. For example the "census" of 1659 records Hobigan as one of the principal Irish names in the barony of Rathcline, Co. Longford, which is adjacent to Co. Roscommon. Even more convincing is the evidence of the Galway Book of Survey & Distribution, wherein we read that in the parish of Addergoole a man called Edward Hopkins in 1676 was styled Edward Obbykin in 1641. I might also mention Edmond Hopkine alias Bokine of Lacka, Co. Galway, who according to the list in the Ormond manuscripts, was transplanted in 1656, as was Honora Hopkin, of Co. Westmeath. Somewhat earlier we find among a list of Mayo clergy, mostly bearing Gaelic-Irish names, Donald MacObichin in the parish of Ballinchalla. I think therefore, it can be accepted that in Connacht, where the present Hopkins population is estimated to be approximately 1000 persons, Hopkins is either a Gaelic-Irish or

at any rate a Gaelicized Norman surname, now spelt Mac-Oibicín.

O'HORA   O'Hora as a synonym of O'Hara is amongst those given by the registrar-general, Robert Matheson, in his official report on the subject. This, however, is no proof that they are in fact true variants of the same Gaelic name, since the absorption of uncommon names by common ones is a phenomenon frequently noticed in this book. A further fact which would point to their identity is that O'Hora is found almost exclusively in north Connacht, the homeland of the O'Haras; and I may add an interesting reference to them in that part of Ulster to which a branch of the O'Haras migrated; in 1606 the O'Horas were employed, in company with the MacDonnells, MacGuinnesses and MacQuillans, to "prosecute" woodkern in Co. Antrim. (This of course, is an isolated case and may have been no more than a misspelling of the name in the Lord Deputy's letter.) On the other hand there is an entirely distinct sept of Ó hEarchadha which, according to Woulfe, is anglicized inter alia as Horahoe, obsolete forms being O'Harroghue, O'Horrochoe, O'Horchoy etc. The latter appears in the "census" of 1659 as a principal Irish name in the barony of Corren, Co. Sligo, and an O'Hurkoy is among the Sligomen who obtained "pardons" in 1592. Horohoe is a well known name in Swinford, Co. Mayo, area. In the list of synonyms referred to above Horoho and Horaho are reported from Swinford as being sometimes ridiculously changed to the English names Harris and Harrison. Neither of the latter, however, is at all common in Connacht, though both are numerous in Dublin and Belfast.

HORE, Hoare   The name Hoare or Hore is now found chiefly in counties Cork and Kerry. It has long association with the city of Cork where Hoare's Bank was an important institution in the early eighteenth century – a good account of this will be found in Journal of the Cork Historical & Archaeological Society, vol. 1, (1892).

It is, however, with Co. Wexford that the name is most intimately associated. It recurs in the "Ormond Deeds", the feodaries, etc., frequently from the year 1247 when the family of Le Hore were in possession of

Tilladavin (parish of Tomhaggard, barony of Bargy). In the thirteenth century also Thomas le Hore held lands in the barony of Bantry, Co. Wexford: this adjoins Co. Kilkenny, in which county Hores were considerable landholders in succeeding centuries; Horetown, Horesland and Horeswood are all place-names in Co. Wexford, attesting the influential position of the family there. They were in Co. Louth too: Walter Hore held estates there in 1404. In the "Ormond Deeds" the name appears as early as 1190, often in the Latin form of Canutus.

Traditionally they are descended from Philipe le Hore, who was one of the Anglo-Norman invaders under Strongbow. In the mediaeval records the name is given variously as Le Hore, La Hore, Le Horhe, the Hore (de Hore is an eighteenth century invention). The derivation of the name is uncertain. Capt. Edward Hoare in his valuable book on the family, referred to in Irish Families, p. 324, mentions several possible derivations: that from the word hore or hoar meaning white or grisly (cf. hoarfrost) is usually considered the most probable but it must be remembered that hore is an Anglo-Saxon or Scandinavian not a Norman word.

In the sixteenth century Hore of Pole-Hore and Hore of Harperstown are included in the contemporary (1598) list of chief gentlemen of Co. Wexford so often quoted in this book. The name appears many times in the Fiants, in almost every case for the Wexford area, recording pardons, which in effect meant the admission of native Irishmen to the ordinary rights of citizens under English law, so far as it was in operation. One Fiant of 1566 does include a horseman called Hore, of Kilmallock, Co. Limerick, but that is an exception.

Coming to more modern times we find Hore given in Petty's "census" of 1659 as one of the principal Irish names in the barony of Shelmalier (which lies between Bargy and Bantry): in the same document two Hoares appear in Co. Cork, one in the city and one in the parish of Fanlobus. A generation later four of the name were in James II's parliament of 1689, for constituencies in counties Wexford and Waterford, and at least one was an officer in his Irish army and seven appear in the list of attainders following the Jacobite defeat.

It cannot be assumed, however, that all Hores in Ireland are necessarily descendants of the long established Anglo-Norman families referred to above. Several came later to this country, for example as Cromwellian officers and as "adventurers": indeed it is stated in Burke's Landed Gentry, that the Co. Cork line descends from two officers in Ireton's army.

Notable Irishmen of the name include Brother Mathew Hore O.F.M., who, with Fr. Fleming, was martyred at Benescha in 1631; Sean de Hóra (c.1716-c.1780), Gaelic poet of west Clare, who, according to O'Curry, was born in Co. Cork; and Philip Herbert Hore, whose valuable history of Wexford fills six large volumes – his voluminous MSS are preserved at St. Peter's College, Wexford. Several of the Cork family were prominent in their day: Joseph Hoare M.P. was created a baronet in 1784, and is remembered for having, though totally blind and 93 years of age, attended the House of Commons in 1800 to vote against the Union.

It should perhaps be added that when found in Connacht the name Hore may well be of quite different origin, because Horahoe, the usual anglicized form of Ó hEarchadha, has to some extent, been absorbed by the simpler Hore. The same name is also sometimes anglicized as Harrihy and from that has riduculously become Harrison and Harris. Co. Sligo rent rolls of the early seventeenth century give the name as O'Harroghue, Horohoe is now very rare, it is often contrasted to Hore. The fact that the late eighteenth century scribe Edmond Hore wrote his name in Irish as Ó Horrochodha, as Dr. Moore has pointed out, suggests that in Co. Roscommon it may be distinct from the Mayo Ó hEarchadha.

(O) HORGAN   This is, and always has been, an almost exclusively Munster surname. The 66 birth registrations for 1890 were all for that province, 40 being in Co. Cork and 21 in Co. Kerry. The 1864 figures are even more striking as of 86 Horgan births registered that year all except two (Dublin and Clonmel) were in counties Cork and Kerry. There are no less than 4 Ballyhorgans in Co. Kerry, all in the barony of Clanmaurice, and the 1901 census records 142 families of Horgan in that county. The most notable person of the name, Rev. Mathew Horgan (1777-1849), P.P. of his native parish of Whitechurch, Co. Cork, was a poet, Gaelic scholar and antiquary. Of course the name occurs occasionally outside the borders of the southern province, e.g. pardon of David O'Horegane, a kern, of Lex (Leix) in 1551. This, however, is probably a mis-spelling of O'Horahan (or O'Hourihan) since a sept so called was located at Dunamase, Co. Leix. This name is Ó hAnradháin in Irish, better known in Thomond where it is anglicized O'Hanrahan.

The Gaelic form of the name, Ó hArgáin, is said to be a corruption of Ó hAnradháin, which is the name of the erenagh family of Ross, Co. Cork, anglicized Hourihane there and Hourigan in Co. Limerick. Synonyms of Horgan used in Munster are Harrigan (Listowel) Horrigan (Kenmare and Mallow) and Organ (Cashel).   Map

HOSFORD   This name is of Cromwellian origin in Ireland: it is believed to be derived from Horseford, a place in Norfolk, England, though some English families so called came from Horseforth in Yorkshire; and the fact that Horsford is sometimes used as a synonym of Hosford corroborates the belief. It is remarkable in two respects: it is found almost exclusively in west Cork and though the rural population has declined in the past century, the Hosfords living in a rural district have markedly increased in numbers.

(Mac) HOSTY, Custy   Woulfe evidently treated the name Custy as obsolete, as he does not give this as one of the anglicized variants of the Gaelic-Irish Mac Oiste (or Mac Coiste), though he does give MacCosty as a form no longer in use. Custy, however, appears in the Clare freeholders, 1821, and is still extant in west Clare to my own knowledge. According to tradition Mac Oiste, normally anglicized Hosty (sometimes Hasty), originated as a surname with Roger (Hodge) Merrick, a Mayo Welshman who was killed in 1276. It was in Co. Galway in the sixteenth and seventeenth centuries: it occurs as MacCusty in the Composition Book of Connought (1585); eight times ad MacCosty(e) and MacCosto in the Galway Book of Survey & Distribution (barony of Dunmore) and many times in the Elizabethan Fiants relating to counties Galway and Mayo as MacHostie, MacHoste, MacCoiste, MacQuist etc., and is still found in its modern form in fair numbers in those counties.

Hasty is mentioned in the Registrar-General's report on synonyms as becoming Hastings both in Co. Armagh and Co. Derry. The rare name McGusty is also presumably an anglicized form of Mac Oiste. For further reference to Hastings see Hestin.

HOVENDEN   Though now very rare this name was formerly much more numerous in Ireland and, moreover, one of considerable note. According to Prof. Hayes-McCoy the family came to Ireland as Scottish mercenaries under O'Neill, but Fr. Paul Walsh says they were an English family which settled in Co. Tyrone under the Great Earl. There is no doubt that they were closely associated with the O'Neills, for one Robert Hovenden married an O'Neill widow, Richard and Henry Hovenden are described in 1594 as foster brothers of the Earl of Tyrone and Henry Hovenden had been the earl's secretary for ten years at the time of the Flight of the Earls in 1607; and in the subsequent Plantation of Ulster we find them classed as "natives" in Co. Tyrone. In 1664 a Hovendon appears in the lists of Co. Armagh householders.

The name Hovenden, though less prominent in Leinster, is also closely associated with Queen's Co. (mod. Leix) where their main seat has been at Tankardstown since 1550. Not far away Egidius Hovenden, of Levediston, Co. Kildare, is described as "gent" in a Fiant of 1557.

In the "census" of 1659 Hovendens appear as tituladoes in four counties viz., Cork, Tipperary, Clare and Down, i.e. only one Ulster county; but in the attainders of Jacobites in 1691 there are two from Co. Armagh, one from Tyrone and one from Queen's Co. Three Hovendens, transplanted in 1657 as Papists were from counties Limerick and Mayo.

In several of the references to which I have referred, and notably in the Ormond Manuscripts lists of seventeenth century army personnel, the name is given as Hovenden alias Ovington; and going back to the fifteenth century, de Offington occurs quite frequently, e.g. in the Ormond Deeds. We do, in fact, find the name in Ireland long before that, as for example David de Offynton, who was Seneschal of Kilkenny in 1295.

Ovington is now almost obsolete but a modern synonym in Co. Derry is Huffington.

There was a twelfth century annalist called Roger de Hovenden, whose work dealt with Ireland. In modern times Robert Hovenden, born at Dunmanway, Co. Cork in 1840, was a landscape and subject painter of note. He was killed in 1895 endeavouring to save the life of a child at a railway crossing.

HOWARD, O'Hure   IVERS   MacKEEVER, MacIvor
The Thomond sept of Ó hÍomhair, in allowing their ancient and honourable name, formerly englicized O'Hever, O'Huar, O'Hywer etc., to be superseded by Howard, assumed one of the most aristocratic of English surnames; but the fact that the form O'Hawrde was used as early as 1542 should acquit them of any snobbish motive in so doing. O'Huer was still in general use in Clare in the seventeenth century — it is listed in Petty's "census" as one of the principal names in the barony of Inchiquin — but now they are all Howards, even the few families around Corofin, who sixty years ago were still called O'Hure, in speech, though officially recorded as Howard. The sept was allied to the O'Deas, though located further north in the county near Mount Callan, and is listed in the "Wars of Turlough" among the principal Thomond septs at the Battle of the Abbey in 1317. It has been stated that certain Ó hÍomhair families who forsook the Irish cause and became of the ascendancy used the name Ivers not Howard. However, Thomas Dineley, who visited Mount Ievers (now spelt Ivers) in 1682, tells us in his diary that its owner Henry Ievers had acquired the place only fourteen years before that, having come to Ireland as a barrister's clerk. He was High Sheriff of Co. Clare in 1673. Before his time Mount Ivers was called Ballinareela. In the "census" of 1659, referred to above, the name, spelt then O'Heever, appears numerous in the barony of Corran, Co. Sligo. O'Donovan in his notes in The Tribes and Customs of Hy Fiachrach states that Ó hÍomhair (descendant of Ivor), the name of a Sligo sept located in the parish of Kilglass on the east side of Killala Bay, had become Ivers in some places at that time (about a century ago). It is not common there now. Ivers is a name which is to be found today also in Co. Louth, but I think it is an abbreviation of MacIvor which is there an alternative form of MacKeever — Mac Íomhair in Irish. Both MacIvor and MacKeever are well known names in counties Monaghan, Tyrone and Derry. It is interesting to note that on a Dungannon jury convened in connexion with the Plantation of Ulster in 1609, 23 of its 24 members had Gaelic-Irish surnames including Edmond MacOwen MacIvor. In the Patent Rolls of that time it occurs as MacEver in Co. Armagh. It has been suggested that the MacKeevers are Mac Éimhir not Mac Iomhair and a branch of the MacMahons with whom the forename Éimhear (anglice Heber) was favoured. MacKeevers appear in the Hearth Money Rolls for Co. Armagh (1664); and one Neile MacKeever was secretary to Shane O'Neill in 1567. Possibly the Iverses of Co. Louth are descendants of one of the Ivers (or Evers) families (relatives of the Taaffes) who were among the leading gentry of Co. Meath in the sixteenth century.

According to Woulfe Howard is used as the anglicized form of the rare surname Ó hOghairt. This would hardly be worth mentioning here were it not for the fact recorded by Matheson that in the Ballymoney area Hogart and Howard are found as synonymous. Woulfe, however, differentiates between Ó hOgairt and Ó hOghairt. I have no first-hand knowledge of these names beyond noting that one Hygyn Hogart was among the muster of captains, archers etc., reviewed at Mellifont Cistercian monastery in 1434.

All the Howards who have been prominent in Irish life were born or lived in Dublin. Four of them were of the family the head of which was created Viscount Wicklow in 1785. Hugh Howard (1675-1737) was a noted portrait painter and collector of pictures; George Edmond Howard (1715-1780), a voluminous author chiefly of legal works, is notable for the fact that he was one of the earliest advocates of Catholic Emancipation. Though not of an Irish family Cardinal Dominic Howard is of interest to Ireland because he brought the head of Blessed Oliver Plunket to Rome, whence it was later transferred to Drogheda.

(O) HOWLEY WHOOLEY   Woulfe equates this name with the Irish Ó hUallaigh, which he suggests may be an abbreviated variant of Ó hUallacháin (Houlihan), O'Houlig occurs in a Fiant of 1581 relating to Co. Cork, where O'Houlihans were and are numerous, but for the most part Howleys are found in north Connacht with some in Galway and Clare. There is an English surname Howley derived from a place of that name, but our Irish Howleys, at any rate those in the west, are not of that descent: the use of the form O'Howley with the prefix O, e.g., in Fiant 5799 relating to Co. Mayo, indicates an Irish origin. In modern times Wholey has been used as a synonym of Howley and this may give a clue to the curious equation of Howley and Wylie in east Clare. The most prominent men of the name Howley have not been of Connacht. John Howley, an officer in Butler's infantry regiment of King James II's Irish army, was presumably from Co. Kilkenny or Co. Tipperary, and Henry Howley (c. 1774-1803), executed for his part in the Robert Emmet rising, was born at Roscrea. Two officers of the name also appear in the army lists to be found in the Ormond manuscripts of 1644 and 1664. Some have been distinguished churchmen: Robert Howley was abbot of Mothel, Co. Waterford, in 1440, and William Howley, P.P. of Fethard, Co. Tipperary, was vicar-general of the archdiocese of Cashel as we know from a sworn anti-papist information of 1744.

In the Clonakilty (Co. Cork) district some O'Driscoll families acquired the agnomen Whooley which has now become a hereditary surname. In the forms Whooley, Whooly, Wholey and Wholy it appears quite frequently in the birth registrations for west Cork since compulsory registration was introduced in 1864.

HOWLIN, Holden   Following the Anglo-Norman invasion at the end of the twelfth century a Welsh family of Huolyn established themselves in an area in the southern part of what is now Co. Kilkenny and in due course became lords of Kilree and other places in the barony of Kells (Co. Kilkenny). There were many early variants of the name such as Holying. Houlyn and Howling, and these became standardized as Howlin. It appears frequently in records such as the Ormond Deeds and Judiciary Rolls from 1306, when Richard and John Houlin were tenants of the manor of Gowran; and later in the Chancery Rolls – in 1536 Edmund Holying, yeoman of Co. Waterford, was pardoned for murder. When the "cen-

sus" of 1659 was compiled Howling was recorded as a principal Irish name both in the barony of Kells and in that of Knocktopher, a location often mentioned in references to the family occurring in the intervening centuries. They had by that time spread into Co. Wexford, where the name was entered as Howlin, and a place was called Knockhowlin. Subsequently some branches of the family began to be called Holden, particularly in the vicinity of the Walsh mountains on the border of these two counties. In the barony of Gowran the place called Howlingstown in the 1659 "census" has since become Holdenstown. Holdensrath, near Kilkenny, is no doubt also named from them, but Holdenstown in Co. Wicklow, near Beltinglass, is given the alias Ballyhalton in a sixteenth century Fiant and has probably no relation to the surname now under consideration. Holden was certainly in use as a synonym of Howlin before 1685 when the will of Thomas Holden of Bennett's Bridge was proved; a few years later we meet the will of Michael Holden of Waterford. Smollet Holden (d. 1813), military music-master and instrument maker in Dublin, was the editor of several musical publications. His son Francis Holden, Mus. Doc., was associated with George Petrie in the collection of Irish airs.

Holden, it must be added, is also an English surname and some Holdens now settled in Ireland are unconnected with those of Howlin origin. The name occurs among the seventeenth century Ulster Plantation settlers; and is also that of a family which came from Lancashire about 1850; in their case the name Holden (quite numerous in the north midlands of England) is a contraction of Holedene.

For a curious gaelicization of the name see under Gildea. Normally it was called Húilín in Irish.

There was a remarkable character born in Tipperary called John "Plumper" Hoolan (1842-1911) an Australian pioneer and Labour politician who figures in many extravagant and amusing parliamentary incidents in Queensland. I have assumed that his family name was originally Howlin; but it may perhaps have been Hoolihan.

MacILHAGGA, Maharg   At first sight these two names would not appear to be variants, but when we remember that MacIlhagga is also found as MacIlharga, MacElhargy and MacIlharg and that in Ulster Mac in speech is frequently abbreviated to Ma the transition becomes intelligible. According to MacGiolla Domhnaigh the Gaelic form is Mac Giolla Chairge, which is common to Galloway in Scotland and to counties Antrim and Derry. Maharg is also written Meharg.

MacILHOLM   Extant variant spellings of this name are MacElholm and MacIlhome. Woulfe describes it as rare and very scattered; but in fact it is one very much associated with a definite and limited area, viz. the country between Enniskillen and Castlederg. That, at any rate, is the case for the past two centuries. If, however, Woulfe is correct in giving Mac Giolla Cholaim as the Gaelic-Irish form, it must be mentioned that in the

Elizabethan Fiants this name occurs in Co. Cavan in the person of Donogh duff Mac Gillacollum; but as, unlike most of the people included in the "pardon" in question, he was a soldier he need not necessarily have been a native of that province, (he is described as of Corananan, an unidentified place).

MacILVANY, MacElvenna   MacILVEEN
MacILWAINE, Kilbane   Though both MacIlwaine (or MacIlvaine) and MacIlveen are names almost entirely confined to north-east Ulster they are different in origin and are, it may be noted, not used as synonyms. The former is Mac Giolla Bháin in Irish, and is of the Hy Fiachrach group, the sept being located in the parish of Dromard, Co. Sligo; but in counties Sligo and Mayo it has become Kilbane and also, by partial translation, White. In 1659, however, it appears in the "census" as MacElveaine among the more numerous names in the baronies of Dromahair and Rosclogher, which are at the northern end of Co. Leitrim. The MacIlwaines and Mac-Ilvains of Ulster are of Scottish descent. MacIlveen, on the other hand, appears to be an indigenous Irish surname, belonging to south Co. Down, viz., Mac Giolla Mhín, mín (mild or gentle) being the root word, as compared with bán (white) in the other name under consideration. MacIlveen and MacIlvean are names of frequent occurrence in the Co. Armagh Hearth Money Rolls of 1664. Dr. William MacIlwaine (c. 1810-c. 1900), a Belfast clergyman, was a poet of some note in the seventies of the last century.

A'nother somewhat similar surname is MacIlvany with its variants MacElvenna, MacElveney and Gilvany. These are Mac Giolla Mheana in Irish. It belongs to north-east Ulster but is not numerous.

IRELAND   This surname is numerous in counties Armagh and Antrim. It is said to have originated in the case of early emigrants from Ireland who thus acquired the Norman name of de Yrlande, some of their descendants returning eventually to this country. In its modern form it occurs in the 1664 Hearth Money Rolls for Co. Armagh, and Samuel Ireland was one of the Poll-tax Commissioners for Co. Louth in 1660.

In mediaeval records we meet more frequently the cognate name le Ireis: its modern form, Irish, was formerly well known in Co. Kilkenny: eight families of the name are in Griffith's Valuation of that county in 1851, in which three Irelands also appear. Ireland is now rare there but fairly numerous in Ulster.

IRVINE, Ervine   IRWIN, Erwin   The best known of the Irvines are those of Irvinestown, Co. Fermanagh. Irvinestown, which lies close to the Co. Tyrone border, was formerly called Lowtherstown and even as late as the beginning of the present century it was described as "Irvinestown or Lowtherstown": the new name first appears officially in the census returns for 1861. The name Lowtherstown itself only dates from the seventeenth century. The lands in question were called Mekarney, Drominshin and Rosquire prior to a formal regrant to Sir Gerald Lowther in 1629. The Irvines who settled there about the same time became a very influential landlord family: in 1878 eight landlords of the name possessed 12,189 acres in Co. Fermanagh, 4621 in Co. Tyrone, 14,352 in Co. Donegal as well as more than 5,000 acres in other counties. In the same year there were 17 landowners named Irwin possessing 29,000 acres between them, most of which lay in Connacht, though seven of them held extensive estates in Fermanagh and other Ulster counties.

I treat Irwin and Irvine together because the two names have been much confused, especially in Ireland. Indeed the first of the Irvines of Irvinestown appears in the "census" of 1659 as Irwin, the titulado of Lowtherstown being recorded as William Irwin. In 1695 "Christopher Erwin of Castle Irwin", Co. Fermanagh, was M.P. for that county; and in 1714 the owner of Castle Irvine signed his will 'Christopher Irwin", while in 1755 the will of his successor to the estate bears the signature "Christopher Irvine". Nevertheless though they have been used to a considerable extent as synonyms in Ulster, even comparatively recently, as the Registrar-General's report published in 1901 shows, the two names are properly quite different in origin. According to Reaney Irvine is taken from a Scottish place-name, while Irwin is derived from the Old-English eoforwine (boar-friend). Woulfe treats them as synonyms, deriving both from the Gaelic Ó hEireamhóin, "a rare south of Ireland surname", and ignores the fact that these are almost entirely British surnames borne by families of planter stock in Ireland. The figures for two years for which detailed birth statistics are available, show how little connexion either of these names (especially Irvine) has with Munster:

	Ireland		Ulster		Connacht		Munster	
	1866	1890	1866	1890	1866	1890	1866	1890
Irvine, Ervine	75	87	70	80	0	2	2	2
Irwin, Erwin	188	137	146	114	15	7	10	12

It is noticeable that notwithstanding the fall in the population the number of Irvines in Ulster increased in the generation covered by these figures.

It is possible that some descendants of the small Gaelic sept mentioned by Woulfe are extant under the name of Irwin; but any references I have found to it relate to Leinster not to Munster. In 1297 and again in 1305 men named O'Hirwen, O'Hyrwin etc., were outlawed and about the same time we find an O'Herewen among the tenants of the manor of Dunkerrin, King's Co. The form O'Hervan occurs in a Fiant as late as 1601.

The two most notable men of the names under consideration were both Ulsterman: William Irvine (b. Co. Fermanagh 1740) who took a prominent part in the American War of Independence; and Thomas Caulfield Irwin (b. Co. Down 1823) who, though almost forgotten now, was regarded in his day as one of Ireland's most distinguished poets. Dr. Alexander Irwin (d. 1779), Bishop of Killala, was from Elphin.   Bibl., Map

IVORY   Although Thomas Ivory (1720-1786), the famous Dublin architect, who designed inter alia the Bluecoat School, was born in Cork, the name has been closely identified with Co. Wexford since it came to Ireland in the seventeenth century. This came about through the grants of land to the disbanded army of Cromwell in 1655. Capt. William Ivorie, or Ivory, of Ludlow's regiment of horse, settled in Co. Wexford. He soon became a leading citizen of New Ross and is so recorded in the "census" of 1659. He was one of the three gentlemen appointed for Co. Wexford to implement the proclamation of Novemver 2, 1678 ordering the disarming of all persons of the "Popish religion" throughout Ireland. His son Sir John, who was an officer in the Duke of Ormond's regiment in 1684 and later in other regiments, was M.P. for Wexford in 1692. There was a Capt. Ivorie in Lord Mountcashel's infantry regiment in James II's Irish army, but his christian name is not recorded and he does not appear in the Jacobite outlawries. A number of wills, nearly all for Co. Wexford, are in the diocesan records.

The name is of French origin – de Iverio or Ivray. The suggestion that it is a corruption of a Gaelic name, and should be written Ó hIomhairín, can be disregarded.

The comparatively modern Griffith's Valuation (1849-1854) records 19 families of the name in Co. Kilkenny, 10 in Co. Waterford and several in the adjacent counties. At the present time it is mainly found in or near Dublin. A very early association of the name Ivory, though not as a surname, with Co. Wexford is St. Ibhar or Iberius (d. c. 500) who is locally known as St. Ivory.   Bibl.

JACOB, Jago   Jacob is a very old surname in England (having, it should be noted, no Jewish connotation). The principal families of the name still extant in Ireland descend from two Cromwellian officers. Capt. Mathew Jacob, who settled at Clonmel in 1655, was the founder of the Co. Tipperary family: he was one of the commissioners under the Poll Money Ordinance of 1661; in 1648 Capt. William Jacob acquired Gigginstown and a large estate in the barony of Forth, Co. Wexford, and was the ancestor of the Jacobs of counties Wexford and Leix. The surname Jacob, however, is to be found in Ireland long before that. As early as 1313 the Justiciary Rolls mention that the name of the Prior of the Island of Roscrea was Yego; in 1311 they refer to a Co. Waterford juror called Griffin Yago, and in 1310 they record the trial of a Co. Meath burglar called Roger Jacob; and

even if in that case Jacob was possibly an ephemeral surname, this cannot be said of Walter Jacob a gentleman of Dollardstown, Co. Kildare, pardoned in 1583, or indeed of the other Jacobs of this county who appear in the sixteenth century Fiants. A little later in 1608, Jacob of Srowlane appears in a list of crown officers for Co. Kildare, at which time Sir Robert Jacob was Solicitor-General for Ireland: he was M.P. for the borough of Carlow in 1613. There are also references from the fourteenth century onwards to Jagoestown (or Yagoestown), a place near Naas, Co. Kildare.

Jago and Jacob are basically the same name – in the now defunct Cornish language Jago is the word for James and in Welsh it is Iago. Jago, indeed, is a surname found in Cork today. In the form of Iago or Igoe, it is not unknown in Co. Roscommon – I do not know whether the local tradition that this family is of Spanish origin is based on anything more definite than the fact that Iago is a Spanish christian name (equivalent to James). It is interesting to observe that the prefix Mac it appears a number of times in the Fiants relating to Co. Roscommon as MacKigoe, McKigog, MagEgo etc. None of these forms, however, appears in the "census" of 1659 for Co. Roscommon which, as the original detailed document is not now in existence and we have only the summary available, does not indicate that they were necessarily obsolete there at the time but only that they were not numerous enough to be included in the lists of "principal Irish names" or important enough to be classed as tituladoes.

Some Jacobs (including the family whose Dublin biscuit factory has a world-wide trade) have been Quakers, a fact overemphasized on account of the career of the ex-Quaker Joshua Jacob (1805-1877), the Clonmel man who founded a strange religious sect. The Leix Jacobs were certainly not all Quakers; if some were it might account for the fact that three of them were attainted as Jacobites, since it is generally believed that the Quakers of that and other parts supported James II because of his favourable attitude on the question of religious toleration. Two of these attainders were reversed under the articles of the Treaty of Limerick. In more recent times a distinguished member of the same family was Arthur Jacob (1790-1874) the noted oculist who was Professor of Anatomy in the Royal College of Surgeons, Dublin, for 43 years. His son Archibald Hamilton Jacob (1837-1901) succeeded him with almost equal distinction.

JOLLEY, Joly   Though rather rare outside Dublin and scattered in location, this name, at least as Joly, is very well known, particularly to readers in the National Library where the Joly Gift forms one of the most important collections there. It was formerly the property of the Royal Dublin Society but was transferred to the National Library when the latter was established in 1877. The donor was Jaspar Robert Joly (1819-1892) who was born in King's County (Offaly) and as well as being a lawyer and a scholar was the owner of a considerable estate in counties Offaly, Clare and Meath. Another notable man of the name was Charles Jasper July (1804-

1901), the astronomer. Julys and Jolleys settled in Ireland at various times. Perhaps the first was Henry Jolly, who was master-gunner in 1595. In the next century, apart from a soldier who appears in the army lists for 1644, we meet a Quaker living at Clonmel in 1680; and the Jolly monument in Fethard (Co. Tipperary) Protestant churchyard recalls the romantic story of the English trooper Robert Jolly and Ellen Meagher which has often been told (see for example, J.R.S.A.I. VII, 179 seq.). His wife Ellen, who had first married a rich Jew, is described as a "faithful Catholic" in the will of the parish priest of Clonmel in 1711. Jully twice appears among the tituladoes in the barony of Burren, Co. Clare, in 1659, but this may not be a synonym of Jolly. I do not think it is in north Clare now. The derivation of the English name is from the French joli and O'Hart says some Jolys in Ireland were Huguenot refugees.   Bibl.

(Mac) KEADY   There are a few instances of the prefix O being used with this name, but it is and was normally Mac Céadaigh. In the sixteenth century Fiants, for example, for one O'Keddy we find 21 MacKeadys, MacKedaghs etc. Of these six are in Connacht (as is O'Keddy), two in Co. Longford, ten in or near Queen's County (Leix) and three in Munster. The last may well be of the once important Corcalaoidhe sept Ó Meicéidigh, a name which was corrupted to Mac Céidigh. The Leinstermen were followers of O'More or of the Fox; while those located in Connacht no doubt belonged to the MacKeady sept of Co. Galway. In 1635 Strafford's Inquisition of Co. Mayo found one MacKeady of note but no O'Keady or Keady. The prefix Mac had been dropped by 1793: in that year there were 34 Keady families in the single Co. Galway parish of Moycullen, none being called MacKeady or O'Keady. In modern times the name Keady belongs (apart from metropolitan Dublin) almost exclusively to counties Galway and Mayo.

The surname Keady has no connexion with the town of Keady in west Armagh

MacKEAG(UE)   This Ulster name is found in all the northern counties especially Co. Down. MacKeag is slightly more numerous than MacKeague. Its Gaelic-Irish form is Mac Thaidhg, i.e., it is the same as MacTeigue except that the T is aspirated. Tadhg, of course, is one of the commonest christian names.

(O)KEAVENEY (O)GUINEY (O)KEEVAN, Kevane (Mac) COVENEY   Ó Géibheannaigh, anglicized as Keaveney, Keveney, Kevany, Geaveny and even Geany in Connacht, is the name of a sept of the Uí Maine descended from Geibheannach, son of a Hy Many chief slain in 971. Co. Galway is still their principal homeland. It is possible that the Guineys of Co. Kerry and Co. Cork are a branch of this sept, though in modern Irish their surname is contracted to Ó Guinidhe; alternatively they may be Ó Duibhne. Their name should be pronounced Gin-ee or Ginny (I have seen it spelt Guinea) not Gy-nie as it is usually called in Dublin, where it is a household

word: the latter pronunciation, I may add, is now quite frequently heard in Co. Limerick. There is also a Mac form of the name, viz. Mac Géibheannaigh which was that of a Co. Fermanagh sept mentioned in the Annals of Loch Cé (1308).

It was almost inevitable that the well known name Kavanagh would absorb other less common names resembling it. To some extent this has happened with Keaveney; still more so with the name Kevane: thus in the 1901 census there were 41 families of Kavanagh in Co. Kerry while there were very few Kevanes, though this is of Corca Laoidhe origin (Ó Ciabháin in Irish). In Connacht Ó Caomháin, recte Keevan or O'Kevane, one of the Hy Fiachrach septs located in Co. Sligo, has widely become Kavanagh, thus obscuring its distinguished origin. Their eponymous ancestor flourished in the ninth century and during the Gaelic period they had the privilege of inaugurating the O'Dowd chieftains. Worse still, some of them, not content with Kavanagh as a substitute, have become Cavendish!

On the other hand, Kavanaghs sometimes abbreviated their name to Kavan, and so to Keavan which is often to be found in late mediaeval and early modern deeds relating to south-east Leinster.

The somewhat similar sounding name Coveney has also been erroneously equated with Keaveney. Coveney is Mac Coibheanaigh, (with which the prefix O is sometimes erroneously used), the name of an Ossory family formerly chiefs of a small sept in the barony of Crannagh (Co. Kilkenny), as in Map.

MacKEE KEYES   Both these surnames are numerous in Ireland: it is estimated that MacKee numbers about 4,500 souls and Keyes (or Keys) some 2,000. MacKee belongs today almost exclusively to Ulster, particularly to counties Antrim, Down and Armagh; and this was equally the case in the seventeenth century, as evidenced by the "census" of 1659, which found them numerous in Donegal as well as in the three north-eastern counties. The name in various spellings (MacKee, MacKey(e), MacKea, MacKeeay and MacKe) was also fairly widespread in Leinster in the previous century: the Fiants, Extents etc., record them in Offaly and adjacent counties as well as in Ulster. At the time of the Plantation of Ulster Sir Patrick MacKee was a prominent Donegal "servitor". The normal form of MacKee in Irish is Mac Aoidh, a variant of Mac Aodha, (see MacCoy).

Woulfe states that MacKee is also used as an anglicized

form of Mac an Chaoich (from caoch, blind), a name adopted by a branch of the O'Reillys of Breffny; he adds, that this is probably also anglicized Keyes. Keys, usually without the second E, is certainly a name found in that part of Ulster. It is also well known as Keyes in Tipperary and Limerick. As Keys and Keyes are common names in England and I have no information regarding families of the name in Munster I cannot say whether they are or are not of Gaelic origin. It may be of interest to add that in the United States the name O'Casey has sometimes been corrupted to Keyse. Reaney mentions no less than five different derivations of the name Keyes in England and Wales. The name MacKee has sometimes been confused with Mackey.   Bibl.

MacKELVEY, MacElwee   KILBOY   CALVEY
These names, with occasional variants like MacElvey, are the modern anglicized forms of Mac Giolla Bhuidhe. The Four Masters under date 1181 mention two leading men of Connacht called Mac Giolla Buidhe (translated by O'Donovan as MacGillaboy). In 1392 Richard MacIlboy was a citizen of Limerick. These are dealt with under Gilbey. Earlier anglicizations such as MacGilleboy were fairly close to the original: one of these, MacIleboy, appears as a principal Irish name in the barony of Upper Iveagh, Co. Down, in the "census" of 1659. In the same source we find Gilbert MacIlwee, a titulado in Letterkenny town. That is in Co. Donegal which, with the adjacent parts of Co. Tyrone is the principal location of MacKelvey, MacElwee etc., today. In The Tribes & Customs of Hy Fiachrach and in O'Donovan's notes thereto Mac Giolla Bhuidhe is placed in the barony of Carra (Co. Mayo) under the O'Gormleys: O'Donovan says, that there the name was anglicized Kilboy. This form of the name is still extant in north Connacht, where it is presumably a distinct sept, not a branch of that located in Ulster.

Other synonyms of MacKelvey reported by local registrars in 1890 were MacCalvey, MacCelvey, MacElvee, MacElvie, MacGilvie, MacKilvie and Kilvey. A few years earlier MacElvea and MacElvoy were recorded. Woulfe gives several other rare variants. It will be observed that MacKelvey is a name with which the prefix Mac has been consistently retained, though the simple Kelvey is occasionally found. The late Mr. J.C. MacDonagh in a map showing the present location of Donegal surnames, which he kindly prepared for me, places MacElwee in Inishowen and MacGilway further south. Here we must take note of the fact that the name Calvey is almost peculiar to counties Mayo and Sligo. Woulfe gives Mac an Chalbhaigh as the Gaelic-Irish form of Calvey, and of MacCalvey, with no indication of the part of the country to which they belong. MacCalvey does not appear in the birth registrations 1864-66.

(Mac) KENDRICK   (Mac) KENDRY   The prefix Mac is usually retained with this name in its homeland, northwest Ulster; the form MacKentrick has been noticed in Co. Cavan. Elsewhere it is more often Kendrick or Kenrick. These are Mac Eanraic in Irish. MacKendrick is to

be distinguished from the Antrim name MacKendry which, according to Woulfe, is a variant of MacHenry. Dr. R. J. Hetherington points out that the alternative origin of this name, viz., the Welsh cynrig, is itself taken from the Old-English cynrie (which means chief or ruler). Neither of these derivations would apply widely in Ireland.

KENNEFICK   For the past four centuries this has been almost exclusively associated with Co. Cork and adjoining parts of Munster. But in the mediaeval period from the end of the thirteenth century many references to people of the name are to be found in records relating also to the city of Dublin and in the Leinster counties of Louth, Kildare and Kilkenny. They came to Ireland soon after the Anglo-Norman invasion, their name, formerly with the prefix de, being taken from a Welsh place-name. It has never been numerous and is now rare. Among the variant spellings in the modern birth registrations is Kenafaque! It occurs as Kenefeake in the Kinsale presentments relating to "Popish inhabitants" in 1712.

(O) KERRIGAN   (O) KEIGHRON   A townland called Ballykerrigan is situated in the parish of Balla, Co. Mayo, while Ballykergan is in the parish of Kilteevogue, Co. Donegal, near Stranorlar. It is in these two areas that Kerrigan families are mainly to be found today. The sept of O'Kerrigan (Ó Ciaragáin in Irish) was one of the Hy Fiachrach group of north Connacht and a branch of this migrated to Co. Donegal; quite a considerable number of the name went as far as Co. Armagh where O'Kerrigans were well established by the middle of the seventeenth century.

As might be expected the name Kerrigan has been confused with Carrigan and Corrigan. The latter occurs in the Westport area of Co. Mayo as a synonym of Kerrigan; and Carrigan is interchangeable with Kerrigan in Co. Fermanagh. Carrigan, however, is etymologically a variant of Corrigan not of Kerrigan.

In Co. Roscommon, and to a lesser extent in counties Galway and Mayo, Ó Ciaragáin was anglicized Comber or Comer, from its supposed derivation from cíor, a comb, though the root word in fact is ciar (black). Comber is used, too, (by pseudo-translation) as an anglicized form of Ó Ciaráin, which is a variant of Ó Céirín (see Kieran) and it is also found as a foreign occupative name of Norman origin.

The surname Keighron (Ó Ciocharáin), that of a small and quite distinct sept which originated in Co. Galway (barony of Longford), has also by a not uncommon process of attraction been changed to Kerrigan in some places, notably Manorhamilton, Co. Leitrim.   Map

KETTLE   COTTLE   Both of these names are Coitil in Irish, Kettle being Mac Coitil and Cottle Ó Coitil. The former belongs to the counties north of Dublin: as MacKetyll it was in Louth in the second half of the sixteenth century and as far back as 1305 Thomas Ketyl was bishop-elect of Down. Cottle is now very rare: it originated as a sept of the Uí Fiachra and is perpetuated in the placename Cottlestown in the parish of Castleconnor in the north-west of Co. Sligo. A few Cottle families are extant in Connacht.

Professor Thomas Michael Kettle (1880-1916) was one of the brilliant young Irishmen who, following the lead of the Redmonds, was killed in action in the First World War.

It should be observed that both these names are also English, Kettle being derived from Old-Norse ketill and Cottle from Old-French cotel.

MacKEVITT This is the form which the better known MacDevitt of Donegal takes in the Oriel country: Mac-Kevitt is found almost exclusively there (i.e. counties Louth, Monaghan and south Down). The substitution of K for D arises from the aspiration of the D (Mac Dhaibhéid for Mac Daibhéid) and the consequent transfer of the final C of Mac. An early anglicization found in the Fiants was MacCaveat.

(Mac) KILCLINE, Clynes The name in Irish is Mac Giolla Chlaoin and it appears as Macgilleclyne and other similar early anglicized forms in the Fiants from 1585 in counties Roscommon and Longford. The place name Ballykilcline in that part of the former, lying between counties Longford and Mayo, indicates the homeland of the sept. Families of the name later became fairly numerous also in the neighbouring county of Leitrim as well as Mayo. The older form Kilcline has now become rare even in counties Roscommon and Mayo, having been superseded by the better known Clynes which is now chiefly found in Leitrim and Longford. Other modern variants are Clyne, Clynne, Clines and Cline. John Robert Clynes (1869-1949) a leader of the Labour Party in England, was born in Co. Mayo.

The famous fourteenth century annalist, John Clyn, was of a Co. Kilkenny family which is perpetuated in the place-name Clinstown. It has no connexion with the Gaelic-Irish family of Clynes, being Cambro-Norman in origin.

(Mac) KILFEDDER The Irish name MacGiolla Pheadair (i.e. son of the servant or devotee of St Peter) has several anglicized forms: Kilfeather, Kilfeder, Kilfether and occasionally Gilfeather – the prefix Mac is not now retained with any of them. The homeland of the sept was Co. Sligo and it has spread into the neighbouring counties of Ulster.

This is not to be confused with Kilfedrick, which is a rare synonym of Kilpatrick.

(Mac) KILGALLEN, Kilcullen There is a marked tendency in the anglicization of Connacht names to make giolla Kil rather than Gil. This is one of the many surnames to which this generalization applies. According to Woulfe the Gallen comes from St Caillin, making the name Mac Giolla Chaillín. As Kilgallen or Kilgallon it is

numerous in Co. Mayo, especially around Swinford, and as Kilcullen it is equally prevalent in the barony of Dromore West, Co. Sligo.

(Mac) KILKELLY As is usual with Irish names beginning with Mac Giolla – this is Mac Giolla Cheallaigh – the Mac is seldom retained in the modern anglicized form when, as often happens in Connacht, the Gil has become Kil. The meaning of the name in this case is son of the follower of St. Ceallach. The family is of noble origin being, like the O'Clerys and the O'Heynes, descended from the famous King Guaire Aidhne, "the Hospitable". Their territory was in the Clanrickarde country at the base of Galway Bay, their principal seat being Cloghballymore, called Clogh in the Composition Book of Connacht. They are described as ollavs of O'Flaherty in history and poetry, having as their stipend certain lands near the modern town of Headford, Co. Galway. Their pedigree is discussed by John O'Donovan in his edition of The Tribes and Customs of Hy Many.

The name appears frequently in the sixteenth century Fiants and in various Connacht records of the seventeenth and eighteenth centuries. The most noteworthy member of the sept was Most Rev. Peter Killikelly, O.S.D., Bishop of Kilfenora and Kilmacduagh from 1744 to 1783. This form of the name is now very rare.

It may be observed that Kilkelly has suffered from the regrettable tendency for comparatively uncommon surnames to be absorbed by more numerous ones somewhat similar in sound: in this case Kilkelly has sometimes become Kelly, notably around Oughterard.   Map

(Mac) KILKENNY, MacElhinney This surname is not taken from the place-name Kilkenny which is Cill Chainnigh i.e. the church of St. Canice. There are occasional examples of its use as a toponymic in mediaeval times, e.g. David de Kilkenny (Bishop of Achonry 1312-1344) but for the most part this surname in Irish is Mac Giolla Chainnigh, i.e. son of the follower of St Canice, and this in the process of anglicization has taken on many variant forms, Kilkenny being one of them. Though hardly any mention of this sept is to be found in the Gaelic-Irish records there is little doubt that they were of the Cenél Eoghain group. St. Canice, whose place of origin was Dromachose in Co. Derry, was alternatively called St. Kenny, which is nearer to the original Irish phonetically. A few cases are on record within the past century of families abbreviating Kilkenny to Kenny. Other forms of the surname as anglicized are MacElhinny, Mac-Elheeny and MacIlhenny with and without the prefix Mac – indeed well over a dozen variants are recorded in the Tudor Fiants and other late mediaeval or early modern records, several of these being still extant. The form Kilkenny was in use before the end of the seventeenth century: James Kilkenny of Co. Leitrim was one of the Jacobites attainted after the defeat of the Boyne. Paddy Kilkenny, a well known wandering piper of a hundred years ago, was born at Clifden, Co. Galway. Kilkenny, though rare outside north Connacht, is quite numerous there: in the year 1866, for example, there were 23 births registered for the name, 21 in counties Leitrim, Roscommon and Mayo, and 2 in Co. Galway. More recent statistics corroborate this. Similarly the returns for MacElhinney, MacIlhenny and their other spelling variants show 26 registrations all (except one in Belfast) in counties Donegal and Derry. Here again the position was unchanged a generation later. These are the counties in which the same names were chiefly found in the sixteenth century.

(O) KILLEEN, Killian MacKILLEN   Ó Cillín, anglicized Killeen, usually without the prefix O, belongs both by historical association and by present day location to the west of Ireland, being found in the three Atlantic seaboard counties, Clare, Galway and Mayo. In successive centuries – 1443 (Four Masters), 1585 (Composition Book of Connacht), 1655 (Book of Survey & Distribution) – Kileens are recorded as residing at or near Ballykileen which is in the parish of Annagh, Co. Mayo, while more than a century later in 1783 the Galway Wardenship Mss. record Killeens as resident at Ballinrobe in the same county. Killeen first occurs as early as A.D. 964 (though probably not a hereditary surname), in the person of Cormac O'Killeen, Bishop of Clonmacnois; in 1106 his namesake was archdeacon of that diocese; in 1026 Conell O'Cilline is recorded as successor of Cronan of Tuamgraney, Co. Clare.

Some families which crossed the Shannon and settled in Co. Westmeath use the form Killian. Woulfe is usually reliable and accurate but I think he may be mistaken in equating Killen with Killeen. Killen is more probably simply Mac Killen without the prefix. Both these belong chiefly to Antrim, the Irish form being Mac Coilín or Mac Cailin, a galloglass family brought from Scotland by the O'Donnells in the fifteenth century. It is true that the enumerators recorded O'Killin as one of the more numerous Irish names in Co. Down in 1659, but they frequently confused the prefixes O and Mac and it is more probable that the family so described were really MacKillens. In north-east Ulster MacKillen may be confused with MacQuillan.

There were several mediaeval ecclesiastical dignitaries in Connacht called O'Killeen. In our own time Dr. John Killeen, Bishop of Port Augusta (now Port Pirie), is remembered for his help in combating the "Black & Tan" campaign. Two Belfast men, Rev. Thomas Young Killen (1826-1886) and Rev. William Dore Killen (1806-1902) were notable as leading Presbyterians; also from Co. Antrim was James Bryce Killen (1845-1916), the Fenian and cofounder with Michael Davitt of the Land League; another Fenian was the New York lawyer Doran Killian; and going back to an earlier insurrection there was John Killen, who was most unjustly hanged in 1803 for his alleged complicity in Robert Emmet's attempt.   Map

(Mac) KILLILEA   Notwithstanding the extent of emigration from the west – no less than eight entire families called Killilea went to America from the single parish of Ahascragh, Co. Galway, in 1850 – this name is now little less numerous in that county and in Co. Ros-

common than it was a century ago. We meet it, especially in Co. Galway, quite frequently in sixteenth and seventeenth century records, such as the Fiants, Civil Survey and Books of Survey & Distribution, under the earlier anglicized forms of MacKillilea, MacGillilea, etc. The latter is near the original Gaelic form, perhaps Mac Giolla Léith as suggested by Woulfe. The substitution of Kil- for Gil- is quite usual, especially in Connacht names.

MacKILLOP   Beyond the fact that this name is Mac Fhilib in Irish Woulfe gives no information about it. It is Scottish in origin being a branch of the Clan MacDonell or MacDonald of Keppoch. It is on record in Ireland from the seventeenth century; I have not found out when it was established here, but it is recorded in the "census" of 1659 among "the principal Irish names with some Scotch" in the barony of Glencarn, Co. Antrim: Antrim, it must be remembered, was not one of the six Ulster counties planted at the beginning of that century. Since then practically all references I have met to it, such as wills, birth registrations etc., have been to Co. Antrim or an adjacent Ulster county. Mother Mary MacKillop, foundress of the Australian order, the Sisters of St. Joseph, came of a Highland Scottish Catholic family.

(Mac) KILLORAN   The Kill in this name, as in most Irish surnames beginning with Kil, was formerly Gil and MacGil, i.e., MacGiolla. In the "census" of 1659 it appears as Gillelorin, one of the principal Irish surnames in the barony of Gorren, Co. Sligo, and that part of the country is the main habitat of the Killorans today. A few are still called Gilloran. Woulfe gives Mac giolla Luaithrinn as the Gaelic form. Luaithrinn being a saint's name.

KILLOUGH   Though as a surname Killough is rarely found outside northern Ulster it is not derived from the Co. Down place-name Killough, but is the form used in Ireland for the Scottish MacKelloch, a sept of the clan MacDonald. It appears in Co. Louth in the "census" of 1659 in the person of Jon Killogh, a citizen of Drogheda. This, however, may possibly be a form of the English name Kellough or Kellow (derived from the place-name Kelloe). Possibly Kellog is an Americanized form of this Kellough. Weekley suggests that it comes from M.E. Cullehog. Killoch is in the current Dublin city directory. There are six Killoughs in or near Ballymena in the telephone directory and the few earlier references to the name I have met are (with the exception of that to Killogh mentioned above) all to persons in that area of north Antrim and Derry. Another similar name occurs in the Dublin Justiciary Rolls of 1311 when John Kellagh was found guilty of burglary and hanged. This, however, may be an ignorant clerk's attempt at a phonetic rendering of Ó Ceallaigh (i.e. Kelly).

(Mac) KILLOUGHRY   This west Clare name might have been passed over in this book as it is rare even in its homeland; but it is one for which Woulfe (who does not mention its origin) gave a Gaelic form not easy to accept viz., Mac Conluacra. Surely this should be a Giolla name, say Mac Giolla Luachaire (from St. Luachair). Killoughry is occasionally shortened to Killoury.

(O) KINAHAN   When Kinahan and Kinaghan are found in Ulster or Louth they are usually variants of the ubiquitous Cunningham, which in Great Britain is a toponymic (from the place of that name in Ayrshire) but has been widely used in Ireland as the anglicized form of Ó Cuinneagáin and Ó Cuinneacháin (see Cunningham). For example George Henry Kinahan (1820-1908), geologist and engineer, was from Co. Down. Kinahan, as a distinct name (probably Ó Coinneacháin in Irish) belongs to the country south of Athlone, comprising the neighbouring parts of counties Offaly, Westmeath and Galway; and there it is mainly found to-day. Pedigrees of the Offaly families are among the records of the Genealogical Office.

KINCAID   Other spellings of this name are Kincaide, Kincade, Kinkaid and Kinkead. It is that of an old and important Scottish sept belonging to Stirlingshire. I have not found the name in connexion with the Plantation of Ulster, but by the 1660's it was well established in that province: it appears in nearly all the northern Hearth Money Rolls, especially in those of Antrim and Derry. One branch settled in Co. Sligo and held extensive property at Collooney up to the time of the Land Acts and the transfer of the great estates from landlord to tenant.

KINCH   This name is of Gaelic origin being the Manx form of Mac Aonghuis (MacGuinness). It may be of longer standing in this country, but the first Irish mention of it I have met is to a soldier in the army in 1644. Subsequent references are mostly to people living in counties Wexford and Wicklow.

KINGSTON, MacCloughry   Kingston or Kingstone, synonymous with MacCloughry in Co. Galway, is a mistranslation – cloch (stone), rí (king) – the Irish form Mac Clochaire is clearly from clochaire, a worker in stone. However, both MacCloughry and Kingston are rare in Connacht; and there is no evidence of their equation in west Cork, the only part of Ireland where the name Kingston is numerous. Modern birth statistics (1864-1890) show that approximately 90 per cent of those registered for Kingston occurred in Co. Cork. Woulfe states that he found Mac Oinseamáin as the Gaelic form of Kingston in west Cork, but one is left to suppose that this is merely a phonetic approximation to the English form. The Co. Cork Kingstons indeed do not claim to be Irish in origin. One family historian states that they came to Ireland between 1625 and 1649 and that many of the Kingstons in England are of families which returned thither from Ireland; another says the first to visit Ireland was Col. James Kingston of William III's army. At any rate since the seventeenth century they

have been one of the Protestant families to be found in strength around Bandon and Drimoleague. In the latter area they have been particularly numerous. It has been stated that about the year 1885 the teacher and every one of the sixty pupils attending the National school of Meenies was a Kingston. This I find to be manifestly an exaggeration. The writer of the article referred to (in the magazine of the united diocese of Cork, Cloyne and Ross) gives examples of the necessity for some Kingston children to be called by the christian name of their grandmother as well as their father, e.g. Richard Sally Sam Kingston and Richard Mary Sam Kingston. The writer of the article in question bewailed the fact that some "interlopers" had recently crept into this Kingston stronghold. Tempora mutantur: some of the Kingston families in Munster are now Catholic.

According to a family tradition recorded in the Genealogical Office, Dublin Castle, but unsupported by documentary evidence, the Kingstons of Co. Longford were originally MacCloughrys from Scotland, seventeenth century Presbyterian refugees who settled first in Co. Donegal, and after 1690 acquired the Co. Longford property of their relatives the Clintons when the latter emigrated to America.   Bibl.

MacKINNEY   This name is numerous in Ulster to-day; it is mainly found in counties Antrim and Tyrone. It is far more numerous now than it was a century ago – in 1866 there were 9 MacKinney births registered and in 1890 there were 42. The reason for this most unusual increase is that there has been a continuous tendency for the Scottish Mackenzie to become MacKinney in Ireland and it has also been used as a synonym of MacKenna. MacKinney is also the name of a sept of the Clan MacKinnon.

(O) KIRBY, Kerwick   The Gaelic-Irish surname Ó Ciarmhaic has been reasonably anglicized Kerwick in Co. Kilkenny, which is the original habitat of the lesser of the septs so called. They were numerous also in Co. Waterford in the seventeenth century. The prefix O, in this case already falling into disuse then, is now quite obsolete. Historically and in respect of modern distribution of population the name belongs to west Munster where in due course it became corrupted to Ó Cearba in Irish and Kirby in English. Up to the twelfth century Ó Ciarmhaic was chief – the Annals of Loch Cé call him king – of Áine (Knockany, Co. Limerick).

The family gradually sank into obscurity but continued to be well represented numerically, not only in Co. Limerick but in Kerry and Cork also. They were found as far south as Kinsale where several of the name were included in the presentments relating to its "Popish inhabitants" in the early eighteenth century persecution. Ballykervick, in the Macroom area, recalls the earlier form of the surname. In more recent times they have spread into Co. Kerry: there are 52 Kirby families in that county in the 1901 census.

It would appear also that a third small sept of Ó Ciarmhaic existed in Connacht; this, however, is not mentioned in the Gaelic treatises on Hy Many and Hy Fiachrach, so the Kirbys and Kerwicks of Co. Galway and Mayo may be descendants of migrants from one of the two septs mentioned above. The records of the Wardenship of Galway indicate that the name in both forms existed there and in the diocese of Tuam in the sixteenth century, and when Matheson made his statistical analysis of the birth registrations for 1890 he found one quarter of those for Kirby (35 in all) were in Connacht. It is somewhat surprising, therefore, on examining the 1864-1866 returns (which average 45 registrations per annum) to find barely ten per cent in Connacht. In both periods the majority of the births were in Munster, (excluding Clare where, however, the name is well known now due to the outstanding success, in Ireland and America of the Kirby brothers of Tuamgraney in the game of handball). Kerwick was almost entirely confined to Co. Kilkenny and adjoining areas.

KIRKPATRICK   (Mac) KILPATRICK   Kirkpatrick is basically a Scottish name formed from a place – Kirkpatrick, i.e. the church of St. Patrick – and most of our Irish Kirkpatricks, especially those to be found in north-east Ulster, are of Scottish descent. Owing to its similarity to the Irish surname Kilpatrick, which can be a form of Gilpatrick or Macgilpatrick (the usual modern form of which is Fitzpatrick), Kilpatrick has been widely substituted for Kirkpatrick. The latest available statistics show that the two names are about equally numerous and both are mainly confined to north-east Ulster. In fact Kilpatrick is unknown as an indigenous family in the Fitzpatrick country (see "Irish Families", p. 145). It was listed in the "census" of 1659 as a principal Irish name in two counties (Antrim and Fermanagh). But all the names classed as Irish in that document are not Gaelic. In the records relating to the Plantation of Ulster we find two Kilpatricks in the Lifford area classed as non-Irish, but on the other hand Owen Macgilpatrick who had 128 acres in Baskill, Co. Donegal is among the "natives". Kilpatricks are fairly numerous today in north Donegal. I have found no evidence to show that these Kilpatricks were of an Irish sept of Mac Giolla Phádraig. In this connexion it is worth remembering that there is also a place-name Kilpatrick in Scotland. Woulfe states that a branch of the Mac Giolla Phádraig (Fitzpatrick) family of Ossory settled in Co. Cavan, but I do not think this can be accepted as the origin of the Ulster Kirkpatricks and Kilpatricks, though the latter (if not the former) were, no doubt, Scottish Gaels: the modern use of MacIlfatrick and MacIlfederick as synonyms of Kilpatrick in Co. Antrim corroborates this. Ferguson lists both Kilpatrick and Kirkpatrick as branches of the Scottish clan Colquhoun. Three Kirkpatricks from Ulster were notable presbyterian clergymen. Some Kirkpatricks have abbreviated their name to Kirk, which in Munster is sometimes used as a synonym of Quirke.

(O) KISSANE, Cashman   (O) CUSSANE, Patterson It is sad that the euphonious Irish name Kissane, the form still used in Kerry, should have been transmogrified into the English word Cashman as has happened in Co. Cork: no doubt Kerry being more inaccessible was less subject to English influence during the period of Gaelic submergence. O'Kissane was still the form used in Co. Cork at the time of the Cromwellian Settlement, as the various seventeenth century records show. In Irish this surname is Ó Ciosáin. Guissane is found in west Clare.

There is another Gaelic name Ó Casáin, that of one of the eight Sodhans, i.e. the septs located in the Hy Many or Uí Maine country which were not of the same race as that group. The best known of the others are O'Mannin, O'Lennon, MacWard and O'Dugan. Ó Casáin was formerly anglicized Kissane but I think this is almost obsolete in Connacht where (especially in the Glenamaddy area) Cussane and Paterson are the modern equivalents of Ó Casáin. The latter can only be explained by the fact that casán means a path, locally pronounced "pat", which is the first syllable of Patterson. The English names Paterson, Patterson and Pattison all denote "son of Patrick".

Both these patronymics are entirely distinct from Ó Caisín (see under Cashin).

(Mac) KITTERICK   Woulfe describes this name both as rare and scattered; but in fact it is by no means uncommon within a comparatively limited area, viz., the old territory of Oriel. Its homeland has always been the country centred around counties Armagh and Monaghan. In the former county a peculiar synonym of the name, viz. Hanson (q.v.) is hard to explain. MacKeterick, one of the numerous variant spellings of the name, occurs in an Ormond army list of 1648 as a triumpeter in Capt. Parsons' troop: nearly all the soldiers in it were English and perhaps this man was in fact a MacGetrick from Galloway in Scotland. It should be mentioned that MacGettrick was a name well established in Co. Sligo a century ago. Alexander MacKitrick was one of the "tenant settlers" in the Clogher area under the Plantation of Ulster: most of the families in that settlement were Gaelic-Irish. The name is formed from the Norse personal name Sitric and it appears in a Judiciary Roll of 1306 dealing with Co. Waterford as MacShitteruk – in Irish it is Mac Shitric. An interesting fact is that Ketrick without the prefix Mac is associated with Westport, Co. Mayo, not with Oriel.

(O) KIVLEHAN   Woulfe states correctly that this name (Ó Cibhleacháin in Irish) is that of a family formerly coarbs of St. Feichin at Fore, Co. Westmeath. He adds that they are now scattered. The fact is, however, that the name is now mainly concentrated in counties Sligo and Leitrim, where indeed members of the sept were already to be found in the sixteenth century, as we know from the Elizabethan Fiants.

(O) KNEAFSEY, Crampsy, Bonar   Ó Cnáimhsighe, a numerous surname in Co. Donegal, belongs almost exclusively to that county, where it is anglicized as above and, more frequently, Bonar or Boner from the fact that the Irish word cnámh means a bone, a case of pseudo-translation. The true derivation is quite different – possibly from an obsolete christian name: Woulfe says it is one of our few matronymic surnames. The 1890 birth registration statistics are significant: 9 registrations for Crampsy or Crampsey, all in Co. Donegal; 38 for Bonar and Boner, all in Ulster and 29 of these in Co. Donegal; while for Kneafsey, Neaphsy and Neecy there were less than 5. A comparison with those of the previous generation shows for 1864 Bonar, Boner, etc., 43 (nearly all Co. Donegal), Cramsey 4 (Donegal) and Kneafsey 5 (all Mayo). The list of synonyms used by emigrants compiled by the Cunard Steamship Company equates Bonar and Boner with Crampsy but does not mention Kneafsey. The Donegal Hearth Money Rolls (1665) have O'Cnawsey and O'Crawsey; and in 1659 the "census" enumerators, who found it numerous in Inishowen (Co. Donegal), wrote it down as O'Knawsie. In that barony there is a townland called Ballycramsie. The only mention of the name in the Annals is under date 1095, when Scannlán Ó Cnáimhsighe was anamchara (confessor) of Lismore. In 1584 Philip MacShane Y Neasy was "one of Lord Viscount Roche's men"; but he may well have been a mercenary from the north, and the name, if it was ever associated genealogically with the south of Ireland, has long been almost unknown there.

(Mac) KNIGHT   Knight is a purely English name and is not common in Ireland. It may occasionally be used as an abbreviation of MacKnight, which is an Irish name, though not Gaelic in origin. MacKnight is a translation of the Irish words mac an ridire meaning son of the knight, an Irish surname adopted by a branch of the Norman family of Fitzsimons, which was located in Co. Meath in mediaèval times. This name in English cannot be distinguished from the Scottish MacKnight which is in Gaelic Mac Neachtain, more usually anglicized Mac-Naughton. The fact that of 39 births recorded for Mac-Knights in the last available annual return 31 were in Ulster (mostly Antrim) suggests that the majority of our MacKnights are of Scottish origin. In the same year the number of Knight births recorded was 13, with no more than 4 in any one province.

No person called Knight has particularly distinguished himself in any sphere of Irish history. James Mac-Knight (1801-1876), a friend of Charles Gavan Duffy, was prominent in the fight for Irish tenant right.

KNOTT   Both Knott and Nott occur in mediaeval Irish records as early as the end of the thirteenth century, e.g. in law cases recorded in the Judiciary Rolls for counties Cork and Tipperary. According to Reaney these are different names, Knott being derived, like Canute, from Old Norse Knutr, thence from Old English cnotta, used of a thickset person, while Nott is from hnott bald-headed or close cropped; Knott may also come from Middle English knot a hill. It is most improbable that any descendants in the male line of any of these early Knotts exist in Ireland to-day, but there are numerous references to the name from the seventeenth century on-wards. In 1666, for example, Isaac Knott was an original member of the Coopers Guild in Dublin. A year later the will of John Knott, a clothier of Dublin, was proved – in 1659 he appears in the "census" of that date as of High Street, Dublin. In 1686 one Daniel Knott, late of Sir Thomas Newcomen's Regiment of Foot, was a pensioner in the Royal Hospital, Kilmainham. As early as 1641 we find the name in north Connacht when Henry Knott, son of an English trader, narrowly escaped death at Sligo in the trouble of that date. It became established there as we know from wills of 1708 (Co. Sligo) and 1729 (Co. Roscommon), and in the Alumni Dublinenses wherein are listed three students of those two counties born 1763, 1777 and 1811. There are also references to the name in another part of the country viz. Co. Offaly (King's County). Joseph son of William Knott is mentioned in a will of 1724 and John and William Knott are listed as tenants at Clonad in 1763. The Quaker wills also record two Knotts as witnesses of a Co. Kildare will in 1734.

Several authors of the name will be found in the catalogues of the National Library of Ireland. The most distinguished of these is Eleanor Knott, the Irish scholar.

KYLE   In his Some Anglicized Surnames in Ireland, Padraig Mac GiollaDomhnaigh makes the surprising statement that Kyle is an anglicized form of the Scottish Mac Suile. It is, however, corroborated by the summary of returns of local registrars, published by Matheson in 1901, in which it is recorded that in the Ballycastle district (Co. Antrim) Kyle and MacSuile were actually used as synonyms by members of the same family. The principal family of Kyle came from Ayrshire to Co. Derry at the time of the Plantation of Ulster and the name has since become numerous in that province, especially in Derry and Antrim. They are in the Hearth Money Rolls of counties Derry and Antrim and as Kylle in those of Co. Tyrone (1663-1669); many Kyles appear in the wills records for the diocese of Derry from 1664 onwards and a smaller number in those of Raphoe, Clogher and also Dublin. It is occasionally found elsewhere, e.g. Henry Kyle who is listed in the parish of Killenawle in the Tipperary Hearth Money Rolls of 1666. A branch of the family became established in the United States early in the eighteenth century: Samuel Kyle settled in Pennsylvania in 1738 and his grandson James Henderson Kyle (1854-1901), a congregational minister, was an American senator of note. In Ireland, apart from the famous rugby footballer Jack (now Dr. John) Kyle, the most noteworthy men of the name have been two bishops: one a Protestant Dr. Samuel Kyle (1770-1848) provost of Trinity College, Dublin, from 1820 to 1831, when he became bishop of Cork and Ross; the other a Catholic Dr. Kyle (d. 1869) vicar-apostolic, Northern District, Scotland.

LAFFAN FANT Laffan is not of Gaelic-Irish origin, but families so called were established in the Ormond country early in the fourteenth century and they appear in Co. Tipperary records, particularly around Clonmel and other places in the south of the county, where they were very numerous during the sixteenth and seventeenth centuries. Later there was the patriot parish priest of Fethard, Archdeacon Michael Laffan (1791-1861) and Most Rev. Robert Laffan, Archbishop of Cashel from 1823 to 1833. Thence also came Sir Joseph de Courcy Laffan (1786-1848), a noted physician. Curtis equates the name MacLeveyn, which appears in the Ormond Deeds in an Inquisition of 1312, with Laffan. The Red Book of Ormond records Henry Laffayn, grantee in the Thurles area, as early as 1293. There were also in the sixteenth and seventeenth centuries several prominent families of Laffan in Co. Wexford; Laffan of the Slade is in the list of chief gentlemen of that county in 1598 and elsewhere he is called MacLaffan of the Sladd. The Mac prefix in that case is extraneous.

Woulfe derives Laffan from the Norman L'Enfaunt. This is known to have taken the modern form Fant, whence Fantstown, Co. Limerick. (Fant, by the way, may have another origin, too, since de la Faunte is a name not unknown in the mediaeval Ormond deeds.) Whether L'Enfaunt ever became Laffan is open to doubt: among all the many references to these two names in mediaeval sources I have met there is not one case of their being equated. Woulfe's opinion was possibly based on the fact that in 1359 the seneschal of Tipperary was named Laffan and in 1374 L'Enfaunt; but these were two different people who succeeded each other in that office and were apparently unrelated. La Font or La Fin, names found in French records, may possibly be the original form of Laffan.

Matheson records Lappin as a synonym of Laffan, but he does not give the district from which it was reported, and it was probably an isolated case. (See Lappin infra.)

LANDERS Other extant forms of this name are Launders and Landry; it derives from the mediaeval de Londres (i.e. of London) and its variants Londra and Londrey. De London was also in use in the thirteenth century. From that time until the present day these names are mainly found in Munster, the former in all the counties of that province except Clare, the latter in Co. Limerick. Landers was listed as a principal Irish name in the barony of Decies, Co. Waterford in the 1659 "census" and statistics indicate that in quite modern times Waterford is the county in which it is most numerous; as Launder we find it in the city of Waterford in 1575: it occurs in the return of householders paying hearth-money in 1665 in ten different parishes of Co. Tipperary; the place Ballylanders is in the south-east corner of Co. Limerick. The earliest reference to the name in Ireland I have met (apart from the Archbishop of Dublin, Henry de Londres, who was papal legate in 1217-21) is in 1260 when an official enquiry was made as to the holding of Daniel Laundry, son of William Laundry "the Londoner" at Clondegad, Co. Clare; and later in the thirteenth century

it appears twice in Co. Kerry, and, to take a modern statistic for that county, there were 23 Landers families in Kerry in 1901; for the remaining county, with which the name is less closely associated, Cork, we must turn to the wills and marriage licence bonds recorded for the diocese of Cork, Ross and Cloyne and various municipal records of the eighteenth century.

London is much rarer though just as ancient as Landers: it occurs as Londown without the de in Dungarvan in 1333.

Though Glanders has been reported as a synonym of Landers in use in Co. Waterford Glanders is according to Woulfe, a form of Gillanders i.e. Mac Giolla Aindréis. Gillanders, alias Mac Landrish, is a Monaghan name; Mac Landrish is found in Rathlin Island.

Lander in England may be derived from the old French lavandier (washerman) and so be a synonym of the surname Lavender, but this alternative origin may be disregarded in Ireland, though Lavender is not unknown in this country: it occurs in Griffith's Valuation of Co. Wicklow (1854).

LANDY None of the authorities on British surnames has dealt with this name, and all Woulfe has to say about it is one word: "Leaindi" — just the modern form written phonetically in Irish. I think it derives from the Norman de la Launde (Launde, a glade). This has been established in counties Kilkenny and Tipperary since the thirteenth century. In one of the earliest references to it, it appears as Landa, John Landa being a witness at Cashel in 1297. William Launde, abbot of St Mary's Dublin, who was granted a royal pension in 1540, is called Laundey in another official document of two years later. Usually we find it as de la Launde, de Launde and Launde, nearly all those, up to 1600, being in counties Kilkenny, Waterford and south Tipperary. Patrick de la Launde was sheriff of Kilkenny in 1337. The most notable family of the name was Lande or de Launde of Keatingstown, Co. Kilkenny, which they held for at least two centuries from 1367. In the seventeenth century they had become Lawndy, Laundy and Landy, but were less prominent in Co. Kilkenny: there were Landy families returned in ten different parishes in Co. Tipperary in the Hearth Money Rolls of 1663-5, and there are three recorded wills of Youghal Lawndys (1686-1697). Modern birth registrations place the Landys mainly in Co. Tipperary. Having regard to their continuous association with the Ormond Country — every volume of the Ormond Deeds contains references to them — it is surprising to find that the only place in Ireland where the Landys or Laundys appear in the summary of the "census" of 1659 is as a principal Irish name in the Co. Dublin barony of Balrothery. Local registrars in the Youghal and Lismore districts report the occasional synonymous use of Landy and Landers: the latter, however, is quite distinct from Landy — see Landers. Landy and Lawndy occur fairly frequently in the eighteenth century Cloyne marriage licence bonds.

(O) **LAPPIN, Delap** Delap is a curious anglicized form

of Ó Lapain, which in its more normal form, Lappin, is now fairly common in Co. Armagh and the adjacent borders of Tyrone and Antrim. Originally a leading sept of Tirconnell (Donegal) their chief was lord of Cenél Enda, but little is heard of them there after 1100. They were well established in Co. Armagh by the beginning of the seventeenth century, but I do not know at what date in the intervening period their migration thither took place. The name occurs frequently as O'Lappin, Delap and De Lappe in the Hearth Money Rolls of Co. Derry (1665), and as Dowlapp and Dulapp as well as O'Lappin in those of Co. Armagh. Dulapp and Dunlapp are found in the Inquisitions for Co. Antrim (1635). Theirs would appear to be one of the earliest hereditary surnames: a family of O'Lappin are mentioned by the Four Masters as tenth century erenaghs of Derry, and one of them, who died in A.D. 957, was Bishop of Raphoe. I am informed by Mr. P.J. Kennedy that the name Delap is found in south Connemara as well as in Mayo. He also mentioned that Penelope (colloquially Penny and Nappy) is traditionally a christian name in this family and still in favour with them.

LARDNER   (O) LARGAN   (O) LERHINAN

In Ireland Lardner belongs principally·to Co. Galway, where I was informed by Mr P.J. Kennedy, the Irish form of it is Ó Lorgnáin from Ó Loirgneáin, which is found in Co.Clare in the anglicized forms Lerhinan and Lernihan. Families of Lardner unconnected with Galway or neighbouring counties are probably of English origin: Lardner is an English name, formerly Le Lardiner, derived from lardiner, meaning a bacon salter and sometimes an overseer of pigs. Another somewhat similar name in Irish is Ó Lairgneáin which O'Donovan states is that of one of the Oriel chiefs, now extant in Ulster but rare, the modern form being Largan.

LARMINIE

The Larminies have only been established as an Irish family since the early eighteenth century and the name is very rare to-day, but it is included here because they were quite numerous in Co. Mayo prior to the Great Famine and from these people came the poet William Larminie (1849-1900). My evidence for the foregoing statement is a rental of the O'Donel estate for the year 1829 in which several tenants called Larminie appear. The founder of the family in Ireland was not a farmer but a London flax dresser who in 1721 leased land in and around Newport, Co. Mayo. He was Samuel Larminie (1693-1757), son of François Larminie of Picardy, a Huguenot refugee. The poet was great-grandson of this Samuel and he was born at Castlebar. In France the name was normally Lerminier and was associated in that country with the weaving industry.

MacLARNON

This is also spelt MacLernon, MacLornan and occasionally MacClarnon. Apart from Dublin, which is comprised of course of families from all the provinces, this name and its variants are rarely found outside Ulster, where it is now numerous. Many Ulster MacLarnons

come, no doubt, originally from Scotland, but quite a number also are of indigenous Irish stock, for the sept of Mac Giolla Earnáin was well established in Iveagh (Co. Down) in the twelfth century. They remained in Ulster, if not in County Down; several appear in the Ulster Inquisitions as lessees and tenants, e.g., Hugh MacLerenan (Co. Down 1616) and Hugh Mac Lyrenan (Antrim 1633). In 1699 Paul and Hugh MacLorrinen, of two different places in Co. Antrim, who had been outlawed as Jacobites, claimed under the articles of Limerick and Galway. In the eighteenth century a similar variant of the name was usual, as evidenced by testamentary records in which MacLornan occurs frequently, but not the other modern forms – these testators are all of Ulster (or Dublin). One of them, Daniel MacLorinon alias MacLorinan, of Tullyboy, Co. Derry, left a small sum of money to be divided equally between his parish priest and the local Protestant clergyman -- surely an unusual bequest in 1745.

(O) LARRISSEY   The Larrisseys are an exception to the general rule that a name is found to-day mainly in the locality where its sept originated. There is no doubt that the sept of Ó Learghusa belonged to the barony of Carra in Mayo: we have the authority of the Book of Lecan and other genealogical tracts for that and we do find it in Connacht as late as 1591 (as O'Larysa in Fiant No. 5611), yet by 1659 Petty's "census" lists Larissy as a principal Irish name in the barony of Maryborough, Queen's Co. (Leix); it occurs in the Hearth Money Rolls of North Tipperary about that time and, coming to the last century, Griffith's Valuation reveals that people of the name were then numerous in Co. Kilkenny, with some families also in the adjacent counties of Leix and Waterford. Of these no doubt was James Larrissey, a prominent member of James Freeney's highwaymen about a hundred years earlier. The obvious inference from the facts given above, and from any other reference to the name which I have met, is that there were two distinct septs of Ó Learghusa, one in Connacht and one in south Leinster, rather than the alternative possibility of a migration from Connacht to Leinster; but I have found no evidence of the existence of a Leinster sept of the name in pre-Norman or even in late mediaeval times.

LAVELLE, O'Mulfaal   (O) MULHALL   (O) HALLEY
Different as they sound in English Lavelle and Mulfaal are

both anglicized forms of the Irish Ó Maolfábhail. This has also been further disguised in some places under the form of Melville, an aristocratic-sounding surname which, as we saw in Irish Families, has also been adopted by some Mulvihils anxious to hide their Gaelic ancestry. Lavelle is the usual form: it is of frequent occurrence in Connacht, particularly in Co. Mayo, where Lawell is a variant of Lavelle. Mulfaal belongs to Co. Donegal: the surname is the same as the foregoing in Irish but is of different and distinct origin being that of a family who descended from Fergus, grandson of Niall of the Nine Hostages, and were chiefs of Carrickbraghy, in the barony of Inishowen. There, however, it has been widely corrupted to MacFael, MacFall and even MacPaul and Paul; when that is the case it is indistinguishable from the Antrim Mac Fall (MacPhail and MacPhoil) which I think is of Scottish origin. O'Mulfoyle is listed in the 1659 "census" as a principal Irish name in the barony of Tirkeerran, which is continguous to Inishowen. The most distinguished of the name was Dr. James Augustine MacFaul (1850-1917), Bishop of Trenton, protagonist of Irish Catholic causes in U.S.A.

The families of Ó Maolfabhail who are now known as Lavelle are of the sept originally seated at Donaghpatrick in the barony of Clare (Co. Galway). Hardiman, writing in 1846, says that the anglicized form Lavelle was then coming into use, the name being at that time normally O'Mullawill (cf. Lawell above). It should be noted, however, that O'Lawell, O'Lowell and O'Lavell appear in the seventeenth century Hearth Money Rolls for Co. Armagh.

Mulhall is never used as a synonym of Mulfaal. It is the name of a Leinster sept, Ó Maolchathail in Irish; it signifies descendant of a follower of St. Cathal or Cahill and was O'Mulcahill in its earlier anglicized form. It is spelt Mulchaell in the 1659 "census" and appears among the more numerous names in three different baronies of Queen's Co. (Leix), which is the place of origin of the sept and also its principal location in modern times. Some of the Halleys of nearby north Tipperary are Mulhalls, though Halley (Ó hAilche) is in fact primarily the name of a small sept located around Templemore and (Ó hAille) of another in Co. Clare whence was named Ballyally, the scene of a small but famous siege in the Cromwellian war. There are several seventeenth and eighteenth century testators named Hally in the will indices for the diocese of Waterford and Lismore.

Michael George Mulhall (1836-1900), author of several statistical works, founded the first English language newspaper in South America.

(O) LAVIN, Hand   (Mac) GLAVIN, Hand   It is advisable to deal with the surnames Lavin (or Lavan) and Glavin together because the Lavin and Glavin (or at least MacGlavin) have both been turned by pseudo-translation into Hand. Laffan, which is the subject of a separate entry supra, is also sometimes confused with Lavin.

Lavin and Lavan taken together are much the most numerous of these, with 42 birth registrations in 1890 and 46 in 1864, almost all of them in counties Mayo and Roscommon. The comparable data for Hand were 28 and 29 births (mostly in or near Dublin); for Laffan 8

and 13 (Limerick, Tipperary, Kilkenny and Wexford); for Glavin 7 and 8 (nearly all in Cork and Kerry).

In the neighbourhood of Clones Hand and MacLave or MacClave (Mac Laithimh) have been used interchangeably.

Edward Hand (1744-1802), a leading figure in the American revolutionary army and later a member of Congress, was born in Co. Offaly.

If we now examine the background of these names we find that Lavin or Lavan, in modern Irish Ó Lámháin, is that of a Roscommon sept who are recorded in the Annals as followers of MacDermot Roe, several being especially prominent in this capacity in the sixteenth century.

The rare MacLavin, when not synonymous with the Westmeath Mullavin (perhaps Ó Maoiléimhín), is Mac or Mag Laimhín the name referred to above as MacGlavin. MacGlavin, however, has become Hand. Glavin without the prefix is Ó Glaimhín, which originated in Connacht as a small Hy Fiachrach sept but is now rarely found outside west Munster, where Hand is never used as a synonym of it.

(O) LEAHY, Lahy   (O) LAHIFF, Lahy   At the present time the name Leahy is very numerous in southwest Munster, and the Fiants, the Ormond Deeds, Petty's "census" and the Hearth Money Rolls all indicate that this was equally the case in the sixteenth and seventeenth centuries, particularly in the counties of Tipperary and Cork. In Irish it is Ó Laochda (laoch means a hero). This Gaelic surname is to be distinguished from Ó Lathaigh. This is anglicized as Lahy and, since Lahy is also a synonym of Leahy — indeed they were formerly practically interchangeable — confusion is inevitable, though the location of a family is of course some guide in this matter. Ó Laithigh is thought to be a corrupt form of Ó Laithimh, which is itself a late form of Ó Flaithimh. This is a Clare and south Galway name normally called Lahiff in English, but sometimes Lahy; there also Lahiff and Flahy have been recorded as synonyms. Flahive, which is phonetically a more correct anglicization of the older form of this name, is now very rare.

There have been two outstanding personalities of the name of Leahy: Edward Daniel Leahy (1797-1875), celebrated as a portrait painter; and Most Rev. Patrick Leahy (1806-1875), the Archbishop of Cashel who built the cathedral at Thurles; he was remarkable both for his scholastic attainments and for his success in reducing intemperance and faction-fighting in his diocese. John O'Lahy (d. 1581) was hanged for his part in arranging the escape of a Jesuit priest to France and refusing to renounce the faith. John Lahiff (d. 1343) was Bishop of Killala and I might add that James Lahiff was an officer in O'Moore's regiment of James II's Irish army. It is remarkable that neither of the names under consideration is to be found in the Jacobite attainders.

In Co. Clare, around Corofin sixty years ago, the Scottish name Guthrie was synonymous with Lahiff: I have not discovered the origin of this.   Map

(O) LEAMY   This is the name of an old Gaelic sept of Upper Ormond. There were 15 families of this in the Tipperary Hearth Money Rolls. At the same time the 1659 "census" names Leany as one of the principal Irish surnames in the barony of Eliogarty, Co. Tipperary, while Leamy is not listed. In this case Leany may possibly be an error for Leamy; however, in the Fiants we find O'Leny and O'Lenie in Munster as well as O'Leamy and O'Leamygh: according to Woulfe Leeney is from Ó Laighnigh while Leamy is from O'Léime or Ó Laomhda. D.F. Gleeson's Last Lords of Ormond has some interesting observations on the retention of land throughout centuries of confiscation by certain families in north Tipperary, among them the Leamys. They were still strong in Co. Tipperary in 1855 when there were 33 householders of the name there; the number is now much smaller.

(Mac) LEAVY   LEVIS   The anomalies revealed by birth registrations are often strange. My own brother-in-law whose name is Tadhg, on getting his birth certificate found that his registered christian name was Tige and that he was officially a female! The man of a Leavy family who was registered as Levi, if he made no effort to change back to Leavy, must have had difficulty in persuading people that he was not of Jewish ancestry. The form Levy, often seen, does perhaps suggest a modification of Levi. Until I came to examine the question I assumed, as Woulfe does, that Levy and Leavy are abbreviated forms of Dunlevy, and perhaps occasionally they are when met with in the Dunlevy country (see IF, pp. 118-119). O'Leavy occurs in the Monaghan Hearth Money Rolls of 1666. In actual fact, however, Leavy is seldom to be found in Ulster and, if not solely confined to Co. Longford and Westmeath is much more numerous there than anywhere else. They are a quite distinct sept, akin to the O'Farrells, their name in Irish being Mac Con Shléibhe which in its earliest anglicised forms appeared as MacEnlieve, MacEnleve, etc., and always in or near Co. Longford. In the O'Clery genealogies, too, we find Genelach Meg Con Sléibhe appropiately presented. In the 1659 "census" it appears as a principal Irish name in the barony of Longford (Co. Longford) in the guise of MacIlleavy.

The O'Levies or O'Leavys who, as surgeons, were among the professional classes to whom lands were assigned in the sixteenth century in the MacCarthy country were presumably a branch of the Longford sept. W. F. T. Butler suggests that this is the origin of the Levis family, well-known in west Cork, since the seventeenth century; but Levis, numerous in West Carbery, is almost certainly of Huguenot origin.

It is perhaps worth adding that there is an English name Leavy, Levy derived from the Old English leofwig meaning beloved warrior, but few if any of our Irish Leavys are of English or Jewish origin.   Map

LEESON   Woulfe suggests that Leeson is the modern form of the name O'Lishane or O'Lyshane, which occurs in Fiants of 1601 for counties Cork and Kerry, and further that these are corrupt forms of Gleeson (Ó Giliasáin). I do not dispute this possibility; but it should be remembered that Leeson is an English name, a fact to which Woulfe does not allude. Its familiarity to Dubliners is due to the well-known Leeson Street, named from the patronymic of the Earl of Milltown. This family, according to Craig, came to Ireland about 1680, made a large fortune as brewers and acquired much property in the area around what is now Dawson Street. The name Leeson is found in Ireland before 1680: four Leesons occur in the lists of army personnel in the Ormond Manuscripts, the earliest in 1644. The name has never become numerous: birth registrations of the last century indicate that it is rare outside Dublin and the neighbouring Leinster counties. A notable Dublin architect was John Leeson (fl. 1830).

LEMASS   In this form this Dublin name is not on record before the eighteenth century. I think it is the anglicized form of the French le Maistre, which was well-known in Dublin business circles in the eighteenth century but disappears after 1845. A Leighlin will of a Carlow le Maistre brings it back to 1731. No records now survive to determine whether these have any connexion with people called le Maistre who appear in our mediaeval documents as far back as 1258. Le Maistre, and also Lemasle, are among the names of Huguenot refugees who settled in Great Britain and Ireland.

Seán Lemass, (1899-1971), a Dublin man, was Taoiseach (Prime Minister) of the Republic of Ireland.

LETT   The name Lett is prominent though not numerous in Co. Wexford. It dates there from the mid-seventeenth century, when Thomas Lett, a Cromwellian "adventurer", obtained lands at Newcastle, Co. Wexford. According to Reaney Lett is a pet form of Lettice, a surname derived from laetitia (joy). That name occurs in Cambridgeshire in 1208 as filius Lete and it would seem possible that Lett might also derive from Old English lete (a watercourse) since Atte Lete is recorded as a mediaeval surname also. Another derivation worth consideration is the Norman de Lette. While not suggesting that the Wexford Letts were necessarily in Ireland in 1302, I may observe that the Justiciary Rolls twice mention John de Leyt as owner of property in Co. Dublin; and perhaps the existence of Adam Leth, a Co. Carlow Inquisition juror in 1307, may also be relevant. From the early eighteenth century references to the name Lett are frequent in all the normal sources of research and almost all these relate either to Co. Wexford or an adjacent county.

A notable member of the Wexford family was Sir Hugh Lett (b. 1876) who was President of the British Medical Association.

(O) LIDDANE, Lydon, Leyden   The three names given above are anglicized forms of the Irish Ó Loideáin, sometimes spelt Ó Lodáin. Lydon is the usual form in counties Galway and Mayo – in 1890, 55 of the 57 births recorded in that year and in 1864, 47 out of 52 were in those two counties; Leyden occurred principally in Sligo and Clare, and Liddane in Clare; in the census of householders compiled for the parishes of Ballinrobe and Moycullen in 1783 and 1793 there were 24 families named Liddane. Ludden is another variant occasionally recorded in Co. Galway. None of these occur, except occasionally, in any part of the country east of the Shannon, apart of course from the metropolitan area of Dublin which is composed of families from all parts of the country. The Annals of Loch Cé record the death of the Abbot Ó Lotáin, "a paragon of piety and learning", in 1216. It is probable that this is an early form of the name under consideration. Two Liddans, of Castlebar, Co. Mayo, are included in the list of Jacobite attainders.

(O) LIDDY, Leddy   Though this name is found in Co. Cavan, usually as Leddy, it belongs historically to Co. Clare, Ó Lideadha being the patronymic of a Dalcassian sept much to the fore in the Thomond wars of the fourteenth century. We meet them also within the nearest sphere of English influence at the same time: Gillecrist and Malaghlyn O'Liddy, for example, were at Limerick in 1314, with other "mere" Irishmen, discharged of all "felonies" etc., on paying a fine. In the seventeenth century it (as Lyedie) is recorded by Petty as one of the principal names in the barony of Corcomroe, Co. Clare, a district some distance from the sept's original habitat in east Clare where it is still extant, though less numerous than formerly. The Annals of Loch Cé spell the name Ó Laidigh, citing two bishops of Killala so called and an archdeacon of Annaghdown, of which parish they were erenaghs. Woulfe states that the Co. Cork name Ó Loidigh (Luddy in English) is a modern variant of Ó Laidigh: he is usually a reliable authority, but I have not found corroborative evidence for this statement. Another early surname which might also have been anglicized Liddy is O Ligda or Ó Lighde: the Annals of Innisfallen, under date 1058, refer to Cairbre Ó Ligda, erenagh of Emly, and have further references to the name in 1122 and 1204; but this must now, I think, be regarded as obsolete. More modern references to the name which I have noticed are all to people belonging to Thomond (Clare-Limerick) or to Co. Cavan. Daniel R. Lyddy, (1842-1887), the American novelist, was born in Co. Limerick.   Map

LILLY, MacAlilly   The sept of Mac Ailghile, formerly anglicized MacAlilly but now usually Lilly, Lilley or Lillie, is a branch of the MacGuires of Fermanagh, and its members to-day are mainly located in its original homeland around Enniskillen, though families of the name are found in other counties bordering on Fermanagh. Its origin is dealt with in several of the old genealogical works such as the Book of Ballymote and Mac Firbis. The surname Lilley (akin to Lely) is well-known in England where it is indigenous; but, though at least four appear in the army list of the Cromwellian and Restoration period, very few of that stock settled in Ireland and it may be assumed that Irish Lilleys are MacAlillys, especially if their families belong to central Ulster.

LIMERICK   As a modern surname this has no connexion with the Irish city but is derived from a French place and first took the form de l'Ambroux, later de Lambrouk; its earlier form in this country was Limbrick. As Limbrick and Limrick it occurs five times in the Co. Derry Hearth Money Rolls of 1665. It is traditionally believed to have come to Ireland from France via Scotland. Occasional examples of de Lumeryk (i.e. of Limerick city) do occur in the thirteenth and fourteenth centuries but this does not appear to have been more than an ephemeral surname.

LINDSAY   Alternative forms of this name are Lindsy and Linsey: they are all numerous in Ulster, especially in counties Down and Antrim. In the former Linchey has also been recorded as a modern synonym. No doubt the majority of these are of Scottish origin – Lindsay is the name of a great Scottish clan: several such were among the settlers in Cos. Tyrone and Fermanagh at the time of the Plantation of Ulster (c. 1608). But it is important to remember that Ó Loingsigh, often anglicized Lindsay in Ulster (Lynch in other provinces) is the name of an important sept whose chief was Lord of Dalriada (north east Ulster) up to the time of the Anglo-Norman invasion: what proportion of Ulster Lindsays are of this descent cannot now be determined. The fact that some MacClintocks changed their name to Lindsay adds to this difficulty. The Armagh Hearth Money Rolls (1664-6) include O'Linsye as well as Linsay and Lindsay, the last two being also in those of Co. Monaghan. O'Linsey, O'Lenshie, etc., occur frequently in the Tudor Fiants, but as they are clearly used synonymously with O'Linche (i.e. Lynch), usually in a Munster connexion, little relevant information can be gleaned from them: in the few cases which relate to Ulster they presumably represent the name now known as Lindsay. A number of Lindsays have held leading positions in Ireland since Robert Lindsay was High Sheriff of Co. Tyrone in 1667, the most important being Thomas Lindsay who, as well as being Archbishop of Armagh from 1714 to 1724 was also appointed Lord Justice in 1714. Perhaps it may be of interest to add that the Anglo-Norman name de Lindesaye occurs as a Dublin juror in the year 1292.   Bibl.

O'LOANE, Lambe   Lambe is a common name in Ireland, being distributed fairly evenly over the four provinces, with of course a preponderance in the city of Dublin which with suburbs comprises almost one fifth of the whole population of Ireland, including the thickly populated Belfast area. Apart from those families called Lambe who are the descendants of Cromwellian and other English settlers, the name, in Irish Ó Luain, has a dual origin in Ireland. First there was the Co. Limerick sept whose chiefs were lords of Deisbeg (Small County barony): they were dispersed soon after the Anglo-Norman invasion and spread throughout Munster, where they are almost invariably known as Lambe at the present day, though a century ago O'Donovan found some then called Loane. The other sept belonged to Oriel, but like their southern namesakes were scattered through their province. They remained fairly numerous in Co. Monaghan, Co. Armagh, Co. Fermanagh and Co. Tyrone at least until the end of the seventeenth century, as the Hearth Money Rolls for those counties attest, and moreover they retained a more Irish name, since the usual forms in Ulster were and are O'Luan, O'Lowan, O'Loan and Loane rather than Lambe.   Map

(O) LOGUE, Leech   The surname Ó Laoghóg (originally Ó Maolmhaodhóg) is numerous in counties Derry and Donegal in its anglicized form Logue. For some reason (or one might almost say without any reason) it has been anglicized as Leech in that part of the country in which it originated, viz. Co. Galway: the family is first recorded as chiefs of a district between Athenry and Athlone, and is still to be found in counties Galway and Clare. In the Athlone area Leech is recorded in the registration statistics as synonymous with Logue, Loogue etc. These also indicate that the name Leech exists in all the provinces. West of the Shannon it is of the Gaelic origin given above; elsewhere it is an old English name which, however, has long been in Ireland – witness, for example, William Leech, alias the Leeche, Provost of Rosponte (New Ross) in 1337, and similar references to be found in fourteenth century Ormond Deeds, in Archbishop Swayne's Register etc. Leech here is an occupative surname, leech meaning physician. O'Donovan states that in the Uí Maine country, in which the Ó Laoghóg territory lay, the name has become Lee; certainly Lee is not unknown there now, but it must be remembered that Lee, as an anglicized form of Ó Laidhigh or Ó Laoidhigh, belongs also to Co. Galway, though to the western part of the country, (see Irish Families, p. 208).

The most prominent member of the sept – from the Ulster branch – was Cardinal Michael Logue (1840-1924) Archbishop of Armagh.

O'LOHAN (O) LOGAN   Lohan is also spelt Loghan and Loughan and these names have been confused with Logan even by families bearing them. A list compiled by the Cunard Steamship Company of the surnames used interchangeably by Irish emigrants to America which equates Logan, Loghan, Loughan and Lohan, is corroborated by Matheson who shows that Loughan and Logan have been noted by local registrars as synonymous in Co. Galway, especially in the baronies of Killian and Tiaquin. Ó Leocháin in Irish, it was apparently sometimes called Logan by the Anglo-Norman officials of the thirteenth century, e.g. in a list of Co. Roscommon inquisition jurors in 1299, which is presumably too early a date to have a reference to a migrant from Antrim (vide infra).

The chiefs of the sept of Ó Leocháin, were lords of Gailenga Mór (now Morgallion Co. Westmeath) until driven across the Shannon by the Anglo-Normans after the invasion. Maurice O'Loughan was Bishop of Kilmacduagh from 1254 to 1283. Many of the humbler members of the sept, however, remained in their homeland, as we know from the Fiants relating to Co. Westmeath. The annalists tell a remarkable story of the miraculous death of the men of Teffia (Co. Meath) as re-

tribution for the slaying by them in 1024 of Cuan Ó Lothcháin, chief poet of King Malachy II.

The name has been ridiculously anglicized as Duck in some places by mistranslation (the Irish word for duck is lacha). O'Donovan, in his notes to The Tribes and Customs of Hy Fiachrach states that there was a sept called Ó Luacháin, located in Easkey (Co. Sligo) whose name became changed to Ó Luachair and that all the families there so called had in turn become Rush (luachair is the word for rush or sedge in Irish). That being so it would appear that the Lohans of Co. Galway are of Meath rather than Uí Fiachrach origin. It is of interest to note that the Inquisitions of the early seventeenth century relating to Co. Fermanagh contain a number of persons called Rush and Ruish.

Logan is found in all the provinces but is most numerous in Ulster where, in Co. Tyrone, it is sometimes interchangeable with Lagan. A number of Logans and O'Louchans (both forms are used) appear in Archbishop Swayne's Register as archdeacons, deans and parish clergy in the diocese of Armagh and Down between 1418 and 1439. Petty's "census" shows that 50 years after the Plantation of Ulster Loggan was among the principal names in four baronies of Co. Antrim. In three of these it is classed as an Irish name, but so also are such obviously non-Gaelic names as Bell, Donnelson, Eccles, Fulton, Hill etc.; and there is little doubt that these Loggans were descendants of Scottish Logans. The most notable of them was James Logan (1674-1751), Lurgan-born Quaker, who was secretary to William Penn and held several important offices in the state of Pennsylvania; his son and grandson were also prominent in American politics.

Another Logan family of non-Irish origin was de Logan: the first of these came to Ulster with the Norman de Manderville and they appear in the Carrickfergus area occasionally in mediaeval documents even as early as 1190, but if they have survived they are now indistinguishable from Logans of Scottish origin.

Cornelius Ambrosius Logan (1806-1853), American actor and dramatist, was of Irish parentage. His daughter, Olive Logan (1839-1909), actress, and his son Cornelius Ambrose Logan (1832-1899), physician and politician, were also persons of note in the United States.

There are four distinct townlands called Loughanstown in Co. Westmeath and one in Co. Meath, which also has a Loganstown. Loughan's Park is near Tuam, Co. Galway. There are many widely separated Ballyloughans, but these are not I think, formed from the surname but from the word lochán (a small lake).

LOMBARD   Lombard is a well known surname in Co. Cork, but rare elsewhere. Its association with that county is commemorated in the place-name Lombardstown. It was introduced into Ireland subsequent to the Anglo-Norman invasion and the family was firmly established in the barony of Muskerry by a grant of Edward III (1369), where they were already in possession of lands. They were still proprietors there in 1641 and at the Restoration they recovered some of the property they lost in the Cromwellian confiscation. A few years later we find one of them an officer in Col. Hon. Nicholas Browne's regiment of James II's army. Gregory Lombard of Buttervant "gent" was one of the jury which in 1603 acquitted William Meade, Recorder of Cork, in defiance of the English authorities' desire to have him convicted of high treason. Another branch settled in the city of Waterford: William Lombard was the first mayor of that city in 1377 and four times held that post, and in the subsequent list of mayors and sheriffs the name Lombard occurs frequently. It is of interest to note that the Charter incorporating the city is dated 1206, but the chief citizen, at first known as provost, was not termed mayor until 1377. Dr. Peter Lombard (1554-1625), Archbishop of Armagh and a theologian of European reputation, was born and educated in Waterford. This family was closely associated with the famous family of Wadding.

The name Lombard originated as a designation of a person from Lombardy, but in the course of time it came to denote a banker and so may be regarded as an occupative not a locative surname. In the Jacobite attainders it appears as Lumbert and Lumpert as well as Lombard.　Map

(O) LONG　(O) LANGAN　(O) LANIGAN　DAWSON

Long, of course, is a common English name and families of le Long came to Ireland very soon after the Anglo-Norman invasion of 1172. Though no doubt English Longs settled in Ireland from time to time since then, the great majority of Irish Longs are not of planter stock, but descendants of one of several Gaelic-Irish septs. First there was Ó Longaigh, for which Long is the only anglicized form extant, the earlier O'Longy being obsolete. The O'Longs of Cannaway were a considerable sept in Co. Cork, holding lands from the see of Cork including Garrane I Long in the parish of Moviddy. They lost their properties in the upheavals of the seventeenth century, but they remained in their homeland in a reduced position and have been numerous in Co. Cork and other parts of Munster down to the present time. The Longs of Killoran, near Templemore, who acquired the Everard estate there and assumed that name, though remaining Papists, lost it later through the machinations of the Dublin banker, Alderman Dawson.

The Dawson family of Ulster came to Ireland at the time of the Elizabethan wars and settled in Co. Monaghan becoming barons of Cremorne and Dartrey. Another Dawson family acquired large estates around Portarlington; and a third got possession of the Glen of Aherlow in Co. Tipperary – hence the appellation Dawson's Table in connexion with the mountain Galtee More.

Another patronymic for which Long has been used as the anglicized equivalent is Ó Longáin which is properly made Longan or Langan in English. This is the name of two distinct septs: the Langans of Co. Mayo, where that name is now chiefly found, are said to be a branch of the Ulster sept of Co. Armagh, now rare in its original habitat but several times mentioned in the Register of John Swayne, Archbishop of Armagh (1418-1439); the family of Ó Longán, who were erenaghs of Ardpatrick, Co. Limerick, and Patrician stewards of Munster (one of

whom was Bishop of Cloyne in the thirteenth century), are now called Long, but in the eighteenth and early nineteenth centuries the O'Longan family of Co. Cork were well known as scribes and poets, the most notable of them being Michael O'Longan (c. 1765-1837), the poet of the United Irishmen. His father was Michael O'Longan (d. 1770) of the well known Croom poetic circle, and his sons Peter, Paul and Joseph were all engaged as Irish scribes. It is probable that the townland of Ballylanigan in the barony of Glenquin, Co. Limerick, was named from the erenagh family of O'Longan, though Joyce derives it from Flanagan, a sept unconnected with Co. Limerick. On the other hand Ballylanigan, near Callan, has a different origin, the family in that case if not O'Flanagan being O'Lonagáin, anglice Lanigan, of Co. Kilkenny and north Tipperary; one of these appears among the outlaws of 1297 and they are numerous there in seventeenth century documents such as Petty's "census" and the Hearth Money Rolls. From this came the celebrated Dr. John Lanigan, (1758-1828) author of The Ecclesiastical History of Ireland.

One other surname remains to be noted in connexion with Long, viz. Fodha. This is simply the Irish word fada, meaning long or tall, written phonetically; it occurs in the modern Co. Waterford birth registrations and is a surname of the adjectival type like Bane, Crone, Lawder, etc., where an epithet has superseded a regular Mac or O name.　Bibl.

(O) LOSTY, Lasty

This ancient name has become Lastly in some places, whence the corruption to Leslie, the form in which it is usually found in Co. Donegal today. The main Leslie families in Ulster, however, are of British origin. Losty in Irish is Ó Loiste; and as such, or as Ó Loisde, it is found in our mediaeval Irish records, e.g., the Annals of Loch Cé, which chronicle the death of John O'Loisde, abbot of Assaroe, Co. Donegal, in 1502. In more than one anglicized form it occurs in the Antrim Hearth Money Rolls of 1669 and also, unexpectedly, in those of Co. Tipperary of a few years earlier.

In any of its forms – Lasty, Losty or Lusty – the name has now become very rare.

(O) LOUGHRAN

Ó Luachráin, (spelt Ó Luchairen in the Annals of Ulster) now anglicized as Loughran, is the name of a distinguished ecclesiastical family located in Co. Armagh. The most noteworthy of them were Thomas O'Loughran (d. 1416), Dean of Armagh; Father Patrick O'Loughran, who, after suffering torture, was executed with the Bishop of Down & Connor in 1612; Father John O'Loughran of the same diocese who died in prison after torture in 1576; and Father Neilan Loughran, O.F.M., of Armagh, another martyr whom the Cromwellians hanged in 1652. Friar O'Mellan, in his journal of the war in Ulster (1641 to 1647), mentions four different O'Loughrans, members of the Franciscan order: the diary is written in Irish and he spells the name O Laochthren. Families of O'Loughran were even then as numerous in Co. Tyrone as in Co. Armagh, a branch of the sept having settled in the former about the year 1430.

Spelling variants of Loughran include Laugheran and Lochrane. One peculiar synonym is recorded by Matheson for the Dungannon district, where Loughran and Early were both used by members of the same family. This is thus explained by Mr. T. Ó Raifeartaigh, in one of the many useful notes he has given me. Loughran was connected popularly with Loughrey; and since Loughrey, he says, is Ó Luatheirghigh (i.e. descendant of the early riser) Early, Mohery etc., became confused with Loughrey and Loughran. Normally, however, Loughrey is Ó Luachra, (see Early). Lutheran has been used as a synonym. Map

(O) LUBY   Luby, in Irish Ó Lúbaigh, was formerly anglicized as Looby, a spelling still used around Athlone and some other places. It is chiefly to be found in Co. Tipperary today, as was the case in 1659 when Petty's "census" listed it as one of the principal names in the barony of Iffa and Offa in that county. Nearby is the place-name Ballylooby in the parish of Galbally. There are 20 families of Looby in the Co. Tipperary Hearth Money Rolls (1665). Lt. William Luby, a Co. Kildare gentleman who joined the army of James II, was consequently outlawed for high treason: he appears to have claimed with success some years later to have this sentence reversed. His descendants became Lube, one of whom (as well as two 1649 officers called Luby) is mentioned by Dalton in his "King James's Army List". The name has been made famous by Thomas Clarke Luby (1822-1901) Young Irelander, Fenian and revolutionary journalist — he was the son of a Protestant clergyman of T.C.D. Catherine Luby, the poetess, was a relative of his. Rev. Thomas Luby (1800-1870), mathematician, who was born in Clonmel, was his uncle.   Map

(O) LUCEY   The Norman name de Lucy was prominent in Ireland in the fourteenth century, for Anthony de Lucy was Justiciar in 1332. It appears in the Gormanston Register even earlier — at Carlingford in 1305. There is no evidence, however, that there are any present-day representatives of de Lucy families and I think we may safely say that our Luceys are all Gaelic in origin, their surname being Ó Luasaigh in Irish. Woulfe says this is a corruption of Mac Cluasaigh but he does not list Mac Cluasaigh as a surname in the appropriate place, so if his statement is correct Mac Cluasaigh must be regarded as quite obsolete. In 1560 one Robert MacClwos of Cork obtained "English liberty" and later in the century several persons called MacCluosse etc., appear in the Fiants: possibly this is the name he had in mind — they were living in or near Co. Cork. O'Lwosie occurs in the same source twice in Co. Cork. As Luosy, alias Lousy, we find it in the Kinsale presentments of 1712 among the "Popish inhabitants" against whom execution was obtained. South-west Munster is almost exclusively its present location: 41 of the 42 birth registrations for Lucey in the 1890 return were in Munster, 33 of these in Co. Cork. Similarly in 1865, 39 of 43 registrations for

the name were in Co. Cork. In 1901 there were 42 families of Lucy or Lucey in Co. Kerry and 21 of Lucid. King, who made an analysis of the 1901 census, states that Lucid is a variant of Lucey, both being Ó Luasaigh in Irish.

LUNDY   Since the compulsory registration of births was introduced in 1864 the name Lundy has been mainly found in Ulster (particularly counties Cavan, Down and Antrim) though some families are located in north Connacht. In the Downpatrick area it has been recorded as a corrupt synonym of MacAlinden but it is improbable that this is the origin of the name in most cases. In 1665 it was quite numerous in Co. Tipperary, as the Hearth Money Rolls attest, and the Lundys were no newcomers to this county then, for in the Ormond Deeds we find John Boy Lundey, a Co. Tipperary witness, giving evidence at the age of 100 years in 1533, and more than a century earlier a cottager of the name is recorded for the same part of the country. In 1297 Gilbert de la Lounde was murdered by O'Mores; in 1307 it occurs as Lunde. Lundy is not given in the standard dictionaries of British surnames and I think the Norman de la Lounde may be accepted as normally the original form of the name in the Tipperary-Kilkenny area. I have no evidence of how it became comparatively numerous in Ulster. Col. Robert Lundy, whose name will be always remembered in connexion with the Siege of Derry, was an Englishman. His subsequent career after his escape from that city is not known — perhaps he settled in Ulster.

(O) LUNNEY   (O) LOONEY   Since the Gaelic name Ó Luinigh has assumed the anglicized form Looney as well as the more correct Lunney we must treat it together with Ó Luanaigh, anglice Looney. The latter is well known in Munster particularly in counties Cork, Kerry and Clare. Brian O'Looney (1837-1901), Gaelic poet and scholar, was a Clareman; John Luony was a Kinsale rapparee who was captured in 1712. Lowney, a name found in considerable numbers in west Cork, particularly in the Castletownbere area, is equated by Woulfe with Looney. According to family tradition, however, it is quite distinct from Looney, being a contraction of Na Labhna i.e. of the River Lowna (mod. Laune), a sobriquet assumed by a branch of the O'Sullivans and retained as a hereditary surname.

The sept of Ó Luinigh was of more importance, at any rate in the mediaeval period. They were once chiefs of Cenél Moen in the barony of Raphoe, whence they were driven across the Foyle into the barony of Strabane; there they became so firmly established that they gave their name to the Munterlooney area in Co. Tyrone. At the present time they are chiefly to be found there and in Co. Fermanagh: usually, as stated above, these families are called Lunney not Looney. Leonard has been reported as a synonym of Lunney in Ulster, and Linney is a rare variant.   Map

(O) LYNAM   LYNAGH   The name Lynam, which is

149

now chiefly associated with Offaly and other midland Leinster counties, appears in its Gaelic-Irish form (Ó Laigheanáin) very early as that of the erenaghs of Ferns: there are eight references to them in the Four Masters, all prior to 1100: Bishop O'Lynan was founder of the Church of St. Peter at Ferns in 1055. The family were also at one time erenaghs of St. Mullins, Co. Carlow. In the Middle Ages they appear frequently in Co. Kildare and Co. Meath, usually in respectable though not prominent positions. By the end of the sixteenth century they were to be found among the leading gentry of that county, being established in the barony of Moyfenrath, which adjoins Co. Westmeath. In 1659 Petty's "census" lists Lynan among the more numerous Irish names in Moycashel, Co. Westmeath. Thirty years later we meet one of the same family as an officer of Dillon's regiment in King James's army, and two spelt Lynham. Two Lynhams of Co. Meath were outlawed for Jacobite activities.

Woulfe states that Lynam has also been used in Offaly as the anglicized form of a different surname, viz. Laighneach, properly Lynagh or Leynagh in English. This is, no doubt, one of those descriptive agnomina which superseded an older surname, the meaning of the word in this case being simply "Leinsterman"; this implies that it was acquired by a Leinsterman outside that province, and the place-name Gorteenlynagh in Co. Mayo has presumably a similar origin. This was probably the case in the thirteenth and fourteenth centuries: the name Leynagh is of frequent occurrence in the Justiciary Rolls in Co. Tipperary and Co. Limerick. John Leynagh was Bishop of Lismore from 1323 to 1354. The same source has occasional references to it in Leinster. Later we seldom meet it outside that province, and the fact that the great majority of the many Leynaghs, Lynaghs etc., to be found in the Tudor Fiants from 1550 are located in counties Kildare and Meath and that a century later Leynagh was one of the principal Irish surnames in the barony of Carbery, Co. Kildare (which adjoins Moyfenrath), particularly as Lynagh or Linagh is still found there, suggests that the usually accepted derivation given above may be misleading, and that the name is in fact, at least in many cases, a corruption of O'Lynan (Lynam). This theory is corroborated by the fact that individual tituladoes in the barony of Carbery are called Lynham in the same document. Moreover the name with the prefix O occurs in the fifteenth century Statute Rolls (temp. Edward IV), where O'Leynaghs are described as "villeins of the Duke of York in Meath".

Although it is improbable that any descendants of the Norman de Lynhams remain today it should nevertheless be mentioned that such a family did exist in the thirteenth and fourteenth centuries in Co. Kildare.

Two men of the name have been prominent in recent times: Major William Francis Lynam (d. 1894), the creator of the humorous character Mick McQuaid; and Edward William Lynam (d. 1950), the distinguished superintendent of the department of maps in the British Museum, whose family belongs to Co. Carlow.

LYNESS   Lyness, with its variant spellings, Lynas, Lynass, Lynis, is a numerous name in counties Antrim and Down today. It appears in the Co. Armagh Hearth Money Rolls of 1664 in three parishes. Strange though it seems Lynas or Lyness has been recorded in recent times as in use in the Newry area as a synonym of MacAleenan.

LYNNOTT   The Lynnotts were one of the powerful Cambro-Norman families which became established in Connacht in the thirteenth century. In 1585 "the lands of the Lynnotts" were of sufficient extent and importance to be mentioned as such in the Composition Book of Connacht with such well-known families as the Burkes and the Barretts, and fifty years later at the time of Strafford's Inquisition of Co. Mayo, five Lynotts are mentioned as landowners, mainly in the barony of Tirawley. But from that on they declined in prosperity and influence. Not one is listed among the "tituladoes" of Co. Mayo in the "census" of 1659 and only one in the eighteenth century appears in the list of Prerogative Wills. Numerically, too, the name has diminished.

It should be added that Livott and Lyvet are sometimes found, at various dates, as corrupt synonyms of Lynnott. Lyvet, however, is a distinct Anglo-Norman name in Leinster (not in Mayo) since the thirteenth century.

(O) MACKEN   (Mac) MACKEN, Macklin
O'Macken (Ó Maicín and sometimes Ó Macáin) and Mac-Macken (Mac Maicín) are the names of two and possibly three quite distinct septs. In that part of the Book of Lecan which deals with Corca Laoidhe Ua Meiccon is given as one of the hereditary proprietors of that region, and O'Donovan in his notes on the text equates this old form with the modern name Macken. It occurs in Munster as O'Makan, O'Mackane, O'Mackine etc., at various dates from 1314 in the Justiciary Rolls (e.g. a "notorious felon", which usually means a native Irishman persona non grata to the Anglo-Norman government) to 1600 in the Fiants (when two of the name from the Corca Laoidhe country received "pardons"). O'Macken, however, is not confined in mediaeval records to the southern province: Leighlin Omakin is mentioned in an official report of 1360 as one of the Leinster enemies of the English king; in Connacht the Four Masters record the death of Thomas O'Maicin, Bishop of Leyney (i.e. Achonry), in 1265; the Annals of Loch Cé mention a Maeilbhrighde O'Maicin, Abbot of Ballintubber in 1225; and the early connexion with Co. Mayo thus indicated is still to be seen in modern birth registration statistics. Neither the Cork nor the Mayo O'Mackens can be regarded as akin to the Mackens of Ulster who are properly MacMacken. In their ancient homeland, the present Co. Monaghan, the name is now usually written Mackin not Macken. John Macken (1784-1823) the Ulster poet, of Co. Fermanagh, was no doubt one of these; but the discarding of the prefix leaves it uncertain from which sept persons of the name found in other parts of the country belonged – one wonders for example was James Macken, who was murdered at Hoggen Gate "in the purlieus of Dublin" in 1567, a Mac or an O. One can be sure he was a "hibernicus" since the official record tells us

that his murderer was pardoned, though found guilty of the crime.

The use of MacEvoy and Macken as synonyms in the Mullingar area is curious, and, since these names have nothing in common, must have arisen through ignorance. Map

(O) MACKEY   Though sometimes used as a synonym of the Ulster surname MacKee, Mackey is properly the normal anglicized form of the Irish Ó Macdha, an Ormond sept whose territory lay in and around the parish of Ballymackey near Nenagh. Though the Co. Tipperary Hearth Money Rolls of 1666 show that there were then some 50 substantial families of the name in the county only one of these, strangely enough, was in the parish named after them. The Fiants of a century earlier prove that even then they had spread into neighbouring counties, particularly Limerick, Waterford, Kilkenny and Offaly. In this case the Fiants have to be used with particular care because in the sixteenth century, as at present, MacKee, with such variants as Mackey, MacKea, MacKehe etc., as well as the more obvious O'Maaky and O'Mackey, were already in use to denote O'Mackey and in some cases were identical with the form used to denote the northern MacKee. The Daniel Mackey who became Bishop of Down and Connor in 1671 was a MacKay. It should also be remembered that many Scottish families named MacKay settled in Ulster and some of these became Mackey.

If the Mackeys have not been very prominent in the political or cultural history of the country, their name is very well known in our·own day in the sphere of sport, since the Mackey brothers of Co. Limerick were among the greatest exponents of the national game of hurling. Captain Mackey was one of the most prominent and active of the Fenian organization: this, however, is a pseudonym and his real name was William Lomasney. James Townsend Mackey (1777-1862), author of a standard work on Irish plants, was the creator of the Trinity College, Dublin, botanical gardens.   Map

(O) MACKLE, Mackell   I do not accept the statement that Mackle is a form of MacGill, though there is no doubt that the two have been used as synonyms in Co. Down: such usage frequently arises from ignorance and has little etymological value. There is in fact good reason to believe that Mackle is an O name, O'Mackell. The Hearth Money Rolls of the northern counties, particularly Co. Armagh, have a number of O'Mackells. It is true that MacKell also appears in them; and this form has become established in counties Armagh and Down as well as the more numerous Mackle. In this connexion we may compare the Limerick name O'Mackessy which similarly became MacKessy as well as Mackessy when the Ó was dropped. As MacKell the name is well-known in Australia.

Mackle is the spelling now almost invariably used in counties Armagh and Tyrone where the name is numerous to-day. A century ago Mackel and Machel were current variants there. MacCahill was found in Co. Cavan, but that was, no doubt, a different Ulster name viz.,

MacCahill (Mac Cathail). Woulfe says this is obsolete: it has in fact become McCole and MacCarvill.

MADDOCK, Vaddock   Better examples than Ballymaddock of the rare place-names formed from English surnames combined with the Irish prefix Bally are Ballyarnott, Ballystokes and Ballytaylor. Maddock is Welsh not English. The change from M to V is normal, Mh being pronounced V. Vaddock (with its synonyms Waddock, Weddick etc., and also Maddox) is a distinct surname — Mac Mhadoc — being that of a family which claims descent from the MacMurroughs and thus to be of Gaelic-Irish not Norman origin. There is good authority for this, including the Book of Leinster. They were formerly called MacVaddock in English, and mediaeval and early modern records contain many references to people of the name and to "MacVadog's country" in Co. Wexford and Co. Kilkenny; and in his official report on the state of the country in 1579 Sir Nicholas Mally speaks of MacEvado, chief of his name. Richard Madock, gent, of Townhely (Tinahely) was a Co. Wicklow Jacobite outlawed under William III.

MAGEOWN   Though Mageown is one of the recorded synonyms of MacGowan, it should be stated that it is also of another origin viz., Mag Eoin or Mag Eoghain, cognate with MacKeown. It is occasionally found in the abbreviated form Geon.

MAGNER   This was originally Magnel. Castlemagner in Co. Cork was formerly Magnelstown. Many Magnels were in Co. Cork in the thirteenth century, as we know from the Justiciary Rolls and similar records; and it is with that county families of the name have been associated ever since. It had become Magner by the sixteenth century and is numerous in the Tudor Fiants. In the next century we find it listed in the "census" of 1659 as a principal Irish name in the Co. Cork barony of Kilmore and Orrery; and three years earlier two of the name were transplanted as Papists from Co. Cork to Connacht.

Maingnéir is used as the Irish form of this name.

MAHAFFY, MacAfee   This name is of Scottish origin, but since the beginning of the seventeenth century it has been numerous in Ulster. In Gaelic it is Mac Dhuibhshíthe. The two anglicized forms given above are the most usual, but it has several other variants such as MacHaffy and MacFie. As MacHaffy it occurs in the Co. Armagh Hearth Money Rolls of 1664; but most records relating to the name find them in Co. Donegal.

John Pentland Mahaffy (1839-1918), provost of Triniy College, Dublin, was famous not only as a scholar but also for his mordant wit. Rev. Daniel MacAfee (1790-1873), a Wesleyan clergyman, was a noted controversialist in his day, especially as an opponent of Daniel O'Connell.

MAJOR   As an Irish surname Major is seldom found outside Ulster, and there mainly in the north-eastern counties of Antrim, Down and Armagh, though in the eighteenth century there were some families of the name in counties Donegal and Derry also. It is a name of some note in England (see D.N.B.). Its earlier forms are Mauger and Mayger, derived not from the Latin major but from the Old-French maugler or old-German madalgar, meaning council-spear. I make this statement on the authority of Reaney. Weekley gives the Teutonic name from which it is derived as Maethelgaer, maethel meaning an assembly. It occurs as Major in Connacht as early as 1287, when John Major was Archdeacon of Tuam, but it does not appear to have become established in Ireland until the seventeenth century, when we find it as an English titulado in the Derry section of the "census" of 1659 and also in the Monaghan Hearth Money Rolls. One such entry is of interest because the occupant of a holding in the parish of Tedavnet was returned as James Major in 1663 and as James Meares in 1665; similarly the English philosopher John Major (c. 1550) was also called John Mair. However the equation of Meares with Major (assuming that these entries refer to the same person) may be a clerical error, for confusion in the entry of surnames in these rolls is not infrequent. Meares is normally a Clare name, Ó Meidhir or Ó Midhir in Irish (see Meere).

(O) MALINN, Millynn   Like so many Irish surnames this has several spelling variants and is consequently apt to be confused with Mallin and with Milne. The sixteenth century Fiants include 14 surnames which could be anglicized forms of the name now under consideration, but the fact that the location of the people referred to is usually in the Carlow-Leix-Kilkenny area renders that unlikely, except in the case of Westmeath references, belong to Malinn, Malinn, Millynn, and those other forms in which the stress is on the second syllable, the parts of counties Monaghan and Fermanagh centred around Clones. MacFirbis and other authorities place the Uí Maelfinde there. First it was anglicized as O'Mulline and O'Molline: this almost inevitably was absorbed by the ubiquitous Mullin as happened in Co. Monaghan; but those families which moved to Co. Westmeath, first as O'Mulline and O'Molline, became Malinn etc.

The modern Irish form of the name is Ó Maoilfhinn.

(O) MALLON, Mellan   These are two variants in English of the Irish surname Ó Mealláin, that of a family chiefly noted as joint hereditary keepers with the Mulhollands (q.v.), of the bell of St. Patrick, otherwise called the Bell of the Testament: frequent mention is made of them in the Annals of the Four Masters, Loch Cé, etc. Their territory was Meallánacht, i.e., O'Mellan's country, which included the present Cookstown, Co. Tyrone, but groups of them were also to be found scattered over the church lands of the Archbishop of Armagh. The sept was a branch of the Cenél Eoghain, from whom the county of Tyrone (Tír Eoghain) got its name. Mallons are numerous today there and in Co. Armagh; it is estimated that there are some 2500 persons of the name in Ireland of whom 80 per cent use the spelling Mallon while the remainder are Mellan and Mellon. The prefix O does not appear to have been resumed to any extent, though it was in common use in the seventeenth century when O'Mellan was recorded in Petty's "census" as one of the principal Irish names in the barony of Dundalk and it occurs frequently also in the contemporary Co. Armagh Hearth Money Rolls. In that century there were a number of distinguished priests of the name, particularly in the Franciscan Order, as the Wadding Papers testify. The best known was Fr. Turlough O'Mellan whose Ulster War Diary (1641-1647) in Irish is "a document of surpassing interest, historically and linguistically". It was at one time ascribed to his brother, another Franciscan.

Rev. Charles O'Mallon was Dean of Armagh in 1444. As early as 1420 it is recorded without the O, when two men named Mallon were appointed tax-collectors for Drogheda by the parliament of that date. Commandant Michael Mallin was one of the leaders of the Rising executed in 1916.

Some families in Co. Tyrone, e.g. around Cookstown, have allowed their true name Mellan to be changed to Mullen, which is that of a sept very numerous in Tyrone and Derry. A few O'Mellans have, more strangely, become Munroe.

(O) MARKEY   This is Ó Marcaigh in Irish, and is a true Oriel surname; for whether we look at early records or consult modern statistics we find it in counties Monaghan or Louth or quite near one of these — though actually the earliest reference to the name I have met records the fact that one Robert O'Markey was outlawed in Co. Tipperary in 1302. The prefix O was still retained in the seventeenth century, e.g. in the Monaghan Hearth Money Rolls, but was already falling into disuse: it appears simply as Marky among the principal Irish names in Co. Louth in the "census" of 1659, and in modern times the O seems to have been completely discarded. In its homeland and in Dublin, Markey has been widely changed to Ryder, in this case a genuine (not, as is so often the case a spurious) translation, for marcach means a horseman. Another synonym reported from the Oriel country is Mark, but not all people so called are Markeys, for Mark is also an English name. It is perhaps worth noting that the list of kern mustered in 1544 by the O'Reilly of the day includes one Thomas Marke.

(O) MARLEY   Probably the best known person of the name was Thomas Marley, Chief Justice of the King's Bench, (d. 1756), who was the grandfather of Henry Grattan. The family to which he belonged stemmed from a Newcastle-on-Tyne merchant whose grandson Anthony Marlay acquired property in Co. Longford about 1675. According to Bardsley the name, variously spelt Marley and Marlay, was taken from a place near Gateshead in England.

The great majority of Irish Marleys, however, are of Gaelic-Irish descent. Woulfe gives us no information about them. He gives Ó Mearlaigh as the Irish form of the name: I cannot accept his tentative suggestion that it is a corruption of Ó Murghaile and having regard to the early anglicized form Marhelly I think Ó Mearthaile is more likely (I have not met the name in Irish). I have no doubt that there was a distinct sept of O'Marley belonging to Oriel. References thereto are frequent in seventeenth century records, e.g. in the Hearth Money Rolls of counties Armagh and Monaghan and in the Dowdall Deeds (chiefly Co. Louth); in the "census" of 1659 O'Marley is listed as a principal Irish name in Co. Armagh.

It is therefore remarkable that in recent times, in fact since compulsory birth registration was introduced in 1864, the location of people called Marley is almost entirely in the north west of the country; in the 1864 to 1866 registrations there are some around Dundalk, but thirty years later there were none in that area, all being in counties Donegal and Mayo.

MARNELL   This is an old family in Kilkenny, a suburb of which is called Marnell's Meadows. In the "census" of 1659 the name in Kilkenny appears as Mornell. It was also found in Co. Tipperary: the sixteenth century "pardons" for that county include Marnells of Killinleigh and Slieveardagh and in the next century the fact that another Co. Tipperary man named Edmund Marnell was transplanted under the Cromwellian régime as an Irish papist is a further indication of their having become hibernicized. In modern times, the name, though not numerous, is still associated with Co. Kilkenny and adjacent areas.

(O) MARRON, Marren   This name is quite numerous. In 1865 58 births were registered for Marren (24) and Marron (34); nearly all the Marrens were in Co. Sligo and most of the Marrons were in the Carrickmacross area of Co. Monaghan. In 1890 there were 31, with the same distinction between Marren and Marron, but the latter were then much more numerous. In the Co. Monaghan Hearth Money Rolls (1663 and 1665) we find O'Maran, O'Marran and O'Meran, while in the "census" of 1659 O'Merran was a "principal Irish name" around Carrickfergus, Co. Antrim. O'Meran appears too in a north Mayo Fiant. In Matheson's list of modern synonyms Mearn is recorded with Marron in Ballymena, Co. Antrim, but this Mearn may be the Scottish Mearns of Kirkcudbrightshire. The Gaelic form of O'Marron is clearly Ó Mearáin. I can find no positive evidence indicating the early history of the sept; it seems probable that there were in fact two septs so called, one in Oriel

and the other smaller one in the Uí Fiachra country – but there is no mention of the latter in The Tribes and Customs of Hy Fiachra.   Map

MacMASTER MASTERSON   The Irish MacMasters are a Breffny sept, of the same stock as the MacGuires of Fermanagh, called Mac an Mhaighistir in Irish in which language maighistear means master. Useful early pedigrees relating to families of this sept will be found in Analecta Hibernica, No. 3. The earlier anglicized forms of the name as recorded in the Fiants were numerous – MacAmaster, MacYmaster, MacMester etc., – and they were found in all stations of life then, as in the next century, mostly in counties Cavan and Longford. By the date of Petty's "census" (1659) they had already for the most part adopted the form Masterson there. Birth statistics show that these two counties are their main location in recent times also. MacMaster on the other hand, which in population totals almost equals Masterson, is now found almost entirely in Antrim and Down, where they are descendants of Scottish settlers.

The important family of Masterson, so prominently identified with Co. Wexford, must be distinguished from the Gaelic Mastersons of Breffny. Coming from Cheshire in England Sir Thomas Masterson was granted lands in Co. Wexford by Queen Elizabeth; in 1583 he was seneschal of the county and liberties of Wexford and constable of the castle of Ferns. His descendants married Catholics and less than a century later we find them defending the castle on behalf of the Confederate Catholics. In the Cromwellian confiscation the family lost their vast estates, which had been greatly increased by a grant of 10,000 acres to Sir Richard Masterson in 1613.

One MacMaster family of Co. Down has been notable in America: Rev. Gilbert MacMaster, D.D. (1778-1854), Presbyterian minister at New York and author of many religious works, and his two sons, Erasmus MacMaster (d. 1866) professor of theology at Chicago, and James A. MacMaster (d. 1886) a convert and leading Catholic journalist. William MacMaster (1811-1887), born in Co. Tyrone, was the founder of Toronto University.   Map

MATTIMOE, Milmoe   According to local tradition in the Boyle (Co. Roscommon) area, the only place in Ireland where the name Mattimoe is established, it is a variant of Milmoe, the homeland of which is in Co. Sligo, a few miles north of Boyle. The evidence available, if not absolutely conclusive, tends to corroborate the oral tradition, which is also supported by the fact that at least one family in the area is known to have used in quite recent times both these surnames concurrently. The extent to which families of the name Mattimoe were found concentrated there in the last century is indicated by the returns in the Tithe Applotment Books of 1835, when there were 13 in the parish of Kilmactranny, 4 in Ballisodare, 2 in Kilronan, 10 in Ardcarne and 14 in Boyle parish. In the 1832 Tithe Applotment Book Mallimo similarly occurs. In the census of the Elphin diocese made in 1749 Mattimoes, Millamoes and Mullamoes are found side by side in Boyle, Ardcarne etc. Col. Cyril M.

Mattimoe, who has done much research on these families, has written a useful and interesting account of this, a copy of which can be seen at the National Library, Manuscripts Department. According to Reaney Mattimoe is an indigenous English name, but in Ireland it could appear to be one of the many English names used as a synonym of an Irish one of somewhat similar sound. If we accept it as synonymous with Milmoe, as I do, then the correct Irish form of Mattimoe is, like Milmoe, Ó Maolmuaidh; and according to MacFirbis there was a minor sept so called, a branch of the Silmurray, located in Co. Roscommon. Neither Mattimoe nor Milmoe was included in Matheson's statistical return for 1890 which records all surnames for which five or more births were registered in that year; the birth registrations for the three years 1864-66 were: Mattimoe 13, all at Boyle; Milmoe 12, at Boyle, Swinford and Sligo.

MAUNSEL   MANSFIELD, Mandeville   Maunsel is one of the many Anglo-Norman surnames which were quite numerous up to the end of the seventeenth century, but are now rare and chiefly confined to the class usually described as landed gentry. It is derived from the Norman-French mancel, i.e. an inhabitant of Maine, or alternatively from le mansel, a feudal tenant occupying a manse farm. In Irish it is called Móinséil. The name occurs frequently as that of people of consequence in all the mediaeval records such as the Ormond Deeds, the Justiciary Rolls, the ecclesiastical registers etc. They were located for the most part in Tipperary and Limerick: in both these counties Mansels held the position of chief sergeant in the thirteenth and early fourteenth centuries. The Fiants show that they were there, and also in counties Cork and Kilkenny, in the sixteenth century, when some ranked as gentlemen and some had occupations such as cottoner and sherman. In the seventeenth century they are still mainly in Co. Tipperary – in fact the 1659 "census" includes Maunsel as one of the principal Irish names in that county where a few years later nine Maunsel families are recorded in the Hearth Money Rolls. Maunsel's Bank (called the Bank of Limerick), founded in 1789, was one of the leading private banks of the period, but it failed in the financial crash in 1820. The spelling is usually Maunsell, but in the Fiants Monshiall, Monshale, Monseall and Monsell all occur, the last of these being still in use. William Monsell (1812-1894) 1st Baron Emly of Tervoe, Co. Limerick, was P.M.G. and Vice-Chancellor of the Royal University. Daniel Toler Maunsell (1835-1875), authority on the Irish Poor Law medical system, was a Co. Limerick man. Dr. Henry Maunsell (1806-1879), co-founder of the Dublin Medical Press, is also worthy of mention.

The name Maunsel is intimately associated with the Irish literary renaissance of the first quarter of the present century, since the firm of Maunsel and Co. Ltd., of Dublin, published works of every writer in that movement. No individual Maunsel, however, was concerned in this undertaking: the name was chosen almost at random, one of the first directors being Joseph Maunsel Hone.

Mansfield, which in Co. Kerry occurs in modern birth registrations as occasionally synonymous with Maunsel, is a name chiefly associated with Co. Waterford. Mansfield was originally Mandeville, the transition stages of the name being Mandefill, Monfield, Monsfield. The Co. Louth parish now known as Mansfieldstown is called Maundervillestown in Archbishop Swayne's Register (1418-1439) and other mediaeval documents. The de Mandeville family – de Magna Villa in the Latin form – is one of those which accompanied William the Conqueror from Normandy and came to Ireland in the wake of the Anglo-Norman invasion. From 1210, when Martin de Maundeville was a witness to the charter of Ratoath, we find the name in the mediaeval records of Co. Meath. In the thirteenth and fourteenth centuries they were established in Antrim: Hugolin de Mandeville was the ancestor of the MacQuillans of the Route. They settled also in counties Waterford and Tipperary: in the latter county the Mandevilles of Castle Annagh and of Ballydine were powerful landed families from the seventeenth to the nineteenth centuries. There is a statue in Mitchelstown commemorating the Fenian John Mandeville (1849-1888).   Bibl.

(Mac) MAY, Mea, Mawe, Mayo   (O) MEE, Mea
The Gaelic-Irish sept of Ó Miadhaigh, whose name was first anglicized as O'Miey and later as Mee, Mea and even May, was located in Teffia (Co. Westmeath), where the place-name Clonyveey (Cluain Uí Mhíadhaigh i.e. O'Mey's meadow) is a memorial of it. A member of it was notorious at an early date when Gilla-gan-máthair Ó Miadhaigh struck off the head of Hugh de Lacy in 1186. As was the case with most of the Irish septs in that area, they were dispossessed by Norman families and remained in their homeland only in humble positions, as we can see from the evidence of the sixteenth century Fiants. Some moved north-westwards: Conor O'Miey was one of the followers of Rory O'Donnell in Tirconnell, and today they are mostly found in Sligo and neighbouring counties, where Mea and Mee are the usual modern forms of the name. Mee, it should be added, is occasionally found as an abbreviation of MacNamee (q.v.).

I think the Mays who appear quite frequently in the Co. Tipperary Hearth Money Rolls of 1666 were Mac Máighe. The pronunciation of this is not far from Mac-Mawe, and Mawe is a synonym of May in use in the part of the country associated with the MacMawes (alias Mac-Maugh, MacMawige etc.). They were a branch of the celebrated Condon family of east Cork and Co. Waterford (v. Irish Families, p. 84) who assumed a Gaelic patronymic. Mac Máighe is an abbreviation of Mac Máigheog. They were sometimes called MacMawe-Condon in English. Barnard May and David May were sovereigns of New Ross in 1287 and 1290; and in 1305 a John Mey was an Inquisition juror at Ardmoyle, Co. Tipperary. Later we find Richard May a tenant of cathedral lands in Co. Waterford in 1427. He was possibly not a MacMay for many of the Mays are of English origin. May is an indigenous English surname and it is also Anglo-Norman. As early as 1210 Ralph de May was proprietor of lands at Ratoath. John Mey (whose register is preserved at Trinity College, Dublin) was Archbishop of Armagh from 1444 to 1456; Sir Algernon May acquired much land in Co. Kilkenny and appears in the Kilkenny Book of Survey and Distribution as a new proprietor in the baronies of Ida and Iverk; and many, presumably of immigrant stock, are often met with in the records of the civic and commercial life of the city of Dublin from 1500 onwards.

George Augustus May (1815-1892), a Belfastman, was a distinguished Irish judge.

MacMayo, also abbreviated to Mayo, appears as a surname in the Book of Survey and Distribution for Co. Mayo and a few years earlier (1647) in the Ormond MSS. we find an army officer described both as Mayo and May.

There are thus at least three different origins for the name May in Ireland and to determine their own background persons of the name must have an authenticated pedigree or at least a firm family tradition.

MEADE, Miagh The use of the English surname Meade by families formerly called Miagh dates from the seventeenth century. Before that they were almost always Miagh or some variant thereof such as Myagh or Meagh. There is no doubt that Miagh is a phonetic anglicization of the Irish Midheach (which means a Meathman). This is proved by, inter alia, the fact that in mediaeval Latin deeds the name is de Midia.

From the beginning of the fourteenth century the Miaghs were among the leading families in Co. Cork and nearly all the many references to them in our mediaeval and early modern records relate to Munster. Though I have found no positive evidence of it I think it may be presumed that they settled first in Co. Meath soon after the Anglo-Norman invasion and thence moved southwards. Mr. John Meade who has made a thorough study of the Meades of Co. Cork (see Bibliography) believes that they came to Ireland from Somerset via Bristol and he has pointed out to me that the arms of the fourteenth century Miaghs of Buttevant were the same as those of the Meades of Bristol. Though Meade certainly is a west of England name, I think it is unlikely that the Co. Cork family in question were Meades of Somerset stock: there would have been no need for them to adopt the surname Miagh. The Co. Cork Judiciary Rolls for 1295 include a case in which one Bernard de Mithe (a variant of de Midia) is definitely described as hibernicus in sharp distinction from men of English stock. I suggest as a probability that they migrated from Meath to Co. Cork and later, having normal trading contacts with Bristol, a branch of the family settled there and after a generation or two Miagh (Latin de Midia) became Meade and subsequently indistinguishable from the native English Meades. The place-name Meadstown (in Co. Cork), however, appears as early as 1577, when in a Fiant of that date it is given as the residence of William Synane, gent. (see Synan).

In the mediaeval period the Miaghs were not confined to Co. Cork. In 1350 Richard, Henry and William de Midia were witnesses to a Durrow deed; in 1415 we find

the name at Carrick-on-Suir; in 1499 a Myagh was sovereign of Kilmallock; and the history of Clonmel abounds in references to the name, especially in the seventeenth century when the majority of them had become Meade. The most notable of these was Sir John Meade (d. 1711), chancellor of Tipperary and ancestor of the Earls of Clanwilliam. This particular family took the side of William III, but there were at least five Meades or Miaghs serving against him as officers in James II's army. In the records of the subsequent outlawries the name appears as Meade alias Meygh. At that period it was most numerous in Co. Limerick and in Cork city, and if not actually numerous in the Kinsale and Youghal districts families of standing so called were long well established there.

Among the many Cork ecclesiastics called Miagh or Meade I should mention Father James Miagh, who was Vicar-Apostolic of Cork and Cloyne from 1610 to 1635, and his relative Father Bernardine Miagh O.F.M. of St. Isodore's. Two well known nineteenth century figures, Sir Richard Meade (1821-1894) of Ballymartle, who distinguished himself at the time of the Indian Mutiny, and Lizabeth Meade (? 1844-1915), novelist, were both of Co. Cork families.

Ó Miadhaigh is an entirely different name: it was anglicized Mee or May (see previous article).   Bibl.

(O) MEEGAN   MEEHAN Woulfe suggests that Meegan (Ó Miadhagáin) is a variant form of Meehan (Ó Miadhacháin) which was dealt with in Irish Families, pp. 224, 225. Although at first sight this would seem improbable, since Meegan is now found almost exclusively in Co. Monaghan and the Oriel country whereas Meehan belongs (apart from Dublin) rather to Munster, Connacht and Donegal, nevertheless I think Woulfe is right: not only because we have the evidence of local registrars that Meehan and Meegan have been used synonymously in Co. Monaghan, but earlier records corroborate their identity: for example in the Tipperary Hearth Money Rolls of 1665-7 there are 8 families of Meehan and as many as 29 of Meegan; similarly the 1659 "census" places several anglicized variants of Ó Miadhachain in Co. Clare and Co. Tipperary and also four families of O'Meehan in Co. Fermanagh, while in the Monaghan Hearth Money Rolls (1663-5) there are a number of entries for O'Meeghan, O'Mighan as well as O'Migan.

MacMEEKIN This name has at least five variant spellings of which the above is the most usual. It is very numerous in Ulster. Woulfe suggests MacMiadhacháin as the probable Gaelic-Irish form, which seems acceptable.

(O) MEENAN This is Ó Mianáin, not to be confused with Ó Mianchain (see Meenaghan, sub Drennan, supra). Meenan belongs almost exclusively to Donegal and adjacent counties. It occurs there in an early record, for an O Mianáin, O'Donnell's tutor, was hanged at Sligo in 1246 with O'Donnell's foster-brother, these men having been left as hostages to Maurice Fitzgerald. Meenan is one of the few names which are as numerous in the 1890 birth statistics as in those of 1865. In the map of Co. Donegal showing family locations, prepared for me by the late Mr. J. C. MacDonagh, Meenan is placed in the district between Rathmullen and Ramelton.

(O) MEERE   In England the name Meer, more usually Meare or Mears is derived from the Old-English mere (lake) or maere (boundary) and occasionally we do find persons called Meeres etc. among the English settlers in Ireland; but these are so few to-day that we may disregard them in this essay. As an Irish name Meere belongs almost exclusively to Co. Clare. In current voters lists it appears in east, west and central Clare; it is frequent in the 1821 forty-shilling freeholders, especially in the barony of Islands; the prefix O was still retained in the seventeenth century for we meet Hugh and Rory O'Meere in an Inchiquin deed of 1627 and in the same Co. Clare estate the Gaelic-Irish form of the name is used in 1693 in the person of Evelin Ni Mire. In the sixteenth century Fiants it is called O'Mire, which is the earliest anglicized form of the Gaelic Ó Midhir. In the case of this name the Fiants must be consulted with caution: O'Mear is used there for the well-known Tipperary name O'Meara. There has been a tendency among some Meere families to adopt Myers as a synonym and when met in Co. Clare Myers is of that Irish origin. When found elsewhere in Ireland (e.g. Meares of Mearescourt, Co. Westmeath), these are English names of French origin being derived from mire a word having two distinct meanings, viz. physician and marsh. As early as 1347 the name appearing as de Meer, and de la Mere, resident in Co. Meath in 1310, is probably the same.

(O) MELLERICK   This name appears in the Annals of Loch Cé as Ó Maolgeric in 1088 and Ó Maelrioc in 1218 in both cases recording the death of poets of outstanding distinction. Woulfe mentions the former and correctly states the modern Gaelic form of the name to be Ó Maoilgheiric which can be accepted, for we find O'Mulgherick in the Fiants as an early anglicized form. This occurs in a list of "pardons" of Inishowen people. The name is rare: in modern times it is associated with Youghal and other places in east Cork where Mullerick and Millerick have been noted as variants of the more usual Mellerick. Woulfe says that in Mayo it has been corrupted to Mulderrig: if that is so it would mean that the family mentioned in the Annals of Loch Cé may still be extant; but I have found no evidence that any of the Mulderrigs of north Connacht are not true Mulderrigs.

MELLOWES   Mellows is stated by Barber to be a variant of Mellis, which, he says, is taken from a place in Suffolk or alternatively from the French personal name Mellisse. Reaney, a reliable authority, while mentioning the English place-name, is of opinion that Mellis (and also Mellish, Malise and other spelling variants) derive from the Irish Maol Íosa ("tonsured servant of Jesus"). This is found in the surname of the archbishop of Armagh (from 1270-

1303) viz., Nicholas Mac Maoil Íosa. O'Dugan in his Topographical Poem names Mag Maoiliosa as chief of a district on the borders of the present counties of Longford and Westmeath; and O'Donovan in his notes thereto says that name is now obsolete there. Woulfe states that it survives in Scotland as Mellis and Malise. Certainly neither of these names occur in any modern records I have consulted; nor does Mellowes, which does not even once occur in the complete birth registrations of three consecutive years consulted, a fair indication that it is not a current Irish surname. Woulfe gives Ó Maoil Íosa as the Irish form of Mellowes, now in use, adding that this is apparently recent. If Mac Maoil Íosa had been chosen in gaelicizing Mellowes it would have been more acceptable.

(O) MELODY   We now regard Melody as almost exclusively belonging to counties Clare and Galway, and indeed it is very rare elsewhere. This sept was located in the north Clare barony of Corcomroe and adjacent part of Co. Galway. Rather surprisingly the first reference I have met to an individual of the name is to Master Gilbert O'Moledy, tenant of a holding in Drogheda, who appears as the victim of a robbery in 1297. In 1448 Cornelius O'Mallady, then bishop of his native diocese, Clonfert, was translated to Emly. Some authorities erroneously call him O'Mullally. The name as O'Meledy, O'Moledy and O'Mulledy appears fairly often in the records of the next two centuries, but always in the midland counties – Longford, Cavan, Meath, Westmeath and Offaly, the sept in this case being originally located at Ballymaledy, near Kilbeggan on the border of the two last named counties. Sir Joseph O'Mulledy, Bart., of Ballinver, attainted in 1642, was of this sept, as was Gilbert Mulledy of Nugent's regiment in James II's Irish army, and also, I think, Capt. Anthony Mulledy; Thomas Melody, an officer in Clanrickarde's regiment was more probably from the Corcomroe family, though I have no evidence of this beyond the district of that regiment's recruitment. Sir Patrick O'Mulledy was Charles II's ambassador to the King of Spain in 1666. Five were outlawed as Jacobites under the names Mulledy and Malladay. There were several other former variants of the name: an Ossory testator, for example, signs his will in 1699 John Mylady, and a Louvain priest is O'Miledy. Mulleady is sometimes found today, while in Co. Cavan an unfortunate corruption has produced Malady as a synonym. There is only one form in Irish, viz., Ó Maoiléidigh.
   A rare form of the name is Mulleda. Harry Shaw Mulleda (1840-1876), the Fenian, was born at Naas.   Map

MacMENAMIN   MERRIMAN, Marmion   (O) MERRY
The Irish surname Mac Meanman takes the anglicized form MacMenamin in Co. Donegal and west Tyrone, where it is numerous, and MacManamon in Co. Mayo. Many Tirconnell names are found in Mayo as a result of considerable migration in the early seventeenth century. MacMenamin must definitely be regarded as a Donegal name. The Annals of Loch Cé record the death of two MacMenamins, nephews of O'Donnell, in 1303 and the

156

name appears in a list of the followers of O'Donnell of Tirconnell in 1601, as well as many times in the records of the diocese of Raphoe. A variant of the name found in north Connacht is MacVanamy (an aspirated form of MacManamy), while in Co. Tyrone it is sometimes abbreviated to MacMenim.

Woulfe gives Merriman as a synonym of MacMenamin. Brian Merriman (1741-1808), author of the much discussed poem "Cúirt a' mheadhon oidhche" is often called Mac Giolla Mheidhre in Irish but it is generally agreed that this is a translation or semi-translation of Merriman (merry man): Brian uses it himself in the poem by way of a humorous translation. O'Donovan, in his Ordnance Survey letter dealing with Brian Merriman's native parish, Feakle, Co. Clare, states that his real name was Mac-Menamin, adding that this was a family of the Clann Choileáin, of which the Macnamaras were the leading sept. An examination of his source, "Caithréim Toirdheabhaigh", makes it doubtful if this Menamin was more than a christian name in the Macnamara family. Frost goes a step farther and calls the poet Brian Merriman Macnamara. Brian's origin cannot yet be stated definitely. Another suggestion is that of Professor James Carney who thinks he was actually of the O'Houlihan sept. MacMenamin is a name having no connexion with Co. Clare, whereas the O'Houlihans or O'Holohans are a Thomond sept; and there is no doubt that Merry and O'Houlihan were used synonymously in the sixteenth century: in a pardon of 1558 for example, Richard Merry, of Callan, Co. Kilkenny is officially recorded as "alias O'Howloughane." This may possibly have been extended to Merriman, though I have met no case where this is expressly mentioned. In one Fiant of 1602 we meet Meryman and O'Marrye together, but this refers exclusively to Co. Down. In mediaeval documents O'Merry etc. occur sometimes in Co. Westmeath, as does Marryman, but most often in or near Co. Waterford which, with south Tipperary, is the original habitat of the sept of Ó Mearadhaigh, now always Merry without the O. In the Gaelic period they were chiefs of Uí Fathaidh in the barony of Iffa and Offa West. O'Merry must be regarded as entirely distinct from O'Meara, though confusion has arisen by reason of the fact that the former was sometimes anglicized as O'Marye.

Modern birth registrations record that Marmion has been locally regarded as synonymous with Merriman in several places in counties Dublin and Meath, and also in Co. Down. Several nineteenth century examples of persons described as Merriman alias Marmion have been noted at the Registry of Deeds. Vicars, in his Prerogative Wills, draws attention to the same equation: wills under Marmion are all eighteenth century probates, mostly for Co. Louth; the Meryman and Maryman entries are all Co. Dublin, the earliest being 1646. In 1602 a John Mareman is mentioned with the St. Lawrences of Howth in a Fiant, and in 1550 one Nyckol Marmyn appears in a Co. Kilkenny Ormond rental. As early as 1302, and thenceforward, we find the name Marmyoun quite frequently in Dublin and neighbouring Leinster counties. I think this was of Norman origin. The name Marmion is uncommon in Ireland to-day. Families so called may be descendants of these Norman Marmyouns,

but it is possible that they are Merrimans whose name has acquired the form now in use. Abbot Columba Marmion, O.S.B. (1858-1923), a spiritual writer of international repute, was born in Dublin.   Map

MERNAGH   Some families omit the final GH and spell their name Merna. It is still found almost exclusively in the same part of the country as it was when it first appears on record, that is in Co. Wexford and the adjacent areas in counties Carlow and Wicklow. So closely, indeed, are persons of the name associated with the Kavanaghs that it is probable that Mernagh, which is a name of the epithet or agnomen class, is in fact an alias for some branch of the MacMurrough Kavanagh sept. Its earlier spelling, e.g. in the sixteenth century Fiants, was Merenagh, which I take to be derived from the Irish adjective meirtneach, meaning dispirited. We know, of course, that nicknames, arising often from a single incident, tended to become permanent surnames particularly where many families of the same name lived in close proximity.

MERRICK   The statement that Merrick in Connacht is a Welsh name is undoubtedly correct so far as the Merricks of Co. Mayo are concerned: the Four Masters, using the form Mac Mibhric, record the death of one of them there in 1237 and another reference to that family was cited in dealing with Hosty (q.v.). Merrick is also an English name, probably derived from the christian name Almeric. Some of our Merricks or Meyricks may be of this origin; several soldiers of the name served in the Royalist army in Ireland between 1641 and 1681, but in the army lists preserved in the Ormond Manuscripts many of the regiments consisted of a mixture of Irish and English personnel. It does not appear to have been considered hitherto that the Merricks of the south of Ireland are of a different origin – Gaelic not Welsh or English: they are probably of the sept Ó Mearadhaigh, now generally anglicized as Merry (q.v.), one of the older forms of which is Mariga. The name is associated with the country comprised of west Waterford, east Cork and south Tipperary: we find it as O'Merrick in a Co. Waterford Fiant of 1600, as Merricke and Myricke in the South Tipperary Hearth Money Rolls of 1666, in the Cloyne marriage licence bonds from 1684, in the business life of Youghal in the 1790's and again in south Tipperary in Griffith's Valuation of 1850.

Two Merricks were transplanted as papists under the Cromwellian régime, one from Co. Limerick and the other from one part of Connacht to another.

The Mac prefix also appears in the Patent and Chancery Rolls in 1356: that was in Co. Kerry, and in 1406 the same record has Patrick Meryk, also of Kerry.

(O) MESCALL MISKELLY   This is a surname with many variants not only in old records but also in modern times. In the birth registrations of the years 1865-1866 it is spelt Mescal, Mescall, Mescill, Meskal, Meskel, Meskela, Meskellm Meskel, Miskill, Miskel, Miskela, Miskele, Miskella, Miskell, Miskle: of the 70 births then registered 39 were in Clare and south Galway and 10 in Co. Limerick, 8 in the area around west Waterford, east Cork and south Tipperary and 6 in Co. Wexford. There were also 14 for Miskelly all in north-east Ulster (see last paragraph of this section below). The current Co. Clare voters' lists show that the name is numerous there but the lists of freeholders in 1821 include only six and it is surprising how few references to the name in any form are to be found in earlier records relating to Co. Clare. Griffith's Valuation of a decade earlier than the birth registrations referred to above found householders of the name also fairly numerous in counties Wexford and Waterford. The name is infrequent in eighteenth century records; in the seventeenth Meskell was a name fairly prominent in the city of Cork and it occurs also in the Co. Tipperary Hearth Money Rolls; and, going back to the Fiants of the sixteenth century we find three of the name in Co. Kilkenny and just one in the Co. Clare area. The earliest reference to it I have found occurs in a Justiciary Roll of 1313 dealing with Co. Limerick.

The indeterminate nature of the facts here collected no doubt accounts for the lack of information given by Woulfe under the head of Ó Meiscill. His treatment of Mac Scalaigh (MacScally or Skally) is misleading: among its anglicized forms he gives Miskelly, Miscella and Miskell. There is however, no doubt that Miscella and Miskella are synonymous with Miskell and · Mescal; but Miskella, which is a name practically confined to north Ulster, may be a northern corruption of MacScally, (q.v.).

MacMILLAN   This well-known Scottish name is numerous in Ulster. It is also used as a synonym of Irish Mac-Mullan. Mac Maoláin is the Gaelic form in both cases.

MILLETT   Modern synonyms of this name are Mellott, Mellet, Millott, Mylotte, Mylot and Milod. As Milot and Milet it appears in the Justiciary Rolls, in Co. Cork 1311, Co. Tipperary 1313 and Co. Kilkenny 1314: Nicholas Milet was a Kilkenny juror in 1356 and later deeds in the Ormond collection indicate that the name was to be found in the Ormond country, both in Tipperary and Kilkenny throughout the following centuries. Two place-names taken from the family occur in the sixteenth century Fiants: Millotteston, Co. Kilkenny, while Ballvilode, mentioned in the Co. Tipperary Civil Survey (in bar. Kilnamanagh), may possibly be of the same origin. None of these appears in the modern Townlands Index, but there is a Ballyvalode in Co. Limerick near the Tipperary border. The association with these counties continues into the nineteenth century: Ossory and Cashel wills, for example, are recorded for Mylod, Millet etc., in the seventeenth and eighteenth centuries and Griffith's Valuation of 1851 lists householders of the name throughout counties Kilkenny and Tipperary. I am informed by Father Walter Skehan, an authority on north Tipperary families, that the majority of Millett families in that area were Protestants in the eighteenth century and he believes they were descended from William Millett of Drangan who appears in the Hearth Money Rolls in 1665 and whose will was proved in 1672. Thomas Millatt, pre-

sumably his son, was a burgess of the Corporation of Fethard in 1707.

Notwithstanding this concentration in the Ormond country it is equally true that, at least since the early seventeenth century, Mellott etc. must be regarded also as a Connacht surname. Several appear in Strafford's Inquisition of Co. Mayo (1635) in the barony of Kilmaine; no less than 13 Mellott householders will be found in the census of the parish of Ballinrobe carried out by Father Francis Burke in 1783; and the birth statistics for 1865 are remarkable: of 15 registered, ten are in Co. Mayo, four in an adjacent Connacht county and only one in Co. Kilkenny. Other years about that time give a similar picture. By 1890 all forms of the name show a considerable reduction in numbers.

Mylot, Milet etc., are diminutives of Miles, which as a rule is derived from the Latin miles (soldier). Families of the name were in Cornwall before they became established in Ireland.

(O) MILLIGAN, Milliken   This surname, which is now almost entirely confined to north-east Ulster, is said to be a variant form of Mulligan (Ó Maolagáin) attenuated to Ó Maoileagáin. Milligan was certainly in north-east Ulster and the adjacent county of Sligo in the sixteenth and seventeenth centuries i.e. the country in which Mulligans were chiefly found. Its earlier form in English was usually Milegan; nowadays Milligan and Milliken are approximately of equal frequency.

Alice Milligan (d. 1953), who was born at Omagh, was a poetess of distinction and a well known figure in the Irish literary movement. Edward James Milliken (1840-1897), also a poet, was best known for his humorous contributions to "Punch," while Richard Alfred Milliken (1767-1815), a Cork attorney, is remembered as the author of The Groves of Blarney and perhaps also for his activities against the insurgents in 1798.

MINCHIN   MINCH   Minchin is a name of considerable antiquity in England where it is found in early mediaeval cartularies: it is derived from the Middle-English word minchen which means a nun (derivation as monk) whence, according to Weekley, comes the well-known Mincing Lane in London.

It has been associated with Ireland since the Cromwellian period when Capt. Charles Minchin purchased estates in the neighbourhood of Roscrea in counties Tipperary and Offaly. The family soon became firmly established in that area: in the 1659 "census" two of them are listed as tituladoes and no less than eight families of the name will be found in the Co. Tipperary Hearth Money Rolls of 1665. Numerous Minchin wills are recorded for the same part of the country from that time until the present day; and Minchins appear as sheriffs of counties Tipperary and Offaly in the eighteenth century and as extensive landowners there in de Burgh's The Landowners of 1878.

The origin of Minch, a name associated with Co. Kildare, is uncertain. Two suggestions have been made: that Minch is an abbreviation of Minchin; and that it is a variant of Minnis or Minnish, which Woulfe makes a Gaelic-Irish surname, viz. Mac Naois, normally anglicized as MacNeice and sometimes MacNish. I do not accept either of these theories, but have no alternative suggestion to offer.

(O) MINOGUE, Minnock   This name belongs primarily to east Clare: the townland Ballyminogue in the parish of Tuamgraney marks the centre of its present location. It is to be found also on the other side of Lough Derg, in the barony of Lower Ormond, where several families were resident when the 1659 "census" was taken. The Bishop of Leighlin who died in 1050, Clerichen Ó Muineóc, described in the Annals of Loch Cé as "tower of the piety of Erin", was perhaps of this sept, though Leighlin is far from Clare; but nearer home was Walter O'Mynok, as he is called in the record of a trial in 1313, acquitted of a charge of stealing cattle near Limerick. In modern Irish the name is Ó Muineóg. Muineóg, according to Woulfe, is a diminutive of manach, a monk, and this derivation, though not generally accepted, would seem to be corroborated by the fact that Monaghan and Mannix, both similarly derived, are recorded by Matheson as synonyms of Minogue. However, from my own intimate knowledge of the district from which these are reported I may say that Monaghan is very rare if not unknown in east Clare; I know one case of Mannix.

In Offaly Ó Muineóg is anglicized Minnock and as such is found there in small numbers today.   Map

MINORGAN   This name, also returned as MacNorgan and Norgan, occurs in Griffith's Valuation (1852) and the Tithe Applotment Books (1828) for Co. Carlow.

MOCKLER   This is the modern form in Ireland of the French Mauclerc (from Norman Malclerc, cf. Beauclerc). As such it is on record in Co. Tipperary at least as early as 1210. In 1356 John Mauclerk was an extensive landowner in Co. Tipperary and from that time on the name is of frequent occurrence in records dealing with that county. It is particularly numerous for the sixteenth and seventeenth centuries, e.g. in the Todor Fiants, Petty's "census" of 1659, Tipperary Hearth Money Rolls, wills etc. There are two townlands called Mocklerstown in Co. Tipperary, both in the barony of Middlethird with which the Mockler family were particularly associated. There were no less than forty Mockler families among the householders of south Tipperary when Griffith's Valuation was carried out in the 1850's and seven in north Tipperary.

(O) MOHAN, Maughan, Vaughan   The Welsh surname Vaughan which is that of some settler families in Ireland — they are on record in various parts of the country since 1540 if not before — is widely used as the anglicized form of Ó Mocháin and its variant Ó Macháin. In Co.

Galway its original habitat, it is called Mohan and sometimes Maughan or Mahan in English, and this in turn has often been changed by attraction to Mahon. Vaughan, indeed, is a rare name in Connacht but quite numerous in the Munster counties of Cork, Limerick and Clare. The town of Ballyvaughan on the Clare side of Galway Bay is stated by O'Donovan in his Ordnance Survey letters following the Four Masters to be Baile Uí Bheachain i.e. O'Behanstown. This I suppose can be accepted, although O'Behan is a midland sept, whereas the sept of Ó Macháin was located a few miles east of Ballyvaughan, which I suggest should be Baile Uí Mhacháin. In addition to this sept – Ó Mocháin or Ó Macháin of Kilmacduagh – another, at one time of considerable importance as patrons of learning, was situated in Co. Roscommon, where they were erenaghs of Killaraght and keepers of the Cross of St. Attracta. It produced a number of distinguished ecclesiastics of whom the most important was Gregory O'Moghan, Archbishop of Tuam from 1372 to 1385 – he died in 1392. The name in various forms occurs very frequently in the Fiants – that of Sheelie ny Donell Ivaghain of Ballymacelligott, Co. Kerry, illustrates the transmutation from Moghan to Vaughan. The great majority of these refer to west Munster or to Connacht. There is none for Co. Monaghan, yet that is the area in which the name Mohan is chiefly found in recent times: Vaughans, as stated above, are mianly in Munster, but they are also fairly numerous in the Belfast area.

Prominent persons of this name have for the most part been of Welsh descent, e.g. Sir Thomas Vaughan who was killed at the battle of Rathmines in 1649 leading Ormond's "Celts"; John Vaughan, deputy escheator in 1640; Henry Vaughan, Ulster Plantation grantee; and another who was an extensive "new proprietor" in the barony of Tirawley, Co. Mayo, in the Cromwellian Settlement: it was a common name among the "adventurers" of that epoch. The Welsh surname is derived from the word fychan meaning "of small stature."

Daniel Vaughan (1818-1879), the brilliant astronomer and mathematician, who died of semi-starvation in Cincinnati, was born near Killaloe, Co. Clare.

Cardinal Vaughan, Archbishop of Sydney, was not of the Irish Vaughans.

The best known of the Mahans was Alfred Thayer Mahan (1840-1914), the naval historian, whose grandparents emigrated to U.S.A. from Ireland in 1802. His father Denis Hart Mahan (1802-1871) was notable both as a soldier and an educator in America.   Map

(O) MOHER   We have here a name of a family or minor sept which has been found from the earliest relevant record till the present day almost exclusively in counties Waterford and Cork, especially in the territory lying between Mitchelstown in east Cork and Lismore in Co. Waterford. The 23 Moher householders in Griffith's Valuation (1851-3) were all in the east Cork barony of Condons.

Woulfe gives Ó Móthair as the Gaelic-Irish form, but Ó Móchair is, I think, preferable. It appears in the "census" of 1659 as a principal Irish name in every barony of

Co. Waterford under the spelling Mogher — in Co. Cork it is there given as O'Mohir.

(O) MOLAN MOLAND These names are now rare, but a century ago there were a number of Molan families in south Tipperary. This is an abbreviated form of Mohalan, i.e. Ó Móthlacháin. In several anglicized variants such as O'Mohalane and O'Mohalaghan it occurs frequently in the Tudor Fiants, always in Munster. About the same time, in 1553, we find Dermot O'Molan a chaplain in Co. Meath, when we also find Molans as clerics and officials in the same area. These are probably Molands. Moland is fairly frequent in Anglo-Irish records, and this appears to be an English name unconnected with O'Molan. It is not unlikely, however, that this final D may have sometimes been added to the Irish Molan, as in the case of Bolan — Boland.

Mac MONAGLE The MacMonagles are numerous in Co. Donegal and in the city of Derry and those found elsewhere have their origin there. The name is also spelt MacMonigle, MacMonegal and MacMonigal. There are several in the Co. Donegal Hearth Money Rolls of 1665 (one appearing, presumably by error, as O'Monigal). Crone considered Alexander MacMonagle (1848-1919) "the doyen of Ulster journalists" worthy of a place in his Dictionary of Irish Biography.

MONTGOMERY Montgomery is a toponymic; the place from which it is derived is not, however, the Welsh county or town but Montgomeri in France. It appears frequently in the records of the Anglo-Norman ascendancy in Ireland in the thirteenth and fourteenth centuries, when they were prominent in counties Dublin, Meath and Louth. One, indeed, had important Irish connexions even before the invasion of 1170, for Arnulf de Montgomeri married the daughter of Murtagh O'Brien in 1100 and their daughter became the wife of Maurice Fitzgerald. As far as I know these mediaeval Montgomery families are extinct in Ireland. The Montgomerys, who from the early seventeenth century to the present day have been so prominent in Ulster, first came to Ireland in 1603. Sir Hugh Montgomery, a Scot from Ayrshire, acquired part of the lands of Con O'Neill with whom he and one of the Hamiltons made a tripartite agreement when they contrived his, O'Neill's, escape from Carrickfergus. The lands so obtained were the nucleus of a chain of estates so large that in 1878 the Montgomerys owned 72,523 acres in thirteen counties, 17,000 being in Co. Antrim, 12,000 in Co. Donegal and 10,000 in Co. Leitrim. The history and pedigrees of the various branches of these families can be studied in detail in the works listed in the Bibliography.

Among the many distinguished persons of the name especially noteworthy are George Montgomery, who was Bishop of Derry, Clogher and Raphoe — his visitation of the diocese of Derry and Raphoe in 1606 is a valuable source for that period and locality; William Montgomery M.P. (1633-1707) of Co. Tyrone, the historian; Hugh Montgomery (1623-1663) 3rd Viscount Montgomery and 1st Earl of Mount Alexander; Co. Dublin born Richard Montgomery (1736-1775), of the American revolutionary army, who was killed in the assault on Quebec; in the nineteenth century there was William Montgomery (d. 1859) a pioneer obstetrician, and in our own day the brilliant and controversial Field-Marshal Viscount Montgomery of Alamein, who came from Co. Donegal. Nor must I omit to mention James Montgomery (1870-1943) whose incomparably witty bon mots are remembered with delight by the Dubliners of his day. Bibl.

MOODY Woulfe informs us that Irish speakers call Moody Ó Muadaigh in that language. He does not mention that Moody is a well-known English name (derived from the Old-English modig, meaning impetuous, brave). In Ireland it is found mainly in Ulster. I think we must reject the idea that it may also be a Gaelic name, although I have actually met one instance of O'Mody in an Oriel document of 1428 contained in Archbishop Swayne's Register. Mody without a prefix is quite commonly found in Irish records as far back as 1297 and following years (in Co. Kildare) and throughout the mediaeval period in (Co. Kilkenny and elsewhere); after 1600 it has become Moody (or occasionally Mudy as in the Antrim Hearth Money Rolls). Some families of the name settled in Ireland at a more recent date. They have never been closely or at all exclusively associated with any particular place or county; the name occurs often in Co. Armagh from 1639 and in Co. Cork from 1637 and the voters' lists indicate that there are now a number of Moody families in Co. Offaly as well as in the north-eastern counties of Ulster.

Probably the best known man of the name was Cork-born John Moody (c. 1727-1812) the noted actor: he was, however, not a Moody by blood, his real name being Cochrane.

(O) MOONAN It may be accepted as correct that Ó Muanáin (anglicized Moonan) is etymologically an Oriel form of the Munster name Ó Maonáin (Moynan); I have no direct evidence that they are genealogically connected, but the fact that in our earlier records, e.g. the fourteenth century Justiciary Rolls and even in the sixteenth century Fiants, O'Monan and O'Monane are the names of Munstermen would suggest that probability. Though Moynan and Moonan do not appear to have ever been used as synonyms, Moynan and Moynihan have been reported as such from Co. Offaly; but Moynihan is almost exclusively a Cork-Kerry surname. Moonan — occasionally Monan — is now found mainly in or near Co. Louth, and as O'Monyne it occurs in the Co. Armagh Hearth Money Rolls of 1664-65.

(O) MORRALLY, Morley This name was also written Morrelly, Morally, but now the English name Morley is almost invariably used as a synonym of it in Mayo. Morally is essentially a Mayo name of which the Gaelic-Irish form is Ó Murghaile. It must not be confused with the Munster Ó Muirthile which, though formerly anglicized Morrally, Murhilla and Murley, is now usually Hurley. That name has no Connacht associations and ninety per cent of the people so called are of Co. Cork or some adjacent area to the east and north of the county.

MORTELL, Martell   Mortell is the usual spelling of this name now, but in the nineteenth century the variants Mortal, Mortall, Mortel and Mortil were recorded. It is synonymous with Martell and has two derivations: either from Martellus, akin to Martin, or it can be a nickname or occupational surname from the Old French martel (a hammer). I have noted references to it in Ireland in every century since the thirteenth, at first almost entirely in Co. Tipperary, where the parish of Mortlestown perpetuates the name; soon after we find it in Co. Limerick around Kilmallock, and later in Co. Cork in the Mallow-Fermoy area. In 1576 Martell of Martellston (presumably Ballymartle) was one of the county jury and in 1652 Martel was one of the most numerous names in the city of Cork. In the Tipperary Hearth Money Rolls of 1666 the family is called Morteel. John Mortall, gent, of Co. Cork was among the Jacobites outlawed after their defeat in 1690. A Mortell was M.P. for Trim in 1560, which is the only instance I have met of any importance outside Munster: this is perhaps the same as Robert Mortell who appears in the Fitzwilliam Accounts as receiver of Customs at Trim in 1560.

(O) MOY   This is a Co. Donegal name. It would appear to be of dual origin. Woulfe gives the Gaelic form Ó Muighe on the authority of The Gaelic Journal. It can be accepted as native Irish because in a return made in 1751 by the parish priest of Stranorlar there were three O'Moyes. On the other hand we find Henry Moy an undertaker in the Plantation of Ulster; about the same time there was a noted English pirate called Lambert Moye: it is possible, of course, that he was of Irish descent. There are seven places in Ireland called Moy, one of which is in Co. Donegal, as well as the river in Co. Mayo, but there is no reason to believe that the surname has a connexion with any of these.

(O) MOYLAN   This is Ó Maoileáin in Irish, an attenuated form of Ó Maoláin which is well known in Munster as Mullane and Mullins. Moylan, too, belongs to Munster, being now chiefly found in Co. Cork, whence came the most noteworthy persons of the name. Brigadier General Stephen Moylan (1734-1811), whom Washington considered one of his ablest commanders, was among the first to enlist in the American War of Independence; he was elder brother of Francis Moylan, "loyalist" Catholic Bishop of Cork from 1786 to 1815. Another Francis Moylan (b. 1775) was a life-long friend of the Abbé Edgeworth in France. Seán Moylan (1888-1957) was a prominent member of the Irish independence movement and Minister for Agriculture at the time of his death.

Unless the Omothlans, Co. Cork robbers fined in

1295 with Ugans and Osynniis, were O'Moylans whose name was so written by the law clerk who recorded the case, I have not found any early references, the first two being a "pardon" to Donaghe O'Moylan of Derryknockane, Co. Limerick in 1586, and another to Daniel Mac-William O'Moylane of Kilbride, Co. Clare, in 1591. It is numerous in the Hearth Money Rolls for Co. Tipperary (1666) — rolls for the other Munster counties are not extant. It does not occur in the summary of the census of 1659 unless O'Meolane, of the barony of Islands, Co. Clare, is the same name in a different form.

MOYLE, Moyles, Miles   These three names are all rather rare, Moyles being more numerous than the other two. It is only since the beginning of the nineteenth century that that is so. Up to 1750 Moyles hardly appears at all while Moyle is met frequently from an early date: for example Hugh Moyle was a Kildare witness in 1235, two of the name were jurors in Waterford in 1312, two brothers Moyle give a pledge at Clonmel in 1457 and Moyles are named among the 1544 muster of kern in all parts of the country, a Moyle of Co. Wicklow was among the men outlawed for participation in the Rising of 1641, and so on in deeds, rolls, fiants, wills, marriage licence bonds, etc. In the latter relating to the Cloyne diocese Moyles, equated with Miles, begins to appear in the eighteenth century. In that and similar cases the name is derived either from the Latin miles (a soldier) or from the forename Milo. In some of the earlier instances Moyle may be the word maol (bald), an epithet which, like rua and láidir eventually became a hereditary surname: this might be expected among the kern; one of them in MacGinness' muster (i.e. from east Ulster) is returned as Rory O'Moyle, but as there is no surname resembling that we may regard the insertion of the O as one of those not infrequent clerical errors which often make the identification of mediaeval and early modern personal and palce-names difficult. An occasional Mac-Moyle has also been noticed.

Birth registrations show that a century ago the name Moyles was quite numerous in Co. Mayo but little known elsewhere, while Moyle was already extremely rare.

Now the names under consideration are not closely associated with any particular part of the country.

(O) MOYNIHAN, Minihan(e)   MINNAGH
It is seldom I find myself in disagreement with Father Woulfe as regards the origin of a sept, but in this case I think he is misleading in the few lines he devotes to Minihan. It is of course quite possible that Minihan may have been used occasionally as a synonym of the surname usually anglicized as Monahan; but it is indisputable that Minihans and Moynihans have the same habitat now, and have always had as far back as records go, i.e. west Cork and Kerry. In the Kenmare Manuscripts it is one of the most numerous names, being exceeded only by MacCarthy, Cronin, Barry, Fitzgerald, O'Mahony and O'Sullivan. In short I consider that Moynihan and Minihan (or Minihane) are both anglicized forms of Ó Muimhneacháin. The sixteenth century Fiants have several refer-

161

ences to O'Moynaghan, Myneghane etc. in Co. Cork; the 1659 "census" gives Minighane as a principal Irish name in the barony of Tulla, Co. Clare and Munnighane in two baronies of Co. Cork; and later records again indicate Munster as their homeland. The brothers Michael and Mortimer Moynihan, associates of O'Donovan Rossa in his Fenian activities, were from Skibbereen.

There is no doubt that there was a sept of some importance of the Hy Fiachrach group called Ó Mionacháin and anglicized Minaghan (and perhaps Minihan), one of whom is mentioned by the Four Masters under date 1220; Knox in his History of Mayo remarks that the name of this sub-chief of Erris was then anglicized Minihan, which implies that it was still extant there at the end of the last century; but Minihan, like Moynihan, belongs now almost exclusively to Co. Cork.

Ó Muimhnacháin is derived from the word muimhneach which means a Munsterman. This word is actually used in the Leitrim-Longford area as a surname omitting the prefix O and the diminutive termination (cf. laighneach a Leinsterman anglice Lynagh). Muimhneach as a surname is variously anglicized Minnagh, Mimnagh and Moyna(gh) but none of these is at all common.

Minnock, a name of different origin, is a synonym of Minogue. Map

(O) MUCKIAN   This family belongs to Co. Monaghan. The O has been dropped with the result that the name as spoken sounds like MacKeen and has sometimes been actually changed to the Scottish name MacKean. Muckian, however, is much more usual than MacKean in counties Monaghan and Down. MacKean and MacKeen are mostly found in counties Antrim and Derry. Muckeyin, a variant of Muckian, recorded at Newry, approximates to the Gaelic-Irish form i.e. Ó Mochaidhean. Another variant is Muckeen.

(O) MULDOON, Meldon   There were originally three distinct septs of O'Muldoon (Ó Maoldúin in Irish). Numerically and historically that of Co. Fermanagh is the most important. They were chiefs of Lurg and prior to their subjugation by the MacGuires about 1400 they ranked as of royal status — in the Annals of Loch Cé, for example, they are styled kings of Lurg. They continued to be of importance in Ulster until the destruction of the Gaelic order in that province in the seventeenth century; as late as 1642, when he was killed at Dungannon, Felim O'Muldoon was a leading man in the insurgent army. The name, which is among the most numerous in Co. Fermanagh in the 1659 "census", is still to be found there in considerable numbers.

It is very rare, however, in the habitat of the second of the septs referred to, viz. Thomond, where in the thirteenth century O'Muldoon of Ogonnelloe was one of the leading Uí Bloid families. Rev. Prof. John Ryan S.J. has suggested to me, and I agree, that the identity of these east Clare Muldoons is hidden under the name Malone, which is quite numerous in that area and is there pronounced Mulloon.

The third of these septs was a branch of the Uí Fiach-

rach, located in the barony of Tireragh, Co. Sligo. O'Donovan writing in 1838 says that they were then nearly extinct. The name, however, is little less numerous in Connacht than Ulster today, being found mostly in Co. Galway. Whether these present-day representatives are of that line or are immigrants from Thomond, I do not know. Two abbots of Clonmacnoise bore this surname.

I have seen the name of Connor O'Muldowne as a tenant in Wexford town in 1551. This is probably Muldowney not Muldoon.

The surname Meldon is an anglicized variant of Muldoon. Austin Meldon (1843-1904), President of the Royal College of Surgeons, Ireland, was of a family descended from the Muldoons of Lurg.   Map

MULGREW, Grew MULCREEVY   An earlier anglicized form of this, O'Mulcreevy, is a fair phonetic approximation of the original Irish Ó Maolchraoibhe. Mulcreevy, however, is now extremely rare, if not extinct, having become Mulgrew in its original habitat, Co. Tyrone. This is no recent change, for O'Mulgrew and O'Mulgrue both occur in the Tyrone Hearth Money Rolls (1664) in the barony of Dungannon, in which document the more usual form O'Mulcrieve also appears. The almost contemporary Petty "census" lists Mulcreevy as a "principal Irish name" in the barony of Dundalk and O'Mulcreve in nearby Orior, Co. Armagh. The intermediate form O'Mulcrew not only occurs in the Elizabethan Antrim Fiants, but as early as 1428 we find one Rory O'Mulcrew in trouble with the Bishop of Dromore. Early seventeenth century documents relating to the Plantation of Ulster have both Mulcreeve and Mulcrew among the "meer Irish".

At the present time Mulgrew is quite a numerous name in several counties of north-east Ulster. Grew, which I take to be an abbreviation of Mulgrew, is not very numerous but is well-known in Co. Armagh. Father Seosamh Ó Dufaigh in The Clogher Record (1959 p. 399) confidently suggests that Grue, which he says is common in the Clones district, is an anglicized form of Mac Riabhaigh; but surely Mulgrue is a more likely origin for Grue and Grew. It is also hard to accept Fr. O'Gallachair's suggestion that MacGrue is an intermediate form of the Tyrone name. MacGrew and MacGreo appear six times in Elizabethan Fiants, four of these being in the west of Ireland and the other two in south-east Leinster; not one is in Ulster. An isolated case in Ulster two centuries later does occur in the Derry wills (Drumrath, 1774). It should also be added that there is a surname Grew derived from the Old-French griu, a crane, but I have found no evidence that any of these settled in Ireland. See Rice.

(O) MULHERN, Mulkerrin, Mulherrin   Mulkerran and Mulhearn are other variants in English of Ó Maoilchiaráin, which signifies descendant of the follower or devotee of St. Ciaran. The form Mulkerrin is almost confined to Connacht, particularly counties Galway and Roscommon; the other forms are now commoner in Ulster. In the seventeenth century Mulkieran was not uncommon in

Co. Armagh and Co. Donegal as we know from the Hearth Money Rolls. The sept, a branch of which became established in south-west Donegal, originated in Co. Roscommon where they were erenaghs of Ardcarne; the Four Masters also refer to one of the name who was slain in 1012 when erenagh of Eaglis Beag (Clonmacnois). They were notable chiefly as ecclesiastics: Denis O'Mulkieran (d. 1224) was Bishop of Elphin and Maelisa O'Mulkieran (d. 1197) Bishop of Clogher. Fr. John Mulcheran, hanged and quartered on December 11, 1589, was one of the many Ulster martyrs.

In America the name is usually spelt Mulherin or Mulherrin.

I may quote here a note I received from the late Mr. P. J. Kennedy of Galway who was very well informed about names in that county. "Mulkerrins is common both in east Galway and south Connemara. It appears to be an anglicized corruption of two distinct Gaelic surnames; Maoil Ciaráin, which one would associate with Kilkerrin in west Connemara, and Maoil Cearraill, which one associates with the parish of Clonkennkerrill near the small modern village of Gurteen. To the writer's knowledge people whose surname was originally Mulkerrill now call themselves Mulkerrin and Mulkerrins".

(O) MULLANY   Older anglicized forms of this name were O'Mulleena and O'Molina, the latter being perpetuated in the place-name Crossmolina in Co. Mayo. Another place in Co. Sligo, not far from Boyle (Co. Roscommon), is Ballymullany also named from this family. No less than four brothers, sons of William Ó Maelenaigh, were among the poets, ollavs and "men of other arts" who took part in a gathering organized by Rory MacDermot and his wife in 1540 as related in the Annals of Loch Cé. (Loch Cé in Co. Roscommon is now called Lough Key). Their present as well as their ancient habitat is in that area. In 1659 we learn from Petty's "census" that O'Mullany was one of the most numerous names in the barony of Boyle, Co. Roscommon.

In modern Irish this name is Ó Maoilenaigh, which Woulfe states is a form of the older Ó Maoilsheanaigh, denoting descendant of the follower or devotee of St. Seanach. This derivation is not accepted by northern scholars who point out that there was a family of Cenél Eoghain called Ó Maoil Enaigh, now extinct and that this form tells against any connexion with St. Seanach.

An Irish-born man of some note of this name was Patrick F. Mullany (1847-1893), who was well known in America under the pen-name of "Brother Azarias".

(O) MULLARKEY ERCK, Herrick   There are several other modern spellings of this name — Mollarky etc. — but Mullarkey is the usual form. It is that of a Tirconnell family which in common with several others from Co. Donegal migrated to Connacht in the wake of the O'Donnells in the seventeenth century, and the name is now almost confined to that province. One of the leaders of the O'Neill-O'Cahan conspiracy against the Ulster planters in 1615 was Edmond Mullarkey, the Provincial of the Irish Franciscans.

The name is Ó Maoilearca in Irish, which probably denotes descendant of a follower or devotee of St. Earc or Erc.

The surname Erck, which in spite of its un-Irish appearance is a Gaelic one, has no connexion with that saint: it is Ó hEirc in Irish and the family so called, which was located on the river Derg in Co. Tyrone, claims descent from Erc eldest son of Colla Uais, fourth century king of Ireland; but these semi-legendary personages are seldom if ever actually the eponymous ancestors of any sept. The name Herrick, when found in Ireland, is probably a synonym of Erck. It occurs in the Donegal Hearth Money Rolls (1665) as O'Harrick. John Caillard Erck (1829-1900) was the editor of a number of important Irish historical documents.

(O) MULLERY   Woulfe equates this with Ó Maolmhuire of Clogher, Co. Tyrone, adding that it is changed to Myles in Mayo. Mullery and Mulry, however, are mainly found in the Connacht counties of Mayo, Roscommon and Galway where Mulry is listed in the "census" of 1659 as one of the principal Irish names in the south of Co. Roscommon. Co. Galway is missing from that document. Mulry is synonymous with the more numerous Mulroy, q.v. The Christian name Maolmhuire is anglicized Myles, and this has also occurred with the surname, though the use of Myles and Mullery as synonyms is not frequent. The Fiants of the sixteenth century contain many somewhat similar names with the prefix Mac; e.g. MacMelery, MacMelmory, MacMulmory, MacMolmoree, MacMoylmurry etc. etc., but these relate to parts of the country remote from the Mullery homeland. From the same source we learn that Gilchrist O'Moylery was one of the men who followed Rory O'Donnell to Mayo in 1603, but to decide what Gaelic surname this represents would not be possible in the absence of further evidence.

(O) MULQUEEN   This is Ó Maolchaoine (from St. Caoine). Mulqueeny, (whence the place-name Ballymulqueeny near Ennis) is a variant. The Dalcassian Mulqueen has in some cases in the Kilrush area been absorbed by Mulligan (though in fact the latter is rare in Co. Clare). The Mulqueens were a noted bardic family in Thomond.

(O) MULRENNAN, Renan   Though now comparatively rare this name was formerly of importance in Connacht being that of one of the four families ranking as royal lords under O'Conor, King of Connacht. Each of these, as well as other families,* had special duties to perform and for his services O'Mulrenan received an annual stipend of 50 cows and 50 pigs. His name in Irish was Ó Maoilbreanainn (i.e. descendant of the servant or devotee of St. Brendan) and he was chief of Clanconnor, a territory in Co. Roscommon centred in what is now the parish of Baslick. References to the name are frequent in the Annals (16 in the Four Masters and 13 in Loch Cé) up to the middle of the fourteenth century, chiefly in connexion with the O'Connors but sometimes as ecclesiastics (of Elphin and Boyle). The home of Roger Mulrennan, an army officer mentioned in the Ormond correspondence of 1664, was Tullymulrennan, Co. Roscommon; and there is a Ballymulrennan near Castlereagh in that county. I may add that there was another small sept of the same name in Tirawley, Co. Mayo, one of the Hy Fiachrach group.

Bernard Mulrenin (1803-1868), a Co. Sligo man, was a painter of distinction. Richard O'Mulrennan (1832-1906), Gaelic scholar and "Nation" poet, was born in Co. Roscommon. The prefix O is seldom retained in modern times with this name which was formerly anglicized Mulbrenin and now has such spelling variants as Mulrennin, Mulrenan; district registrars' reports from Co. Donegal show that Renan is used as an abbreviated form of it. The form Mulbrandon is found in Co. Clare. Renan does not appear to have been used as a synonym of Reneghan.   Map

(O) MULSHINOCK   Though this is a rare name it has many spelling variants such as Mulshinoge, Multinock, Mulchinock, Mullshenogue and Mulshenagh; it is Ó Maoilsionóg in Irish and belongs almost exclusively to counties Kerry and Cork. I have not found it in mediaeval records but it occurs in the 1659 "census" in Mallow town and in 1714 Father Thomas Mulshinoge, "a very old man then", was parish priest of Kinsale; elsewhere in the two counties mentioned men of the name were recorded as landholders. William Pembroke Mulchinock (1820-1864) the Young Ireland poet and author of The Rose of Tralee, was himself a Tralee man. King's "Kerry" gives biographical details of several Mulchinocks in that county, the earliest being born about 1750. Little known arms are recorded for Mulchinock in the Genealogical Office. It is perhaps worthy of mention that Anthony Mulshinogue, a Co. Cork Catholic, was exempted from the Cromwellian transplantation to Connacht because he was a medical doctor.

(O) MULVANY, Mulvenna   (O) MULVEY   Before the destruction of the Gaelic order in the seventeenth century the sept of O'Mulvenna was located in O'Cahan's country (Co. Derry): they were hereditary ollavs to O'Cahan (O'Kane). Mr. T. Ó Raifeartaigh, remarking that the first Ó Maoil Mheana mentioned in the Annals (Annals of Ulster 1164) was fourteenth in descent from Eoghan, son of Niall of the Nine Hostages, says that the name is probably associated with the river Meana (now the Main), which flows into Lough Neagh at Randalstown, and that, if so, the name would mean "devotee of the Meana". William Hennessy, translating the Annals of Loch Cé calls Ó Maelmhenaigh (i.e. O Maoilmheana as it is written to-

day) O'Mulvany; but in Ulster it is always Mulvenna now, and this was the spelling, with the prefix O, in the 1659 "census". By that time, however, they were no longer to be found to any extent in their traditional homeland, but were numerous in the adjacent county of Antrim – in the barony of Glenarm, which includes that part of the county least affected by the upheavals of the seventeenth century. Modern birth statistics indicate that Mulvany is the usual form of the name outside northern Ulster.

From south Ulster (Co. Cavan) came Rev. Thomas Mulvany (1849-1892), distinguished as priest, university professor and poet in Canada. Another who was a poet of some note in that country was Rev. Charles Pelham Mulvany (1835-1885). The best known of the name were two artists, father and son, Thomas James Mulvany (c. 1770-1845), an original member of the Royal Hibernian Academy, and George Francis Mulvany (1809-1869), director of the National Gallery of Ireland; the former's other son, William Thomas Mulvany (1806-1885), was an engineer and scientist of note, both in Ireland and Germany. All the four last named were born in Dublin. Dr. Reeves considered that Mullanfy (earlier O'Mullanfuy, Irish Ó Maolainbhthe) is a metathesized form of Mulvany.

Mulvey is recorded in the birth registration returns as having been used as a synonym of Mulvany. Mulvey, however, is actually an entirely different surname, being that of two distinct septs viz: Ó Maoilmhiadhaigh and Ó Maoilmheadha. The former, of Co. Leitrim, was of considerable importance and there are many references to this sept in the Annals, particularly those of the Four Masters and Loch Cé. They are of the same stock as the MacRannals and the O'Farrells and were chiefs of Tellachebhellan and Muintir Eolais, in south-west Leitrim. Practically all the references to the name I have met related to Co. Leitrim. The other sept mentioned above was also located west of the Shannon, on the Atlantic coast of Co. Clare near the modern town of Miltown Malbay.   Bibl., Map

MUNROE   This well known Scottish name, gaelice Mac an Róthaic, is traditionally believed to be Irish in origin. It has also been used as an occasional synonym of Mulroy (Ó Maol Ruaidh) in the barony of Tirawley, Co. Mayo, the homeland of that Hy Fiachrach sept.

(O) MURNANE, Marrinan   WARREN
(O) MURNAGHAN   Murnane and Marrinan, with some other spelling variants, are basically the same name, being anglicized forms of the Irish Ó Murnáin which Woulfe states is itself a corruption of Ó Mananáin, a Thomond name derived from that of the ancient seagod Manannán. Presumably he did not make this statement without evidence but I have found no corroboration of it. The Fiants of the last quarter of the sixteenth century contain no O'Manannan but have a number of entries for Marrinan, O'Marnane etc., all in counties Limerick, Kerry and west Cork. One of these referring to Conogher MacShane Iwarrynane shows how the name became

*The other royal lords were O'Finaghty, O'Flanagan and MacGeraghty. Particulars of the duties and functions of the chiefs of the principal Connacht septs subject to O'Conor are given in "Linea Antiqua" –military: MacBrenan, MacDermot, MacDockry, O'Flinn and O'Hanly; naval: O'Flaherty and O'Malley; household: O'Beirne and O'Teighe (Tighe); steward of the jewels was O'Kelly and chief poet O'Mulconry.

Warren, an English surname widely adopted in place of Marrinane by members of that sept in the period of Gaelic depression.

It must not, however, be assumed that all Warrens in Ireland are of this origin. Outside south-west Munster most persons of the name Warren are the descendants of Anglo-Norman or later settlers. Their surname was at first de Warenne (from La Varenne in France, according to Reaney.) The principal Anglo-Norman families of Warren settled in the Pale and acquired considerable estates in counties Meath, Kildare and Offaly — there are four places called Warrenstown in these counties, for which in the sixteenth and seventeenth centuries Warrens are recorded as sheriffs, M.P.'s etc. They suffered in the Jacobite cause — no less than seven of the name were officers in James II's Irish army. Eight of the name Warren were outlawed as Jacobites; the lists contain no Marrinan or Murnane. Richard Warren (1705-1774) of the Corduff, Castleknock, family, a colonel in the Irish Brigade, rescued Prince Charles after the failure of the 1745 expedition; he eventually became Governor of Belleisle. Perhaps the most distinguished of these families was that of Bellaghmon, Co. Kildare, which after the Treaty of Limerick went to France where in due course Edward Warren (d. 1733) was admitted to the nobility of that country. His sons and grandsons served in the French and Austrian armies with distinction. Their present representative is Comte Edouard de Warren who is a hereditary Papal duke. The Warrens of Warren's Court, Cork, baronets since 1784, originally de Warrenne, came to Ireland in the seventeenth century. De Burgh's The Landowners of Ireland (1878), lists ten Warrens possessing 17,000 acres, nearly all in Co. Cork.

Murnaghan (Ó Muirneacháin in Irish) has no connexion at all with Murnane: it is a rare surname belonging almost exclusively to Ulster.

MacNABOE, Victory   MacNABB   The surname Victory, synonymous with MacNaboe, though often written Mac na Buadha in Irish (buadha is genitive case of buaidh, victory) is not in fact derived from the word, but is Mac Anabadha (possibly from anabaidh, premature). The earlier anglicized form of this name, MacAnaboy, which is now obsolete, is clearly from Mac Anabadha and not from Mac na Buadh. Victory and MacNaboe are chiefly associated with Co. Cavan. MacNabb, a quite distinct name (Mac an Abbadh — abbot), is Scottish.

MacNABOOLA   This name was formerly more numerous than it is today. It has always belonged almost exclusively to north Connacht. It appears as MacNabuolly in the Co. Sligo Hearth Money Rolls (1662). Woulfe gives the Irish form as Mac Con na Buaile, but Buaile should be Búille as it refers to the place Boyle. In Co. Leitrim, where MacNabola is perhaps the more usual spelling, the strange use of Banbo synonymously with MacNaboola has been noted. Benbow is an English name originally meaning an archer.

MacNAMEE   MacNamee is Mac Con Midhe in Irish, which means son of the hound of Meath. The principal sept so called is of Ulster, where they were hereditary poets and ollavs to the O'Neills. The poems of at least six of these are among the manuscript Gaelic-Irish poetry which has come down to us from the middle ages. The best known of them are Giolla Brighde Mac Con Midhe (c. 1260) and Brian Mac Angus MacNamee, chief poet to Turlough Luineach O'Neill who died in 1595: he was one of the last of the "classic poets". There was a branch of this Ulster sept who were erenaghs of Comber on the river Foyle in the deanery of Derry, and they are recorded as such as late as 1606 when Bishop Montgomery's survey of the diocese was made. Just about that time the Ulster Plantation records show MacNamees among the natives of Co. Tyrone and later in the century the name appears in Charles O'Neill's regiment in James II's Irish army. Tyrone and Derry, it may be said, are the counties where the name is chiefly found in modern times. That was not the case in the seventeenth century. Petty's "census" found them most numerous in Co. Leitrim and in the previous century the Fiants show them to have been in Leitrim and the other parts of Connacht bordering on Ulster, as well as in Derry and Donegal. The Annals of Loch Cé tell us that in the thirteenth century the chief of Muintir Laoideacháin on the border of Connacht and north-west Leinster was Mac Con Meadha, which W. M. Hennessy, the editor of that work, equates with Mac Con Midhe: nevertheless the annalist does write the former when referring to west Leinster and Connacht and the latter in the case of Ulstermen. Later references confirm its connexion with the West, e.g. in Carew's list (1602) of Clare gentry and their castles we find Teige oge MacConmea of Neadenurry, this, however, may well be an error for Mac Conway (vide Irish Families, p. 93). Fr. Kelly, in his notes to Cambrensis Eversus, states that the sept of MacNamee was seated beside the Shannon in the barony of Kilkenny west (Westmeath); and, coming to quite modern times, in 1875 the Conmees of Kingsland were among the leading gentry of Co. Roscommon. As the name MacNamee is now extremely rare in Connacht it may be assumed that survivors of the sept in that province have become Conmee, which in turn has been widely absorbed in the well-known surname Conway.

NAPPER   TANDY   The names Napper and Tandy

are closely associated by reason of the prominence of James Napper Tandy (1740-1803), the United Irishman, and I will deal with them together here. They have much in common, both families being Protestant settlers owning neighbouring estates in Meath. Tandy, also spelt Taundy, occurs several times in the fourteenth century in counties Kilkenny and Wexford and there was a landowner of the name in the vicinity of Navan, Co. Meath, mentioned in an Inquisition of 1618. Napper, also spelt Naper, occurs occasionally in mediaeval Irish records. Jordan le Naper, who died in 1284, had a life tenure of the "bailiwick of the sergeancy" of Connacht. In 1593 Sir Robert Napper, of a well-known west of England family, and afterwards Chief Baron of the Exchequer, Ireland, was made Commissioner for Ecclesiastical Causes; he married a sister of Sir William Petty. From him descended the principal family of the name, viz Napper or Naper of Loughcrew, Co. Meath, a number of whom served as High Sheriffs of that county between 1671 and 1911; two were Meath M.P.s and others occupied official positions, legal, administrative and military during the seventeenth and eighteenth centuries. A Captain Napper, of Col. Ingoldsby's regiment, obtained the Meath estate following the disbandment of the Cromwellian army, and by 1660 was appointed a Poll Money Commissioner for Meath with others of the local gentry. The Meath Book of Survey and Distribution shows that about the same time the Tandys' property was not far away in the parish of Kells, and an Inquisition of 1695 finds the estates of the two families adjacent. In 1878 Major James Napar (so he spelled his name) of Loughcrew owned 18,863 acres of prime Meath land, but Thomas Tandy of Jonesbrook had a mere 623 acres in the same county. References to both Nappers (or Napers) and Tandys occur frequently in testamentary and other records of the seventeenth and eighteenth centuries. Both these Meath families had branches in Co. Wexford.

According to Reaney, Naper and Napper are synonyms of Napier, which is derived from Old-French le napier (nappe means a tablecloth). Reaney does not give the derivation of Tandy, which Bardsley states is equivalent to Dandy, a pet form of Andrew. Naper has been recorded as synonymous with the much more numerous Napier in Co. Down, where Neper and Neeper have also been similarly used. Both Napper and Tandy are rare names in Ireland today.

(O) NEARY, Nary   In Irish Ó Naradhaigh, formerly anglicized O'Nary and O'Nery, the prefix O has but seldom been resumed in modern times with this name, now usually called Neary. The form Ó Naraighe was formerly used, e.g. Fr. Nicholas O'Naraighe, O.F.M., Provincial from 1504 to 1508. Apart from the metropolitan area of Dublin the only county outside Connacht in which it is at all numerous is Co. Louth; in Connacht it is one of the more numerous surnames, especially in counties Mayo and Roscommon. Edmond O'Nary, of Clongreagh, Co. Roscommon, is mentioned in the sixteenth century Composition Book of Connacht as a man of importance, and in the Fiants and Monastic Extents of that time

many others of the name appear in counties Roscommon and Leitrim, and a few also in counties Kildare and Meath: presumably Donal boy O'Nare, "idleman," who in 1546 was pardoned for various offences, including the murder of one John Vale, was one of these. He is described as a kern in another contemporary document. For the meaning of "idleman" see App. III. Rev. Cornelius Nary (1658-1738) author of many works, was born in Co. Kildare: he held a high ecclesiastical position in Germany, was head of the Irish College in Paris, in 1703 declined the appointment of Bishop of Kildare and became a notable figure as parish priest of St. Michan's, Dublin.   Bibl.

NEESON   Though at first sight this name appears to be English and though Woulfe suggests that it is the Scottish MacNee, it has been shown by the late Dr Seamus O'Ceallaigh and others to be in fact Irish Gaelic in origin. I have certainly found it in the Hearth Money Rolls (1659 to 1665) of both Tyrone and Monaghan as an O name (O'Neason etc). Family tradition derives it from a variant of Mag Aonghusa (Mac Gennis) viz. Mac Aonghusa, which, however, is often anglicized MacNeece. The change from Mac to O could have occurred through the tendency in Ulster to slur the prefix Mac and the influence of the spoken word on orthography. Presumably the reason Woulfe suggested Mac Niadh rather than Mac Neidhe, which he makes a Connacht sept (probably a branch of the Mulconrys) is that Mac Neidhe in Connacht has not been anglicized as Neeson and that Neeson is found almost exclusively in north-east Ulster. In this connexion birth registration statistics for Neeson are interesting: in 1865 the figure was sixteen, all in Ulster, mainly in counties Antrim, Down, Armagh and Monaghan; in 1890 it was seventeen, also all in Ulster, chiefly in Co. Antrim.

It is perhaps worth adding that Nason is a not uncommon surname in Co. Cork, where Neason occurs in marriage licence bonds in 1765 and 1777. I do not know the origin of Nason there. Neither Neeson nor Nason appears in any of the standard works on British surnames, which strengthens the belief that Neeson is an indigenous Irish name.

MacNEILL, MacGreal   There is no doubt that the Mac-Neills of Antrim and Derry, so numerous there today, are the descendants of the Scottish Gaels from the Western Isles who settled in the north of Ireland long before the time of the Plantation of Ulster. MacNeill and Mac-Quillan, chiefs of territory in Clandeboy, are recorded in the Annals as submitting to Con O'Neill in 1471. The first of them came as galloglasses and as such they were employed as far west as the borders of Connacht at least as early as 1346 when, the Four Masters tell us, Mac-Neill cam, a Scottish galloglass captain, was killed in the service of O'Rourke. Most of the MacNeills today are Protestants, as were Dean Hugh MacNeill (1795-1879), the noted Antrim-born anti-Catholic preacher in England, Sir John Benjamin MacNeill (1793-1880) builder of Irish railways, and John G. Swift MacNeill (1849-1926) M.P.

professor in the National University and author of many historical and constitutional works.

In the Glens of Antrim they remained Catholic: thence came Eoin MacNeill, the distinguished historian who was co-founder of the Gaelic League.

I have personally little doubt, though there is not general agreement on the point, that the MacGreals of Mayo and Leitrim, who were formerly called MacNeill, are of the same galloglass origin. Woulfe mentions a MacNeill sept of the Uí Fiachrach: true, it did exist – MacNeill was one of the chieftains of Carra (Co. Mayo) – but even by the thirteenth century they were enfeebled; none of them, according to the Mayo historian Knox, were among the freeholders of the sixteenth century, and O'Donovan declares that in his time they were extinct. On the other hand we know that Scottish MacNeills penetrated not only into Leitrim but into Mayo also, the two counties in which the name MacGreal is now principally found.

The use of the form MacReill (later MacGreal) for MacNeill presents no difficulty – the transition from internal N to R is not abnormal, (cf. MacNeilis – MacGrelish or Luimneach – Limerick). In any case the identity of the two names is not questioned – they appear as aliases in the sixteenth and seventeenth centuries, e.g. in the Mayo Book of Survey and Distribution which shows many 1641 proprietors of the name. The point at issue is whether they were Hy Fiachrach MacNeills or of Scottish Gaelic origin. As I have said I think the weight of the evidence points to the latter.

MacNeill is one of the few names identical in Irish and English (except that in Irish the E is accented). MacGreal is Mac Réill or more often Mag Réill.

MacNEILLY, Neely   (Mac) CONNEELY   We have here to consider two quite distinct Gaelic surnames – Mac an Fhilidh and Mac Conghaile – which in their earliest anglicized forms were almost indistinguishable. In the sixteenth century Fiants, for example, we find the former as MacAnellye and the latter as MacEnelly as well as MacNely. The modern form of Mac Conghaile is Conneely, which is so essentially a Connacht name that every one of the 92 births registered in 1890 took place in Connacht, and 89 of these were in Co. Galway; and the birth indices for 1864 to 1866 show an almost identical preponderance of Co. Galway registrations. A century earlier it was also numerous in south Mayo. It will thus be seen that Conneely is among the more numerous Irish surnames. They represent an ancient west-Galway sept, which according to John O'Donovan was not the same as Ó Conghailaigh of the Sil Anmchadha in the south-eastern part of that county. In his edition of Iar-Connacht Hardiman in a note on Coneely (Mac Conghaile) relates a tradition that several of the sept were by magic metamorphosed into seals. This, he says, not only resulted in these animals being seldom if ever killed there but also in the name Coneely being sometimes changed to Connelly and Connolly. This change, we know, did occur to some extent but whether ever for the reason suggested I do not know.

Mac an Fhilidh, on the other hand, is the name of an Ulster sept, numerically inferior to Mac Conghaile but not without its distinguished representatives: the Four Masters describe Giollachriost Mac an Fhilidh, who died in 1509, as a learned poet. The name means son of the filidh or file: this word, which in modern Irish denotes simply a poet, had formerly a more specialized meaning, a file being a professional poet with a well-defined privileged position in the Gaelic system. The principal family of the name in Co. Donegal in modern times is that of Mountcharles, from which came Father Charles MacNeely (1816-1870), a noted parish priest in the diocese of Raphoe.

(O) NELIGAN   King's analysis of the 1901 census for Kerry indicates that there were then 34 Neligan families in that county and as we know that the name is also in Co. Cork it is remarkable that it does not find a place in the almost contemporary statistical return prepared by the Registrar-General, since this purported to indicate every name for which 5 or more births were recorded in the year. In 1864 there were 8 Neligan registrations and in 1865 twelve, nearly all in counties Cork and Kerry. As far back as the sixteenth century it occurs in Kerry and Cork records, but it is not to be found in the Annals or the genealogical treatises, consequently little is known of its origin. The earliest references I have found suggest that it originated in south Leinster. In 1315 Richard Nelgan, a follower of the Kavanaghs, is mentioned as an interpreter on the occasion of Richard II's intercourse with the Irish chiefs. At the end of the next century we find John Neligan a merchant in Kilkenny and Nicholas Neligan a householder in the same city. Ballynelligan is a place near Lismore. John Moore Neligan (1815-1863), a physician who wrote a standard text book on medicines, was born at Clonmel. Rt. Rev. Moore Richard Neligan (1863-1922), noted Anglican bishop, was Irish born. The father of Emile Nelligan (1879-1941) the French-Canadian poet, was an emigrant from Ireland. Woulfe gives Ó Niallagáin, which is derived from the christian name Niall, as the Irish form of Neligan.

MacNELIS, Grealish   GREALLY   The substitution of R for N, resulting in this case in the form Grealish as a synonym of MacNelis, was discussed in the article on MacNeill.

The G of Grealish comes from the prefix Mag (a form of Mac), Mag Riallghuis (pronounced Magreelish) being a corrupt form of MacNiallghuis, whence MacNelis, the form peculiar to Co. Donegal, and Nellis, which is more usual in adjacent counties. Though the latter is also in Mayo, in Connacht it is nearly always Grealish. There are, even in our own time, several other variants: for example in Ulster MacGreallish, MacEnealis and Manelis have been noted; four parish priests called MacNeilis are mentioned in Maguire's History of the Diocese of Raphoe. Turning to earlier centuries we find MacNeilus and MacNellus among the more numerous names in the 1659 "census" for Co. Donegal; in 1609 one Neal MacGnellus was a Lifford juror; in Bishop Montgomery's survey of the diocese of Raphoe at the same date Bernard MacNellus is among the clergy specially mentioned – he was curate of Glencolumbkille and we are told he "paints cleverly and speaks Irish, Latin and English well". The family were associated with that Donegal parish for, as we learn from the Annals of Loch Cé under the year 1530, they were coarbs of Columcille there.

Grealy or Greely is sometimes found as a synonym of Grealish. Woulfe gives Mag or Mac Raghallaigh as the Irish form of it, but adds no further information. It probably is different from Grealish but I have not discovered its origin. It is exclusively a Mayo-Galway surname and Grealys or Greallys living elsewhere can no doubt trace their descent from a Connacht family.   Map

NEVILLE, O'Nee, Needham
O'KNOWELL, Knowles, Newell   The name Neville has a French or Norman appearance and it is true that among the Anglo-Norman invaders and settlers of the late twelfth century were one or more families called de Neville who acquired lands in south-east Leinster and are frequently mentioned in all relevant records. In Co. Wexford especially they were prominent in local affairs: for example, Lawrence Neville was Bishop of Ferns from 1480 to 1503 and Robert Nevyll was a notable burgess of New Ross in 1511. Thomas Nevill who claimed to come within the articles of the Treaty of Limerick was from Rathmore, Co. Kildare. There were Nevills in Clonmel in 1688 but whether these and the two officers of the name in James II's army were of this Norman stock I do not know.

We can be sure that the Nevilles of counties Limerick and Cork, the only part of the country where they are now numerous, are Gaels in disguise; during the period when it was fashionable not to be Irish they allowed the patronymic Ó Niadh to be represented in English by the aristocratic sounding Neville. In the Topographical Poems the Gaelic form is given as Ó Neidhe, and in his notes thereon O'Donovan, calling the form Neville a "whim", mentions that the family were keepers of St Patrick's bell at Knockpatrick, Co. Limerick. A distinguished modern representative of the Nevilles was Dr. Neville of Blackrock College, who became Vicar-Apostolic of Zanzibar in 1913 and laboured in tropical countries with much success for 30 years.

The surname Ó Niadh which means "descendant of the hero" (nia), is not uncommon also in Connemara where, however, it is never anglicized Neville but takes the form Nee (sometimes spelt Knee) which is an approximately correct phonetic rendering of Niadh. In Mayo the majority of Nees have adopted the English sounding surname Needham.

Neville has also been used as a synonym of Nevin (see next article). It may be added that it is never interchangeable with Newell. That is Ó Tnúthghail in Irish. This was a minor sept located on the border of the modern counties of Kildare and Meath and the name was first anglicized as O'Knowell, whence the modern Knowles. As Newill it appears in the Hearth Money Rolls for Co. Tyrone (1664). Both Newell and Knowles are, of course, also common English surnames. Three men called Knowles, relatives of Richard Brinsley Sheridan, of whom James

Sheridan Knowles (1784-1862) is the best known, were distinguished in various branches of literature in the nineteenth century. Three Newells, too, all from the Belfast area, are noteworthy: one Edward J. Newell (1771-1798) admittedly only as an informer, but Alexander Newell (1824-1893) was a distinguished scientist and Hugh Newell (b. 1830) an artist of repute in America.   Map

(Mac) NEVIN   The MacNevins have a very distinguished record. MacCnáimhin, the name of a sept of the Uí Maine, appears frequently in the Annals from 1159 onwards in its Co. Galway homeland. The chief resided at Crannagh-MacNevin in the parish of Tynagh, near Loughrea, and the family held considerable property there until quite recent times. Hugh MacKnavin, Chief of the Name, who is described as alias MacKelly, was hanged in 1602 for his participation in the resistance to Elizabethan aggression.

They were famous both as poets and physicians. Three of the name (Gilpatrick, Lucas and Patrick) are represented by long poems in the Book of Magauran. The most celebrated of the physicians was William James MacNevin (1763-1841) of 1798 fame; his uncle Baron MacNevin (c. 1723-1790), who emigrated to Austria, was physician to the Empress Maria Theresa. In the 19th century Thomas MacNevin (1814-1848) was a distinguished member of the Young Ireland party.

In modern times the name is scattered; in the form of Navin (occasionally Knavin) it is chiefly found in Co. Mayo. In west Clare it has been lamentably changed to Neville.   Map

MacNICHOLAS   The name MacNicholas is almost entirely confined to families belonging to Co. Mayo, where the Gaelic form Mac Nlocláis has sometimes also been anglicized Clausson. They are said to be a gaelicized branch of the Norman de Burgos. The inquisitions of James I's reign show that they held extensive estates then around Bohola in the barony of Gallen and the Book of Survey and Distribution records them as 1641 proprietors in the adjacent barony of Clanmorris. The name is prominent again in Co. Mayo in the persons of Most Rev. Patrick MacNicholas, Bishop of Achonry from 1818 to 1852, and Most Rev. Dr. MacNicholas O.P. (1879-1950), Archbishop of Cincinnati, who was born at Kiltimagh.

A misunderstanding might arise from the fact that MacNicholas is given in the 1659 "census" as one of the principal Irish names in Co. Waterford, but the explanation of this is probably the interchangeability then of Mac and Fitz, these people being FitzNicholases of different stock: the name MacNicholas was certainly to be found in the south-eastern portion of the country, as it occurs several times in lists of tenants and jurors in Co. Wexford in the 16th century, as does FitzNicholas in similar sources for Co. Waterford.   Map

NIXON   Nixon is numerous in Ulster, especially in counties Antrim and Fermanagh. The most notable immigrant family of the name settled in Co. Fermanagh in 1609. Fifty years later we find Nixson listed in Petty's "census" as a principal name in two baronies of that county. No doubt more than one Englishman of the name settled in other counties in the seventeenth century: there are, for example, three Nixons in the Co. Tipperary Hearth Money Rolls of 1665. Testators of the name are numerous in the Prerogative wills from 1677 to 1811: 27 are Nixon, of which ten were of Co. Fermanagh or neighbouring Ulster counties and nine of Dublin; as Nickson six of the nine are of Co. Wicklow. In Griffith's Valuation (1853) there are five Nixons in Co. Wicklow. Of similar derivation is Nix (i.e. son of Nicholas or Nick) i.e. Mac Niocais, a patronymic adopted by some families of Woulfe in Co. Limerick. The Registrar-General's report of 1909 indicates that at that time Woulfe and Nix were in the Newcastle, Co. Limerick, district used synonymously, while in another case they were combined to make the surname Woulfe-Nix. The best-known person of the name is the controversial Richard Nixon, who was President of the U.S.A. from 1969-1975.   •Bibl.

(O) NOONE   There are a large number of Noones in north Connacht but, apart from the metropolitan area of Dublin (where families from all the provinces are represented), the name is rare elsewhere. They are a sept of the Uí Fiachrach with traditional descent from Niall of the Nine Hostages. Their main territory lay in the present parish of Calry near Sligo town. They are still in Sligo and also in counties Mayo, Roscommon and Galway, especially in the baronies of Kilconnell and Clonmacnowan (Co. Galway). Rather surprisingly there is no mention of them in the Composition Book of Connacht but fifty years later in Strafford's Inquisition of Mayo (1635) the name occurs several times, in each case as landholders in the barony of Murrisk.
    According to O'Donovan the name in Irish is Ó Nuadháin; Woulfe states that Lambe is used as a synonym of it (presumably from its similarity in sound to an uain, of the lamb). Lambe, however, is a recognized substitute for Ó Luain (see Loane, supra).   Map

(Mac) NORMOYLE   Woulfe gives Mac Confhormaoile for this, meaning son of the hound of Fermoyle. We know from National Library MS. G. 841 that this was a suggestion made by Richard Foley and accepted by Fr. Woulfe. I think it is correct: the form MacEnormoyle appears in a Fiant of 1603. Formaoil is the obsolete name of a castle in Co. Clare, the county with which Normoyle is mainly associated; the form Normile is more usual in the adjacent county of Limerick.

NORRIS   This name as le Norreys (i.e. the northman) is very frequent in Irish records since the thirteenth century. It came into special prominence with the arrival of Sir John Norris, who was responsible for the terrible massacre at Rathlin Island in 1575. He became President of Munster in 1584 and was succeeded by his brother Thomas in 1597. Another brother, Henry (d. 1599), is

favourably mentioned by the Four Masters. The name is now found in considerable numbers in all the provinces except Connacht. Some curious synonyms of it have been reported by local registrars, e.g. Nowry in Co. Derry, Nurse in Co. Kerry and Northbridge in west Cork. These three names are very rare in Ireland: Nurse and Nourse are normal synonyms of Norris in England; Northridge is an English name denoting residence at the north ridge.   Bibl., Map

(O) NYHAN   Other forms of this name still occasionally found are Nihan and Nihane; while Nahane and Neehane are in the lists of Linen Board premiums for 1896 for the parish of Ballymoney. The influence of the usual anglicized spelling has resulted in it being now generally pronounced Nye-han; but only a generation ago it was always Nee-haan (Neehane) in its native homeland, viz south-west Cork, so that the Irish form Ó Niatháin, given by Woulfe, is probably correct, though his conjectural identification of it with Ó Niadh and Ó Niadhóg seems far-fetched. He says he found no early instances, but in fact it occurs twice in the Justiciary Rolls for Co. Cork as early as 1295 when Neivin O'Nyhyn was charged with "harbouring felons" and soon after a William O'Nyhyn appeared in another law case.

ODELL   Though pronounced Odle not O-dell by the family, this is, or was, frequently writen O'Dell as if it were a Gaelic name, especially in the eighteenth century though the Gaelic order was then at its lowest ebb; but in fact it was basically rather a Catholic than a Gaelic submergence, for those Gaelic families which had accepted Protestantism were not ashamed of their Gaelic origin, so perhaps the gaelicization of the English name Odell is understandable in Ireland. It has been chiefly connected with Co. Limerick. According to their own family record the senior branch (now seated at Kilcleagh, Moate, Co. Westmeath) obtained their extensive estates in Co. Limerick by a patent of 1667. There were, however, people of the name, presumably relatives, well established in Co. Limerick some time before that: apart from army officers, we find in the 1659 "census" John Odell, gent, resident at Pallice (parish of Ballingarry), and Edward O'Dell, gent, near Askeaton. The former was one of the Inquisition jurors for the barony of Connello in 1644 – of the 46 jurors named for that barony only six are not of old Limerick Gaelic or Norman families. This man's name is also spelt Odle. He was among the gentlemen appointed as officers to lead the militia to be raised in Co. Limerick in 1659 and later he was High Sheriff of Limerick in 1677 and 1679. References to the name are numerous in eighteenth century records, chiefly in Co. Limerick; but a number of wills in the Waterford diocesan archives show a connexion with that part of Munster, while the Kenmare (Browne) rentals indicate that Odells were strong farmers in Kerry also.   Bibl.

ODLUM   The older form of this name, Adlum, has been recorded in comparatively recent times in Co. Offaly. This, as Adelem (later Adlam), is on record in England since the twelfth century: it is derived, according to Reaney, from the Old-German adelelm (noble protector). As Odlum it appears in Ireland in the seventeenth century: Thomas Odlum was one of 29 soldiers disbanded from Ormond's own troop in 1662 (in one place the name is spelt Oldum presumably by a mistranscription). The family settled in King's Co. (Co. Offaly) and there are many Oldum wills listed from 1735, the testators up to 1800 being variously described as "farmer" and "gent" and all of that county. Three Odlums are in the Earl of Charleville's King's Co. rental of 1763. Later they were found also in Co. Leix, but Griffith's Valuation of the 1850's and modern voters' lists confirm that they are very definitely of Co. Offaly ever since they first came to Ireland. The name is very well known in the flour milling industry.

ORR   The surname Orr is a toponymic, being derived from the parish of Orr in Kirkcudbrightshire, Scotland. Its association with Ireland is comparatively modern — Apart from an officer in Ormond's army (1646), not necessarily an Irishman, the earliest reference I have found to it in Ireland is 1655: this relates to a shopkeeper called Thomas Orr, who lived in Church Street, Dublin. A family of Orr settled in Co. Tyrone in the same century probably earlier than 1655 since many families of Orr are recorded as resident in Co. Derry and adjacent areas only ten years later. Orr figures among the commoner of the Scottish names in Ulster being widely distributed in the three north-eastern counties and in east Tyrone. From Co. Antrim came the two United Irishmen, William Orr (1766-1797) who was hanged, unjustly as was generally thought, and James Orr (1770-1816) who, though he took part in the Insurrection of 1798, escaped that penalty. The latter was the author of the popular poem "The Irishman". Andrew Orr (1822-1895), from Coleraine, was also a poet, whose "In Exile" was written after he had emigrated to Australia. Orrs from the north of Ireland have also been prominent in the United States: Orrville in Anderson County, South Carolina, is named from them. James Laurence Orr (1822-1873), who was governor of South Carolina and speaker of the House of Representatives, was notable for his attempts at compromise in the Civil War period: his family had emigrated from Ulster in 1730. Alexander Ector Orr (1831-1914) born at Strabane, Co. Tyrone,

was the pioneer of subways and rapid transit in New York city.

PALMER   Palmer is a name of Norman origin — Old-French le paumer, i.e. the palmer or pilgrim. It is of very frequent occurrence in Anglo-Norman records in Ireland from the thirteenth century. In those early times it was not associated with any particular part of the country, and few Irish Palmers of the present day can claim descent from these mediaeval immigrants. Families of the name were definitely established as landed proprietors both in Kerry and in Meath (later Kildare) in the seventeenth century. Today it is fairly numerous only in east Ulster and in the city of Dublin.

Palmer has sometimes been used as an anglicized form of Ó Maolfhoghmhair (Mullover, alias Milford); but it is essentially an English name. There are 57 Palmers in the Dictionary of National Biography, only two of whom have Irish connexions: one a British colonial politician who happened to be born in Ireland and the other the celebrated Dublin beauty Eleanor Ambrose (c. 1720-1818), who married Sir Roger Palmer of Mayo and Dublin.   Map

MacPARLAND, Bartley   MacFARLANE   MacParland is the most usual modern spelling of the surname MacParthaláin: MacParlan, MacPartland and MacPartlin being variants of it, while MacFarland and MacFarlane are also so used. The latter is, however, usually of Scottish origin, and is very numerous in counties Tyrone and Armagh, where in the baronies of Orior and Upper and Lower Fewes MacParlan was listed in the "census" of 1659 as a principal Irish name. It also occurs frequently in the Armagh Hearth Money Rolls of 1664. In the sixteenth century the name appears chiefly in Co. Leitrim where, with Armagh (MacPartlan and MacFarlane), it is principally found today. In some cases it has been changed to Bartley. The city of Dublin is, of course, disregarded in all such cases as the metropolitan area is composed of inhabitants from all the provinces.

Parthalán, the forename from which the surname is formed, is regarded in modern usage as the equivalent of Bartholomew, which is fairly popular as a Christian name, being that of one of the twelve Apostles. Parthalán is a great figure in mythological prehistoric Ireland: tradition makes him a native of Grecian Sicily and the leader of the invasion of Ireland 300 years after the Flood.

Owen MacPharlon, dean of the diocese of Kilmore, appears in a list of leading Catholic dignitaries in Co. Leitrim compiled by the High Sheriff in 1744; the priest hunters also mention a Father Parlon of Armagh.

Six scribes or poets called Mac Parthaláin are included in the catalogue of Irish Mss in the British Museum. The best known of these was Diarmuid Bacach Mac Parthaláin (fl. 1485).   Map

PARLE   Although at the present time we have both Pearls and Perrills in Co. Clare, which are presumably variants of Parle, the latter is, and has been as far back as it is recorded in Ireland, almost exclusively connected with Co. Wexford. Although an early reference (1570) shows one Edmund Perle of Brittas, Co. Wicklow, to have been a galloglass, those of the name who appear in records have been almost uniformly of what we call now the strong farmer class, e.g. Thomas Parle, of Cowlesheiken, Co. Wexford, who was killed in a quarrel in 1563. Griffith's Valuation (1852-3) indicates that there were nearly 90 families of Parle in Co. Wexford at that time, mostly so spelt, though a few are returned as Parl, Parrel and Parrell. A curious spelling recorded at Gorey in 1725 is Parolz: the same man is also given as Parole. The name is derived from Pierre (Peter) with diminutives el and in forming Perrel and Perrin, the latter more usual in England.

(Mac) PATRICK Patrick as a surname, even in Ireland, is usually of Scottish origin: Patrick, also called Mac-Patrick, is a sept of the clan Lamont. Both are fairly frequent in the Ulster Hearth Money Rolls. Patrick is more numerous in Ulster than in the other provinces. Though Scottish names may be expected there it is probable that some of the Ulster Patricks are descendants of families formerly called Mulpatrick (Ó Maol Phádraig). O'Mulpatrick, now practically obsolete, was listed as a principal Irish name in the "census" of 1659 both in east Fermanagh and in the Granard district of Co. Longford. O'Mulpatrick, however, appears more often in Munster in early records: it was the name of the erenagh family of Mungret, Co. Limerick: as far back as 1306 an O'Mulpatrick has a Cork juror and Munster Mulpatricks figure in the Elizabethan Fiants, as indeed do MacPatricks, though the latter are located mainly in Queen's County and Wexford in that voluminous source. These, however, were probably Fitzpatricks. That is possible also in the case of the fifteen families called Patrick who are in the Co. Tipperary Hearth Money Rolls of 1664. One, Rory MacPatrick, is definitely stated in the Ulster Plantation documents relating to Co. Armagh to be a native Irishman not a planter. The earliest reference I have met to Patrick as a surname is in Archbishop Alen's Register to a canon of St. Patrick's in 1229, but his name may have been ephemeral; in 1256 it is quite definitely a surname in counties Wicklow, Carlow and Waterford.

(Mac) PEAKE Woulfe briefly describes this as a rare west Ulster name, but in fact it is still fairly numerous in counties Tyrone and Derry and was formerly quite common there as the Hearth Money Rolls, diocesan wills etc. attest: in the 1659 "census" MacPeake appears as one of the principal Irish surnames in the barony of Loughinsholin, i.e. the part of Co. Derry adjoining Co. Tyrone. Their association with north Ulster is also perpetuated in the place-name Ballymacpeake in the same barony. The long list of Ulstermen who followed Rory O'Donnell to Connacht in 1603 includes two MacPeakes, Dermot and Manus; Owen Callowe MacPeake and Owyne Peake, yeomen, Irishmen who received "pardons" about the same time, were from the Co. Tyrone area. It must also be

remembered that the records show that there were quite a number of Peakes (without the prefix Mac) in other parts of Ireland whose origin was different: there is an English name Peake of the toponymic type and derived from the word peak (hill). Probably Philip Peake, Marshall of the Four Courts in 1655 was of this stock. The Mac-Peake family of Belfast are notable for their activities in the field of Irish traditional music.

PELLY Authorities differ as to the origin of this name: Reaney says it is a diminutive of Peter; Weekley's explanation is le pelé (the bald man). A further possible derivation is from de la Pelle — Richard de le Pelle appears in the Justiciary Rolls as a Co. Cork lessee in 1307, but it is hardly likely that he is the ancestor of the present day Pellys in Ireland, who for the most part belong to families located near Ballinasloe and other places in south Galway, where they are on record for many centuries. In 1656, Susanna, widow of Thomas Pelly of Coolecartan, Co. Galway, was one of the persons transplanted under the Cromwellian Settlement; and the Books of Survey & Distribution, which record landholders of the next generation, have a number of references to a Peter Pelly's acquisition of lands in Co. Roscommon. (In this connexion it is interesting to note that in 1878 a Mr. Pelly owned 1,510 acres of good land in Co. Roscommon.) A Peter Pelly, possibly the same man, obtained lands in the parish of Clooney, barony of Corcomroe, in that part of Co. Clare which adjoins Co. Galway, part of the property owned by the O'Connors in 1641. It should be added that at the same time one Peter Pelly appears in the Armagh Hearth Money Rolls (1664-65).

In recent times the name appears frequently in church records both as priests and nuns.

PEOPLES This Donegal name is an example of the more absurd type of pseudo-translation — it arose from the similarity of the sound of the word daoine (people) and the duibhne of O'Duibhne, anglicized Deeney. Both Peoples, also spelt Peebles, and Deeney are mainly found in the barony of Raphoe. In 1631 Hugh Peoples of Carnetellagh acquired the lands of Ballehebestocke, Co. Antrim and the name as Peoples, Peables, Pebbles, Pebles and Pheables appears frequently in the Co. Antrim Hearth Money Rolls (1669).

PEPPARD, Pepper   Known when they first came to Ireland as de Pipard and Pipard this Norman family was one of the most important in that part of the country which was subjugated after the invasion of 1172. In 1185 Gilbert de Pipard obtained a grant of all Oriel; in 1192 Peter de Pipard was a witness to the grant by King John "Lord of Ireland", to Walter Pincerna (i.e. Butler), and a few years later he was Justiciar of Ireland; in 1226 we find William FitzRoger Pipard holding the barony of Ardee (Co. Louth) from the crown. In 1302 Rulf Pipard, Baron of Ardee, had to surrender his estate there to the King since he was unable to defend this "outpost" against the MacMahons: it was about this time that Oriel became divided into Irish Oriel (Co. Monaghan) and English Oriel (Co. Louth). From the beginning of the thirteenth century to the end of the seventeenth the Peppards were closely connected with Co. Louth both as territorial magnates and also as burgesses of Drogheda: for example the attainders following the Jacobite defeat in 1690 include the mayor, two aldermen and three burgesses of that town, all named Peppard. Two Peppards were in Bellew's regiment of King James II's army, which was mainly recruited in counties Louth and Meath. Drogheda is close to Co. Meath and in that century many Peppards were found there as well as in Co. Louth; in fact Peppard is recorded in Petty's "census" as one of the principal Irish names in Co. Meath in 1659 (English officials thus regarded it as Irish).

The name Peppard has, as might be expected, sometimes become Pepper; this tendency was especially marked in the last century, but it is not entirely a modern innovation as the townlands of Pepparstown in the Ardee (Co. Louth) and Kells (Co. Meath) areas attest. There is a Peppardstown in Co. Tipperary (Cashel district) and Peppard's Castle near Gorey. The Peppards have long association with Co. Wexford as well as with the country north of Dublin: Richard Pipard, a tough Norman knight, built his thirteenth century Co. Wexford castle on church lands in defiance of the protests of his bishop. In the sixteenth century Peppards were mine owners in Co. Wexford.

Though, as I have said, Pepper has been fairly widely used as a synonym of Peppard it must not be assumed that all Peppers in Ireland are Peppards, since Pepper is itself an indigenous English surname, which Peppard (derived from a French place-name) is not. George Pepper (fl. 1820-1840), American dramatist, was presumably a Peppard, since he was born at Ardee.

There is a fine collection of deeds and other Peppard family papers in the National Library of Ireland.   Map

PEYTON, Payton, Patten, Patton   Apart from a few families named from English place-names or, in the case of Paton and Patton, alternatively from a diminutive of the personal name Patrick, the surnames at the head of this section are derived from the Irish Ó Peatáin. This in its place of origin – near Ballybofey in Co. Donegal – was first anglicized as O'Pettane and later became Patton. Murtough Ó Peatáin whose death in 1178 is recorded by the Four Masters, was of the Cenél Moen, so he too came from the barony of Raphoe. In Connacht the anglicized form is usually Peyton, which is mainly found in Co. Mayo. This branch of the sept appears to have followed the O'Donnells from Donegal in the early seventeenth century. The prominent landed family of Laheen, Co. Leitrim, however, descend from an English clergyman, Rev. Thomas Peyton, who became Dean of Tuam in 1625. Among the more prominent men of the name in Ireland were Christopher Peyton, who carried out the Desmond Survey which bears his name in 1586 and Sir John Peyton, surveyor general (ordnance) 1684.   Bibl., Map

(Mac) PHILBIN   This is a Connacht name borne almost exclusively by families belonging to Co. Mayo or adjacent parts of Galway and Sligo. In the Composition Book of Connacht (1585) Clanphilbin is described as a sept of Burrishoole and its head as Chief of the Name: long before that, though not of Gaelic origin, they had become completely hibernicized and were reckoned by the annalists as a sept. Hardiman, quoting O'Ferral's Linea Antiqua states that the family of Philips or MacPhilbin of the Lower Owles (Burrishoole) was a branch of the Burkes. In a note to the Annals of the Four Masters (1355) O'Donovan remarks that MacPhilbin was one of the chiefs of Sil Anmchadha, i.e. the O'Madden country in east Galway: and he was undoubtedly of Burke ancentry. In his Notes to The Tribes and Customs of Hy Fiachrach O'Donovan tells us that Clanphilbin of Erris were of different stock, being a branch of the Barretts. He adds that MacPhilbin lived at Doon Castle, four miles from Westport. It would seem impossible now to distinguish between the different MacPhilbins of Connacht, since the barony of Erris borders on that of Burrishoole. The information given in the Annals of Loch Cé complicates rather than elucidates the point, for that work records the death in 1579 of Gilladubh MacPhilip, lord of the Leitir (i.e. Litir MacPhilip, which is in Co. Sligo).

When English came to be used in the records, e.g. the Fiants of the sixteenth century, MacPhilbin was often written MacPhilip and the further transition to the English surname Philips was inevitable in the period of Gaelic and Catholic submergence. In 1635 Strafford's Inquisition found MacPhilbin one of the most numerous surnames in Co. Mayo – it was exceeded only by Barrett, Burke, MacGibbon and Prendergast – while the synonym MacPhilip only occurs three times in that document. MacPhilip appears in the "census" of 1659 as a principal name in several counties besides Mayo (where the form MacPhilbin is not mentioned); but this may elsewhere be regarded as one of the many ephemeral surnames formed from the father's christian name and seldom hereditary: in Co. Tipperary indeed it is given as an alias of Fitzphilip.

Philip Phillips (d. 1787), Bishop of Achonry and later Archbishop of Tuam, was no doubt a MacPhilbin, as were the three Philips officers in James II's Irish army. There are four persons called Philips or Phillips in Crone's Concise Dictionary of Irish Biography, of whom only Judge Charles Phillips (1786-1859) would appear to be of MacPhillbin origin. Dr. William Philbin is the present Bishop of Down and Connor.   Map

PIGOT This well-known English name, often spelt with two Gs and/or two Ts, is derived, as also is Pickett, from a form of the Christian name Peter. It has been fairly prominent in Ireland since the sixteenth century: the first Pigot I have met with is Nicholas Pigote who was appointed governor of Dublin Castle in 1546 (another of the name filled the same post in Elizabeth I's reign). Another was an alderman in 1591 and since then there have always been Pigots in Dublin. In 1563 John Pigot obtained a grant of the lands of Dysert and other places in Co. Leix and since that time the Pigot or Pigott family (they spell it both ways) have been associated with Queens Co. (Leix) as extensive landowners and sheriffs of the county. The "census" of 1659 and the list of Poll Money Commissioners which accompanies it contain many Piggotts, mainly in Queen's Co., not only as titula-does but actually among the "principal Irish names" in the barony of Maryborough. The others mentioned in that document were of Cork or Limerick; and modern statistics show that more than half the Pigots of the present day came from counties Cork and Limerick or Dublin.

Though many of the Pigots mentioned in Irish records were soldiers or officials working in the English interest, the classing of Piggot as an Irish name in the "census" of 1659 is not without some justification for (apart from the affiliation of early Picots) we find many Pigots obtaining "pardons", beginning with David Ro Pigot of Ballyclohy, Co. Cork, in 1573; later on two Piggotts were among the outlawed Jacobites; and in the last century there was John Edward Pigot (1822-1871) poet and Young Irelander, who was the son of a Cork man, Judge David Richard Pigot (1797-1873). The name is also in-gloriously associated with the Parnell forgeries case.

The obsolete form Picot occurs frequently in medi-aeval records: one in the Justiciary Rolls of 1306 relating to Co. Limerick is of special interest here because Simon Picot appears (on a charge of robbery and murder) with fifteen other men all of whom bore Mac or O names.

MacPOLIN POLAND, Polan Woulfe's suggestion that Poland and Polin are variants of the same name must be taken with reserve. Polin and MacPolin are found now almost exclusively in counties Armagh and Down, and MacPolin is in the 1664-5 list of Co. Armagh households. Poland on the other hand is essentially an Offaly name, even if it is occasionally used as a synonym of Polin in Ulster. We can accept the derivation of Polin and MacPolin from Paulin, a diminutive of Paul; I have yet to find authoritative evidence for the derivation of Poland. Monsignor MacPolin of the Maynooth Mission to China was prefect-apostolic in Korea during the second World War.

PORTER Porter is of course a well known English name but having regard not only to its numerical strength in Ireland to-day but also to its prominence in every aspect of Irish life since the Anglo-Norman invasion it must certainly be included in this series. Indeed there are few names which occur more widely in every kind of Irish record, legal, testamentary, diplomatic, military, medical and ecclesiastical (both Catholic and Protestant). These represent a wide distribution territorially. I will take a few examples. There were five Porters among the Jacobites outlawed following the final defeat of James II in 1691: these came from counties Meath, Kildare, Tipperary and Waterford; wills are most numerous in the diocese of Derry, Raphoe, Cork, Waterford and Dublin; of the eleven Porters included in Crone's Concise Dictionary of Irish Biography five were born in the Derry-Donegal area, three in Dublin, two near Belfast and one in Meath – perhaps the most remarkable of them was Rev. James Porter (1753-1798) Presbyterian Minister who was publicly hanged for his part in the United Irish-men's insurrection of 1798 and whose son Alexander Porter (1796-1844) became an American senator of note; in one volume of the Ormond Deeds covering the years 1350 to 1413 there are thirteen Porters (mostly called le Porter, i.e. the doorkeeper, mainly in counties Tipperary and Kilkenny. The place-name Porterstown is to be found in Counties Meath, Westmeath, Kildare and Dublin, while Portersland and Portersgate are in Co. Wexford. It is not possible here to do more than touch briefly on some aspects of the subject but this brief note will indicate that there is an exceptional amount of Porter material to be found in the usual sources for Irish historical and genealogical research.

POTTER Potter is a name of obvious derivation: it means simply a maker of pots. It appears in Dublin as le Poter in a number of cases in the thirteenth century. It was, however, not common in the mediaeval period, but from the sixteenth century on it became more numerous and is found now in all the four provinces. Judging by such tests as diocesan wills, Fiants, Hearth Money Rolls, marriage licence bonds and other legal records it would appear that counties Cork, Tipperary, Galway and Down are the parts of the country where the name is mainly found – apart, of course, from the city of Dublin which is composed of people from all the provinces; but the frequent references in the Fiants to Potterstown in Co. Kildare indicated that the family was once well established there, though there is now no place so called in the townland and parish lists of Kildare or any other county.

Most notable people of the name have been English; but Thomas Joseph Potter (1828-1873), author and professor at All Hallows College, was Irish, and more recently we have Archibald Potter, the distinguished composer, and Maureen Potter, the comedienne, to keep Potter prominent as an Irish name.

O'PREY Woulfe makes this name a corruption of a' Phréith. The word préith is given in Dinneen's dictionary, meaning cattle-spoil and being both m. and f. in gender: no doubt it is a little used loan-word from the English "prey". Professor M.A. O'Brien tells me that O'Prey is derived from the Pictish predhae and that it occurs in the genealogies dealing with the very part of Co. Down in which it is now to be found.

Though the name is not included in Matheson's statistical list for 1890 (giving all surnames for which five or more births were registered in that year) earlier birth records indicate that it was formerly more numerous. In 1866, for example, there were 15 registrations, all in Co. Down or Belfast: most of these were entered as O'Prey, but the variants O'Pray, Prey and Preay also appear.

PRIOR   Woulfe describes this name (Mac an Phríora in Irish) as scattered. This is quite true of earlier times, but for the past hundred years families of the name have been largely concentrated in and around Co. Cavan. Of 21 births registered in 1866, sixteen were in Co. Cavan and three in Co. Leitrim; in 1890 ten of the fifteen registrations were in Co. Cavan and four in Connacht (mainly Co. Leitrim). In the records of earlier centuries references to the name in that area are infrequent; in the seventeenth and eighteenth centuries we find many Priors, MacPriors, MacInpriors and MacGilpriors, most of whom belonged to the Queen's Co. (Leix), with a lesser member in the Kavanagh country (counties Wexford and Carlow) and a few in Co. Cork. No doubt the Priors who appear in mediaeval records of Dublin and Limerick as clergy, jurors, artificers etc., during the thirteenth to fifteenth centuries were of Norman not of Gaelic-Irish stock. Of the Irish variants given above the obsolete Mac-Inprior is a simple rendering of Mac and Phríora; Macgilprior is Mac giolla an phríora, denoting son of the prior's follower or servant. The townland of Ballymac-prior in Kerry would appear to indicate the existence of an influential Prior family of Gaelic stock in that county, while Priorstown in Co. Louth is another suggestive place-name; but this and other townlands (Priorsfarm, Priorspark, Priorsweir, Priorswood, Priorswarren) may well have been named from the office not the surname. On the Longford side of Co. Cavan some families formerly Prior have become Fryer and Friary. Thomas Prior (1679-1751), one of the founders of the Royal Dublin Society, was of the Rathdowney, Co. Leix, family which continued to be prominent in the county until recent times.

(O) PRUNTY, Bronté   Prunty is the modern form of the name better known to the world as Bronte. The form Brunty is also used today in Co. Armagh. Ó Proinn-tighe is the form now used in Irish. It has been stated that this is derived from the word proinnteach (refectory), but facile derivations from modern Gaelic words must be accepted with caution. It could be Ó Proinntigh or Ó Pronntaigh meaning descendant of the bestower or generous person. It is an Ulster Gaelic surname appearing in the seventeenth century Co. Monaghan Hearth Money Rolls as O'Prounty, chiefly in the barony of Cremorne and in those of Co. Armagh (barony of Lower Fees) as O'Prunty. In the Fiants of the previous century it is spelt O'Prontye. Hyde in his Literary History of Ireland expresses the opinion that the ancestor of the three famous women novelists Charlotte Bronte (1816-1855), Anne Bronte (1820-1849) and Emily Jane Bronte (1818-1848) was Patrick O'Prunty, the Ulster Gaelic poet; their father was Rev. Patrick Bronte, who was the son of Hugh Prunty, a small farmer in Co. Down.

PUNCH   POYNTZ   The name Punch is of Norman origin, being derived from the Latin-Norman forename Poncius, which became Pons or Ponz in France and Poyntz and Ponce in Ireland before it assumed its present form. As such it is to be found in Irish records as far back as the thirteenth century in Dublin and Co. Kildare; while Poynstown, Co. Kildare, (now Punchestown, famous for the annual point-to-point race meeting held there) occurs in the Justiciary Rolls for 1300. References to the name, however, are not numerous before the seventeenth century when they begin to be more frequent. Dr. John Ponce or Punch (1603-1672) is mentioned as of Co. Waterford in Ware's "Writers"; in 1631 Rev. John Punch O.F.M. a native of Co. Cork, was rector of the Irish College, Rome; in 1649 Rev. Nicholas Punch was procurator of the Jesuit school in Limerick. Subsequently Punches appear often in the records of Cork city and county (especially Macroom) and Limerick.

The family of Poyntz of Co. Armagh came to Ireland at the time of the Plantation of Ulster at the beginning of the seventeenth century. Poyntzpass, between Newry and Portadown, is in Co. Armagh. The name as Pointz and Poyns occurs in the Inquisitions (c. 1630) relating to counties Antrim, Down and Tyrone as well as Armagh.

There were several families of Poyntz in Kerry in the second half of the eighteenth century, when they were influential in the town of Tralee. Mr. Basil O'Connell informs me that the Poyntz families now to be found in America sprang from this group.

PURDON   This name was once very prominent both in Co. Cork and Co. Clare. According to the family pedigree they came from Cumberland and settled in Co. Louth in the first half of the sixteenth century. The pedigree, however, needs revision as it confuses Tulla in Co. Clare with Tulloe (alias Tullagh) Co. Limerick. Any connexion they had with Co. Louth was shortlived: in 1570 Simon Purdon of Tallaght, Co. Dublin was granted a pension on account of being lamed in the Queen's service. He was the ancestor of the Purdons of Co. Clare: they became established there at least a generation before the Cromwellian upheaval, for another Simon Purdon, who held the position of governor of Co. Clare, was born at Tinerana in 1655. They were there in the "census" of 1659. Another early reference is to one Morris Purdon who was Co. Limerick agent to George Courtney, the well known Munster "undertaker". This Purdon died in 1638. Twenty years later Petty's "census" records John Purdon as titulado of Tullo in the parish of Lismakeery, Co. Limerick, while two more of the name were tituladoes at Ballyclogh, Co. Cork, and Major Purdon was at Buttevant with his troop: he was an officer in Inchiquin's army and is presumably the John Purdon of Tullo mentioned above. According to Canon Begley this family was of the Catholic gentry of Co. Limerick, but they did not suffer transplantation; one of them, Sylvester of Tullo, served in James II's army and suffered forfeiture as a Jacobite but his estate was restored in 1698. From the end of the seventeenth century Purdons were associated mainly with Co. Cork and were fairly numerous: the Cloyne marriage licence bonds include 26 Purdons in little more than a century from 1683; and the register of students of Dublin University has 36 of the name, mostly from Co. Cork, the earliest being born in 1645. There are many references to the name in such collections as the Ormond, Orrery and Inchiquin papers, now in the Manuscripts Department of the National Library of Ireland. It is now more numerous in Antrim and Down: there it has sometimes been used synonymously with Purdy.

PURTILL   Woulfe states that Purtill is derived from a place called Porthill, forming the surname de Porthill. I have met no instance of this in any mediaeval or modern record; nor is Porthill or Purtill to be found in the standard works on British surnames such as Reaney, Bardsley and Weekley. In Ireland, at any rate Purtill and Purtell are forms of Purcell. Its variants Purshell and Purscell, found in some seventeenth century documents, could have become Purtell in speech and subsequently been so written. This is corroborated by a Fiant of 1601 in which we find Robert Reogh Purtell, Garret Purcell and William FitzJohn Purcell all resident in the same part of Co. Limerick; and coming to modern times the return of Clare freeholders for 1821 has thirteen Purtills in the barony of Moyarta and only one Purcell. Official records of the Registrar-General show that some families in Co. Clare have used Purcell and Purtill synonymously. I can also add from local knowledge that Purtill is currently pronounced Purcill in Co. Clare. As Purtill the name was formerly numerous in Co. Tipperary: there were seventeen householders so called in South Tipperary at the time Griffith's Valuation was carried out in 1850 and Edmund Purtil of Cahir, Co. Tipperary, is mentioned in the British Museum catalogue of Gaelic manuscripts (1865). Purcell, which is numerous in Clare as well as in most counties of Munster and Co. Kilkenny, is dealt with in Irish Families (pp. 248-249), where many famous men of the name are mentioned: as Purtill it has not been prominent.

PYNE   Woulfe equates Pyne and also Fyan with Payne deriving them from the Latin paganus; but Reaney, the best authority on English names, distinguishes between Pyne and Payne. The latter, he states, is from paganus, the former having several different origins viz. (1) Old French pin, nickname for a tall, upright man, (2) atte pyne, i.e. dweller by the pine or at the place called Pyne or (3) from the French place Le Pin. In Ireland families of the name have been located mainly in Co. Cork with a few in Co. Clare and some other Munster counties. I have not met any early mediaeval instance of it, but it has been in this country continuously for some four centuries, at least since Robert Pyne was the Earl of Ormond's attorney in 1599. In modern times we find

some of them among the Catholic farming and trading community, but for the most part they have been of the Protestant gentry class, often holding official positions: thus Henry Pyne was one of the commissioners appointed to survey the property in Co. Tipperary to be allotted to Royalist officers after the Restoration; Henry Pyne was a Poll-Money Commissioner for Co. Cork in 1660 and 1661 and in the next generation Chief Justice Sir Richard Pyne was a prominent figure in the administration. Many also appear in the army lists, though not in that of James II. Some 20 Pyne wills, nearly all in counties Cork and Clare, are recorded, but the originals of these were for the most part lost in the destruction of the Public Record Office in 1922.

The name Fyan, with its variants Fynes and Foynes, is dealt with earlier in this volume.

QUALTER   This name is a curtailed form of the MacWalter in use in north Galway and Mayo. It is a branch of the de Burgo or Burke group. MacWalter was also found in connexion with other great Hiberno-Norman families, e.g. the Butlers, but does not appear to have persisted as a surname except in Connacht. O'Calter, found in the Armagh Manor-court Rolls of 1625-27, is not to be equated with Qualter, but is a variant of O'Colter. Qualter, similarly derived, is also a Manx name where it normally takes the form Qualtrough.

(O) QUANE, Quaine   (Mac) QUAN   Quane, alias Quain(e), Quan etc., has for several centuries been principally identified with east Munster – Co. Waterford, east Cork and south Tipperary. By origin, however, it appears to belong to Co. Sligo: at any rate O'Donovan in his notes to The Tribes and Customs of Hy Fiachrach says that Ó Cuain (anglicized as Quaine and occasionally Quaid) was the name of a sept located at Dooncoy in the parish of Templeboy. Here it may be observed that in the "census" of 1659 MacQuan appears as one of the principal names in Co. Monaghan; but since Quan when synonymous with Quane is an O name, and having regard to O'Donovan's observation on the interchangeable use of Quane and Quaid it may be presumed that this MacQuan should be equated with the Monaghan sept of MacQuaid. In this connexion reference should be made to the name Qua. This occurs in the Co. Armagh Hearth Money Rolls of the 1660's, and Mr. George Paterson, curator of the Armagh County Museum, tells me that there are still families called Qua in the parish of Lough-gilly.

In the Fiants it is sometimes difficult to distinguish between Quane and Quin, several of the entries being spelt O'Quene and O'Queyne. These, however, usually represent the name now called Quin or Quinn, the pronunciation and spelling Quain being a comparatively modern innovation; and those which are unmistakably Quane in the sixteenth century Fiants and Inquisitions relate with one exception to places in or near Co. Waterford, as do most of the few other references I have noticed of a later date e.g. a number of wills proved in the diocese of Waterford between 1699 and 1758 in the names of Quan, Quean, Quane and Quoan.

There is a place called Templequain in the parish of Rathdowney, Co. Leix: this is not derived from the surname Ó Cuain but denotes "the church of St. Cuan".

The best known persons of the name were nearly all born in Co. Cork. Three were medical men: Dr. Jones Quain (1796-1865), author of Elements of Anatomy, a standard text-book; his brother Richard Quain (1800-1887) and near relative Sir Richard Quain (1816-1892) equally distinguished medical authors and practitioners; also Sir John Richard Quain (1816-1898), the judge. William Quain (1851-1896), Dublin-born American judge, was a founder-member of the Theosophical Society.

(Mac) QUEALE   Except by people who favour an English accent this name is pronounced Quail and indeed is usually so spelt, Quayle also being used as a variant. It is generally regarded as of Manx origin (Manx being one of the Gaelic linguistic group) and is Mac Fhail in that language – i.e. son of Paul. It is found today chiefly in Dublin and Belfast. In the records of the former it appears intermittently from the end of the sixteenth century: in 1583, for example, John Quell was warden of the Carpenters Guild and somewhat later Patrick Quayle was a foundation member of the Guild of St. Patrick (the Coopers), while others of the name occur in seventeenth century Dublin church and trade archives. In Ulster the first reference I have noted is to Thomas Quayle, occupying tenant at White Abbey, Co. Antrim, in 1670. Mac Fhail does not seem to have been used as the Gaelic form in Ireland and the question arises whether our Queales and Quails are immigrants from the Isle of Man or of earlier Irish stock. It is not improbable in the case of Queale families who trace their background to Connacht, that this name is an anglicized form of Mac Céile (see MacHale in 'Irish Families, p. 170).

In the Composition Book of Connacht compiled in 1585, considerable space is devoted to MacKeally Chief of His Name, the territory of which he was lord being in Co. Leitrim. In 1635, when Strafford's Inquisition of Co. Mayo was taken, three MacKeales were returned as landholders in the barony of Tirawley.

Some of the persons called MacCaell, MacKaill and similar variants mentioned in the sixteenth century Chancery Rolls and Fiants were of north Connacht (Mayo, Roscommon and Leitrim); others were associated with midland counties. Very few similar names with the pre-fix O are to be found there or in other mediaeval and early modern sources. O'Kaill appears occasionally but usually in south and east Leinster where they are probably of a family of Ó Caollaidhe (see Queally). Keal, Kayle etc., also occur both in Connacht and Leinster, while there was a Keayle at Kinsale in 1712, but these are only isolated instances. Except when used as an abbreviated form of Queally, Queale is quite definitely a Mac not an O name; and in this connexion it may be observed that there are families called MacQuail extant in Ireland today.

O'Kaill and variants also occur a few times in the Hearth Money Rolls (1663-1666) for several Ulster counties.

(O) QUEALLY, Kealy, Kiely   Much confusion is inevitable in regard to the names Kealy, Keeley, Kiely, Keily and Queally. The birth registrations in 1890 for these names combined amounted to 110, Keily and Kiely accounting for 46 (chiefly in counties Waterford, Limerick and Cork), Keeley for 36 (chiefly counties Galway and Wicklow), and Kealy for 18 in Co. Kilkenny; the form Queally is used in Co. Waterford. In 1659 Quelly and O'Quelly were enumerated as principal names in Co. Clare – the celebrated Dr. Malechy O'Queally, Archbishop of Tuam, was of that sept. The various forms beginning with K were then numerous in counties Limerick and Tipperary and in the midland counties of Leinster. The Keeleys of Co. Galway are probably of the sept Ó Caella in Irish, but possibly Ó Cadhla: Ó Cadhla, called O'Kealy by Hardiman in his notes to O'Flaherty's book Iar-Connaught was chief of Connemara up to the time of the Anglo-Norman invasion of Connacht. Dr Lynch in his Cambrensis Eversus gives "Ó Cadhla sive Quaelly". Hardiman says that the Co. Waterford name Kyley (i.e. Kiely today) is of another race and sept, Ó Caella in Irish, but that notable worker in the Gaelic revival, Patrick O'Kiely from Ring (d. 1948), always wrote his name Ó Cadhla. In the Ormond Deeds, in which these names appear frequently in different spellings, O'Kyally occurs in Co. Tipperary while members of the Kilkenny sept are called Kaaly, O'Kaylly, O'Kealy, O'Kaille etc., which are presumably Ó Caollaidhe in modern Irish. As already mentioned in Irish Families, Kealy in counties Kilkenny and Leix has tended to become absorbed in the ubiquitous Kelly (O'Kelly was in fact one of the Seven Septs of Leix). Examples of this will be found in Vol. IV of Carrigan's History of the Diocese of Ossory.

(O) QUIGG, Fivey, Twigley   The name Fivey presents a remarkable example of the absurd pseudo-translations which have disguised some fine Gaelic-Irish surnames. I am informed by Fr. Ó Gallochair that in the case of Fivey this arose from the fancied resemblance of the Coig in Ó Coigligh to the word cúig (i.e. the numeral five). Ó Coigligh is normally anglicized Quigley. A similar statement regarding Fivey is made by Padraig MacGiolla Domhnaigh in his Some Anglicized Surnames in Ireland: he adds that Quigg, Twigg and Twigley are also anglicized forms of Quigley, and mentions that there are three septs of the name in Ulster — located in Inishowen, Co. Donegal, in Loughinsholin, Co. Derry, and in south Monaghan. Quigg and O'Quigg occur quite frequently in the seventeenth century Hearth Money Rolls for counties Derry and Antrim; and it appears from birth registrations that these abbreviations are still fairly widespread in Co. Derry and adjacent areas. O'Quig is listed as a "principal name" in the "census" of 1659. It is not unknown also as a Mac name: one James MacQuigge, whom the writer of a Gaelic manuscript now in the British Museum describes as a "vulgar pedant", was notorious in Ulster about the year 1815. In the form of Fivey the name belongs principally to Co. Down. Those who adopted it appear to have been well-to-do in the eighteenth century; three, all born in that county (the earliest in 1761) were students of Dublin University; and two relevant Prerogative wills may be mentioned, those of Thomas Fivey of Loughbrickland, Co. Down (1767) and William Fivey of Dublin (1775).

Fives, a surname found in counties Waterford and Cork, is, I think, of English origin, probably an abbreviation of Fiveash.

Mac QUIGGIN, MacGuiggin, MacGuigan   The form MacGuiggin is now much more numerous than MacQuiggin, though the latter was the usual variant in the sixteenth century when the anglicization of Irish names became general for official purposes. As such it appears several times in the Fiants in counties Fermanagh, Down and Armagh and once in Co. Tyrone as O'Quiggin. It is, however, Mac Guaigín in modern Irish and is definitely not an O name. MacGoogan (also MacGookan) of Co. Antrim (MacGuagáin) is basically the same. According to Woulfe there are modern forms of MagEochaidhín (also anglicized MacGookin, MacGuckian etc.), and Mac Eochagán respectively: as the latter is normally Geoghegan I am reluctant to endorse that statement. True MacGuigan and Geoghegan have been reported as interchangeable in south Down, but that is no evidence of original identity. I think in fact that having regard to the extent to which names have been corrupted in the course of time and to their many variant spellings, it is now impossible to distinguish definitely between MacGuiggin, MacGuigan, MacGuckian and their numerous variants, which are still to be found in considerable numbers in the Ulster counties mentioned above. In addition to the numerous variants beginning with G and Q the following have also been noted: Mac Wiggin, Mac Wiggan, Wigan, Fidgeon, and Pidgeon.

(O) QUILL   This name is Ó Cuill in Irish. It is that of a sept almost exclusively belonging to counties Cork and Kerry. It is not very numerous today and appears but seldom in the records. So far as seventeenth century and subsequent records are concerned this is partly accounted for by the fact that Ó Cuill has been made Woods by one of those mistranslations so common in the anglicization of Gaelic-Irish surnames: if translated at all it should be Hazel, since coll — genitive cuill — has that mean-

ing, whereas wood is coill — genitive coille — (cf. Mac-Quilly). The chief family of Ó Cuill is mentioned in An Leabhar Muimhneach in the section devoted to the pedigree of Mac Carthy Mór; MacFirbis, however, says that they are of the same stock as the O'Sullivans. In his notes to O'Dugan and O'Heerin's Topographical Poems O'Donovan tentatively identifies Ó Cuill of Kilnamanagh as the modern Quill. They were a distinguished literary family, two of whom were thought worthy of an obituary notice in the Annals, viz. Cinnfaelidh Ó Cuill, "chief poet of Munster" (d. 1048) and another Cinnfealidh Ó Cuill (or Kinealy O'Quill) who died in 1507: the latter was Chief of His Name. The one Quill in the Jacobite attainders of 1692 is described as of Dublin city.

(O) QUILTY, Kielty   As Quilty or O'Quilty this anglicized form of Ó Caoilte is a Munster name, mainly found in Co. Limerick, but also in Tipperary and Waterford, both at the present time and in the seventeenth century. As O'Kilte — no christian name, described simply as hibernicus — it appears in a Co. Limerick Justiciary Roll of 1313. Other early anglicized forms are O'Caltie and O'Kiltie. In Offaly Quilty and Kielty are found together; but for the most part Kielty is associated with counties Roscommon and Galway. In some cases Kielty has been changed to Woods in the mistaken belief that it derives from coillte (plural of coill, a wood). A similar error has resulted in Kielty becoming Small in Co. Tyrone, in this case the supposed Irish word being caol (slender). The name MacQuilty is occasionally met in Co. Antrim: I have not discovered its origin, but it is presumably unconnected with O'Quilty, but may be a case of the substitution of Mac for O.

QUINLISK   According to Woulfe, Grimes is used in west Mayo as a synonym of Quinlisk, as well as of Grehan etc., elsewhere. Quinlisk, the usual modern form, belongs to north Tipperary and Offaly; Conliss and Cunlisk are variants occasionally found in western and southern counties. The Annals of Loch Cé give the Irish form of the name as Ó Cuindlis (referring to the slaying in 1342 by the O'Concannons of the "eminent historian" Domhnall Ó Cuindlis) which, the editor W. M. Hennessy remarks in a note, is more correct than the Four Masters' form Ó Coinleasg. It appears as O Cunlis in several lists of bishops: in Lynch's De Praesulibus Hiberniae the bishop of Clonfert from 1448 to 1463 is described as "Cornelius O Cunlis alias O Ruculy sive (ut est in Annalibus Hibernicis) O Moelachlain". Murchadh Ó Cuindlis (fl. c. 1400) was the scribe of The Red Book of Munster and part of The Yellow Book of Lecan.

(Mac) QUINN, MacGuinn   There is a surname Mac-Quinn derived, like O'Quinn, from the personal name Conn (genitive Cuinn). It is rare both as MacQuinn (a Kerry name) and also as MacGuinn, the form of Mac Cuinn found in Co. Sligo and other parts of Connacht. Maghnus Mac Cuinn is mentioned in the Annals of Loch Cé among the leading men killed at the battle of Desertcreagh in 1281, which resulted in a victory for the Cenél Eoghain over the Cenél Conaill. Most of these of course were Ulsterman – O'Donnells, O'Boyles etc., but at least one prominent Connacht name – O'Flaherty – was among them.

It should be mentioned that the west Ulster name Ó Coinne, anglicized Cunnea in Co. Donegal and Conney in some other parts of Ulster, has been changed to Quinn by some Co. Donegal families, affording a good example of an uncommon surname being absorbed by a common one.

(O) QUIRKE MacGURK The name Quirke is found only in families of Munster origin: the great majority of these belong, and have belonged for many centuries, to Co. Tipperary. In the eleventh and twelfth centuries, before the Anglo-Norman invasion, the leading family of O'Quirke – Ó Cuirc in Irish – was of kingly rank, ruling as it did over a considerable territory in the barony of Clanwilliam in south-west Tipperary, then known as Muscraighe Cuirc, (Muskerry Quirke) and sometimes called Quirke's country. An early form of the name in English was O'Curk: the Archbishop of Cashel was charged in 1295 with having sheltered a robber named Murchad O'Curk (and was acquitted). Carew in 1592 calls them O'Kirke. As Quirke, Quoyrke and Cork the name is of frequent occurrence in the records of Clonmel, and there are many families of Quirke in the Co. Tipperary Hearth Money Rolls of 1664-1666.

In that century we also find them located in Connacht, for two Quirkes of Co. Galway were transplanted thence as Irish Papists under the Cromwellian régime. Quirkes were in Ormond's army in 1649 and in the Irish army of the 1670's (more than half of whom were of English birth) and again 20 years later in James II's army. The most noteworthy was the Dominican Father Thomas O'Quirke, a priest of exceptional eloquence who was chaplain-in-ordinary to the Supreme Council of the Confederation of Kilkenny. Another Dominican Father Quirke was prior of St. Saviour's, Limerick, in 1527.

Somewhat strangely, since the name is a simple one both in Irish and English, a remarkable number of synonyms have been used for Quirke. These include Oates (by mistranslation – oats in Irish is coirce), Kirk and Quick in Co. Cork, and MacCarthy in north Connacht (perhaps by reason of its southern origin). The great majority of people called Kirk or Kirke, who are numerous in Ulster but not elsewhere in Ireland, are of British stock.

MacQuirke is also found both in the Fiants and today, but this has no racial connexion with O'Quirke, being a mis-spelling of the Ulster surname MacGuirk or MacGurk. The latter is the more usual modern spelling. Woulfe states that in Irish it is Mag Cuirc or Mac Cuirc and thus philologically akin go Ó Cuirc, both, he thinks, being derived from the forename Corc (corc is a middle-Irish word meaning heart). I prefer, however, to accept Mr. T. Ó Raifeartaigh's view that MacGuirk has no philological connexion with Ó Cuirc, the spelling in the genealogies being Mac Oirc. He mentions that Ballygurk, near Magherafelt, is called Baile 'ig Oirc in Irish. He further tells me that the family, who were of the Cenél Binnigh, descended from Niall Naoighillach, were hereditary joint keepers of St. Colmcille's bell (now in Edinburgh Museum). The name appears frequently in the Hearth Money Rolls both for Co. Armagh and Co. Monaghan: it is now chiefly found in Co. Tyrone and in Belfast. The parish of Termonmahuirk of which they were erenaghs, is in the barony of Omagh, Co. Tyrone, in the extreme north-west of the arch-diocese of Armagh. The MacGuirks were hereditary tenants of the archbishop there until the property was lost in 1624 following the Plantation of Ulster. A notable member of this family, born there in 1622, was Fr. Brian MacGurk: at the age of 90 he was captured by the notorious priest-hunter Dawson and died in prison the next year. Further afield is another place the name of which commemorates the family – Carrickmacguirk, near Granard.

RACKARD This name is so well-known on account of the fame of the Rackard brothers as Wexford hurlers that it will surprise many people to learn that it is quite rare even in Co. Wexford. It is in fact a fairly modern form of MacRichard and MacRickard, which themselves began as ephemeral surnames formed from the Christian name of some member of one of the great mediaeval Irish families, in this case probably the Anglo-Irish Butlers but possibly the Kavanaghs. The name was well established in Co. Wexford at the beginning of the nineteenth century, for Griffith's Valuation lists three families in the barony of Bantry and six in the barony of Forth (two of the latter being spelt Rackward in that document) and the Tithe Applotment Books of the previous generation corroborate this.

(O) RAFTER, Raftiss, Wrafter Woulfe gives Ó Reachtabhair as the Gaelic-Irish form of this name and says that it is a variant of O'Raftery. In this, no doubt, he is right in cases where families of the name are located in Mayo and adjacent parts of Connacht. Birth indices indicate that about one-third of the people so called belong to Connacht. The other two thirds however (ignoring metropolitan Dublin whose population is made up of families originating in all four provinces) are associated with a midland area centred in Kilkenny. Though I can cite no traditional evidence for the existence of a distinct O'Rafter sept in that part of the country, there are many small septs unrecorded by the genealogists, and the existence of such a sept is much more probable than the alternative possibility that a large section of a Mayo sept migrated to Co. Kilkenny. Some evidently did move northwards to Donegal as the annals of that county contain the name O'Raghter.

Apart from a reference in a 1295 Judiciary Roll to a John Orathcor, cattle thief, whose dwelling place may have been in Co. Cork and who was probably not an O'Rafter at all, the earliest mention of the name I have found is to Thomas Raghtour, burgess of Kilkenny in 1518, of which city Thomas Raghtor was sovereign (or mayor) in 1589. It occurs also in Co. Kilkenny with the prefix O, e.g. in the person of Shane O'Raghtore, who received a "pardon" in 1597. In 1659 Rafter is recorded as a "principal Irish name" in Co. Leix, and Raghter in the barony of Kilkea, Co. Kildare, which adjoins Co. Leix, and in the same so-called census James Rafter is listed among the chief citizens of Kilkenny. Wills and other sources confirm the association of the name Rafter with Kilkenny since the seventeenth century. For example, three Rafters appear in the lists of Jacobite outlawries, two of Kilkenny city and county, one of Naas. A little later, in 1713, Ignatius Raffter, of Kilkenny city, was one of the Catholic gentlemen licensed to carry a sword, a gun and a case of pistols. In the nineteenth century Griffith's Valuation indicates that it was numerous in counties Kilkenny, Offaly and Leix, especially Kilkenny. There we find the synonym Raftiss accounting for more than a third of the 32 householders listed. This has a particular interest because it illustrates the pronunciation of the final slender R in the Irish language as it was spoken in Co. Kilkenny a century ago – a sound something between R and Z.

Though it has an English appearance in its modern anglicized forms of Rafter and Wrafter, no such indigenour English surname appears to exist and it may therefore be taken as reasonably certain that all persons in Ireland so called are of native Irish origin.

RANKIN   Though Mac Rancan was the chief of a sept in Westmeath in the thirteenth century and that name would presumably be anglicized MacRankin or Rankin, it appears to be obsolete there. Rankin is a numerous name in Derry and adjacent counties. There it is of Scotch origin, Rankin being a branch of the Clan Maclean of Coll. The name appears in the records of the early seventeenth century Plantation of Ulster in the parish of Artea, Co. Tyrone, and an Inquisition of 1629 shows that one William Rankin was in possession of land at Magherybeg, Co. Donegal, at that date. In the Hearth Money Rolls later in the century (1663-69) there are five of the name in those for Co. Antrim, five in Co. Donegal and two in Co. Derry, but none in Co. Tyrone. The name Rankin is formed from the diminutive of the Christian name Randolph.

(O) RATIGAN   The above is the usual spelling of this name: other forms are Rattigan, Ractigan, Ratican, Rattican and Rhatigan. The accepted Irish form is Ó Reachtagáin, – cf. the Gaelic poetess Máire Ní Reachtagáin (d. 1733) – but in the Irish charters copied into the Book of Kells (printed in the Miscellany of the Irish Archaeological Society) it appears twice as a Mac name – Mac Rechtogain and Mac Rectacan – which O'Donovan in his notes thereto says is anglicized Rattigan. These charters are of the 12th century but the probability is that Mac Ratigan had already become a hereditary surname. However, by the sixteenth century it was definitely an O name as the Tudor Fiants show. It so appears also in the Four Masters (for A.D. 1488).

This family were coarbs of St. Finnen in the parish of Clooncraff (Co. Roscommon). This lies between Elphin and Athlone. Testing their modern location by birth registrations of the second half of the last century I find it to be an area centred at Clooncraff and spreading into the adjoining counties of Galway, Mayo and Westmeath. It may be of some interest to mention that the number of Ratigan etc. births in 1865 was 26; in 1890 it was 9. Map

RAWLEY, Raleigh   From before the year 1600 the Rawleys of Co. Limerick appear frequently in such records as the Fiants, and as the majority of these are described as of Rawleystown, it must be assumed that they were well established there at that date – Rawleystown, I may add, was also called Ballynrawley. Even then the family name was sometimes given as Raleigh, which is now the usual form there. About the same time Richard and G. Raleigh, stated to be English descent, acquired a considerable property from the Fittons in the parish of Knockainy, which, like Rawleystown, is near Kilmallock, in the barony of Smallcounty, Co. Limerick. If the name de Ralleye can be accepted as a mediaeval form of Rawley it was at Knockainy as early as 1307, as we know from the report of a law case in the Justiciary Rolls. Rawley appears in the "census" of 1659 as a principal Irish name in that barony with eleven families, while in the same document one Garrett Ralagh is listed as a titulado in the neighbouring Co. Limerick barony of Owney. There are some Raleighs in the Hearth Money Rolls for Co. Tipperary (1665). Rawleys and Rawleighs, too, are to be found among the testators in Limerick and also in Cashel wills of the seventeenth and eighteenth centuries, for the family spread into Co. Tipperary. Today they are mainly found in Co. Limerick. It would appear that in the early years of their association with Ireland the Rawleys were established also in Leinster, for Daniel Rawley of Tullaghanemore, Queen's Co. (Leix), was transplanted as an Irish papist in 1657 and then obtained 200 acres in Connacht; and as early as 1597 we find another Daniel Rawley among a number of Co. Kildare Irishmen who obtained "pardons". It is of interest to note that this man was given the alias of Donell O'Rhawley, which would suggest that his family was not of English descent at all or else that the official who compiled the list made a not very uncommon error.

(Mac) REA, Ray, MacCrea   WRAY, Ray   It has

already been mentioned in Irish Families (p. 165) that Rea is used as an abbreviation of MacRea, which has long been more often written MacCrea. This is the Scottish form of our Mac Raith, usually Mag Raith in Irish and anglicized in Ireland as MacGrath or Magrath. As the name Rea is now much more common in Antrim and Down than elsewhere in Ireland it is probable that most of our Reas are Scottish in origin. However, they are not newcomers, for the place-name Ballymacrea (bar. Dunluce, Co. Antrim) and an occasional mention in the Fiants (1600-1601) prove that they were established there before the Plantation of Ulster — which in any case did not include Antrim and Down. At the same time it must be recalled that there were Ulster Plantation settlers called Rea in Co. Cavan.

Rea can also be an abbreviated form of Reagh (spelt also Reaugh, Reogh, Reigh etc., in mediaeval documents). This, like Roe, Bane, Begg etc., is an epithet (Riabhach i.e. swarthy or grizzled) which superseded a surname. That being so it is only to be expected that it should be found in widely separated places, the greatest number being in the Kilkenny-Wexford area and in Co. Cork.

In Co. Cork and Co. Limerick we get O'Rea (with variants O'Ree, O'Ria, O'Reigh) frequently occurring in the Fiants of 1550-1600 and figuring as a principal Irish name in the barony of Owney, Co. Limerick in 1659. This is presumably Ó Riabhaigh, formed from the adjective riabhach referred to above. The Irish name Rea is sometimes phonetically written Ray.

The Rhea family in America, of whom Congressman John Rhea (1753-1832) was the best known, came from Co. Donegal. Rheatown and Rhea County, Tennessee, are named after them.

Then again there is the surname Wray. This is occacionally, like Ray, used as a synonym of Rea, but in Ulster there is a well known family of Wray, with branches in counties Donegal, Derry and Antrim, who came from Yorkshire as Elizabethan settlers some time before the Plantation of Ulster was contemplated.

According to Reaney, Rae is a Scottish form of Roe. Ray (also written Rea) as an English name is formed from atte rea, i.e. at or near a stream. As Ray the name is on record in Ireland in 1392 when John Ray of Rayestown, Co. Meath, was a party to the transfer of land.

Thomas Matthew Ray (1801-1881), secretary to O'Connell's Repeal Association, was born, lived and died in Dublin.   Bibl.

REAP, Reapy   These are variants of the same surname, Reap being the more usual form. It belongs exclusively to Co. Mayo (Ballina and Claremorris), while Reapy is found also in Co. Galway. Reap is pronounced Rape and occasionally so spelt. I have not been able to discover the form in Irish: Ó Reabaigh has been suggested.

(O) REDDAN   Reddan (Ó Rodáin in Irish) is certainly a Clare name by origin: in mediaeval times O'Reddans officiated as stewards to the Dalcassian chiefs O'Brien and MacNamara. Until the upheavals of the seventeenth century they were in possession of considerable estates

in the parish of Kilfinaghta in east Clare. On a tombstone there, dated 1619, the name in the Latin inscription is written Rodan, while in an Inquisition of the previous year it is O'Ruddan. In a deed of 1542 relating to the same part of the county one of the witnesses is O'Brien's steward, O'Rodan. In 1661 we find O'Ruddanes in the neighbouring parish of Quin side by side with their relatives the MacLysaghts, on whose present land, not far away, there is a Reddan's Quay.

The name is well known in our own time in literary and legal circles in Dublin where it is spelt Reddin. I asked one of this family were they from Co. Clare or from Donegal — where O'Rodans were numerous (in the barony of Inishowen) at the time of the 1659 "census" — but was told that they have been in the city of Dublin for give generations and have traced no further back. Daniel Reddin, who was concerned in the rescue of Allen, Larkin and O'Brien at Manchester in 1867, was a Dublin man. The association with Leinster is evidently of long standing: there was a Reddan family of Co. Leix from whom no doubt the place Reddanswalk was named and Fr Peter Redan, S.J. (1607-1651), the learned author, was born in Co. Meath.

It should be stated that Reddan is not used as a synonym of Redehan which is quite distinct from it.   Map

(O) REIDY MULREADY   Members of the Dalcassian sept of Ó Riada are to be found in considerable numbers in all the three counties of west Munster, particularly Clare and Kerry; in 1659 the "census" enumerators found them chiefly in counties Kerry and Limerick. The Four Masters under date 1129 describe the chief of the sept as king of Aradh, a designation applied to the O'Donegans up to 1100 and to O'Brien in the fifteenth century.

Matheson states that in 1890 Reidy occurred in birth registrations as a synonym of Roddy (q.v.), though there is no relation between the names. Reidy, however, does not appear ever to have been treated as interchangeable with Reddy or as an abbreviation of Mulready, which is a rare name belonging to a sept of the Uí Maine, located in the southern part of Co. Roscommon bordering that part of east Galway known as Keogh's country, from which in fact they were gradually displaced by the MacKeoghs. They are still to be found in that part of Connacht and in Co. Clare. William Mulready (1786-1863), famous painter and designer of the first postage envelope, was born in Ennis.   Map

(O) RENEHAN, Ronaghan   This is an O name, Ó Reannacháin in Irish, but in English the prefix was dropped at an exceptionally early date: not only does it appear (as Ronaghan) in the 1659 "census", where it is given among the principal Irish names in the barony of Tiranny, Co. Armagh, but in the Fiants nearly a century earlier, in which Renaghan of Carlingford, Co. Louth, appears, the O is also missing. It is a rare name today, but there are Renehans in Co. Cork and a few other places and Ronaghans in Co. Monaghan.

Rev. Dr. Lawrence Renehan (1797-1857), a Tipperary man, was President of Maynooth College and author of a standard work in Irish church history: he was the donor of the Renehan collection of manuscripts to that college.

The use of Ferns or Feerons as a synonym of Renehan has been recorded in Co. Offaly – a case of mis-translation: raithneach means fern. Fern, however, is an occasional synonym of Ferran (Ó Fearáin) q.v.

REVILLE   There was a Roger Rivel in Co. Kilkenny in 1305 and in 1544 Pyers Revell was one of the kern in Lord Power's muster for service in England. But the name does not appear in Irish records with any frequency until the seventeenth century when it begins to occur regularly in Co. Wexford. By 1659 it was sufficiently established and numerous enough there to be returned in the so called census of that date as a principal Irish name in the barony of Bargy. Two centuries later it was still definitely of Co. Wexford: Griffith's Valuation lists over 40 families in the county, but they had ceased then to be concentrated in the one barony. Though Reville can thus be regarded as a naturalized Irish surname, it is still far more common in England: Marshall in his bibliography of family history lists works on Revells in five different English counties and also in Wales. Three different derivations of the name are given by Reaney and Weekley: Latin rebellus, whence French revel and font-name Revel; a reveller; and French place-name Rievaulx. As a surname in France it is Réville, cf. Albert Réville (1826-1900), the Protestant theological writer.

RIDGE   It is not claimed that this is an anglicized form of any Gaelic-Irish surname: even if Woulfe is correct in suggesting that it is an attempted translation of Mac Iomaire it is not Gaelic, since, as Woulfe points out, Mac-Iomaire is merely an attempted gaelicization of Montgomery. Nevertheless, it is remarkable that Ridge is almost entirely confined to Co. Galway or areas adjacent thereto. I have consulted the birth registrations for several different years in the past century and in every case all the births occurred in Co. Galway, chiefly in Connemara. One is almost forced to the conclusion that this is one of those rare cases where the descendants of one or two settlers so multiplied as to become quite numerous in a comparatively small area in the course of three centuries. This is known to have happened in the case of Gorham in Co. Galway, where, however, it has been for a considerably longer period than Ridge.

John Ridge, presumably an Englishman, was clerk of the council, Connacht Presidency, in 1619. Strafford's Inquisition of Co. Mayo records the purchase in 1652 by a John Ridge "esquire" of a large property in the barony of Kilmaine from Viscount Mayo. In 1641 the will of another John Ridge, of Abbeytown, Co. Roscommon, was proved: this is perhaps the same John Ridge who is listed among the Co. Sligo proprietors of 1633-36 as an extensive landholder. And yet another John Ridge is recorded in the Dunsandle rentals as lessee in 1689 of 310 acres in the barony of Leitrim, Co. Galway. The name continues to appear in later records but is less prominent after the end of the seventeenth century.

RIDGEWAY   This name came to Ireland in the person of Sir Thomas Ridgeway (d. 1631), later first Earl of Londonderry, who came of an old Devonshire family. He was a member of the Council of Ireland in 1606 and took a very active part in the organization of the Plantation of Ulster: he obtained for himself 2,000 acres in Co. Tyrone and a relative also acquired a large estate in Co. Cavan at the same time. His nephew, Capt. John Ridgeway was very prominent in opposition to the 1641 insurgents. As an Ulster family they died out, but a younger branch settled in Queen's Co. in the seventeenth century. Two of these appear in the "census" of 1659 as tituladoes in Kilkenny city. They later became influential in Waterford – an interesting account of the very extensive export trade of Henry Ridgeway from that port for the year 1792 will be found in Analecta Hibernica, No. 15 (p. 376). The name is not at all numerous but is still found in counties Dublin, Leix (Queens Co.) and Cork. Sir William Ridgeway (1852-1926), archaeologist and scholar, and William Ridgeway LL.D. (1765-1817), author of State Trials in Ireland, were two men of distinction.

(O) RIGNEY, Reaney, (Mac) Reyney   RAINEY
The origin and location of Rigney can be definitely stated. In Irish it is Ó Raigne and it is almost exclusively confined to families belonging to Co. Offaly, where the sept was associated with that of MacCoghlan in the barony of Garrycastle. This form Ó Raigne is undoubtedly a variant of Ó Raighne, which is mentioned by the Four Masters as of Garrycastle in 1542, and all the relevant Fiants from that date till the end of the century relate to the same county. At that time the name also occurs with the prefix Mac as MacRegnie and MacCrayney. Father Paul Walsh accepts O'Donovan's derivation of the place-name Clonyrina (in the barony of Rathconrath) as Cluain Uí Raighne, i.e. Reaney's or Rigney's meadow. Reaney does not seem to have been adopted as an anglicized form of the name in the Offaly-Westmeath area, but it is usual in Co. Mayo where the G in this name is always aspirated. Reaney is also a Yorkshire name – it is now wrongly pronounced Reeney there, we are told by P.H. Reaney, the author of A Dictionary of British Surnames. He differentiates it from Rainey (equated with Rennie) which, like Ó Raighne, derives from a form of the Christian name Reynold. Rainey is Scottish and is very numerous in the two north-eastern counties of Ulster.

(O) RING   WRENN   Rinn, Rynn, Reen and also Wrenn are other variants of the Irish Ó Rinn. This is the name of two distinct septs whose present day descendants are still to be found in the territories occupied by them in the Gaelic period. Neither is now very numerous, but that of the barony of Imokilly in east Cork accounts for 75 per cent of people of the name. Imokilly is the anglicized form of Uí Macaille, a tribe or population group of which the O'Rinns were a branch.

Members of minor septs do no appear frequently in official mediaeval records until the time of Henry VIII and Elizabeth I when the Fiants covered the whole country. Prior to that the Anglo-Norman jurisdiciton at

181

its zenith extended over only half the country and scarcely touched more than the fringe of Ulster. A curious case is recorded in the Justiciary Rolls of 1307 for Co. Cork: Elena Ryng with a number of men was convicted of having castrated a cleric called Stephen O'Regan for continuous intercourse with the wife of a man absent in military service. The name occurs in those rolls of that period in Co. Cork, but does not appear in Co. Roscommon until the sixteenth century, though from native sources it is known to have been there from an early date.

There is a place-name Rynn in the parish of Mohill Co. Leitrim, and the surname Rynn has been found there. The English surname Wren or Wrenn is derived simply from the bird. The Wrenns of Litter, Ballylongford, Co. Kerry were settlers from England: they claimed close relationship to Sir Christopher Wren, the famous architect.

In our own time the name Ring is very familiar to all who follow our native games, as Christy Ring of Co. Cork for many years had an almost fabulous reputation as a brilliant hurler. See Rynne.

RINGROSE   The tradition in this family is that the name was originally Rose and that in 1560 Queen Elizabeth presented a ring to Richard Rose of Hampshire or Dorset as a reward for distinguished military service, as a result of which the surname became Ringrose. Weekley offers a less romantic derivation, viz., Ringroe, wroe from Middle-English wra meaning a nook or corner. Both he and Bardsley describe Ringrose as a Yorkshire name. Whatever its origin in England may be it is on record in Ireland since the seventeenth century and closely associated with east Clare. The first Ringrose to settle there was Col. Richard who was well over 100 years old when he died in 1707: he is said to have been the grandson of the Elizabethan soldier. He is described as of Mynoe (near Scariff), Co. Clare, and there are quite a number of references to Ringroses in that area in wills, leases, rentals, etc., from the year 1699 onwards though it is rare there now.

That remarkable character Basil Ringrose (d. 1686), who was both buccaneer and author, was an Englishman. A young Irishman of the name, Comdt. Ringrose of the Irish army, attained fame as an outstanding performer in international jumping contests.

(O) RODDY, Ruddy, Redehan   (O) REDDY REID Though dissimilar in those anglicized forms, Roddy and Redehan are basically the same name – Ó Rodocháin, the earliest form becoming abbreviated to Ó Rodaigh in Leitrim and attenuated to Ó Roideacháin in Mayo. In the latter county the variant Ruddy is also quite usual today. Reddington, more usually for Mulderrig, has superseded Redahan in some parts of Connacht. O'Rody seems to have been more usual than O'Rodahan at the end of the sixteenth century. As O'Rody it is familiar to students of the seventeenth century in the person of Tadhg O'Rody, who in 1683 contributed the description of Co. Leitrim to the Dublin Society's chorographical survey. He was of the family which had for centuries been coarbs of St. Cullen of Fenagh, one of whom, another Tadhg, was prominent in that capacity in 1515, as we learn from the Book of Fenagh. The same source tells us that he called himself O'Rodachae, the eponymous ancestor being Rodachae. There is a townland called Tir Roddy in the parish of Taughboyne, Co. Donegal, named from a family of O'Roddy who were erenaghs there. Canon Maguire in his book Diocese of Raphoe describes them as a leading sept of the Uí Bhreasail branch of Muintir Banna (son of Niall of the Nine Hostages). If that is correct they are distinct from the Leitrim O'Roddys: from them, no doubt, stem the Roddy and Ruddy families now located in Donegal and other parts of Ulster. The only O'Roddy in the Jacobite attainders hailed from nearby Co. Tyrone.

Apart from what has been said above it is easy to be led astray in dealing with the name Roddy, because there was a sept of the Uí Maine called Ó Rodaigh and this was sometimes attenuated to Ó Roidigh, resulting in the occasional use of Reddy as a synonym of Roddy. Reddy, however, is I think in most cases a distinct surname: it occurs in such records as the Ormond Deeds in south-east Leinster, where it is chiefly found today and where are Ballyreddy in Co. Kilkenny and Reddysland just over the county border near New Ross. Richard Reddy, who was outlawed in 1659, was a Jacobite of some note: he is described as of Kilkenny city. John Reddy, who was hanged in 1750, was the man who initiated the famous James Freney into the Kellymount gang as a highwayman. Rede, however, which is the Norman le Rede (the Red) and modern Reid must not be confused with O'Reddy. The English name Reid or Reade is very numerous in Ulster, when not that of a settler family in Ireland it is used as a synonym, but semi-translation, of Mulderrig (dearg, red).

ROE, Rowe   ORMOND   MacENROE   The surnames Roe and Rowe are now fairly numerous: in the year 1890 there were 42 births registered, 21 for Roe and 21 for Rowe, two-thirds of them in each case being in Leinster; the three years 1864-1866 averaged 60 (37 Roe, 23 Rowe) with a similar Leinster preponderance. By way of comparison we may take the following ten names having a similar birth rate – Bergin, Bermingham, Cusack, Dinneen, Gormley, Grogan, Lawless, Quirke, Scannell, Tuohy, while another ten, taken again almost at random, had just half the foregoing – Bannon, Brett, Dowdall, Fitzmaurice, Gaynor, Lanigan, Moylan, Nash, Tynan, Woulfe. While not to be classed as rare these numbers are samll compared with say, Murphy 1386 or (O) Sullivan 975. If we turn now to the returns for 1659 (which, of course, cannot be regarded as having the accuracy of modern statistics but are of great value when only an approximation is required) we find the name – spelt Roe, Rowe, Ruoe – extremely numerous in Co. Cork, especially in the baronies of East and West Carbery, and also in counties Limerick, Tipperary, Kilkenny, Kildare, Meath, Carlow and Wexford. A curious equation appears in the 1659 "census" for East Carbery, Co. Cork, where Buoige and Dinane are included in the Roe total. Possibly this was a clerical error. The 1665 Hearth Money Rolls for Co. Tipperary include no fewer than 60 householders of the name. The chief reason for the subsequent diminution was that even as late as the seventeenth century Roe was not as a rule a true surname: it was an epithet (cf. O'Conor Roe) like Reagh, Oge, Bane etc., which Petty's enumerators treated as a surname. Nevertheless it has been perpetuated as such in a number of cases. It must be remembered, too, that Rowe and Roe are also indigenous surnames in England, occasionally brought to Ireland by settlers at various times. Fynes Moryson, for example, mentions a Capt. Roe who commanded Elizabeth's troops in Co. Louth.

The old Gaelic-Irish surname Ó Ruaidh was at first anglicized O'Rooe etc.: this belongs to west Waterford and east Cork and so appears in sixteenth century records such as the Fiants, but it has since been corrupted to Ormond — Ormond, i.e. east Munster, (Urmhumhan in Irish), formerly embraced the greater part of Co. Kilkenny and it is merely a coincidence that the name Roe is associated chiefly with that area. It is found there at least as early as 1348 when landholders of the name are recorded at Knocktopher, Co. Kilkenny, while in 1375 Adam and David Rowe were parliamentary collectors for Kilkenny.

Another name which is sometimes abbreviated to Roe is Mac Conrubha, normally modernized as MacEnroe. This is the name of a Breffny sept in counties Leitrim and Cavan.

An interesting character of the early seventeenth century was Sir Thomas Roe, under whom the first Irish settlement in America was made in 1612 — it was later dispersed. I do not know his origin. Four eighteenth and nineteenth century alumni of Trinity College, Dublin, are noteworthy: two were clergymen, viz., Rev. Peter Roe (1778-1842), a famous preacher, and Rev. Richard Roe (1765-1853), a pioneer in stenography; and two were medical men, viz., George Hamilton Roe (1795-1873), who made his reputation as a physician in London, and Samuel Black Roe (1830-1913), a celebrated army surgeon who was twice sheriff of his native Co. Cavan — the others were from counties Wexford and Leix. Another notable surgeon, not of T.C.D. but of Queen's College, Galway, was Dr. William Roe (1841-1892).

Of the three great distiller families of Dublin, Power, Jamesoon and Roe, the last named may be mantioned here on account of the fact that a large part of the fortune they made, when the distilling of Irish whiskey was more profitable than it is in this competitive age, was spent on the restoration of Christ Church Cathedral, as the Guinness family devoted theirs to a similar purpose on the other Cathedral, St Patrick's. The Jameson family was of Clacmannan, Scotland, and came to Ireland in the mid-eighteenth century. Guinness and Power were treated of in Irish Families.   Map

(O) RONAN, Ronayne   Historically there were several small septs of Ó Rónáin. By the sixteenth century all but one of these were displaced and their surviving representatives scattered. In Co. Dublin they were erenaghs of Clondalkin and were landholders in that area up to the end of the thirteenth century. Thomas O'Ronan, Abbot of Ballintubber in 1416, was no doubt of the Uí Fiachrach sept, and so possibly was the family of Floskagh, Dunmore, Co. Galway. John Ronan, an officer in Tyrone's regiment of James II's army, was probably of the midland sept whose head was a chieftain in the barony of Granard until dispossessed by the O'Farrells in the thirteenth century. John O'Donovan says that in his time (about a century ago) they were unknown there.

The only one now at all numerous in its original habitat is that of Co. Waterford and east Cork. In Decies and Coshmore & Coshbride, the two Co. Waterford baronies contiguous to Co. Cork, Ronane was one of the principal names in the 1659 "census"; the location of the majority of the name in the Elizabethan Fiants corroborates this, as do the 1666 Hearth Money Rolls of south Tipperary; and the seven Ronans outlawed as Jacobites a generation later were all from counties Cork and Waterford. The most notable person of the name, Joseph Philip Ronayne (1822-1876) M.P., Young Irelander, railway engineer and wit, was a Co. Cork man, as was Judge Stephen Ronan (1848-1925). The see of Ardfert was twice occupied by an O'Ronan.   Bibl., Map

(O) ROONEEN   This has several variants, viz., Ruineen, Runian, Roonian, Roonien, and has also, as was inevitable, been much absorbed by the better known Rooney. Under all these forms Ó Ruanaidhín belongs almost exclusively to the area lying between Manorhamilton, Co. Leitrim, and Ballyshannon in the south of Co. Donegal.

ROSSITER   The Rossiters were one of the earliest families from England to be established in Ireland after the Anglo-Norman invasion; they first landed in fact in 1170. They came from Rawcester or Rochester in Lincolnshire — Woulfe makes a slight error in placing that village in Staffordshire — and from that time to the present day they have been identified with Co. Wexford being seldom found elsewhere — the Dublin Rossiters came to the city from Co. Wexford. In 1357 Robert Rowcester made good his claim to the advowson of Rathmacknee, Co. Wexford, claiming that the church had been built by his forbears, as was the castle of Bargy. The family was dispossessed of Rathmacknee in 1653, but the name was among the most numerous in the barony of Forth, Co. Wexford, in 1659. Among the numerous Rossiters who have held prominent positions in the county of Wexford the most notable was Michael Rossiter, Bishop of Ferns from 1698 to 1709.   Bibl., Map

(O) ROWAN   (O) RUAN, Rouine   (O) ROGAN
The name Ruane presents little difficulty; it is that of a sept of the Uí Maine (Ó Ruadháin in Irish) whose modern representatives are numerous in the Uí Maine, or Hy Many, country in east Galway. In north Connacht Ó Ruadháin, formerly Ó Ruaidhín according to O'Donovan, was the name of a distinct Uí Fiachrach sept, located around the parish of Robeen, Co. Mayo, and still there, as Ruane, when he visited the place in 1840.

William Hennessy, editor of The Annals of Loch Cé, says that Ó Ruadháin was then (1871) anglicized both as Rowan and Roughan, not mentioning Ruane. Birth registration statistics of a much later date show nearly 80 per cent of Ruanes to be in Co. Mayo and the remainder in Co. Galway, whereas the Rowans were scattered throughout the four provinces. Even in the sixteenth century this was the case, for the name under the variants Rowan, O'Rowane, O'Rowhan, O'Rowghan, O'Roan, O'Roen and O'Rwan occurs frequently in the Fiants relating to counties Clare, Galway, Cork, Kilkenny, Wexford, Wicklow, Kildare and Leix. In south-east Leinster some Rowans were a branch of the O'Morchoe sept, as witness the pardon dated 10 June 1584 to "Moriertagh O'Morchoe alias O'Rowane of Ballinvalle in the Moroes, Co. Wexford, gent." The Annals, Inquisitions and Books of Survey and Distribution all agree in placing the O'Rowans as people of property and importance in the barony of Gallen, Co. Mayo, and other contiguous territory, but eighteenth and nineteenth century sources of information make it clear that Ruane is the form finally adopted in English by most of these families.

Rowan, though now rather less numerous than Ruane, is historically a name of importance and the fact that it can be of several different origins is confusing. In addition to the two septs of Ó Ruadháin already mentioned Ó Robhacháin of Thomond has become Rowan. This small sept was never very prominent, but they are recorded as accompanying the O'Gradys in the unsuccessful attack on Ballyalla Castle in 1642, when all but one of their number were killed: they were hereditary stewards to the O'Gradys. They survive in east Clare as Rohan as well as Rowan. In west Clare and south Connacht the variant Ó Ruaidhín (Rowine, Rouine and Ruine) is not uncommon.

In addition to the many variants in the Fiants given above, O'Roghan also appears in Clare and Tipperary; in the "census" of 1659 O'Roughane is given as a principal name in the barony of Bunratty (east Clare) and Roughane in the barony of East Carbery (Co. Cork). William Roghan was conformist Chancellor of the diocese of Cashel in 1564. Woulfe states that the Rowans or Roughans of Clare were an ecclesiastical family connected with monasteries as far afield as Swords and Lismore, and the Four Masters record the death in 988 of Ó Robhacháin, successor of St. Colmcille on Iona Island, though this man lived at a time when surnames were very rarely fixed. There have certainly been a number of distinguished churchmen of the names now under consideration, such as Felix O'Ruadhain, Archbishop of Tuam, who was one of the Irish prelates at the Lateran Council in Rome in 1215; judging by the positions they occupied they were presumably of the Uí Fiachrach or Uí Maine (Connacht) septs, though occupancy of the see of Kilmacduagh could possibly point to Thomond as well as Uí Maine. In all seven different members of the sept were bishops of Connacht dioceses. Woulfe derives Ó Ruadháin from ruadh red; the surname is probably not connected with St. Ruadhan of Lorrha.

The most famous Rowans were Archibald Hamilton Rowan (1751-1834), the United Irishman, and his relative Sir William Rowan Hamilton (1805-1855), the astronomer and mathematician. A notable member of the Tralee, Co. Kerry, family was Ven. Arthur Blennerhassett Rowan (1800-1861), antiquary and genealogist; while from Antrim came two officers of the British army called Rowan who distinguished themselves in the Napoleonic wars.

Finally it should be observed that Rowan is found indigenous in England being an abbreviated form of the better known Rowantree or Rowntree. There was also the Norman Rohan and de Rohan, but it is improbable that the few mediaeval families in Ireland so named have any surviving descendants called either Rohan or Rowan. It has been suggested that William Rohane, of Moclerstown, Co. Tipperary, whose will was made in 1762, was one of these. Dr John Roan, the Protestant Bishop of Killaloe from 1675 to 1693, who was relentless in his persecution of the Catholic bishop (Dr. Molony), also spelt his name Rohan.

O'Rogan, sometimes confused with O'Roghan, has no connexion with Rowan or Ruane: it is the name (Ó Ruadhagáin in Irish) of an Oriel sept of considerable importance in the baronies of Armagh and Iveagh (Co. Down) up to the end of the twelfth century when it sank into comparative obscurity. They did not die out, however. In 1550 the O'Rogans of Kenelerte (mod. Kinelarty, Co. Down) are mentioned in a Chancery Roll. They were in Co. Westmeath in 1402, for the Annals relate that Ruaidhri Ó Ruadhagáin was attacked by the Galls (i.e. the English) there in that year. One appears in a list of the principal followers of O'Donnell in 1601; and several appear in northern Hearth Money Rolls later in that century. It is found today in all the provinces in small numbers, the majority being in Ulster.

(O) ROWLEY, Rowland   If the Connacht family of Ó Rothláin were constrained by circumstances to adopt a well known English surname as the anglicized form of theirs one would expect Roland or Rowland rather than Rowley. Rowland indeed does appear in Connacht, for example in the person of Dr. Rowland, Warden of Galway in 1597 and Bishop of Kilmacduagh; but O'Donovan in his notes to The Tribes and Customs of Hy Many, having stated that the chief of the sept, who was "not penurious of cattle", was seated in the parish of Easkey, on the east side of the river Easkey (Co. Sligo), goes on to say that its modern representatives were in his time (c. 1850) always Rowley, never Rowland. However, today one meets Rowlands as well as Rowleys in Co. Mayo. In his notes to O'Dugan's Topographical Poem, O'Donovan places the family of Ó Rothláin "now Rowley" in the parish of Kilshesnan, barony of Gallen, Co. Mayo, where in fact their chief was in early mediaeval times lord of Coolcarney. In the Annals of Loch Cé we are told that Ó Rothlain "the master" died in 1337, but his homeland is not indicated: the fact that this is not mentioned in Annals of Ulster suggests, though it does not prove, a western rather than a northern origin.

I have mentioned that Rowley is an English name. John Rowley, mayor of Derry and Ulster Plantation agent for the London Company, was of a Cheshire family, and another Rowley was the "undertaker" member for

Derry in the 1641 Parliament. Admiral Sir Joshua Rowley (c. 1730-1790) was of that family; the other notable seaman of the name, Admiral Sir Josias Rowley (1765-1842) is said to have been a Leitrim man.

The Norman name de Roleys occurs in the early Ormond Deeds, but I think that family did not survive in Ireland.

(O) ROYAN   This is a form of Ó Ruadhain (see Ruane) fairly numerous in north Connacht. The townland of Gortyroyan near Ballinasloe is Gort Uí Ruadháin in Irish, indicating that Royan was once a synonym of Ruane in the Uí Maine country also. As might be expected Royan has sometimes been altered to Ryan in Co. Mayo and Co. Roscommon.

A somewhat similar name, Ruvane, belongs almost exclusively to south Mayo. I cannot say for certain, but I suggest that it is yet another form of Ó Ruadháin.

RUSH   This name is found mainly in two widely separated areas and in these its origin is entirely different. The greater number are in the Oriel country. There it is Ó Ruis: it appears both as O'Rush and O'Ruse in the Monaghan Hearth Money Rolls of 1663-65, and as O'Rush in those of Co. Armagh. Denis Carolan Rushe, author of The History of Monaghan, says that it is Ó Fuathaigh in Irish; and it has also been stated that one of the anglicized forms of Ó Fuada (normally Foody or Swift) is Rush. If there is any basis for these statements such equations were rare. O'Ruis, on the other hand, can be supported both by the pedigree in an Lebor Gebála of Ó Rois of Oriel and by the evidence of the Hearth Money Rolls; similarly in the Fitzwilliam Accounts (1561) we find Thomas O'Rushe as official letter carrier; Tadhg O'Rushe, kern, appears in the Co. Dublin Fiants (1566); and in 1582 two husbandmen of the name are recorded in Co. Wicklow. Five different families – spelt Rush, Rushe, Ruish and Ruishe – appear in the Inquisitions for King's County (Offaly), 1623 to 1629.

The surname Rush is also found in north Connacht where it is a pseudo-translation of the Uí Fiachrach Ó Luachra; luachair is the Irish word for rush or sedge. This sept, correctly and usually anglicized as Loughry, belongs to the barony of Tireragh, Co. Sligo.

It should perhaps be added that there is an English surname Rush, but it is unlikely that many Irish Rushes are of that origin. It should be remembered that the derivation of Loughrey mentioned by Mr. T. O Raifeartaigh (in the article on Loughran, q.v.) is not the common one.

(O) RYALL, Real   Other variants of these are Riall, Ryle and Rile. As all these are almost invariably found in Munster, it is difficult to accept Woulfe's statement that this name – Ó Raghaill in Irish – is an abbreviated form of Ó Raghaille, i.e. O'Reilly, because O'Reilly is a Breffny name. If it must be equated with any other name O'Rahilly would appear more likely since it belongs to Co. Kerry as does Ryall: the census of 1901 records 21

families of the name in Co. Kerry. It occurs in one of its variant forms, always without the prefix O, in many records from the present time back to the seventeenth century – e.g. birth registrations, Griffith's Valuation, diocesan wills, Dublin University register etc., and I have not met any instances outside Munster except a few in Leix and Offaly. In the sixteenth century the O is still retained and the name is more like O'Rahilly, for it occurs in the Fiants as O'Rahill and O'Raghill (in counties Cork and Limerick). The inconsistency of spelling names at that period, due to the unfamiliarity of many recording officials with the Irish language, may lead to some confusion: O'Reile and O'Reale for example may be meant for O'Reilly but in such cases the homeland of the person in question is often a help in identification.

According to de Burgh's The Landowners of Ireland, 1878, the Rialls of Clonmel possessed extensive property in Co. Tipperary prior to the Land Acts. According to Weekley in England Ryall is an occasional derivative of Riulf (Anglo-Saxon Riewulf).

Judge Patrick Real (1847-1928) of Queensland, was born at Pallas, Co. Limerick.

RYNNE   Rynne is a Clare name. Its origin is not certain but the weight of the evidence points to it coming from Mac Bhroin of Connacht, not from Ó Rinn of Cork.

ST. LAWRENCE   The distinguished family of St. Lawrence has been in possession of, and resident at, Howth Castle, Dublin, from 1177 (when their ancestor, a comrade of the famous de Courcy, came to Ireland) until the present time, though on the death in 1909 of William Ulick St. Lawrence, 4th Earl of Howth, the property – and with it the name and arms of St Lawrence – passed to the female line which is now known as Gaisford-St Lawrence. The head of the family was first known as Lord of Howth: in 1461 they became Barons Howth and in 1767 Earls of Howth. Though from the early seventeenth century their record was for several generations consistently loyalist and Protestant, they are now prominent in the Catholic aristocracy of Ireland.

The name is also to be found among the farming community in east Clare.   Bibl.

SALMON   SAMMON   (O) BRADDEN   Though

basically distinct Sammon is sometimes found as a variant of Salmon in Connacht and Clare. There Salmon is of Gaelic-Irish origin, being an anglicization of Ó Bradáin, which is derived from the Irish word bradán meaning a salmon, and in counties Donegal and Leitrim is rendered Bradden and Bradan, and this in turn has sometimes been made Fisher in English in the Glenties district. This is not to be confused with Breadon and its variants Bredon and Breydon, which are formed from an English place-name and were first made de Brdeon. This, I think, can be equated with the Bredan given in the 1659 "census" as a "principal Irish name" in the barony of Maryborough, Queen's Co. The name Salmon is fairly numerous and is found in all the provinces. In Leinster it is mainly centred in and around Co. Leix – when Griffith's Valuation was made in 1850, there were 34 Salmon householders there and 14 in the adjacent county of Offaly. In the midlands it is often of English origin: Salmon, is a corruption of Seaman, a name which is self-explanatory. The Sammons settled in counties Kildare and Dublin before the Elizabethan influx: they are on record there at least as early as 1529. By 1659 they were so well established in Co. Kildare that Petty's enumerators ranked them as Irish in his "census". Some of the evidence I have found would suggest that they were not of Gaelic stock, but the fact that one Hugh Samon, a follower of Lord Howth in 1555, is described as alias MacYbradane, proves that some at least of the "lower orders", if not the titulado class, were Gaelic-Irish.

The best known of the name was Rev. George Salmon, D.D. (1819-1904), Provost of Dublin University and distinguished mathematician.

SANDS, Sandys   Numerically Sands (in that form) may now be regarded as predominantly an Oriel name, as such tests as birth registrations and voters' lists of Co. Armagh and adjacent areas will show. The most prominent family of the name, however, is Sandys of Co. Kerry, who claim descent from a Cromwellian officer, grantee of lands in that county about 1650, but the name was in Ireland about a century before that. One Nevill Sands of Dublin was appointed surveyor-general in Ireland in 1565; William Sandes was deputy for the clerk of check in 1588 and another William Sandes was an attorney of the Exchequer Court in 1625. Of the 37 Irish-born students of Dublin University named Sandes (19) Sandys (16) and Sands (2) at least one – John Sands – was born in Co. Westmeath thirty years before the Cromwellian family was established in Kerry. Nearly all the nineteen called Sandes were born in Co. Kerry; the earliest of this spelling, born in 1671 in Queen's Co., was a relative of the Kerry family. The synonymous form Sandys belonged mainly to Dublin though it was also in Co. Roscommon: two were high-sheriffs of Co. Roscommon in 1682 and 1788, and one of Co. Longford in 1767. The many references to this name, in one of its three forms, which are to be found in a variety of Irish records from the seventeenth to the mid-nineteenth century indicate that it was associated principally with counties Kerry, Roscommon, Leix (Queen's Co.) and Dublin, but during the past two centuries Sands has become much more numerous than its variants – this may be due to immigration from Britain to Ulster but the name was certainly there three centuries ago since it appears then in the Hearth Money Rolls for Tyrone and Antrim. The name became closely identified with Ulster when the "H-Blocks" hunger striker, Bobby Sands, died soon after being elected M.P. for Fermanagh-S. Tyrone. The statement that Sandes is an anglicized form of O'Shaughnessy may be disregarded; this belief arose from the fact that a Shaughnessy of Co. Limerick, where the name is pronounced Shannesy, called himself Sandes; but his family reverted to their true names a generation later. The origin of the name, which has of course no connexion with O'Shaughnessy, is from the Old-English sand and it denotes a dweller near the shore or a sandy place.

SAUL, Sall   This name, now usually spelt Saul and rather rare today, was formerly Sall and Sale, the latter being identical in pronunciation (cf. Wale – Wall). It was de la Salle (i.e. of the hall) in its native Normandy, and that form was used, as well as de Salle and Sal, in the earliest records we have of it in Ireland – the first I have met is 1275. From that on it is of fairly frequent occurrence, for the most part in south Tipperary and Waterford, but also in Co. Meath, where the family is listed in 1598 as among the chief gentlemen of that county and where the place-name Salestown in the parish of Dunboyne indicates their connexion therewith. A number of the references occur in Dublin city records e.g. Isaac Sale, master of the weaver's guild in 1705. The more numerous Munster branch, some of whom spread into Co. Kilkenny, were particularly associated with Cashel: there was born the best known of the name, Rev. Andrew Sall (1612-1682), rector of the Irish College at Salamanca and later Superior of the Jesuit order in Ireland, who in the last years of his life very publicly renounced the faith and joined the Church of England. This he did at Cashel, where some 30 years earlier Father James Sall O.F.M. was executed, for his refusal to do the same, by the Cromwellians in 1647. Another Franciscan, Dr. Saul of Waterford, was author of one of the earliest declarations against the doctrine of the English reformers under Henry VIII.

The order of the de la Salle Brothers has no direct connexion with the family under consideration, having been founded in France in 1680 and established in Ireland in 1875.

SAVAGE   There are many people called Savage in Ireland, the number at present being estimated at 2,500, more than half of whom are in Ulster. The great Co. Down family of Savage – Savage of the Ards – was planted there by de Courcy as early as 1177. From that time until the end of the seventeenth century they were a force in the northern province. Though at first at enmity with the native Irish and holding their possessions with difficulty, they gradually became absorbed in the Irish nation. When the Four Masters have occasion to mention the name they give it as Mac an tSabhasaigh, thus accepting it as hibernicized. (Woulfe does not mention this but gives Sabhaois and Sabháiste as the modern Gaelic forms). In 1482 Sir Roland (Janico) Savage, Lord of Lecale, was seneschal of Ulster, but twenty years later he had become one of the "English great rebels", and at the end of the century Dymmok lists Lord Savadge of the Ards among the important Ulster rebels of 1599. Ninety years later again we find no less than thirteen of them serving as officers in James II's Irish army. Most of these were in northern regiments; but not all, for branches of the family had settled in the Ormond country. The history of the family is well told in the two books mentioned in the bibliography.

Some families of Savage are of quite different origin as this surname was adopted as the anglicized form of the Gaelic Ó Sabháin, a small south Munster sept first called O'Sawan in English, which became Savin and was later changed to Savage.

It may be of interest to add that in places as far apart as Belturbet, Dundalk and Nenagh, Sage has been occasionally used as a synonym of Savage.

The poet John Savage (1828-1888), a leading United Irishman and Fenian, and Marmion Wilard Savage (1803-1872), a novelist of repute, were both born in Dublin. Bibl., Map

SCADDAN   Though this name has not been dealt with by O'Donovan, Woulfe, Matheson or any other authority on Irish surnames it is on record in this country since 1299 when an entry in the Justiciary Rolls records that one Martin Scadan was concerned in a Tipperary trespass case. One of the name was a juror in the county in 1312 and in 1314; another was pardoned at the same time for a murder for which he had been found guilty. In the Ormond deeds it occurs frequently, from the beginning of the fourteenth century, as also does the place-name Scadanstown which was in the Clonmel area: I say was, as this place is not to be found in modern lists of townlands or parishes. It is noticeable that in no instance I have met does the prefix O occur with this name; and, since in the mediaeval records O and Mac were rarely omitted from Gaelic surnames, it is probable that, notwithstanding its Irish appearance, Scaddan is not a Gaelic-Irish name. It was formerly often spelt Scadan, and scadán is the Irish word for herring, but that may be regarded as a coincidence.

SCAHILL   O'Dugan in his Topographical Poem, written about 1365, refers to Mac Sgaithghil (i.e. Mac Scahill) as "of beautiful studs" and as "over Corca Mogha" (i.e. Corcamoe) from which territory O'Donovan in his notes states the Scahills were dispossessed before 1170 by the Concannons. Corcamoe may be equated with the present parish of Kilkerrin in east Galway. Modern statistics indicate that Co. Galway and to a lesser extent Co. Mayo are still its main location, though it is not very numerous even there. The Mac prefix was in the course of time changed to O, but neither prefix is now used, the name being plain Scahill.

(O) SCALLAN   The theory that Scallan is a southern form of the Ulster name Scullin or Scullion is hardly tenable. The latter was an erenagh family of the diocese of Derry, and it is true that the northern Ó Scolláin has occasionally been anglicized as Scallon, but Scallan has always been mainly associated with Co. Wexford. In the "census" of 1659, for example, ten families of Scallan and nine of Skallan are recorded in the barony of Forth. Griffith's Valuation of two centuries later records 22 householders in that barony and 72 in the whole county.

Mac SCALLY, Skelly   MESCALL   Though fairly numerous now in counties Roscommon and Westmeath, little is known about the origin of this name. It appears as MacSkally, MacSkelly and MacScally in the Fiants of the sixteenth century in Westmeath-Longford-Roscommon area. This distribution is corroborated by the "census" of 1659. O'Skelly occurs in the Fiants in Co. Cork, but in this case it is almost certainly a variant of O'Scully. According to Woulfe, Ó Scalaidhe and Ó Scolaidhe are basically the same. Mac Scalaidhe is the Irish form of the midland MacSkelly or Skelly. Only one of the name, Bartholomew Skelly a merchant of Drogheda, appears in the Jacobite attainders of 1692 and following years. Woulfe again equates the surname Miskella with MacSkallly. I do not know what evidence he had of that; but on the other hand it is a fact that Miskella has been used as a synonym of Meskell or Mescall which is quite distinct viz: Ó Meiscill, a rare name belonging to counties Cork and Limerick.

(O) SCURRY, Scarry   There are two Irish names anglicized as above: Ó Scurra, one of the six "Sodhans" of Uí Maine, and Ó Scoireadh of counties Waterford and Kilkenny. Scarry and Scurry seem to have been used indifferently as anglicized forms in both those areas. In the latter Scarry appears quite frequently around Callan where David Scarry was a merchant in 1519 and others of the name were farmers there later in that century; Scarry is found in Waterford to-day, while the lexicographer and grammarian, whose works are in the manuscript department of the British Museum, is called James Scurry in English and a century ago Waterford births were registered as Scurry. At that time the registrations in the Uí Maine country (in Connacht) were spelt Scarry and several families so called are resident in east Galway at the present time.

SEMPLE   The obvious derivation of this name from the adjective simple is only applicable to Scottish families: in England it is a toponymic, a corruption of the French St. Pol, first called de Sancto Paulo and Seintpoule and later Sampul. It occurs as Sempill in the "census" of 1659 among the property holders in the town of Letterkenny, Co. Donegal. It is of fairly frequent occurrence in records of the provinces of Ulster from the mid-seventeenth century, but I have not met it earlier than that, except in the case of Sir James Sempil who was an official dealing with land matters in Co. Cork in 1612. It is now fairly numerous in Co. Antrim, but elsewhere scattered and rare.

SEXTON, Shasnan   Sexton, which is a common English surname, is used as the anglicized form of Ó Seasnáin. A less corrupt anglicization of it was Sisnane, which is the form found in the 1659 "census" in Co. Cork. Woulfe gives Shasnan as a synonym still extant but this is now very rare. Matheson records Tackney as a synonym in the Cootehill (Co. Cavan) area: this is not to be equated with the Kerry surname Tagney or Tangney – Ó Teangana in Irish. Sexten is given in the same 17th century "census" as one of the principal Irish names in Co. Clare, where with Limerick city, it is chiefly found to-day. The name is intimately associated with that city: eight Sextons have been mayors there, the most notable of whom was Edward Sexton (1535) arraigned as "of Irish blood and corrupt affection to traitors" (i.e. the Irish who resisted English aggression) but still a friend and favourite of Henry VIII. In 1489 the Sextons and the Galweys are recorded as responsible for repairs to St. Mary's cathedral, a part of which was known as Sexton's chapel. Capt. Sexton (whose Christian name is not given in the articles) was one of those of its defenders specially excluded from the amnesty after the siege of 1651; three of the family were officers in King James II's army. Centuries earlier the name was famous in the literary sphere in the person of Colm or Colman Ó Seasnáin (d. 1050), the Thomond poet. The notorious "discoverer" George Sexten, secretary to Lord Chichester and in 1606 escheator of Ulster, who obtained vast grants of land in the Plantation of Ulster, was, I think, an Englishman. Thomas Sexton (1848-1932) a notable orator, was one of the ablest of the Parnellite M.P.'s; he was born in Waterford.   Map

SHACKLETON   The Shackletons were one of the most notable Quaker families in Ireland. Their famous school at Ballintore, Co. Kildare, where Edmund Burke was educated, was founded by Abraham Shackleton, a native of Yorkshire, in 1726. His son Richard Shackleton and his grandson Abraham Shackleton carried on the school with success. His daughter, Mary Leadbeater (1726-1826), the author of poems and essays, left a valuable account of rural life in the eighteenth century. Sir Ernest Shackleton (1874-1922), the Antarctic explorer, was of the same Co. Kildare family.   Bibl.

(Mac) SHANLY, Ganly   The Gaelic form of this name, Mac Seanlaoich, presumably connotes son of the old hero. It occurs quite frequently in the Annals up to the fifteenth century as that of a sept located in the MacBrennan country in east Roscommon and Leitrim. The Four Masters describe Donncahy son of Murray MacShanly who died in 1404 as "a wealthy farmer of Corcoachlann (one of the three tuathas of Connacht) and chief servant of trust of the King of Connacht"; frequently also it occurs in the Fiants of the next century in Leitrim, Roscommon and Longford; and in the 1659

"census" MacShanly is one of the principal names in Co. Leitrim, where it is also most numerous today, though the prefix Mac is rarely retained now. Three Shanleys served as officers in O'Gara's regiment in King James II's Irish army and about the same time William Shanly was M.P. for Jamestown, Co. Roscommon, in the "Patriot Parliament" of 1689. Four Shanleys from east Connacht counties were outlawed as Jacobites in the following decade. Like so many other leading Catholic families the MacShanleys sank into comparative obscurity in the eighteenth century and have not since been prominent in the public life of this country. In America, Dublin-born Charles Dawson Shanly (1811-1875) had a considerable reputation as a poet.

Ballymacshanly in Co. Leitrim is named from a leading family of the sept. There the variant form Mac Sheanlaoich was also used. This was first anglicized as MacGanly, and as such appears in the 1659 "census" in considerable numbers in that part of Co. Westmeath which adjoins Co. Roscommon. Subsequently the prefix Mac was dropped and present day representatives of the sept are called Ganly (and sometimes Gantley in Connacht). Patrick Ganly (1809-1899) was a distinguished geologist who did very valuable work in connexion with Griffith's Valuation.   Map

(O) SHARKEY   Sharkey is a name now to be found located in considerable numbers in various parts of the northern half of Ireland, chiefly in counties Roscommon, Donegal, and Louth. It originated in Tyrone. As O'Serky as well as O'Sharky it appears in the seventeenth century Hearth Money Rolls of Co. Monaghan; but the prefix O, dropped in the eighteenth century, has not been resumed to any extent. It is of interest to note that the only name in the sixteenth century Fiants which can be equated with this is O'Sherkott (also written O'Skerkott) then in Co. Sligo and Co. Meath. In the form Ó Sergoid this occurs in the Annals of Loch Cé where the death of John Buidhe O'Sergoid, chief priest of Trinity Island, who was drowned in that lake in 1578, is recorded. This probable identification is corroborated by the use of Sharket as a synonym of Sharkey, as evidenced by the birth registration statistics published by Matheson at the beginning of the present century. Though now numerous, references to families of Sharkey etc. are rare in our records: it does not even appear in Petty's "census" of 1659.

The Gaelic form is Ó Searcaigh: Séamus O'Sharkey, Gaelic poet of the O'Naghten circle in the 1720s, wrote a love poem based on the fact that his surname derives from the Irish word searc (i.e. darling).

(O) SHEENAN   Woulfe equates Sheenan with Synan, but I think Sheenan must be regarded as the similar name of an entirely different sept, viz., Ó Síonáin. It has long been found in Co. Tyrone and adjacent areas. The Registrar-General's report shows that it has been to some extent absorbed by Shannon in the Clones district.

(O) SHEERAN   There are five modern spelling variants of this name, Sheeran and Sheerin being the most numerous. The information available about it is puzzling. Six Fiants between 1550 and 1600 record persons of the name O'Sherin, O'Shirine etc., all belonging to Co. Cork, while there is one O'Shearan in Leinster. Yet by 1659, when Petty's "census" was taken, O'Sheerin and O'Shearing are numerous enough in counties Fermanagh and Donegal to be classed as principal names there, and indeed one O'Sherin appears at Lifford, Co. Donegal, as early as 1608. In 1665 we find Sheeron and Sheerin in the Hearth Money Rolls for Co. Monaghan. Eighteenth century wills indicate that the name was to be found also in counties Westmeath, Limerick and Dublin, but none are from Co. Cork diocese. Similarly in the next century the statistics available place it in all the provinces except Munster – Griffith's Valuation records as many as 56 families in Queen's Co. (Leix). The obvious conclusion to be drawn from these facts is there was a sept of Ó Sírín in Co. Cork, now extinct, and another in Ulster which has spread throughout that province and into the adjacent parts of the neighbouring provinces.

Father Thomas O'Sirin O.F.M. (d. 1673) of St. Anthony's, Louvain, edited and published many valuable ecclesiastical works, including MacColgan's Acta Sanctorum and Fleming's Collectanea Sacra. Woulfe suggests that Syron or Syran may be MacSeartúin (the Gaelic patronymic of the Prendergasts in Kerry): the name Syron belongs to Co. Mayo.

(O) SHELLEY, Shally   The Irish surname Ó Sealbhaigh is usually called Shelley in English in Munster and Shally in Co. Galway where families of the name are now found. It has, however, no historic connexion with Connacht. The sept is one of the Corca Laoidhe, originally located in south-west Co. Cork and, though it had spread by the sixteenth century north-eastwards to Co. Tipperary and even counties Kilkenny and Waterford, it is with Co. Cork any distinguished persons of the name were associated. The five mediaeval O'Shelleys who were bishops of Cork are no more than mere names to us, but Augustine Ó Sealbhaigh (d. 1182) Bishop of Waterford, appears to have been a noteworthy prelate, while Domhnall Ó Sealbhaigh (d. 1140), erenagh of Cork, is the subject of particular praise by the Four Masters.

In Co. Tipperary the name was as early as the sixteenth century anglicized rather unfortunately as Shallowe. In Co. Clare it is not uncommon today as Shalloo.

Shelley is also an English name. The celebrated English poet Percy Bysshe Shelley was not of Irish ancestry.   Map

SHERLOCK   The Sherlocks are usually regarded as one of the great Anglo-Norman families which established themselves in Ireland following the invasion of 1170. The name, however, though then not yet fixed as a hereditary surname, is found in English records of a date prior to the Norman Conquest, the original Anglo-Saxon form being, according to Reaney, scir locc i.e. bright haired. Subsequent to their arrival in Ireland their history follows the normal Hiberno-Norman pattern: ac-quisition of lands, tenure of high office, gradual estrangement from England, refusal to accept Protestantism after the Reformation, loss of estates in the Cromwellian Settlement, adherence by the survivors to the Jacobite cause (twelve of them being outlawed as a result), final submergence under the Penal Code and, after Catholic Emancipation, gradual emergence from obscurity in company with, and indistinguishable except by name from, their compatriots of Gaelic-Irish origin.

References to the name in various archaic spellings such as Scherlog, Scurlok, Scurlageston (Co. Meath) etc. are very frequent in all mediaeval and early modern records relating to the Leinster counties from Louth to Kilkenny – Scurlock, indeed, is still occasionally found today: it is retained in two townlands called Scurlockstown in Co. Westmeath. There was also a distinguished branch of the family located in Co. Waterford, their seat being at Butlerstown. Of these Rev. Paul Sherlock, S.J. (1595-1646), Superior of the Irish College at Salamanca, was perhaps the most noteworthy. Others of the name worthy of individual mention are Sir John Sherlock, Ormondist commander in the Cromwellian war, Rev. Martin Sherlock (c. 1747-1797), Protestant Archdeacon of Kilkenny, who had a great reputation as a travel author, and John Sherlock, born in France of Irish parents about 1770, who took part in the Bantry Bay expedition of 1796.

SHERRARD   Several men of this name have been prominent in England, their native country. In Ireland it has been mainly associated with Co. Derry from the seventeenth century to the present day. Two Sherrards, David and William, were among the thirteen famous apprentice boys whose unofficial action led to the subsequent successful resistance of the siege of Derry in 1689.

(Mac) SHERRY, (O) Sherry, Sharry   It was stated in Irish Families, p. 17, that MacSherry (MacShiarie, MacShera etc.), was an alias of the Hodnett family, perpetuated in the place-name Courtmacsherry, Co. Cork; and also that MacShera was used as a surname by some branches of the Macgilpatrick (or Fitzpatrick) sept.

The Sherrys and MacSherrys of our own time, who are located for the most part in Monaghan and adjacent counties, do not stem from either of these sources. Like Dunleavy, Colgan and several other names of northern septs, Sherry appears both as a Mac and an O name in many records – Annals, Fiants, 1659 "census" etc. – from the twelfth to the seventeenth century, as MacSherry and O'Sherry. The sept whose chief, Giolla Pádraig Mac Seiridh, was described as King of Dal Buinne in 1130 is referred to by both forms, and it can be accepted that there was only one sept of the name in southern Ulster, located in the Oriel territory. Petty's "census" records both MacSherry and O'Sherry (with spelling variants) as numerous in counties Armagh and Monaghan, the names being treated as synonymous in the barony of Armagh. A little later we find O'Sherry only in the 1664 Hearth Money Rolls of Co. Monaghan; but in the aggregate Mac was more commonly used than O with this name. The ambiguity continued until finally the disuse of the Gaelic prefixes became general. In this connexion the reader, should he contemplate doing detailed research, is reminded that in the sixteenth century Fiants most of the MacSherrys are of Co. Cork (i.e. Hodnetts) and a few are Fitzpatricks of Ossory.

Prominent individuals of the name are mostly men of the mediaeval period, e.g. Macgrath MacSherry, Bishop of Ardagh (d. 1230). The latest in the Annals is Richard MacSherry who was killed at the battle of Muintir Eolais (Co. Leitrim) in 1473. Dr. MacSharry, Apostolic Vicar at Port Elizabeth (1896), was an outstanding Irish churchman in South Africa.

Finally we may notice the somewhat comical use of Foley as a synonym of MacSherry or MacSharry in Co. Roscommon. The name is Mac Searraigh in modern Irish and searrach, genitive searraigh, is the Irish word for a foal! This Foley has even become Feley in adjacent parts of Co. Leitrim and so might possibly be confused with Feeley (q.v. under Fehilly).   Map

SHERWIN   Woulfe equates Sherwin with Sharvin i.e. Ó Searbháin. The two names have been reported as used synonymously in Co. Dublin in quite recent times. The small sept of O'Sharvan belonged to Co. Roscommon. Sherwin is also an English name derived from the old-English sceran (to cut) and wind (wind). An Edmond Sherwine of Creenagh appears in a Co. Cavan Inquisition of 1640. At the same time we find Christopher Sherwan, of Ballyowen, Co. Dublin, yeoman, taking part in the 1641 rising. Two Sherwins were 1798 United Irishmen – one a Dublin silversmith, the other a goldsmith and pawnbroker. There are a fair number of Sherwins in Dublin to-day but elsewhere the name is rare, as also is Sharvin.

(O) SHEVLIN   Although we know from the Four Masters that the principal sept of Ó Sibhlen (now Ó Seibhleáin) was located in Offaly and was of considerable importance there prior to the Anglo-Norman invasion in the twelfth century, their descendants are no longer found in that part of the country. There was also an Uí Fiachrach sept of the name in Mayo where the name is still extant; and it is not unknown in Co. Donegal. It has a long standing association with Co. Donegal, for we meet two of the name among the followers of Hugh O'Donnell in 1601 – the spelling of the name in that Fiant is O'Syvelane and O'Shevlin is in the Hearth Money Rolls for that county (1665). It is also in those of Co. Donegal. Thirty years earlier we find it as O'Shevelan in a Co. Fermanagh Inquisition. However, the majority of Shevlins and Shevlans of modern times are located in the Oriel country, particularly around Carrickmacross in Co. Monaghan: indeed it was well established there in the seventeenth century, for it appears as O'Shevlin, O'Shevlan and O'Shavlan in the Co. Monaghan Hearth Money Rolls of 1663-65, and as Shevelin in a list of recruits to Lord Blayney's company of Col. Thomas Dongan's regiment, c. 1670, mostly from Co. Monaghan. Present day forms

are Shevlan, Shevland, Shevlane, Shevlin, Shivlin and Shovelin. The prefix O, dropped during the period of Gaelic and Catholic submergence, has not been resumed to any extent.

(O) SHINE   Apart from the fact that Woulfe gives no information about this name beyond stating that it belongs to Munster and is Ó Seighin in Irish, it is numerous enough to merit an article; I have also to correct a wrong impression which a passing reference to it would give. I referred to it as a Thomond surname. We do find it in Clare, but that is not its original nor its main location to-day, which in fact is Cork and Kerry. I do not find reference to them in the seventeenth century unless John Shyhane of Kilfinnan in the 1659 "census" may be one (it is more probably for Sheehan); but in the next century there are a number of wills recorded for people of the name in counties Cork and Kerry, and also in the eighteenth century, five Shines appear in the Kenmare estate manuscripts.

Weekley mentions a Welsh name, Shinn or Shine, but in Ireland – at any rate in Munster – this may be disregarded. Shine is definitely an Irish surname, from which the prefix O has long been dropped. Woulfe's derivation of Ó Seighin from a word meaning wild-ox is not accepted: it is probably from old-Irish seigéne, small.

SHINKWIN   (O) SHINNICK   Both these names belong to Co. Cork but in spite of a superficial resemblance they are quite distinct. Shinkwin derives from the English Jenkin which was gaelicized as Sinchín or Seinchín and this in turn was re-anglicized Shinkwin. Nevertheless it should be mentioned that the Four Masters, under date 1013, mention an anchorite called Ó Seinchinn with, however, no indication of his homeland; but if this ever became a hereditary surname it must have died out, unless it is an early form of Ó Scingin, the name of an erenagh and literary family of Ardcarne, Co. Roscommon: it is of the Uí Fiachra and has no connexion with Co. Cork – to-day it survives in Co. Cavan as Skinnion (q.v.) which according to Matheson has been changed to Delahide. Shinnick, on the other hand, is the name of a small sept of Corca Laoidhe, and Co. Cork is the only part of Ireland in which there is any considerable number of them to-day. Shinnick, too, is misleading for, the Shinnock and Shinagh and other similar variants, it has been widely used as a synonym of Fox in Connacht.

SHIPSEY   This name is very seldom found outside counties Cork and Waterford. It has been associated with Co. Cork (particularly the Skibbereen area) since the mid-eighteenth century. The first I have met is a Cork marriage licence bond of 1735. The tradition that it is derived from the two words ship, sea, spoken by a shipwrecked sailor is too far fetched for serious consideration. I think it is merely a variant of the English surname Shipside (ship - sheep, side - side of hill).

SHORTALL   Neither Bardsley nor Reaney include the name Shortall in their dictionaries of British surnames. Woulfe says that it is derived from the Anglo-Saxon scork-hals, i.e. short neck, a nickname. Woulfe says also that the Shortalls probably came to Ireland early in the reign of Edward I of England, but actually references to them in this country are to be found even earlier than that: in the Gormanston Register, for example, a Schortal of Kells is mentioned in the year 1243. The name, variously spelt Shortals, Schortals, Scortals, Scortal etc., appears in every principal record relating to Co. Kilkenny from that time onwards. The family became powerful and influential, so much so indeed that in a notarial instrument of 1532 we find James Sortals described as "captain of his nation" like any Gaelic-Irish chieftain. In 1537 an Inquisition jury reported that Lord Shortell, alias Sortall, "useth the same exactions" as the Earl of Ossory. The tomb of Shortalls, "Lord of Ballylorcan", was set up in St. Canice's Cathedral, Kilkenny, in 1507; and in 1552 James le Shortales is described in a Chancery Roll as Lord of Ballielorcan. Their principal castles were at Ballylorcan and Castle Idough. In 1659 there were 16 families of Shortall in the barony of Gowran, six in the barony of Crannagh and six in Kilkenny city. Their proportion of the population is now considerably less.

Sebastian (or Stephen) Shortall (d. 1639), Abbot of Bective, Cistercian monk and poet, was born in Co. Kilkenny.

Carrigan's History of the Diocese of Ossory gives much detailed information about the various families of Shortall in Co. Kilkenny.   Map

SHORTEN   Shorten is not an English name. Woulfe regards it as a variant of the well-known Shortall. As Shortaun it occurs in the 1642 attainders for Co. Wexford in the person, however, of a Co. Limerick man. For the past two centuries Shorten has been almost exclusively a Co. Cork name. It is now numerous there, especially in Cork city.

SIGGINS   The name is on record in Ireland since the thirteenth century but is not of Gaelic origin, being derived from the Anglo-Saxon personal name Sigen. The family is commemorated in five place-names in Co. Wexford (Sigginstown etc.), and also in the better known Jigginstown in Co. Kildare, all still extant as well as others such as Siggensmede now obsolete. It is clear from the earlier references that it was at first somewhat scattered, several of these being to Munster (including William Sygne, who was mayor of Cork in 1402), but there was a Siggins (then Sygyn) who held land in Co. Wexford as early as 1250 and it is with that county they have been mainly associated. Sigen of Sigenstown was counted among the chief gentry of Co. Wexford by Sir Arthur Chicester in 1608; fifty years later Edward Siggins, of Sigginstown, Co. Wexford, was among those transplanted under the Cromwellian regime. We know from the Civil Survey that he was an "Irish Papist" and held some land in the parish of Clonmines. Their adhesion to the old faith and consequent transplantation to

Connacht led to their extinction as members of the landed aristocracy; and the name has since become rare. Some families of Siggins, however, are still to be found in Connacht and also in Co. Kildare.

SIMMS   This has been a well known name in Ulster since the early seventeenth century. Though more numerous in Co. Antrim than elsewhere it has also a close association with east Donegal, whence comes the family of the recent Protestant archbishop of Dublin.

Several of the name were prominent United Irishmen: Robert and William Simms of Belfast were two of the founders of the Society, and Thomas Simms, a Dublin merchant, who joined in 1792, was sponsored by Oliver Bond. The name is derived from the Christian name Simon, of which Sim is a diminutive; it is thus etymologically the same as Simpson which, however, statistics show to be three times as numerous as Simms both in Great Britain and Ireland. Like Simms, Simpson is mainly found in Co. Antrim.

SINNOTT   This name is also spelt Synnott, especially by families which have migrated to Dublin from Co. Wexford. They have been in Co. Wexford since the beginning of the thirteenth century: the earliest reference I have seen is 1247, when Richard, son of John Synod, was in possession of Ballybrennan, in the barony of Forth, which remained their principal estate. Fr. Nicholas Synnot, who wrote an interesting account of the barony of Forth in 1680, enumerates 23 landed gentry of the name having estates in the south-eastern part of the county: they have often been referred to as the most numerous of the various Anglo-Norman families which settled in Co. Wexford after the invasion of 1170, and for four centuries they not only possessed extensive estates but also held many important public positions. Their stock multiplied as well as prospered, for in the "census" of 1659 Sinnott is listed as a principal Irish name in the barony of Forth and in the town and liberties of Wexford.

They were remarkable for their constant loyalty to the crown, which stood them in good stead until the seventeenth century, when the advent of Cromwell, and later the victory of William III over their lawful sovereign James II, greatly reduced their properties and influence. David Synnot was governor of Wexford at the time of the famous siege in 1649. He was killed in the defence of the town and Fr. Richard Sinnott was one of the eight priests massacred on that historic occasion. Col. Oliver Synnot was the emissary of the Duke of Lorraine in his negotiations with Ormond in 1650. Two Synnotts were officers in James II's army and eight of the name were attainted in 1691-2.

Fr. Patrick Sinnett (fl. 1600) was tutor to O'Sullivan beare, the historian, who gratefully commemorated him in a Latin poem. Whether he was from Co. Wexford I do not know. James Sinnott (1800-1884) noted performer and teacher of traditional Irish music was born at Bree, in that county. The name is occasionally found elsewhere, e.g. Matthew Sinnett, a householder at Ballinrobe in 1783.

An old Forth alliterative jingle relating to the Wexford families of Norman and Fleming origin, attaching a descriptive epithet to each, is quoted in the article on Devereux. In it Sinnott is called "shimereen", i.e. showy. Bibl., Map

SKILLEN   This name is numerous in Co. Down and rare elsewhere. Skilling is a variant of it. Authorities differ as to its origin – it is either Norse or English. O'Hart's statement that it is an anglicized form of Ó Scealláin (i.e. Scallan) can be discounted. I have found no early examples of it in Irish records.

(O) SKINNION   This name has now become very rare, but it was formerly of considerable importance. Originally the family were erenaghs of Ardcarne in Co. Roscommon, and a branch migrated to Tirconnell where they were ollavs and historians to the O'Donnells before the better known O'Clearys acquired that position. There are a number of references to both these branches in the Four Masters and other annals up to 1402. The late sixteenth century Fiants find them as O'Skynin etc. still at Ardcarne. Coming to the last century, birth registrations locate them in Co. Leitrim and also Co. Cavan, where they were also established under the alias of Delahide: this is an example – not of extraordinary anglicization, for Skinnion is an anglicization of Ó Sgingín – but of the absurd synonyms sometimes adopted, in this case presumably from the connexion of skin and hide! Another variant which a century ago was more numerous than Skinnion was Skinnan or Skinnon.

SLANE   It is assumed that this name is derived from the place in Co. Meath. It was not numerous enough to be included in Matheson's statistical list but in the first three years of compulsory registration (1864-66) there were 34 Slane or Slain(e) births, mostly in or near Tyrone.

(O) SLATTERY   The original territory of the Dalcassian sept of Ó Slatarra was at Ballyslattery near Tulla, Co. Clare (now known as Newgrove) and it is in east Clare the name was most numerous in the seventeenth century: this is also the case today, but now the name is found in almost equal numbers in the adjoining counties of Limerick and Tipperary. In the mediaeval period the O'Slatterys were supporters of the Macnamaras in the Thomond wars, particularly in the famous Battle of the Abbey in 1317.

In modern times a distinguished member of the sept, Dr. Michael Slattery (1782-1857), who was a graduate of Trinity College, Dublin, was President of Maynooth College and subsequently Archbishop of Cashel for 25 years.   Map

(O) SLEVIN, Slavin, Slamon
Both the forms Slevin and Slavin are found today in about equal numbers, chiefly in Ulster, 18 of the 25

births registered for the name in 1890 being in that province. Ó Sléibhín, which is said to be derived from the Irish word sliabh (a mountain) was the name of a branch of the Cenél Eoghain in Ulster, famous in the early mediaeval period as poets. Giolla Comhghaill Ó Sléibhín, chief bard of Ulster, was associated with King Malachy in the northern resistance to Brian Boru; other Ulster poets of the name about the same time are mentioned by the Four Masters, as well as one who was chief poet of Oriel in 1168. Though seldom met with in historical records after that time, they evidently did not sink into obscurity since as late as 1514 we find in the Ormond Deeds a judgement of the Liberty Court of Tipperary in which Terrelagh O'Slevin, together with an O'Donnell, is described as "pure Irish of the Irish nation" when charged with acquisition of lands contrary to statute; and again in the Survey of Co. Fermanagh made in 1603 Munter Slevine are cited as "carbes" (coarbs) of Kiltierney in the barony of Lurg.

It would appear that by the middle of the next century families of the name had become established in the midlands since Slevin is included among the principal Irish names in the barony of Farbill, Co. Westmeath, in the 1659 "census". The name occurs at approximately the same date in the Hearth Money Rolls for Co. Armagh, Co. Donegal and Co. Tyrone. The forms used are O'Slavin, O'Sleaven, O'Sleivan, O'Sclevin and O'Slamman.

Slamon is occasionally used in Co. Offaly, in the neighbourhood of Birr, as a synonym of Slavin.

The second Chief Herald of Ireland, Gerard Slevin, retired in 1981.

(Mac) SLINEY, Sleyne   This was formerly written Sleyney and when first used as a surname carried the prefix Mac: the Fiants of 1569 and 1583 mention two MacSleyneys, both of Ballygeany, Co. Cork. It is not, however, a true Gaelic-Irish surname, as it was the Gaelic patronymic adopted by the Norman Fitzstephen family of Co. Cork. It has always been rare outside that county and the adjacent parts of Co. Waterford: in the latter it has sometimes been spelt Sleaney. Another form of the same name is Sleyne, which was borne by a notable bishop of the penal times, John Sleyne of Cork and Cloyne. I presume that Sline, well known in the Dublin commercial world, is the same: Cork and Ross wills of the eighteenth century include those of Slyne and Sline. The Christian name to which the Mac was first prefixed must be obsolete – the suggestion that it was Stephen would imply that L was substituted for T, which is unlikely.

It has been stated that Sleyne is basically the same as Slevin. I think this is not the case. O'Donovan states that this name was an Irish patronymic (Mac Sleimhne) assumed by the Co. Cork Norman family of Fitz Stephen, one of whom was Bishop of Cork from 1701 to 1709. Gams gives his name as Skyne, which is an error for Sleyne. Gerlad MacSleyney (1568) and David MacSleyney (1584) are among the Co. Cork Elizabethan pardons. Synonyms of this name found today are Sliney, Slyne and occasionally MacSliney. They are all rare.

(O) SLOANE, Sloyan (O) SLOWEY

Sloyan or Sloyne (a rare Mayo name) and Sloane (of east Ulster) are both stated by Woulfe to be anglicized forms of Ó Sluagháin, an abbreviated form of Ó Sluaghadháin, which is derived primarily from the Irish word sluagh, a host, legion. He further suggests that it is a variant of Ó Sluaghadhaigh (Slowey) of west Ulster, which is now a rare surname but was of importance in early mediaeval times. In north Connacht Maelpatrick O'Slowey, who died in 1015, is described by the Four Masters as "sage of Ireland". After 1200 references to both these names are very infrequent until we come to the seventeenth century: from then on Sloane is closely connected with Co. Down. In 1659 the census enumerators found Slowan one of the most numerous Irish names in the barony of Newry, while one Alexander Sloane is returned as a titulado in the barony of Kinelarty. Sir Hans Sloane (1660-1753) was born near there, and is famous as the man whose amazingly extensive and valuable collection formed the nucleus of the British Museum: his family in Co. Down is said to have been of Scottish origin — their name would suggest that it was one of those Gaelic families which originated in Ireland and migrated to Scotland before the era of authentic history. In the seventeenth century it spread into counties Armagh and Monaghan, and in modern times has become a very numerous name in the Belfast area and also in Dublin. It is well known in America, not only in the person of Tod Sloan (1874-1933), the famous jockey (whose ancestry is unknown to me), but also Samuel Sloan (1817-1907), railway pioneer, and William Milligan Sloan (1850-1928), historian, who were of Ulster families.

Slowey has become Molloy in counties Cavan and Monaghan though the elision of the C in Mac and aspiration of the S.

SMITHWICK

This name is usually associated with Kilkenny on account of the well-known brewery there, but in fact since Col. Henry Smithwick obtained an extensive estate in the barony of Duhallow, Co. Cork, under the Cromwellian Settlement, the family has been established in that county as well as in the Carlow-Kilkenny area. The "census" of 1659 shows Col. Henry Smithwick to be still in active command of his regiment, stationed at that time in Drogheda, and in the same document and also in the lists of poll money commissioners (1660-1661) we find a Henry Smithwick in Co. Carlow, while in 1665 he and his son, another Henry, are parties to a transaction relating to land in Co. Kilkenny in which they had an existing interest. Again in 1673 and 1678 one of these Henry Smithwicks was appointed a commissioner to carry out the act providing for the disarming of Catholics. This family frequently appears in our records e.g. in the Orrery Papers. Somewhat later they became considerable landowners in Co. Tipperary. William Smithwick appears as a J.P. in north Tipperary in 1715 and 1727, and by the end of the last century one branch had been long established at Portroe on the Tipperary side of Lough Derg. In 1878 they owned 1150 acres there and another branch possessed over 2000 acres in Co. Kilkenny. The fact that the will of Dorothy Smithwick was proved in the Cork diocesan court in 1642 indicates that at least one family of Smithwick was in Ireland before the Cromwellian upheaval.

(O) SNEE

In England Snee is a variant of the better known Sneyd, but it is safe to assume that this is not the origin of the name when it is found in Ireland, particularly in Connacht, for Ó Sniadhaigh (anglicized Snee) is that of a distinguished Mayo sept, many of whose members are still in their ancient homeland, mainly around Swinford. Clement O'Snee, Bishop of Achonry from 1209 to 1219, was a notable ecclesiastic.

SODEN

This family, of which I have found no trace prior to the transactions under the Acts of Settlement and Explanation, has since multiplied considerably. Thomas Soden thus obtained the lands of Lislakely in Co. Sligo at that time and immediately afterwards acquired the nearby Grange property from the grantee Thomas Park. Soden of Grange appears as a titulado in the 1659-60 "census" and James Soden of Grange was one of the Protestant gentlement attainted under James II. Testamentary records for Co. Sligo from 1699 show that persons of the name were extensive property owners in Co. Sligo up to the middle of the eighteenth century, after which they seem to have become less prosperous though more numerous. By 1864, when general registration of births came into force, they were still found in Co. Sligo but were mainly located in or near Co. Cavan. In some places e.g. Kells, the name has been curiously equated with Saurin (q.v.). Reaney and Weekley agree that Soden is derived from Soudan, a corruption of Sultan, and is thus a surname of the nickname class.

(O) SOLAN, Solahan

I can advance no evidence to prove it conclusively, but I have little doubt that Solan is an abbreviated form of Solahan i.e. Ó Sóchlacháin. This Connacht family were erenaghs of Cong, Co. Mayo, an earlier anglicized form of the name being O'Soghlaghane. One of these, Donlevy Ó Sóchlacháin, was a renowned harpmaker in the thirteenth century. The modern location of families of Solan, viz. mainly Mayo, corroborates my view.

A very similar name, Souloughan, occasionally found in Co. Cavan, is not to be equated with Solahan or Solan, as it is a synonym of Sullahan (Ó Súileacháin) which, however, has now been almost entirely absorbed by the ubiquitous Sullivan.

John Sologhan was joint controller of the ports of Cork and Kinsale in 1402. His origin is not known.

(O) SORAHAN SAURIN

This name, also spelt Soraghan and sometimes abbreviated to Soran, is, and since the seventeenth century has been, associated almost exclusively with the counties of Monaghan and Cavan. It is frequent in the Hearth Money Rolls of Co. Monaghan (1663-1665) as O'Soraghan, and sixty years before a Fiant recorded it somewhat further north at

Tullaghoge, Co. Tyrone, in which county an Inquisition of 1632 also found it. It is rather surprising, therefore, to find the name occurring in Co. Waterford in 1312 when Henry O'Sourehan was accused of theft there, but found not guilty.

Saurin (de Sauverne) a Huguenot surname has, as far as I know, never been used as a synonym of Soran; but it has been reported from the Kells area as synonymous with Soden (q.v. supra). The Saurins were extensive landlords in counties Tipperary and Kilkenny a century ago, but the best known men of the name, e.g. William Saurin (1757-1839), the notable lawyer, were associated with Belfast.

MacSORLEY   This name is numerous in Co. Tyrone but rare outside Ulster. The Gaelic form MacSomhairle comes from a Scandinavian personal name and the first bearing it to come to Ireland were of the Scottish clan MacDonald. (MacSorley, it should be added, is also a sept of the Scottish clan Cameron.) In 1211 Ranal MacSomhairle, Lord of Argyle, invaded Ireland, landing in what is now Co. Derry, and another such invasion followed in 1258; later numbers of the clan came to Ireland as galloglasses and subsequently settled in the north of the country. The MacSorleys and the Mac Donnells of Co. Antrim became very closely allied and were a powerful element in the Ulster resistance to England up to 1600. Though the great majority of the many references to MacSorley to be found in Irish records over the centuries relate to Ulster we do meet them occasionally elsewhere: for example John MacSawerley, a harper of note, was a landholder at Kilmallock, Co. Limerick, in 1571; four Mac Sorley families are in the Co. Tipperary Hearth Money Rolls of 1664 and another MacSorley family migrated from Co. Armagh to Co. Mayo in 1795. Alexander MacSorley was one of the Catholic martyrs: he was hanged at Derry in 1615. Patrick MacSorley, editor of The Irish Exile, (1850-51) was prominent among the Young Irelanders transported to Australia.

SPAIGHT   This name, though not numerous, is well known in Limerick and Co. Clare. The first settler, James Spaight, came from Kent to Co. Derry, but his grandson Thomas established the family in east Clare in the reign of Charles II and soon became a person of importance: he was high sheriff of the county in 1697 as was his grandson nearly a century later. Spaight is one of the most prominent names in the commercial life of Limerick city. The name is derived from the Middle-English word speight, meaning a woodpecker.

(O) SPILLANE, Spollan   SPELMAN   The surname Ó Spealáin is of dual origin. One sept so called possessed territory in the barony of Eliogarty (Co. Tipperary) in early mediaeval times but were dispossessed by their neighbours the O'Dwyers of Kilnamanagh and were subsequently to be found chiefly in counties Cork and Kerry, which is their principal location today. Though the majority of them did settle there, various families of

Spillane, as they were called in English, were widely scattered over the country. In 1540 a group of them was to be found at Bective, Co. Meath. In 1659, in addition to the three southern counties of Munster, the name (spelt Spollan in that case in the "census") was also in Offaly, where that variant is still found. The place-name Ballyspellane occurs both in Co. Kilkenny and Co. Tipperary; Ballyspillane is a parish in the Midleton area of Co. Cork and this place-name is also found near Killarney.

The other Ó Spealáin sept is of the Uí Fiachrach: this belonged to the parish of Kilglas, Co. Sligo. When John O'Donovan was conducting his researches a century ago he found the name there as Spillane, but today in Connacht it is invariably anglicized as Spelman. This form is peculiar to Connacht and is quite numerous in counties Galway, Mayo and Roscommon. The most notable man of this sept is Cardinal Spelman (b. 1889), Archbishop of New York.   Map

SPRING   In dealing with Rice of Co. Limerick 'Irish Families, p. 257) reference was made to the Spring-Rice family. The Springs came to Ireland from Suffolk towards the end of the sixteenth century. It has been stated that the connexion of the two families arose from the marriage of Stephen Rice of Mount Trenchard, Foynes, Co. Limerick, with the daughter of Thomas Spring in 1785; it is of interest, therefore, to record the fact that in a Fiant of 1599 a Kerry lady is described as Elizabeth Rhise alias Springe. Thomas Springe became controller of wines at Limerick in 1579. Thomas Springe (presumably the same man) was appointed Constable of Castlemaine Castle in 1584 and a Springe was M.P. for Kerry in 1585. The Springs in fact became firmly established in Kerry, intermarrying with the Brownes (Kenmares) and other leading aristocratic families of west Munster. One at least – Edward Spring of Killaghagh, Co. Kerry – was transplanted to Connacht as a papist in 1656, but the majority remained in Kerry: King gives the number of Spring families in the county according to the 1901 census as eight.

SPROULE   At the present time this name is usually spelt as above throughout Ulster; Sproulle, Sproul, Sprowle and Sprool are also current variants. The older spelling was Spruell: two "tituladoes" so called appear in the barony of Raphoe, Co. Donegal, in the "census" of 1659. As Sproule it is still found there. The name is very rare outside Ulster and the adjacent parts of some Connacht counties. Co. Tyrone is its main location.

STAFFORD   Like many other surnames formed from association with an English town or village and introduced into Ireland at or soon after the Anglo-Norman invasion, Stafford has become numerous in its adopted country while it is scarce in its former habitat. The de Staffords (who according to tradition were from Buckinghamshire not Staffordshire) settled in Co. Wexford in the thirteenth century and are still mainly to be found there. Their principal seats were Ballymacarne and Bally-connor. They figure in every account I have seen of the leading gentry of Co. Wexford from 1345 to 1878. Much interesting information regarding them will be found in Hore's monumental History of Co. Wexford. Of individuals of the name, while not forgetting Sir Francis Stafford, member of the Council of Ireland in 1598, or Richard Stafford, member of the Supreme Council of the Confederate Catholics in 1646, I am inclined to regard Lieutenant Thomas Stafford as the most important, even though he was on what we would call the wrong side: not indeed for his own military distinction but because he is, it is generally agreed, the author of a famous book, that most interesting contemporary account of Sir George Carew's campaigns in Munster in the closing years of the sixteenth century which was published later (in 1636) under the title of 'Pacata Hibernia.

The Stafford connexion with Co. Mayo, where at one time they had considerable property, was not of long duration: they are listed as new proprietors in the post-Restoration Book of Survey & Distribution and did not remain there in an influential position very long.

The Staffords of Ulster were for the most part really Macastockers. The Irish surname Mac an Stocaire (son of the trumpeter) was for some strange reason anglicized as Stafford. They were still called MacStocker in English in the 1660s when the Hearth Money Rolls were compiled.

The Stafford family figures in the old Co. Wexford rhyme quoted in the article on Devereux.   Map

STAPLETON, Gaule   (Mac) GILL, Magill
STACKPOOLE   The Stapletons are a Norman family which took its name from an English village, but coming to Ireland in the wake of the Anglo-Norman invasion of 1170 settled in counties Kilkenny and Tipperary and became hibernicized. Some branches of it adopted a Gaelic patronymic, viz., Mac and Ghaill (son of the foreigner: Irish gall) which in due course was anglicized Gall, Gale and Gaule. Gale was formerly pronounced Gall (cf. Wale – Wall, Sale – Saul). Both names, Stapleton and Gaule, are still well represented in the south-eastern counties in the proportion of approximately 2 to 1. 300 years ago, when Petty's "census" was taken, they were then comparatively more numerous than today, but in similar proportions as the enumerators recorded for Gaule 17 families in the barony of Ida and 9 in Lower Ormond, while Stapleton families numbered 34 in Eliogarty and 20 in Middlethird baronies. In the Ormond Deeds we find them frequently mentioned under both names, one of the earliest being Robert de Stapleton, who was sheriff of Waterford in 1287. An interesting sidelight on the Reformation policy of Henry VIII, as compared with his Protestant successors, was the granting of a pension to Elicia Gaalle, a "displaced nun" of Co. Kilkenny in 1540. They penetrated into north Leinster too, for we find them at Drogheda in 1423 and in 1428 John Gale was one of a party of O's and Mac's who plundered the Prior of Fore (Co. Westmeath) of livestock and goods. A number of Gaules are among the "old proprietors" in the Co. Kilkenny Book of Survey and Distribution. The adjective gallda formed from gall gave the epithetic sur-

name Gault which occurs often in seventeenth century Inquisitions for northern counties.

Some of the Stapletons were called Gallduff (gall dubh, black foreigner) notably Fr. Theobald Stapleton, alias Gallduf, (1589-1647) whose Catechismus vel Teagasc Críostuí (in Latin and Irish) was published in Brussels in 1639: he was captured by Cromwellian soldiers in the cathedral at Cashel and put to death on the spot with another priest called Stapleton. Like so many of the hibernicized Norman families the leading Stapletons espoused the Jacobite cause and were forced into exile by its defeat. John Stapleton, of Thurlesbeg, Co. Tipperary, settled at Nantes where an Irish colony was established; his son John Stapleton was ennobled as Comte de Trèves. The French departmental archives contain records of many naturalizations of Irish-born Stapletons during the first half of the eighteenth century. Of the same stock was Brigadier-General Walter Valentine Stapleton (d. 1746) of the Irish Brigade, who in his youth had distinguished himself in 1690-91 at the siege of Limerick (where his relative, Col. Stapleton the deputy-governor was killed in a sortie) and later again at Fontenoy; he was fatally wounded at the battle of Culloden.

John O'Donovan, in his introduction to the Topographical Poems of O'Dugan and O'Heerin, refers to the adoption by the Stapletons of the name Gaule; nevertheless the Galls or Gaules of Gallstown, Co. Kilkenny, are of different origin. O'Donovan (whose mother was of that family) states that they were called Gall or Gall-Burke, Walter Gall de Burgo being M.P. for Co. Kilkenny in 1650. His son William became Count Gall von Bourckh of the German Empire and other sons served in the Spanish and Austrian armies.

Mac an Ghaill, the Irish patronymic of the Stapletons is a variant of Mac an Ghoill, usually anglicized MacGill or Magill. As is usual with MacG names the composite Mag form (i.e. Magill) is the one generally used in east Ulster, while the full prefix is retained (MacGill) in west Ulster. In 1659 Petty's "census" enumerators found the name, which they recorded as MacGill, very numerous in Co. Antrim, especially in the barony of Glenarm; the same document gives Gill, without the prefix, as common in Co. Longford. Those MacGills and no doubt the present day Magills of Co. Antrim are descendants of Scottish mercenary forces – or should I term them professional soldiers – the Clann an Ghaill, as they were called. MacGills from Scotland were also among the new proprietors introduced by the Plantation of Ulster.

MacGill (written Magill in sotth-east Ulster) is undoubtedly often merely an abbreviation of one of the many surnames beginning with Mac Giolla. Gill, without the prefix, is approximately the same in numerical strength: 1890 and 1864-1865 (average) registration statistics record 65 (73) Magill, 19 (18) MacGill and 61 (84) Gill births. Gills are more numerous in counties Mayo and Galway than elsewhere, Co. Longford being its principal location outside Connacht now as in the seventeenth century. The founder of the well-known publishing firm M.H. Gill & Son, Michael Henry Gill (1794-1879), was born in Co. Offaly. His son and successor Henry J. Gill (1836-1903) was a Nationalist M.P. The poet and novelist Patrick MacGill is a Co. Donegal man.

Fr. Hugh MacGoill, O.P., of the convent of Rathmore, hanged at Waterford in 1653, was one of the many Catholic martyrs of the seventeenth century. Woulfe states that Mac Goill is a rare Galway name now anglicized Giles. The name MacGuill is well known in Co. Louth and Co. Armagh today and is listed in the "census" of 1659 as one of the principal Irish names in the barony of Orior, Co. Armagh. It is probably Mag Cuill in Irish, i.e. son of Coll.

The Gaelic patronymic Gallduv mentioned above in connexion with the Stapleton family was also adopted in some cases by the Stacpooles. First known as de Stakbolle (from the place in Pembrokeshire) they came to Ireland from Wales in the thirteenth century and were prominent among the Anglo-Normans of the Pale in the mediaeval period. By the end of the sixteenth century they had become more numerous in Co. Clare than elsewhere; and up to quite recent times Stacpoole was one of the leading landlord names in that county. One important branch remained Catholic: this is now represented by the Duc de Stackpoole of Tobertynan, Co. Meath.

A branch of the Clare family went to Cork city early in the eighteenth century and prospered as merchants. They spelt their name Stockpole. One of them married David Aikenhead, apothecary, and their daughter was Mother Mary Aikenhead, foundress of the Irish Sisters of Charity, whose centenary was commemorated by the issue of a special postage stamp.

STEPHENS   In Ireland a family called Stephens may be of various origins. If not of comparatively recent immigration from England, as a number of those in Leinster and Ulster are, they could be of Norman stock, descendants of some FitsStephen, a name much in evidence in mediaeval Munster and Ormond records; or they might be true Gaels of the small sept of MacGilstefan (Mac Giolla Stiofáin), which Woulfe says belongs to Leix. The only instance I have met of a person of the name is one Shane MacGilstefan, of Kiltevan, who was among a number of Co. Roscommon men "pardoned" in 1582. It is probable that any survivors of this sept in Connacht are now called Stephens. It is in north Connacht the name Stephens is chiefly found today, apart from the metropolitan area of Dublin. MacStephen is of frequent occurrence in sixteenth and seventeenth century Connacht records such as the Composition Book of Connacht, the Fiants, Strafford's Inquisition and the Book of Survey and Distribution for Co. Mayo, where the place-name Garan MacStephen also occurs. I have yet to ascertain whether, as may possibly be the case, they were in fact MacGilstefans, or, as I think more probable, a branch of the Barretts of that province.

Two Irishmen called James Stephens are noteworthy, viz. James Stephens (1825-1901) Kilkenny born co-founder of the Fenian Brotherhood; and James Stephens (1882-1951) the poet. John Stevens, who kept an interesting diary of his experiences in Ireland in 1689, though he was a Catholic and an officer in James II's army, was not an Irishman.

(O) STRAHAN, Strain, Shryhane   There are two slightly different forms of this surname in Irish – Ó Sraitheáin and Ó Srutháin, both as Strahan and Strain (Co. Down) found now in Ulster in fair numbers. The sept was of Tirconnell where they were erenaghs of Conwall in the barony of Kilmacrenan, Co. Donegal. Sitric Ó Sruithen is mentioned by the Four Masters as such in the year 1204. The Annals refer to them as followers of the O'Donnells with whom, however, at the end of the sixteenth century they were at loggerheads.

Another anglicized form the name met with today in Co. Tyrone is Shryhane. Stuffaun recorded at Cappoquin, Co. Waterford, is presumably another snynonym. It is mentioned by Matheson among the curious cases reported to him by the local registrars: two full brothers were registered respectively as Sruffaun and Bywater, the latter being evidently a supposed translation of the Irish word sruth, a stream.

STRITCH   Though English in origin, being derived from an old form of the word street, this name may now be regarded as Irish. It is especially identified with Limerick and neighbouring territory. Between 1377 and 1650 the name Stritch or Stretch appears more than fifty times in the lists of Limerick mayors and baliffs (as the sheriffs were formally called).

In 1650 the last of these Catholic mayors, Thomas Stritch, was so prominently concerned in the successful resistance to the siege during that year that on the final surrender he was excluded from the amnesty and executed. Fr. Andrew Stritch, who died in prison in 1585, was a Limerick priest. In 1587 we find one Richard Stritche of Limerick preferring a claim to certain mills at Clonmel which he stated had been in the possession of his family for 300 years. Indeed the Stritches appear frequently in east Munster and south Leinster records from 1325 onwards and were formerly almost as closely connected with Clonmel and that area as with Limerick. One of these was Bishop of Waterford and Lismore (1735-1739); another was Bishop of Emly (1695-1718). A notable priest was Fr. John Stritch, Jesuit missionary in South America and the West Indies 1650 to 1655. The Stritches did their part also as soldiers; in addition to Thomas Stritch mentioned above, in the next generation there were three officers in King James's Irish army. Some of the seven Stritches outlawed as Jacobites subsequently recovered their property.

The Stritches, who in the "census" of 1659 are classed among the more numerous and more influential Irish families in the barony of Bunratty, Co. Clare, have so far become reduced in numbers that the name does not find a place in Matheson's birth registration returns. The name, however, does survive in east Clare, particularly in the parishes of Killaloe and Ogonnelloe.

In recent times a very well known man of the name was Cardinal Stritch, Bishop of Toledo, U.S.A., who died in Rome in 1958.

(O) SUGRUE   SIGERSON   The surname Sugrue is

almost entirely confined to Kerry – the 1901 census records some 800 persons of the name in that county and the 1890 registration returns show that 22 out of 23 births were in Co. Kerry, the odd one being in the adjacent county Cork. In 1659 it appears under the form Shagroe as one of the more numerous names in the barony of Iveragh, Co. Kerry. The seventeenth and eighteenth century writers on the subject give the O'Sughrues a similar location and describe them as a branch of the O'Sullivans, who used the forename Sigfrid from very early times. Their principal seats were Fermoyle (retained until quite recently) and the Castle of Dunloe, which passed into the hands of the O'Mahonys. The fact that the Gaelic Ó Siochfhradha is derived from the Norse Sigefrith is, of course, not evidence of Norse origin (cf. MacManus and O'Heever). The most distinguished member of this sept was most Rev. Dr. Charles Sugrue, Bishop of Kerry from 1797 to 1824. His name is spelt Sughrue in the manuscripts of the Wardenship of Galway, where he was Apostolic Visitor in 1816-17. One of the best known of the protagonists of the modern Gaelic revival is a Sugrue, though he is little known as such, his identity being hidden under the pseudonym An Seabhac. To him I am indebted for the information that there are two curious Sugrue nicknames which have given rise to what almost amount to surnames: muintir an tsneachta (people of the snow) appear in the Fiants as Itnaghty and Entnaghty and are still called the Sneachtas in English; while muintir na sméar is another example, the modern use of which was to be found in the person of Norry Blackberry living at Cahirciveen 80 years ago. He mentions that the name Sugrue should rightly be pronounced Shugrue in English as it appears from the 1659 reference given above to have been in the seventeenth century. A number of the 1864-1866 birth registrations are spelt Shugrue. I may add that I have heard it so pronounced in Munster.

The surname Sigerson is also derived from the Norse forename Sigfrid or Sigrid. It has been made illustrious in Ireland by the family of Dr. George Sigerson (1839-1925), himself a distinguished scientist and poet, whose wife was a novelist and his daughter Dora Sigerson (1870-1918) a poetess of considerable merit. The Sigersons have been established in Ireland at least since the sixteenth century. Sigerson of Halveston was one of the "constables" of Co. Kildare in 1608 and there was a family of the name at Ballinskelligs, Co. Kerry, in the eighteenth century. Thomas and Edward Segerson, both of Co. Kerry were attainted as Jacobites in 1692. There were eight Segerson families in Co. Kerry in the census of 1901. As Seagerson the name occurs in the Co. Armagh Hearth Money Rolls of 1664-5.   Map

SUPPLE   While never numerous the Supples are very much in evidence since the first of them came to Ireland with Strongbow in 1171. There is scarcely an extant record, particularly those dealing with counties Limerick and Cork, which does not mention them. Though I have never had occasion to make an exhaustive search for them references I have noted from time to time occupy a full page of a large ledger. This, however, is not the place for a detailed account of them.

They lost much of their property in the Desmond wars of the sixteenth century. The Supples of Castletown, Co. Limerick, were transplanted as papists under the Cromwellian régime, and at least one from Kilcolman, Co. Cork, was outlawed as a Jacobite, but others held on and the family never ceased to be one of substance in west Munster.

The name occurs as Soople in Co. Roscommon, which is in accordance with the local pronunciation of it.

George Supple of The Nation, who emigrated to Australia after the Rising of 1848, was implicated in an extraordinary murder trial in which he was condemned to death three times, but the sentence was finally commuted. He died in New Zealand about 1900.

SWANTON   Though this is an English name derived from a place in Norfolk it has become closely identified with west Cork since the seventeenth century. There are no less than twelve references to Swantons in the Fifteenth Report of the Irish Record Commission (1825) all of the seventeenth century, including a Connacht certificate.

The name occurs frequently in the Cork and Ross wills and in the marriage licence bonds for the same diocese from 1690. Practically all the fairly numerous Swanton births of the nineteenth century were registered in Co. Cork; in 1853 Griffith found as many as 58 Swanton families in west Cork and in 1878 there were seven of the name among the larger landowners of Co. Cork, owning between them 11,750 acres. A few Swantons do appear in our records elsewhere e.g. a sheriff of Co. Kildare in 1675. The most notable of the Co. Cork family were those who distinguished themselves in France. James Swanton (c. 1760-1828), who at the age of twelve was adopted by his uncle the abbé Swanton, served in Berwick's regiment of the Irish Brigade and afterwards as a colonel in the French army. Hilaire Belloc was his grandson. His son Armand (c. 1785-c.1830) was also an officer in the Irish Legion; he was said to be the handsomest officer in the French army.

SWAYNE SWAN   These two names have been much confused but Swan, except where it occurs as a synonym of Swayne, is of much later introduction into Ireland than Swayne. The latter is quite frequent in mediaeval Irish records from 1297, when Walter Swayne was coroner of Offaly, for the most part in Leinster from Co. Kildare to Co. Louth (one of Ardmoyle, Co. Tipperary in 1297 was an exception). The first I have noted is Laurence Sweyn mentioned in an Offaly charter of 1288. Swan became numerous from the middle of the seventeenth century, being found from that time until the present day (apart from Dublin the population of which is made up of people from all the provinces) mainly in Ulster. Swan is now much more numerous than Swayne which cannot be identified with any particular county or area.

These English names have several different derivations

– from Old-English swán (peasant), swan (the bird), Old-Norse svein (servant) etc., etc. Dr. Douglas Hyde considered that some Irish Swaynes are actually Mac-Sweeneys.

SWIFT A few examples of this name are to be found in Irish mediaeval records, e.g. in 1297 there was a monk of Baltinglass called Thomas Swyft and in the same year another of the name was indicted for attempted robbery of corn from the archdeacon of Leighlin. The famous Swift family (Dean Jonathan Swift 1667-1745) came from England early in the seventeenth century.

Swift, by pseudo-translation, has been used for Foody (Ó Fuada) in Connacht and for Fodaghan (Ó Fuadacháin) in Ulster. According to O'Donovan the Swifts of Co. Mayo are Ó Huada as well as Ó Fuada.

SYNAN, Sinon This name, formerly very prominent in Co. Cork, is still extant in Co. Clare where it is also spelt Shynane. According to the article on the Synans of Doneráile listed in the Bibliography the family burial place of Kilbolane in west Cork dates back at least to 1492; it records the arms (the blazon is unfortunately not given) with motto 'confido in Domino et non morie-mur". The Sinons are one of the few Munster families described in the Spanish archives dealing with Spanish knights of Irish origin as "illustre".

The only Irish manuscript in which I have seen the name is that relating to the foundations of the Irish Franciscan province (see Analecta Hibernica VI 202) where Nioclás Sionán is mentioned as Provincial in 1629. It occurs several times in the Fiants between 1573 and 1603 as Shynan and Shynane, all in Co. Cork and mostly Doneraile. In none of these cases is the prefix O used with the name. This supports the traditional belief that the name Synan is of Norman origin. I do not accept Woulfe's statement that Ó Sionáin denoting Synan is a variant of Ó Seanáin (Shannon).   Bibl.

SYNGE In England this name is also written as it is pronounced – Sing. It has only been in Ireland since the beginning of the seventeenth century and never became at all numerous though it is worthy of note that as many as eleven Synge marriage licence bonds are recorded in Co. Cork between 1681 and 1739. I include it here because of the eminence of so many of the family. Territorially the name has been very scattered. The first I know of was born in Co. Louth; the main family came from Shropshire in the person of George Synge (1594-1652) who was Bishop of Cloyne; in 1792 the will of Edward Synge of Syngefield (Co. Offaly) was proved; in 1878 de Burgh recorded eight Synges with considerable estates in eight different counties; today it is found in Co. Wicklow and Dublin. The Edward referred to above was a clergyman, and it is as Protestant ecclesiastics that the Synges, apart from John Millington Synge (1871-1909) the playwright, have been most prominent. Five of them were bishops: dealing with another Edward

Synge (1649-1751), Archbishop of Tuam, the Dictionary of National Biography says of him "as the son of one bishop, the nephew of another, himself an archbishop and the father of two other bishops, his position in ecclesiastical biography is probably unique". Yet another Edward Synge, prebendary of St. Patrick's, preached a remarkable sermon in 1733 advocating relaxation of the anti-Catholic penal laws.   Bibl.

TALBOT When More Irish Families was published in 1960 the Talbots of Malahide had the record unique among Hiberno-Norman families of being in possession of the same property in unbroken male descent from the time of the invasion of 1170 to the present time – already nearly 800 years with every prospect of continuance. However, in 1973 the property was acquired by the Dublin County Council as a public amenity. Having regard to this, to the fact that the name is still well represented in Ireland (apart from the Malahide family) and to the number of members of its various branches who have played a notable part in the history of the country, it should certainly have been included in Part II of Irish Families. Several of the most famous Talbots were actually born at Malahide, Co. Dublin, e.g. the three sons of Sir William Talbot, Bart., (d. 1623) of Carton, Recorder of Dublin and M.P. for Kildare, viz., Most Rev. Peter Talbot, S.J. (1620-1680), Archbishop of Dublin, who died in Newgate prison after being arrested for alleged complicity in the "Popish Plot", and his brother Richard Talbot (1630-1691), better known as the Duke of Tyrconnell, James II's Lord Lieutenant. Another pair of brothers, also born at Malahide, but whose reputation was made outside Ireland, were Thomas Talbot (1771-1853) the Canadian statesman, who founded many towns including Port Talbot, and Admiral Sir John Talbot (1769-1851). Richard Talbot (c. 1709-1752) 3rd Earl of Tyrconnell, whose father was attainted as a Jacobite and lost his estates in Co. Louth, joined the French army as a boy, rose to the rank of brigadier and later represented France as ambassador at Berlin: he went with Prince Charles Edward (the "Young Pretender") to Scotland in 1745, as did his relative George Anthony Talbot, a naval captain and ardent Jacobite who later became a privateer. One of their minor titles was Baron of Talbotstown. Talbotstown is the name of a barony in Co. Wicklow and there is also a small place so called in Co. Wexford. Talbot's Inch and Talbotshill are both in the Kilkenny area while Mount Talbot, the seat of another branch, is near Roscommon. Some of the other branches are the Talbots of Robertstown, of Dardistown and of Agher (Co. Meath), of Balgard and of Templeogue (Co. Dublin(. Less prominent perhaps as leading gentry, they were also numerous in counties Kildare and Wexford as M.P's, J.P's etc., while more than a dozen of the name served as officers in James II's army, Mark Talbot being one of the signatories of the Articles of Limerick in 1691. Going back to mediaeval times we find many references to the name in civil and ecclesiastical records, as Talebute, Taleboth etc.; but Sir John Talbot, four times Lord Deputy between 1414 to 1449, and his brother Richard Talbot, Archbishop of Dublin from 1418 to 1449, were English Talbots, relatives of the Earl of Shrewsbury, who, it may be mentioned, was descended from the same Norman ancestor as the Irish Talbots. In our own time the most celebrated man of the name was the saintly Matt Talbot (1856-1925), a Dublin labourer.

It is not possible to do justice to so eminent a family within the limits of a page or two, but enough has been said here to indicate their importance and the reader anxious for more detailed information is referred to the family history listed in the Bibliography.   Bibl., Map

TALLON   The Tallons have been influential in the Pale since the Anglo-Norman invasion and today are seldom found outside the counties of east Leinster. They settled first at Nurney in Co. Carlow, where by the fourteenth century they had so far become hibernicized as to be included in official reports among submitting chiefs, one being described as "Englishman and rebel". They were early in Co. Louth also: William Talloun was mayor of Drogheda in 1354. By the fifteenth century they were already found in Co. Dublin, at least in a subordinate capacity, for the Statutes of Henry VI specifically mention one of them as a husbandman in that county in 1459; and in the sixteenth century they were still holding lands in the Hacketstown area of Co. Carlow and at Templeton, Co. Wexford, they had spread northwards into counties Dublin, Meath and Louth. In Meath especially they had become one of the more influential families; the place-name Cloontytallun is called after them; in 1586 Edward Tallon was one of the gentlemen in the "rising out" of the barony of Skreen and a few years later Tallon of Wilkinstown was one of the principal gentry of the county. In the next century the "census" of 1659 includes Tallon among the principal Irish names in Co. Louth (barony of Dundalk), and it also appears among the Catholic burgesses of the city of Armagh in 1688. In Irish the name is written Talún.   Map

(O) TALTY   (O) TALLY   Talty is essentially a Co. Clare name and when met elsewhere will be found to be of Clare origin. While accepting Ó Tailtigh as the Gaelic-Irish form, as given by Woulfe, I think he is wrong in saying that it is a metathesized form of Ó Taighligh, the older form of which is Ó Taichligh (as, e.g., in the Four Masters and Topographical Poem of O'Dugan and O'Heerin). That name belongs to Tyrone and Fermanagh and appears to have no connexion at all with Clare. Ó Taithligh is anglicized as Tally, Tilly and Tully. Tully, it is true, is found in Galway, the county nearest to Clare, but there it is always an abbreviated form of MacAtilla (see Irish Families, pp. 278, 279).

(O) TANGNEY   Almost every reference to this name which I have met relates to Co. Kerry. Such references are rare enough, but occur occasionally from the time of the Elizabethan Fiants to modern birth registrations and voters' lists. It is Ó Teangna in Irish. The 1901 census shows that there were fifty families of Tangney in Co. Kerry at that date. At one time some Killarney families were called Tangley, which may be regarded as a corrupt synonym of Tangney.

(O) TANNIAN   The Gaelic-Irish form of Tannian used in the Annals of Loch Cé is Ó Tanaidhen. In 1406 Diarmuid O'Tannion was one of three prominent Connachtmen who assassinated the king of the day. There are some families of the name in Co. Galway today, the name being little known outside Connacht.

(Mac) TANSEY   Woulfe found no early form of this name, but stated that in the spoken language it is rendered as Ó Blioscáin by a supposed translation of the English word tansy (an aromatic herb). If so he should surely have written Ó Brioscáin, since the Irish word for tansy is brioscán, blioscán being an artichoke. However, I think there is no doubt that the correct Irish form of Tansey is Mac an Tánaiste, i.e. son of the tanist. This is supported by the inclusion of the surname Tanist as one of the principal Irish names in the barony of Corren, Co. Sligo, in the "census" of 1659: south Sligo and the adjacent part of north Roscommon is the principal location of Tansey families in more recent times. As MacEtanestie it occurs in a Connacht Fiant of 1588.

(O) TARPEY, Torpey   The Tarpeys are still to be found mainly in that part of the country to which they belong historically and traditionally, namely north Connacht. Farranyharpy (Fearann uí Tharpaigh) in the parish of Skreen, Co. Sligo indicates their original homeland. Connmach O'Tarpy was Bishop of Leyney (Achonry) from 1220-1227, and references to members of the sept in mediaeval records relate to Co. Sligo. By the seventeenth century they had spread into other Connacht counties and in 1652 Thomas oge Tarpey was one of those who refused to sign the articles of surrender of Galway; the Franciscan Father Francis Tarpey, who was a professor of note at Louvain, was educated at Galway (c. 1627) as well as at Rome; and at the present time there are some families of the name around Gort and Ardrahan.

Another sept of the same name Ó Tarpaigh was counted among the followers of O'Leary of Corca Laoidhe. The name is rare there now; in Munster it is better known as Torpey. As such it occurs three times in the Co. Tipperary Hearth Money Rolls of 1665-7.   Map

TARSNANE   I can offer little information on this name to which Woulfe devotes just two words viz. "Ó Tarsnáin, Tarsnane", i.e. no derivation, no old anglicized form, no location. At least I can state that it is a west Clare surname. It appears among the Clare freeholders in 1821 and following years and in all the west Clare birth registrations that I have consulted. A somewhat similar name is Tarsany or MacTarsany, but that has no connexion with Co. Clare: it appears in the Co. Armagh Hearth Money Rolls of 1664. Judging from nineteenth century birth registration statistics Tarsany and MacTarsany are no longer extant in Ulster.

TAYLOR   The name Taylor is wholly English in origin: this is not one of those cases where a Gaelic-Irish family has adopted, by translation or phonetic attraction, an English surname as a synonym of their own. Nevertheless, though there can be no doubt that the majority of our Taylors are immigrants of comparatively recent date, the name has long been very numerous in Ireland: it was in Dublin and the south-eastern counties as far back as the thirteenth century and the existence of the place-name Ballytaylor, near Ballymoney, shows that it was well established in Co. Antrim by the seventeenth century, which is confirmed by the Hearth Money Rolls where it also appears twice as MacTaylor. A perusal of the record of the Prerogative Wills, which begins in 1536, shows that Taylors settled in many places outside Ulster. The most notable of these settlers was Thomas Taylor who came to Ireland with Sir William Petty in 1653 and became a Commissioner of the Court of Claims; much valuable manuscript material relating to the seventeenth century land settlements thus remained in the family at Bective Castle, Co. Meath. The present title of Marquess of Headfort dates from 1800, that of Earl of Bective from 1766. The earliest of the wills referred to above is 1583, Co. Meath; from 1600 to 1650 they relate to residents in counties Cork and Waterford; thereafter many of the testators are of Dublin. Modern birth registrations find them in all the provinces, the majority being in Ulster. An approximate present day estimate puts the number of Taylors in or near Belfast as 5,000, in Dublin as 2,000; in the rest of the Republic barely 500.

Apart from Francis Tailor (d. 1621), the Dublin alderman who was one of the Catholic martyrs for the faith – and perhaps I should mention the four Co. Dublin Taylors who were outlawed for their participation in the Rising of 1641 and two in the Jacobite outlawries – no one of the name has been prominent in the Irish national struggle; though Walter Shawe-Taylor (1832-1912) of Castletaylor, Co. Galway was notable in the closing stages of the Land War as one of the few really enlightened landlords of the time. John Sydney Taylor (1795-1841), chiefly famous for his authorship of the poem "The Burial of Sir John Moore", was born in Ireland, as were several other writers and soldiers named Taylor. Jeremy Taylor (1613-1667), Bishop of Down, was one of the most distinguished of Irish Protestant churchmen. Probably the best known of the name born in Ireland was George Taylor (1716-1781), one of the signatories of the American Declaration of Independence.   Bibl.

(O) TEAHAN   (O) TEGAN   This name is also spelt Teehan. It is Ó Téacháin in Irish. Woulfe, in his very brief note, states that it originated in Co. Roscommon. I have found no evidence of this. It occurs in the Elizabethan Fiants as O'Taughan in Co. Kerry, where in its modern form it is chiefly found today. In 1901 there were 79 families of Teahan in Co. Kerry, according to the census of that date. The most remarkable man of the name was of that county, viz. Dr. Gerald Teahan, who was Bishop of Kerry from 1787 to 1797 and was appointed Archbishop of Cashel but resigned before taking office. He died in 1797. He carried out the apostolic visitation to the Wardenship of Galway in 1794. In the "census" of 1659 Tehan is recorded as one of the principal Irish names in two baronies of Queen's Co. (Leix), viz. Maryborough and Ossory. It seems likely that there it was synonymous with Tegan or Tagan (Ó Taghgáin) which occurs in the same document in the barony of Ikeathy, Co. Kildare, as a principal name. In support of this suggestion I may mention that Tehan also occurs in the birth registrations for Queen's County in the returns for 1864-1866, especially in the Mountmellick area, where there is a townland called Ballytegan.

TEELING   This is one of the few important families whose leading branches have consistently remained Catholic and still retained a place among the landed gentry. Though not Norman in origin themselves the Teelings came to Ireland following the Anglo-Norman invasion and have been prominent in the life of the country, particularly Co. Meath, through the centuries. Almost every important record – Ormond Deeds, Dowdall Deeds, Justiciary Rolls, Ecclesiastical Registers, Fiants, Inquisitions, Wills etc. etc. – contain references to the Teelings from the middle of the thirteenth century, not only to men of eminence like William, lord of Syddan and the many owners of the Mullagha property, but also to minor clergy and even to gaelicized outlaws. The Syddan family are extinct. All the most notable men of the name were of the Mullagha branch: they include Thomas Telyng (Teeling), who having joined the Rising of Silken Thomas Fitzgerald, was implicated in the assassination of Archbishop Alen for which he suffered torture and death in 1535; the brothers Bartholomew (1774-1798) and Charles Hamilton Teeling (1778-1850), the former hanged as a leading United Irishman, the latter arrested as such but not executed. The Teelings have a distinguished military record in Ireland for which they suffered outlawry and confiscation both in the Cromwellian period and as Jacobites in the next generation, and also abroad, serving as they did in the armies of France and Spain.

(O) TEEVAN   I cannot accept the suggestion that

Teevan is a form of the Co. Sligo name Tivnan, i.e., according to Woulfe, Ó Teimhneáin, which became Tynan in Leix and Kilkenny. Teevan on the other hand is an Ulster name (possibly Ó Téimheáin in Irish) found principally in or near Co. Cavan. Teevan occurs in the Monaghan Hearth Money Rolls – in the parish of Errigal Trough in 1663. As O'Tewan we meet it as a tenant of Maguire in Co. Fermanagh in 1594.

In 1878 the Teevan family of Enniskillen owned extensive estates in counties Donegal and Fermanagh.

TEMPEST   Woulfe ignores the well-known and distinguished English name Tempest and simply gives a Gaelic-Irish form viz., Mac Anfaidh. I presume he had some authority for this: I have not discovered it. The pre-Christian Maol Anaithe can hardly be so regarded. The first of the name I have found in Ireland is Sir Thomas Tempest, who was Attorney-General in 1640. John Tempest was sheriff in Drogheda in 1659; and in the interesting and long drawn out case arising out of the will of Lord Chancellor Eustace in 1665 one Michael Tempest appears as the guardian of the petitioner, Maurice Eustace. The name has attained prominence as the surname of the Marquesses of Londonderry: their real name, however, was Vane to which Tempest was added.

TERRY   Terry has been a notable name in the county and city of Cork since the thirteenth century – in the city, between 1500 and 1646, shortly after which date the Cromwellian régime put an end to Catholic corporations, they held the position of mayor 22 times. (For the pedigree of this family see Bibliography.) Like the Goulds, Coppingers and other citizens successful in business, branches of the Terry family moved out into the surrounding countryside and are found as 1641 freeholders in the barony of Barretts. Some of them, indeed, were resident in the adjacent barony of Barrymore as far back as 1297. Other former spellings of the name were Tyrry, Tirry and Therry. In one case, pardon to Gilleduff Philippi O'Terry, a Co. Tipperary man, in 1585, the prefix O would imply that it is a Gaelic-Irish surname. It is true that the Gaelic surname Mac Toirdealbhaigh had been anglicized, inter alia, as Terry but that is a Mac name which appears in 1540 as MacTerye in Co. Meath and elsewhere. The normal form of Terry in Irish was Tuiridh, a phonetic rendering of the Anglo-Norman Terri which is itself an abbreviation of Teorrus or Theodoricus. This is no doubt the origin of most of our Terrys, including James Terry (1660-1725) of Limerick, who was Athlone Herald (i.e. Deputy Ulster King of Arms) under James II after he had been supplanted by William III: his heraldic manuscripts, preserved in the British Museum, have been of considerable value in reconstructing the Irish heraldry of the past.

In addition to their prominence in the civic affairs of the city the Terrys of Cork have produced several distinguished churchmen. Fr. William Tirrey, O.S.A. the author of a religious work to which the Cromwellians objected, was hanged, drawn and quartered in 1654; another William Tirry was Bishop of Cork and Cloyne from 1622 to 1640, and Rev. John Joseph Therry (1790-1864) reputed to be the first priest to visit Queensland, was the "patriarch of the Church" in New South Wales, in which colony another of that name, Sir Roger Therry (1800-1874) was attorney-general and judge. Before he went to Australia he was a notable advocate of Catholic Emancipation.   Bibl.

TESKY   This is a Palatine surname introduced into Ireland at the time of the German Palatine settlement in Co. Limerick in 1709.

(O) TEVLIN   I have not found the Gaelic form of this name: it may be Ó Teibhlin on the analogy of Ó Seibhlin for Shevlin. The suggestion that Tevlin may be a local form of Shevlin seems unlikely etymologically; but before rejecting this it should be borne in mind that the area in which the name Tevlin is almost exclusively found is adjacent to that of Shevlin. The Tevlins are located in Co. Cavan and in north Meath, especially around Kells. In the former it is also spelt Tevelin. James Tevlin (1798-1873), poet and schoolmaster, was a Co. Cavan man.

MacTIGUE, Teague, Tighe   (O) TIGHE   MacTigue and Tighe are the two most usual anglicized forms of the surname Mac Taidhg, other variants being MacTeague and MacTague. Teague is the form generally used in Ulster, but MacTeague, with the prefix, is commoner in Co. Donegal and MacTague occurs chiefly in Co. Cavan. The MacTigue and Tighe forms, found in Connacht, are more numerous: Co. Mayo is their principal habitat. There was, however, no actual sept of Mac Taidhg: like MacShane, MacTigue as a surname came into being in a number of places independently, and was at first an ephemeral appellation formed from a father's Christian name which at some period became fixed.

Ó Taidhg, on the other hand, was a genuine patronymic which, in fact, belonged to as many as four distinct septs, whose present day representatives, where they survive, are now either Tighe or have become MacTigue or Mac Teague by attraction. An example of this is to be seen in the case of Donnchadh Ó Taidhg, Archbishop of Armagh from 1560 to 1562, whose name appears in some records as Donal MacTeague. He was presumably of the Ulster sept of Ó Taidhg of Oriel origin, erenaghs of Termonkenny, Co. Down, located also in Feara Li (barony of Coleraine). James Tighe (1795-1869) was of this sept. There were three other Ó Taidhg septs. Before the Anglo-Norman invasion an Ó Taidhg was chief of Imail, a territory in what is now Co. Wicklow, subsequently occupied by the O'Tooles. Then there was the sept located in Connacht in the country of the O'Connors, to whom they were akin: they are frequently mentioned in the Annals and O'Teige is described in a manuscript written by Donogh O'Mulconry in 1228 as chief of the household of the King of Connacht. Lastly the Thomond sept whence came Tadhg Ó Taidhg, Bishop of Killaloe, whose death in 1083 is recorded by the Four Masters. I wonder was John O'Tayg, of Cnockanveegh, Co. Tipperary, from whom 30 sheep value 8d. each were stolen in 1307, one of these. The Justiciary Rolls, which so often afford an interesting picture of life in mediaeval Ireland, do not in their relation of this case help to answer this question, which might equally be asked about Thomas O'Taig, an Ormond tenant at Carrick in 1444. The use of Taddeus in Latin documents to denote the surname tends to increase confusion between Mac and O: thus Fr. Patrick MacTeig, O.P. is called simply Patricius Taddeus in a processus datariae relating to the see of Kildare in 1620.

The name Tighe presents a good example of pseudo-translation of Irish surnames: Kangley, a rare Breffny (Cavan) name is Mac Ceanglaigh in Irish: ceangail is the Irish verb for tie, hence Tighe has been used as a synonym of Kangley!

The best known family of Tighe in Ireland, that of Woodstock, Co. Kilkenny, is unconnected with any of those mentioned above. The first of these came from Market Deeping in England and, becoming sheriff of Dublin in 1649, M.P. in 1656 and three times mayor, was the ancestor of a long line of sheriffs, D.L's and M.P's. One of these, Henry Tighe (d. 1836), M.P. for Inistioge, was the husband of Mary Tighe (née Blatchford) (1772-1810), a poetess whose works went into six editions.

(Mac) TIMLIN   Woulfe describes this as the name of a Welsh or Anglo-Norman family long settled in Co. Mayo. They certainly settled in Mayo and became completely hibernicized, for they appear in the Mayo Book of Survey and Distribution as "the sept of Tomilins" in the barony of Tirawley, where they were among the papist proprietors in 1641. I do not think, however, that they can be included in the category of those Anglo or Cambro-Normans who settled in Connacht after the invasion at the end of the twelfth century, because as late as 1600 we find them in Co. Donegal (as the Elizabethan Fiants attest) and very soon after that several of the name were among the followers of O'Donnell when he migrated from Tirconnell to Mayo.

The name in its modern form, Timlin, belongs almost exclusively to Co. Mayo.

TIMMONS, MacTomyn   The individual members of Clann Toimin, a branch of the Barretts of Tirawley, were called Mac Toimin in Irish and MacTomyn in sixteenth century documents in English. MacFirbis places the family of Tomin amongst those of Welsh origin. Occasionally O was erroneously substituted for Mac e.g. Fr. Eugene O'Teman O.F.M. one of the martyrs under the Cromwellian régime. The name is said to have become Timmons, but this is very rarely found in Connacht in modern times and O'Donovan considered that Toimin was a clan or group name only. Timmons or Timmins is now associated with Co. Carlow and adjacent counties. It has been there at least as far back as 1420 when William Tomyne was a parliamentary collector for Co. Kildare. In 1552 it occurs as Tomyne in Co. Kildare and in 1558 under the gaelicized guise of Patrick Rwo MacTommyn in Co. Wexford. In 1659 Tomin was listed in the "cen-

sus" as a principal Irish name in two baronies of Co. Carlow. (Wicklow is missing from the document). Bally-timmin is the name of a townland in the same part of Co. Carlow. Timmons in Co. Wicklow and Carlow may thus be the modern form of the earlier O'Timon (i.e. Ó Tiomáin), which is on record there in the Tudor Fiants. This is quite unconnected with the family of similar name in Connacht. It should be added that Timmons is now seldom found outside Leinster, whereas Timon (or Tymon) is the form current in Connacht. Some confusion in these names is thus inevitable. In 1798 Edward Timmins of Cullentragh was active on the side of the insurgents. Dr. John Timon C.M. (b. 1797), Bishop of Buffalo, was a prominent educator in U.S.A.: he was the son of James Timon or Timmons, who emigrated from Co. Cavan in 1796.

(O) TIMONY   (Mac) TIMPANY, Tumpane   We may ignore the statement that these two names are basically the same: without the prefix Mac or O (which indeed are scarcely ever seen with either of them to day) they are occasionally used as synonyms; but they are in fact distinct. Timpany, which also takes the form Tempany and Tenpenny, is Mac in Tiompánaigh, tiompánach being a player of the musical instrument known as the timpane. Early anglicizations of this were Mac Tympane and Mac-Itempanye, the names of sixteenth century families dwelling with the O'Preys and the Savages in the Ards, Co. Down. It is very rare now in any form; the shortened form Tumpane is found in modern times in north Tipperary.

Timoney, on the other hand, is fairly numerous in the stretch of country covering adjacent parts of counties Donegal, Tyrone and Leitrim. We find it in another Ulster county in 1665: it appears several times as O'Temmany in the Armagh Hearth Money Rolls. The Co. Donegal Gaelic poet Tadhg Ó Tiománaidhe so wrote his name and we may accept that as the correct Irish form. In the same document one householder is returned as O'Timpany but the fact that there the prefix is given as O not Mac is not significant.

(O) TOHILL   The name of the Co. Derry sept of Ó Tuathail has seldom become O'Toole, but is anglicized Tohill. O'Donovan found this as Toghill a century ago, and this form is perpetuated in the parish of Desert-toghill, which indicates their location.

On the other hand in the south Toohill and Twohill are in fact variants of O'Toole: these forms are found in counties Cork and Waterford; in the latter Towell is a more numerous variant. See Toal.

(O) TOLAN, Toland, Toolan   Ó Tuathaláin in Ulster, the province of its origin, is now usually Toland, while in Mayo it is Tolan, though a century ago in Mayo it was Toolan. This is the natural pronunciation having regard to the Irish form and indeed it was so called in its homeland, the barony of Tirhugh, Co. Donegal, when Petty's "census" was taken in 1659: in that document the prefix O, now discarded, is retained. The O'Toolans migrated, like many other Donegal families, to Mayo with some of the leading O'Donnells in 1602; but many remained, as is proved by the Hearth Money Rolls of 1665 in which as O'Toolan and O'Twolan the name occurs frequently. In the Book of Lecan the sept appears as cenel Tulán. It was however, found in Co. Sligo long before that. Petrus Ó Tuathaláin was vicar of Killaspugbrone in the barony of Carbury in 1306; and a Fiant of 1594 includes an O'Tolan of Co. Sligo. According to O'Donovan's editorial note in the Annals of the Four Masters the Tolans went to Mayo in the seventeenth century with the O'Donnells; he adds that in Achill the name became Thulis.

(O) TONER   Though this name is derived from the Norse forename Tomar, that of a Scandinavian king of Dublin in the tenth century, the sept of Ó Tomhrair is a truly Gaelic one. It was not unusual when Gaels married women of Norse stock to baptize some of the children by Norse names (Manus, whence MacManus, is the best known example of this). In the case of Ó Tomhrair (anglice Toner) we meet the not uncommon substitution of N for R and vice versa in the anglicization of proper names (cf. MacNelis – MacGrelish or Luimneach – Limerick). The Toners were a family of the Cenél Eoghain, who possessed territory on the shores of the Foyle near Lifford. In the course of time they moved eastwards into Co. Derry and thence to Co. Armagh, where Toner appears in Petty's "census" (1659) and the Hearth Money Rolls (1664) among the principal Irish names of that county and where it is today most numerous. It appears in the arch-diocese of Armagh two centuries earlier in the person of Patrick Othonyr, an obdurate priest who is reported in 1435 as continuing after seven years to defy a sentence of excommunication. John Thonor (or Thonery) was Bishop of Lismore from 1554 to 1565. Excluding the capital city of Dublin, where names from all provinces are of course found, it is rarely met outside Ulster.

The church of Killodonnell in Co. Donegal should properly be called Killotoner since it is named after an O'Toner not an O'Donnell. The Four Masters mention a priest of Clonmacnois (A.D. 1011) called Ó Tomhrair. Woulfe states that Ó Tomhnra, anglice Tonra and Tunry, is a variant of Ó Tomhrair, and places this family in Mayo and Sligo; O'Donovan gives both Toner and Tonry as modern synonyms of Ó Tomhrair.   Map

TONGE   This name is pronounced by the families so called to sound like tonj, though those who erroneously make it sound like tongue are basically correct since it is derived from the English word – either, Reaney states, from residence on a tongue of land or from a propensity to chatter: Weekley also mentions it as a toponymic, from a place called Tonge. The present pronunciation was not universal a century ago, as we find it returned in birth registrations as Tong as well as Tonge, and in the list of graduates of Dublin University one is given as

Tonge and another as Tonge alias Tongue. The latter was born in England in 1652. From that date on the name as Tonge is of fairly frequent occurrence in Irish records, principally in Co. Wexford (New Ross) and other east Leinster counties. It is, however, mainly in English records it is found and in the index to the publications of the Historical Manuscripts Commission Tonge and Tongue are equated.

The most notable man of the name in Irish history is associated with Ulster not Leinster: he was Miles Tonge, who was one of the men who cut the boom at the siege of Derry in 1689.

(O) TORMEY   This name originated in Annaly and from the earliest times of which we have records down to the present day the name O'Tormey has been associated with Co. Longford and the adjacent counties of Westmeath and Cavan. Gillaíosa Ó Tormaigh, Bishop of Ardagh from 1232 to 1237, was of sufficient importance to be mentioned by nearly all the annalists. References to the name in the Elizabethan Fiants relate to the O'Reilly and Nugent country in Cavan and Westmeath, and modern statistics place it in the area running eastwards from Granard in Co. Longford.

TORRENS TORRANCE TARRANT   Apart from the fact that Thornton is an occasional synonym of Torrens in Co. Derry and of Tarrant in Co. Cork there is confusion regarding the three names at the head of this article since they are sometimes used synonymously and in some cases have, and in others have not, a common origin. Richard Foley (N.L. MS. G. 841) says Tarrant is an anglicized form of Ó Taráin; Ewen and Bardsley (not referring to Ireland) say it is an English toponymic: both these statements may be right. Again Ewen says Torrance is a Scottish toponymic and Black confirms this. Nevertheless Torrance is definitely a variant of Torrens which is a numerous name in Co. Derry. Griffith's Valuation lists 51 house- or landholders there in 1858 with 17 in neighbouring Co. Donegal, and these I have assumed to be originally Ó Toráin; Elrington Ball, however, in his Judges of Ireland states that the Torrens family of Derry are of Swedish descent.

For the individual bearing one of these names the problem of deciding from which origin his ancestors came can only be solved, if at all, by arduous research. All I can do in this brief article is to record the facts given above to which I might add that present day statistics show that Torrens is very numerous in Co. Derry and that Tarrant, also spelt Torrant and Torrent is mainly found in Co. Cork (but not in the western part of that county). Reaney does not include any of the names in question in his dictionary of British surnames.

Fianlly it would perhaps be of interest to mention Sir Robert Torrens (1814-1884), author of the Australian Torrens Act, which introduced a new system of simplified land title registration and was subsequently adopted by sixty other countries, who was born in Cork. The river Torrens, in south Australia, was named after his father, Co. Robert Torrens.

TOSH   This name is met quite frequently in north-east Ulster. It is simply an abbreviation of the Scottish Makintosh, Mac an Toisich, i.e. in Irish Mac an Taoisigh (taoiseach, chief or leader).

(O) TOUGHER, Tooher (Tucker)   Records of the sixteenth centuries and also modern statistics corroborate Woulfe's statement that Ó Tuachair is the name of two quite distinct septs, one originating in the Ely O'Carroll territory (north Tipperary and south Offaly) and the other belonging to, though not originating in, north Connacht. (They came from Ulster and are mentioned in the Annals there as early as 1126.) In modern times the anglicized form of the name of the Connacht sept has usually been spelt Tougher and Togher, while the other tends to be Tooher, which is very numerous in Co. Offaly at the present time: Toher is common to both. In both areas this Gaelic-Irish name has sometimes been disguised by being changed first to Tooker and then to the English Tucker. There is, however, no real consistency in these differences of spelling; and when we look, for example, at the "census" of 1659 we find both Tougher and Toher listed as principal Irish names in King's County (Offaly). A century earlier when the anglicized forms of Gaelic surnames began to come into regular use, especially in official records, many variant spellings occur such as O'Tuogher in Co. Tipperary and O'Twoghir in Offaly.

TRANT   Though Woulfe counts the Trants of Norman origin and states that they took their name from Trent in Somerset, England, the tradition that they were in fact Ostmen (Scandinavians) of one of the pre-Norman Shannon settlements is to some extent supported by the absence of the particle de with their name in early mediaeval records, e.g. the Justiciary Rolls, where they appear frequently as Trawent, sometimes Trewent and once as le (not de) Trewent. Apparently Woulfe did find the form de Trente but this could be a different surname unconnected with Trant. All these Trawent and Trewent records relate to Co. Kerry with which county they have been closely associated since the thirteenth century. In the 16th century the name often appears in the barony of Clanmorris; in 1592 Richard Trainte was sovereign of Dingle, while one of them went to Spain after the battle of Kinsale with O'Sullivan Beare's son. In the 17th century they were particularly prominent as Jacobites. Sir Patrick Trant, Bart, a colonel in King James' Irish army, in which four other officers of the name are listed, was, with eleven others of the name, outlawed and his extensive estates in Kerry and other counties were confiscated. His daughter Olive Trant (1675-c.1755) was the wife of the Prince d'Auvergne; she was also the mistress of the Duke of Orleans and was well known in her day as a worker in the Jacobite cause in France. Another of the same family Chevalier Thomas Trant, son of Dominic Trant of Ballintlea, Dingle, was an officer in the Irish Brigade who left France about 1780 to fight on the American side in the War of Independence in which he played a notable part. He was later ruined as a result of his efforts on behalf of the French monarchy at the time of the Revolution and died in Ireland in 1794. Another soldier of Dingle stock also educated in France was Sir Nicholas Trant (1769-1839), who distinguished himself in Portugal in the Peninsular War.

There were 21 families of Trant in Co. Kerry in the 1901 census and all the births recorded in 1866 and in 1890 were in that county. Trant was one of the most numerous names in the barony of Corcaguiney in 1659. Bibl., Map

(O) TUBRIDY   Though Tubridy is the usual form of this Co. Clare name, which is Ó Tiobraide in modern Irish, its synonym Tubrit, also found in Clare, seems to be nearer the earlier anglicized form. The earliest I have met — O'Tybryth — is in the Justiciary Rolls of 1311 (not in Clare in that case but in Co. Carlow). In the sixteenth century we meet Tubridd, Tubbred and Tibrud. Nevertheless the terminal third syllable is nearer the original which occurs in such records as the Book of Lecan, the Book of Ballymote and in the MacFirbis genealogies, in the form of Ua Tipraide and O Tipraite. It was never numerous in any century but the current Co. Clare voters lists show that it is far from dying out.

TUMULTY   I accept Woulfe's Gaelic forms of this name viz. Ó Tomaltaigh and Mac Tomaltaigh, but it can hardly be described as rare and it certainly is inaccurate to locate it in south Leinster. An analysis of birth registrations for several years shows that it is seldom found outside the Oriel country i.e. south Down, north Louth and Co. Monaghan. It appears too in the Hearth Money Rolls of Co. Monaghan of 1665 (in 1663 it appeared as Tomoly) but it was not numerous enough to be listed as a principal Irish name in any barony in the "census" of 1659. Bernard Tumulty, the nineteenth century Drogheda poet and scribe, wrote his name Brian Ó Tumultaidhe.

The name is on record also in Co. Roscommon and east Galway in the mediaeval and early modern period, where it has since strangely been corrupted to Timothy. This probably a small sept distinct from the O'Tumultys of Oriel, deriving from Tomaltach, chief of Moylurg from 1169 to 1206. In the sixteenth century Mac Tumulty occurs much more frequently than O'Tumulty. In the Fiants, for example there are thirteen Macs and only three O's with this name (there are seven variations of spelling with MacTumulty) ten of those belonged to the Connacht sept and the other three to Leinster counties adjacent to Connacht. Two with the Mac prefix are in the Composition Book of Connacht (1585) and none with O.

Two prominent ecclesiastics of Elphin and Athlone (1284 and 1410) are mentioned in the Annals of Loch Cé; and a third appears in the state papers as Canon of Elphin in 1296. None of these has the prefix Mac. In the next century we find the O'Tumultys allied by marriage to the leading O'Kellys of Uí Maine; and Fr. P.K. Egan states that the name is still extant in the barony of Moycarn.

(O) TUNNEY   A branch of the Cenél Conaill located on the borders of Co. Sligo and Co. Donegal. In modern times the name has been mainly associated with Mayo especially the Swinform area. Tonnach from which the name Ó Tonnaigh is derived, means billowy, from tonn, wave.

(O) TUOHY, Twohig   (O) TOWEY, Tuffy   The sept of Ó Tuathaigh is a branch of the Uí Maine, formerly seated at Aughrin, Co. Galway. O'Donovan states that the modern form of the name is Tookey; but from his time till now Tuohy is very much more numerous. It is a fact that families called Tuohy, Touhy, Twohy etc., are for the most part now to be found in Clare and south-east Galway. Co. Galway is missing from the "census" of 1659: that enumeration places them chiefly in Co. Tipperary – in Kilnamanagh and Owney and Arra, the baronies adjacent to Thomond. It is in Co. Tipperary, too, that the name appears most frequently in seventeenth and eighteenth century documents such as Hearth Money Rolls, leases, court cases and the like. Already by the middle of the sixteenth century it had become quite numerous in Co. Cork, too. There the form Twohig is now used in English, just as Ó Cobhthaigh (Coffey elsewhere) is called Cowhig in that county. Patrick J. Twohey (b. 1865), a notable piper, was the son and grandson of Co. Galway men, also pipers of note, who, however, according to O'Neill's Irish Minstrels and Musicians bore the name Twohill in English. I have not met another example of Twohill (i.e. Ó Tuathail or O'Toole) being changed to Touhey or Tuohy. Twohill is usually found in Co. Cork. Dr. Charles Tuohy was Bishop of Limerick from 1814 to 1828.

Towey is reported as having been occasionally used as a synonym of Tuohy, but in north Connacht at any rate Towey is a distinct name, being the anglicized form of Ó Toghdha. There, especially in Co. Roscommon, it is numerous. There is not much historical or genealogical information available about the name. Ó Toghdha was chief of Bredagh, a small territory lying in the parishes of Moygawnagh and Kilfian, barony of Tirawley, Co. Mayo, the sept being a branch of the Hy Fiachrach. Towey is the usual modern form of the name; the rarer Tuffy is a synonym.   Map

TURKINGTON   This English name is included here because of its close association with one particular county, viz. Armagh, where it is now numerous. It was there in the seventeenth century as we know from the Co. Armagh Hearth Money Rolls, though not then numerous.

TUTTY TUTHILL   I have found no evidence to support Woulfe's statement that Tutty is an anglicized form of Ó Tuataigh which, he says, ia a variant of Ó Tuathaigh (Tuohy). The occurrence of O'Thouty, (probably a clerical error for O'Touthy) in a Fiant (Co. Tipperary 1585) can hardly be regarded as a link with Tutty. As Tutty it occurs but rarely in our records and never, to my knowledge, before the Cromwellian period when two

Londoners of the name appear among the "adventurers" for Irish land.

Tutty is included in the list prepared by the Registrar-General in 1891 as used synonymously with Tuthill. Tuthill is an English toponymic, quite distinct from Tohill (q.v.). It first appears in Ireland in the army of the 1640s. Families of the name acquired property in Co. Limerick and several other parts of the country under the land settlement of the Cromwellian and Restoration periods: they retained their place among the landed gentry during the three following centuries. John Tuthill's unedifying part in the 1817 Limerick election is still remembered.   Bibl.

TWAMLEY   This is a name of English origin, derived from a place called Twemloe in Cheshire. It has been located in Co. Wicklow since the beginning of the eighteenth century.

TWEEDY   Tweedie is a sept of the Scottish clan Fraser. It may be a coincidence that one of the earliest Tweedys to be on record in Ireland, Patrick Tweedy, was a lieutenant in the regiment of the army stationed at Carrickfergus, under the command of Capt. Alexander Frazer. That was in 1678. There was a Tweddy in Ulster some fifty years earlier, when, in 1629, Walter Tweddy and a number of other men, mostly Gaelic-Irish, obtained leases of "planted" lands in Co. Cavan. The name has never been numerous in Ireland and, except in Dublin, is little known outside Ulster, where it has been mainly found in counties Cavan and Armagh. There is a Ballytweedy in Co. Antrim but this is one of many misleading place-names – the tweedy is not taken from the surname Tweedy.   Bibl.

(O) TYNAN   Tynan, occasionally spelt Tinan and Tynnan, was formerly O'Teynane and O'Tyvnane; the last approximates phonetically to the Irish form Ó Teimhneáin. It is originally a Leix surname, and is found in that part of the country today in considerable numbers, as was the case in 1659 when Petty's "census" was taken: at that time the name was also numerous in the adjacent part of Co. Kilkenny (barony of Galmoy), and in 1665 eleven families of Tynan appear in the Hearth Money Rolls for various parts of Co. Tipperary. The Fiants, which are the best guide we have to population distribution in the sixteenth century, show that counties Leix and Kilkenny were equally their habitat at that period.

The most noteworthy person of the name was Katherine Tynan (1861-1913), poetess and novelist.   Map

TYRRELL   Very shortly after the invasion of 1170 the Anglo-Norman family of Terrell or Tirrell, which had gone from France to England with William the Conqueror, came to Ireland, obtaining a grant of the greater part of the barony of Fertullagh in Westmeath as well as the lordship of Castleknock in Co. Dublin. There or thereabouts they have remained since, appearing in the records down the centuries in every walk of life but always with representatives in the highest ranks of society. In the Ormond Deeds and other mediaeval records the name occurs frequently from the year 1176 onwards, the most prominent of the many mediaeval officials of the name being Hugh Tirrell, who was seneschal of Ulster in 1224.

In some sixteenth century records, e.g. Dowling's Annals and the Fiants, the name is given as MacTyrrell: this is not to be taken as indicating that there was also a Gaelic sept of the name but merely that many families of the name had become assimilated in the Irish nation by that time. While not becoming hibernicized so completely as other Norman families more remote from the Pale, they were typical of the powerful "Old English" Catholic families which in the seventeenth century were identified with the Confederation of Kilkenny, opposition to the Cromwellian régime, and later support of the Jacobite cause.

Tyrrell's Pass in Co. Westmeath got its name from the victory won there in 1597 by Capt. Richard Tyrrell, one of O'Neill's ablest commanders; in that year was born Edward Tyrrell (d. 1671) superior of the Irish College, Paris, and official agent of the Confederation of Kilkenny in France. In the next generation Dr. Patrick Tyrrell O.F.M., Bishop of Clogher from 1676 to 1688, afterwards Bishop of Meath, was closely associated with St Oliver Plunket, and nine Tyrrells were officers in King James II's Irish army, including two in Sarsfield's own regiment.

In modern times Professor Robert Yelverton Tyrrell (1844-1914), was a celebrated classical scholar and poet; the Rev. George Tyrrell (1861-1909) was the author of religious books for the publication of one of which he was excommunicated.   Bibl., Map

UNIACKE, Garde   Few names are more closely identified with one county than Uniacke is with Co. Cork; and this association is especially close with Youghal and its vicinity, in which there are two townlands called Mount Uniacke. The connexion with Youghal dates back at least till 1386 in the person of Thomas Unak, and in 1357 a Thomas Unack, perhaps the same person, is described in a patent roll as of Cork. From the fourteenth to the nineteenth century records relating to Co. Cork abound in references to the name (those I have noted alone occupy a whole page of a very large ledger): for the most part these were landed gentry or leading burgesses of Youghal, some of whom suffered as Jacobites in 1690, though one, who is called MacUnacke in a Fiant of 1587, is there termed labourer. This Mac prefix however, has no Gaelic significance. The origin of the name is in some doubt. Richard Foley, who knew that part of the country intimately, in a note on Woulfe's treatment of the name says: "Father Woulfe says it is taken from their place of residence — not their Irish place, however, because that was Baile Uí Mheirgin, half way between Youghal and Killeagh. The reference may apply to some place of theirs in England. They are called Garde. The first to be styled Uniacke (in thirteenth century) was

Bernardus Unak". Woulfe gives the Gaelic-Irish form of the name as Doingeard, making the obsolete anglicized form Donnarde, derived from the Middle- English atten yeard from residence in an enclosure.

Though I have not met a modern case of the synonymous use of Uniacke and Garde there seems to be little doubt that in Co. Cork, where in Ireland the name Garde is mainly found, families so called are of the same stock as the Uniackes. There is also an English surname Garde derived from the word guard. A branch of this from Kent is said to have settled in east Cork in the seventeenth century, but as stated above Gardes in that area are mainly Uniackes. Mr. P.J. Kennedy told me that the name Uniacke is to be found in the parish of Kilconierin (near Loughrea, Co. Galway) where it is believed to be a corruption of Mac Sheonaic, i.e. son of Jonathan (de Burgo).

John Fitzgerald Uniacke, who emigrated to Australia about 1820, wrote accounts of exploration surveys in that continent in which he had taken part.   Bibl.

(Mac) VALLELLY   (Mac) VARRILLY   The name Vallelly is quite numerous in Co. Armagh but rare elsewhere, though it is found in Co. Galway and I have met an isolated case of it in Co. Clare. As might be expected it is a name which lends itself to spelling variants: including these there were 18 birth registrations in 1866 and 9 in 1890, almost all in or near Co. Armagh. Woulfe did not know the Irish form of the name; and Mac Giolla Domhnaigh says it is Mac Imhaile, mentioning that a seventeenth century anglicization of it was MacEvalley. I question this because the forms found in the Armagh and in the Monaghan Hearth Money Rolls of 1664-1665 are MacIlvallely, MacIlvelluly and the like, while in the "census" of 1659 MacIlvalluly is given as one of the principal Irish names in Co. Armagh. The Il in these is undoubtedly an abbreviation of Giolla. To go further than Macgiolla would be guess work on my part at this stage. The Gaelic form given by Mac Giolla Domhnaigh is probably an attempt to write it phonetically as he heard it and cannot be regarded as authentic; he does, however, tell us the interesting fact that the numerous Vallelly families living in the parish of Ballymyre, Derrynoose, Kilclooney and Lisnadill (all in south County Armagh), though in many cases unrelated, have one thing in common, namely that the great majority of the people so called are red- or sandy-haired.

In Connacht Vallelly and Varrilly have been reported by the local registrars as in use synonymously in the Clifden and Westport districts. According to Woulfe, Varrilly, Verrelly and Varley are anglicized forms of Mac an Bhearshuiligh. Varrily is certainly a Connacht name. In the Connacht birth registrations for 1865 there are 14 Varillys (no variants) but no Vallally. Further confusion may possibly arise from the fact that Varrelly has also been used as a synonym of Farrelly.

MacVEAGH   The spelling MacVeigh is now more usual than the older MacVeagh; and MacVey is also found.

The name is very numerous today in north-east Ulster; and in the seventeenth century it is mainly recorded in Antrim, Armagh and Donegal as MacVagh, MacVaugh, MacEvagh and occasionally MacBey. Two MacVeaghs of Co. Down were prominent Jacobites. Prior to that, however, references to persons of the name relate almost exclusively to Connacht, all the counties in that province being represented. Its origin there is obscure. The name – Mac an Bheatha in Irish – is not dealt with in the Hy Many or Hy Fiachrach books or in any of the genealogical compilations. A Mac Beatha, who took part in the battle of Clontarf in 1014, is mentioned in the Annals, but this name is probably an ephemeral pre-surname appellation. It survived as a surname, however, as Fr. Patrick Macabeath was Bishop of Ardagh in 1541. (It should be observed that he was also called MacMahon.) Mac Bheatha is now the Gaelic form of the Scottish MacBeth and it is not unlikely that many of the Ulster MacVeighs are of that stock. In modern times MacVeigh has been confused with MacEvoy in Ulster; e.g. in the case of Fr. Peter MacVe (d. 1792), President of the Irish College, Louvain. O'Connell in his Schools and Scholars of Breffni says that he was actually a MacEvoy and that some of the eighteenth century Kilmore diocesan registers have MacVe as the Latinized form of MacEvoy. In addition to MacAvey (a synonym in Co. Sligo) the substitution of the aristocratic Vesey for MacVeigh has been noted in Co. Mayo, in which county Vahy is also similarly recorded, though normally Vahy is equated with Fahy, the well known Connacht surname dealt with in Irish Families. Flower, quoting Skene, states that Mac Beatha (Scottish Mac Bheatha) was the name of the hereditary physicians of Islay and Mull and shanachies to the MacLeans. He adds that they were of Irish (O'Neill) descent and great collectors of manuscripts. They were called MacBeth, Beton and MacVeagh in English. He mentions four such who flourished in the sixteenth century. Cardinal Beaton, his uncle and nephew were all ornaments of the Scottish Catholic Church at that time.

John MacVeigh, prominent in the Insurrection of 1798, was executed at Baltinglass.   Map

VEALE, Calfe   Almost all Irish people of this name belong to Co. Waterford families. It is less common now than it was in the seventeenth century when it appeared among the principal names in the barony of Decies. Petty's "census" lists it as an Irish name and, like Power in the same county, it may well be so calssified. It appears in mediaeval records very soon after the Anglo-Norman invasion and occurs repeatedly in the Ormond Deeds from the year 1294 onwards. Walter le Veele was Bishop of Kildare from 1300 to 1322. He is also called Calfe. In several documents both le Veele etc. and Calfe are used to denote the same person. The name is Norman in origin: le veel i.e. the calf. The form Calfe was the more usual in Leinster, where it died out but is perpetuated in the place name Calfestown, Co. Kildare. In Irish the le has erroneously become de and de Bhial is the normal form of it in Co. Waterford in modern Irish.   Bibl.

VERDON   Though comparatively rare now, from the Anglo-Norman invasion till the end of the seventeenth century Verdon was a name of great importance in Leinster, particularly in Co. Louth where at Verdonstown and other places their principal estates lay. They shared the fate of many other great Hiberno-Norman Catholic families after the Jacobite defeat, when John Verdon, titular Baron of Clonmore, was attainted. His ancestor Bertram de Verdon, who came to Ireland with Prince John and was appointed seneschal of the Pale, was granted the barony of Dundalk; his grandson founded the Grey Friary of Dundalk in 1313. At that time they were at the zenith of their power and defeated the great Justiciar Wogan himself in battle in the year 1312. Bartholomew Verdon represented Co. Louth in the parliament of 1420. In addition to the three references given in the Bibliography much useful information on the de Verdons will be found in Dalton's History of Drogheda. A branch of the Verdon family was settled at Kilmallock and Limerick in the sixteenth century, where they held many important civic offices: one of these appears in the Jacobite attainders for Munster.

The family were originally from Verdun in France, whence they went to England with William the Conqueror. In Irish they were called de Bheardún which is simply the Norman de Verdun gaelicized.   Bibl., Map

MacVICKER   This name, with its variant spellings MacVicar and MacVickar, is fairly numerous throughout Ulster but very rare elsewhere in Ireland. The MacVicars are a sept of two Scottish clans, Campbell and MacNaughton, and our Irish MacVickers are mostly of this descent. There was also, I believe, in the seventeenth century a small branch of the MacMahons of Oriel called MacAvicear, and in the 1601 Fiants relating to counties Limerick and Kerry we meet the names MacVycare and MacYvicare, but it is unlikely that direct descendants of these people now survive. The Gaelic form is clearly seen in MacAvicear and MacYvicare i.e. Mac a' Bhiocaire (son of the vicar).

MacVITTY   Variant spellings of this name recorded by Matheson are MacVeity, MacVity, MacVeety and Mavity, but the total number of people in Ireland bearing these names is small. Formerly it was prominent in Co. Longford where John MacVitty was high sheriff in 1773. If

Woulfe is correct in giving the Gaelic form of the name as Mac an Bhiadhtaigh it is etymologically akin to Betagh and Beatty (q.v.)

WADDING   The pre-eminence of Father Luke Wadding (1588-1657), an outstanding figure in the history of the Catholic Church as well as of Ireland, creates the impression that the Waddings were a Waterford family. Such indeed was the case, but only from the middle of the fifteenth century when a branch, from which Father Luke came, was established there. The Waddings, however, had settled in Ireland 250 years earlier: coming with the Anglo-Norman invaders they soon acquired estates in Co. Wexford, in the baronies of Forth and Bargy. Their chief seats were Ballycogley and Ballyrane, and they were also influential citizens of the town of Wexford. Having throughout the mediaeval period been continuously prominent in Wexford and adjoining counties as ecclesiastics, county and municipal officials, members of Parliament etc., they shared the fate of almost all the great Catholic families in the seventeenth century. The Cromwellian confiscations resulted in Richard Wadding of Ballycogley and John Wadding of Bannow being transplanted to Connacht, where the former got 499 acres and the latter 216; but they did not prosper in their new environment. Richard Wadding had been treasurer for Co. Wexford under the Confederation of Kilkenny. The Cromwellian régime did not completely expel the Waddings from their homeland: we find Lucas Wadding Bishop of Ferns in 1687 — he was notable as a writer of carols — and a Richard Wadding in Bagnall's regiment of James II's army. The Jacobite débâcle, however, finally ruined them.

The Wadding family of Waterford is remarkable for the number of its members who became distinguished ecclesiastics on the Continent in the seventeenth century. After Father Luke Wadding (whose countenance became well known in Ireland on account of the postage stamp issued to commemorate his tercentenary) the most notable were Rev. Peter Wadding S.J. (1580-1644), chancellor of the Universities of Prague and Gratz, and Rev. Michael Wadding (d.c. 1650) author of theological works in Spanish — he was known as Miguel Godinez in Spain.

Apart from works relating particularly to the career of Father Luke Wadding, Hore's History of Co. Wexford contains much information relating to the various branches of the family; and in this connexion the valuable Wadding family manuscript (National Library MS. 5193) should also be mentioned.   Bibl., Map

WADE   Wade has two distinct origins. One is native Irish i.e. MacWade (as a variant of MacQuaid) which is sometimes abbreviated to Wade; the other is English derived in some cases from the old-English wadan (to go) and in others from the Norman-French de la wade (of the ford). The former (MacWade) belongs to the Oriel country; the latter is found in all the provinces and is on record in Ireland since the thirteenth century. One of the earliest

references to landowners or tenants of the name is to John Wade of Ballymore-Eustace, Co. Kildare, and for some time after that they are to be found in several Leinster counties. When we come to the seventeenth century we meet them also in Co. Waterford: in the "census" of 1659 they appear there both as a "principal Irish name" and one also as a titulado — clearly not to be counted in the same category since in 1650 this man was a Justice of the Peace. Another held that position at Kinsale in 1712 at the time of the presentments of "Papists" under the penal laws. The same diversity existed in Co. Galway: in telling me of certain tenant families of Wade in east Galway Mr. P.J. Kennedy stressed that these are not to be confused with a Cromwellian landlord of the name at Aughrim nearby. Another prominent Cromwellian was Captain Samuel Wade who settled in Ormond; but his family died out within a century. The name Wade is equally prominent among extensive landowners in modern times: de Burgh records them in 1878 in counties Galway, Roscommon, Cork, Tyrone and Meath. It is with the last that the Wades of this class have been mainly associated, though the testamentary records of dioceses in all parts of the country list many Wade wills and so indicate both their ubiquity and their prosperity. In those of Derry MacWade occurs. The only MacWade in the Elizabethan Fiants was of Co. Cork.

Probably the most distinguished of Irish Wades was Field-Marshal George Wade (1673-1748) who was notable as an engineer as well as a soldier; in other fields Joseph Augustine Wade (1796-1845), composer, and Walter Wade (d. 1825) pioneer in scientific botany are worthy of mention. Father Walter MacWaid, whose name appears in a Franciscan manuscript as Mac Ubháid, was Observant Provincial, 1567-1587.

WAFER, Weafer   The second of these two variants is now the more usual in Dublin, while Wafer as well as Weafer is still found in Co. Wexford, with which county it has been mainly associated in modern times. Earlier, however, it belonged rather to the midlands of Leinster; there, particularly in Co. Meath, the name occurs frequently in mediaeval records. In the Patent Rolls, for instance, it appears 13 times between 1303 and 1427, all in Leinster but none in Co. Wexford. The earliest reference I have met is dated 1292 when William Wafre, also called le Wafere, was a tenant at Corbally, Co. Meath. In the sixteenth century the connexion with Co. Wexford begins to appear, for an official despatch of 1536 describes Peter Waffre as a "King's enemy" in that county. But the name was still to the fore in Meath and we find it in all classes of society. Nicholas Wafer, for example, was one of the kern recruited in Meath for service in England in 1544; in 1598 the Wafers are named among the leading gentry of Co. Meath, while one Waffer, of Ballemoy in the barony of Ballighkeen, is so described in a similar list for Co. Wexford.

In some places the name is said to have been changed to Weaver but I have seen no evidence of this. Such a change would be etymologically wrong, since Weafer and Wafer derive from an old word waferer i.e. a maker of eucharistic wafers.

WALDRON WELLESLEY, Wesley COLLEY

As a surname Waldron has two distinct but analogous origins. In the form in one case of Mac Bhalronta and in the other of Mac Bhaildrin it was a Gaelic-Irish patronymic assumed by one of the great Norman families which came to Ireland in the wake of the Anglo-Norman invasion of 1170. At the present time seventy-five per cent of the people called Waldron came from Connacht families, particularly those belonging to counties Mayo and Roscommon. The Connacht Waldrons are said to be a branch of the Costelloes — MacCostello is of course itself a Gaelic-Irish patronymic assumed by the de Angulos. As MacWaldrin (which is phonetically approximately the same as the Gaelic form Mac Bhaildrin) and later as Waldrum, Waldron etc., we meet them in the official records relating to counties Mayo, Roscommon and Leitrim, and also in the Irish annals, throughout the centuries, the last in a prominent position being Most Rev. Peter Waldron, Bishop of Killala from 1814 to 1834.

In Leinster the patronymic Mac Bhalronta was assumed by a branch of the Wellesley family. Waleran, an Old-German forename, was much in use by the mediaeval Wellesleys, and in accordance with the usual practice in such cases the Gaelic name assumed became fixed. As a surname Waleran is of frequent occurrence in English as well as in Irish mediaeval records, so that it cannot be assumed that all Walerans, Walronds etc. who were in Ireland in the thirteenth and fourteenth centuries were Wellesleys, since Wallerans came over from England during that period in various capacities, e.g. Robert Wallerand, who was Bishop of Ferns from 1305 to 1312.

The Wellesleys were more prominent in Irish public life under that name than as Waldrons from the time Wallerand de Welleselegh was appointed a justice itinerant in 1243 until the death of Arthur Wellesley (1769-1852), better known as the Duke of Wellington. It must be admitted that that famous soldier, unlike his elder brother Richard Colley (1760-1853), Earl of Mornington and Marquis of Wellesley, as a British statesman was no friend of Ireland, notwithstanding his Irish birth and background. The Wellesley family had been at Dangan, Co. Meath, since 1174 and some of them became sufficiently hibernicized to appear quite frequently in sixteenth century records as obtaining "pardons" like their Gaelic neighbours; and Father Walter Wellesley O.S.A. was Bishop of Kildare from 1529 to 1539.

On the failure of the male line in the eighteenth century their property, and with it their name, passed to the Colleys of Castle Carbery, Co. Kildare, to whom they were closely related. These Colleys came to Ireland in the reign of Henry VIII. In 1796 the Wesleys, as they were then called, reverted to the earlier form of their name. The abbreviation of de Wellesley to Wesley was already well established in the sixteenth century. In the Fiants of that time 25 different members of the families of Dangan, Naragh and Blackhall are mentioned, some of them several times: 18 of the 25 are in the form of Wesley and only 7 are called Wellesley. Edward Wesley, Catholic Bishop of Kildare (1683-1693) used that spelling.

For a note on Colley as a Gaelic-Irish name see Appendix I.

WARKE   This name is an English toponymic derived from a place in Northumberland. It is now quite numerous in Donegal and Derry where it was found in the seventeenth century as the Hearth Money Rolls attest.

(Mac) WARNOCK   This is an ancient name belonging to Co. Down. It appears as Macgillavearnoge in a Fiant of 1592 relating to that county, i.e. Mac Giolla Mhearnóg in Irish. Warnock occurs frequently in the Hearth Money Rolls for Fermanagh and Donegal: in the latter it appears in the more Irish form MacIlvarnock. It occurs in nearly the same form in Scotland — MacGilvernock and MacIlvernock, e.g. in the Valuation Rolls of Argyle, 1751. This is a sept or branch of the clan Graham of Menteith.

WAUGH   Though better known in the north of England and the Scottish border, this name is numerous enough in Ireland to be considered in this book. It may be regarded here primarily as an Ulster family: they are to be found in the Hearth Money Rolls of counties Monaghan, Antrim and Derry (1664-69). The Waugh arms inscribed (1751) on a tombstone in the parish of Muckamore, Co. Antrim, are those of a lowland Scottish family from Roxburghshire. In the Donegal Hearth Money Rolls MacWaughe occurs, suggesting a Gaelic origin for the name, but Waugh is unquestionably derived from the Old-English word walh meaning foreign, and MacWaughe may be a clerk's attempt to write MacVeagh: the MacVaghs who appear in the contemporary "census" are certainly MacVeaghs. In recent times outside of Ulster and Dublin the name Waugh is rare: a few are to be found in counties Cork and Offaly. At Carrick-on-Shannon Vagh and Vaugh (but not MacVagh) are recorded as synonyms of Waugh.

MacWEENEY MAWHINNEY   There is no doubt that MacWeeney is Mac Mhaonaigh, the earlier form of which was MacMaenaigh, the name of a sept of Moylurg in the modern Co. Roscommon. This is close to Leitrim where the MacWeeneys (excepting those who have migrated to Dublin) are mainly to be found to-day. However, some confusion must arise from the fact that the Ulster name usually spelt Mawhinney is also Mac Whinney, for which many synonyms have been recorded by local registrars:

among these are MacQuinney and MacWeeny. The latter is very rare in Ulster and is normally a variant spelling of the Connacht MacWeeney. Some of the synonyms of Mawhinney are interesting. In the Lisburn area it has been made Mawhannon: this in turn was called Bohannon and in Co. Antrim became Buchanan, which of course is the name of a well known Scottish clan. The Buchanans of Omagh are of Scottish origin. It has been suggested that the Irish form of Mawhinney is Mac Shuibhne is a variant of Mac Suibhne (MacSweeney). The "census" of 1659 records 15 families of MacWynny and Mac A Vynny in Co. Fermanagh; both of which can be equated with the modern Mawhinney and not with MacWeeney.

WEIR WARE   The Ulster surname Weir is the modern form of Mac an Mhaoir (pronounced Macavweer) formerly anglicized MacMoyer; it was borne by a Co. Armagh family noted in history as the hereditary keepers of the celebrated Book of Armagh. The last of these was Florence MacMoyer (d. 1713) of Ballymoyer who earned an unenviable reputation as a perjured witness for the prosecution at the trial of St Oliver Plunket. Eugene MacGillaweer, who was Archbishop of Armagh from 1206 to 1216 was, however, of a different Armagh sept, viz. Mac Giolla Uidir (see MacClure).

Weir has been, by mistranslation, used as a synonym of Ó Corra (Corry). In Co. Westmeath the name has become Wyer, e.g. Mathew Daly Wyer (1853-1891), poet and prominent member of the Pan-Celtic Society. Two Westmeath men who were outlawed as Jacobites were returned respectively as Wyer and Weyre.

Ware, on the other hand, is English in origin. Of the Ware families in Ireland the best known are Ware of Woodfort (settled in Co. Cork 1588), and that of Dublin-born Sir James Ware (1594-1666), historian and one of the greatest of Irish antiquaries, who succeeded his father as Irish auditor-general; his son, Robert Ware, was notorious for his anti-Catholic views and for his tampering with Sir James Ware's manuscripts. Hugh Ware (c. 1772-1846), born in Co. Kildare, was a prominent United Irishman in the field in 1798 and afterwards a colonel in Napoleon's army.

De Ware is occasionally met in early Hiberno-Norman records.

WELDON, Veldon, Belton   This name is derived from a place in England and first appears in Ireland in the early fourteenth century. Richard de Welleton was in possession of property in the city and county of Dublin in 1320 and in 1333 Henry de Weldoun appears as an inquisition juror at Carrickfergus. The family, however, has had little connexion since then with Ulster, being settled in Counties Dublin, Louth and Meath. In the latter they gave their name to the townland Veldounstown, Veldon being up to the seventeenth century a more usual spelling than Weldon: Veldon indeed is still found around Dublin, and Belton is numerous there but this variant is of comparatively modern introduction. The most prominent family of the name Weldon is not descended from the early settlers; four Weldon brothers came to Ireland about 1600 and acquired considerable estates in Queen's Co. (Leix) at Ratheenderry and in Co. Kildare around Athy. They soon became influential and within a generation we find them as M.P's and sheriffs of Co. Kildare. A descendant of theirs is remembered for his disinterested action in faithfully holding for the Catholic Graces their estates during the period of the Penal Code. The Weldons were, however, for the most part Catholics: one, of the Co. Louth Weldons, was a member of the Catholic Confederation in 1646 and two from other Leinster branches were officers in James II's army.

In our time there have been two literary figures named Weldon. I have already referred to John Weldon alias Brinsley MacNamara (Irish Families, p. 47); the other was Bob Weldon, Gaelic poet of the Comeraghs, who died about 1925.

WHITAKER   This is the most usual modern form, but there are several variant spellings in use, including Whiteacre, which reveals the derivation of the name. It appears in the Patent Rolls as de Whiteacre at Drogheda in 1403 and at Trim in 1408; Robert Whytacre was Bailiff of Drogheda in 1305 (he is also called Quitaker in the Justiciary Rolls) and there are several other mediaeval references to men of the name in or near Meath. Griffith's Valuation and other modern sources find the name still in the midland counties, but from the seventeenth century it becomes increasingly well known in Ulster. In 1636 Thomas Whitaker was mayor of Carrickfergus and a generation later the name occurs occasionally in the northern Hearth Money Rolls. It is now fairly numerous in Ulster and also in the city of Cork, but its absence from eighteenth century Cork records shows that its connexion with that city is not of long standing.

WHITNEY   This is an English name which as de Whiteney appears in Co. Louth as early as 1297. It has never been numerous. In modern times, apart from Dublin, where there are a number of families of the name, it has been chiefly found in Co. Longford and Co. Wexford.

WHITTY   Reaney gives three alternative derivations for this, all from Old-English, including the one accepted by Woulfe viz. atte wytheg (the white enclosure). It has been in Co. Wexford and Co. Waterford for many centuries and from 1305 occurs frequently in records relating to those counties. They possessed, and probably built, the castles of Ballyhealy, Baldwinstown and Ballyteige in Co. Wexford, the last named being the seat of the principal family of the name. By 1659, when Petty's "census" was taken, Whittys were very numerous in Co. Wexford, 27 families being recorded in the baronies of Forth and Bargy. When Griffith carried out his Valuation two centuries later he found more than 150 Whitty householders in Co. Wexford, and this is corroborated by the official birth registrations which began in 1864. There is an armorial monument to Walter Whitty (d. 1630) in the church at Kilmore, Co. Wexford. Robert Whitty was convicted of "high treason" in 1715 – his crime being espousing the cause of the "Old Pretender". Two Co. Wexford men, Michael James Whitty (1795-1873) and his son Edward Michael Whitty (1827-1860), were pioneers in the sphere of journalism. Ellen Whitty (Mother Mary Vincent of the Australian Sisters of Mercy) (1821-1892), pioneer nun, was also born in Co. Wexford.

In Ulster there are some families of Whittey (sic), presumably descendants of MacWhitty and Mawhitty householders who appear in the Hearth Money Rolls for Co. Antrim (1669).

WHORISKEY, Caldwell, Hiskey, Houriskey WATERS
The English name Waters, which is derived in some cases simply from the word water and in others from the Christian name Walter, is often of Cromwellian origin in Ireland; it has also been used as the anglicized form of: –

(a) Mac Con Uisce (from cú, hound, uisce, water), formerly MacEnuske, a minor sept of Farney (Co. Monaghan) attached to the MacMahons.

(b) Mac Uaitear: this was sometimes only an ephemeral surname formed from a father called Walter. It occurs in the Fiants, chiefly in Leinster, as MacWater. MacWatters and MacQuatters are found today as well as Waters.

(c) Ó Fuaruisce. This and Ó Fuarghuis (O'Fworishe in a Co. Roscommon Fiant of 1591) are the Irish forms of the name now phonetically anglicized Whoriskey and erroneously "translated" Walters.

(d) Ó hUaruisce: this is basically the same as the foregoing (c) and is properly Houriskey in English. Caldwell and Coldwell as well as Waters have been used in Ulster as anglicized forms in this case. Horish, a synonym of Caldwell in the Clogher area, is of similar origin. From Co. Cavan Caldwell is reported as synonymous with Colavin. This is an entirely different name, viz. Mac Conluain, a family of the Uí Fiachrach originating in north Connacht. An earlier form of this name is MacColwan.

(e) Ó hUisce and Ó hUiscín – Waters, Hiskey, Heskin and even Hoskins in English – are found in Connacht, but these forms are presumably corruptions of one of the foregoing.

(For the Waters family of Co. Cork see Bibliography.)

WILLMORE, MacLiammóir   This name is very well known in its Gaelic form because of the international reputation of the Irish actor Michael MacLiammóir. Bardsley equates Willmore with the English name Wilmer, but, though I have not met any near-Gaelic anglicized form of the name, I cannot state for certain that it is not Irish in origin: it occurs in Co. Tyrone in 1596, when Anne Willmore received a "pardon". The Fiant in question (no. 5996) is somewhat unusual and is worth quoting in full: "Pardon to Hugh, earl of Tyrone, and all the sons, brothers, kinsmen, followers. tenants and servants of the said earl, dwelling in the country of Tyrone, Henry Hovenden, gent, Robert Hovenden, his son, Francis

Mountfort, John Baeth and James Gernon, gentlemen, Rob. Benett, Anne Willmore, George Cawell and Edm. Barrett, and all other persons dwelling in the country of Tyrone".

At any rate it was definitely in a remote part of Ireland as far back as Elizabethan times. It may be of interest to mention that Willmore occurs in a list of Latin equivalents of fourteenth century English surnames, printed by Ewen, as de Salicosa Mara. Always a rare name it occurs occasionally as Wilmor as well as Willmore in comparatively recent times in Dublin.

WOGAN, Ogan   Though not numerous, representatives of this family are still to be found in Ireland, for the most part in Dublin and Co. Louth. As an Irish family it dates from 1317, when Thomas Wogan was granted Rathcoffey, Co. Kildare. He was the son of the famous Sir John Wogan, who came to this country as Justiciar in 1295. Sir John was great-grandson of Gwgan, a scion of the ancient Welsh royal race. He himself was in possession of lands in Co. Kildare before 1317 as we learn from the Red Book of Ormond. His sons Walter and John were members of the Irish judiciary between 1318 and 1328. In 1347 Thomas Wogan complained to the king of the hardships of the English in Ireland; Richard Wogan was Chancellor of Ireland with an intermission from 1441 to 1446 during the feud between the viceroy Ormond and Archbishop Talbot. In fact it was not until the seventeenth century that we find them definitely ranged on the Irish side: even then we must regard them as primarily Catholics and royalists – and so Jacobites – rather than consciously Irishmen. Their devotion to the faith is personified in Fr. Nicholas Wogan O.F.M. who was contemptuously hanged by his cincture in 1650. This should perhaps be qualified by the reflection that William Wogan (1678-1758), who was secretary to the Lord Lieutenant, the Duke of Ormond, in 1710, was the author of Church of England religious works and – a more striking contrast – Thomas Wogan (a Welshman) was one of the 1649 regicides; Charles I's life had previously been saved by Col. Wogan of Rathcoffey at the battle of Naseby. As Jacobites in Ireland they appear as high-ranking officers in James II's army and one, John Wogan, was M.P. for Co. Kildare in the "Patriot Parliament" of 1689. It was after the death of James II, when like so many of his adherents they had migrated to France, that those romantic Jacobite figures, the brothers Chevalier Charles Wogan (1698-1754) and Chevalier Nicholas Wogan (1700-1770) come on the scene. The former, who was in the Irish Brigade of the French army and later in the service of Spain, is celebrated for his part in the rescue from Innsbruck of Princess Clementina Sobieski. Nicholas, who like his brother followed the "Young Pretender" in 1745, was naturalized in 1724. Richard Hayes in his Biographical Dictionary of Irishmen in France, says he was "out" in 1715 and was pardoned on account of his youth. He does not mention 1745 as the D.N.B. does. Several of the Wogans were men of distinction in France: the last of the ennobled house was Baron Tanneguy de Wogan who died in Paris in 1906. At home Robert

Wogan (fl. 1768-1782) and Thomas Wogan (d. 1781) earned a reputation as miniature painters.

Other modern forms of the name Wogan are Ogan, Ougan and Oogan, all found in counties Louth and Dublin. As Ogan and Owgan it appears in the 1659 "census" (7 families) in the barony of Shelbourne, Co. Wexford; and I have seen Ugan as far back as 1295 when William Ugan was with many O's and Mac's in Co. Cork pardoned for all felonies except killing an Englishman. I have found no reliable evidence that Ogan has been used for Hogan. The name is written Úgán in Irish (pronounced Oogawn) and is derived from the Welsh gwgan, diminitive of gwg, a scowl or frown.   Bibl., Map

WYER   In the note on Weir Wyer was briefly mentioned as a Westmeath name, i.e. as a variant of Weir, which in that county is not an anglicized form of Mac an Mhaoir (as Wyer is) but a mistranslation of Ó Corra (see Corry and O'Curry) or sometimes an English name. The form Wyer has long association with Co. Westmeath: Hugh Wyre of that county was one of the Irish Papists transplanted to Connacht under the Cromwellian régime in 1656, and Wyer is listed in the "census" of 1659 as a principal Irish name in the barony of Moycashel. That is the barony contiguous with Co. Offaly, where Wyer is a numerous name at the present day, as is also Weir. In those two counties Weir and Wyer have been often used synonymously: Weir indeed, is tending to supersede Wyer.

WYLIE, Wiley   This is a numerous and predominently Ulster surname and one which despite a fall in the country's population in the last hundred years has not decreased during that time. In 1865 fifty-five births were registered for Wylie, Wiley and Wyley, 54 of which were in Ulster (mainly Counties Antrim, Armagh and Tyrone); in 1890 there were 51 births registered for Wylie, Wiley, Wilie and Wily, 49 in Ulster, chiefly in Co. Antrim. The name is English in origin (Bardsley says it is a toponymic, being taken from the village of Wyly in Wiltshire). There was a miller called Richard Wylly of Castletowncooley, north Louth, in 1449, but I have met no evidence to indicate that his descendants survive and are now called Wylie. In Pynnar's Survey in 1618-19 John Wylie is recorded as a lessee on the Fort Cunningham estate; and the families now widespread in the north of Ireland appear to have been introduced at the time of the Plantation of Ulster. Little is heard of them in the seventeenth century, though there are several of the name in the Hearth Money Rolls of Counties Antrim, Tyrone and Donegal, but subsequently the testamentary records of the northern diocese prove a number of them to have been people of substance. It should be mentioned that O'Wyle occurs twice in the Derry Hearth Money Rolls (1663). If this is to be equated with Wylie the O is probably a clerical error.

The name is to be found also to-day in east Clare, where the form used for it in Irish is Ó hUallaigh (see Howley), but whether there is a traditional basis for this or it is merely guesswork I have been unable to ascertain.

WYSE, Wise   Though actually of old west of England stock we may fairly regard the Waterford family of Wyse as being in the Anglo-Norman category, since they descend from Andrew Wyse who came to Ireland in 1170 with Strongbow and acquired land in Co. Waterford, where they remained as extensive landholders for seven centuries; these lands included Ballynacourty, near Dungarvan. The manor of St. John's on the outskirts of the city, with which they were identified almost up to our own time, came into their hands later; and it is a noteworthy fact that, although they were afterwards remarkable for the uncompromising adherence to the old faith, they actually obtained full possession of these monastic lands, of which they had formerly been tenants, as a result of the Reformation. Their intimate association with the city of Waterford dates from the fifteenth century: in 1452 Maurice Wise was mayor and from then till Cromwell's time, when Catholics were debarred from office, they held this position 15 times, and again in 1688 during the short respite under James II. The operation of the penal laws caused many of the family to seek service abroad and several were distinguished officers in the Irish Brigade in France in the eighteenth century. At home the family managed to retain a part of its property and in 1757 Thomas Wyse, still hereditary lord of the Manor of St. John, was one of the founders of the Catholic Committee which took the first active steps towards the ultimate achievement of Catholic Emancipation. His great-grandson, another Thomas Wyse (1791-1862) was an outstanding figure in the same cause: he married Letitia Bonaparte, a niece of Napoleon, and eventually became Great Britain's ambassador to Greece. His son, William Charles Bonaparte Wyse (1826-1892), born at Waterford, was a poet of distinction. A branch of the family, known as Wyse Bonaparte, settled in Provence and was admitted to the nobility of France.

The name has in recent times become rare, though in 1659 it was recorded as one of the principal Irish names in the barony of Galtire, Co. Waterford.   Bibl., Map

YOURELL, Uriel   Though this is a rare surname it is spelt to-day in several ways — as above, Eurell etc.; and formerly there were also other variants such as Irriel which appears in the Elizabethan Fiants as the name of a Westmeath gentleman, seated at Laghanstown. Several other Fiants of the late sixteenth century also cite persons called Uriell etc., domiciled in Co. Westmeath, and in the Description of Ireland, written in 1598, Uriell of Balromen is listed among the principal gentlemen of Co. Westmeath at that date. They seem to have lost this prominent position by 1659 as they do not appear among the tituladoes of that county in the "census" of that date.

Yourell is one of our few toponymics, being de Oirghilla in Irish, i.e. of Oriel. It was in fact in the eastern part of Oriel, viz. Louth, that this Norman family first settled after the invasion. As Uriell, Eryell, Yriel etc., often with the prefix de, it is frequent in records relating to counties near Dublin from 1263 onwards. I do not know when they became established in Co. Westmeath: probably at the beginning of the fifteenth century when James Uriel was Chief Baron of the Exchequer in Dublin. In 1540 William Urielle was appointed a collector for the barony of Corkaree, Co. Westmeath. The Westmeath Book of Survey and Distribution records one Oliver Uriell as a proprietor in 1641 in the parish of Portnashangan in that barony.

Surprisingly it is found as of Galway city in the list of Irishmen outlawed as Jacobites after 1691 in the person of John Erell. In the same document it appears also as a Christian name – Irriell Farrell of Co. Roscommon.

Another part of the country remote from its homeland in which it has been found is Co. Clare (1655) and Dermot F. Gleeson in his Last Lords of Ormond mentions that Uriel, formerly Iriel, is a surname still to be found in the Ormond country to-day.

APPENDIX I

This appendix consists of additional information on names which were the subject of articles in the first volume of the Irish Families series. At the head of each entry the relevant page reference to the latter (IF) is given. S indicates the page reference to The Surnames of Ireland.

ATHY   The Red Book of Ormond records two tenants named de Athy in Co. Kildare in 1311. IF49, S42.

BALFE   Balfe does not appear in Reaney's Dictionary of British Surnames. It is an anglicization of the Irish adjective balbh meaning dumb or stammering: it is therefore a name of the epithet type which eventually became a hereditary surname. Families of Balfe were established in Meath before the fourteenth century and were among the leading gentry of that county, two being M.P.s for Kells in 1585 and 1613. As early as 1293 in a deed in the Ormond collection Walter, son of David Balf, is concerned in a transaction relating to 60 acres of arable land at Ballchaunegane. IF288, S11.

O'BEIRNE   O'Beirne is also found in Co. Kildare where it is not of the Connacht sept of the name but a synonym of O'Byrne. IF54, S16. Map.

(Mac) BRADY   A Catholic descendant of Hugh Brady, first Protestant Bishop of Meath, Edwin James Brady (1869-1952), had an adventurous life in many lands and was the author of some fine sea ballads. He was born at Carcour, New South Wales. The modern use of the prefix O instead of Mac with this name is erroneous. IF58, S24, Map.

O'BRIEN   The accepted date for the birth of Brian Boru is 941, not 925 as stated by the Four Masters. According to Eleanor Hull's History of Ireland (p. 201) the first O'Brien to adopt the surname was Donogh Cairbre (1194-1242), son of Donal, who submitted to Henry II. Murrough O'Brien (d. 1551) was first Earl of Thomond; Murrough of the Burnings (d. 1674) was sixth baron Inchiquin. IF62. S27, Bibl., Map See Bryan.

(O)BRODER   Amplifying the brief mention in Irish Families of the Co. Galway sept of O'Broder, the existence of two townlands called Ballybroder (in the parishes of Kilmeen and Loughrea) should be mentioned. Mr. P. J. Kennedy tells me that he knows more than 30 families of the name in the area between Galway and the Shannon. IF64, S27, Map.

(O)BROLLOGHAN   This is a cognate form of (O) Brallaghan (in Irish O Brolachain) which is dealt with in Irish Families (p. 59) and Map. It is included here because I am indebted to Mr. W. Maxwell-Brodie for much useful (and to me new) information relating to the O'Brologhans of the Western Highlands of Scotland, who were of the same stock as the O'Brologhands of Derry and whose name has been anglicized as Brodie in modern times. IF59, S28, Map.

BROWNE   Referring to the Brownes of Connacht mention should also be made of John Browne, the first high sheriff of Mayo (1583). He was of the family already at that time well established at the Neale, in the barony of Kilmaine. His descendants who became, in the senior line, Barons of Kilmaine and, in the junior, Earls of Altamone, have since been closely associated with Co. Mayo. Seated at Westport the 3rd Marquis of Sligo (5th Earl of Altamont) was, prior to the land legislation of the late nineteenth century, owner of an estate of 114,000 acres.

Ulysses Browne (1705-1757) should be described as Field-Marshal Maximilian Ulysses Browne: he was son of Col. Ulysses Browne, of Camus, Co. Limerick. George Count de Browne (1698-1792) was yet another famous Continental soldier of the Camus family. IF64, S28, Map.

BUCKLEY   The variant spellings of Bohely and Bucaile both occur in the returns of Irish Jacobites outlawed after the defeat of James II. IF65, S29

BURKE   Sir John Davis said in 1606: "There are more able men of the surname of Bourke than of any name whatsoever in Europe." IF66, S30. Map

As Curtis and other modern scholars have shown, O'Donovan and his contemporaries were wrong in describing William de Burgo, Strongbow's famous successor in Connacht, as William FitzAdelm de Burgo. IF66, S30. Map.

BUTLER   Professor Edmund Curtis in his History of Mediaeval Ireland, shows that the MacRichard Butlers were actually the ancestors of the later Earls of Ormond, and that at least two branches of the Butlers were patrons of Gaelic-Irish leanring and great collectors of Irish manuscripts.

To the list of distinguished persons of the name that of Sir Theobald, commonly called Sir Toby Butler, should be added. He was attorney-general in the reign of James II and the framer of the Treaty of Limerick on the Irish side; he made a memorable speech in 1703 against the Anti-Popery Act. IF67, S31. Map.

Mac CANN Rev. Prof. John Ryan rejects the usually accepted derivation of this name and states that it is derived from cana, wolf-hound. IF71, S36. Map

MacCARROLL Father Aubrey Gwynn, Proceedings of the Royal Historical Society (Vol. X), referring to the four notable archbishops of Cashel named MacCarroll says that the evidence he has found suggests that they did not belong to the sept of O'Carroll of Ely, as has been thought hitherto, but to a distinct sept of MacCarroll, located in some part of the territory covered by the present counties of Carlow, Kilkenny or the eastern part of Co. Tipperary. John O'Donovan, in his notes to O'Heerin's Topographical Poem makes it clear that there was a distinct O'Carroll sept whose chief was lord of a territory extending from Kilkenny city northwards to the boundary of the present county of Leix.

Rev. Anthony Carroll S.J. was a cousin, not a brother, of Archbishop John Carroll. IF74, S38. Bibl.

MacCARRON CAREW The name MacCarron is now almost exclusively associated with Ulster, especially Counties Donegal and Derry, and in the "census" of 1659 it is confined to that province. Statistics of two centuries later give a similar picture: for example in 1865 there were 48 births registered for MacCarron (including some minor spelling variants) and 5 for Carron, all these being in Ulster; there was one Carroon – in Co. Westmeath. Other years for which figures are available corroborate this. In earlier records, however, from 1100 to 1600 it appears frequently as that of a sept on what is now the barony of Kilkenny West (Co. Westmeath). The Four Masters call the head of the sept Chief of Maol an tSinna, i.e. Chief of the Shannon, their territory lying on the Westmeath side of the river. In 1578 Hobbert MacCarron of Killenefaghna, Co. Westmeath, was as "chief serjeant of his nation" confirmed in the possession of the lands in that county (including Kilmacaron) which of old belonged to the "chief of the nation of MacCaron".

Carron, without the prefix Mac, is a different name: it is of Norman origin, formerly de Carron but later altered to Carew. The best known was Sir George Carew, Elizabethan President of Munster, and implacable enemy of the Irish. The name, however, was not confined to the landlord class: it was numerous among the ordinary householders of Co. Tipperary in 1666 as shown by the Hearth Money Rolls and is still found there. John Edward Carew (1785-1868), sculptor, was born at Waterford. IF153, S38. Map.

COLLEY COOLEY Though usually regarded as an Anglo-Irish name, Colley is also an anglicized form of the Gaelic-Irish Mac Cúille or Mac Giolla Chúille. The sept so called was of Connacht and there are many references to members of it in the sixteenth century Fiants relating to counties Roscommon, Galway and Clare. In the "census" of 1659 Colly appears as a principal name in the barony of Ballintubber, Co. Roscommon. In the Fiants the spelling of the surname is usually MacColly, MacCollie etc., and it appears only once as MacCooley. IR 288, 550.

COLLINS A very well known name in Australia is Tom Collins, which in fact was the nom-de-plume of Joseph Furphy (1843-1912). He was well known under his own name also, so much so that "furphy" became a word in current Australian speech, signifying a rumour without foundation. (Joe Furphy was not himself a desseminator of rumours, but the water-carts his firm manufactured, which were in use all over the country and were called furphies, were frequently the meeting-place of gossips.) His father was a tenant farmer at Tanderagee, Co. Armagh, who emigrated in 1840. The surname Furphy is very rare. It occurs occasionally in the modern birth registers for Co. Armagh and also in the Co. Armagh Hearth Money-Rolls of 1664-5. Professor M.A. O'Brien has suggested to me that the name is probably Ó Foirbhte, derived from the adjective foirbhthe, meaning complete or perfect. IF101, S51. Map.

(O) CONNOLLY Father P. O'Gallachair, who is an authority on Clogher history and families, has commented on the fact that I did not mention the O'Connolly sept of Devenish in Irish Families: the omission was due to my belief that they were now extinct and that the Connollys of the diocese of Clogher are all of the Farney stock. The reader specially interested in the Connollys of Co. Monaghan and adjoining areas is recommended to read Father O'Gallachair's notes on the subject in the Clogher Record (II. i. pages 172-189, 1957). IF87, S55, Bibl, Map.

(Mac) CONNULTY This is a form of the Donegal name MacAnulty, peculiar to Co. Clare.

O'CONNOR I am informed by a member of the family that General Sir Luke O'Connor V.C. was of the O'Conor Roe branch, not the O'Conor Sligo. IF88, S55, Bibl, Map

CONSIDINE There was a Norman family of de Constentine, one of whom founded the Priory of the Blessed Virgin Mary at Tristernagh (Westmeath) in the early thirteenth century. They had no connexion with the Considines of Thomond, a branch of the O'Briens. IF92, S56. Map.

(Mac) COSTELLO(E) COSTLEY CUSHELY CASSERLEY Dr. Reeves, writing in 1850, noted the adoption of the name Costelloe for the Donegal surname then known as Cushely and previously O'Cassaly. Muntercassely (Uí Chasalaigh) are recorded in the 1609 inquisition on Armagh church lands as a sept located in the Glenaul area. Casly is the spelling used in the lists of Jacobite outlaws. Cushley and Costello are recorded by Matheson (1901) as synonymous in the parish of Magherafelt, Co. Derry. Cushelly, Cushley or Cuskley (Mac Giolla Choiscle) is a north Ulster surname. Costley is more often a variant of this than of Costello, but the similarity of sound accounts for its occasional use as a synonym of the latter. It should be added that Cuskley is found today in Co. Offaly, as it was in 1601 in the earlier anglicized form of Mac-gilkuskley.

Another name which may be confused with these is Casserley i.e. Mac Casarlaigh, which has long association with Co. Roscommon and now (without the prefix Mac) is found there and in the adjoining county of Galway. This confusion is the more likely because in Co. Roscommon some families so called spell the name without the R, viz. Casseley. Cumumhan Mac Casarlaigh is mentioned by the Four Masters as one of the Connacht chiefs slain at the battle of Athenry in 1249 and another of the name was a canon of Tuam in 1462. IF96, S60. Map.

CROKE The Crokes were in Co. Kilkenny before the fifteenth century: I have found a record of them there in 1324 and in Co. Tipperary in 1299; as early as 1241 there was a William Croc or Crok of Crokeveyl in Burke's country. The Most Rev. William Croke was Archbishop of Cashel as stated in the second edition of Irish Families. IF289, S65.

CRONE Some families of this name (I am informed by Sir Henry Blackall), including the Crones of Byblox, Doneraile, Co. Cork, are of Pomeranian origin: Daniel Crone of that country figures in a list of Protestant immigrants who were made denizens of Ireland (temp. Charles II). IF19, S66.

CUFFE Cuffe is used as an anglicized form of three distinct Irish surnames, viz., MacDhuibh a variant of MacDuibh (anglice MacDuff), O'Duirnín (usually Durnin) by supposed translation, and occasionally even of Ó Cobhthaigh (Coffey). Neverthless the name should not have been included in Appendix C of Irish Families because it is also an indigenous English surname. It appears fairly often in Irish historical records, but almost always in the person of some English official, soldier or settler. It is the family name of the Earls of Desart. Hugh Cuffe, one of the undertakers of 1589, obtained 12,000 acres of the Desmond lands at 1d. per acre.

(Mac) CUNNEEN (O) CUNNEEN. As the prefixes Mac and O have in the case of this name been entirely dropped there is little except family tradition to indicate to which of these quite distinct septs a Cunneen of today belongs. They both derive from coinín (rabbit) – I do not accept the suggestion that it is from cano, wolf cub. There are two O Coinín septs – of Thomond and Offaly both called Rabbit and Cunneen. That of

Thomond is recorded as taking part in the battle of Loghrasha in 1317. Mac Coinín was sub-chief to O Caithnid (O'Caheny or Canny) in the barony of Erris, Co. Mayo. There are four references to them in The Tribes and Customs of Hy Fiachra. IF105, S69, Map.

(O) CURRAN Referring to the distribution of this name in the seventeenth century it is of interest to note that it is one of the most numerous in the Co. Tipperary Hearth Money Rolls of 1665-7 with 73 householders. King's analysis of the 1901 census for Co. Kerry indicates that there were then 142 families of Curran or Currane in that county. IF106, S71, Bibl., Map.

O'CURRY In addition to the main Thomond sept of Ó Comhraidhe another of the same name was located in Co. Westmeath, where they were chiefs of Moygoish. Father Paul Walsh has pointed out that Curristown (now Belmont) was outside the true O'Curry country. Dr John Curry (c. 1710-1780) of Dublin, was notable as an eminent physician, as a historian and as the organizer of the first Catholic Committee during the Penal Code period. Families of the name belonging to south-west Cork are probably representatives of the minor Corca Laoidhe sept of O'Curry. Currie is Scottish; a branch of the clan MacDonald. IF107, S166. Map.

(Mac) CURTIN John Joseph Curtin (1885-1945), a very notable Prime Minister of Australia, was the son of a Co. Cork man. He was a cousin of William O'Brien M.P. and related to the Nagles of Kilconway Co. Cork. IF107, S71, Map.

CUSACK A name which should have been mentioned in the article on Cusack is Michael Cusack (1860-1907) co-founder of the Gaelic Athletic Association: he was born in Co. Clare. IF108, S72, Bibl., Map.

(O) DEVLIN Mr T. Ó Raifeartaigh informs me that the O'Devlins of Co. Sligo are still extant, and even numerous in counties Sligo, Leitrim and Cavan, but the name there has been widely changed to Dolan. IF115, S81, Bibl., Map.

DINNEEN DINAN   The list of synonyms used by emigrants which was compiled by the Cunard Company shows that Dinan, Dinane and also Denning were equated with Dinneen, and Matheson's Synonymes corroborates this in the case of Dinan. Dinan, also spelt Dynan, is certainly a Munster name now and primarily of Co. Cork, and it appears as such in the "census" of 1659. Woulfe, however, differentiates Dinneen and Dynan, giving Ó Daghnáin as the original Irish form of the latter. IF117, S82, Map.

(O) DOHERTY In Munster Doherty is often not Ó Dochartaigh but Ó Dubhartaigh: this is more corectly anglicized Doorty in west Clare. In Oriel Dorrity is an occasional synonym. IF117, S84, Bibl., Map.

(O) DOLAN The generally accepted form in Irish today

is Ó Dubhláin (mod. Ó Dúlain) as given by Woulfe and others. I have little doubt that in the first edition of this work and in Irish Families I was wrong to accept that as its supposed derivation. In fact O'Doelan, later Dolan, derives from Ó Dobhailen, the name of a family on record since the twelfth century in the baronies of Clonmacowen, Co. Galway, and Athlone, Co. Roscommon, in the heart of the Uí Maine country and quite distinct from Ó Doibhilin (Devlin). There has been a movement north-eastwards so that now the name Dolan is numerous in counties Leitrim, Fermanagh and Cavan as well as in counties Galway and Roscommon, but see Devlin (supra) for the name Dolan in those counties. IF118, S84.

MacDONAGH   Mr. J. C. MacDonagh, who collected much useful information regarding the Connacht sept of MacDonagh, considered that while the MacDonaghs of Thomond are undoubtedly a branch of the main Co. Sligo sept, those of Co. Galway are of different stock, viz. an offshoot of the O'Flahertys of Connemara. IF122, S84, Bibl., Map.

MacDONNELL   Professor Edmond Curtis states that the MacDonnells were brought to Mayo by the Burkes in 1399; and that by the sixteenth century they were quite numerous in Leinster.

Mr. Ó Raifeartaigh reminds me that the Antrim surname MacDonnell is a pitfall for the unwary. Up to our own time the local Irish pronunciation of the name was in accordance with the spelling 'Ac Dhomhnaill, with the aspirated D silent, and so was sometimes anglicized McConnell and even O'Connell. Hence a MacConnell from, say, Ballymena, is quite likely to be a descendant of the lords of the Isles rather than of a less famous sept. IF119, S85, Bibl., Map.

MacDOWELL   MacDubhghaill (dubh, black; gall, foreigner) is the Irish form of the name of the Scottish family of MacDugall which came from the Hebrides as galloglasses and settled in Co. Roscommon where Lismacdonell locates them. It is now mainly found in north Ulster, largely due to more recent emigration.

Peter and Allen Dowell were tituladoes in the parish of Shankill, barony of Roscommon, in the census of 1659. Lismacdowell is in the adjoining pairsh. Col. Luke Dowell was one of the Co. Roscommon Jacobites. His son Denis, outlawed under William III, was wrongly returned as Donnell. Patrick MacDowell (1799-1870), a sculptor of note, was born in Belfast. Benjamin McDowell (1821-1885) of Trinity College, Dublin, was a famous "character" who might be regarded as the prototype of the "absent-minded professor." IF129, S89, Map.

(O) DOWNEY DOHENY MULDOWNEY In addition to the principal sept of O'Downey dealt with in Irish Families, the name Downey is also used as an abbreviation of Muldowney. It so occurs in south Down in nineteenth century returns, as do Dawney, Gildowney, and Macgilldowney. The last two, of course, are properly synonyms of MacEldowny not of O'Muldowney.

Ó Maoldhomhnaigh, as stated in Irish Families, is the Gaelic form of Molony. The same name, but with the D unaspirated (i.e. Ó Malodomhnaigh) is anglicized Muldowney. This is presumably of the same origin as Molony. O'Molony and O'Muldowny were formerly used synonymously: for example Malachy O'Molony, Bishop of Kilmacduagh from 1570 to 1610, was also referred to as Muldowney; and in the "census" of 1659 Mullowny and Muldowny are returned as one name in the barony of Fassadinin, Co. Kilkenny, where families so called were then fairly numerous. They have been associated with Kilkenny continuously since then.

In the south of Ireland Dawney and Downey are often found as synonyms of Doheny (the Gaelic form of which, according to Woulfe, is Ó Dubhchonna), a name familiar to students of nineteenth century history in the person of Michael Doheny (1805-1863) the Young Irelander. This sept was one of the Corca Laoidhe and has always been associated with Cork and neighbouring counties. IF128, S89, Bibl., Map.

(O) DRISCOLL   In the Miscellany of the Celtic Society (1849) John O'Donovan gives extensive notes and extracts from documents relating to the sept of O'Driscoll. Including Gaelic poems on the family these fill 125 pages of the book. IF129, S90, Bibl., Map.

(O) DUFFY DUHIG   This, in Irish Ó Dubhthaigh, is a numerous name in all the provinces except Munster. Modern statistics show that it is now the most numerous name in Co. Monaghan.

The variant Duhig occurs in Munster. Sir James Duhig, the late Archbishop of Brisbane, was born at Limerick in 1871. He held that position for 46 years. His predecessor, the first Archbishop, Robert Dunne (1830-1917), a native of Ardfinnan, Co. Tipperary, held it for 30 years. The first bishop was James Quinn, appointed in 1859. He was so successful in promoting Irish emigration to Australia that his critics sarcastically suggested changing the name of Queensland to Quinnsland. IF130, S92, Bibl., Map.

DURACK   The Duracks from Co. Clare were perhaps the greatest of pioneer pastoral families in Australia. The story of their 2½ years trek across the continent (1883-1885) makes enthralling reading. IF35, S94.

O'DWYER   Interesting information on this sept will be found in Glankeen of Borrisoleigh, by Rev. M. Kenny, S.J. In Chapter III he deals with Edmond O'Dwyer (Eamonn a' Chuíc). Michael Dwyer died in 1825, not in 1815 as stated in Irish Families. IF133, S94, Bibl., Map.

EDGEWORTH   The Ábbe Edgeworth was a cousin of Richard Lovell Edgeworth, not his nephew as stated thus in earlier editions of Irish Families. IF290, S96, Bibl.

(Mac) EGAN   An early example of the form Hegan is to be seen in the signature (Owen Hegaine) of Owen Mac Egan in a letter he wrote in 1602, which is quoted in Pacata Hibernia. For pedigree and notes on MacEgan see Tribes & Customs of Hy Many, Appendix E. IF133, S96, Bibl., Map.

EMMET Earlier examples of the name in Ireland are: William Emett of Capangaran, Co. Tipperary (Cashel and Emly will 1672), and Robert Emmett of Dungarvan (Waterford will 1661). IF290, S99, Bibl.

ESMONDE Father John Esmond was one of the five Co. Wexford priests who, with two Franciscan brothers, were put to death by Cromwellian soldiers at Wexford in 1649. An interesting account of how the Esmonde estate escaped forfeiture will be found in the Williamite Confiscation by J.G. Simms (pp. 41-42). IF287, S100, Map.

FAGAN While the fact that Fagan is in most cases of Norman origin is accepted, Rev. Professor John Ryan disagrees with the statement, made by Fr. Woulfe and in Irish Families, that Ó Faoghagáin is a variant of Ó hAodhagán (O'Hagan) and other scholars concur. They say it is a distinct sept of eastern Airghialla (Oriel). There Fagan, Fegan, Feighan and Feehan are numerous and much confused; probably these all derive from O'Faodhagáin. IF137, S102, Bibl., Map.

(O) FAHY Father Anthony Fahy (1805-1871) was a famous Irish priest in Argentina. The Fahy Institute in that country was founded to commemorate him. IF137, S102, Bibl., Map.

FAY Fay (de Fae) has been used as a synonym of Fahy. W. G. Fay, of the Abbey Theatre, stated that his grandfather was William O'Fahy of Tuam, Co. Galway. W, G. (Willie) Fay died in 1947; Frank Fay was born in 1870 not 1879). See O'Fee. IF291, S105.

FERRITER The name Ferriter appears in Alan's Register (Co. Dublin) as early as 1260 and in The Justiciary Rolls in Co. Kerry in 1295. IF291, S108, Map.

MacFIRBIS Among distinguished men of the name we might include Giolla Íosa Mór Mac Firbis, the main compiler of the Book of Lecan (1417). O'Donovan's notes to the Tribes and Customs of Hy Fiachra will be found useful; O'Farrell's History of Co. Longford may also be consulted. IF292, S109.

FITZPATRICK Much information on the Fitzpatricks will be found in Corrigan's History of the Diocese of Ossory; Vol I. IF145, S110, Bibl., Map.

FITZSIMONS, Eddery Referring to the FitzSimons of Co. Mayo it is of interst to note that while in 1585 the Composition Book of Connacht has only one reference to them under their Gaelic patronymic, in the Strafford Inquisition, made fifty years later, they are called MacRuddery, MacEruddery etc. in 22 entries, the name Fitzsimon not being used at all. One of its synonyms in that document is Ediry, a surname which as Eddery is extant today, though rare. Eddery is not mentioned in Woulfe's Sloinnte. IF291, S110, Map.

(O) FLAHERTY There is a great deal of information about the O'Flahertys throughout Hardiman's edition (1846) of Roderic O'Flaherty's book Iar-Connaught, particularly pages 309-437 thereof. IF145, S110, Bibl., Map.

FLOOD THYNNE Some Floods are of English extraction, but in Ireland they are mainly O Maoltuile or Mac Maoltuile, abbreviated to Mac anTuile or MacTuile, anglicized MacAtilla or MacTully as well as Flood. Tuile means flood, but probably it is here for toile-gen of toil, will, i.e. the will of God. See Floyd.

O'Thina is reported from Co. Galway (Cong district) as entered in a birth registration by a family usually called Flood. The Irish in this case is Ó Tuine, for Ó Tuile, which is a colloquial contraction of the original form (see Irish Families p. 279).

O'Thina has no connexion with the surname Thynne.

This Co. Clare name is there pronounced Tyne and was formerly so spelt, e.g. Dermot O'Tine of Kilshanny (the homeland of this Irish sept) whose outlawry as a Jacobite was reversed in 1699. It is Ó Teimhin in Irish, and has no connexion with a similar English name pronounced Thin. A notable member of the Clare sept was Andrew Joseph Thynne (1847-1927) who as lawyer, politician and soldier was a prominent figure in Queensland, Australia, for more than forty years. IF278, SIII.

(O) FLYNN John Flynn (1880-1951) Presbyterian missionary (with an Irish Catholic background) is regarded by the Australians of all creeds as one of the finest men their country has produced. He founded the Flying Doctor Service and was known as "Flynn of the Inland." IF148, S112, Map.

(O) FRIEL Rev. Professor John Ryan, S.J. has pointed out that the chief point of interest about the O'Friels is that they are nearest in blood to St Colmkille, for they alone are in the direct line from his brother. IF152, S115, Map.

GALLWEY Referring to the origin of the name, James Grene Barry states (J.R.S.A.I. xxiv, 338) that it was assumed by the descendants of John De Burgo (Burke), known as John of Galway, who, after his gallant defence of Baal's Bridge, Limerick, against the O'Briens, was knighted by Lionel, Duke of Clarence in 1361. His descendant, Sir Geoffrey Galwey (d. 1636) was notable for his uncompromising opposition to Carew, when Mayor of Limerick. IF292, S118, Bibl.

(O) GEARY Another Co. Limerick form of Ó Gadhra (in Connacht O'Gara) is Guiry. IF155, S121.

(Mac) GILMARTIN Kilmartin is a synonym of Gilmartin, the two forms being equally numerous today, mainly in east Connacht. Both forms (with the Mac retained) are among the principal Irish names in Co. Fermanagh in the 1659 "census." IF223, S125.

(Mac) GILROY Norman Thomas Gilroy, Archbishop of Sydney, created a cardinal in 1946, the first native born Australian to be so honoured, comes of a family which emigrated from Ireland. His Eminence is uncertain where they were located. Birth registration statistics 1864-1890 indicate that the name was mainly associated with north Connacht IF134, S125, Map.

(Mac) GORMAN, O'Gorman There are ten townlands called Gormanstown lying in Cos. Kildare, Meath, Westmeath, Wicklow, Limerick and Tipperary and two called Gormanston in Cos. Dublin and Meath. Gormanston in the parish of Stamullen, Co. Meath, appears as Villa Macgorman in a cartulary of Llanthony of c. 1200. IF162, S132, Map.

MacGOWAN, Mageown Though Mageown is one of the recorded synonyms of MacGowan it should be observed that it is also a surname in its own right — MacEoin or Mag Eoghain in Irish and cognate with MacKeown. It is also found in the abbreviated form Geon.IF164, S133.

(O) GRADY Many of the Gradys of Mayo and Roscommon are Greadys — Mag Riada in Irish, corrupted in the spoken language to Ó Griada. In Co. Tipperary Grady is often Gready in disguise, the Irish form there being Ó Greada. This, no doubt, is the original of the names to be assimilated to better known ones of a similar erous in the barony of Middlethird (Co. Tipperary) in 1659. There is a constant tendency for uncommon names to be assililated to better known ones of a similar sound: thus Gready tends to become Grady, as does Graddy in Kerry. IF165, S134, Bibl., Map.

MacGRATH Caithréim Thoirdhealbhaigh (The Wars of Turlough) was written by John MacGrath, son of the Clare poet, Rory MacGrath, about 1365. IF165, S135, Map.

GRATTAN There are four families of Grattan in the Co. Tipperary Hearth Money Rolls (1665-67). Mac Grattan and MacGretton are to be found in current Irish directories. IF165, S135, Bibl.

GRAY, Colreavy, Gallery Mr. Philip MacGuinness has given me convincing evidence to show that the name anglicized Colreavy and Culreavy, as well as Gray, in in Irish Mac Cathail Riabhaigh not Mac Giolla Riabhaigh. The latter is normally anglicized MacAreavy. In Clare it was first MacGillereagh. The Compostion Book of Connacht and other late sixteenth century souces refer to MacGillereagh of Cragheene, chief of his name: this has now been abbreviated to Gallery. IF293, S135.

GREENE This well known English name does duty in Ireland for a number of Irish names. Houneen, MacGreen, Fahy, MacAlesher, MacGlashan, Greenan and Guerin. It is also an O'Sullivan agnomen, glas.

The form MacGrainna was in use as early as the sixteenth century: it appears as MacGrina and Magrina in a list of the followers of Rory O'Donnell in 1602.

Séamus MacGrianna is the doyen of living Gaelic writers. The name MacGreene, as well as Greene, is fairly numerous in west Clare. I do not think this is MacGrianna: I suggest that it is Ó hUaithnín, first made Green by translation and later erroneously given the prefix Mac.

On page 53 of Irish Families the name of the Co. Limerick historian is given as James Greene Barry: his second name was Grene not Greene. The Grenes of Grene Park, Cashel, are a well-known Co. Tipperary family. IF185, S136, Bibl.

GRIFFIN Mr. Basil O'Connell's genealogical researches have led him to believe that Maurice Griffin, the Gaelic poet, was of a Co. Monaghan family which migrated to Co. Kerry in the eighteenth century. IF167, S137, Map.

O'GROWNEY This corrupt form of the name Mac Carrghamhna i.e. MacCarron is of long standing,as six families called O'Growney appear in the Co. Tipperary Hearth Money Rolls of 1665-57.

The name O'Growney was in general use in English in the mid-seventeenth century. It is one of the few names given with the prefix O in the Tipperary Hearth Money Rolls, in which six householders so called appear. IF153, S138, Map.

(O) GUINAN It is perhaps of interest to mention that Griffith's Valuation of 1854 records the fact that there were then twenty housholders called Guynan in King's Co. (Offaly) eighteen of which were in the barony of Ballycowan. IF313, S139.

MacGUIRE Hugh MacGuire and Warham St Leger were slain at the battle of Carrigrohane, near Cork, in 1600. IF167, S140, Bibl., Map.

GWYNN There were families of Gwynn in Ireland before the Cromwellian era. As early as 1570 Richard Gwynne, gent, obtained a lease of monastic lands in Co. Kildare, the conditions (as given in the Fiant of that date) being that he should maintain an English archer, not sublet to any tenant of Irish blood and not charge coyne. The same source indicates that a year later a soldier called Maurice Gwyne was pardoned for slaying Nicholas Barnwell with his sword in a Dublin cemetery, while in 1587 another Gwynne was granted the wardship of a County Longford O'Farrell. Later Fiants (for 1602-3) exemplify in the person of John Gwynn the extent to which plurality of church livings was then carried: he was presented to four in three different dioceses — Cashel, Ossory and Lismore. In the next generation another south of Ireland clergyman, Rev. Arthur Gwynn, who was rector of several parishes, was the cause of contention between Strafford and Lord Cork. They were well established as landowners in Co. Tipperary before 1659 as Petty's "census" shows; and there were Gwynn wills proved in both Cloyne and Lismore dioceses before the end of Charles II's reign. IF294, S141,

(O) HAGAN While it is not incorrect to give Ó hAodhagain as in Irish form of O'Hagan, Mr T. Ó Raifeartaigh tells me that the usual form in Ulster is now Ó hAgáin in Irish, which was originally Ó hÓgain. He has also pointed out a slip on my part on page 169 of Irish Families where (9 lines from end of page) Hugh O'Neill should read Hugh O'Donnell as correctly printed on page 120 ibid: IF169, S141, Map.

(O) HALLORAN According to family tradition Sylvester O'Halloran and the rest of that distinguished Limerick family were of the Co. Galway not of the Thomond sept.

In the O'Halloran arms (Plate XIV of IF) for martlets read mullets. IF170, S143, Bibl., Map.

HAMILTON The town of Manorhamilton in Co. Leitrim was not mentioned in Irish Families. For information on the notorious "Hamilton gallows" there see Meehan's book on the Confederation of Kilkenny. Much useful information on the family will be found in O'Grady's book on Strafford.   IF295, S143, Bibl.

(O) HANLEY, Henley Since the end of the seventeenth century Henley, Henly, Hendley and Henely have been used in Munster, especially in Co. Cork, as variant forms of Hanley.   For Hennelly in Co. Mayo see under Fennelly. IF171, S145, Map.

(O) HANNON Patrick Hannan (1842-1925), who was born in Co. Clare, discovered the Kalgoorlie goldfield in Western Australia which contains "the richest square mile of gold in the world." The supply of water to this goldfield, which entailed an engineering undertaking of great magnitude, was conceived and carried out by Charles Yelverton O'Connor (1843-1902), who also built Fremantle Harbour. He was born in Co. Meath. IF172, S145.

O'HARE O'Hare is one of the few surnames which resisted the general tendency in the eighteenth century to discard the O and, even before the propaganda of the Gaelic League and the resurgence of 1916-1921 resulted in widespread resumption of the prefixes Mac and O, the O'Hares outnumbered the Hares and Haires by three to one. The great majority of these were descendants of the Oriel sept of Ó hÍr (sometimes called Ó hÉir) — who were akin to the O'Hanlons and seated in the barony of Oriel (Co. Armagh) where, with the adjacent counties of Antrim, Down and Louth, they are still chiefly found.

O'Hare and Hare are stated by Woulfe to be used as synonyms of O'Hehir (Ó hAichir). Such an equation, if it ever occurs, is in fact very rare, any Hares belonging to counties west of the Shannon being properly MacGarrys, whose name was mistranslated from its supposed derivation from the Irish work girr-fhiadh, a hare. Haier, however, found in west Clare, is probably a synonym of O'Hehir.

The name Hare is indigenous in England and quite common there, but very few Irish Hares are of that origin. IF155, S146.

HARRINGTON As late as 1659 Ungerdell or Hunger-dell was the form of this name in common use in Co. Cork. It appears thus in the "census" of that date among the principal Irish names in the barony of Kinalmeaky. IF174, S148, Map.

HAY The name Hay (i.e. Norman de la Haye) is on record in Co. Wexford since 1182. It has now become Hayes in most places. IF176, S150.

(O) HEALY James Healy (1830-1900), has been described as the first black American bishop. Actually he was only one quarter black his father, Michael Healy, being an Irish immigrant and his mother a mulaltto slave.

In the Tralee and Killarney areas of Co. Kerry Healy is usually a synonym of Kerrisk or Kerrish in Irish Mac Fhiarais i.e. son of Ferris. Woulfe thinks the eponymous ancestor was Ferris O'Helie. In Co. Clare Mac Fhiarais is anglicized Kierse. IF176, S151, Bibl., Map.

(O) HEAVY, Heaphy In the sept map in Irish Families O'Heavy is placed in Co. Armagh. This was a misprint for O'Heany. Heavy is a name now found in small numbers in all the provinces except Ulster. Its origin is obscure. The earliest instance I have found of it is a husbandman of Thisteinagh, Co. Westmeath in 1601. The cognate surname O'Heaphy (Ó hEamhthaigh) belongs of old to Cos. Waterford and Cork. IFMap, S152.

HENRY I am indebted to Mr. T. Ó Raifeartaigh for the information that the Ulster Henrys have other potential origins besides the one I gave in Irish Families: they can be Ó hAiniarraidh, an Oriel sept, or Mac Enri, a Síol Eoghain family of the Bannside. IF136, S155, Bibl., Map.

O'HIGGINS Ambrosio O'Higgins, Viceroy of Peru, was created Baron de Ballenary by the King of Spain in 1788 and Marquis of Ossorno in 1792. He usually styled himself O'Higgins of Ballinar (not Ballina), though the prefix O appears to have been resumed by him officially only in 1788. He founded, among other towns in Peru, San Ambrosio de Ballenar. It has been frequently stated that he was born near Summerhill, Co. Meath, in which vicinity there is a townland called Ballina; but Vicuna McKenna and other writers, including the author of the article in the Dictionary of National Biography, give no authority for this. Statements in this D.N.B. article cannot be accepted without verification. It says, for example, that O'Higgins sent money to Father Kellett, P.P. of Summerhill, for his impoverished relatives. There was, in fact, never a parish priest of Summerhill of that name; there was a Protestant rector of Agher (which includes Summerhill) named John Kellett, but he was not appointed till 1808, seven years after the death of Ambrosio O'Higgins. Perhaps the remittance was actually made by his son Bernardo. At any rate the statement, which presumably has some foundation, bears out the belief that this O'Higgins family had a connexion with Summerhill. Presumably also the tradition that he was employed as a page or postillion by the Countess of Bective has some factual basis, though that lady was not so called till long after Ambrosio had gone to Spain. The Summerhill estate belonged to Sir Hercules Langford, whose daughter and heiress married Sir John Rowley in 1671. In 1754 Jane Rowley (Langford) married Sir Thomas Taylour, M.P., of Kells, who was created Baron Headfort in 1760 and Earl of Bective in 1766. This explains the anomaly in the tradition that O'Higgins was in the employment of Lady Bective of Summerhill.

I think we may accept the suggestion that his emigration to Spain was due to a relative of his being a prominent ecclesiastic there (confessor to King Carlos III) and that for a time he studied for the priesthood in that country. Thence certainly he went to South America at the age of 41.

The most recent and most scholarly of his biographers, Riccardo Donoso, in a work published by the University of Chile in 1941, says (p. 46) that in 1761 Don Ambrosio obtained a certificate of nationality in which he was stated to be a Roman Catholic, resident in Cadiz, son of Don Carlos O'Higgins and Margaret O'Higgins of Ballenary, in the diocese of Elphin, Ireland. None of his biographers appears to have been aware of the existence of further and more conclusive evidence that Don Ambrosio was in fact born at Ballinary, Co. Sligo, of a family of standing long established there. In the Genealogical Office, Dublin Castle, which as the Office of Arms was established in 1552, there is an original contemporary sworn affidavit (not made by an O'Higgins) to that effect (G.O. MS. 87, fo. 169): this and another (G.O. MS. 165, fo. 396 et seq.) corroborating it are prosaic documents free from the pretentious and verbose language which characterizes some of the eighteenth century claims to "nobility."

Mehagan in his book O'Higgins of Chile, published in 1913, states that Ambrosio's father migrated from Co. Sligo to Co. Meath, where he became a tenant farmer, thus accounting for this family's connexion with the two areas. Though not necessarily relevant it is perhaps of interest to mention that Sir Hercules Langford of Summerhill, Co. Meath, acquired much land in north Connacht in the seventeenth century as the Mayo Book of Survey & Distribution testifies. His name does not appear, however, in the S. & D. Books for Sligo and Roscommon. Ballinary is on the Roscommon border of Co. Sligo.

There is no doubt that a branch of the O'Higgins family of Connacht was established at Kilbeg, Co. Westmeath, at least as early as 1550, as we know from a Funeral Entry of 1638. Their connexion with the midland counties in the sixteenth century is corroborated by the Fiants; and in the next century Petty's "census" of 1659 lists the name Higgin as numerous both in King's and Queen's Counties (Offaly and Leix). IF181, S157, Bibl., Map.

(O) HOEY HAUGH HOUGH   Ó hEochaidh (O'Hoey) is the name of a Meath sept, as well as of the once royal family of Ulidia. The O'Hoeys were of primary importance in Ulster till subdued by their kinsmen — the MacDunlevys about the year 1300. There are, however, Hoeys in Ulster of planter stock. These are also called Huey. Ó hEachach (Haugh) and Ó hEochach (Hough) are etymologically variants of Ó hEochaidh, but they must be regarded as racially distinct. Haugh belongs chiefly to Co. Clare and Hough to Counties Limerick and Tipperary. The use of Hoey as a variant of Haughey (q.v.) is very rare but Hoy is recorded as having been so used. IF200, S159, Map.

(O) HOGAN   Rev. Professor John Ryan states that the O'Hogans of north Tipperary were of the Muscraíghe and distinct from the Dalcassin Hogans of Co. Clare. IF182, S159, Map.

HOLLAND, Holian   Mr. P. J. Kennedy told me that he knew families called Holland in the vicinity of Loughrea and Craughwell who were formerly Holian. Whether this is an anglicized form of Ó hAoláin (usually Hyland) or a distinct Gaelic surname, Ó hÓileáin, I do not know. Not far away, in the Aughrim and Ballinasloe area, there are, he says, Hollands who are traditionally descendants of disbanded Williamite soldiers settled on the Trench estate. Tradition ascribes a similar origin to the Cookes and Howards of that district. Both these names in that part of the country, however, have a more distinguished origin as we have noted elsewhere. IF183, S160.

(O) HORAN   The Offaly name Haughran (Ó hEachráin) has been often changed to Horan. IF183, S161, Map.

(O) HUSSEY   I learn from Professor James Carney that the death of Eochaidh Ó hEoghusa (Eoghy O'Hussey), ollav or chief poet successively to Cuchonnacht MacGuire and his two sons, took place in 1612. He was born in 1569 or 1570.

The town of Dingle (Daingean Uí Chúis) is said to be named from a family of Hussey. Rev. J. O'Connell (Archivium Hibernicum xxi, pp. 5 and 20) shows that the name occurs in the Annates of Kerry as Hosse and Hussye in 1473-5, and this appears to be the first recorded mention of it in Kerry. He says that de la Cousa was gaelicized as Ó Cúis, sometimes becoming O'Cushe in English speech which was modified Hosse and Hussey. According to An Seabhac, Husae is the normal Gaelic form of Hussey in Coraguiny (the barony in which Dingle lies) and he thinks it unlikely that Ó Cúis could ever have been a synonymous form of Husae. It has been suggested to me, as a possibility, by the placenames section of The Ordnance Survey that a surname Ó Cúis, now obsolete, may once have been found there and that, after the coming of the Norman Husseys to that area, Ó Cúis may have been anglicized as Hussey and both names subsequently through confusion gaelicized Husae. There would thus appear to be no evidence available at present to determine from whom (or possibly even from what) the town of Daingean Uí Chúis got its name. IF184, S165, Bibl., Map.

(O) KANE, O'Cahan, Kyan   This name has been corrupted to Kyan in Co. Wicklow where, according to Rev.

Edmund Hogan S.J. and other authorities, a leading branch of the O'Cahan sept of Co. Derry were settled in the eighteenth centry at Ballymurtagh. Of this family was Esmond Kyan who was executed (half an hour before pardon arrived) for his part in the 1798 Insurrection. He was one of the few insurgents with previous military experience. The name Kyan is quite distinct from Kyne. IF191, S187, Bibl., Map.

(O) KENNEDY Since Irish Families and More Irish Families were published the election of Senator John Fitzgerald Kennedy as President of the United States of America, the first man of Gaelic-Irish ancestry on both sides to hold that office, calls for fuller treatment of the O'Kennedy sept than was given there.

In Irish Families no mention was made of that small O'Kennedy sept which was one of the Uí Maine or Hy Many group located in Connacht (of the same stock as the O'Dorceys or Darcys and the O'Loughnans), because it was of minor importance especially having regard to the numerical strength of the Ormond O'Kennedys and the power and prominence of their chiefs. The latter were descended from Cinnéide, nephew of Brian Boru, the greatest of the kings of independent Ireland, who was killed at Clontarf in 1014 during the battle which finally destroyed the power of the Norsemen (or Danes as they are often called) in Ireland. The surname came into being in the eleventh century as Ó Cinnéide, which was later anglicized O'Kennedy. Cinnéide was also the name of Brian Boru's father, who was King of Thomond. The prefix O', which was discarded in the period of Gaelic and Catholic depression under the Penal Code imposed on the country in the seventeenth and eighteenth centuries by its English conquerors, has seldom been resumed in modern times, leaving the name simply Kennedy. This is now one of the most numerous surnames in Ireland.

The principal sept of O'Kennedy, of this Dalcassian descent, originated in Thomond, in that part of County Clare where their name ι perpetuated in the parish of Killokennedy, near Killaloe. They are generally stated to have been driven thence by the O'Briens and the Macnamaras at an early date, and they certainly prospered and multiplied in their new territory on the other side of the Shannon in Ormond (Co. Tipperary), for as early as 1159 the Four Masters, who have many references to the family after 1300, describe the then chief as Lord of Ormond. There they became undisputed lords of that country: they appear, for example as a "nation" of importance in an Ormond deed of 1336. The sept was subdivided into three, the chiefs thereof being called respectively O'Kennedy Finn (fionn, fair), O'Kennedy Roe (rua, red) and O'Kennedy Don (donn, brown). Their history can be read in Dermot F. Gleeson's admirable book The Last Lords of Ormond. Nevertheless they were not without influence in Thomaond after their migration, for we find Donal O'Kennedy as Bishop of Killaloe from 1231 to 1252.

In due course they spread eastwards from Ormond so that by 1659, when Petty's "Census" was taken, Kennedys were numerous throughout County Tipperary and had settled in considerable numbers as far east as the city of Waterford. The name in that document is also spelt Keenedy, Kenedie, Kenady, Kenedy etc. In this connexion it may be noted that the name of the American publisher mentioned in Irish Families (p. 198) is spelt Kenedy not Kennedy. At that date there were 36 families called Kennedy in the baronies nearest to that city. This is interesting because this area is close to Stokestown and Dunganstown, the homeland of the President's ancestors: his great grandfather, Patrick Kennedy, was baptized there on October 18, 1829, son of James Kennedy, his mother's maiden name being Maria Handrick of the same place, which brings them back to the end of the eighteenth century. The name Handrick, also spelt Hanrick, Henrick and Hendrick (Ó hEanraic in Irish) is associated with this same district in south Wexford and is very rare elsewhere.

Place-names give some indication of O'Kennedy location. Mount Kennedy, the seat of the baronet family of Kennedy, and Newtownmountkennedy, a small town in County Wicklow, lie some distance from those parts of the country chiefly associated with the name; but most of the place-names embodying the surname O'Kennedy are found in one of their homelands. In addition to Killokennedy (cill, kil, church), which has already been mentioned, there is Garrykennedy (garraí, garry, garden) in Upper Ormond and Coolkennedy (cúil, cool, corner or nook) also in north Tipperary. There is, too, a place in south County Waterford called Ballykennedy (baile, bally, home or place).

Several Kennedys were officers in James II's Irish army and fought at the Battle of the Boyne in 1690, and in other less disastrous engagements during the Williamite War. As a result of their loyalty to the Stuart and Catholic cause seventeen of the name were outlawed after the Jacobite defeat and their lands were confiscated in consequence. The majority of them were from County Tipperary and from the city of Dublin. Some, of course, had lost their lands a generation earlier in the debacle under the Cromwellian regime. These, when they did not go to the Continent to become the forerunners of the famous Wild Geese, disdaining to work as labourers for the new "upstart" proprietors, had to seek a dangerous living as rapparees or tories: as such they usually met a premature death, as for example Daniel Kennedy, for whose head, set up as a warning over the gate of Carlow Castle, an English officer received a reward of £20 (a large sum then) in May 1657.

In contrast to this melancholy but not inglorious picture it may be added that, before the Land Acts had transferred ownership from the landlords to the occupying tenants, there were 19 Kennedys listed in de Burgh's Landowners of Ireland, 1878, a book which gives particulars of all landlords in possession of considerable estates at that date. Of these, however, only two were seated in a part of the country traditionally associated with the name. Those who remained at home, and at the same time retained the faith and national spirit of their forbears, had to be content with a more humble position in the country.

An interesting sidelight on the Irish origin of the Scottish Kennedys is given by Dr Handley in his Irish in Scotland (p. 7). Writing at the end of the 15th century the Scots poet Dunbar calls his fellow bard (Kennedy) an Irish beggar, and their dispute reveals the extent to which the Irish language was then prevalent in south-west Scotland. IF198, S176, Bibl., Map.

(O) KENNY In Co. Leitrim Kenny has to some extent absorbed the local name Keeney. This, spelt also Keeny, Keany, Keaney, is fairly numerous in Co. Leitrim and south-west Donegal. Woulfe gives the Irish form of Keany as Ó Cianaigh or perhaps more correctly Ó Caoinnigh; he lists elsewhere Mac Éanna, anglice MacKeany, as a Wexford-Carlow surname and regards it as now hardly distinguishable from MacKenna. Mac-Keany, however, is found in Co. Fermanagh as synonymous with Keany. I find MacEanny in a Co. Roscommon Fiant of 1593 and I am inclined to think that Keany (Keeney etc.) is a Mac not an O name, the K, as in Keegan, Keogh and many others, being the C of Mac carried over to a proper name beginning with a vowel or silent F. I put this forward, however, as a probability, not as an authenticated fact.

Kenney is usually merely a variant spelling of Kenny, but it is also the name of some English immigrant families. One of these, by a coincidence, settled in the homeland of O'Kenny of Uí Maine. IF199, S176, Map.

(Mac) KEOGH The present Irish spelling of this name is MacEochaibh. Formerly in Munster it was MagCeoch or MacCeoch which was retained while Gaelic survived there as the vernacular. IF199, S177, Map.

(O) KERNAGHAN Shown in the mediaeval sept-map in Co. Donegal, this name now belongs to Co. Armagh and also the adjacent parts of Co. Antrim, where it is often spelt Kernohan. Another variant Carnaghan, formerly much more numerous than at present is phonetically nearer the original Irish Ó Cearnacháin (derived from cearnach, victorism). Map.

KICKHAM Charles James Kickham was of Mullinahone. There is a verbatim report of his trial in 1865 in the Fenian Trials series in the library of Dáil Éireann. IF296, S178.

(Mac) KIERNAN, Kernan In his Ordnance Survey letters (Co. Cavan) O'Donovan gives a pedigree of this family. Kernan is a variant. Senator Francis Kernan, mentioned in Irish Families should be so spelt. Kernan is also a synonym of Kernaghan. IF273, S179, Map.

(Mac) KILROY In the town of Roscommon and its vicinity Kilroy takes the form Kilroe, which is a truer anglicization of Mac Giolla Ruaidh (ruadh, red). IF134, S182.

(O) KINNANE This, in Irish Ó Cuinneáin, is a Thomond name mainly found in north Tipperary with occasional variants Quinane and Guinnane. The latter also occurs in west Clare, where, however, it can be a

mis-spelling of Goonane, but is normally a variant spelling of Ginnane, the usual form in Clare. Woulfe derives Ó Cuinneáin and Ó Cuineáin from the forenames Conn and Conan. IF106, S184.

(O) LAVERTY Variants of Laverty are Lafferty and Laherty, the Irish form of which is Ó Laithbheartaigh (in modernized spelling Ó Laifeartaigh). Both O'Lafferty and O'Laherty occur in the Elizabethan Fiants relating to Co. Donegal. IF145, S190, Map.

LAWLESS Though the surname Lawless is formed from the Old English word laghles meaning an outlaw, it may, as far as Ireland is concerned, be regarded as falling in the Anglo-Norman category. Outlawe was itself a not uncommon surname in Ireland in the middle ages, e.g. Roger Outlawe, prior of the Hospital of St. John of Jerusalem in 1337, and Henry Outlawe, sovereign of Kilkenny in 1312. From soon after the invasion the name (written Laweles, Laghles, Lachles, Laules etc). appears frequently in mediaeval records up to the end of the sixteenth century throughout Leinster and Munster, particularly in Co. Kilkenny. One branch settled in the city of Kilkenny in the fourteenth century: Walter Lawless was mayor of Dublin, his family being landowners at Cabra and elsewhere near the city. Petty's "census" of 1659 indicates that in the seventeenth century they were fairly numerous in Co. Kilkenny and the Dublin area. Dublin is one of the places where the name is chiefly found today. The other is Co. Mayo. As early as 1285 Thomas Laghles was Constable of Connacht, and about that time Sir William Lawless obtained from the Barretts a considerable tract of country in and near the parish of Killala (Co. Mayo).

In addition to the notable persons of the name referred to in Irish Families mention should also be made of Valentine Lawless, 2nd Baron Cloncurry (1773-1852) who was a member of the United Irishmen in 1798 and a protagonist of Catholic Emancipation.

Mount Lawless in Australia is named after the Irish family which was one of the great pastoral pioneers of Queensland in the 1840's. IF297, S191, Bibl.

(O) LENNON Since the 4th edition of Irish Families was published John Lennon, an outstanding member of the Beatles group, assassinated in 1980, has become well known outside Ireland not only as a talented musician but also for his connection with the peace movement. I should also mention another John Lennon (b. Co. Down 1768), whose daring feats with his ship Hibernia are part of American history 1812-14. IF209, S194.

LYONS The family of Lyons of east Cork, who were physicians to the Roches of Fermoy, are called O'Leighin in B.M. MS. Egerton 92. IF124, S202, Bibl., Map.

(Mac) LYSAGHT Three of the name from Co. Clare were in King James II's Irish army and three were outlawed following the defeat of the Catholic cause. The name is of frequent occurrence in the Co. Clare

Inchiquin Manuscripts: it fills nearly a column of the index under several variant spellings. MacGillysaghty was the usual form up to mid-seventeenth century, after which both Mac and Gil were generally dropped. Such abbreviation at that period was normal, cf. Carrig. IF215, S202, Bibl., Map.

(O) MADDEN In addition to pedigree and useful notes thereon O'Donovan in his edition of the Tribes and Customs of Hy Many, Appendix B, has a long note on O'Madden arms. The probability of the Maddens of Maddenton, who came to Ireland from Oxfordshire in the sixteenth century, being actually of Irish origin; is also considered there. IF216, S203, Bibl., Map.

(O) MALONE Rev. Professor John Ryan S.J. has pointed out to me that the alleged close connexion of the O'Malones with the O'Connors of Connacht did not exist, being the result of a pedigree which was a forgery. For the suggestion regarding the origin of the Malones of Co. Clare see Muldoon. IF220, S206, Map.

(O) MANGAN, Mongan The Munster Mangans (in Irish Ó Mongáin) have been long enough established in Co. Limerick to have a townland (in the parish of Drom-colliher) called after them viz. Ballymongane. This is also the name of a townland in the parish of Kilnamona, Co. Clare. The Ulster sept, which, as erenaghs of St. Caireall, gave its name to the parish of Termonomongan in Co. Tyrone, appears to be now almost extinct. There are twelve families of Mangan in the Hearth Money Rolls for Co. Tipperary (1665-1667). Charles Mongan (1754-1826), son of Dominic Mungan or Mongan, a Co. Tyrone blind itinerant harper, became a Protestant and having assumed the surname Warburton was appointed successively Bishop of Limerick and of Cloyne. Three brothers named Warburton (viv. 1810-1894) were of sufficient importance to be included in Crone's Dictionary of Irish Biography. Though of Offaly they were not in the direct line of the family of Garryhinch in that county, who were very extensive landowners. Mangan arms will be found in plate XX of the later editons of Irish Families.

MANNIX, (Ó) Manahan A sept of the Corca Laoidhe still mainly found in south-west Cork. The Irish form Ó Mainchín (manach, monk) is more usually anglicized as Mannix, which is sometimes used for Minogue in east Clare.
    O'Mannis is a seventeenth century scribe's error for MacMannis, which shoud be equated with MacManus. It has no connexion with the Munster surname Mannix. There is thus a consequential error in the earlier editions of Irish Families Arms Plate XX. In the seventeenth century there was much confusion on the part of record clerks between Mac and O. For example, in the "census" of 1659 in several baronies of Co. Clare the O'Connors are widely returned as MacConnor; and at the end of the century we find MacGuire appearing in the Jacobite outlawries as O'Guire.

(O) MEEHAN It was stated in Irish Families that two

O'Meehans were bishops of Achonry, the authority for this was Analecta Hibernica VI; the subsequently published British Handbook of Chronology corrects this the name of the first being Thomas O'Maicin not Ó Miach-áin. IF224, S212, Map.

MILLEA MILEY In treating these names in Irish Families as anglicized forms of Ó Maolaoidh of Connacht I followed Woulfe. Further research shows that almost every record in which they appear relates to Leinster mainly Co. Kilkenny or an adjacent area. Among these are Fiants of 1575, the "census" of 1659, Ossory and Prerogative wills of the eighteenth century and Griffith's Valuation of the nineteenth. It would seem unlikely therefore that the Irish form of these midland families is Ó Maolaoidh; but I am unable as yet to suggest the correct alternative.
    When Millea occurs in Connacht it is probably a corrupt form of (O) Malley, Mullee being the usual anglicized form of Ó Maolaoidh there. IF225, S216.

MOLLOY, Slowey The use of Molloy as a synonym of Slowey in the Cavan-Monaghan area of Ulster is explained by the elision of the c and the aspiration of the S. in the spoken form of the Irish Mac Sluaghaidh. IF225, 309, S275.

(O) MORAN MORRIN The arms recorded at the Office of Arms as O'Moran and illustrated in Plate XXI of Irish Families belong to families now usually called Moran but more correctly Morahan. This is Ó Murcháin in Irish, a sept of east Offaly. This name has also been anglicized as Morrin and as such it appears in the "census" of 1659 as very numerous in five different baronies of counties Offaly and Kildare, sometimes bracketed by the enumerators with Moran, from which they even then found it indistinguishable. A century earlier it occurs frequently in that area in the Chancery Rolls and Fiants as O'Moran. Further complication is the modern equation of Moran with MacMoran or MacMorrin, a sept whose pedigree (as Mac Moruinn) is given in the Fermanagh genealogies of O'Luinin.
    Arms for the family of Moran of Ballinamore Co. Leitrim, are recorded at the Office of Arms, viz. azure on a mount proper two lions combatant or supporting a flagstaff also proper therefrom a flag argent. Mr. T. Whitley Moran has made a study of the O'Mornas of Connacht.
    It should perhaps be added that there is an English surname Morrin of French origin. IF228, S221, Bibl., Map.

O'MORE The transplantation of the remnants of this sept to Kerry after their subjugation in Leix, may account for the frequency of this name More there now. IF228, S221, Bibl., Map.

MORRIS Michael Morris, Lord Killanin, President of the International Olympic Committee (1972-1980), is grandson not grandnephew of Michael Morris, the first holder of the title. IF231, S222, Bibl.

MORRISSEY While Dr. St. J. Brooks (J.R.S.A.I. lxii, 50) and Dr. D. F. Gleeson (J.R.S.A.I. lxxi, 132 and The Last Lords of Ormond, pages 12, 15) both agree with my opinion regarding the origin of the Morrisseys of Co. Waterford and south Tipperary, it should be stated that the sixteenth century Ormond Deeds and Fiants and also the "census" of 1659 indicate the presence of O'Morrisseys there who may have been Gaels or families of Norman stock who assumed the prefix. IF231, S222.

MacMORROW, MacMorry In the Manorhamilton area this predominantly Leitrim name is now usually written MacMorry. IF237, S222, Map.

(O) MULLIGAN MOLOHAN MULQUEEN The name of Hercules Mulligan, George Washington's confidential correspondent, should be added here. He was born at Coleraine in 1740 and died at New York in 1825. For James Venture Mulligan (1837-1907), born at Rathfriland, Co. Down, one of the most notable of Australian explorers, see Australian Encyclopaedia Vol. VI, p. 195, and Logan Jack Northwest Australia, Vol. II, p. 465. In some parts of the west Ó Maolacháin has become Mulligan by absorption; but in west Clare is found anglicized as Molohan and Mullihan which approximate phonetically to the Irish original. IF233, S227.

(O) MULVIHIL Sir Henry Blackall reminds me that the Mulvihils of Knockanira, Co. Clare, altered their name to Mulville. There are pedigrees of this family in the Genealogical Office. IF234, S229, Map.

MURRAY Sir Terence Aubrey Murray (1810-1873), who was born in Limerick, was a pioneer pastoralist in Australia and built at Canberra the house later converted into the official residence of the Govenor-General. One of his sons Sir John Hubert Plunket Murray (1861-1940) was notable for his care of the natives during his long term of office as governor of New Guinea; the other, Professor Gilbert Murray (1866-1957), of Oxford University, was celebrated as a Greek scholar. IF236, S230, Map.

O'NAGHTEN O'Donovan has valuable pedigree and notes on O'Naghten in The Tribes and Customs of Hy Many, Appendix G. For collection of O'Naghten poems see Analecta Hibernica No. 3, page 227. This O'name has no connection with the Scottish MacNaughton. IF237, S231, Map.

(Mac) NALLY This name appears under the form Knally as a principal Irish name in Co. Westmeath (Rathconrath barony) in the "census" of 1659. IF239, S232.

MacNAUGHTON, Mac Cracken The well known Antrim and Down name Mac Cracken is a corrupted form of the Scottish MacNeachtain. Henry Joy Mac Cracken (1767-1798), who commanded the United Irishmen at the battle of Antrim, was executed in Belfast his native city. The name MacNaughton has no connexion with

O'Naughton, for which see O'Naughton. IF237, S232.

(O) NEYLAN Referring to the article on O'Neylan of Co. Clare it should be added that other forms of this name, found chiefly in Co. Galway, are Nilan, Niland and Nyland. IF240, S236, Map.

(O) NOLAN As Knowlan and Knowland this name is noted in the "census" of 1659 as numerous in Longford and in the adjacent baronies of Co. Westmeath. IF242, S237, Map.

(O) NOONAN, Neenan The numerous Munster surname Noonan has to some extent absorbed the rather rare Clare name Neenan (Ó Naoidheanáin) which, however, is still found in the western part of that county. IF245, S237, Map.

PARSONS Some Irish families called Parsons may be of Gaelic origin. In the Tudor Fiants we frequently meet MacEparson, MacParson etc. In Scotland this name became MacPherson. IF298, S242.

(O) PHELAN Edward Joseph Phelan was a native of Co. Waterford not Dublin, as stated in the earlier editions of Irish Families. IF245, S245, Map.

PRENDERGAST The Prendergasts who assumed the Fitzmaurice name were also caleed MacMaris. Sir Henry Sidney so terms them in a despatch of 1576. IF248, S247.

PRESTON The Gormanston Register, compiled by Sir Christopher de Preston in 1397-8, and continued subsequently in different hands, was published by the Royal Society of Antiquaries Ireland, in 1916. Both text and introduction provide a mine of information regarding the early history of the Prestons in Ireland and contain many useful references to the Berminghams and other families to whom the Prestons were related. A good account of the Preston family will be found in the Introduction to the Gormanston Register. IF299, S248, Bibl., Map.

MacQUAID This name as MacQuaid, Mac Quade and MacQuoad appears frequently in the Hearth Money Rolls for Co. Monaghan and for Co. Armagh (1664-1667). In Irish it is MacUaid (son of Wat). IF249, S249.

(O) QUIGLEY In the entry on Quigley in Irish Families no reference was made to an Ulster sept of the name. That in Inishowen should have been mentioned: in the "census' of 1659 Quigley is the fifth most numerous name in that barony. IF249, S251, Map.

(O) RAFFERTY Mr T. Ó Raifeartaigh has given me the following note: "Etymologically Ó Robhartaigh and Ó Raithbheartaigh (both spellings found) are unrelated. The former is clearly from robharta (a flood tide), hence presumably the three fishes in the arms. The latter is rath plus bheartach (prosperity wielder). There were three O'Ravertys on the Hearth Money Rolls of 1663 in my native parish, but O'Raverty could come from either Irish form." There are twenty entries for O'Raverty in the Co. Armagh H.M. Rolls. IF252, S253, Map.

(O) REGAN Referring to the reference to Teige O'Regan in Irish Families I have not discovered the dates of his birth and death. Wood-Martin says "he was about 70 years old in 1690." I have been reminded that he distinguished himself not at the siege of Limerick but at the sieges of Charlemont and Sligo.

The pronunciation of the name of President Reagan as Raygan is in consonance with that of much of Munster where Ó Raogáin rather than Ó Riagáin is more usual Irish form. IF255, S256, Map.

ROCHE The place-name Rochestown occurs six times in Co. Wexford, twice each in Counties Cork and Kilkenny and once each in Counties Limerick, Tipperary, Kildare, Meath, Westmeath and Dublin; in the last named there is also a Rocheshill. Roche's Street in Limerick commemorates the particular association of the family with that city. IF258, S259, Bibl., Map.

RUSSELL Though his activites were associated with Ulster, Thomas Russell, the United Irishman mentioned in Irish Families, was not an Ulsterman: he was born at Mallow of a family long associated with Co. Kilkenny. IF300, S263.

SCULLY SCULLION Scully is used sometimes in north Connacht as a synonym of Scullion or Scullin (Ó Scolláin). Scullin is now rare, but Scullion is fairly numerous in north-east Ulster. The O'Scullions were erenaghs of Ballyscullion in the deanery of Rathlowry, diocese of Derry.

James Henry Scullin (1876-1953), one of Australia's most notable Prime Ministers, was born in that country of a Catholic Irish family – his father was from Derry.

Five other Australian Prime Ministers were of Irish birth or parentage, viz, Joseph Benedict Chifley (1885-1951), who was son of Patrick Chifley and Mary Ann Corrigan (a native of Co. Fermanagh) and grandson of another Patrick Chifley, of Thurles, Co. Tipperary; Francis M. Forde (P.M. 1945) whose family came from Ballinaglera, Co. Leitrim; Joseph Aloysius Lyons (1879-1939) from Co. Galway; John Joseph Curtin and Arthur Fadden (see Curtin and Fadden supra). IF263, S266, Map.

(O) SHEEHAN It was Dr. Michael Sheehan (1870-1945), late Archbishop of Sydney, who was associated with Ring College and the revival of the Irish language, not Richard Sheehan, Bishop of Waterford, as stated in Irish Families. IF267, S270, Map.

(Mac) SHEEHY Apropos of the character of the Mac-Sheehy galloglasses it is on record that Manus ne Cleggan MacShehe, captain of galloglasses, received £7.15.6½ Irish as "head money" for the head of Mallanchy (MacClancy) chief of his name, one of O'Rourkes chief allies, in 1539. IF268, S270, Bibl., Map.

SHIELS William Shiels (Barry Fitzgerald) was not a brother of George Shields (recte Shiels). IF269, S271, Map.

(O) TOOLE The O'Tooles of Connacht are, according to Hardiman, of dual origin: O'Toole of Inisturk a branch of the O'Malleys, O'Toole of Omey descended from immigrants from the Leinster sept. IF276, S288, Bibl., Map.

TORRENS According to Elrington Ball (Judges in Ireland) the Torrens family of Derrynane are of Swedish descent. IF307, S288.

(Mac) TRAYNOR While MacCreanor is the form of the name which occurs in the Co. Armagh Hearth Money Rolls of 1664, in the Co. Monaghan rolls of like date it is MacTreanor. IF278, S289.

USSHER In Irish Families a brief note on Ussher was placed in Part IV (the Anglo-Irish section) as were several other families, e.g. Rothe, Ledwich, Henebry, who, being of Norman origin, feel that they should have been included with the Hiberno-Normans in Part II, i.e. those who came to Ireland during or immediately after the invasion and remained in this country permanently.

The Usshers are certainly of Norman origin. Parr, who wrote the life of the celebrated Primate James Ussher in 1686, states that they were originally Nevills and that one of these Nevills, having come to Ireland with John, took the surname Ussher from the official position he held under that king. There is no doubt that several persons of the name are recorded as being in Ireland during the early thirteenth century. Tradition links up these individuals with the Ussher family which produced so many distinguished Irishmen. John Ussher, who then lived in Yorkshire, was appointed Constable of Dublin Castle in 1307: he died in England. It can be confidently stated that Arland Ussher, "merchant, of Dublin" in 1420, was this John's descendant and the pedigree is authenticated from him down to the present day.

Referring to the notable men of the name briefly mentioned in Irish Families the life of Most Rev. James Ussher (1581-1636)—who was, for thirty years archbishop of Armagh not Dublin – is fully dealt with, both as churchman and author, in the Dictionary of National Biography, though his change from the bitter anti-Papist outlook of his middle years to the tolerance of his old age might be more emphasized; Sir William Ussher (b. 1651) was Clerk of The Council and superintended the publication in 1602 of the first printed version in Irish of the New Testament (that of William O'Donnell), while his father, John Ussher (1529-1590), the mayor of Dublin, was responsible for the publication of the first book ever printed in the Irish language.

Additional names which might well be included are: Sir Thomas Ussher (1779-1848), son of Henry Ussher the astronomer, who conveyed Napoleon to Elba and refused to testify that the emperor was mad; Capt. Arthur Ussher (1693-1768), of the Co. Waterford branch, veteran of nine campaigns under Marlborough and famous for killing his colonel in a duel for which he was acquitted by the Duke; and perhaps Harry Ussher (1883-1957), of Eastwell, Co. Galway, who has been called "the last of the Harry Lorrequers." A branch of the family has been established in South America for nearly two centuries: it still flourishes and has produced several priests prominent in Argentina. In connexion with Armagh it is of interest to add that in the new corporation of that city under the charter of 1613 the sovereign and three of the twelve burgesses were Ushers.

A few families bearing the old Connacht surname Hession (or Hussian) have changed their name to Ussher, which in such cases is really Ó hOisín. Another anglicized form of this Gaelic surname is Hishon, which is found in Co. Tipperary. The name Ó hOisín occurs in the Annals relating to the eleventh and twelfth centuries in all the provinces except Ulster. Bibl.

WALL Though the name Wall is now rare in Connacht and Ulster, it should be mentioned that families of the name were well established in the western province in the sixteenth century and compilers of the Composition Book of Connacht treated them as an Irish sept, naming Water Wale, alias the Fealtach, of Droughtie Co. Galway as chief of the name. IF280, S295, Bibl., Map.

WILDE In addition to the family of Sir William and Oscar Wilde, the origin of which is given in Irish Families, the name was found in Ireland as de Wylde at a much earlier date: there are references to it both in the Pale and in Co. Limerick from 1295 onwards.

Oscar Wilde was born in 1854, not 1856, the year given in the Dictionary of National Biography and elsewhere. IF303, S300.

APPENDIX II

Anglo-Norman surnames formed from trades, employments, personal characteristics and nationality taken from mediaeval Irish records and still found in Ireland. (Many families so called are, however, of post-mediaeval introduction).

le Archer
le Bailiff (Bailey)
le Baker
le Barbour
le Blak(e)
le Blound (Blunt)
le Boucher (Butcher)
le Brette
   Broun (Browne)
   Burgeys (Burgess)
le Botiller (Butler)
le Campion
le Carpenter[1]
le Carter
le Clerke[2]
le Collier
le Comber[3]
le Cooke[4]
le Cousin[5]
le Croker
le Cuirteis (Curtis)
le Devenish
le Draper
le Dyer
l'Enfant (Fant)
le Engleys (English)
l'Ercedekene (Archdeacon)
le Fauconer (Falkiner)

le Fereter
le Fisher
le Fleming
le Forester(al)
le Francis
le Franklyn
le Ganter
le Gardener
le Glover
le Grant
le Harpur
le Hayward
le Hunt(er)
le Large
le Lawles(s)
le Leche
Lightfot
le Lombard
le Long
le Marchant
le Mareschal (Marshall)
le Mason
le Mercer
le Miniter
le Noble
le Norreys
le Parker
le Paumer (Palmer)

le Petit (Petty)
le Piper
le Poer (Power)
le Potter
le Proude (Prout)
le Ragged
le Rede (Reid)
   Roussel (Russell)
   Sauvage (Savage)
le Serjeant
le Shepherd
le Skynner
   Smithe[6]
le Steward (Stewart)
le Tanner(e)
le Taylour
le Toukere (Tucker)[7]
le Ussher
le Vyneter
le Wakeman
le Waleys (Walsh)
le Warner
le Webbe
le White
le Wilde
le Woodeman
le Wyse
le Yong (Young)

[1] See MacAteer in text.
[2] Most of our Irish Clarkes are O'Clery by origin.
[3] Comber is also an anglicized form of O Ciaráin and Ó Ciaragáin.
[4] In Connacht Cooke and MacCooke are usually for MacDhabhóc, a branch of the Burkes. MacCooge was the seventeenth century form there; MacCooke is quite frequent in the Hearth Money Rolls of the north-eastern counties
[5] See Cussen in text.
[6] Smith, especailly in Co. Cavan, is now usually an alias of MacGowan.
[7] Tucker is also an anglicized form of Tougher or Toher (Ó Tuathair). Tougher is now a Mayo name.

APPENDIX III

The following are the commonest English, Scottish and Welsh surnames found in modern Ireland. The majority of them are concentrated in and around Belfast. The figures show the estimated approximate present population of each.

In the case of names marked with an asterisk * a considerable proportion of the population figure may be ascribed to persons of Gaelic stock whose Irish patronymic has been changed at some period: thus many Smiths are really MacGowans, Clarkes are Clerys and Kings Conrys. This is true also of several others not so indicated — some Grahams, for example, are Grehans, Armstrong may be Lavery, Burns Byrne, and occasionally Dickson is a synonym of Deehan; but in such cases the relevant proportion is small. For further information on this point see *Irish Families* Appendix A. The sign † indicates that the name so marked is dealt with either in the text of this volume or in *Irish Families*.

*Smith	30,000	*†Ferguson	5,500
†Brown(e)	20,000	*†Morrow	5,500
*†Murray	18,000	Young	5,500
Wilson	15,000	†Mitchell	5,500
*†Campbell	14,000	Walker	5,000
*†Clarke	14,000	Gordon	5,000
Johnston(e)[1]	14,000	Craig	5,000
*†Hughes	13,500	Hall	5,000
*†Martin	13,000	Watson	5,000
Thom(p)son	13,000	Hill	5,000
White	12,000	Irwin[2]	5,000
Stewart and Stuart	10,500	†Gray	4,500
Burns	9,000	Black	4,500
Robinson	9,000	†Morris	4,500
Reid	8,500	†Morrison	4,500
Graham	8,500	†Montgomery	4,500
*†King	8,500	†MacClean and MacLean	4,250
Bell	8,000	Stevenson	4,250
*† Cunningham	8,500	†Davis	4,250
Anderson	7,000	Wright	4,250
*†Rogers and Rodgers	7,000	†Beatty	4,250
†Hamilton	7,000	Jackson	4,250
Miller and Millar	7,000	†Russell	4,250
† Allen	7,000	Dickson and Dixon	4,250
Boyd	6,500	Gibson	4,000
Patterson	6,500		
*Green(e)	6,500	The returns for the following well known	
Jones	6,500	Irish names are given here as a basis of comparison:	
† Taylor	6,500	Murphy	55,000
Wallace	6,000	O'Brien and Brien[3]	30,000
†Kerr	6,000	Fitzgerald	13,500
Armstrong	6,000	Clancy	4,250
*Woods	5,500	Coffey	4,250

[1] Johnson (c. 2, 500) not included. [2] Irvine (c. 3,000) not included. [3] Bryan and MacBrien not included.

APPENDIX IV

Explanation of Technical Terms used in Text

Adventurer. A person who subscribed ("adventured") a sum of money for the equipment of an army to suppress the Rising of 1641 on the security of lands to be confiscated from Irish porprietors.

Aspiration. The addition of the letter H to a consonant, thereby modifying its sound, e.g. BH = V. (Cf. PH in English, which gives the sound of F).

Barony. A territorial divison next in order of size to the county, each county comprising from 5 to 20 baronies according to its extent.

Betagh. This term (from the Irish biatach, food-provider), called betagius in mediaeval Latin, was applied to Irish "villeins" under the Norman régime (see entry on Beatty).

Brehon. (Irish breitheamh, genitive breitheamhan) a judge. The terms Brehon Law and Brehon System refer to the Gaelic legal system in force before the Norman invasion: this system was not completely superseded until the seventeenth century.

Census. The so-called census of 1659 was not a complete census of population in the modern connotation of the word. There is a difference of opinion as to its exact purpose: it was carried out in connexion with the hearth-money tax.

Coarb. The following passage is quoted from J.F. Kenney's Sources for the Early History of Ireland p. 747:
By the eleventh century ... in the average church the abbot, generally known as the comarba (coarb), "heir," of the saintly founder, or, if it were not the saint's principal establishment the aircinnech (erenagh), "head," had become a lay lord, whose family held the office and the church property from generation to generation. In some cases, apparently, all trace of a church-establishment had disappeared, except that the incumbent claimed for his lands the termonn of the ancient monastery, those prievelges and exemptons which had from of old been accorded to ecclesiastical property; but generally the comarba or aircinnech maintained a priest.

Eclipsis. The suppression of a consonant at the beginning of a word by the insertion before it of another consonant of the same class, e.g. M before B (labials), D before T (dentals).

Erenagh. See Coarb supra.

Fiant. This is short for "Fiant litterae patentes." Fiants were warrants to the Chancery authority for the issue of letters patent under the Great Seal. They dealt with matters ranging from commissions for appointments to high office and important government activities to grants of "English liberty" and "pardons" to the humblest of the native Irish.

File. A poet.

Gaelic. This word in Ireland has no relation to Scotland. As a noun it is used to denote the Irish language; as an adjective to denote native Irish as opposed to Norman or English origin.

Galloglass. (Irish gallóglach). A heavily armed mercenary soldier, usually but not always of Scottish origin.

Gavelkind. "A system of tribal succession by which land, on the decease of its occupant, was thrown into the common stock, and the whole area re-divided among the members of the sept." (O.E.D.)

Idleman. This word is used in the Fiants etc. as the equivalent of a gentleman, as opposed to workman.

Kern. (Irish ceithearnach). An Irish soldier, lightly armed.

Ollav. A professor or learned man; a master in some art or branch of learning.

Pale, the. The district centred on Dublin under the full control of the government of the King of England. It varied greatly in extent as the power of the English waxed and waned. At the end of the fifteenth century it comprised only Co. Dublin and parts of Louth, Meath and Kildare.

Pardon. In Tudor times this was equivalent to immunity from the effects of anti-Irish legislation, only in some cases being an actual pardon for a specific offence.

Shanachie. (Irish seanchaidhe). An antiquary, story-teller.

Tanist. Heir presumptive to a chief, lord or dynast.

Termon. See Coarb supra.

Titulado. In a general way this denotes the principal proprietor in a townland or a street. For a note on the specialized meaning of the term see R.C. Simington, Analecta Hibernica, No. 12, p. 177.

Townland. The territorial sub-divison of a parish, each townland greatly varying in size, commonly averaging from 250 to 400 acres. The term has no relation to a town or city.

Undertaker. A person, usually English, who, as a

condition of obtaining a grant of lands confiscated from Irish proprietors, undertook to plant thereon English or Scottish settlers in place of the dispossessed occupiers.

Wild Geese. A term applied to Irish exiles to the Continent of Europe in the seventeenth and eighteenth centuries. Originally denoting those who became soldiers in continental armies it was later extended to refer to their descendants.

APPENDIX V

A Bibliography Of Works
Relating To The Irish Abroad

The following selective list only includes works of a general character. There are also, of course, many books dealing with Irish activity in limited areas (e.g. the very useful diocesan histories) and with individual Irishmen abroad. Many of these will be found in the bibliographies included in some of the undermentioned works.

Adams, William Forbes: Ireland and Irish emigration to the New World from 1815 to the Famine. Yale University Press, 1932.

American-Irish Historical Society: Journal. Vol. 1– Boston (later New York), 1891–1941.

– The Recorder: the bulletin of the American-Irish Historical Society New York, 1902–(In progress).

Berardis, Vincenzo: Italy and Ireland in the middle ages. With an introduction by John Ryan, S.J., Dublin, 1950.

Blanke, Fritz: Columban and Gallus. Urgeschichte des schweizerischen Christentums. Zurich, 1940.

Cleary, P. S.: Australia's debt to Irish nation-builders. Sydney, 1933.

Cullen, Rev. J. H.: Young Ireland in exile. The story of the men of '48 in Tasmania. Dublin, 1928.

Davin, Nicholas Flood: The Irishman in Canada. London and Toronto, 1877.

Denvir, John: The Irish in Britain from the earliest times to the fall and death of Parnell. London, 1892.

Dunaway, Wayland F.: The Scotch-Irish of Colonial Pennsylvania. The University of North Carolina Press, 1944.

Durack, Mary: Kings in Grass Castles (Australia). London, 1959.

Gibson, Florence E.: The attitudes of the New York Irish toward state and national affairs, 1848-1892. Columbia Univ. Press, 1951.

Gougaud, Dom Louis: Christianity in Celtic lands, a history of the churches of the Celts, their origin, their development, influence, and mutual relations. London, 1932.

– Gaelic pioneers of christianity. The work and influence of Irish monks and saints in continental Europe (VIth-XIIth cent.) Translated from the French by Vistor Collins. Dublin, 1923.

– Les saints Irlandais hors l'Irlande: études dans le culte et dans la devotion traditionelle. Louvain and Oxford, 1936.

Guerin, Thomas: The Gael in New France. Montreal, 1946.

Hackett, James Dominick: Bishops of the United States of Irish birth or descent. New York, 1943.

Handley, James Edmund: The Irish in Scotland, 1798-1845. Cork, 1943.

– The Irish in modern Scotland. Cork and Oxford, 1947.

Handlin, Oscar: Boston's immigrants: a study in acculturation. Revised and enlarged edition. Harvard Univ. Press, 1959.

Hayes, Richard: Biographical dictionary of Irishmen in France. Dublin, 1949.

– Ireland and Irishmen in the French Revolution. With a preface by Hilaire Belloc. 1932.

– Old Irish links with France. Some echoes of exiled Ireland. Dublin 1940.

Irish Manuscripts Commission (Dublin): Various publications, notably Analecta Hibernica, No. 4–Rev. A. Gwynn, S.J.: The Irish in the West Indies. No. 22–Eilish Ellis: State-aided emigration to Canada. Jennings, Rev. Brendan, O.F.M.: Irishmen in Spanish Flanders. Dublin 1961.

Kiernan, T. J.: The Irish exiles in Australia. Dublin, 1954.

McDonald, Sister M. Justille. History of the Irish in Wisconsin in the nineteenth century. Washington, 1954.

McGee, Thomas D'Arcy: A history of the Irish settlers in North America: from the earliest period to the census of 1850. Boston, 1852.

McNeill, Charles: Publications of Irish interest published by Irish authors on the Continent prior to the eighteenth century. Dublin, 1930.

Maginnis, Thomas Hobbs: The Irish contribution to America's independence. Philadelphia and Dublin,

1913.

Marshall, W.F.: Ulster sails west. The story of the great emigration from Ulster to North America in the 18th century. Belfast, 1944.

Meehan, Rev. C. P.: The fate and fortunes of Hugh O'Neill, Earl of Tyrone and Rory O'Donnell, Earl of Tyrconnell: their flight from Ireland, and death in exile. 3rd ed. Dublin, 1885.

Mooney, Rev. Canice, O.F.M.: Irish Franciscan relations with France 1224-1850. Dublin, 1951.

Moran, Cardinal Patrick F.: History of the Catholic Church in Australasia from authentic sources, containing many original and official documents. Sydney, 1894.

Murray, Thomas: The story of the Irish in Argentina. New York, 1919.

Myers, Albert Cook: Immigration of the Irish Quakers into Pennsylvania, 1682-1750, with their early history in Ireland. facss. Swarthmore (Pennsylvania), 1902.

O'Boyle, Rev. James: The Irish Colleges on the Continent. Their origin and history. Dublin, 1935.

O'Brien, Michael J.: George Washington's associations with the Irish. New York, 1937.
 — A hidden phase in American history. Ireland's part in America's struggle for liberty. New York, 1919.
 — Pioneer Irish in New England. New York, 1937.

O'Callaghan, John Corenlius: History of the Irish Brigades in the service of France, from the Revolution in Great Britain and Ireland under James II, to the Revolution in France under Louis XVI. Glasgow, 1870.

O'Donnell, Elliot: The Irish abroad. A record of the achievements of wanderers from Ireland. London, 1915.

O'Kelly, J. J.: Ireland's spiritual empire. Dublin, 1952.

O'Rahilly, Cecile: Ireland and Wales. Their historical and literary relations. London, 1924.

Quigley, Rev. Hugh: The Irish race in California and the Pacific coast. San Francisco, 1878.

Roberts, Edward F.: Ireland in America. Foreword by Claude G. Bowers. New York and London, 1931.

Solomon, Barbara Millar: Ancestors and immigrants: a changing New England tradition. Harvard Univ. Press, 1956.

Stewart, Herbert Leslie: The Irish in Nova Scotia: Annals of the Charitable Irish Society of Halifax (1786-1836). Kentville, N.S., 1949.

Tommasini, Fra Anselmo: Irish saints in Italy. Translated with some additional notes by J. F. Scanlan. London, 1937.

Waddell, Helen: The wandering scholars. London, 1927.

Walsh, James: The world's debt to the Irish. Boston, Stratford; Dublin, 1926.

Walsh, Micheline: Spanish Knights of Irish origin, 3 vols. Dublin, 1960-1970.

Wittke, Carl: The Irish in America. Louisiana State Univ. Press, 1956.

Ulster

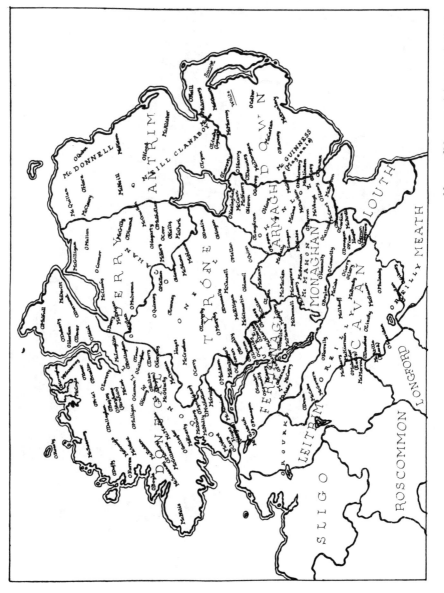

Names of Norman origin are underlined.

Munster

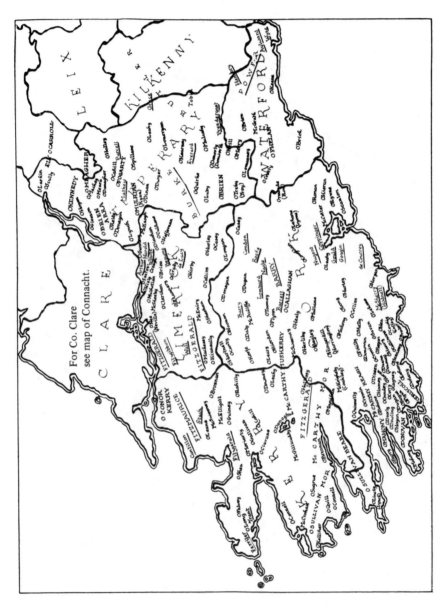

Names of Norman origin are underlined.

Leinster

Names of Norman origin are underlined.

Connacht

Names of Norman origin are underlined.

INDEX OF NAMES IN MAPS

In this index, as in the maps, all Mac names are given Mc.
(Mc and M' are, as mentioned elsewhere, merely abbreviations of Mac)

O'Rynne: Cork.
Sarsfield: Dublin.
Savage: Down.
O'Scanlan: Cork, Fermanagh and
  Galway.
O'Scannell: Sligo.
O'Scully: Tipperary.
Segrave: Dublin.
O'Sexton: Limerick.
O'Shanahan: Clare.
McShane: Tyrone.
O'Sexton: Limerick.
O'Shanahan: Clare.
McShane: Tyrone.
McShanley: Leitrim.
McSharry: Cavan and Leitrim.
O'Shaughnessy: Galway.
O'Shea: Kerry.
McSheedy: Clare.
O'Sheehan: Limerick.
McSheehy: Limerick.
O'Shelly: Cork.
O'Sheridan: Cavan and Longford.
McSherry: Cork and Armagh.
O'Shiel: Donegal.

Shortall: Kilkenny.
O'Shryhane: Donegal.
Sinnott: Wexford.
O'Slattery: Clare.
McSolly: Louth.
O'Sonnohan: Sligo.
O:Spelman: Sligo.
O'Spillane: Tipperary.
Stack: Kerry.
Stafford: Wexford.
O'Sugrue: Kerry.
O'Sullivan: Kerry.
McSweeney: Cork, Donegal and
  Kerry.
Sweetman: Kilkenny.
Taaffe: Lough and Sligo.
Talbot: Dublin.
Tallon: Carlow.
O'Tarpey: Sligo.
O'Tierney: Mayo.
Tobin: Kilkenny and Tipperary.
O'Tolleran: Mayo.
O'Tomelty: Tyrone.
O'Toner: Donegal.
O'Toole: Wicklow.

O'Toomey: Cork.
O'Towey: Mayo.
O'Tracey: Galway and Leix.
Trant: Kerry.
O'Trehy (Troy): Tipperary.
Tuite: Westmeath.
O'Tuohy: Galway.
O'Tynan: Leix.
O'Tyne: Clare.
Tyrrell: Westmeath.
McVaddock: Wexford.
McVeagh: Armagh.
Verdon: Louth.
Wadding: Wexford.
Walsh: Wexford.
Wall: Limerick.
McWard: Galway.
McWeeney: Roscommon.
White: Down and Sligo.
Wogan: Kildare.
Woulfe: Limerick.
Wyse: Waterford.

INDEX